W. H. Irwin and Co.

City of Hamilton Twelfth Annual

Alphabetical, General, Street, Miscellaneous and Subscribers' Classified Business Directory

W. H. Irwin and Co.

City of Hamilton Twelfth Annual
Alphabetical, General, Street, Miscellaneous and Subscribers' Classified Business Directory

ISBN/EAN: 9783744756853

Printed in Europe, USA, Canada, Australia, Japan

Cover: Foto ©Andreas Hilbeck / pixelio.de

More available books at **www.hansebooks.com**

A. F. FORBES,

STOCK AND SHARE BROKER,

Railway, Municipal Debentures Bought and Sold.

NO. 2 MERRICK STREET.

HENRY HARDING,

PLUMBER, GAS AND STEAM FITTER,

Baths, Water-Closets, Forcing Pumps, Marble Wash Stands, Porcelain Slabs, Gas Fixtures, Globes and Shades.

Copper Cylinder Boilers, Galvanized Iron Boilers, etc., all the latest improvements in ventilation.

North-west cor. James and Cannon sts.—No. 119 James st. N.

HAMILTON COFFEE TAVERN COMPANY,

(INCORPORATED).

GORE COFFEE TAVERN,

13 Hughson st. north, next Times office.

ARCADE COFFEE ROOM,

Alexandra Arcade, adjoining the Market.

Meals at all Hours,

With Tea, Coffee and Cocoa, etc., at low prices.

ADAM BROWN, President. ALFRED POWIS, Secretary.

☞ Patrons will please observe that all orders for the Hamilton City Directory bear our name, and that our agents are not authorized to receive money or goods in anvance payment for subscriptions.

CITY OF HAMILTON

TWELFTH ANNUAL

Alphabetical, General, Street, Miscellaneous and Subscribers' Classified Business

DIRECTORY

FOR THE YEAR MARCH, 1885, TO MARCH, 1886,

TO WHICH ARE ADDED

DIRECTORIES OF DUNDAS, WATERDOWN, ANCASTER

AND THE VILLAGES AND POST OFFICE LOCALITIES OF

THE COUNTY OF WENTWORTH.

PRICE, . - $2.50.

W. H. IRWIN & CO., COMPILERS AND PUBLISHERS.

Printed at the Office of A. McPherson, 51 North James St., Hamilton, Ont.

PREFACE.

The publishers, in presenting their TWELFTH ANNUAL EDITION of the City of Hamilton Directory, gratefully acknowledge the support awarded them, and assure their patrons, the great majority of whom they are happy to know are personal friends or acquaintances, that as in the past, so in the future, every means in their power will be exerted to make the work as thorough and reliable as it is possible for a compilation of this kind to be. Every house has been visited by our agents, and if errors are discovered we solicit a lenient criticism. The present volume contains about 12,000 names and addresses which is in excess, considering the population of the city, of the average Directory number. Wishing our patrons a favorable year, we take our leave, hoping in due time to request their support for the THIRTEENTH edition of this book.

☞ Several of our patrons complain that certain persons are in the habit of constantly borrowing Directories, and when most needed they are not to be found. The best remedy for this evil is not to permit the book to leave your premises. Every business man requires the book and can afford to purchase it.

W. H. IRWIN & CO.

March 1st, 1885.

W. H. IRWIN & CO.,

Directory Publishers and Publishers' Agents

The oldest established Directory publishing firm in Ontario, and excepting Messrs. Lovell & Son, of Montreal, in the Dominion. During our long experience we have compiled this class of work for all the cities of Ontario and Quebec with the exception of Montreal; a large number of the counties of Ontario; the Eastern Townships of Quebec, and compiled the Messers. Anderson's Ontario Directory published in 1869. This experience authorizes us to state that our compilations are as complete as any of the publications of this kind can be. While avoiding all redundancy; cramming the book with matter foreign to the character of this class of books, nothing is omitted that should be included in the legitimate contents of the Directory. Please see list of our publications on page 390.

—Address—

12 MACNAB STREET SOUTH, HAMILTON, ONTARIO.

GENERAL INDEX.

ADVERTISERS' INDEX.

BOOTS AND SHOES,

—ON THE—

SQUARE,

—AT—

GEO. HENDERSON'S,

45. Macnab street north. 45.

MARKET SQUARE.

HAMILTON DIRECTORY, 1885-6.

TWELFTH ANNUAL EDITION.

W. H. IRWIN & CO., Compilers.

Abbs John A, clerk, 19 Macab n
Abell Daniel W, machinist, 19 Grove
Abey Jarvis, boilermaker, 19 Devonport
Abram Frederick, tailor, 50 Wilson
Abraham Charles, commission merchant, 14 Charles, h 17 Park s
Accident Insurance Co, of North America, Seneca Jones, agent, 59 James n
Acheson John, 91 Wellington n
Acheson Joseph, machinist, 20 Lower Cathcart
Acheson Wm, salesman, bds 91 Wellington n
Acklan Robert, carpenter, Wentworth n
Ackland Robt, patternmaker, 85 Bay n
Ackworth Mrs Mary, (wid John) 182 Napier
Acres Wm, hats and furs, 12 King e, h 44 Hunter w
Adam James, plumber, 22 Hughson n
Adam James, bookkeeper, cor Hughson and King Wm
Adam Mrs Mina, (wid James) 16 Hunter e
Adams George, stove mounter, 107 East ave n
Adams James, laborer, 79 Hannah e
Adams James, packer, 83 Mary
Adams Manufacturing Company, J E Martin, manager, wringers, mattresses, etc, 114 James n
Adams Peter, tailor, 135 Hunter e
Adams Thomas, sailor, 74 Barton e
Adams Thos, carpenter, 18 Inchbury n
Adamson, Miss E, r 303 McNab n
Adcock John, machinist, 70 Hughson s
Adcock Mrs, Garth, s of Concession
Addison James, (W Addison & Sons) bds 94 Wellington s
Andison Mrs John, 113 Rebecca
Addison Kobt, carpenter, 15 Charles
Addison Thos, laborer, 30 Hess n
Addison William sr, (W Addison & Sons) 90 Wellington s
Addison Wm sr, (W Addison & Sons) 90 Wellington s
Adrian Mrs, bds 140 Main e
Ætna Insurance Co, of Hartford, W F Findlay, agent, 25 James s
Aged Women's Home, Miss McFarlane, matron, 115 Wellington s

Ahern Robert, polisher, 8 Spring
Aikin James, butcher, Wentworth n
Aikin Wm, blacksmith, 34 Wellington n
Aikins Mrs Mary, (wid James) bds 150 Bay n
Aikins Robert, scale maker, 38 Stuart e
Aikins Wm, machinist, 150 Bay n
Ailes James, manager Knights of Labor co-operative store, h 80 Bay n
Ailles Rich, bricklayer, 2 Margaret
Ainsborough John H, moulder, 367 Catharine n
Ainslie Mrs Eliza, 76 Napier
Ainslie James, tanner, 230 King William
Ainslie Wm, trunk maker, 25 Markland
Aird John, carpenter, bds Dominion hotel
Aitchison Alex W, chief fire brigade, 89 Main w
Aitchison & Co, (Wm and David) planing mills, 56 and 58 Main w
Aitchison David (Aitchison & Co) h 9 Bay s
Aitchison J W, com traveler, 33 Caroline n
Aitchison Thos A, bookkeeper, 68 Hannah w
Aitchison Wm, (Aitchison & Co) h 33 Caroline n
Aitchison Wm, hotel, 93 Bay n
Aitken Mrs Christina E, (wid Samuel M) 39 Jackson w
Aitken E P, clerk, 39 Jackson w
Albery Wm, shoemaker, 157 John n
Albins Wm, machinist, 195 East ave n
Alder Robert, teamster, 184 King Wm
Alderman Wm, laborer, 5 Harriet
Alderson, George W, plasterer, 30 Bay n
Aldous J E P, organist, 84 James s
Aldrich William, laborer, 141 Wood e
Aldridge Fred, printer, 60 Lower Cathcart
Aldridge James, shoemaker, 7 Ferguson ave
Aldridge Thomas, shoemaker, r 74 Emerald n
Alexander A, accountant, court house, h Wentworth cor Stinson
Alexander Albert E, clerk, Concession cor Hilton
Alexander, Mrs Christina, 12 New
Alexander Douglas, law student, Wentworth s
Alexander Ernest, clerk G T R, cor Stinson and Wentworth
Alexander Frederick, laborer, 353 John n
Alexander, Henry, sawyer, 91 Picton e
Alexander Mrs Isabella, 153 John s
Alexander James, carpenter, 45 Queen n
Alexander John, leather and findings, 13 and 15 King w, h Concession cor Hilton
Alexander John, moulder, 105 East ave n
Alexander S H, clerk, Wentworth s
Alexander Thos, bartender, 12 New
Alexander Wm, bartender, Royal hotel
Alf John, moulder, bds 41 John n
Alford Wm, china, 11 McNab n
Alhambra saloon, Smith & Findlay, proprs, James cor Merrick
Allen Mrs Agnes, 47 Queen n
Allen Edward, blacksmith, 135 Wood e
Allan Fred, grocer, 53 Hunter e
Allan George, telegraphist, 138 Cannon e

Allan George, moulder, 56½ John s
Allen Mrs George, 104 Barton e
Allan Mrs George, 84 John n
Allan George R, printer, 24 Locomotive
Allan Mrs Helen S, (wid Thos S) 64 Queen n
Allen Henry, boilermaker, 28 Simcoe e
Allan Jas, moulder, 41 Chisholm
Allen James, carpenter, 47 Catharine s
Allan James R, 39 Magill
Allan Mrs Jane, 163 King Wm
Allan John, machinist, 129 Park n
Allan John, lithographer, bds 64 Queen s
Allen John, grocer, 55 Hunter e
Allen John, carpenter, 47 Catharine s
Allan Mrs Maggie, (wid Adam) 54 Young
Allen Martin, laborer, 128 East ave n
Allen Michael, shoemaker, 55 Hunter e
Allen Patrick, laborer, 75 Catharine n
Allen Paul L, bds 13 Bold
Allen & Provan, (Robert Allen and David Provan) new and second hand dealers, 14 and 16 King Wm
Allen Mrs Rachael (wid Osborne) 178 King Wm
Allen Richard, bootmaker, 116 King w
Allen Robert, (Allen & Provan) h 33 Hughson n
Allen Robt, carter, 11 Kinnell
Allan Mrs Susan (wid Wm) bds 39 Magill
Allan Steamship Line, J B Fairgrieve, agent, 59 James n
Allen Thomas jr, telegrapher, 10 Simcoe e
Allen Thomas sr, fitter, 10 Simcoe e
Allen Thomas, builder, 143 West ave n
Allen Thomas, dyer, 18 Strachan w
Allan Thos, shirt cutter, bds 64 Queen s
Allan Wm, contractor, 14 Barton w
Allan Wm, carpenter, 136 King Wm
Allan Wm R, blacksmith, 63 Locomotive
Allardice Geo R, stone cutter, 229 Main w
Allardice R A & Co, furniture manfrs, 86 Merrick
Allardice R A, (R A Allardice & Co) bds St Nicholas hotel
Allardice T C, cabinetmaker, bds Commercial hotel
Allcock Henry, brickmaker, 197 Main w
Allingham Robt, laborer, 291 King w
Allins Eli, whitewasher, Pearl s
Allison Mrs B, (wid William) 10 Liberty
Allison Caleb, bartender, 51 Stuart w
Allison House, W Y Allison, propr, 51 Stuart w
Allison Oliver, moulder, bds 53 Gore
Allison Thomas, machinist, Ferguson ave n
Allison Wm Y, propr Allison House, 51 Stuart w
Alliss Joseph J, laborer, 106 Simcoe e
Almas Adam, laborer, 50½ Hunter e
Almas A E, barber, 50½ Hunter e
Almas Charles, barber, Walnut n, h 15½ Hunter e
Almas H F, barber, bds 50½ Hunter e
Almas John, farmer, 47½ Catharine s
Almond John, clerk, 200 King w

Almond Mrs Mary, (wid David) dairy, 200 King w

All Saints' Church, Queen cor King

Ambrose Mrs Alexander, 199 Hughson n

Ambrose A W, barrister, 199 Hughson n

Ambrose Mrs Charles, 27 Maria

Ambrose Miss E, 47 Walnut s

Ambrose E H, law student, 20 Augusta

Ambrose E S, clerk Bank of Hamilton, 27 Maria

Ambrose Robert S, music teacher, 20 Augusta

Ambrose Walter, salesman, 92 Bay s

Ambrose W J, clerk, bds 27 Maria

American Bracket Co, John N Barnard, manager, 145 King w

American Express Co, J P Johnson, agent, 18 James s

American Hotel, F W Bearman, propr, King cor Charles

American M E Church, Rev J B Roberts, pastor, 80 John n

American Nail Works Co, foot Queen n

Ames Jonathan, (L D Sawyer & Co) 6 West ave s

Amess James, contractor, 125 King e

Amess Samuel, carpenter, 125 King e

Amey Thomas, carpenter, 123 Rebecca

Amor Albert, laborer, bds 14 Victoria ave s

Amor Mrs Isabella (wid David) bds Robinson

Amor James, undertaker, 3 Queen s

Amor Mrs Nancy, (wid John) 22 Guise

Amor Wm, excise officer, 9 Queen n

Amos James S, 48 Catharine n

Amos Miss L, dressmaker, Thomas C Watkins, 30 King e, h 109 Hughson n

Amos Robert, salesman, 155 Bay n

Anchor Steamship Line, George McKeand, agent, 57 James n

Ancient Order United Workmen Hall, 14 McNab s

Anders John, brushmaker, 12 Steven

Anderson A A, manager Hamilton and Dundas street railway, hd Queen s

Anderson A C, (A C Anderson & Co) h 94 Catharine n

Anderson A C & Co, wh jewelers, 55 King e

Anderson Alex, blacksmith, 25 Florence

Anderson Alex, 42 Hunter w

Anderson Alexander, laborer, 39 John n

Anderson Mrs Annie (wid Gilbert) 180 Napier

Anderson & Bates, (J N Anderson, M D, F DeWitt Bates, M D, oculists and aurists, 34 James n *see card*

Anderson Charles, stonecutter, Aikman's ave

Anderson David, machinist, bds 127 John n

Anderson George, carpenter, 15 Murray e

Anderson George, carpenter, 69 Queen n

Anderson Henry, machinist, Herkimer

Anderson James, laborer, 99 Victoria ave n

Anderson James, M D, 192 Macnab n

Anderson James, carpenter, 69 Vine

Andrews James, mech supt, Ontario Cotton Mills, 264 Macnab n

Anderson James, laborer, Brock w
Anderson James, stonecutter, 4 Emerald n
Anderson James, blacksmith, 43 West ave n
Anderson J E, com traveler, 7 O'Reilly
Anderson John, bookkeeper, 192 McNab n
Anderson John sr, 24 Caroline n
Anderson John jr, carpenter, 24 Caroline n
Anderson John, laborer, 283 Hughson n
Anderson John, waiter, 90 Rebecca
Anderson John F, moulder, 113 Hess n
Anderson J N, M D, (Anderson & Bates) 34 James n, res Burlington
Anderson Peter, laborer, 32 Strachan e
Anderson Robert, bookkeeper, 17 Pearl s
Anderson Mrs Samuel, 58 East ave n
Anderson Thomas, machinist, 33 Lower Cathcart
Anderson Thomas, baker, 170 Macnab n
Anderson Walter, bookkeeper, 114 Market
Anderson William, crimper, 7 O'Reilly
Anderson William, pumpmaker, 17 Liberty
Anderson Wm, machinist, 97 Victoria ave n
Anderson W J, butcher, James st market, h King e
Andrew James, printer, 99 Wellington n
Andrew Robert, spinner, 99 Picton e
Andrews A W, laborer, 62 Catharine s
Andrews Mrs Eliza, (wid John) 75 Peter
Andrews Mrs G, 315 Hughson n
Andrews James, carpenter, 264 Macnab n
Andrews Mrs Jessie, (wid Edward) 12 Murray e
Andrup Hans, shoemaker, 26 Tisdale
Angle Job, laborer, 354 King e
Angle Samuel, laborer, 326 King e
Angold Harry, machinist, 66 East ave n
Angus Andrew, (Robert Evans & Co) h 42 Duke
Angus H R, salesman, 36 Jackson w
Angus James jr, hats and furs, 24 King w, h 44 Duke
Angus James sr, 42 Duke
Angus John, patternmaker, 112 Bay n
Angus Robert, 36 Jackson w
Angus Wm, tinsmith, 64 Hess n
Angus Wm, letter carrier, St Paul's cottage, James s
Anketell Mrs Margaret, 89 Young
Annick Mrs Mary Ann (wid Jacob) rr 106 McNab n
Anson Alfred, cigarmaker, 106 Ferguson ave n
Anstey Charles, letter carrier, 31 Alanson
Anstey Wm, shoemaker, 103 Victoria ave n
Anstey W W, plumber, 100 John n
Ante Otto, watchmaker, bds 97 Hess n
Anthony A J, plasterer, 137 Picton e
Antunovich Pietro, mariner, bds 304 James n
Appleby Edward, stove mounter, Hannah w
Applegarth Miss Elizabeth, bds 63 Wellington s
Applegate Thomas, laborer, 156 Hughson n
Appelgate Thomas sr, cabdriver, 170 Hughson n

Appleton Thomas, gardener, 88 Wilson
Appleton Thomas, pawnbroker, 89 James n
Appleyard John, machinist, rr 103 Catharine n
Arcade Coffee Room, (Chas Lambert, manager), 20 Arcade
Archer G C, cutter, bds Commercial hotel
Archibald John, fitter, bds 48 Murray w
Archibald Robert, foreman GTR, 48 Murray w
Archibald Robert, brakesman, 226 Macnab n
ArchibaldThos,laborer,105 Maria
Argyll Terrace, 14-18 Herkimer
Arkell Arthur, miller, 111 Macnab n
Arland & Bro, (Henry and Patrick) boots and shoes, 62 King e, h 67 Park n
Arland Michael, 119 Bay n
Arless Mrs Henrietta, confectioner, 103 John s
Armtrust Lincoln, clerk, 105 King w
Armitage Mrs Ann, (wid James) 38 Strachan e
Armitage Mrs Harriet, (wid George) 11 Spring
Armitage Mrs Mary (wid Wm) dressmaker, 35 Bay n
Armitage Thomas, machinist, 129 Emerald n
Armour John, 79 Jackson w
Armour Robert, civil engineer, 79 Jackson w
Armstrong Albert, bartender, 1-3 Cannon e
Armstrong Mrs Arthur, 70 Ferguson ave
Armstrong Charles, cartage agent, N & N W R, 33 James n, h Wentworth s
Armstrong Charles, cigarmaker, h 3 Cannon e
Armstrong Edward, clerk Dominion hotel
Armstrong Edward, laborer, 175 Mary
Armstrong Fergus, station master G T R, 16 Park s
Armstrong George, watchmaker, bds 36 Bay n
Armstrong Geo H, clerk P O 109 Main w
Armstrong Mrs Hannah A (wid Geo) 109 Main w
Armstrong & Haw, (Thos Armstrong, Lawrence Haw) proprs Dominion hotel, 80 King w
Armstrong Henry, bookkeeper, h mountain top
Armstrong Isaac, grain buyer, 95 Market
Armstrong James, painter, 6 Liberty
Armstrong James, plumber, 58 Robinson
Armstrong J J, foreman, 104 Wellington s
Armstrong John sr, 36 Bay n
Armstrong John, plumber, 36 Bay n
Armstrong John, baker, bds Victoria hotel
Armstrong John, printer, 261 King Wm
Armstrong John, carpenter, 7 Walnut n
Armstrong Joseph, grain buyer, bds 95 Market
Armstrong Mrs, 319 Macnab n
Armstrong Matthew, 49 Robinson
Armstrong Nelson, 36 Bay n
Armstrong Peter, wagon maker, 33 Mary, h 22 Catharine n
Armstrong Robert, 153 West ave n
Armstrong Miss Sarah, 130 Park n
Armstrong Thomas, (Armstrong & Haw) 80 King w
Armstrong Walter, painter, 194 John n

Armstrong Wm, com traveler, 32 George
Armstrong Wm, foreman cotton mills, bds 175 Mary
Armstrong William, laborer, 20 Florence
Armstrong William, tailor, 290 York
Arnett Ed, painter, bds 33 Peter
Arnett Fred, tailor, 18 Chisholm
Arnett Joseph, painter, Greig
Arnold Mrs Caroline (wid Francis) 164 James n
Arnold Stanley, upholsterer, 87 Lower Cathcart
Arnold Wm, polisher, 68 Wilson
Arnott Mrs Wm, Concession
Arrol James, moulder, 309 Macnab n
Arrol Robert, second hand dealer, 47 York
Arthur C, butcher, King e
Arthur Humphrey M, rr 81 Caroline n
Arthur John, polisher, 60 Victoria ave n
Arthur John, porter, Wentworth n
Arthur Mrs Mary (wid John) 347 James n
Arthur Samuel, builder, 16 Elgin
Arthur Thomas, carpenter, 250 King e
Arthur James, laborer, 20 Mary
Ashbaugh Fred A, com traveler, 91 Napier
Ashbaugh R R, Central hotel, 135 King e
Ashburn Wm, laborer, 56 Tom
Ashby George, cabinetmaker, 115 John s
Ashby Wm, foreman gas works, 108 Bay n
Ashton Walter, clerk, bds 41 John n
Ashton Wm A, nailer, part 33 Locomotive
Askew Geo, shoemaker, 257 Mary
Aspell William, clerk, 118 Maria
Astels J W, foreman W Silver jr, bds 48 James n
Astle Samuel, machinist, 32 Railway
Asylum for the Insane, Bidwell Way, bursar, mountain top
Atkin Samuel, clerk, 28 Victoria ave n
Atkins Isaac, sailor, 16 Margaret
Atkins J H, barber, 8 Hunter e
Atkinson Bros (W G and W H) manfr stationers, 35 King e and 66 James n
Atkinson C C S, bds Commercial hotel
Atkinson John, com traveler, bds 34 Bay s
Atkinson Joseph, painter, 32 Wilson
Atkinson Richard, shoemaker, 101 Wellington, h 124 West ave n
Atkinson Mrs Susan (wid John) 44 Catharine n
Atkinson Wm, 3 Bay s
Atkinson W G (Atkinson Bros) h 3 Bay s
Atkinson W H (Atkinson Bros) h 45 Charles
Atlantic House, A Ruthven, propr, 29 McNab n
Attle John, tinsmith, 90 Florence
Attwood M W & Son (M W and J A) watchmakers, 88 King w h 44 Pearl
Atwell Harry, porter, Burlington n
Audette David, clerk, 5 Ferrie e
Audett Isaiah, blacksmith, 38 Barton e
Audette Joshua, laborer, 23 Inchbury s
Audley Mrs Helen, bds 8 Locke s
Auld Wm, watchman, 184 Jackson w
Austin Edward H, carpenter, 198 Emerald n
Austin James, blacksmith, 9 Robert e

Austin Peter, carpenter, Murray e
Austin Thos B S, letter carrier, 84 Emerald n
Avis Richard, laborer, Queen s
Awtey Arthur, shipper, 274 King e
Axford George, butcher, 149 Wilson
Ayers Wm, carpenter, 179 Emerald n
Aylett Samuel, gardener, 77 Caroline s
Aylwin Mrs Fanny T (wid Horace) 24 Macnab s
Aylwin H C, clerk, 24 Macnab s
Aynsley Joseph J, green grocer, 153 King e
Babb James, melter, 69 Catharine n
Backus Mrs Nora, r 256 Macnab n
Backus Thomas, shoemaker, 97 John s
Baddams William, laborer, 154 Emerald n
Badeau Joseph, jr, shoemaker, 101 Ferrie e
Badeau Napoleon, shoemaker, 77 East ave n
Badger James, shoemaker, 37 Crooks
Baghot Chas, com traveler, Ray s
Baghot Mrs Hannah (wid Samuel P) 46 Hess n
Bagnall Robert, 129 Wellington n
Bagwell Geo M, supt job dept *Times*, 29 Robinson
Bagwell J B, 21 Park n
Baikie Charles. barber, bds 124 Cannon e.
Baikie Mrs E, dyer, 132 McNab n
Baillie John, bookkeeper, 82 Merrick
Baillie John, salesman, 56 Walnut s
Baillie J E S, letter carrier, P O
Bailey Mrs Annie (wid Henry) 162 Market
Bailey Mrs Anne (wid Henry) 74 Peter
Bailey Mrs. Charlotte, 47 Peter
Bailey George, lamplighter, 90 Emerald n
Bailey George M, restauranteur, 32 Merrick
Bailey John, market gardener, Wentworth n
Bailey Samuel, carpenter, Bruce
Bailey Thomas, carpenter, 44 East ave n
Bailey Walter, 141 Main w
Bailey Wm G, miller, 52 Hunter w
Bain Alex, gardener, 20 Victoria ave n
Bain Alex, cabman, 214 Main e
Bain Andrew, salesman, 214 Main e
Bain & Colville, machinists, Mary cor Cannon
Bain James (Bain & Colville) h 151 West ave n
Bain James, grocer, 255 York
Bain John, cabman, bds 214 Main e
Bain Mrs Margaret (wid Patrick) 183 Main e
Bainbridge John, policeman, bds 60 James s
Baine Henry, grocer, 60 Cherry
Baine John, laborer, 201 Mary
Baine Mrs M (wid Thos) 84 King w
Baine Mrs Margaret, 185 Main e
Baine T J, propr west end music store, 84 King w, h 51 Wellington s
Baine Thos, cellarman, bds 143 Bay n
Baine Thos H, hotel, 60 Cherry
Baines James, machinist 40 Magill
Baines Wm F, foreman G T R, 40 Magill
Baird A L, law student, 68 Catharine s
Baird C C, grocer, 39 Wellington n, h 34 Mary
Baker A E, jeweler, bds 14 Blythe

Baker Alfred H, watchmaker, 64 Herkimer
Baker Alfred, laborer, 318 King w
Baker Edward (J D Pennington & Co) cor Kelly and Wellington
Baker Edward J, foreman, 90 Park n
Baker Geo, laborer, 318 King w
Baker Frank, laborer, 7 Devonport
Baker Hugh C, manager Ontario department Bell Telephone Co, 1 Hughson s, h 3 Herkimer
Baker H C, (Standard Whip Co) 23 Spring
Baker James, 55 Napier
Baker John, laborer, 154 Hughson n
Baker J P, night station master, bds 44 Murray w
Baker Josiah, carpenter, 14 Blythe
Baker Ralph, salesman, 14 Blythe
Baker Robert, laborer, r 256 Macnab n
Baker Rev Thos, Congregationalist, 3 Bold
Baker Thomas, baker, 170 O'Reilly
Baker Thos, engine cleaner, 7 Devonport
Baker T W, clerk, Main w
Baker Stephen, laborer, 127 Rebecca
Baker Wm, supt Hamilton Street Railway, 196 Bay n
Baker Wm, shoemaker, bds 97 John s
Baker Wm, laborer, 318 King w
Baker W C, commission agent, 26 James s
Balch Thomas, machinist, 5 Picton w
Bale James, bookkeeper, 83 Emerald n
Bale Joseph, shipper, 130 Victoria ave n
Bale Thomas, machinist, 72 Hughson n
Bale Thomas, com traveller, 83 Emerald n
Bale Thomas, mason, 58 Hughson n
Bale Walter, bookkeeper, 114 Victoria ave n
Balfour James, architect and building superintendent, Wentworth Chambers, 25 James s, h Hannah w, nr Bay
Balfour Peter, city assessor, Hannah w of Bay
Balfour St Clair (Brown Balfour & Co) h 40 Duke
Ball Fred, moulder, 82 Lock n
Ball Robert, laborer, 310 Hughson n
Ball Wm, baker, 84 Park n
Ballantine Wm, laborer, 102 Bold
Ballantyne Thomas, plumber, 52 and 23½ York
Ballentine Adam (Adam Ballentine & Bros) 119 John s
Ballentine Adam & Bros, grocers, 115 John s
Ballentine A L (Adam Ballentine & Bros) 119 John s
Ballentine R B (Adam Ballentine & Bros) 119 John s
Ballard W H, inspector public schools, 241 King w
Balmer Stephen, laborer, 41 Peter
Bampfylde Chas H, manager Dundurn Park, 62 Main w
Bampfylde Charles H, salesman, 39 Bay s
Bampfylde John P, agent, 38 Victoria ave n
Bampfylde Robt J, com traveler, 62 Main w
Bamrick John, laborer, 24 Mulberry
Bangarth William, confectioner, 14 York
Bank of British North America, D G McGregor, manager, 5 King e

Bank of Commerce, E Mitchell, manager, King, cor Hughson

Bank Federal, J M Burns, manager, 2 James s

Bank of Hamilton, E A Colquhoun, cashier. 17-19 King w

Bank Merchants', J S Meredith, manager, King cor John

Bank of Montreal, J N Travers, manager, James cor Main

Bank Stinson, A H Moore, manager, 10 Hughson n

Bankes Wm, artist, 15 Inchbury n

Bankier P M, law student, Ham Prov and Loan Chambers

Banks Mrs Catharine (wid John) bds 145 Duke

Banks Louis, laborer, 145 Duke

Baptist Church (Colored) 106 Macnab n

Baptist Missions, Herkimer and Wentworth n

Barber A N, 55 Emerald s

Barber Bristol, brickmaker, 317 King w

Barber B F, clerk P O, 14 Augusta

Barber Wm, gardener, 90 Queen s

Barclay Mrs Ann (wid John) 45 Hannah e

Barcley Wm, carpenter, Clark ave

Barclay Wm, piano maker, 75 Wellington s

Bard Thomas, glassblower, 283 James n

Bardwell Jas, machinist, 51 Ray s

Barker Daniel, carpenter, 57 Burlington w

Barker Hiram (Barker & McBrien) h 25 Cherry

Barker Holten, carter, 357 James n

Barker James, fruit dealer, 83½ John s

Barker John P, clerk G T R, 20 Picton e

Barker & McBrien (Hiram Barker, David McBrien) painters, 33 James s

Barker Robe.t, laborer, 15 Macauley w

Barker Robert, woodworker, 195 Wellington n

Barker Samuel, general manager N & N W R, h Bellevue, hd John s

Barker Wm R, fireman, 144 Jackson w

Barlow Charles, foreman, 76 Catharine s

Barlow George, clerk, 76 Catharine s

Barlow John, laborer, 245 York

Barnard Alfred, bookeeeper, 181 Main w

Barnard Henry, merchant, 110 Catharine s

Barnard James T, sec treas Hart Emery Wheel Co, 1 West ave s

Barnard John N, manager American Bracket Co, 19 Locke s

Barnard P B, staple and fancy dry goods, 36 King w, h 229 King w

Barnard Robert, laborer, bds 44 Catharine n

Barnes Mrs A (wid Thomas) 31 Mary

Barnes C W (W C Barnes & Son) h 146 King William

Barnes & Haskins, wine merchants, 7 Arcade

Barnes Henry, brass moulder, 71 Market

Barnes John, livery stable, 21 Hughson n, h 35 Lower Cathcart

Barnes Thomas, Main e

Barnes W C (W C Barnes & Son, h 146 King Wm

Barnes W C & Son (Barnes W C, C W Barnes) stained glass works. 22 Hughson n

Barnfather W C, engineer, 92 Barton e

Barnfather D, cigar maker, 92 Barton e
Barnhart Charles, barber, 130½ Macnab n
OFFICE 2
Barr Andrew, butcher, 330 King Wm
Barr Mrs Barbara (wid Peter) 133 Ferguson ave
Barr Miss Eliza, 124 Jackson e
Barr George, carpenter, 52 West ave n
Barr G D, salesman, 50 Hannah w
Barr Geo, vice-pres Reid & Barr manuf Co, h 34 Catharine n
Barr John, clerk, bds 88 Rebecca
Barr John A (John A Barr & Co) h 38 Victoria ave s
Barr John A & Co, chemists and druggists, York cor Macnab
Barr Lettlelus B, 20 Ray n
Barr Mrs M, 317 James n
Barr Wm, 188 Main e
Barr Wilson, clerk G T R, 88 Rebecca
Barrett Charles, tailor, bds 53 Park n
Barrett Daniel, laborer, 124 Maria
Barrett Mrs Elizabeth (wid Wm) 52 Robert
Barrett Mrs Ellen (wid Richard) 68 Vine
Barrett Patrick, tinsmith, 143 Catharine n
Barrett Robert, laborer, 83 Young
Barrett Robert, machinist, 143 Catharine n
Barrett Thomas, laborer, 85 Robert e
Barrett T J, excise officer, bds 44 Main w
Barrett Wm, painter, 126 James n
Barringer Wm, 86 Rebecca
Barron Alex, grocer, 65 Pearl n
Barron James, policeman, 79 John n
Barry Mrs Daniel, Rob Roy hotel, 89 John s
Barrow Ernest, surveyor, Wilson e of Wentworth
Barry James, laborer, 201 Catharine n
Barry James, freight checker, bds 156 Mary
Barry John, barrister, 75 Herkimer
Barry John, painter, 53 Hannah e
Barry Joseph, artist, 49 Augusta
Barry Samuel, traveler, bds 62 Cannon e
Bartholomew James, moulder, 185 Hughson n
Bartle James, lamplighter, 43 Allison
Bartlett Cameron, accountant Bank of Hamilton, 117 Macnab s
Bartmann Adam, tailor, 3 O'Reilly
Bartmann George, tailor, Walnut s, cor King, h 77 Jackson e
Bartmann G W, cutter, 84 Wellington s
Barton David, bookkeeper, 21 Young
Barton George M, barrister. 4 James n, res Dundas *see card*
Barton King, law student, res Dundas
Barton Terrace, e s Wellington nr Barton
Basquel John, tobacco roller, 174 Rebecca
Basquel Michael, moulder, 174 Rebecca
Bassett H D, repairer of sewing machines, 99 King e
Bastien Louis H, boat builder, 267 Bay n
Bastien H L, boat builder, 265 Bay n
Bastedo Walter, furrier, 156 Cannon e
Bateman E W, baker and confectioner, 200 King e, h 27 Victoria ave n
Bateman Fred, laborer, 160 Hunter

Bateman Patrick S, blacksmith, 33 York, h 71 Wellington s
Bateman Wm, baker, 78 Queen s
Bateman Wm, laborer, 94 Florence
Bates Alfred, carpenter, 270 Mary
Bates David, teamster, 92 George
Bates Edward, upholsterer, 136 and 138 King w
Bates F DeWitt, M D, (Anderson & Bates) 34 James n, res Burlington
Bates James, clerk, 28 Gore
Bates Mrs Mary (wid James) 28 Gore
Bates Philo D, gardener, Wentworth n
Bates Thomas P, clerk, 144 Wellington n
Batstone John, baker, 185 Emerald n
Battershinn Mrs Sarah (wid John) bds 17 Margaret
Batterton Richard, stonemason, 6 Locomotive
Battram E, fruiterer, 122½ King e
Battram H S, clerk, 74 Wellington n
Battram Sylvester, shoemaker, 18 West ave n
Batty Robert, moulder, 104 Simcoe e
Batzner William, teamster, 35 Macauley w
Bauer Albert, artist, 12 Main e
Bauer Mrs Henry, wine vaults, 14 Main e
Bauer James, laborer, bds 65 Park n
Bauer J M, proprietor Walker House, king, cor Ferguson ave
Bauer Mrs Margaret (wid Michael) 174 Napier
Bauman J W, music teacher, bds Commercial hotel
Baxter And B, butcher, 56 Caroline s, h 96 Bold
Baxter George, teamster, 83 Bold
Baxter James, teamster, 96 Bold
Baxter Richard, clerk, 16 Colborne
Baxter Thomas, wire worker, 169 King e
Baxter Wm, tailor, 132 Victoria ave n
Bawden Aaron, brickmaker, Canada
Bawden Harry, crystal palace view hotel, cor Peter and Locke
Bawden John, brickmaker, 80 Canada
Bawden Mrs Margaret (wid John) Peter cor Locke
Bayley John, blacksmith, 114 Picton e
Baylie Wm, laborer, 70 Lower Cathcart
Baylis Alfred, grocer, Copp's block, King e
Baylis John, gardener, 46 Hannah e
Bayne James, machinist, bds 25 Queen n
Bayne John, moulder, 158 Napier
Bayne Peter, carpenter, 25 Queen
Bazzard Geo, R R agt, 33 King w
Beach George, com traveler, 91 Hunter w
Beadmore Thomas, brass finisher, 37 Chisholm
Beal John, baker, 60 Maria
Beale Thos, laborer, 26 Peter
Beam Frederick, tailor, 80 Main e
Beard Edwin, laborer, 29 Wellington n
Beardwell James, carpenter, Tiffany
Beare Henry, laborer, 55 Catharine n
Beare Josiah, moulder, 72 Maria
Beare William, milk driver, 261 James n
Bearman F W, American hotel, King cor Charles
Beasley M C, conductor N W R, 103 Main e
Beasley Thomas, city clerk, Main e

Beasley Thos, conductor, 76 Elgin
Beasley R S, 103 Main e
Beaton Mrs Hortense (wid Donald J) 58 Catharine s
Beattie John A, salesman, 31 Robinson
Beatty A O M, teller Federal bank
Beatty Edward, laborer, 244 York
Beatty Charles, customs broker, 235 Macnab n
Beatty John, melter, 70 West ave n
Beatty Oliver, hotel, 300 James n
Beatty Oliver, jr, clerk P O, 300 James n
Beatty Thos, laborer, 111 Jackson e
Beatty Thomas, boiler maker, 300 Hughson n
Beatty William, engineer, 141 Ferguson ave
Beauford John, carpenter, 128 Park n
Beaumert Fred, hatter, 198 Barton e
Beaver George, Western hotel, 225-7 York
Beavers Thomas, laborer, 40 Macauley w
Beck Mrs Eliza (wid George) 22 Ray n
Becker George, jeweler, bds 169 King Wm
Becker Henry, laborer, 331 Catharine n
Beckerson Elijah, laborer, 55 Hess n
Beckerson John, laborer, 16 Mill
Beckerson Matthew, teamster, 48½ Walnut s
Beckerson Richard, laborer, 178 York
Beckett H C com traveler, 134 Hughson n
Beckett J & G, flour and feed, 22 Macnab n, h 46 West ave
Buckingham Edward, laborer, 43 Little William
Beckman John, laborer, r 281 King w
Beddie Alex, stonecutter, 156 West ave n
Beddoe Joseph, shoemaker, 11 Elgin
Beddoe Thomas D, manager Ham Forging Co, 164 Main w
Bedlington Henry, com traveler, 3 Victoria ave n
Bedwell Dan'l A, cutter, 2 Hilton
Beedom Simon, laborer, 113 Jackson e
Beer Francis, butcher, 123 King e
Beer J S, butcher, Burlington n
Beer Isaaiah, contractor, 35 Murray e
Beeston Samuel, laborer, 31 Kelly
Begg Andrew, laborer, 83 East ave n
Begg Geo, clerk, 130 King Wm
Beggs Geo, bartender, King Wm
Begley Alex, laborer, 113 Napier
Begley James, laborer, 286 Macnab n
Begley Mrs M G (wid Andrew) 9 Strachan e
Begley Morris, conductor, Aikman's ave
Behen Jeremiah, glassblower, 7 Ferrie e
Belau Anthony, tailor, 81 Caroline s
Belknap C M, lumber merchant, 17 Colborne
Belnap William H, tinsmith, 81 Catharine n
Bell Adam, tailor, 22 Cannon w
Bell Mrs Agnes (wid Matthew) 57 Wilson
Bell Alex, laborer, 267 York
Bell Edward, shoemaker, 230 Cannon
Bell Fred, shoemaker, 161 Wellington n
Bell George F, law student, 100 Market
Bell George M, machinists, 20 Macnab n, h 51 Ray s

Bell Mrs Hannah (wid John) 80 Catharine s
Bell Miss I, teacher, Coll Inst Catharine s
Bell John, machinist, Maple
Bell Mrs Nathaniel, 67 Colborne
Bell Samuel (McNair & Bell) h 29 East ave n
Bell Telephone Co, city office 1 Hughson s, K J Dunstan, agent
Bell Telephone Co, (Ontario department) 1 Hughson s, Hugh C Baker, manager
Bell Thomas, engine driver G T R, bds 32 Locomotive
Bell Thomas S, civil engineer, 100 Market
Bell William, barrister, Wentworth Chambers 25 James s, h hd Stinson s
Bell Wm, machinist, 117 Robinson
Belleville Evangelist, laborer, Poulette
Bellhouse Mrs Agnes (wid Wm) 90 James s
Bellhouse P M, purser, 90 James s
Bellhouse W A, accountant Merchant's bank, 115 Catharine s
Belling Charles, 42 Peter
Belling George W, carpenter, 274½ Hughson n
Belling James, manfacturing jeweler 21 York, h 42 Peter
Belling Thos, jeweler, 42 Peter
Belz Henry, tailor, 33 John s, h 20 Upper Cathcart
Belz Lawrence, laborer, 20 Upper Cathcart
Benner Richard, com merchant and ins agent, 7 Main e, h 6 Main e
Bennett Charles, 13 Mulberry
Bennett F, messenger Bank of Hamilton
Bennett George, carriage trimmer, bds 70 Hughson s
Bennett Henry, foreman Tuckett's, 20 Napier
Bennett Henry, printer, 60 East ave n
Bennett, J J, engineer, 165 West ave n
Bennett Joseph, laborer, bds 70 Hughson s
Bennett Louis, waiter, 51 Mary
Bennett Patrick, laborer, 332 Hughson n
Bennett Robert, blacksmith, 48 Kelly
Bennett Robert, moulder, 166 Catharine n
Bennett Samuel woodturner, 3 George
Bennett Samuel, brassfinisher, 268 Bay n
Bennetto Mrs Mary (wid John) 39 Lower Cathcart
Bentis Mrs Caroline (wid John) 80 Locke n
Benton Mrs Amy (wid John) 99 Maria
Berchell W D, stockkeeper, bds 62 Cannon e
Bergmann Rev R (Roman Catholic) 25 Sheaffe
Bernard Isaac, tanner, 231 Ferrie e
Berrie W A C, clerk Royal hotel
Berry Charles, carpenter, 39 Chisholm
Berry James, grocer, 32-4 Guise
Berry John, 56 Guise
Berry Philip, teamster, 56 Guise
Berry Samuel, carpenter, 370 John n
Berry William, harness maker, 24 Aurora
Berryman Albert, telegraph operator G T R, 147 Bay n
Berryman James, shoemaker, 195 Bay n
Berryman Robert, wool and com merchant 1 Market, h 122 Catherine s
Berryman William J, laborer, 93 Tiffany
Bertram Jas, tobacco worker, Pine

JOHN FINAGIN,

MERCHANT TAILOR,

The Choicest in Foreign and Home Goods from the best available markets.

Gents' Furnishings of the finest quality always on hand

140 KING STREET EAST,

Copp's Block, Hamilton, Ont.

Sign of "THE LION." Inspection Invited.

GOOD WORK. PRICES LOW.

EXCELSIOR PRINTING HOUSE

JAS. A. HARVEY, PROP.,

26 MERRICK ST., HAMILTON, ONT.

ALBERT BRUNKE,

FURRIER

And Dealer in Hats, Caps, and Furs.

All kinds of Furs made to order and neatly altered and repaired.

30 and 32 York St. HAMILTON, ONT.

Best Alfred, gardener, 140 Duke
Best A C, salesman, 145 Hunter w
Best James, laborer, r 205 Catharine n
Best Joseph, porter, 141 Main w
Best Thomas, laborer, r 205 Catharine n
Best Thomas N, 78 Market
Betecone Donald S, com traveler, 45 Walnut s
Betcone William, 45 Walnut s
Bethune Edward, bookkeeper, 63 Catharine n
Bethell Charles, 168 Emerald n
Bettles Thos, caretaker, Arcade
Betts Joseph, bookkeeper, 80 Market
Betzner William, laborer, 288 Macnab n
Beulah Suburb, mountain foot, south Concession
Bevan Charles, laborer, Maple
Beveridge John, laborer, 229 Ferrie e
Beveridge John, carpenter, New
Bevis William, machinist, 54 Steven
Bews Bros, (W D and John T) merchant tailors, 74 King e, h 25 Victoria ave n
Bews James, shipper, 239 Barton e
Bews W H, news agent, bds 52 Hunter e
Bews William, 52 Hunter e
Bewicke David, printer, 22 Macnab s
Bezanson E D, photoghapher, 42 James n
Bible George, 188 John n
Bible Robt, 34 Ray s
Bickell D, com traveler Orr, Harvey & Co
Bickle John, carpenter, 5 Inchbury s
Bickle John W, grocery broker, 11 Main e, h 37 Bold
Bicknell James (Fuller, Nesbitt & Bicknell) h 31 Nelson ave
Bicknell Jas sr, accountant, 31 Nelson ave
Bigelow R O, builder, 79½ John n
Biggar A C, carpenter, bds Victoria hotel
Biggar George, M D, 206 King e
Biggar S D, law student, 68 Catharine s
Biggar W A, bartender, Franklin House
Bigley Jas, laborer, 95 Simcoe e
Biglow John J, grocer, 48 York
Bilakewitz Joseph, wagon maker, bds 121 Jackson w
Billings John, 3 Jackson w
Billings W L, M D, Maple ave
Billington G T, farmer, Wentworth s
Billington John, shoemaker, 97 York
Bilton George, soda water manufacturer, 87 Mary
Bilton Geo & Co (Geo and W) soda water manufacturers, 62 Cannon e
Bilton Mrs Matilda, 62 Cannon e
Bilton Wm, soda water manufacturer, 62 Cannon e
Bingham G S, M D, King cor Ferguson ave
Bingham John, laborer, 103 Maria
Binkley John, farmer, 2 Crooks
Binkley Lewis E, bookkeeper, 2 Crooks
Binnington Robt, laborer, 6 Inchbury n
Bird John, machinist, 139 John n
Birely E L, clerk, 184 Main e
Birely G F (Reid Goering & Co) h 184 Main e
Birely Lewis D, 54 Charles
Birely Mrs N F, 184 Main e
Birkenthal Rev Dr Herman, Rabbi Jewish Synagogue, 27 Hannah e
Birkett Wm, sec treas Dundas Cotton Mills, 4½ Bay s

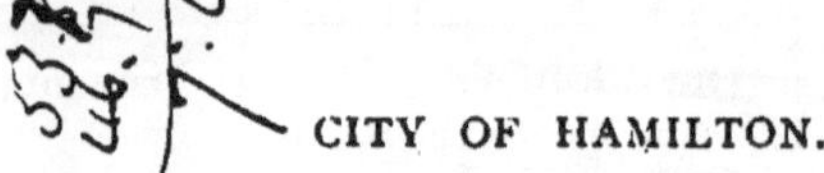

Birnie William, miller, 78 Hughson s

Birrel Michael, porter, 55½ Walnut s

Birrell Wm, foreman Farmers' Dairy Co, 70 Vine

Bisby G H (Long & Bisby) 54 John n

Bishop Chas, laborer, 82 Markland

Bishop J B, tinsmith, 30 King William

Bishop's Palace, Roman Catholic, 25 Sheaffe

Bismarck August, hotel keeper, 84 King e

Bissonnette Alfred, moulder, 143 Hughson n

Blaase Carl, hotel keepet 112 James n

Blachford Chas D (Blachford & Son) 47 King w

Blachford Mrs Elizabeth (Blachford & Son) 47 King w

Blachford & Son (Mrs E Blachford, Chas D Blachford) undertakers, 47 King w

Black Mrs Ann, 48 Cannon e

Black Charles, hardware, Copp's Block, King e, h 107 Main e

Black George (manager G N W Telegraph Co) h 41 East ave s

Black James, laborer, 374 Catharine n

Black James, conductor G T R, Barton w

Black John, brushmaker, 48 East ave n

Black John, butcher, cor Park and Barton

Black Thomas, cutter, A S Vail & Co

Blackbrough Wm J, carpenter, 41 Pearl s

Blackburn Charles, weaver, 383 John n

Blackburn Charles, carder, 251 Hughson n

Blackburn Thos, engine driver, G T R, 50 Inchbury n

Blackburn Wm, wheelright, 142 Barton e

Blackley David, accountant, 11 Main e, h 36 Victoria ave n

Blackman Chas, porter, 78 Locke n

Blackmore Fred, laborer, bds 1 Wood Market Square

Blackwitch Frank, laborer, 9 Sophia s

Blaicher P C, (R N Taylor & Co) h 108 Main w

Blain John, painter, 272 Macnab n

Blain William, laborer, 46 Ferrie e

Blair Alex, cigar maker, bds 31 Bay n

Blair Mrs Elizabeth (wid Samuel) 52 Caroline s

Blair J B, excise officer, bds Dominion hotel

Blair Robert, grocer, cor Wilson and Ferguson ave

Blair Wm, carpenter, 76 Victoria ave n

Blair Wm, 220 Main e

Blake George, laborer, 225 Cannon e

Blake Jas, grocer, n w cor Mary and Simcoe

Blake John, teamster, 29 Wood e

Blake Mrs, 13 Barton w

Blake Mrs Mary A, bds Duke

Blake Patrick, laborer, 13 Barton w

Blake William, butcher, James street market, h 44 Ferrie w

Blakeley John, salesman, 104 Victoria ave n

Blakeley Robert, watchman, 104 Victoria ave n

Blakeley Robert, salesman, 104 Victoria ave n

Blakeley Robert, ruler, 104 Victoria ave n

Blakely Wm, carpenter, 104 Victoria ave n

Blakely Wm J, policeman, 65 East ave n
Blakemore Arthur, brass finisher, 61 Hannah e
Blanchard Mrs Caroline (wid Josiah) 37 Robert
Blanchard Wm, 37 Robert
Bland Jonn H, barber, 16 Hughson n
Bland Robert, laborer, 22 Liberty
Bland RobtC,machinist,68Cherry
Blandford Henry, picture framer, 50 King e, h Wentworth cor Main
Blandford R, clerk, Mary cor Robert
Blankstein Henry, carpenter, 154 Duke
Blanney Mrs Robert, 45 Park n
Blasdell John W, carpenter, Locke s
Blatz Leo, tailor, 1 O'Reilly, h 81 Hannah e
Bleeze Henry, machinist, 201 John n
Blizzard James, laborer, 312 Macnab n
Bliss Henry C, patent medicines, 117 Catharine s
Blondin Moses, engineer, 351 Hughson n
Bloomer Andrew, laborer, 34 Picton e
Blowes Mrs Catharine, 364 James n
Blowes Isaac, laborer, 344 James n
Blowes Samuel, glassblower, 6 Wood e
Blue Henry, laborer, 33 George
Blumenstiel Isaac, (Blumenstiel & Labitzky) bds 34 King Wm
Blumenstiel Joseph, second hand dealer, 49 John s
Blumenstiel & Labitzky, cigar manufs, 114 John s
Board Geo S, blacksmith, 130 Jackson w
Board John E, tobacco roller, 31 Railway
Boardman George, 4 Park s
Boam A P, cabinet maker, 152 Mary
Bodden Edward, painter, 93 Ferrie e
Bodden Edward, painter, 97 Picton e
Bodden, W H, bricklayer, 129 Macauley e
Bodley W J, second-hand dealer, 34 York
Boggess James H, second-hand dealer, 28 York
Boggess Nathan, machinist, 173 East ave n
Boggess T, second-hand dealer, 19 King Wm, h 7 Upper Cathcart
Boice Mrs Wm, 50 John n
Boles Robert, laborer, 78 Caroline n
Boligan John C, grocer, Locke s corner Maine
Bolter Thos, salesman, bds 31 Bay n
Bolton Charles, carpenter, 199 John n
Bolton Richard, laborer, 109 Caroline n
Bolton Thomas, laborer, 38 Walnut s
Bolton Wm, carpenter, r 205 Catharine n
Bolton Wm, teamster, 348 Hughson n
Bolton Wm, tinsmith, 31 Catharine n
Bolus Edward, pattern maker, 42 Stuart e
Boneny Lewis, laborer, 112 Strachan e
Bowen Stephen, laborer, 114 Strachan e
Bond John, laborer, Herkimer
Bond Henry,teamster,358 John n
Bonds John, clerk P O, 96 Victoria ave s
Boniface Peter, tinsmith, 58 Lower Cathcart

Bonny H P, clerk, 308 King e
Booker Albert H, bookkeeper, bds 88 Jackson w
Booker Chas G, merchant tailor, 2 King William, h 88 Jackson w
Booker Henry, machinist, 304 Macnab n
Booker John, traveler, Wilson, e of Wentworth
Booker W D, sec treas Victoria Mutual Fire Insurance Co, h 88 Jackson w
Boond Arthur, foreman file works, 153 Main e
Booth Chas, heater, 153 Locke n
Booth Frank, bookkeeper, 54 Tisdale
Booth George, engine driver, bds 73 Stuart w
Booth John, porter, r 55 Lower Cathcart
Booth Patrick, shoemaker, 39 Young
Booth Robert, 179 East ave n
Boothby Henry, engrosser, hd Queen s
Boothman Frederick, mariner, 48 Burlington w
Boothman Capt Thomas, 49 Macauley w
Boreham Benjamin, laborer, 23½ Chisholm
Borland John, laborer, 8 Tiffany
Boswell Wm, gardener, Herkimer w of Garth
Bottle Thomas, 84 Hughson n
Botts Miss, dressmaker, 140 Main
Boult Alfred, fitter, r 71
Boulter Thomas, clerk, bds Temperance Dining Rooms
Bourne Arthur, telegraph operator, bds 75 Wellington n
Bourgue Charles, brushmaker, 174 Wilson
Boustead Edwin, commission agent, 9 King w
Bovaird James, carriage builder, 124 Wellington n
Bow Robert, tinsmith, 85 Hughson n
Bowden Thos, laborer, 136 Bay n
Bowditch Alfred, clerk, 28 Main w
Bowen Elijah, engineer, 289 Macnab n
Bowen James, tobacco roller, 86 Hess n
Bower Eric, shoemaker, 118 Emerald n
Bower John, lithographer, 29 Macnab s
Bowering & Pain (Robt Bowering, Albert Pain) butchers, 89 King w
Bowering Robt (Bowering & Pain) 89 King w
Bowers Mrs Margaret (wid Jonathan) 222 Hughson n
Bowes, Jamieson & Co (John G Bowes, James Jamieson) iron founders, King e, Tisdale and King Wm
Bowes John G (Bowes Jamieson & Co) h 40 East ave s
Bowes John, dentist, 9 James n, h 10 Park s
Bowes Samuel, machinist, 3 Evans
Bowes Miss Sarah, 142 Wellington n
Bowker Thos, fruiterer, 46½ York
Bowles Mrs, 330 Hughson n
Bowman Mrs Annie (wid Joseph C) bds 44 Jackson w
Bowman D B, 12 King Wm, h 46 Queen s
Bowman J W, salesman, 44 Jackson w
Bowman & Moore (Wm Bowman, J H Moore) hardware, 54 King e
Bowman Wm (Bowman & Moore) h 56 Hunter w
Bowron Addison, tinsmith, 52 Wellington n
Bowron Bolton, tinsmith, 53 Victoria ave n

Bowstead Edwin, broker, bds 95 Catharine n
Bowstead, Wm, sr, foreman D Moore & Co, 95 Catharine n
Bowstead William, pattern maker, 95 Catharine n
Boyd Alex, painter, 155 Cannon e
Boyd Andrew, laborer, 1 West ave n
Boyd C E, com traveler, Orr, Harvey & Co.
Boyd David, cooper, 27 Catharine n
Boyd Mrs Ellen, 5 Strachan w
Boyd Mrs Mary (wid Alex) 23 Barton e
Boyd James, plasterer, 3 West ave n
Boyd Robert, hatter, 155 Cannon e
Boyd Mrs Susan, 375 John n
Boyd Wm, fireman, 42 Sheaffe
Boyes Francis D, checker G T R, 33 Bay n
Boylan Wm, laborer, 41 Ray n
Boyle Arthur, druggist, 254 York
Boyle Mrs Ellen (wid Edward) 143 Park n
Boyle Hilda, agent, 43 Catharine n
Boyle Mrs Johanna (wid Timothy) 319 York
Boyle John, Dundurn hotel, 287, 289 York
Boyles Albert, shoemaker, 44 Hannah w
Boyne Julian, bds 5 Bold
Boys' Home, Stinson
Brace John, nailer, 64 Locomotive
Brace Joseph, shoemaker, 95 Walnut s
Bracken Michael, bricklayer, 3 Picton w
Bracken Michael, glassblower, 321 James n
Brackenbury Robert, 41 Hannah w
Brad George, lather, 159 Victoria ave n
Bradfield Charles W, salesman, Macnab n
Bradfield Mrs Hannah (wid Thos) 102-104 Bay n
Bradford Henry, laborer, 69 Park n
Bradley Mrs C, 55 Little Wm
Bradley John (Flatt & Bradley) h Catharine n
Bradley John, contractor, 5 Cherry
Bradley John, cabinet maker, 113 Macnab s
Bradley Thomas, butcher, 45 Little William
Bradley Wm, blacksmith, 298 King w
Bradshaw George, 93-5 York
Bradt Harry, plater, 78 Victoria ave n
Bradt Mrs Rhoda (wid Samuel) 78 Victoria ave n
Brady Michael, laborer, 40 Strachan e
Brady Patrick, laborer, 20 O'Reilly
Brady Thomas, coal inspector, 235 Hughson n
Bragg Wm, yardsman G W R, 221 Catharine n
Braid Alex (How & Braid) h 204 King w
Braid Henry, foreman, 77 Catharine s
Braid Henry, jr, shoemaker, 96 Emerald n
Braid W, com traveler, 98 James s
Braidwood William, foreman, 15 Wood w
Bramford William, plasterer, 38 Liberty
Brand George, laborer, 59 Florence
Brandon George, broommaker, 5 Evans
Brannigan George, brickmaker, Main w

Branston James, bricklayer, 48 Ray n

Brant George, foreman, bds 58 Vine

Branton Albert, porter, bds Golden's hotel.

Brass Benjamin, printer, 6 Hilton

Brass James, laborer, 127 Hess n

Brass Mrs Margaret (wid Peter) 8 Hilton

Brass Peter, architect and valuator, 52 Hunter w, h 49 Bay s *See card*

Brass William, carpenter, 92 Market

Bratt Charles, teamster, bds 28 Catharine

Braund Mrs Eliza, 46 Florence

Bray Mrs Elizabeth (wid Geo W) 221 Main w

Bray George, carriage trimmer, 221 Main w

Bray Josias, notary public, etc, 34 James n, h 10 Emerald s

Brayley & Dempster (Jas Brayley, C H Dempster), builders' and saddlers' hardware, 49 King Wm

Brayley James (Brayley & Dempster) h Barton

Brazier Henry, barber, 19 York

Breay Henry P, fireworks maker, 213 Main w

Brechin Hugh C, spinner, 89 East ave n

Bredon Edward R, music teacher, bds 84 Merrick

Breeze William, laborer, bds 35 Napier

Breheny Edward, shoemaker, 155 King e, h 7½ Walnut

Breheny John, shoemaker, 106 Jackson e

Bremen Steamship Line, Wm. Herman, agt, 16 James s

Bremner Charles, grocer, King cor Walnut, h 82 Herkimer

Bremner James, grocer, 248, 250 King w

Bremner Wm, contractor, 102 Jackson w

Brennan C J (J & C J Brennan, h 5 Market

Brennen H S (M Brennen & Sons) h 192 Main e

Brennan J & C J, family grocers, 5 Market

Brennan James, (J and C J Brennan) h 160 Napier

Brennen J S, (M Brennen & Sons) 34 Victoria ave n

Brennen Joseph S, carpenter, 34 Victoria ave n

Brennan John, carpenter, 208 Hughson n

Brennan John, machinist, 131 Barton e

Brennen Michael, (M Brennen & Sons) h 192 Main e

Brennen M & Sons, (Michael, H S and J S) sash, door and blind manfrs, 63-67 King Wm

Brennan Mrs Sarah (wid James) 75 John n

Brennan Wm, 76 Mary

Brend Henry, gilder, bds 177 Main w

Brend Wm, fitter, 177 Main w

Brenston William, telephonist, 44 Florence

Brent Geo W, clerk bank of Hamilton, bds 61 George

Brenton Sydney, polisher, 215 John n

Brenton William, glass moulder, 268 McNab n

Brethour & Co, dry goods and clothing, 188 and 190 King e

Brethour Joshua, (Brethour & Co) h 188 King e

Bretermitz Julius, tailor, 114 Napier

Brettingham George, fitter, 101 Caroline s

Brewster George, fireman, 144 Catharine n

Briar James, lather, 175 King Wm

Brick John, lithographer, 100 Jackson e
Brick Robert, machinist, 98 Jackson e
Brick Mrs Sarah (wid Timothy) 105 Hunter e
Brick Thomas, carter, 22 Cherry
Bridges John, laborer, 337 King w
Bridgman A, law student, bds 26 Main w
Bridgwood Mrs Charlotte, 71 Locomotive
Bridgwood Geo, wagon maker, 291 King w
Bridgewood James, fruit dealer, 33 Catharine s
Bridgwood Wm, laborer, 74 Ray s
Brierley Richard, druggist, 14 King e, h 83 Jackson w
Briers Thos, painter, 41 Markland
Briggs G C & Sons, (G C, W S and W A) patent medicines, 25 King w, h 1 Bay s
Briggs Mrs Hannah K (wid Edmund) bds 87½ Jackson w
Briggs Miss Mary Ann, 87½ Jackson w
Briggs Samuel, supt Hart Emery wheel co, h Park s, bet Duke and Robinson
Briggs Thomas, laborer, 103 Simcoe e
Bristol George E, (Lucas, Park & Co) h 51 Bay s
British America Assurance Co, fire and marine, A F Forbes, agent, 2 Merrick
British Empire Mutual Life Assurance Co, M A Pennington, agent, 30 James s
British & Foreign Marine Insurance Co, (Liverpool) W F Findlay, agent, 25 James s
Britt Charles, laborer, 133 Emerald n
Britt Edward, real estate and labor agency, 109½ King w
Britt Wm, cutter, 109½ King w
Britt William, shoemaker, 110 Macnab n
Britton Robt, machinist, 14 Sophia n
Brizzi Gustave, moulder, 22 East ave n
Broad George, carpenter, 60 Wellington n
Broadbent Geo, machinist, 191 Cannon e
Broadbent Hiram, agent, 141 King w
Broadbent Mathew, engineer, court house
Broadbent Thomas, machinery broker, 141 King w
Broadbent Thos and George, machinery brokers, 141 and 164 King w
Broadfield George E, (J S McMahon & Co) h Emerald cor Hunter
Broadley John, carpenter, 64 Hannah w
Broatch Wm D, engineer, 90 East ave n
Brock George, bottler, 75 Robert
Brock James, whipmaker, 33 Chisholm
Brockelsbey Rich, confectioner, 112 James n
Broderick M A, grocer, 164 John n
Broderick T, shoemaker, bds 153 John n
Brodie John, clerk, 189 Wellington n
Brohman Francis, brewer, 15 Harriet
Bromley Wm, barber, 77 Hunter w
Broomer Andrew, mariner, bds 9 Picton w
Brooks Mrs Charlotte (wid Lucien H) 76 Jackson w
Brooks Egbert H, brakeman, 135 Wellington n
Brooks George, boxmaker, 61 Jackson e

Brooks John, wood turner, 139 Hunter w
Bronson J T, hotel keeper, 52 John s
Brooke Thos, pensioner, 68 Ray s
Brooks Wm, bookkeeper, 52 Hess n
Brooks Wm, foreman roofing department, Thos Irwin & Son, Castle Brooks, Beulah
Broughton Jas, fireman G T R, 18 Inchbury s
Brower George G, machinist, 10 Victoria ave n
Brown Adam, (Brown, Balfour & Co) h 13 Herkimer
Brown Alfred, machinist, Wentworth n
Brown Arthur, gardener, Wentworth n
Brown, Balfour & Co, (Adam Brown, St Clair Balfour) wholesale grocers, 5 James s
Brown Benjamin, laborer, 1 Robert w
Brown Mrs Bridget (wid Michael) 155 Macnab n
Brown Edward, mariner, 7 Picton w
Brown Mrs Eliza (wid John) 106 Queen n
Brown Mrs Eliza (wid Jas B) bds 82 Robinson
Brown Mrs Eliza (wid Michael W) 12 Park s
Brown Mrs Esther, Wentworth n
Brown Frederick, laborer, 116 John n
Brown Charles, salesman, 12 Market sq
Brown Charles, machinist, 132 York
Brown Mrs Christina (wid Andrew) bds 199 Main w
Brown Crozier, laborer, 2 Barton Terrace, Wellington n
Brown David, builder, 11 Barton e
Brown Duncan, bookkeeper, 157 Mary
Brown George, livery, 89 John n
Brown George, 73 Park n
Brown George M, laborer, 342 James n
Brown Henry, bds 210 John n
Brown H K, shipper, 13 Herkimer
Brown Herbert, machinist, 27 Little William
Brown Horace, laborer, 137 James n
Brown Horace, teamster, 35 Barton w
Brown James, carpenter, r 51 Young
Brown James, York
Brown James, hide inspector, 5½ Victoria ave n
Brown James H, clerk, 13 Herkimer
Brown John, machinist, 81 Hess n
Brown Mrs John, 36 Macauley w
Brown John, Brewery Lane, John n
Brown John, blacksmith, 68 Caroline n
Brown John, machinist, 81 Hess n
Brown John M, machinist, 33 Railway
Brown J C, clerk Bank of Hamilton
Brown John E, tanner and whip lash maker, 9 East ave n
Brown Joseph, mason, 204 Robert e
Brown Joseph B, vinegar manf, 46 Herkimer
Brown J W, blacksmith, bds 28 King Wm
Brown J W, foreman, 140 Mary
Brown O J, teacher, 26 Main w
Brown Robert T, machinist, 79 Hess n
Brown Samuel, salesman, 105 King w
Brown Sidney, laborer, 130 Locke n

Brown Thos, teamster, 63 Canada
Brown Thomas E, 94½ Catharine n
Brown Walter, insurance agent, 2 Merrick
Brown William, bds 55 York
Brown Wm, tailor, 18 Pearl n
Brown Wm, shoemaker, 20 Emerald n
Brown Wm E, bookkeeper Brown, Balfour & Co, 32 Jackson w
Brown, salesman, bds 105 King w
Browne E (E Browne & Son) Arkledun, John s
Browne E H (E Browne & Son) h Arkledun, John s
Browne E & Son, forwarders and coal merchants, foot of Macnab n
Browne Edmund, builder, 45 George
Browne Mrs Jane (wid James) bds 180 Napier
Browne J B, asst mgr Hamilton Vinegar Wks Co, Herkimer
Browne John, blacksmith, 116 York, h 68 Caroline n
Browne's Wharf, E Browne & Son, props, ft Macnab n
Brownfield F, accountant Bank B N A, 30½ Jackson w
Bruce Alex, M A (Bruce, Burton & Culham) h 36 Duke
Bruce, Burton & Culham, (Alex Bruce, MA, Warren F Burton, J A Culham, M A) barristers, Canada Life Chambers, 1 James s
Bruce F C (John A Bruce & Co) h 39 George
Bruce John A (John A Bruce & Co) bds Royal hotel
Bruce John A & Co (J A & F C) seed merchants, 37-9 King w
Bruce Miss M L, 89 Park n
Bruce Ralph, law student, 36 Duke
Bruce Walter, bds 10 Stuart e
Bruce Wm, solicitor of patents and engrosser, 14½ King e, h mountain top *see card*
Bruce Wm C, clerk, 26 Main w
Bruce Wm P, 26 Main w
Brugger James, carpenter, 72 Hess n
Brumley John, barber, 51 Rebecca
Brundle John, tinsmith, 70 Hughson s
Brundle James, tinsmith, 70 Hughson s
Brundle Joshua, letter collector, 43 Caroline n
Brunke Albert, furrier, 30-2 York *see advt*
Brunswick Saloon, James C Macpherson propr, 7-9 King William
Brunt Arthur S, barber, 13 George
Brunt Edward, stovemounter, 277 Bay n
Brunt Samuel, carpet beater, 7 George
Brunt Wm, carpet beater, 7 George
Brunt Wm, barber, 13 George
Bryant Henry (Bryant & Post) 133 John s
Bryant James F, plasterer, 77 Victoria ave n
Bryant & Post, grocers, 133 John s
Bryce Robert, 12 Railway
Brydges Thomas, laborer, 204 East ave n
Buck Nicholas, tailor, 89 Catharine n
Bucke John J, clerk, 89 Catharine n
Buckingham George, laborer, 225 King e
Buckingham Isaac, plasterer, 108 Macnab n
Buckingham Mrs John, confectioner, 84 John s

Buckingham John, laborer, 84 John s
Buckingham Levi, moulder, 144 Duke
Buckingham Thomas H, boilermaker, 242 Mary
Buckingham William, butcher, 276 a James n
Buckley H E & Co, 94 Macnab n
Buckley Benjamin, laborer, bds 250 York
Buckley Daniel, laborer, Duke
Buckley Dennis, laborer, 163 John n
Budge Robt, laborer, 83 Canada
Budgen Owen, milk pedler, 265 James n
Buggy Arthur, tobacco roller, 37 Peter
Buchanan Mrs Agnes (wid Isaac) 95 James s
Buchanan Caleb, printer. 6 Elgin
Buchanan J G, city editor *Times*, 18 Young
Buchanan Simon, carpenter, 174 Emerald n
Buchanan W W, managing editor *Canadian Royal Templar*, bds St Nicholas hotel
Buchner Ira, tailor, 55 Mary
Buick David, watchman, 329 Barton e
Bull Geo H, clerk P O, 77 Jackson w
Bull J Eldon, salesman, 38 Wellington s
Bull John, laborer, 50 Wellington n
Bull T J, publisher, bds 52 Park n
Bull Richard, insurance agent, Jamas cor Merrick, h 14 Hunter e *see card*
Bull Stephen, laborer, 286 King w
Bulley Robt, tailor, 48 Caroline s
Bunt Wm, laborer, bds 143 James n
Bunbury H T, clerk 1st Division Court, 12 James s, h Park cor Herkimer

Buntin Mrs Alexandrina (wid Wm) 21 Jackson w
Buntin James, painter, 172 Catharine n
Buntin, Gillies & Co, wholesale stationers, 41-3 King w
Burchill Mrs Mary (wid Samuel) 61 Peter
Burdett Edward, brushmaker, 44 Robinson
Burdett Francis, brush manufacturer, 101 Macnab n
Burdett Joseph, brushmaker, bds 72 Queen s
Burfoot John, engineer, bds 55 York
Burgess Alfred, laborer, 310 King William
Burgess Chas, laborer, Duke
Burgess Jacob, fruit dealer, 21 John s
Burgess James, hotel, 74 John s
Burgess James, bookkeeper, 86 Wellington s
Burgess John, musician, 15 Lower Cathcart
Burgess William, laborer, 75 Young
Burgess Wm, machinist, 108 East ave n
Burke Miss Bridget, 54 Cherry
Burke Geo A, varnisher, 44 Canada
Burke Mrs John, 70 East ave n
Burke Michael, laborer, r 7 Picton w
Burke Patrick, laborer, 279 Macnab n
Burke Wm, dairyman, 70 Garth
Burkholder & Co. machinists, 14 Jackson e
Burkholder, D J, wool dealer 143 King e, h 149 King e
Burkholder Harlam (Burkholder & Co) 149 King e
Burkholder Herbert (Burkholder & Co) 18½ Walnut s
Burkholder John, engineer, 88 Catharine s

Burkholder Michael, Wentworth n
Burkholder R C, printer, 8King William, h Wentworth n
Burlinghoff Jacob, laborer, Wood w
Burn J J, porter G T R, 35 Macauley e
Burn James, laborer, 35 Macauley e
Burn W S, sec Stone Manuf Co, telephone communication, res Chedoke, mountain top
Burner Samuel, gardener, King e
Burnett James, laborer, 10 Picton e
Burnett Louis, laborer, 205 Hughson n
Burnett Wm, glassblower, 348 a James n
Burniston Edward, carpenter, 97 Elgin
Burniston Wm, carpenter, Tiffany
Burniston Wm, 97 Elgin
Burns Rev A, D D, LL D, governor Wesleyan Ladies' College, 57 King e
Burns Adam, 16 Hannah w
Burns A L, painter, 21 West ave s
Burns Mrs Catharine (wid Daniel) 46 Peter
Burns Chas, laborer, 42 Ray s
Burns D A, salesman, 16 Hannah w
Burns Edward, lumber dealer, 72 James n, h mountain top
Burns Mrs Eliza, fancy goods, 96 King e
Burns Mrs Elizabeth (wid Andrew) Lochearn
Burns Felix, driver Express Co
Burns Fred, salesman, 45 Wellington s
Burns G D, clerk, 16 Hannah w
Burns H, clerk, bds Court House hotel
Burns James, machinist, 108 Cannon w
Burns James, porter, 160 Market
Burns Mrs Jane, 17 East ave n
Burns J M, manager Federal Bank, h Argyll Terrace, 14 Herkimer
Burns Mrs John, bds 54 Jackson e
Burns John, brakeman, bds 49 Stuart w
Burns John, fitter, bds Lochearne
Burns John, printer, 96 Elgin
Burns John, moulder, bds 17 East ave n
Burns John, laborer, 37 Little William
Burns John, laborer, 54 Hughson s
Burns Joseph, laborer, 65 Walnut
Burns Mrs Margaret (wid John) 165 Catharine n
Burns Mrs Margaret (wid William) r 61 Jackson e
Burns Martin, machinist, 98 Barton e
Burns Mrs Mary (wid Andrew) 154 John n
Burns Matthew, laborer, 187 Bay n
Burns Patrick, laborer, 56 Wood e
Burns Patrick, glassblower, Ferrie e
Burns Robt, laborer, Robinson
Burns Robt, heater, 46 Peter
Burns Robt, 93 Main w
Burns S F, clerk, bds Court House hotel
Burns Thomas, laborer, 79 Cherry
Burns Thomas, clerk P O
Burns Wm, helper, bds 165 Catharine n
Burns Wm, tailor, 139 Victoria ave n
Burnstein Max, button hole maker, bds 56 Gore
Burrell Thos, fireman G T R, 11 Tom
Burrow, Stewart & Milne (Wm Burrow, Charles Stewart, John Milne) stove and scale manufacturers, Cannon cor John

Burrow Richard, machinist, bds 49 Stuart w
Burrow Wm (Burrow, Stewart & Milne) h 197 Hughson n
Burrows Fred, clerk, 75 West ave n
Burrows Hy, laborer, 126 Hunter e
Burrows Mrs J C, 260 Bay n
Burrows John, laborer, 209 York
Burrows John C, contractor, 36 Hunter w
Burrows Thos, auctioneer, 78 James n, h 48 West ave n
Burrows Thomas jr, clerk, 48 West ave n
Burrows Wm, tailor, 162 Rebecca
Burrows Wm, carpenter, 53 Robinson
Burshaw Miss Rebecea, boarding, 129 Rebecca
Burt John, caretaker, 15 Mary
Burt John R, moulder, 45 Wellington n
Burt Mrs Mary (wid James) 223 Barton e
Burt R B, L D S, dentist, 128½ King e, h 223 Barton e
Burton George, engraver, 20 Murray e
Burton James, cabinet maker, 226 Cannon e
Burton John, com traveler, bds 23 Main w
Burton Richard, carpenter, bds 41 John n
Burton Warren F, Bruce, Burton & Culhan) h 240 King e
Busby Henry, hubmaker, 209 Wellington n
Buscombe Edwin, builder, 52 Inchbury n
Buscombe John H, caretaker, r Synagogue, Hughson s
Buscomb Samuel, shoemaker, 148 Wilson
Buscombe Samuel, shoemaker, 58 Tisdale
Buscombe Richard, bricklayer, 33 Inchbury n
Buscombe Wm, bricklayer, Dundurn
Bush Mrs F, grocer, 43½ Walnut s
Bush Hiram E, pump manuf, 16 Market, h 42 Market
Bush Thomas, Mountain ave Beulah
Buskard Jeremiah, blacksmith, 105 Ferrie e
Buskard Robert, carriage maker, 124 King w, h 8 Bay n
Bustin Henry, piano maker, Robinson
Buston Samuel, laborer, 31 Kelly
Butcher Robert, carpenter, bds 85 King w
Cutler Alfred, carriage builder, 105 King w
Butler David A, laborer, bds 2 Main w
Butler Daniel, carpenter, 27 Simcoe e
Butler Mrs Elizabeth (wid James) 109½ Hess n
Butler Mrs Helen (wid Patrick) 51 Caroline s
Butler Mrs James, 81 Walnut s
Butler Patrick, laborer, 51 Caroline s
Butler Mrs Sarah J (wid George) 2 Main w
Butler Solomon, tinsmith, 143 Ferrie e
Butler Thos H, clerk, 18 Wilson
Butler Thomas, laborer, 109 Wood e
Butler Thomas, blacksmith, 88 Bold
Butler Walter, wood turner, 85 Lower Cathcart
Butler William, brakesman G T R, 17 Mill
Butler W, clerk Bank of Hamilton, bds 61 George
Butterfield John, stonecutter, 25 Tisdale
Butterworth Edward, clerk, 37 Robert

Butterworth John, carpenter, 16 Blythe
Buttrey Leonard, finisher, 77 West ave n
Buxton William, pattern maker, bds 112 Bay n
Byer William, fitter, 50 Locomotive
Byfield Edward, teacher, bds 241 King w
Byrens Geo C, carpenter, 36 Magill
Byrens James M, carpenter, 41 Catharine n
Byrens John, clerk, 54 Jackson e
Byrne Mrs Mark, 51 Ferguson ave
Byrne Miss Mary, dressmaker, 89 Bay n
Byrne Thomas, bookkeeper, 89 Bay n
Byrne Valentine, laborer, Barton w
Byron Thomas, broommaker, 126 Hannah e
Caddocks John, harness maker, 56 John s
Caddy John H, 22 Main w
Caffrey John, moulder, bds 82 Hughson n
Cahill A R, clerk Merchants' bank, 101 King e
Cahill Edwin D (Carscallen & Cahill) h 101 King e
Cahill James, police magistrate, 101 King e
Cahill John, blacksmith, 6 Barton e, h 36 Picton e
Cahill Joseph, glassblower, 306 Hughson n
Cahill Michael, glassblower, 125 Ferrie e
Cahill Michael, cigar maker, bds Commercial hotel
Cain Edward, laborer, Wentworth n
Cain Thomas, shoemaker, 136 Emerald n
Calder A & Co, druggist, 58 York
Calder Alexander (A Calder & Co) h 92 Merrick
Calder John (John Calder & Co) h 98 Hughson s
Calder John & Co, wholesale clothing, 57 Macnab n
Caldwell Charles, moulder, 34 Jackson e
Caldwell Joseph P, moulder, bds Victoria hotel
Caledonian Fire Insurance Co, M A Pennington, agent 30 James s
Caledonian Hall, 14 James n
Callaghan George, butcher, 47 Cannon w
Callaghan John, laborer, 91 Jackson e
Callaghan John, car driver, end Catharine n
Callaghan John, laborer, 12 Picton w
Callahan Mrs Mary, 42 Guise
Callan James, laborer, 40 West Ave n
Callan James, laborer, 71 Young
Callanane John, Western hotel, 81 Stuart w
Callihan John, 12 Stuart e
Callon Mrs Thomas, 25 Barton e
Callowhill Henry, tinsmith, 126 Jackson e
Cambdin John R, butcher, 40½ Ferguson ave
Cameron A D, barrister, Hamilton Prov and Loan Chambers, 1 Hughson s, h 21 Victoria ave n
Cameron Andrew, conductor G T R, 109 Hess n
Cameron Charles, laborer, 16 Strachan w
Cameron Duncan, fireman, 155 Main w
Cameron Duncan, com traveler, 155 York
Cameron D M, stenographer, Hamilton Prov and Loan Society, 11 Main e

Cameron Frederick, shoemaker, 152 John n
Cameron H D, treasurer Hamilton Prov and Loan Society, 74 Emerald s
Cameron James, moulder, 61 Tisdale
Cameron John, laborer, 213 Wellington n
Cameron John, moulder, 153 York
Cameron John, shipper, 1 East ave n
Cameron John, manager Life Ass of Canada, h 6 Main e
Cameron John A, fitter, 193 Wellington n
Cameron John R, managing editor *Spectator*, 155 Main w
Cameron William, blacksmith, bds 39 James n
Cameron William, brakeman, bds 49 Stuart w
Cammell, agent, 47 Caroline n
Cameron William, hotel, 153 Catharine n
Campaign Frank, laborer, 62 Chisholm
Campaign James, laborer, 29 Simcoe w
Campaign Wm, policeman, 245 Macnab n
Campbell Albert, moulder, 27 Sheaffe
Campbell Alexander, chemist, 24 Liberty
Campbell Alexander, grocer, 54 York
Campbell, Alex, policeman, 140 Barton e
Campell Alex, laborer, 36 Wellington n
Campbell A J, agent Victoria Mutual Fire Ins Co, 22 Spring
Campbell Calvin, cook, 43 Park s
Campbell Mrs Catharine, 79 Young
Campbell Mrs Christabella (wid John) 28 Margaret
Campbell Colin, tailor, 52 Jackson e
Campbell Donald, cabinet maker, 120 Locke n
Campbell Donald, policeman, 52 Magill
Campbell Donald, carver, bds 79 Young
Campbell Donald D, clerk P O, 80 Hunter w
Campbell Edward, moulder, bds 28 Margaret
Campbell George, 39 Hannah e
Campbell Henry, storeman, 152 Rebecca
Campbell James, bds 9 Napier
Campbell Mrs James, 50 West ave s
Campbell John, machinist, 324 John n
Campbell John, moulder, 59 Wellington n
Campbell John, watchman, 48 Cherry
Campbell John (Campbell & Pentecost) h 53 Jackson w
Campbell John, merchant, 30 Wellington s
Campbell John, packer, 378 James n
Campbell John D, enameler, 20 Canada
Campbell Joseph, laborer, 51 Locomotive
Campbell Kenneth, laborer, 114 Bold
Campbell Mrs Lilly (wid Daniel) 53 Jackson w
Campbell & Pentecost, (John Campbell, Albert L Pentecost) importers of staple and fancy dry goods, 43 Macnab n
Campbell P S, teacher, 40 Emerald s
Campbell Robt, potter, 108 Jackson w
Campbell Robt, 111 Main w
Campbell Robert, carpenter, 6 Picton w

Campbell Robt W, potter, 190 Main w

Campbell Sewer Pipe Co, Henry New, secy-treas, end Jackson w

Campbell Mrs Susan (wid Wm) 154 Main w

Campbell Thomas, moulder, 49 Wellington n

Campbell Walter P, foreman *Times* office, 78 John n

Campbell William, mason, bds 30 Wellington s

Campbell William, car checker, 256 Bay n

Campbell Wm, laborer, bds 7½ Florence

Campbell W R, clerk, 78 John n

Canada Business College, R E Gallagher, principal and proprietor, arcade, 31 James n

Canada Clock Co, Adam Rutherford, manager, 26, 28 and 30 Lower Cathcart

Canada Felt Hat Co, n e cor Wellington and G T R

Canada Glass House, J C Smyth, manager, 59 King e

Canada Guarantee Co, Seneca Jones, agent, 59 James n

Canada Life Assurance Co, A G Ramsay, managing director and president, R Hills, secretary, King cor James s

Canada Mutual Telegraph Co, C J Jones, manager, 8 James s

Canada Ready Print Co, 3 Hughson n

Canada Transit Co, W J Grant, agent, 33 James n

Canadian Bank of Commerce, E Mitchell, manager, King cor Hughson

Canadian Express Co, J P Johnson, agent, 18 James s

Canada Millers' Mutual Fire Insurance Co, Seneca Jones, sec, 59 James n

Canadian Oil Co, C J Williams, propr, office, 18 Macnab n, refinery, Wentworth n

Canadian Pacific Railway, W J Grant, city ticket agent, arcade, 33 James n

Canadian Pacific Railway, (Ontario division) And Frew, agent, 31 King e

Canadian Piano Stool Co, Thomas Wavell, manager, 12–14 Hughson s

Canary James, laborer, r 69 Cherry

Canary Michael, laborer, 84 Simcoe e

Canary & O'Brien, hotel, 157 James n

Canary Patrick, laborer, 67 Strachan e

Canary Thomas, (Canary & O'Brien) 157 James n

Canary Thomas, cab driver, 57 Kelly

Canham Alfred, laborer, bds 143 Bay n

Cann Ferdinand, clerk, bds 20 Stinson

Cann Mrs Samuel, 77 Hughson n

Canning George, plasterer, 128 Jackson e

Canning George sr, builder, 49 Wellington s

Cannon George M, plater, 225 Barton e

Cannon James, hairdresser, 83 James n

Cannon John, fitter, Barton w

Cant Joseph, clerk bank of BNA, John cor Robert

Canty John, laborer, 36 Ferguson ave

Canute Joseph, 163 Macnab n

Capes John, tailor, 46 Maria

Capes Thomas, fireman, 81 John n

Capes Mrs Thomas, 46 Maria

Capherne Charles, marble cutter, 251 John n

McKAY BROTHERS,

—IMPORTERS OF—

STAPLE AND FANCY DRY GOODS,

Carpets and House Furnishings.

NOTED HOUSE FOR

Carpets, Oil Cloths, Lace Curtains

AND GENERAL HOUSE FURNISHINGS,

Corner King and John Sts. **HAMILTON.**

ANDERSON & BATES,

EYE and EAR SURGEONS,

34 JAMES STREET NORTH,

HAMILTON, - - ONTARIO.

CROSS EYES STRAIGHTENED.

Exclusive attention given to the treatment of Eye and Ear Diseases.

OFFICE HOURS---9 A.M. TO 4 P.M.

JOSEPH HERRON,

MERCHANT TAILOR,

Opposite the Wesleyan Ladies' College,

82 KING STREET EAST, HAMILTON, ONT.

Carberry Right Rev James Joseph, D D, O P, S T M, Bishop of Hamilton, the palace, 25 Sheaffe
Cardwell John, plasterer, Caroline s
Cardwell John, laborer, Greig
Cardwell Wm J, laborer, bds 82 Caroline n
Carey Chas, confectioner, 99½ York
Carey Lincoln, waiter, bds 159 James n
Carey Miss Mary, 26 Young
Carey William, ice dealer, Wentworth n
Carey William, (Southam & Carey) Bay cor Markland
Carle Peter, bender, bds 122½ James n
Carless Edmund, laborer, 132 Wood e
Carless William E, carter, 136 Macauley e
Carlisle Geo, refrigerator manfr, 44-46 Caroline n
Carlson Carl, bds 106 Robinson
Carlson C G, tailor, 44 York, h 106 Robinson
Carlyon Walter, blacksmith, 21 Queen n
Carlyon Wm M, painter, bds 21 Queen n
Carmichael George, cab driver, 180 Hughson n
Carmichael Rev Hartley, rector ch of Ascension, 71 Hannah w
Carmichael John, laborer, 151 Mary
Carmichael John H, shoemaker, 9 York
Carnahan John, brushmaker, 60 Hannah e
Carnegie Peter, merchant tailor, 77 James n
Carney John, moulder, bds 124 Rebecca
Carney —, shoemaker, bds 55 York
Carnochan William, tinsmith, bds 103 York
Carnotta Julia, 229 James n
Carpenter A E, contractor, 111 Hughson n
Carpenter Bros, (John O and Thos B) family grocers, 9 Market sq, h 157 Napier
Carpenter C & Co, hardware, 53 York
Carpenter Charles (C Carpenter & Co) 12 Hess s
Carpenter Chas, Main e
Carr Aaron, messenger Meriden Britannia Co, 89 Napier
Carr Edward and Daniel, flour and feed, 91-93 King w
Carr Geo, plater, 46 Steven
Carr John, shipper, 94 Robinson
Carr Mrs M A E (wid Samuel) 1 Hunter e
Carr Robert, laborer, 48 Peter
Carr Robert, laborer, 25 Strachan w
Carr's Direct Hamburg Steamship, Wm Herman agent, 16 James s
Carrier Nicholas, shoemaker, 150 Wellington n
Carroll D T, proprietor Carroll's American Watch House, 31 James n, h Rebecca
Carroll James, bricklayer, New
Carroll James, r 103 Hunter w
Carroll John, moulder, 224 Hughson n
Carroll John, engineer, 112 Queen n
Carroll Joseph, laborer, 158 Hughson n
Carroll Matthew T, bricklayer, 128 Bold
Carroll Maurice, 80 Young
Carroll Michael, shoemaker, 80 Young
Carroll Nicholas, laborer, 31 Wellington n
Carroll Mrs Nicholas, 109 King William

Carroll Patrick, laborer, 243 Hughson n
Carroll Peter, carpenter, 276 Mary
Carroll T J, watchmaker, 104 Rebecca
Carroll Wm, polisher, 93 Elgin
Carroll Wm, tobacconist 92½ James n
Carruthers John, flour and feed, 15 King Wm, h 76 Mary
Carscallen & Cahill (Henry Carscallen, Edwin D Cahill) barristers, 7 King w
Carscallen Henry (Carscallen & Cahill, 243 Main e
Carse P D, gents' furnisher, King cor Mary, h 38 West ave n
Carson Albert, tailor, 49 Steven
Carson A, carpenter, 115 King William
Carson Charles, cigarmaker, 259 King Wm
Carson George, laborer, 9 Devonport
Carson Henry, shoemaker, 230 York
Carson Henry, cigarmaker, bds 39 Tisdale
Carson James, moulder, Maple ave
Carson John, laborer, 70 Tisdale
Carson Joseph, bus driver, American hotel
Carson Joseph, grocer, 331 James n
Carson Martin, 39 Tisdale
Carson Rice, stonemason, 17 Railway
Carson Rev W W, pastor Centenary Church, 107 James s
Carter Charles, laborer, 133½ Ferrie e
Carter Charles, laborer, 31 Peter
Carter Esau, harness maker, 194 King Wm
Carter James, bricklayer, 53 Lower Cathcart
Carter James, plasterer, South w 6
Carter Stephen, blacksmith, 56 Florence
Carter Thomas, engineer, Ferrie e
Carter William, plasterer, 82 Macnab n
Carter W H, clerk G T R, bds 97 James n
Cartmell Henry, tailor, 11 Wentworth n
Cartney John, blacksmith, 203 Hughson n
Cartwright Charles, laborer, 27 Ferrie e
Cartwright George, blacksmith, 44 Tisdale
Case A C, farmer, King e, nr toll gate
Case Albert, engineer, 23 Liberty
Case Egbert J, milk pedler, 183 King e
Case George, blacksmith, 13 George
Case H N, postmaster, res Postoffice
Case H Spencer, druggist, 50 King w
Case Mrs Mary (wid George) 13 George
Case Wm H, M D, 113 King e
Case Wm I A, M D, 113 King e
Casey James B (Casey & Sons) 86 Main e
Casey M E (Casey & Sons) 86 Main e
Casey & Sons (W J P, J B and M E) sash, doors and blinds, etc, and lumber merchants, 72 Main e
Casey Wm (Casey & Sons) 86 Main e
Cash & Co, mantles, 8 James n
Cash John, laborer, 127 Napier
Cashion David, moulder, 70 Locomotive
Cashmere Timothy, laborer, 66 Hannah e

Castell Jas, policeman, 73 Duke
Cassell Levi, manager Burlington Glass Co, 288½ James n
Cassels Thos, coachman, Queen s
Cassidy Hugh, laborer, 31 Strachan e
Catchpole Arthur, laborer, 114 East ave n
Catchpole George, umbrella maker, 13 Rebecca
Catchpole George, salesman, Concession
Catchpole Mrs Hannah (wid Wm) 35 Florence
Catchpole John, clerk P O, 82 Bay s
Catchpole Richard, fancy goods, etc, 3 Arcade, h 99 King w
Catchpole Samuel, bookkeeper, 99 King w
Catchpole Wm, machinist, 33 Florence
Catharine Owen, melter, 67 Catharine n
Cathcart Thomas, baker, 28 Wellington n
Catlin James, laborer, 41 Little William
Catton Walter, car repairer, 123 Ferguson ave
Cauley Brian, tobacconist, 112 King e
Cauley John, 77 Young
Cauley Thos, laborer, 93 Hughson n
Causewell Alfred, painter, 284 King w
Centenary Meth'st Church, Rev W W Carson, pastor, 10 Main w
Central Drug Store (J Philp, MD, prop) cor Hess and York
Central Fire Station, A W Aitchison, chief, 34 Hughson n
Central School, Hunter w
Cesar John, laborer, 7 Sophia
Chadwick, John A, manf spun sheet metal ware, 173 James n, h 202 John n
Chagnon Emery, turner, 147 West ave n
Chamberlain J F, foreman R M Wanzer, 136 Mary
Chambers Mrs Elizabeth (wid David) 173 Bay n
Chambers Mrs Elizabeth, dressmaker, 202 King w
Chambers James, conductor G T R, 193 Bay n
Chambers --, dyer, 234 Barton e
Champ Wm S, paymaster G T R, 36 Wellington s
Champagne Joseph, harness maker, 102 Catharine n
Chancery Chambers, 8, 10 Hughson s
Chanter Robert, engine driver, 91 Robinson
Chanter Robert W, carpenter, 91 Robinson
Channell Wm, bartender, 4 King w
Chapman Charles, clerk, Herkimer
Chapman Mrs Fanny, 18 Herkimer
Chapman George L, moulder, bds 10 Locomotive
Chapman Jesse (Wm Chapman's Sons) h 49 King w
Chapman John, laborer, 130 Rebecca
Chapman John, laborer, 107 King Wm
Chapman Joseph, plasterer, 17 Upper Cathcart
Chapman Joshua, engraver, 10 Locomotive
Chapman Samuel, druggist, 108 James n
Chapman's Sons Wm, funeral emporium, 49 King w
Chapman Stephen, laborer, 123 Catharine n
Chapman Walter, moulder, 60 Pearl n
Chappel H C, tinsmith, 186, 188 James n

Chappel John, tinsmith, 154 James n
Chappell Mrs Sarah (wid Henry) 69 Queen n
Chappell Wm, bricklayer, 131 Cannon e
Chapple Thomas, foreman, 170 Rebecca
Charlesworth Alfred, shoemaker, 57 Emerald n
Charlesworth Alfred, engineer, 1 Caroline s
Charlesworth Franklin, clerk, 1 Caroline s
Charlesworth Martin, 1 Caroline s
Charlesworth W G, clerk G T R, 1 Caroline s
Charlton B E, president Hamilton Vinegar Works Co, limited, h 52 John n
Charlton Joseph, glassblower, 274 Bay n
Charters James, fitter, 68 West ave n
Charters Thomas, laborer, 320 King w
Chatley Mrs Elizabeth (wid Jesse) 32 Crooks
Chatto Robert, teamster, 5 Vine
Cheesman Alfred, laborer, Breadalbane
Cheesman Jas, brickmaker, 330 King w
Cheeseman John, brickmaker, 303 King w
Cheesman Samuel, brickmaker, West st, King w
Cheesman Thos, brickmaker, 330 King w
Cherrier Emile, butcher, 305 James n
Cherrier F L, grocer, 15 Market sq, h Mary cor Barton
Cherrier J R, grocer, 105½ York
Chesnut Mrs Jane (wid T G) 143 James s
Chesnut T H, clerk, bds 143 James s
Chester Mrs Sarah (wid Arthur) 181 King Wm
Cheyne James, carpenter, 9 Hunter e
Chidley Alfred, machinist, 24 Tisdale
Chidley Thomas, bds 281 King Wm
Child Wm, bookkeeper, 36 Bay n
Children's Industrial School 77 George
Childs Frederick, brickmaker, Garth, h 220 Hughson n
Childs George, carpenter, 18 Harriet
Childs George, moulder, 137 John n
Childs John W, laborer, 82 Mulberry
Childs Wm H, machinist, 7 Mill
Chilman I C, baker and confectioner, 119 King w
Chilman Mrs M (wid Isaac C) 35 Bold
Chilman Wm H, baker, 17 Margaret
China Arcade, 182 King e
China Palace, 46 King e
Chisholm James, B A, (Jones McQuesten & Chisholm) 107 Hughson n
Chisholm James, builder, 114 Macnab n
Chisholm Mrs Janet (wid Wm) 80 Caroline s
Chisholm Robert, 113 Macnab n, h 20 Ray s
Chisnel Robert, 11 Hunter w
Chisnel Roderick, cooper, 15 Hunter w
Chiswell Wm, moulder, 125 Emerald n
Chittenden C S, D D S, dentist, 8½ King e, h 69 Bay s
Choate Z B, carpenter, 32 Hughson s
Christ Church Cathedral, Rev C H Mockridge, D D, 68 James n

Christian Isaac, printer, 24 Erie Ave
Christian Mrs Jane (wid John) 187 Main e
Christian John, porter, 9 Upper Cathcart
Christie James, carpenter, 151 York
Christie John, blacksmith, 225 Catharine n
Christie Robert, superintendent L D Sawyer, 54 East ave n
Christopher Oliver, laborer, 194 Robert e
Church of Ascension, Rev HartleyCarmichael,rector,John cor Maria
Church of the Ascension cemetery, York
Church of Ascension Mission, 114 Wellington s
Church of the Evangelical Association, 98 Market
Church Samuel, laborer, 221 Macnab n
Church Thos, moulder, 173 Mary
Churchill Hugh, laborer, 77 Macauley e
Citizen's Insurance Co (Accident Branch) Richard Bull, agent, 55 James n
City Hall, James n
City Hospital, Barton cor Victoria ave
City Laundry, Joseph Jeffrey, proprietor, 60 Main w
City of London Fire Insurance Co, Richard Bull, agent, James cor Merrick
Clapham John, plasterer, 157 Hunter w
Clapham Samuel, plasterer, bds Commercial hotel
Clappison Thomas C, bookseller and stationer, 92 James n, h 69 Herkimer
Claringbowl Fred, watchmaker and jeweler, Copp's Block, King e *see advt*
Claringbowl William, gardener, 77 Wellington s
Claringbowl Wm jr, laborer, 77 Wellington
Clark Adam, plumber, 36 James s, 142 Main w
Clarke Adam, machinist, 50 Hess n
Clark Adam, steam fitter, 262 James n
Clark Alex, stonecutter, 80 Emerald n
Clark Charles, clerk, 44 Main w
Clarke Chas, laborer, Herkimer
Clark Christopher, hatter, 215 Hughson n
Clark Mrs David, 46 Victoria ave s
Clark Mrs Elizabeth (wid Hutchinson) 77 Hughson n
Clark Frank, laborer, 47 Young
Clark Fred, galvanizer, 108 Maria
Clark George, machinist, 5 Hess n
Clarke Fred, boots and shoes, 260 King e, h 157 Duke
Clark George, car driver, 238 Bay n
Clark Henry, publisher, 110 Bold
Clark James, stove mounter, 109 Park n
Clarke James, carpenter, 284 Hughson n
Clark James, bds 87 Lower Cathcart
Clark John, butcher, 75 Park n
Clark John A, druggist, 34 King e, h 46 Victoria ave s
Clark John B, puddler, Greig
Clarke John D, editor *Times*, 104 Jackson w
Clarke Joseph, salesman, 73 Cannon w
Clark Joseph, mason, bds 55 York
Clarke Joseph M, tailor, 128½ King e, h 72 Maria
Clark Miss Mary, dressmaker, 127 King e

Clark Nelson, laborer, 198 Robert e
Clarke O S, clerk Bank of Hamilton
Clark Peter, laborer, 131 Simcoe e
Clark Richard, moulder, 22 Elgin
Clark Thos, laborer, 46 Ferrie w
Clarke Thomas, butcher, 212 James n
Clark Wm, machinist, bds 93 Caroline n
Clarke Wm, laborer, Hess s
Clark Wm, painter, 138 Rebecca
Clarke W H, manager Troy laundry, 7 Market Square, h 151 Duke
Clarke William H, machinist, Wellington n
Clarke —, machinist, part 145 Main w
Clarkson Mrs Grace (wid Wm) 28 Strachan e
Clayton Mrs Harriet (wid Wm) 56 Ray s
Clayton Henry, lithographer, 108 Rebecca
Clayton John, painter, 18 Hughson n, h 23 Crook
Clear Wm, machinist, 126½ Cannon e
Cleary Edward, shoemaker, 82 Hughson n
Cleary Hiram, shoemaker, 18½ Mulberry
Cleary James, laborer, 50 Jackson e
Cleary Rev M J (Roman Catholic) 25 Sheaffe
Cleary Stephen, searcher customs, 284 James n
Clegg John, laborer, 17 Tom
Cleghorn Mrs Sarah (wid William) 34 Walnut s
Clelland Mrs C, 280 Mary
Clement Miss Katie, 76 Napier
Clement Miss Mary, 76 Napier
Clement Miss Rebecca, bds 76 Napier
Cliff Wm H, printer, 52 Pearl n
Clifford John, machinist, 34 Queen n
Clifton John W, engine driver, G T R, 32 Locomotive
Clifton Joseph, laborer, 326 James n
Cline John J, salesman, 101 Emerald n
Cline R M, fish dealer, 194 King e
Climie J D, boots and shoes, 28 King e, h 33 East ave s
Climie Robert H, 91 Market
Cline Arthur, hackman, 135 Locke n
Cline John J, grocer, 103 Emerald n
Cline J P, marble works, 16 Cherry, h 10 Baillie
Cline Thomas, fireman, 99 Emerald n
Clinton Joseph, printer, 153 Macnab n
Clinton Wm, pattern fitter, 153 Macnab n
Clohecy Robert, carpenter, 18 Emerald n
Clohecy Thomas, harness maker, 59 Merrick, h 112 Macnab n
Cloke John G (John Eastwood & Co) h 79 Mary
Cloney James, laborer, 177 Bay n
Close F R, clerk, 169 King William
Close John, carpenter, 169 King William
Clough Charles, brakeman, bds 73 Stuart w
Cloughley John, melter, 132 Bay n
Clucas Charles, builder, 123 Cannon w
Clucas John, builder, 123 Cannon w
Clucas Wm, builder, 125 Cannon w
Clunas Wm, machinist, 68 Locomotive

Clushman John, moulder, 57 Tisdale
Coadey Mitchell, bus driver, Franklin house
Coates H M, letter carrier, 142 Hughson n
Coates John, milkman, 78 Young
Cobb David, laborer, 120 Macnab n
Coburn Henry P (L D Sawyer & Co) s e corner Park and Hannah
Cochner Francis, laborer, 53 Locomotive
Cochner Mrs, 53 Locomotive
Cochrane J M, M D, resident physician, City Hospital
Cockburn Thos, wireworker, 19 Locomotive
Coddington Wm H, hatter, bds Victoria hotel
Code James R, law student 36 Bay s
Coffer Robert, machinist, bds 168 West ave n
Coffey John W, lather, 37 Railway
Cogon Rev Solomon, 65 Catharine n
Cohen Mark, insurance agent, 50 Victoria ave s
Coiley William, lithographer, 86 Park n
Colbeck Heny, assistant postmaster, res mountain top
Colbeck Joseph, provisions, 66 Hess n
Cole A H, billiardist, Royal hotel
Cole John, 67 Bold
Cole Joseph, laborer, 16 Chisolm
Cole Mrs Susan (wid George) 8 Elgin
Coleman Alex, laborer, Sheaffe
Coleman Alfred, carpenter, 135 Emerald n
Coleman Andrew, teamster, 53 Sheaffe
Coleman Chas, laborer, 108 George
Coleman Rev Francis, Methodist, 121 Napier
Coleman George, painter, 126 East ave n
Coleman James, tabacco worker, bds 95 King e
Coleman Richard, moulder, 121 Park n
Coleman Richard, com traveler, 90 Jackson w
Coles Robert D, com traveler, 189 Macnab n
Coles W B, ledger keeper, Stinson's Bank, 189 Macnab n
Collegiate Institue, Main cor Caroline
Collett George, machinist, 10 Magill
Collier Mrs Mary A (wid Thos) 115 Bay n
Collingwood Henry, laborer, 116 Macnab n
Collins Edward, painter, 317 York
Collins E S & Co, sign painters, 9 James n
Collins E S (E S Collins & Co) bds 48 James n
Collins E W, com traveler, 12 John n
Collins E W & Co, painters, 8 John n
Collins Frank (E S Collins & Co) bds Franklin House
Collins George, carpenter, 154 Wilson
Collins Geo W, bricklayer, Herkimer nr Locke
Collins James, carpenter, 63 Steven
Collins John, foreman Thompson's lumber yard, 146 Queen n
Collins Rev J H, pastor Emerald st Methodist Church, 45 Emerald n
Collins Joseph, glassblower, bds 97 Strachan e
Collins Matthew, carder, 77 Emerald n

Collins Thos, potter, 70 Canada
Collins William, 120 Queen n
Collins Mrs, Wentworth n
Collis Geo, coppersmith, 76 Markland
Colquhoun E A, cashier Bank of Hamilton, Barton Cottage, h mountain crest
Colville Charles (Bain & Colville) h 6 Wilson
Colvin John, grocer, 138 James n
Colvin Patrick, 340 Hughson n
Colvin Peter, grocer, York
Colville W, clerk G T R, 22 Hess s
Colville William G, salesman, 22 Hess s
Colwell George, machinist, 21 Gore
Collyer A T, hat manf, 176 King e, h mountain top
Collyer Samuel, grocer, 337 York
Comfort Daniel, paper bag manf, 71 Hunter w
Commercial Chambers, 20 James s
Commercial Hotel, Luke Doyle, prop, cor York and Park
Commercial Union Assurance Co (London. Eng) Payne & McMeekin, agents, 97 Jas n
Commerford Peter, 259 James n
Complin George W, bookkeeper, 24 Queen s
Conbrough Malcolm, laborer, 341 John n
Conder Alfred, fireman, bds 50 Wilson
Confederation Life Association, Seneca Jones, agent, 59 James n
Congdon Richard, bricklayer, 76 Main w
Congo David, porter, 57 Lower Cathcart
Congregational Church, Rev John Morton, pastor, Hughson cor Cannon
Congregational Sunday School, 119 Hunter w
Conian Joseph, conductor, 18 Walnut s
Conklin Mrs Thos, 125 Hunter w
Conley Bernard, teamster, 13 Kelly
Conley Charles, printer, 10 West ave n
Conley James, grocer, 13 Kelly
Conley Michael, r 22 Kelly
Conlon Patrick, laborer, 93 Macauley e
Conley Philip, varnisher, 13 Kelly
Conley William, laborer, bds 93 Murray e
Connell & Cross, dressmakers, 78, 80 John s
Connell D C, gardener, 98 Cherry
Connell James, dairyman, 130 Catharine n
Connell John, bricklayer, Clark ave
Connell Louisa (Connell & Cross) h 78 John s
Connell Owen, laborer, 117 Walnut s
Connell Patrick, laborer, 67 Hannah e
Connell Wm, finisher, 10 Wellington n
Connolly Bernard, brakeman, bds 49 Stuart w
Connolly Christopher, boiler maker, 282 Mary
Connolly James, grocer, 13 Elgin
Connolly John, r 110 Young
Connolly Lawrence, teamster, 25 Guise
Connor Frank, carriage maker, 146 Duke
Connor James, machinist, 97 Hess n
Connor Jeremiah, laborer, foot Caroline n
Connor John, sawyer, 9 Chisholm
Connor Kennedy, shoemaker, 31 Picton e
Connor Mrs Mary A (wid Wm) 123 Cannon w

Connor Patrick, laborer, bds ft Caroline n
Connor Peter, teamster, 233 Mary
Connor Thomas, printer, 123 Cannon w
Connor William Henry, laborer, 9 Mill
Connors Dennis, gardener, 88 East ave n
Connors Ed, baggage master G T R, 24½ Inchbury n
Connors James, tobacco roller, bds 56 Park n
Connors James, burnisher, 62 Tisdale
Connors Jeremiah, laborer, 30 Alanson
Connors John, carter, 50 Jackson w
Connors John, dairyman, 50 Jackson w
Connors John, conductor GTR, 124 Hess n
Connors John, laborer, 55 Erie ave
Connors John, laborer, 213 Mary
Connors Patrick, laborer, 37 Strachan e
Connors Patrick, laborer, 325 John n
Connors Patrick, boat builder, 354 John n
Connors Thomas, carpenter, 56 Robinson
Convent Mount St Mary, King cor Ray
Conway Bartholomew J, excise officer, 14 Colborne
Conway James, machinist, 259 Wellington n
Conway Michael, glassblower, 80 Macauley e
Cook Adam (Ennis & Cook) mountain brow
Cooke Andrew A, trimmer, 34 Bay n
Cooke Charles, 34 Bay n
Cook Charles, hotel keeper, 29 Main e
Cook David (Cook & Mitchell) Franklin House
Cook Edward, painter, bds 168 York
Cook Mrs Eliza (wid Edward) Duke
Cook George, potter, bds 51 Park
Cook Geo, carpenter, 81 Locke n
Cook George, watchman, 22 Crooks
Cook Henry, baker, 53 Peter
Cook Henry, baker, 50 Ray n
Cook James, painter, Duke
Cook John, hotel keeper, 118 Market
Cook Joseph, butcher, 222 Jas n
Cook Louis, moulder, 17 Sheaffe
Cook & Mitchell, (David Cook, Mrs L Mitchell) proprs Franklin House, King cor Park
Cook Richard, civil engineer, 21 Gore
Cook Samuel, carpenter, 92 Simcoe e
Cook Thos, (James Stewart & Co) h 40 Main w
Cook Thomas, fireman, 49 Sheaffe
Cook Wm, plumber, bds 54 Queen s
Cooke William, caretaker market, 126 Hunter w
Cook Wm, coachman, Concession
Cook Wm, (J M Williams & Co) h cor Main and Park
Cook William, painter, 168 York
Cook Wm, machinist, 163 West ave n
Cookson Thomas, machinist, 107 Napier
Coombs Benjamin, laborer, 27 Macnab s
Coombes George, builder, 119 Rebecca
Coombes George, moulder, 56 Maria
Coombs Isaac, pattern maker, 53 Caroline s
Coombs James, shoemaker, 55 York

Coombes Jesse, laborer, 191 Main w
Coombes Wm, moulder, 138 Jackson w
Cooney Elwood, laborer, 25 Elgin
Cooper Alfred, clerk, 173 John n
Cooper A B, 20 James s
Cooper Albert R, printer, 41 George
Cooper Chris, carriage painter, 41 George
Cooper Geo, laborer, Garth
Cooper G W, blacksmith, 39 Alanson
Cooper H G & Co, carriage builders, 6 Park s
Cooper Hamilton (H G Cooper & Co) h 84 Main w
Cooper Henry, laborer, Garth
Cooper James, hair dresser, 82½ King w, h 25 Augusta
Cooper John C, manf baby carriages, 4 Magill
Cooper J T, salesman, bds 34 Bay n
Cooper Miss Mary, seamstress, 85 King w
Cooper R C, grocer, 31 Macnab n, h 11 East ave n
Cooper Richard, salesman, 11 East ave n
Cooper Wesley, laborer, 51 Little William
Cooper Wm, laborer, 51 Stuart e
Cooper Wm H (H G Cooper & Co) h 6 Park s
Cooper Mrs —, 73 Victoria ave n
Co-Operative Printing Co, 92 King e
Copeland George S, rope manfr, 204 Wellington n
Copeland John, carpenter, 6 Devonport
Copeland Thos, carpenter, 48 Robinson
Copeland Wm, cabinet maker, 48 Robinson
Copp Anthony jr, clerk, West Lawn, York

Copp Anthony sr, (Copp Bros) h West Lawn, York
Copp Bros, founders, York cor Bay
Copp Samuel, clerk, bds West Lawn, York
Copp Wm J, (Copp Bros) h Concession
Copperdale —, brewer, 46 Market
Coppins John, tailor, 13 Harriet
Coppley George C, bookkeeper, 90 Hess n
Corbett Patrick, hat finisher, 107 Strachan e
Corbett Timothy, Greig
Corcoran Denis, carpenter, 51 Young
Corcoran E J, bookkeeper, bds 21 Hunter w
Cormack Mrs Kate (wid John) 20 Ray s
Cornell Fred, plasterer, 12 Cherry
Cornell S W, (Hyslop, Cornell & Co) h 96 James s
Cornell Mrs Thomas, Robinson
Corner Robert, shoemaker, 182 King e
Cornish Morris, salesman, 14 George
Cornley Wm, laborer, 49 Locomotive
Corporation Weigh Houses, 366 John n, Macnab cor Stuart and Market sq
Corridi Mrs Mary A (wid Cæsar) 102 Robinson
Corridi Peter, bookkeeper, 102 Robinson
Corrigan John, laborer, 249 John n
Corrigle John, carpenter, 175 Cannon e
Corey Benjamin R, 18 Herkimer
Corey Mrs Catherine (wid John) boarding, 9 Park s
Cosgrave Patrick, laborer, 29 Simcoe e
Cosgrove Mrs Margaret (wid Wm) bds 199 Bay n
Cosgrove Patrick, 103 Ferrie e

Cosgrove William, sewing machine agent, 50 Hunter e
Costello Edward, laborer, 67 Cherry
Costello Patrick, baker, 56 Queen s
Costie William, carpenter, 3 Liberty
Cotter James, tailor, 171 Macnab n
Cotter John, carter, Head
Cotton Herbert, plasterer, 67 Young
Cotton John, builder, 2 West ave n
Cottrell Samuel, bricklayer, 41 Hannah w
Cottrell Samuel, gardener, 9 Stinson
Coughlin Daniel, carpenter, 79 Cannon w
Coughlin Michael, laborer, Victoria ave n
Coughlin Patrick, laborer, 249 Catharine n
Coughlin Thomas, laborer, 110 Walnut s
Coulson Geo S, grain dealer, 46 Catharine n
Coulson Wm, bookeeeper, bds 127 John n
Coulter David, policeman, 385 John n
Coulter Mrs Henry, 193 Cannon e
Coulter Robert, shoemaker, 87 King e
Coulter Robert, gardener, bds 103 King w
Coulter Samuel, shoemaker, 109 Bold
Counihan Gerald W, barber, 4½ King William, h 95 Wellington n
Counsell C M, banker, 14 James s, h 1 Herkimer
Counsell George S, county clerk, Court House, h 89 Jackson w
Court House, Main cor John
Court House Hotel, Wm Gowland, prop, 55-57 John s
Coutts Archibald, saloon and livery, 30-32 Cannon w
Coutts John, pattern maker, 39 Stuart e
Coutts Wm, laborer, 10 Mill
Cousins John, carpenter, 140 Hess n
Cousins John, messenger Bank Commerce, 8 Ferguson ave
Couturie Elyeor, shoemaker, 33 Mulberry
Couturie John, shoemaker, 33 Mulbery
Coventry Mrs E M, 15 Barton w
Coville Mrs Jane (wid Robert) 39 Bold
Cowan Andrew, clerk, 91 East ave n
Cowan Charles, 44 Cannon w
Cowan James S, clerk, 85 Cherry
Cowan John, carpenter, 34 Ferrie w
Cowan Mrs Lucy (wid Peter) 278 King w
Cowan Robert D, 44 Cannon w
Cowan William, platelayer, 234 Bay n
Cowil Peter G, salesman, 87 Cherry
Cowil Robert, carpenter, 275 Macnab n
Cowie Mrs, bds 50 Hess n
Cowing Henry, machinist, 150½ Rebecca
Cox Alfred, cork manufacturer, 157 Wellington n
Cox Alfred J, cork manufacturer, 157 Wellington n, h Murray e
Cox Andrew J, 78 Caroline s
Cox Mrs Ann (wid James) dressmaker, 147 King Wm
Cox Barnet, shoemaker, Smith ave
Cox James, salesman, 44 King w
Cox James, baker, bds 105 James
Cox James A, salesman, 6 Macnab s

Cox John, coffee and spice manufacturer, 25 Pearl s
Cox John, carpenter, 168 Wilson
Cox Thomas, cutter, 147 King William
Cox Wm, pork curer, James st market and 139 King w
Cox Wm, laborer, bds 168 Park n
Cox Wm, laborer, bds 3 Inchbury s
Cox —, laborer, bds 21 Locomotive
Coy Charles, harness maker, 52 Stuart e
Coyne John, laborer, 116 Bold
Craft H W, salesman, 126 Jackson w
Craft Wm, pork butcher, 50 York
Craig Alex, caretaker Burlington Cemetery, York
Craig David, machinist, 8 Kinnell
Craig Mrs Francis (wid Andrew) 3 Little Peel
Craig John, carpenter, 108 Florence
Craig Joseph, vet surgeon, 22 Market, h 34 Market
Craig Robt, tool keeper, G T R, 3 Little Peel
Craigie George, clerk, h mountain top
Craigie W, clerk G T R, mountain top
Crane Jasper G, bds 29 Robinson
Crankshaw Wm John, bookkeeper, 180 John n
Craven Geo, blacksmith, Duke cor Locke
Craven John, blacksmith, Duke cor Locke
Craven Rev J J, Roman Catholic, 244 King e
Crawford A B, clerk, 38 King w
Crawford Mrs Elizabeth (wid Patrick) 27 Elgin
Crawford George, candy maker, 38 King w
Crawford Henry, carpenter, 27 Elgin
Crawford Henry, candy maker, 38 King w
Crawford James, confectioner, 38 King w and 20 Market Square
Crawford John, moulder, 43 Pearl n
Crawford Samuel, grocer, 132 King w, h 42 Pearl n
Crawford Wm, bridge inspector, 92 Park n
Crawford Wm, bricklayer, 131 Napier
Crawford W P, excise officer, 93 Wellington n
Crawford —, shoemaker, bds 55 York
Crawford —, bookkeeper, bds 15 Main w
Crawley Fitzowen sr, machinist, 40 East ave n
Crawley Fitzowen jr, machinist, 40 East ave n
Crear Donald, tailor, 140 John n
Crerar A H, clerk, head Macnab s
Crerar John (Crerar, Muir & Crerar) county attorney, Merksworth, h Macnab s
Crerar Peter, carpenter, South w
Crerar P D, M A (Crerar, Muir & Crerar) h 149 James s
Crerar, Muir & Crerar (John Crerar, John Muir, MA, P D Crerar, MA) barristers, Hamil-Prov Chambers, 1 Hughson s
Crites G A, Star Augur Manf Co, 68 Mary, h 12 Erie ave
Creel Henry, 169 Macnab n
Creighton Mrs (wid David) 255 Hughson n
Cresswell Miss Rebecca, 164 Jackson w
Crews Rev Albert C, pastor Hannah St Methodist church, 100 Caroline s
Crilly Patrick, merchant tailor, James cor Gore

Cripps Charles, bricklayer, 52 Steven
Cripps Daniel, bricklayer, 25 Steven
Cripps Joseph, laborer, 228 Cannon e
Crisp Alfred, clerk P O
Crisp Mrs Elizabeth (wid Alfred) Erie ave
Crisp Mrs Elizabeth (wid Thos) 92 Bold
Crist Alfred, glassblower, 67½ Barton w
Crist Samuel, glassblower, 245 James n
Critchley William, teamster, 70 Hughson n
Croal George, blacksmith, 67 Emerald n
Crockford George, jeweler 4 Canada
Crockett William, ruler, Rebecca
Croft John, laborer, 50 Markland
Crofton Edward, grocer, 265 John n
Crofton Edward, painter, 24 Elgin
Crofton Walter, moulder, 73 Robert
Crombie Mrs Elspit (wid Francis) 16 Wellington n
Crombie William, barber, 33 Park n, h 16 Wellington
Crombie Wm, cutter, 37 Park s
Cronk John, moulder, 44 Catharine n
Cronn John, teamster, 102 Jackson e
Cronyn Daniel,carter,249James n
Crook John, bookkeeper, 113 Wellington n
Crook John, tobacco roller, bds 7 Park s
Crooker W H, 150 York
Crooks Alex, dairyman, 60 Hannah w
Crooks John, laborer, 116 Queen n
Crooks Mrs Mary (wid Richard) Barton w
Crooks Mrs M C, 35 Hughson
Crooks Richard, bartender, 96 King ,William
Crooks R W, teamster, 219 Barton e
Crooks Thomas, hotel, 96 King w
Cross Arthur, tea dealer, 152½ Rebecca
Cross Miss Harriet, bds 78 John s
Cross Moses, teamster, 105½ Jackson e
Cross Mrs Thomas, 16 Guise
Cross Thomas, wrecker, bds 352 John n
Cross William, laborer, 16 Guise
Crossland Edward F, laborer, bds 93 Cherry
Crossland Geo, laborer, 131 Macauley e
Crossland Walter, cigar maker, 93 Cherry
Crossley Irving, dry goods, 4 Felson ave
Crossley James, dry goods, 147 James s
Crossley John, dry goods, James cor King Wm, h 73 Herkimer
Crossley William, dry goods, 73 Herkimer
Crossman Adam, butcher, 124 Bay n
Crotty Patrick, carpenter, 247½ Mary
Crowe Alfred, machinist, 161 Mary
Crowe Thomas, machinist, 122 Wilson
Crowe Robert, machinist, 113 Robinson
Crowley Wm J, dealer, 7 Macnab s
Crowser C, buckle manf, 64 John s, h 43 Queen s
Crowther Wm T M, music teacher, 172 Macnab n
Crozier Richard, laborer, 108 Jackson e
Croy Wm B, com traveler, 109 Bay n

Cruikshank A S, teacher, 110 Cannon w
Cruickshanks John, policeman, 134 Cannon e
Cruickshanks John, stonemason, 167 Hunter w
Cruickshank Robert, builder and contractor, 47 Maria
Crystal Palace View Hotel, Harry Bawden, prop
Cuckow Edwin, packer, 15 Grove
Cuff, Robert C, butcher, 309 York
Culchin John, hostler Franklin House
Culham Joseph A, M A, (Bruce, Burton & Culham) h 55 East ave s
Culhane P J, bill poster, 42 Cannon e
Culhane Stephen, bill poster, 42 Cannon e
Cullen Arthur, laborer, 28 Ferrie e
Cullen Mrs Mary, laundress, 98 Bold
Cullen Michael, laborer, 82 Macauley e
Cullinan Nicholas, laborer, 99 Caroline n
Cullinan Nicholas, laborer, bds 215 Hughson n
Cullum Alby, moulder, 2 Ferguson ave
Cullum David, carpenter, 2 Ferguson ave
Cullum David, plumber, 93 West ave n
Cullum William, laborer, 126 Picton e
Culp Isaac H, machinist, 18½ Walnut s
Culp Jacob, wheelmaker, 229 Mary
Cumbers Wm, 174 Hughson n
Cummer C H, traveler, 89 Wellington n
Cummer E S, Supreme sec I O F, 3 Ferguson ave
Cummer John H (P Grant & Sons) h 89 Wellington n
Cummer Wm L (P Grant & Sons) h 123 Bay n
Cumming Bros, grocers, 108 James n
Cumming John, cutter, 121 King w
Cumming Wm (Cumming Bros) 108 James n
Cummings James, tax collector, 158 Main e
Cummings John, laborer, 74 Market
Cummings Maurice, laborer, r 183 Bay n
Cummings Maurice, laborer, 33 Simcoe e
Cummings, Patrick, laborer, 245 King e
Cunard Steampship Line, W J Grant, city ticket agent, Arcade, 33 James n
Cunningham Arthur, fireman, 42½ Cannon w
Cunningham E B, 87 Cannon e
Cunningham Samuel, conductor, 120 Cannon e
Cunningham Wm, teamster, 39 Burlington n
Cunnington Wm, hatter, 232 Barton e
Cunnison James, 77 Wellington n
Curell Daniel, blacksmith, 74 Elgin
Curell J G, barrister, 34 James n, h 140 Cannon e
Curno Joseph, carpenter, 183 Victoria ave n
Curran John, stovemounter, 328 King William
Curran John, printer, 39 Tom
Curran Michael, laborer, King e
Curran Patrick, laborer, 33 Wood e
Curran Robert, dyer, 85 John n
Curran Rev Wm, rector St Thomas' Church, 91 James

Currie Donald, carpenter, 93 Wilson
Curry George, laborer, 76 Bold
Curry Wm, laborer, 47 Cannon e
Curry Wm D, engine driver, G T R, 123 Queen n
Curtain Wm, laborer, 134 King e
Curtis Thomas, tailor, 28 O'Reilly
Curtis Wm, 87 Park n
Curtis —, 42 James n
Cusack Mrs Elizabeth (wid Patrick) 79 Elgin
Cusack Mrs Jane (wid Wm) 11 Mulberry
Cuseck Wm, laborer, 105 Caroline n
Cusha Mrs Mary, 71 Hannah e
Cussen Michael, laborer, Ferguson ave n
Custom House, 35 Stuart e
Cuthbertson Alex, grocer, 210 King w
Cutler Charles, carpenter, 277 King e
Cutler F A, cabinet maker, 126 Main e
Cutt James, cutter, 87 Hunter w
Cuttriss Edward W, carpenter, 59½ East ave n
Cuttriss George, wood engraver, 138 Main e
Cuttriss Mrs Mary Ann, dressmaker, bds 138 Main e
Cuzner Mrs James, tailoress, 68 King Wm
Cuzner John, shoemaker, 15 York
Cuzner Luke, tinsmith, 13 Lower Cathcart
Dabb Mrs Christina, 29 Peter
Dabbs Mrs Mary (wid Charles) r 51 Young
Dack E & Son, boots and shoes, 23 Arcade
Dack Samuel, laborer, bds 35 Napier
Dake Michael, hotel keeper, 228 James n
Dallis Donald, polisher, 44 Vine
Dallas Mrs E, 5 West ave s
Dallas Harry, com traveler, 94 Victoria Ave s
Dalley E A (F F Dalley & Co) h 34 Elgin
Dalley F F & Co (F F, E A and M) patent medicines, 99 James n
Dalley F F (F F Dalley & Co) h 42 Jackson w
Dalley W R G, bookkeeper, 8 Young
Dallyn Mrs Ann, 170½ James n
Dallyn Charles, hair dresser, 33½ James n, h 90 Elgin
Dallyn F E, bookkeeper, h 90 Stinson
Dalrymple James S, salesman, 132 Main e
Dalton Andrew, moulder, 15 Hess s
Dalton James, laborer, 199 Mary
Dalton Patrick, laborer, 261 Hughson n
Dalton Thomas S, boat builder, 59 Robert
Daly Edward, laborer, 13 Macauley w
Daly Hugh, whip maker, 8 Augusta
Daly James, 87 Murray e
Daly John, yardsman, G T R, Barton w
Daly John J, grocer, 72 Napier
Daly Nicholas, laborer, 346 James n
Daly Timothy, engine turner, G T R, 32 Inchbury n
Daly William, laborer, 27 Simcoe
Daly Wm, tailor, 52 Wood e
Dame Paul, fish pedler, 216 James n
Dampier Miss Mary, 189 York
Danahy Edward, shoemaker, 215 James n
Danforth Benjamin M, nailer, 51 Caroline n

Danger John, hostler, 67 John s
Daniels Benoni, merchant, 1 Young
Daniels Geo, fireman G T R, 35 Inchbury n
Daniels Mrs Jane, r 128 Macnab n
Darby Alfred W, laborer, 39 Little William
Darby Richard G, machinist, 25 Little William
Darche R, conductor, 145 Robert e
Darling —, 105 King w
Darling Albert G, brickmaker, Maple
Darlington Mrs Thomas, 142 Rebecca
Daubreville Fred, scale maker, Mill
Daubreville Ferdinand, hostler, Court House hotel
Davey Wm, 36 West ave n
Davey Wm M, laborer, 119 Park n
Davey —, laborer, 29 Queen s
Davidson Alexander, gardener, 99 Hannah e
Davidson Charles A, finisher, 17 Spring
Davidson Duncan, laborer, St Mary's Lane
Davidson Mrs Elizabeth (wid James) 60 James s
Davidson Enos, bookkeeper, bds Market
Davidson Mrs Isabella (wid John) 66 Caroline s
Davidson James, jeweler, 5 James n, 62 Herkimer
Davidson James H, com traveler, 32 Main w
Davidson John, salesman, 26 Main w
Davidson John, collector, 166 Bay n
Davidson Mrs Margaret (wid Robt) teacher, 66 Duke
Davidson T L, bookkeeper, h 78 Maiket
Davidson Thos, clerk, 45 Duke
Davies Benjamin, confectioner, 25 Arcade, h 25 Young
Davies Chas, salesman, 25Young
Davies Edmund, music teacher, 40 Barton e
Davis Alex T, train despatcher, G T R, 21 Bay n
Davis Alfred J, brickmaker, 193 Main w
Davis Mrs Ann (wid William) 7 Canada
Davis Archd, printer, 124 Main e
Davis Calvin, reporter *Spectator*, 124 Main e
Davis C A, Dentist, 68 King e, h 44 Emerald s
Davis Frank, bds Aikman's ave
Davis Fred, watchmaker, Main e
Davis George, confectioner, 77 Cannon w
Davis H H, bookkeper, Wentworth s
Davis Hy, carpenter, 190 Wilson
Davis Horace K, clerk, bds 44 East ave s
Davis Isaac, helper, 76½ East ave n
Davis J H (J H Davis & Co) h Wentworth s
Davis J H & Co, wool, grain,etc, 9 John n
Davis James, market clerk, bds 44 East ave s
Davis James G, 239 Main e
Davis Mrs Jane (wid Joseph) 194 King w
Davis Mrs Jane (wid James) bds 68 Jackson w
Davis Mrs Jane (wid Evan) 25 Young
Davis J M, machinist, 19 West ave n
Davis John, crockery, 51 Macnab n and 6a York
Davis John, fish and game, Arcade, h Aikman's ave
Davis John, brickmaker, 193 Main w

Davis John A, 81 John n
Davis John E, machinist, 102 Barton e
Davis Jonathan, 194 Main e
Davis Joseph, butcher, 41 Stuart e
Davis Mrs M, 20 Maria
Davis & McCullough (W R Davis, J D McCullough) watchmakers and jewelers, 12 King w
Davis Nicholas, waiter, bds 125 Mary
Davis Nicholas H, 64 Jackson w
Davis Peter, master mariner, 41 Maculey w
Davis Robert, freight checker, bds 156 Mary
Davis Samuel jr, market clerk, 60 Catharine s
Davis Samuel, 44 East ave s
Davis Sewing Machine, W S Lumgair, agent, 115 James n
Davis Mrs Susan (wid John) 44 Main w
Davis Thomas, agent, bds 25 Young
Davis Thomas E, clerk, Wentworth s
Davis T E, bricklayer, 90 Wilson
Davis T M, com traveler, 73 Wellington s
Davis Walter, laborer, Aikman's ave
Davis Walter, clerk, bds 44 East ave s
Davis Warren, stonecutter, 81 John n
Davis William, laborer, 266 Mary
Davis William, blacksmith, 76¼ East ave n
Davis William, barber, bds 16 Wellington n
Davis William, clerk, 16 Wellington n
Davis W R (Davis & McCullough) h 68 Jackson w
Daville Mrs Charlotte 53 Macnab s
Davison Alfred, cigar maker, bds 98 West ave n
Davison Charles (Davison & Modlin) h 12 Lower Cathcart
Davison Mrs Clara (wid Thomas) music teacher, 6 Kelly
Davison & Modlin (Chas Davison, John Modlin) 98 James n
Davison Wm, tailor, 26 Locke s
Dawdy Luther, porter, bds American hotel
Dawe Geo, blacksmith, 35 Magill
Dawe Wm, letter carrier, P O
Dawes Thomas, forgeman, 110 Market
Dawson Donald, tax collector, 144 Hunter e
Dawson George, finisher, 24 Hunter e
Dawson John, laborer, 121 Caroline n
Dawson Meredith, letter carrier, 8 Concession
Dawson —, pedlar, 6 Tisdale
Day Mrs Charlotte (wid F T) 51 Wellington s
Day Edward, laborer, 129 Picton
Day Frank, clerk, 51 Wellington s
Day John, shoemaker, 280 James n
Day Joseph, porter, 66 West ave n
Dayfoot P W, 219 Main e
Day R J, 74 Murray e
Dean Francis, brickmaker, King w
Dean Henry, dyer, 280 Macnab n
Dean John, laborer, 7 Little Wellington
Dean Wm, shoemaker, 58 Peter
Dean W H, com traveler, 3 Caroline s
Debus Mrs Annie (wid Wm) 183 Napier
Defour Alfred, provisions, 133½ James n
Degan Joseph, shoemaker, 156 Victoria ave n
Degarmo Mrs Martha (wid Elias) 128 Cannon e

DeLacey Frederick, saloon, 19 Hughson n
Delaney James, laborer, 7 Strachan w
Delorme C, carriage maker, 31 John n, h 53 Catharine n
Delorme Cyprian, carriage maker, 130 Macnab n
Dempsey George, washaline manufacturer, 47 King Wm, h 112 Main w
Dempsey John C, clerk, P O, bds 112 Main w
Dempster C H (Brayley & Dempster, h 13 Young
Demun Hiram, plasterer, 34 Augusta
Dennis Chas, laborer, bds 16 Margaret
Dennis George H, carter, 72 Jackson e
Dennis James, boots and shoes, 212 King e
Dennis John, painter, 52 Canada
Dennis W H, teacher Canada Business College
Dennison G H, clerk, 78 Hughson n
Denroche Edward, carpenter, 15 Lower Cathcart
Dent Joseph, upholsterer, 101 Hannah e
Depew Edward, salesman, bds 99 Emerald n
Derby Henry, bookkeeper, 5 Ontario
Derby Joseph, grain buyer, 113 West ave n
Derby Wm, buffer, 5½ Chisholm
Dermody Mrs Ann (wid Patrick) 151 Main e
Dermody Frank, bread pedler, 151 Main e
Dermody John, baker, 151 Main e
Dermody Wm, laborer, 300 John n
Derrick T J, tobacco roller, 46 John n

Des Brisay Rev Lestock rector All Saints Church, 126 Market
Desmond John, laborer, 181 Bay n
Destiveler Edward, telegraphist, Royal hotel
Deutscher Paul, hotel, 23 John s
Devine James, carpenter, Ferguson ave n
Devine Mrs Jane (wid Edward) 182 Catharine n
Devine John, moulder, 102 Victoria ave n
Devine Morris, moulder, 207 Hughson n
Devonport Thomas, gardener, 11 Bay n
Dew Charles, laborer, bds 73 Stuart w
Dew George, laborer, 76 Bay n
Dewar Mrs Emily (wid Plumer) 31 Jackson w
Dewart Wm, laborer, 30 Wellington n
Dewey Daniel (D Dewey & Son) 15 George, h 11 Caroline s
Dewey D R, manager Canada Ready Printing Co, 11 Caroline
Dewey D R & Co, coal dealers, 12 James s
Dewey D & Son (Daniel and John) ice dealers, 15 George
Dewey John (D Dewey & Son) bds Franklin House
DeWitt E A, butcher, 183 Cannon e
Dexter David, managing director Federal Life Assurance, h 31 East ave s
Dexter George M, canvasser, 150 John n
Diamond Andrew, machinist, 208 Victoria ave n
Dick David, fireman, 132 Victoria ave n
Dick George, laborer, 80 Cannon w

Dick John, laborer, bds 180 Napier
Dicker Mrs Frances, 59 Young
Dicker William, shoemaker, 83 King e
Dickie Thomas, salesman, res Dundas
Dickinson Benj, laborer, 89 Hunter w
Dickinson Mrs Mary (wid Chas) 4 Ferguson ave
Dickinson Thomas, 252 James n
Dickson Edgar H, porter, G T R, Greig
Dickson George, principal Collegiate Institute, 33 Bold
Dickson John, laborer, 7 Park s
Dickson Robert, carpenter, 111 Hess n
Dickson M C, ass't general freight and passenger agent N & N W R R, h 78 Ferguson ave
Dickson William, carpenter, 62 Duke
Dill Mrs Julia (wid Wm) Queen s
Dillabough E H, M D, 18 Gore
Dillabough Josef, journalist, 30 Gore
Dillon Andrew, hotel, 21 John n
Dillon James, hotel, 262 Macnab n
Dillon James, grocer, 201 John n
Dillon John, grocer, 159 Bay n
Dillon John, machinist, 36 Ferrie w
Dillon Michael J, hotel, 162 and 164 Bay n
Dillon Patrick, laborer, 17 Murray e
Dillon Patrick, laborer, 93 Hannah e
Dillon Wm, laborer, 167 Bay n
Dillon Wm, moulder, 66 John n
Dilworth James, laborer, 39 Wood w
Dingle J A, butcher James street market, h mountain top
Dingle Jas, butcher, 135 John s
Dingle Wm, machinist, 88 Wellington n
Dingle Wm, potter, bds King w
Dingwall Alex, stonecutter, 162 Hughson n
Dingman Norman J, excise officer, 6 Mulberry
Dingman Peter, shoemaker, 71 Locke n
Dingwall James M, fitter, 93 Napier
Dinsse Henry, clerk P O
Disher Mrs Amy, 24 Hunter e
Dittrick Fred, bender, 167 East ave n
Ditty James, tinner, 60 Steven
Dixon Bros (Wm and James) wh fruiterers, 33 King e
Dixon Charles J, clerk, 68 Queen s
Dixon Herbert, customs officer, 4 Hess s
Dixon James (Dixon Bros) h 37 East ave s
Dixon John (Dixon & Morton) h 58 Emerald n
Dixon John, druggist, 9 Park s
Dixon John, carpenter, 23 Napier
Dixon John, knitted goods, 115 York
Dixon & Morton (John Dixon, Wm Morton) fruiterers, 52 King w and 28 James s
Dixon Thomas, 59 Napier
Dixon Wm, machinist, 27 Cannon e
Dixon Mrs Wm, sr, 58 Emerald n
Dixon Wm (Dixon Bros) h 35 East ave s
Doak Simeral, blacksmith, 34 Hunter e, h 22 Young
Dobie John, 25 Hannah e
Dobson John, stovemounter, 213 Bay n
Dodd Mrs, 111 King Wm
Dodd George, piano finisher, 48½ York, h 49 George
Dodd Mrs George, dressmaker, 48½ York

Dodd Mrs Jane (wid Wm) 107 Robinson
Dodd Robert F, valuator, 82 Hunter e
Dodd Wm, bds Maple Leaf hotel
Dodd Wm, feather dyer, 74 Merrick
Dodds Wm, stonemason, 51 Cherry
Dodman Frederick, bookkeeper, bds 38 Caroline s
Dodman James, grocer, 69 Hunter w
Dodson Bros (J & R Dodson) brassfounders, 92 Macnab n
Dodson Fred, painter, 61 Victoria ave n
Dodson Hector, lashmaker, 183 Bay n
Dodson James, brassfounder, 55 Victoria ave n
Dodson Joseph, printer, 118 Catharine n
Dodson J R, brassfinisher, 161 West ave n
Dodson Wm, painter, 29 John n
Dodson Wm, jr, painter, 65 Victoria ave n
Dodson Wm, sr, carpenter, 65 Victoria ave n
Doherty Arthur, grocer, 245 King w
Doherty Burnet, carpenter, 8 West ave n
Doherty Mrs Esther (wid George) 2 Park s
Doherty Hugh, mariner, 294 Macnab n
Doherty James, printer, 8 West ave n
Doherty John, laborer, 58 Locke s
Doherty Michael, laborer, 72 Stinson
Doherty Patrick, moulder, 119 Victoria ave n
Doherty Peter, laborer, 108 Simcoe e
Doherty Thomas, coffee and spice mills, 63 Cannon e
Doherty Thomas Daniel, bds 63 Cannon e
Dolan John, teamster, 109 Ferrie e
Dolman David, laborer, Herkimer
Dolman John, mariner, 45 Burlington w
Dolmheirn —, laborer, 15 Harriet
Domestic Sewing Machine, Hargrove & Sons, agents, 118 King e
Dominion Hat Co, John Tunstead, manager, 210, 212 King e
Dominion Hotel, Armstrong & Haw, proprietors, 80, 84 King w
Dominion License Office, Richard Mackay, inspector, 14 Hughson s, h 100 James s
Dominion Plate Glass Ins Office, David McLellan, agent, 84 James n
Dominion Shirt Factory, S G Treble, proprietor, 2 King e
Dominion Steamship Line, David McLellan, agent, 84 James n
Dominion Suspender Manuf Co, W L Doran, prop, 28 John n
Domville A E, clerk, bds 121 John n
Domville C K, mech supt GTR, 121 John n
Domville Frederick J, mech engineer G T R, 114 Rebecca
Donahue Dennis, laborer, 296 Macnab n
Donahue Stephen, laborer, r 61 Jackson e
Donald Alexander, bottler, 65 Sheaffe
Donald James, engineer, bds 228 York
Donaldson Hugh, carpenter, bds 60 James s
Donaldson J G, laborer, bds 146 Rebecca

Donaldson John, engineer, 19 Caroline s
Donaldson John, engineer, 51 Maria
Donaldson Mrs M (wid William) 27 Young
Dondero Joseph, fruiterer, 85 James n
Donnelly Luke, cabinetmaker, 47 Ray n
Donnelly Mrs Jane (wid John) 49 Cherry
Donnelly Patrick, laborer, 277 Hughson n
Donnelly Patrick, laborer, 245 John n
Donohue A, shoemaker, 10 Wentworth n
Donohue Jeremiah, moulder, 190 King Wm
Donohue Michael, tinsmith, 116 West ave n
Donovan Andrew, laborer, 63 Burlington w
Donovan Cornelius, inspector separate schools, 74 Maria
Donovan Cornelius, moulder, 133 York
Donovan Jeremiah, shoemaker, 97 Young
Dovovan Michael, hackman, 13 Hunter w
Doody Mrs Mary, 271 Macnab n
Doolittle Chas, vice-pres Ontario rolling mill, 46 Bay s
Dora James, laborer, 20 Little Market
Doran Bros (M & W) vinegar manfrs, 31 Stuart w
Doran Mrs Mary (wid Peter) 11 Hess n
Doran Michael (Doran Bros) bds cor James and Stuart
Doran William (Doran Bros) 203 James n
Doran W L (Dominion Suspender manuf Co) h 59 John n
Dormer Carl, Concession cor Caroline
Dornan Joseph, machinist, 298 James n
Dorning Geo, laborer, 8 Little Market
Dorning Wm, carter, 154 Napier
Dossett Joshua, polisher, Ferguson ave, n of track
Dossett Wm, polisher, 35 Peter
Doston Alex, tobacco roller, 111 Herkimer
Doubeville Fred, polisher, 14 Mill
Dougall Andrew, machinist, 135 John n
Dougherty Michael, shipper, 75 Stinson
Douglas Robt, moulder, 15 Devonport
Douglas Stewart, cigar maker, bds 4 Duke
Dowrie David C, letter carrier, 4 Concession
Dow David, plasterer, 31 Bold
Dow George, plater, 155 West ave n
Dow Henry (H & J Dow) h 18 Canada
Dow Henry & John, wood and coal dealers, 45 Main w
Dow John, laborer, 75 Emerald n
Dow John (H & J Dow) h 41 Hess s
Dow Moses, plasterer, 18 Canada
Dow Robt, plasterer, 36 Ray s
Dow Wm, moulder, Garth
Dow Wm, bookbinder, 18 Canada
Dowd John, laborer, 87 Simcoe e
Dowd Wm, laborer, 145 Bay n
Dowden James, whitewasher, 42 Jackson e
Dowden James, whitewasher, 28a Catharine
Dowe John, cooper, bds Victoria hotel
Dowie David, builder, 61 Queen s
Dowle Frank, clerk G T R, 320 Macnab n
Dowle Richard, clerk G T R, 230 Macnab n

Dowler Mrs Ellen (wid Wm) groceries, 223 James n
Dowley Ed, boilermaker, 5 Sophia
Dowling —, salesman, bds 34 Bay n
Dowling Albert, machinist, 239 Cannon e
Dowling Mrs Mary, fancy goods, 85 John s
Downing Edward, carpenter, 176 Jackson w
Downing P J, whitewasher, 148 Hughson n
Downs Charles, stationer, bds 17 Kelly
Downs Daniel, blacksmith, 17 Kelly
Downs Wm, photographer, 17 Kelly
Dowrie David C, letter carrier, 4 Concession
Dowrie John, carpenter, 84 Bold
Dowrie William, carpenter, 59 Queen s
Doyle Anthony, laborer, 111 Maria
Doyle Brian, detective, 165 Mary
Doyle Cornelius, moulder, 102 Wellington s
Doyle Daniel, carriage maker, 57 Merrick, h 58 Duke
Doyle Daniel, wagon maker, 58 Duke
Doyle Mrs Ellen (wid John) 23 Wood w
Doyle James, mariner, 287 Bay n
Doyle J E, grocer, 220 James n
Doyle John, laborer, 29 Railway
Doyle Luke, Commercial hotel, York cor Park
Doyle Mrs Mary (wid Patrick) 73 Cherry
Doyle Mallick, baggage master, 91 Strachan e
Doyle Owen, carpenter, 131 Jackson w
Doyle Patrick, tailor, 24 Little Market
Doyle Thomas, laborer, 369 Hughson n
Doyle William, laborer, 15 Wood e
Doyle Mrs William, 54 Stuart e
Drake A E, foreman cotton mills, 190 Macnab n
Drake Henry, laborer, 106 Florence
Drake R F, gunsmith, 50 Tisdale
Drake Wm, shoemaker, 208 John n
Drayton Wm (W Drayton & Co) h 51 Hunter e
Drayton W & Co, fruiterers, 6 King w
Drenin Mrs Ann (wid Wm) 42 Hughson n
Dressel John A, hotel, 41 Macnab n
Drever Thomas, carpenter, 351 John n
Drever Thomas, laborer, 308 Macnab n
Drew Alfred F, carpenter, Herkimer
Drew Charles, tinsmith, 30 Napier
Drew Mrs Lydia (wid Thomas) 30 Napier
Driscoll John, laborer, 46 Robinson
Drope Henry T, printer, 129 Market
Drope Mrs Jane, 74 Napier
Drummond George, accountant Bank of Montreal, 48 Hunter w
Dryden James, laborer, bds 9 Hess n
Dryden Wm, teamster, 355 John n
Dryland Albert E, lithographer, 15 Mill
Dryland Mrs Margaret (wid John) 15 Mill
Drysdale Alex, agent Chicago & Alton Railway, 181 Main e
Drysdale Mrs Sarah, 182 Napier
Dublin Joshua, whitewasher, 28 Augusta

Duclos Charles, laborer, 12 Simcoe e
Duff Charles (J Duff & Son) 142 York
Duff John (J Duff & Son) 142 York
Duff John & Son, grocers (J Duff, Charles Duff) 144 York
Duff Mrs, 22 Mulberry
Duff W A H, barrister, Victoria Chambers, 31 James s, h mountain top *See card*
Duffield Alfred, plasterer, 176 Wilson
Duffield Mrs Jane (wid Samuel) bds 92 Bay s
Duffield Mrs Mary A (wid William) 141 York
Duffield W S, bookkeeper, 141 York
Duffy Mrs Bridget (wid Thomas) 128 York
Duffy Edward, 12 Locke n
Duffy Mrs E, fancy goods, 53 Macnab n
Duffy Fred, clerk Dufferin house
Duffy James, machinist, 87 West ave n
Duffy James, dyer, bds 23 Murray w
Duffy Mrs Jane (wid John) 83 Peter
Duffy John, laborer, 187 Hughson n
Duffy John, clerk, St Nicholas hotel
Duffy John, 38 East ave n
Dufty John, gardener, Wentworth
Duffy John, hatter, 68 Ray n
Duffy Michael, moulder, 252 Hughson n
Duffy Patrick, 72 Locke n
Duffy Patrick, blacksmith, 70 Ray n
Duffy Peter, Dufferin hotel, 55 Macnab n
Duffy Thomas, moulder, Greig
Duffy Thomas, carpenter, 48 Stuart e
Dufton James, bricklayer, 138 Barton e
Dugal Alfred, shoemaker, 116 Catharine n
Duggan Arthur, brickmaker, 14 Chisholm
Duggan Jas C, tailor, 26 Ferrie e
Duggan James E, clerk, bds 125 Market
Duggan Mrs Margaret (wid John) 64 Robert
Duggan Mrs Margaret (wid John) laundress, 81 Hunter w
Duggan Mrs Mary, Aikman's ave
Duggan R J, barrister, Canada Life Building, 1 James s, h Wentworth, cor Stinson
Duggan Thos A, clerk, 125 Market
Dumfrie James, laborer, 38 Cannon w
Dummer Harry F, fireman, 14 Simcoe e
Dummer Mrs Phœbe (wid Henry) 182 Macnab n
Dummer William, laborer, 182 Macnab n
Dun, Wiman & Co, mercantile agency, Geo J Williams, manager, Hamilton Provident Chambers, 3 Hughson s
Dunbar Alex, moulder, bds Court House hotel
Dunbar Charles, moulder, 75 Hunter e
Dunbar Charles E, moulder, 44 Cherry
Dunbar John, porter, 65 Cannon e
Dunbar Michael, carpenter, 4 Chisholm
Dunbar Patrick, carpenter, 3 Chisholm
Duncan Mrs Alice (wid Charles) 39 Charles
Duncan Bros (Henry and Chas) wh teas and coffees, 71 King e
Duncan Charles (Duncan Bros) h 16 Wilson

Duncan David, machinist, Maple
Duncan Edward, laborer 1 Dundurn
Duncan George, merchant, 155 Main e
Duncan Henry (Duncan Bros) h 25 Wellington s
Duncan Lithographing Co, R Duncan, prop, James cor Market sq
Duncan Mrs Margaret (wid Alex) 25 Jackson w
Duncan Robert (R Duncan & Co) h Charles cor Jackson
Duncan Robert & Co, booksellers and stationers, James cor Market sq
Duncan Thomas, machinist, 62 Hess n
Duncan William, gardener, 147 Duke
Dundin Wm, laborer, 43 Inchbury n
Dundun Mrs Day, 62 Maria
Dundun John, 54 Robert
Dunford Thomas, laborer, Maple
Dunkerley John, driller, 69 Queen n
Dunlop David, saddler, 95½ John s, h 30 Young
[illegible] John, [illegible] Park n
Edson Mrs A E, 151 James n
Edwards Benjamin, confectioner, 100 and 102 King w
Edwards Charles, clerk, 136 Barton e
Dunn Alex, prop St Nicholas hotel, 35 James n
Dunn George J, laborer, 69 Pearl s
Dunn John, glassblower, bds 23 Murray w
Dunn John, laborer, Barton w nr Locomotive
Dunn John, traveler, 190 Hughson n
Dunn John, laborer, 13 Wood w
Dunn John (Russell & Dunn) 190 Hughson n
Dunn J S, tea and sugar broker, Ham Prov Chambers, 1 Hughson s, h 11 West ave s
Dunn Lawrence, laborer, 366 James n
Dunn Mrs Mary, 86 Macnab n
Dunn Matthew, stonecutter, 58 Hess n
Dunn Stephen, foreman R O Mackay, 394 James n
Dunn Thomas, laborer, r 256 Macnab n
Dunn Wm G (W G Dunn & Co) merchant, h Queen s cor Main
Dunn W G & Co, Canada coffee and spice mills, 57 Main w
Dunnett A W, brakeman, 135 Ferguson ave
Dunnett EH clerk PO, 103 Elgin
Dunnet George, moulder, 97 Wilson
Dunnett Henry, painter, 117 Hughson n
Dunsmoor Wm, porter, 149 Duke
Dunstan Kenneth J, city agt Bell Telephone Co, 1 Hughson s, h 159 James s
Dunstan R J, com traveler, 165 James n
Durand Alex, carpenter, 122 Wellington n
Durant Mrs Sarah (wid Daniel) 54 Florence
Durdan William, engineer, 270 Bay n
Durfey John A, laborer, 50 Emerald n
Durham Daniel, axemaker, Mill
Durham Joseph, bds 44 Mulberry
Durphey Dyer, carpenter, 38 Bay n
Durphey John, carpenter, 76 Locke n
Durrand Alex, carpenter 119 Wellington n
Durward John M, marbleized slate manr, 15 Vine
Duston William, weaver, 38 Picton e

Duval H C, barber, 20 John s, h 73 Jackson e

Dwyer Mrs Harriet (wid Alex), 4 Jackson e

Dwyer James, undertaker, 124 James n

Dwyer John, laborer, 22 O'Reilly

Dwyer John, moulder, bds 105 James n

Dwyer Michael, shoemaker, 130 Young

Dwyer Michael, machinist, 98 Elgin

Dwyer Michael, moulder, 41 John n

Dwyer Michael, 63 Hannah e

Dwyer Patrick, undertaker, 63 Hannah e

Dwyer C E, traveler, 111 Victoria ave n

Dyer E L, salesman, 214 King e

Dyer Wm, laborer, 7½ Florence

Dyer William J, bookkeeper, 62 Canada

Dyke John, laborer, 7 Little Peel

Dynes Alex, salesman, 49 Ferguson ave

Dynes J V, clothier, 64 King e

Dynes Richard, moulder, 49 Ferguson ave

Eadie Miss Ann, 3 Wilson

Eager Henry A, clerk P O, 80 Jackson w

Eager Henry T, salesman, 80 Jackson w

Eager Morley P, clerk, 80 Jackson w

Eager Mrs Sarah (wid Joseph B) 25 Hunter w

Eaglesham James, porter, 19 Cannon w

Eaglesham William, gardener, Wentworth n

Eardley E, bookkeeper, bds 13 Bold

Earl Wm, laborer, 57 Canada

Earle Mrs M A (wid Charles) 45 York

Earles Patrick, laborer, 44 Guise

Early Edward, huckster, Argo

Early John, laborer, 38 Charles

Easson John, broom maker, 73 Napier

East Henry, bricklayer, Wilson e Wentworth

Easter Fred (Easter & Purrott) res mountain top

Easter & Purrott, paper hangers, 81 James s

Easter Samuel, saloonkeeper, 23 James n

Easterbrook Elias, steward, City Hospital, Barton e

Easterbrook Mrs Elias, matron, City Hospital, Barton e

Eastwood Frederick, laborer, bds 11 Picton w

Eastwood John (John Eastwood & Co) Main e Hamilton

Eastwood John & Co, booksellers and stationers, 16 King e

Ecclestone E A, foreman, Ontario Cotton Mills

Ecclestone Eugene, grocer, 169 Wellington n

Ecclestone James, tailor, 80 Victoria ave n

—manager, Hamilton Providen[illegible] Chambers, 3 Hughson s

Dunbar Alex, moulder, bds Court House hotel

Dunbar Charles, moulder, 75 Hunter e

Dunbar Charles E, moulder [illegible]

Eckerson & Millman (J J Millman, proprietor) 76 King w

Eckerson N G, photographer, 124 King e, h 70 Stinson

Economical Mutual Fire Insurance Co (Wm Strong, agent, Arcade, 33 James n

Ede Mrs Louisa (wid Wm) bds 37 Queen s

Ede Wm, clerk, 127 Cannon w

Ede William, clerk, 68 Catharine s

Eden John, laborer, 102 Hannah

Edgar David, lumber merchant, 8 Locomotive
Edgar Francis, carpenter, 129 Macnab n
Edgar John, mail driver, bds 79 Main e
Edgar Robert, laborer, 8 Little Peel
Edgar Wm, lumber merchant, 43 Victoria ave s
Edgar William, carpenter, 63 Park n
Edgecombe Mrs (wid Orlonda) 139 East ave n
Edick Alonzo, laborer, 232 James n
Edick L A, foreman Ontario Cotton Mills Co
Edison Electric Light Co, A J Lawson, manager Canada Life Building, 1 James s
Edison Lamp Factory, C F Stillwell, superintendent, 26 King William
Edmondson George, butcher, 157 York, h 124 Napier
Edmonstone John, conductor, G T R, 58 Napier
Edmund E, bookkeper, 95 Bay s
Edmunds John, hostler, 170 Park n
Edson Mrs A E, 151 James n
Edwards Benjamin, confectioner, 100 and 102 King w
Edwards Charles, clerk, 136 Barton e
Edwards Charles P, boots and shoes, 104 King w and 24 James n
Edwards Miss Esther, milliner, 122 James n
Edwards John, hatter, 143 Wellington n
Edwards Miss Mary, Murray e
Edwards Robert, tinsmith, 18 Napier
Edwards Thomas, laborer, 35 Kelly
Edwards Vincent, baker, 52 Pearl s
Edwards W A, architect, 9 James n, h 142 Hunter e
Edwards W J, carpenter, 32 West ave n
Edwards Mrs 250 Barton e
Edworthy Frederick, butcher, 83 Bay n
Edworthy Lewis, pattern maker, 13 Park s
Egan Edward, machinist, 34 Locomotive
Egan James, com traveler, 171 Park n
Egan S F, 39 Mulberry
Egan Thomas, fitter, 120 Cannon w
Egener Adolph, excise officer, 111 Market
Egener Charles, machinist, 45 Cannon e
Egener Erederick, Wellington nr Barton
Egg Charles H, clerk G T R, 63 Colborne
Egg John, butcher, Barton e
Eickoff Chas, cigarmaker, 4 Little Peel
Eisenberg Isaac, tailor, 49 Catharine s
Eland Henry, laborer, 113 Robinson
Elden Alex, machinist, 19 Crooks
Elder Francis, tailor, 81 Lower Cathcart
Elder Geo, clerk, 19 Crooks
Elder William, shoemaker, 227 Cannon e
Elfving J, basket maker, 196 East ave n
Ellen Henry, bricklayer, bds 23 Wilson
Ellsworth Jacob F, grocer, Herkimer cor Caroline, h 59 Cathcart n
Ellsworth James, carpenter, 59 Lower Cathcart
Ellicott John M, com traveler, 17 Walnut s
Ellicott R, assessor, 17 Walnut s

Elliott George, teamster, 106 Elgin
Elliott Henry, butcher, bds Kinge
Elliott Henry E, cutter, Burlington s
Elliott James, agent, 1 East ave s
Elliott J, barber, 65 King w
Elliott John, 90 Caroline n
Elliott Robert, photographer, bds 56 Gore
Elliott R H, furniture, 17½ York
Elliott Samuel, watchman, 92½ Victoria ave n
Elliott Simon, watchman, 94½ Victoria ave n
Elliott Thomas, engineer, 37 Macauley w
Elliott William, butcher, 106 Elgin
Elliott Wm, moulder, 8 Bay s
Elliott Mrs, ft Caroline n
Ellis Mrs Caroline (wid James) 7 Mill
Ellis D G, broker, 8, 10 Hughson s, h 64 Wellington s
Ellis George, 263 York
Ellis George D, salesman, bds 263 York
Ellis Henry E, salesman, 263 York
Ellis John, laborer, Burlington n
Ellis Thomas, laborer, 186 Jackson w
Elmslie Geo S, bookkeeper, 40 Market
Elrington H J, printer, 44 Hughson n
Elrington William, laborer, 44 Hughson n
Elvin William, com traveler, 74 Napier
Elwell John, moulder, 63 Ray s
Elwell Thomas, laborer, 14 Railway
Elwell Joseph, laborer, 14 Railway
Elz Mrs Magdalene (wid Philip) 106 Walnut s
Emberson Alfred, coal oil dealer, r 192 King Wm
Emberson Joseph, carter, 192 King Wm
Embling Joseph, laborer, 136 Jackson w
Emboden Charles, laborer, 75 Robinson
Emerald Street Methodist Church, Rev J H Collins, pastor, 41 Emerald n
Emerson Wm, 63 Jackson e
Emery John W, scalemaker, 5 Kelly
Emory C VanNorman, homœpathic physician, 18 Main w
Empey C P, com traveler, bds St. Nicholas hotel
England Frank, hairdresser, 45 James n, h 19 Spring
England Richard, grocer, 63 Stuart w
England Robert, second hand dealer, 87 York
England Walter, barber, 138 King Wm
English John, carpenter, 137 York
English Richard, nail cutter, bds 23 Murray w
Ennis Charles, piano tuner, 59 Walnut s
Ennis & Cook (James Ennis and Adam Cook) printers, 24 Main e
Ennis George, cabinet maker, 24 Canada
Ennis James (Ennis & Cook) h 206 King Wm
Ennis James, laborer, 13 Burlington e
Ennis Wm, shoemaker, bds 56 Erie ave
Enwright George, moulder, bds 24 Caroline n
Enright Miss Maggie, dressmaker, 174 Bay n
Enright Maurice, laborer, 25 Simcoe w
Enright P J, clerk G T R, 70 Bay n

Equity Chambers, 12, 14 Hughson s
Erdman Charles, milk pedler, 153 Wellington
Erly Thomas A, agent, 111 Park n
Erskine Presbyterian Church, Rev Thomas Scoular, pastor, 71 Pearl n
Erskine —, student, bds 105 King w
Erwood Joseph, teamster, 28 South e
Estress Miss Sarah, 67 John n
Etherington Walter, carpenter, 79 Canada
Elthier Joseph H, hairdresser, 13 Gore
Eustace James, brakeman, bds 103 King w
Evans Mrs Ann, 103 West ave n
Evangelical Lutheran Church, Gore cor Hughson
Evans Charles, lamplighter, 65 Young
Evans & Co, merchant tailors, 6 John n
Evans Danford, com traveler, 84 Hess n
Evans Edward, boarding, 17 Main w
Evans Francis, blacksmith, 112 Locke n
Evans Jas, hostler, Court House hotel
Evans Jonn D (P Grant & Son) 121 Bay n
Evans L, salesman, 137 Hnnter e
Evans M T, brewer, 64 Maria
Evans O C, window shades, 113 James n
Evans Rees, printer, 28 Caroline n
Evans Robert (Robert Evans & Co) h 50 Charles
Evans Robert & Co (Robert Evans, Andrew Angus) seedsmen, Macnab cor York
Evans Robert (Evans & Co) h 37 James s
Evans Mrs Sarah (wid Robert) 139 Macnab n
Evans Thomas, laborer, 100 Park n
Evans Thomas, varieties, 91 King e
Evans Wm, foreman Bell Telephone Co, 29 Park s
Evans Wm, planing mill, 72 Caroline n, h 34 Picton w
Evans Wm B, gas meter maker, 154 Bay n
Evans Wm, bricklayer, George
Evans Wm, marble cutter, 17 Sophia n
Evel James (Semmens Bros) h 100 Cannon w
Everton Nathan, laborer, 175 Napier
Ewing Mrs Jane R (wid Alex) 60 Bay s
Exley Thomas, printer, 171 Hunter w
Eyres Levi, laborer, bds 230 Bay n
Eyatt John, teamster, 295 King w
Fagan Mrs Eliza (wid Wm) 67 Ray s
Fagan Francis, rope maker, 134 Ferrie e
Fahey John, shoemaker, 47 Hess s
Fahey Johnston, bartender, Rob Roy Hotel
Fair —, laborer, Maple
Fair Thomas, laborer, 187 Wellington n
Fairbairn Mrs Sarah, grocer, 319 James n
Fairbank Henry, York, w of tollgate
Fairchild Theodore B, hotel, 128 and 130 King w
Fairchild's Hotel, T B Fairchild, proprietor, 128-130 King w
Fairclough D J, printer, 158 Market
Fairclough James, carpenter, 158 Market

Fairclough Wm E, musician, 158 Market

Fairgrieve Hugh, consulting engineer, bds 40 Market

Fairgrieve J B, coal merchant and ship engineer, 59 James n, h 61 Macnab s

Fairgrieve J C, clerk, 23 Victoria ave n

Fairhurst Richard, wire weaver, 138 Hunter w

Fairley Joseph, carpenter, 210 Mary

Fairley & Stewart, (Wm Fairley and James Stewart) plumbers and gasfitters, 18 John n

Fairley Wm (Fairley & Stewart) h 210 Mary

Fairweather W G, grocer, 263½ Macnab n

Falls James, switchman, 241 Bay n

Falconer James, carpenter, 85 Hunter w

Fallahee Thomas, laborer, 230 Catharine n

Fallahee James, laborer, 60 Strachan e

Fallahey James, gardener, 21 Steven

Fallis William, watchman, 21 Liberty

Fanagh John, laborer, r 61 Jackson e

Fanning Michael, 70 Locke s

Fanning Thomas, grocer, Robinson, cor Locke

Fardy Wm, printer, 30 Murray w

Farish Frank, whipmaker, 38 Augusta

Farmer Arthur, pedler, bds 139 King w

Farmer Bros, photographers, 8-10 King w

Farmer F N, hay and straw dealer, 56 Jackson e

Farmer T D J, law student, bds 178 King w

Farmer James F, blacksmith, 125 John s

Farmer J H (Farmer Bros) h hd Queen's

Farmer Thomas, photographer, 27 Florence

Farmer Thos, law student, 178 King w

Farmers' & Traders' Loan Association Æ Jarvis, manager, 36 King e

Farmer William, F, watchmaker, 56 York

Farmer Mrs William, 18 Hunter e

Farmer William, plumber and gasfitter, 110 James n

Farmer William, photographer, 35 King w, h 124 Victoria ave n

Farmer William, watchmaker, 87 Merrick

Farr E, plasterer, 45 Steven

Farr Charles, nickle plater, bds 173 East ave n

Farr James, bricklayer, 80 Mary

Farr John, carter, 165 Mary

Farral Benjamin, lithographer, bds 23 Barton e

Farrar David, policeman, 11 Strachan e

Farrar Wm, manager Oak Hall, 89 Mary

Farrell Charles, salesman, 103 Cherry

Farrell James, laborer, 328 James n

Farrell Joseph, fireman, 76 Mary

Farrell Thos, laborer, 64 Market

Farrell Thomas, glassblower, 325 James n

Farrow E H, clerk, 89 Hess n

Farrow Thos, carpenter, 89 Hess n

Farthing John, laborer, 100 Victoria ave s

Faulkner J H, mason, 33 Queen n

Faulkner John B, bricklayer, 8 Canada

Faulknor Geo, builder, 157 Napier

Faulknor Joseph, brickmaker, Hunter w, near Garth, 157 Napier
Faulknor Joseph, builder, 157 Napier
Faulknor Robert J, bricklayer, 57 Queen s
Faulknor Thos, builder, 157 Napier
Faulks Robert, carpenter, 190 East ave n
Faustman Charles, cooper, 45 John n
Faustman Ernest, cooper, 45 John n
Fawkes Mrs Elizabeth K (wid Wm) 79 King w
Fearman Edward, plasterer, 172 Mary
Fearman F C, pork dealer, 72 East ave s
Fearman F W, pork packer, 17 Macnab n, h 58 Stinson
Fearman R C, pork packer, 58 Stinson
Fearman W J, bookkeeper, 58 Stinson
Fearnside Edward, gardener, 302 King William
Fearnside John H, letter carrier, 48 Main w
Fearnside Thomas, 302 King William
Fearnside Wm, 302 King William
103 Main w
Fish R, spinner, 85 Simcoe e
Fisher George, harnessmaker, 207 King e
Fisher George F, harnessmaker,
Feasel George, gardener, 95 Hunter w
Feast Henry, car driver, 184 James n
Feast Mrs Mary (wid Alfred) 114 Cannon w
Feast Mrs Mary (wid Samuel) 73 Main w
Feast Miss Sarah A, dressmaker, 73 Main w

Featherstone R, butcher, 227 James n
Feaver Miss Susan, hotel, 12, 13 wood market sq
Feaver Thomas, butcher, r 111 West ave n
Feaver W J, bartender, 19 Queen
Federal Life Insurance Co, David Dexter, managing director, James cor Vine
Fee Thomas, hackman, 9 Margaret
Feidenheimer Philip, baker, Ray s
Fell Arthur, machinist, 104 Hunter w
Fell Henry K, foreman, 13 Rebecca
Fell James, teacher, bds 67 Hunter w
Fell John, machinist, 47 Macauley w
Fell John H, laborer, 6 Spring
Fell Mrs Martha (wid Joseph) 67 Hunter w
Fell William, engraver, 4 Market sq
Fell Wm F, machinist, 46 Pearl s
Fenton C J, dry goods, 83 John s
Fenton David, clerk, 77 Walnut s
Fenwick Edward J, com traveler, bds 32 George
Fenton James, bailiff, r 62 Hannah e
Fenton P J, policeman, 152 Wellington n
Fenton Philip, grocer, 52 Young
Fenton Philip, jr, clerk, h 62 Young
Fenton Mrs Mary (wid James) 103 Rebecca
Fenton Samuel, shipper, 15 Sophia n
Ferguson Alex, messenger customs, 33 Stuart e
Ferguson H, chemist, 178 King w
Ferguson J D, bookkeeper, 55 King e
Ferguson John, shoemaker, 56 Erie ave

Ferguson John M, dyer, Mary
Ferguson Mrs Margaret (wid James) 92 Bay s
Ferguson Richard, tailor, 43 Robinson
Ferguson Robert, printer, 38 Market
Ferguson Thomas, ,shoemaker, 1 Walnut s
Ferguson Wm, teamster, 167 Macnab n
Ferguson Wm, cigar maker, 22 Simcoe e
Ferguson Wm, fitter, 123 Picton e
Ferguson Wm, tailor, 7 Walnut s
Fernihough Henry, packer, 127 Macnab n
Ferres & Co, hardware, 38 Jas n
Ferres James, hardware, 78 Jas s
Ferrie Campbell, accountant, 12 Queen s
Ferrie Mrs Emily (wid John) 12 Queen s
Ferrie Mrs Harriet (wid Robert) 14 Ray s
Ferrie Hughan, 12 Queen s
Ferrie Robert, 12 Queen n
Ferrie R B, clerk, 14 Ray s
Ferris Peter, policeman, 55 Wellington s
Fickle Augustus, packer, 60 Wood e
Fickley Gottlieb, shoemaker, 35 Cherry
Fickley Wm, moulder, 36 Canada
Fiddler Samuel, sailor, 33 Tom
Field Frank, 69 Victoria ave s
Field John, crockery, 176, 174 James n
Field Mrs John, Main e
Field Mrs Mary J (wid Richard) 17 Caroline s
Field Wm J, 9 Caroline s
Fielding Chas W W, letter carrier, 77 King w
Fielding George, warper, 133 Wood e
Fielding James, laborer, 37 Robinson
Fielding John, fireman, bds 25 Murray e
Fielding John S, draughtsman, 77 King w
Fielding Joseph, hatter, 77 King
Fielding Joseph M, moulder, 77 King w
Fielding Wm M, com traveler, 77 King w
Fields Mrs Ellen, 59 Catharine n
Fields Miss Hattie, 69 Victoria ave s
Fields Charles H, barber, 234 James n
Filgiano Frederick, clerk G T R, 115 Bay n
Filgiano Henry E J, clerk, P O, 195 Cannon e
Filgiano T Le P, dentist, 4 James n, h 286 James n
Filiatrault Javide, tobacco roller, 10 Upper Cathcart
Filiatrault Poutien, foreman Tuckett's, 14 Napier
Finagin Edward, painter, bds 160½ Macnab n
Finagin Frederick, clerk, 160½ Macnab n
Finagin John, merchant tailor, Copp's block, King e, h 160½ Macnab n
Finagin Patrick, hack driver, 62 Wellington n
Finch Bros (Wm H & T S) staple dry goods, 18 King w, h
Farrell Thos, laborer, 64 Market
Farrell Thomas, glassblower, 325 James n
Farrow E H, clerk, 89 Hess n
Macauley e
Finch W H, sr, foreman Copp's foundry, 225 Victoria ave n
Finchamp Wm, moulder, 10 Locke s
Findlay David, moulder, 338 Hughson n
Findlay G S, salesman, 23 Young
Findlay H H, com traveler, 32 East ave s

Findlay James, slate roofer, Concession
Findlay James, shoemaker, 59 Jackson e
Findlay Patrick, laborer, bds 6 Tiffany
Findlay W F, accountant and insurance agent, Wentworth chambers, 25 James s, h 132 John s
Findlay Mrs Wm, 66 Victoria ave n
Finlayson Alex, salesman, 117 Young
Finlayson George, salesman, 72 Bay s
Finlayson George, baker, 7 Hunter w
Finlayson John, saddler, 134 Cannon e
Finn Thomas, laborer, 73 Barton e
Finton Samuel, laborer, 105 Napier
Fire Insurance Association, J T Routh, agent, 16 James s
First Methodist Church, Rev A Langford, M A, pastor, King cor Wellington
Firth James, blacksmith, 172 Emerald n
Fisett Miss M B, milliner, 47 Macnab n
Fischer Harris, button hole manf, 103 Main w
Fish R, spinner, 85 Simcoe e
Fisher George, harnessmaker, 207 King e
Fisher George F, harnessmaker, 26 Blythe
Fisher Horace, machinist, 71 Napier
Fisher James, stovemounter, 57 Chisholm
Fisher Jas, laborer, bds 50 Florence
Fisher Mrs Julia (wid James) 11 Bold
Fisher Mrs, Main e
Fisher Mrs Mary (wid Fred) Maple
Fisher Robt, painter, 50 Florence
Fisher Samuel, laborer, 28 Chisholm
Fitch Wm, boilermaker, bds Victoria hotel
Fitt Henry, cabinet maker, 10 Tom
Fitzgerald Duncan, sheriff's bailiff, Court house
Eitzgerald Mrs Ellen (wid John) 105 Walnut s
Fitzgerald Francis, barrister, 10 King w, bds 29 Bay n *see card*
Fitzgerald George, laborer, 190 Hunter w
Fitzgerald James, laborer, 179 Bay n
Fitzgerald Lawrence, boilermaker, 317 Macnab n
Fitzgerald Miss Mary, 37 James s
Fitzgerald Mrs, 215 Cannon e
Fitzgerald Patrick, 72 Tisdale
Fitzgerald Robt, clerk P O, bds 29 Bay n
Fitzgerald Thomas, laborer, King e
Fitzgerald Wm, flour mills, Market, h 29 Bay n
Fitzgerald Wm jun, clerk, 29 Bay n
Fitzgerald William J, finisher, 45 Young
Fitzgerald Mrs Julia (wid Patrick) 19 Aurora
Fitzmorris Robert, moulder, 42 Cherry
Fitzpatrick Mrs Catharine (wid Martin) 17 Napier
Fitzpatrick John, clerk, 77 James s
Fitzpatrick John J, painter, 112 Macnab n
Fitzpatrick M & Co, painters, 33 York
Fitzpatrick Mrs Mary (wid Hugh) 17 Pearl
Fitzpatrick Peter, carpenter, 121 Mary

Fitzpatrick P E J, bookkeeper, 77 James s
Fitzsimmons Henry, coachman, Inglewood, James s
Flack Mrs Lucy (wid Thos) 63 Caroline s
Flagley Mrs Geo, r 104 Macnab n
Flahaven John, painter, 225 Catharine n
Flaherty Francis, laborer, 129 Jackson w
Flaherty James, laborer, 115 Cherry
Flanagan —, stove polisher, bds 60 Bay n
Flanagan Michael, laborer, 22 Little William
Flanders C W, brakeman, 96 East ave n
Flanery Edward, moulder, 136 West ave n
Flanigan James, blacksmith, bds 39 James s
Flatt & Bradley, lumber merchants, cor Wellington and Barton
Flatt J I, (Flatt & Bradley) res Millgrove
Fleck Alexander, painter, 6 O'Reilly
Fleck Geo, laborer, 64 Pearl s
Fleming Burnett, laborer, 25 Stuart e
Fleming Hunter, stonecutter, bds 56 Gore
Fleming John, laborer, 110 Young
Fleming John, grocer, Barton e, cor Emerald
Flemming Mrs Susan (wid Wm) bds 123 Queen n
Fletcher Mrs Catherine (wid Joseph) 112 Napier
Fletcher Rev Donald H, pastor Macnab st Presbyterian ch, 58 Macnab s
Fletcher Mrs Eliza, 303 Macnab n
Fletcher George, moulder, bds 189 York
Fletcher George, bds 57 Wilson
Fletcher Geo, moulder, bds 7½ Florence
Fletcher James, manf jeweler, 22 Macnab s, h 65 Steven
Fletcher John, fitter, 30 Simcoe
Fletcher Joseph, shoemaker, 53 Ray n
Fletcher Joseph, carpenter, 9 Florence
Fletcher Mrs Mary Ann (wid Chas) Barton w
Fletcher Peter, laborer, King w
Fletcher Wm, laborer, New
Flett George, tailor, 30 Catharine s
Flett Mrs Margaret A (wid James) 102 Market
Flight James, stonecutter, 82 Emerald n
Flitcroft David, teamster, 95 Caroline n
Flitcroft Wm, blacksmith, Hess s
Flock Mrs Catharine (wid Wm) 24 Magill
Flockton John, fireman, 23 Simcoe w
Flood W, clerk, 60½ Tisdale
Flooks William G, letter carrier, 48 Wellington s
Flowers Albert, moulder, bds Victoria hotel
Flowers Henry, hostler, 49 Macnab n
Fluke Hugh, salesman, bds 57 John n
Flynn Daniel, laborer, 336 Hughson n
Flynn Daniel, stove mounter, 23 Stuart e
Flynn Edward, laborer, Greig
Flynn James, laborer, 32 Magill
Flynn Mrs Jane (wid James) 40 Charles
Flynn John, baker, 112 Cannon w
Flynn John, laborer, 53 Walnut s
Flynn Matthew, engineer, 260 York
Flynn Michael, 50 Walnut s.

Flynn William, clerk P O, 128 Young
Fobert Peter, tinsmith, 49 Young
Forster A C, tailor, 75 Merrick
Fogwell Mrs Mary (wid William) 45 Cannon
Fokt Louis, presser, bds 167 Catharine n
Foley Daniel, laborer, 114 Cherry
Foley Maurice, moulder, 107 Walnut s
Foley Michael, car driver, bds 49 Stuart w
Foley John, cooper, 34 Aurora
Foley Timothy, laborer, 119 Hannah e
Foote Charles C, superintendent Meriden Works, 10 Victoria ave n
Foquet Mrs Mary Ann (wid Richard) 34 Charles
Foquett Charles, laborer, 17 Barton e
Forbes A F, stock and share broker and insurance agent, 2 Merrick *See card*
Forbes Alex, hatter, bds Walker House
Forbes Alex, potash manf, 181 Wellington n
Forbes David, laborer, 47 Little William
Forbes George, teamster, 3 Kelly
Forbes George, fireman, 186 King William
Forbes John, cigar box manuf, 78 Mary
Forbes Robert, 80 Maria
Ford Mrs Henrietta (wid Joseph) 145 Main e
Ford James, health inspector, 269 John n
Ford John, 79 Barton e
Ford Joseph, clerk, bds 145 Main e
Ford Nehemiah, painter, bds 233 Mary
Ford T A, hair cutter, 68½ James n
Ford Thomas, baker, 88 Bay n
Ford Thomas, machinist, 75 Cannon w
Ford Wm, salesman, 34 Canada
Ford Wm, hair dresser, 117 James n
Ford —, whitewasher, 95 King e
Foreman George, moulder, 49 John
Foreman James, brakeman, 98 Victoria ave n
Foreman John, bookkeeper, 197 Cannon e
Foreman John, laborer, Dundurn
Foreman Mrs Mary (wid Wm) 16 Liberty
Foreman Peter, shoemaker, 197 Cannon e
Foresters' Hall, 108 James n
Forester James, laborer, 243 Bay n
Forrest Mrs Amanda (wid William, 128 John s
Forrest James, porter G T R, 243 Bay n
Forrest James, locksmith, 139 John s
Forster A M, brass founder, 173 James n, h 91 Murray e
Forster Clarence, wood turner, 97 East ave n
Forster John H, farmer, 44 Wellington s
Forster Sydney, wood turner, Smith ave
Forster Wm, wood turner, 128 Emerald n
Forster Wm C, artist, bds 42 Jackson w
Fortier Charles G, collector Inland revenue, 1 Vine, h 237 King w
Fortier Wilson, com traveler, 237 King w.
Forsyth Wm, tinsmith, 29 Murray e
Fossett Mrs, 168 Hughson n
Foster Arthur H, clerk, bds 7 Caroline n

Foster C H, merchant, 79 East ave s
Foster Chas, food inspector, 38 George
Foster C P, photographer, bds Franklin House
Foster Mrs Elizabeth (wid Edware) 127 Picton e
Foster Mrs Ellen (wid James) 72½ Elgin
Foster Frederick G, florist, 53 Charles
Foster George, fireman, bds 72½ Elgin
Foster George, glassblower, bds 43 Macauley w
Foster Henry, mechanic, bds 169 King e
Foster James, cutter, 7 Caroline n
Foster James G, plater, 6 Wellington n
Foster J F, plumber, 61 Strachan e
Foster John, fishmonger, 100 James n
Foster Joseph, engine driver G T R, 118 Locke n
Foster Leonard, potter, Main w
Foster Martin, laborer, 8 Mill
Foster Matthew J, carpenter, 111 Walnut s
Foster O H, clerk, 7 Caroline n
Foster Thomas, foreman clock works, 138 Wellington n
Foster T K, merchant tailor, 62 James n, h 32 Queen n
Foster Wm, moulder, 85 Cherry
Foster W W, manager Young Bros, 43 Lower Cathcart
Fotheringham John, wood worker, 38 Wilson
Foulis Wm, packer, 152 Duke
Foulkes Thomas J, barber, 91 York
Fox Andrew, millwright, 36 Locomotive
Fox Mrs Ann, 26 West ave s
Fox, Caleb, laborer, bds 19 Florence
Fox Mrs Eleanor (wid George) 18 Ray n
Fox George, purser, bds 26 West ave s
Fox James, tinsmith, 149 Main e
Fox John, 19 Florence
Fox John S, cabinet maker, 81 West ave n
Foxton John, carpenter, bds 9 Park s
Foxton John, laborer, 9 Ontario
Fowel Mrs Isabel, 35 Burlington
Fowkes Thomas, dry goods, 11 King Wm
Fowler Benj, laborer, 8 Ontario
Fowler Henry, shoemaker, 142 King Wm
Fowler John, tailor, King e
Fowler Walter, moulder, 180 Victoria ave n
Fowler Wm, foreman H S R R, 225 Hughson n
Fowles Thomas, teamster, 326 Macnab n
Foyster Fred, tobacco roller, 39 Peter
Frainor Frank, gardener, Main e
Francis Wm, pedler, 30 Young
Franey Thos, blacksmith, Duke
Frank Emil, letter carrier P O
Frank George E, carpenter, 306 Macnab n
Franklin House (Cook & Mitchell, props) King cor Park
Franklin Richard, machinist, 114 Wood e
Franklin Thomas, 8 Erie ave
Franks Charles, glue manf, 329 Catharine n
Franks C B, engineer G T R, Maria
Franks James, painter, 137 East ave n
Franks James G, bookkeeper, 45 Catharine n
Franks & O'Neil, painters, 114 King Wm
Franz Henry, presser, bds 167 Catharine n

Franz Henry C, tailor, h 167 Catharine n
Fraser Abner, bookkeeper, 80 Merrick
Fraser Alex, salesman, 145 Hughson n
Fraser Alexander (Fraser & Johnston) Burlington s
Fraser Mrs Ann (wid John) 81 Hunter e
Fraser Donald, tailor, 9 Little Peel
Fraser George, 24 Strachan w
Fraser James, moulder, 75 Duke
Fraser & Johnston (A Fraser, F Johnston) wholesale saddlery, 18 John n
Fraser Louis, shipper, 145 Hughson n
Fraser Robert S, cutter, 81 Hunter e
Fraser Peter, spring bed manf, r 63 King Wm
Fraser Thomas, laborer, bds 59 Locomotive
Fraser Thomas, butcher, 69 Napier
Fraser Wm (Fraser & Inches) h 211 King Wm
Fraser William G, laborer, 36 Jackson e
Fraser & Inches, grocers, 18 John s
Frazer John A, machinist, 211 King Wm
Frawley Michael, laborer, Jones
Frawley Thomas, laborer, Jones
Frazer Thos, butcher, 67 Napier
Frazer William, grocer, 211 King Wm
Free Henry, engineer, 302 Hughson n
Freeborn Edward, bds 42 Wilson
Freeborn George, laborer, 370 Catharine n
Freeborn John, laborer, Clark ave
Freeborn Joseph, laborer, 40 Barton w
Freeborn Thomas, laborer, Clark ave
Freeborn Thomas, shoemaker, 22 Napier
Freed Augustus T, editor *Spectator*, 14 Hannah w
Freed James, gardener, Aikman ave
Freed John B, traveler, 24 South e
Freel Thomas, laborer, 126 Ferrie e
Freeman Elijah, land and insurance agent, 7 Caroline s
Freeman Mrs Grace (wid Chas) 96 Bay s
Freeman Moss, laborer, 30 Gore
Freeman P W, wood dealer, 1 Ferguson ave, h 13 Grove
Freeman Mrs S B, Maplehurst, 161 James s
Freeman Steven, laborer, 53 Chisholm
Freeman W H, wood and coal and builders' supplies, 169 James n, h 80 Elgin
Freeth John jr, teamster, 99 Catharine n
Freeth John sr, 99 Catharine n
French George, gardener, 23 Maria
French George S, bookbinder, 23 Maria
Frenton I E, tailor, bds 150 Wellington n
Fretman Joseph, glassblower, 311 Macnab n
Frew Arch, agent C P R, 31 King e
Frewing Fred, plasterer, 288 King e
Fricker Walter, stove driller, 137 West ave n
Frid Geo, brickmaker, 221 Main w
Frid Mrs Sarah (wid Wm) 2 Robinson
Friday Geo, laborer, 40 Sheaffe
Frier Wm, dry goods, 61 Catharine n

Froelich Nicholas, bricklayer, 77 Bold
Frost W S O, clerk Bank of British North America, bds 54 Hunter w
Froud John, coachman, 88 Hughson n
Fudge Geo, engineer, 308 King w
Froud Wm, bds 126 Queen n
Fuere Richard, laborer, r 256 Macnab n
Fuerd Thos, laborer, 14 Guise
Fullen Frank, laborer, 227 King e
Fuller Albert A, 54 Hunter w
Fuller Andrew, heater, 73 Stuart w
Fuller, Edward, lamplighter, 173 Wood e
Fuller Henry, tailor, r 74 Emerald n
Fuller Henry H, barrister, 98 Bay s
Fuller John, gardener, Main e
Fuller, Nesbitt & Bicknell (V E Fuller, J W Nesbitt, James Bicknell) barristers, 20 James s
Fuller Richard, contractor, 73 Emerald s
Fuller Samuel B, policeman, 120 Wilson
Fuller Mrs Thos B, 75 Jackson w
Fuller V E (Fuller, Nesbitt & Bicknell) h 34 Queen s
Fulton Thos, laborer, r 79 Pearl n
Fulton William, laborer, 103 York
Furey Thos, nailcutter, 89 Ferrie e
Furlong Edward, barrister, 11 Main e, h 46 Duke *see card*
Furlong Moses, hack driver, 295 Macnab n
Furlong Thos, laborer, 286 Hughson n
Furmidge Peter, butcher, 180 James n
Furmidge Samuel, moulder, 180 James n
Furmidge Thos, carriage builder, 180 James n
Furneaux Edwin, carpenter, 21 Emerald n
Furniss Edmund (Furniss & Son) 51 York
Furniss & Son (Edmund & Spencer) marble cutters, 49 York
Furniss Spencer (Furniss & Son) 51 York
Furniss Wm, marble cutter, 9 Tom
Furnivall Thos G, tailor, 25 Pearl n
Fursdon Charles, moulder, 94 Robert
Fursdon Thomas, laborer, 109 Simcoe e
Gadsby Francis E, shoemaker, 37 Markland
Gadsby James, bookbinder, 37 Markland
Gage Andrew, butcher, 37 Queen n
Gage A W (A W Gage & Co) h 38 East ave s
Gage A W & Co, wh jewelers, 57 King e
Gage Mrs Catharine, 2½ Chisholm
Gage George, boots and shoes, 58 King e
Gage & Jelfs, barristers, 55 John s
Gage R R (Gage&Jelfs) Main e
Gage Samuel, laborer, 18 Crooks
Gage Mrs, bds 122 Market
Gagnier Mrs Oliver, hotel, 390 James n
Gahagan Henry, laborer, 40 Guise
Gahagen John, machinist, 33 Kelly
Gahagen M C, whip maker, 33 Kelly
Gahagen Michael, shoemaker, 33 Kelly
Gain Mrs Annie (wid John) 62 Robinson
Gair Matthew, piano finisher, 114 Caroline s
Gainy Mrs, 19 Steven
Galbreaith David B, customs officer, 116 Main e

Galbreaith Newton D, grocer, 104 King e, h 17 Main e
Gale Mrs Mary Ann (wid Edward) 77 Cherry
Gales Richard, barber, bds 63 Rebecca
Galicio Wm, bds 85 Hughson
Gallaghan John, carpenter, 281 John n
Gallagher Charles F, com traveler, 74 Mary
Gallagher George, boiler maker, 37 Inchbury n
Gallagher James, watchman, 113 Walnut s
Gallagher Michael, shoemaker, 74 Lower Cathcart
Gallagher R E, principal and proprietor Canada business college, Arcade, 31 James n, h 120 Market
Gallagher Robert, tailor, 124 John s
Gallivan Daniel, tanner, 137 Main e
Gallivan Dennis, laborer, 33 Margaret
Gallivan Michael, laborer 33 Margaret
Galtrey John, laborer, 33 Stuart e
Galvin John, machinist, 282½ King e
Galvin Patrick, porter, 282½ King e
Gant Jesse, barber, 282 James n
Gardener Alex, carter, Caroline s
Gardener Mrs Eeuphemia (wid Andrew) Maple
Gardiner John, letter carrier, 290 King William
Gardiner Herbert F, editor *Times*, 4 Bold
Gardner D W, salesman, 290 King William
Gardner George, conductor, 192 John n
Gardner James, bookkeeper, bds 42 Vine
Gardner J P, shoe cutter, 17 Steven
Gardner, Wm, scale maker, Bold
Gardner Wm, musician, 365 James n
Garland James, painter, 29½ Park n
Garland Louis (Garland & Rutherford) h 14 Park s
Garland & Rutherford (Louis Garland, Andrew Rutherford) druggists, 6 King e
Garner Geo, 18 Hunter e
Garner James, finisher, 178 Jackson w
Garner Mrs Mary, dressmaker, 111 John s
Garner Wm, fruit dealer, 168 King w
Garratt James, timber inspector, 22 James s, bds Allison House
Garrett James, moulder, 22 Devonport
Garrett John & Co, boot and shoe dealers and manufacturers, 55-57 King w
Garrett Thomas, moulder, 138 Macauley e
Garrick Mrs Ann (wid David) 146 King w
Garrick David J, novelty emporium, 146 King w
Garriock James, mason, 189 King e
Garriock Mrs James, confectioner, 189 King e
Garrison John, engine driver, 114 Cannon e
Garriety Samuel, porter, customs, 58 Ray n
Garrow Thomas, 60 Ray n
Garty John, 18 Hannah w
Garson James, engineer, John s
Garson James, carpenter, 126 John s
Garson David, brushmaker, 70 Main w
Gartland James, laborer, 23 Railway
Garton William, shoemaker, Herkimer

Gartshore Alex, iron founder, Stuart w, h 43 Charles
Garvey Mrs Mary (wid Michael) 48½ Augusta
Garvin William, machinist, 5 Little William
Gaskell Mrs Isabella, 256 Barton e
Gaskin James, engine turner, Jones
Gaston Thomas G, wire weaver, 16 Inchbury s
Gas Works Office, 91 Park n
Gataman Henry, moulder, bds 32 John n
Gatenby William, tailor, 128 Bay s
Gates A R, accountant, 121 Bay s
Gates Frederick W, president Hamilton Gas Co, 7 Herkimer
Gates F W jr, injector and railroad velocipede manuf, 22 James s, h 148 Bay s
Gates George E, clerk, 7 Herkimer
Gates H E, clerk, 7 Herkimer
Gates Joseph, detective, 30 Elgin
Gauld Rev John, Presbyterian, 64 Duke
Gauld John J, law student, 64 Duke
Gausby John D (Mackelcan, Gibson & Gausby) h 23 Main w
Gavey James, scale maker, 149 Jackson w
Gavey James, laborer, 204 Catharine n
Gaviller Alex, 21 Herkimer
Gaviller Edwin A, M D, 8 Park s
Gavin Mrs Margaret (wid Patrick) 40 Mulberry
Gay Mrs Catharine (wid James) bds 40 Pearl n
Gay James, bookkeeper, 66 Hughson s
Gay James P, clerk G T R, 40 Pearl n
Gay John B, bookseller and stationer, 78 King e, h 98 Cannon w
Gay Mrs Walter, 98 Cannon w
Gayfer Harry, manager A Murray & Co, 79 Wellington s
Geary John, gardener, 58 Young
Geary Michael, gardener, King e
Gebhard Jacob, shoemaker, 76 Wilson
Geddes James, car checker, 67 Ferrie e
Geddes J G, general ticket agent, 205 Main e
Geddes Mrs Mary, 290 John n
Gee Arthur, tailor, 18 Mary
Gee James, fitter, Greig
Gee John, laborer, 64 Steven
Gee Philip, laborer, 104 West ave n
Geiger Albert, baker, 218 King w
Geiger E A, sec Hamilton Commercial College, 216 King w
Geiger Henry H, hotel, 216 King w
Geiger Wm, flour and feed, 220 King w
Geiser Frank, brewer, bds 63 York
Geiss Ennis, machinist, bds 98 Bay n
Geiss Henry, wood turner, 4 Elgin
Geiss Wm, machinist, 98, 100 Bay n
Geiss Wm, woodturner, 4 Elgin
Geldart Geo H, picture frames, 131 King w, h 42 Barton w
Geldart Wm, brassfinisher, 42 Barton w
Gell Wm, second hand dealer, 17 King Wm
Gelson Robert, ass sec Y M C A, bds 16 Wellington n
Germania Hall, Jobert Jahn lessee, 33 John s
Germania Hotel, Robert Jahn prop, 22 John s
Generou Anthony, shoecutter, 37 King w

Gentle John, 20 Margaret
George Mrs Eliza (wid Wm) Duke
George Richard, shoemaker, 55 Emerald n
George Robert, tailor, 102 John s
George Mrs Robert, fancy goods, 102 John s
Georgian Bay Transportation Co, W J Grant, agent, 33 James n
Gernflau George W, miller, bds 287 York
Gerrie John W, chemist and druggist, 30 James n, h 5 Caroline s
Gerrie Wm, moulder, 253 Catharine n
Gerry Elbridge, hatter, 159 West ave n
Ghent Frederick, clerk, bds 89 Main e
Ghent S H, clerk county court, deputy clerk of the crown, court house, h 89 Main e
Gibb Albert, paper box manf, 120, 122 King Wm
Gibbons James, gardener, 90 Robert
Gibbs Mrs Elizabeth (wid Rev Samuel Y) 56 Jackson w
Gibson David R, mason, 64 Victoria ave n
Gibson Hamilton, printer, 23 Steven
Gibson John, carpenter, Garth
Gibson J G, conductor, 5 Ferguson ave
Gibson J M, M A, L L B, M P P (Mackelcan, Gibson & Gausby) h 102 Main w
Gidley Mrs Sarah (wid John) 23 Ferguson ave
Gilchrist Mrs Agnes (wid James) 86 Market
Gilchrist James, carpenter, 72 Elgin
Gilbert Alfred, machinist, 32 Wilson
Gilbert David, laborer, 166 Hughson n
Gilbert Ed, laborer, 27 Markland
Gilbert E S, laborer, 88 Florence
Gilbert Mrs Harriet (wid Roswell) 87½ Jackson w
Gilbert H J, clerk, 31 Gore
Gilbert John T, machinist, 56 Pearl s
Gilbert Thomas, bds 27 Markland
Gilbert Thomas, laborer, bds 103 York
Gildon Henry, grocer, 51 Wellington n
Gill Matthew, boiler maker, 102 Ferrie e
Gill Robert, boiler maker, 247 John n
Gill Mrs (wid Joseph) 232 King Wm
Gillam Henry, laborer, 367 Hughson n
Gilland Wm, moulder, Garth
Gillard Henry H, 134 Hughson n
Gillard John (W H Gillard & Co) h 26 George
Gilliard Mrs Maria (wid Henry) 12 Liberty
Gillard W H (W H Gillard & Co) h Concession
Gillard W H & Co, wh grocers, 5 Hughson s
Gillesby William, grain and wool merchant, 6 John s, h Wentworth s
Gillesby William F, clerk, bds Wentworth s
Gillespie Alex, clerk, 9 Emerald s
Gillespie Mrs Ann (wid Thomas) 139 York
Gillespie David, second hand dealer, 160 York, h 6 Greig
Gillespie George H (Gillespie & Powis) h 9 Emerald s
Gillespie Hugh, grocer, 263 Macnab n
Gillespie Hugh, 31 Ferrie w
Gillespie John, machinist, 195 Hughson n

Gillespie John, clerk, bds 9 Emerald s

Gillespie & Powis (George H Gillespie, Alfred Powis) insurance agents, tea and coffee brokers, 31 King e. *See adv, page 2*

Gillespie Samuel, contractor, 247 King William

Gillespie William, whipmaker, 27 Mary

Gillespie William, pattern maker, 8 Simcoe e

Gillett Edward, cashier, Wellington cor Stinson

Gillies Alex, com traveler, 40 Hunter

Gillies Mrs Catharine (wid Geo) 66 Charles

Gillies David (Buntin, Gillies & Co) h 66 Charles

Gillis Edward, clerk, bds 33 Wellington s

Gillies George, printer, bds 71 Vine

Gillies H N, com traveler, bds temperance dining rooms

Gillies William (W Gillies & Co) 159 York

Gillies William, steward house of refuge, 71 Vine

Gillies W & Co, grocers, 159 York

Gilligan Joseph, glassblower, 64 Wood e

Gilmer Oliver, clerk, 22 Hess n

Gilmore John, cabinet maker, 90 Hunter w

Gilmore John, organ builder, 88 Market

Gilmore Mrs Louisiana (wid Dan) 123 Park n

Gilmore Mrs Sarah (wid Robert) 141 Main e

Gilmore Thos H, cabinet maker, 54 Queen s

Gilmore Wm, auctioneer, bds 90 Hunter w

Gilmore Wm, shoemaker, 92 Rebecca, h Wellington n

Gilmore Wm, butcher, 140 Main e

Gilmore Wm, shoemaker, 65 Wellington n

Gilmore Wm J (Johnston & Gilmore) 90 Hunter w

Gimblett Robert, shoemaker, 107 Jackson e

Girls' Home, Mrs Scott, matron, 77 George

Girouard Mrs Margaret (wid Candid) Barton w

Girouard Wm, laborer, Barton w

Gitchell D W, 73 East ave s

Givin Wm, accountant, 35 Robert e

Glackin Thomas, cutter, 155 John n

Glasgow Major John, 65 Vine

Glasgow & London Insursurance Co, Wm Strong, agent, Arcade, 33 James n

Glass Galbreith, shoemaker, bds 63 Wellington n

Glass George, shoemaker, 6 Evans

Glass James, shoemaker, 136 Hunter w

Glass Mrs Sarah (wid George) 164 Rebecca

Glass Thomas, moulder, 87 Elgin

Glass Wallace, moulder, 40 Wellington n

Glassco A W, com traveler, 120 Hughson s

Glassco Charles merchant, 102 Hughson s

Glassco Frank, clerk, 102 Hughson s

Glassco G T (W H Glassco & Sons) h Park cor Robinson

Glassco H W (W H Glassco & Sons) h 109 Bay s

Glassco John T (Macpherson, Glassco & Co) Macnab cor Markland

Glassco W H (W H Glassco & Sons) h 102 Hughson s

Glassco W H & Sons, wholesale hatters, 11 King e
Glassford John, fireman, 118 Cannon e
Glassy Edward, miller, bds 156 Rebecca
Glazier Edward, porter, Bank of Montreal
Gleason Dennis, agent, 80 Market
Gleason Miss Mary, dressmaker, 202 James n, h 45 Murray
Glebe Henry, tailor, Wilson
Gleeson Mrs Mary (wid John) bds 83 Pearl n
Gleeson Mrs Mary, 189 Bay n
Gleeson Michael, boiler maker, 26 Inchbury n
Gleeson Patrick, carpenter, 83 Pearl n
Gleeson Wm, laborer, 139 Ferrie e
Glendon Wm, bookkeeper, 81 Catharine s
Glenn Richard, carter, 129 Wood e
Glenn Mrs Robert, 29 Stuart e
Glennie Wm, com traveler, 54 Victoria ave s
Globe Newspaper, J H Mattice correspondent and agent, 70 James n
Glover Alexander, dairyman, King e
Glover Daniel, bricklayer, 84 Queen s
Goddard Andrew, engineer, 60 Hughson n
Goddard Mrs Emma, 119 Hess n
Goddard John, laborer, 33 Crooks
Goddard Nathaniel, fish dealer, 204 King w
Godfrey William, baggageman, 133 Rebecca
Godard William W, com traveler, 107 Market
Goering George, hotel, 17 John s
Goering Henry, hotel, 61-63 York
Goering Mrs J W, 54 West ave
Goering Wm (Reid, Goering & Co) h West ave cor Stinson
Goff Edward, traveler, 254 Barton e
Golden Miss Mary, 22 Wilson
Goldsmith Rev Thomas pastor St John's Church, 19 West ave s
Gold F M, clerk, G T R, 62 Cannon
Gold J A, piano maker, Aikman's ave
Gompf John, brewer, 360 John n
Gompf William, teamster, Brewery Lane, John n
Gonell T S, excise officer, bds American hotel
Good John, clerk, bds 113 Main w
Good Martin, cabinet maker, 153 Mary
Goodale James, laborer, 82 Bold
Gooddall George, laborer, 7 Wood Market Square
Goodfellow John, painter, 116 Cherry
Goodfellow Walter, pattern fitter, 179 Cannon e
Goodfellow Wm, stovemounter, 181 Cannon e
Goodman Abe, carpenter, Wentworth n
Goodman Frank, stove mounter, 84 Caroline n
Goold Henry J, Maple Leaf hotel, 13 Market Square
Goold Roland, printer, bds Maple Leaf hotel
Goodram Wm, harness maker, 12 Little Market
Goodwin Alfred J, porter, 5 George
Goodwin Richardson A, porter G T R, bds Temperance hotel, Stuart e
Goodwin W D, moulder, Clark ave
Goodwin Wright M, telegraph inspector G T R, 41 Jackson w

Goodwin Wm, watchmaker and jeweler, 77 John s
Goodyer Wm, maltster, 103 Mulberry
Gordon Edwin, butcher, James st, res mountain top
Gordon James, clerk P O
Gordon J S, clerk Bank of Hamilton
Gordon Peter, moulder, 20 Mulberry
Gordon Robert, clerk, 227 Mary
Gordon Robert, carpenter, 72 Wellington s
Gordon Robert, clerk, 221 Mary
Gordon Thomas, shipper, 87 Locke n
Gordon Walter, moulder, 1 Little Wellington
Gordon Wm, cooper, 82 Rebecca, h 32 Catharine n
Gordon W J F, builders' supplies and coal, 108 James n, h 32 Catharine n
Gore John, letter carrier, 122 Cannon w
Gore Coffee Tavern, 11 Hughson n and Alexandra Arcade, 31 James n
Gore St Methodist Church, Rev James Vanwyck, pastor, John cor Gore
Goring Charles, carpenter, 141 Wellington n
Gorman Hugh, porter G T R, 76 Hannan w
Gorman John, laborer, 244 Mary
Gorman John, teamster, 339 John n
Gorman Mrs Mary (wid Patrick) 121 Hunter e
Gorman Peter, blacksmith, 162 King w, h 164 Market
Gorman Philip, moulder, bds 129 Rebecca
Gormley Joseph, glassblower, 282 John n
Gorvin John, sewing machines, 99 James n
Gosnay Jas, filesmith, 139 Main e
Gottorft F, marble cutter, 118 York
Gough Fred, foreman, 164 Ferguson ave
Gould D H, shoemaker, 162 James n
Gould Jacob, joiner, 11 Grove
Gould James, foreman Hurd & Roberts 41½ Pearl n
Goulding Arthur, caretaker Hess st school, 83 Hess n
Goulier Trifler, tobacco roller, bds 95 York
Gourlay Miss Helena, 156 Napier
Govier Mrs (wid James) 16 West ave n
Gow James N, salesman, 98 James s
Gow Mrs Whilelmina (wid Wm) 134 Hunter e
Gowanlock Robert, engine driver G T R, 90 Locke n
Gowland Wm, propr Court House hotel, 55 and 57 John s
Graban John, laborer, bds 119 Napier
Gracie Charles H, laborer, 108 Young
Grace James, woodworker, 217 Barton e
Grace Mrs Mary (wid Lawrence) 203 Mary
Grace Pierce, melter, 156 Bay n
Grace Thomas, wood dealer, 258 Hughson n
Graham Alexander, grocer, 292 John n
Graham C W, salesman, 39 George
Graham D, fireman, 59 Victoria ave n
Graham Daniel, carpenter, 64 Colborne
Graham David, laborer, bds 11 Strachan e
Graham David, gents' furnishings, 3 James n, h 53 Hunter w
Graham Donald, fireman, 127 Cannon e

Graham Duncan, laborer, 66 Emerald n
Graham Mrs Ellen (wid Robert) 44 Burlington w
Graham George, tailor, 101 Hess s
Graham Henry, bartender American hotel
Graham James, shoemaker, 123 East ave n
Graham John, grocer, 317 Barton e
Graham John, cigar maker, Wilson e of Wentworth
Graham John, 13 Little William
Graham John H, clerk, bds 26 East ave n
Graham Misses, hairworkers, 42 James n
Graham Richard, dyer, Herkimer cor Queen
Graham Robert, laborer, bds 173 Macnab n
Graham Wm, grocer, 107 Cannon w
Graham Wm, barber, bds 178 James n
Graham Wm, teller Bank of British North America, Burlington
Grand Trunk, City Passenger Agency, Chas E. Morgan, agent, 11 James n
Grand Trunk Station, Stuart w
Granger Harry, agent, 71 Caroline n
Granger J C, pedler, Ashley
Grant Mrs Annie (wid Thomas) 7 Hunter w
Grant A R, water inspector, 47 Alanson
Grant Mrs Augusta, 284 Bay n
Grant Col C C, 151 John s
Grant Mrs David, 25 Simcoe e
Grant John, moulder, bds 41 John n
Grant Mrs John, 110, 112 Jackson e
Grant P & Sons (James M Lottridge, John H Cummer, Wm L Cummer) brewers, Bay cor Mulberry
Grant Mrs Peter, King cor Wentworth
Grant P H, salesman, King cor Wentworth
Grant R C, agent, 276 King e
Grant S W, bookkeeper, 284 Bay n
Grant William, printer, 288 John n
Grant W J, city ticket agt N & N W, M C and C P R R's, Arcade, 33 James n, h 13 West ave s
Grant Mrs George, 25 Simcoe e
Gray Mrs Elizabeth (wid Daniel) 104 Macnab n
Gray Henry, locker customs, 37 Strachan w
Gray Mrs Janet (wid James) 9 Hess n
Gray John, laborer, 134 Picton e
Gray John, laborer, 57 Stuart e
Gray Patrick, laborer, 23 Locomotive
Gray Richard, 64 Emerald n
Gray Robert, laborer, 288 Hughson n
Gray Robert, conductor G T R, 105 Bay n
Gray Wm, mason, 19 Sheaffe
Grey W J, com traveler, 143 Catharine n
Grey Wm, foreman G T R, 134 Cannon w
Grayson George, spring maker, 26 Caroline n
Gray —, salesman, bds 34 Bay n
Grayson Walter, clerk, bds 78 Market
Greasley —, gardener, 92 East ave n
Great North-Western Telegraph Co, George Black, manager, 18 James s
Green Mrs A (wid Richard) 66 East ave s

Green Edward, laborer, bds 78 Bold
Green Edwin, furniture, 86 King w, h 124 York
Green Fred A, (Storm & Green) 31 Elgin
Green George, butcher, 78 Bold
Green George, laborer, Oak
Green George, laborer, 123 Hess n
Green Harry, merchant, 63 Hughson s
Green Horace, millwright, 192 Robert e
Green James, laborer, 174 Victoria ave n
Green Joseph, bookkeeper, 66 East ave s
Green Mrs John, 145 Main w
Green Mrs Richard, 289 James n
Green Richard, trader, 30 Guise
Green R H (John McPherson & Co) h 89 Hughson s
Green Thomas A, mariner, 168 Ferguson ave
Greene T J C, barrister, 31 James s
Green William, laborer, 108 Strachan e
Greenaway James T, sailor, bds 170 Ferguson ave
Greenaway Job, foreman vinegar works, Wilson e of Wentworth
Greenaway Mrs Susan (wid Thomas) 170 Ferguson ave
Greenaway Thomas, moulder, 66 Hughson n
Greenhill Mrs Isabella (wid David) bds 50 Hunter w
Greenhill Walter W, saddler, 92 Queen s
Greening B & Co, wire mills, 41-3 Queen n
Greening John, agent, 73 Vine
Greenfield Joseph, bailiff, 77 Elgin
Greening Samuel O, (B Greening & Co) h 63 Queen n
Greening T B (T B Greening & Co) h 17 Hess s
Greening T B & Co, teas and coffees, 23 King w
Greening Thomas, moulder, 89 Hughson n
Greenless Malcolm, tinsmith, bds 9 Park s
Greenles James, moulder 35 Stuart e
Greenley James, carpenter, 66 Pearl n
Greenway Francis J, ornamenter, 54 Pearl n
Greenway Henry, laborer, 105 Hess n
Greenwood James R, hatter, 161 East ave n
Greer D Geo, real estate agent, 20 James s, h 13 Duke
Greer Mrs John H, teacher, 9 Murray w
Gregg Jeremiah, laborer, 191 Wilson
Gregg Miss Mary, 13 East ave n
Gregory S E, commission merchant, 55 Catharine s
Greig Geo, gardener, Burlington n
Greig Henry G, 149 John s
Greig John, stationer, 2 York, h 119 Queen n
Greig John jr, salesman, 119 Queen n
Grey Andrew, checker G T R, 86 Caroline n
Grey Henry, customs officer, 37 Strachan w
Grey Robert, laborer, bds 350 James n
Grey Mrs S F (wid James) 7 Cannon w
Greig W, machinist, bds Victoria hotel
Gribbon Thomas, carpenter, 157 Macnab n
Griffin Andrew, letter carrier, P O
Griffin Dennis, machinist, bds 198 James n
Griffin Mrs Harriet (wid Absalom) bds 7 Caroline s

Griffin Henry, 38 Jackson e
Griffin H S, M D, 15 Walnut s
Griffin Mrs Julia (wid Michael) 48 Jackson e
Griffin Justus A, (Griffin & Kidner) h 106 Barton e
Griffin & Kidner, (Justus A Griffin, Frank Kidner) printers, 47 King Wm
Griffin Miss Maggie, dressmaker, 48 Jackson e
Griffin Michael, machinist, bds 161 Catharine n
Griffin Patrick, laborer, 121 Cannon w
Griffin Mrs Thos, 28 West ave n
Griffin William, mariner, 55 Burlington w
Griffin Mrs, 34 Wilson
Griffiths Edwin, laborer, 104 Queen n
Griffith Mrs Elizabeth, 228 Hughson n
Griffith Robert, com traveler, 143 John s
Griffith Samuel, porter, 59 Emerald n
Griffith Mrs Margaret (wid Evan) 12 Upper Cathcart
Griffith Wm (Wm Griffith & Co) 139 James s
Griffith W & Co (W Griffith, Henry Griffith and John Lennox) wh boots and shoes, 53 King w
Griffith —, engineer, bds 208 Macnab n
Griffiths Thos, laborer, Tiffany
Griffiths Tunis B, ticket agent G T R, 6 Ray s
Grigg Alfred, clerk, Concession
Grigg Mrs Janet (wid Edwin) 24 Catharine s
Griggs Chris S, policeman, 37 Locomotive
Grill Lawrence, laborer, foot Caroline n
Grimes Miss Bridget, dressmaker, 73 Merrick
Grimes Joseph, laborer, Concession
Griner W B, glassblower, 42 Macauley w
Gross James, carpenter, 221 Barton e
Grossman Augustus, music dealer, 24 West ave s
Grossman Julius, music dealer, 22 West ave s
Grossman P, music dealer, 49 James n, h 168 Main e
Grotz Adam, nailer, 66 Locomotive
Grover G A, supt American Express Co, 18 James s
Grover Joseph, gardener, bds 1 Wood Market Square
Groves James, blacksmith, 138 West ave n
Groves John, laborer, bds 17 Barton e
Groves John, brakeman, 19 Lower Cathcart
Groves Samuel, blacksmith, 37 York, h 125 East ave n
Grundy C J, gardener, 5 Clark ave
Guarantee Company of North America, Seneca Jones agent, 59 James n
Guardian Fire and Life Assurance Co of London, (Eng) Gillespie & Powis, ag'ts, 31 King e
Guenther George F, tailor, bds 31 Bay n
Guerin Michael, laborer, 128 Queen n
Guerin R C, clerk G T R, 257 Macnab s
Gugel Wm, shoemaker, 122 Rebecca
Guillet Nap, tobacco roller, 87 King w
Gully Joshua, Woodbine hotel, 28 Merrick
Gully J T, grocer, Wentworth n
Gully Thomas G, soda water manf, 41 Sheaffe

Gully W S, hotel, 39 Mary
Gundy F, traveler, bds 62 Can-Cannon e
Gunn Donald, painter, 143 Victoria ave n
Gunn Edmund, bookkeeper, 70 Bay s
Gunn R L, accountant, clerk Ninth Division Court, Court House, h 28 Hannah e
Gunner Wm, tea dealer, 71 Catharine n
Gurner Henry, bricklayer, 120 Jackson e
Gurney Charles (E & C Gurney & Co) h John s
Gurney E & C Co (Limited) (Charles Gurney, John H Tilden, E Gurney jr) stove manufactures, 36-42 John n
Gurney Mrs E, hd John s
Gurney & Ware, scale manfs, cor James and Colborne
Guthrie Thomas, poulterer, 125 Rebecca
Guttridge Joseph, boarding, 304 James n
Guy Hugh, brewer, 10 Guise
Guyette Joseph, porter, 65 Cherry
Gwyder Richard, whitewasher, 84 Macnab n
Haas Gottlieb, nurseryman, 104 Catharine s
Hacker George G, manager W J Waugh, 30 George
Hackett John, polisher, 95 Hunter e
Hackett Michael, polisher, bds 95 Hunter e
Hadley Mrs L, 256 Hughson n
Hafner John, glassblower, 270 James n
Hahnau John, bricklayer, 80 Markland
Haigh Richard, bookbinder and paper boxes, 60 King w, h 3 Canada
Haight H B, yard master N & N W R, 45 Ferguson ave
Haines Alfred, potter, 25 Margaret
Haines Mrs Harriet (wid Amos) 173 Napier
Haines James B, conductor, 126 West ave n
Haines Mrs Sarah (wid John) 179 Napier
Haines Thomas P, machinist, 58 Wilson, h 23 Wellington
Halcrow James, gauger customs, 235 James n
Halcrow Wm, mason, 235 James n
Hale Henry, laborer, 251 Macnab n
Halford Hardy J, barber, 55 John s, h 90 John n
Hall David, blacksmith, 3 Locke s
Hall Edward, hatter, 91 Locke n
Hall Mrs Edward, music teacher, 91 Locke h
Hall Mrs Harriet, 178 Napier
Hall Henry, teamster, 231 Main w
Hall Herbert, fireman, 93 Murray e
Hall James, moulder, 51 John n
Hall John, locomotive foreman G T R, 176 Bay n
Hall John, cabinet maker, 178 Napier
Hall John, laborer, 78 Main w
Hall John, pattern maker, 167 John n
Hall John, 40 Wilson
Hall John T (McCallum & Hall) h 178 Napier
Hall Mrs, 69 Hannah w
Hall Mrs Margaret (wid James) 231 Main w
Hall Mrs Mary, 181 King e
Hall Robert, inspector Landed Banking & Loan Co, e s Wentworth nr Main
Hall Robt jr, burnisher, Wentworth s
Hall Thos, fitter, 13 Inchbury n

Hall Thomas, 93 Locke n
Hall Thomas, engine driver, 89 Elgin
Hall Wm, wood turner, Beulah
Hall Wm, dairyman, 39 Wood e
Hall Wm G, traveler, 21 West ave n
Hall —, moulder, bds 55 York
Hallett Fred, bds 46 Magill
Halliday Christopher, laborer, 134 Macnab n
Halliday Frank B, com. traveler, 109 Catharine s
Halliday John, laborer, 82 Walnut s
Halliday Wm (Reid & Halliday) 131½ Main e
Hallisy Wm, policeman, 117 Jackson e
Halloran J E, livery, 68 John n
Halloran James W, grocer, 48 Peter
Halloran Timothy, laborer, Brock e
Halm Rev M S (Roman Catholic) 25 Sheaffe
Halson Mrs Robert, 39 Robert
Halter Joseph, butcher, 21 Little William
Ham Thomas (Ham & Wilson) 64 Lower Cathcart
Ham & Wilson (T Ham, J Wilson) stoves and tinware, 33 York
Hamburgh Frank, weaver, 223 Catharine n
Hamburgh William, carpenter, 254 James n
Hamen Gerty, laborer, bds 104 Market
Hamill John, laborer, 138 Locke n
Hamill Henry, gardener, 69 Duke
Hamill Henry, gardener, Wilson
Hamilton Mrs A E, 37 Rebecca
Hamilton, Alex, clerk, 64 Ferguson ave
Hamilton A & Co, druggists, King cor James
Hamilton Alex (A Hamilton & Co) h 104 Main w
Hamilton Alex, jr, bookkeeper, 104 Main w
Hamilton Andrew, ledger keeper Ham Prov & Loan society, 41 Bay s
Hamilton Mrs Ann (wid Francis) 134 Locke n
Hamilton Branch Bible Society Depository, Donald McLellan, 28 King w
Hamilton Bridge and Tool Co, C Teiper, manager, foot Caroline n
Hamilton Charles, foreman Thos McIlwraith, foot Macnab
Hamilton Cigar Co, Reid, Goering & Co, proprietors, 102 King e
Hamilton Club, J B Young, sec, 2 Main e
Hamilton Commercial College, M L Rattray, principal, James s cor King w
Hamilton Cotton Co, J M Young, manager, 184, 204 Mary
Hamilton and Dundas Express Office, P E Webber, manager, Bowen
Hamilton and Dundas St Railway, A A Anderson, manager, 16 Main e
Hamilton Ebenezer, clerk, 104 Main w
Hamilton Mrs Emily (wid Jos) 105 James s
Hamilton Mrs Frances (wid John) 32 Breadalbane
Hamilton Gaslight Co, Thos Littlehales, engineer and manager, 91 Park n
Hamilton Glass Works, 306 Hughson n
Hamilton George, stonecutter, 30 Tisdale
Hamilton George E, com traveler, 101 King w

Hamilton Gun Works, J Holman, proprietor, 79 James n

Hamilton Homestead Loan and Savings Society, I A Studdart, sec, court house

Hamilton Hopkin, moulder, 71 Colborne

Hamilton House Building Co, R L Gunn, sec, Court House

Hamilton Industrial Works Co, Jno Kinleyside, manager, Bay n cor Murray

Hamilton Iron Forging Co, foot Queen n

Hamilton James, druggist, 104 Main w

Hamilton James, laborer, Jones

Hamilton James, tobacco presser, 140 Jackson w

Hamilton James, agent The Shedden Co, 9 King w, h 64 Ferguson ave

Hamilton James H, ,carpenter, 81 East ave n

Hamilton John H, clerk, 101 King w

Hamilton John J, clerk G T R, 64 Robinson

Hamilton John M, porter, 51 Stuart w

Hamilton Laundry, Miss Annie Callaghan, propr, 36 Merrick

Hamilton Michael, laborer, 17 Burlington w

Hamilton Mrs Martin, 69 Walnut s

Hamilton and Northwestern Railway, Maitland Young sec, 115 Main e

Hamilton Orphan Asylum, 115 Wellington s

Hamilton Packing House, Thomas Lawry, propr, 14, 16 Macnab s

Hamilton Pottery, Robert Campbell, propr, 46, 48 Locke n

Hamilton Powder Co, James Watson, resident director, 69 James n

Hamilton Provident and Loan Society, H D Cameron, treas, King cor Hughson

Hamilton Protective Collecting Association, F R Ghent, sec, room 9, court house

Hamilton Robert, 258 Bay n

Hamilton Robert, stonecutter, bds 56 Gore

Hamilton Robert J, 101 King w

Hamilton Straw Works, John McArthur, propr, Ferguson ave n

Hamilton Street Railway, 41 Stuart w

Hamilton Universal Labor Agency, J B Dayfoot, 182 King e

Hamilton Vinegar Works Co (limited) B E Charlton, pres, Wm Marshall, sec-treas and manager, 5, 7 Wellington n and 85, 87 James s

Hamilton Whip Co (limited) W J Lavery, pres, T D Murphy, vice-pres, sec-treas and manager, 81 Mary

Hamilton William, carpenter, 81 Locomotive

Hamilton Mrs, 4 O'Reilly

Hammel Samuel, bds Dominion hotel

Hammill Charles, teamster, bds 94 Hunter e

Hammill Henry, teamster, 94 Hunter e

Hammill S R, teamster, 94 Hunter e

Hammon Mrs Matilda (wid Henry) boarding, 51 Park n

Hammond Mrs B, 43 Stuart e

Hammond D N, carpenter, 50 West ave n

Hammond James, grocer, 209 John n

Hammond John, laborer, 57 Mary

Hammond R, whitewasher, 51 Chisholm
Hammond Samuel R, coachman, 75 Jackson w
Hammond Wm F, shoemaker, 46 Young
Hampson Charles, hatter, bds 130 Cannon e
Hampson James, pattern fitter, 126½ Emerald n
Hampson John, shoemaker, 161 King William
Hampson John E, com traveler, 71 Victoria ave n
Hampson Mrs Mary (wid James) 21 Lower Cathcart
Hampton Harry J, machinist, 56 Hughson s
Hancock Edward, carpenter, r 241 Bay n
Hancock James, whipmaker, 61 Maria
Hancock John, bricklayer, 24 Wellington n
Hancock Joseph, 22 Hannah e
Hancock Oliver, tobacconist, 110 King w
Hancock Samuel R, laborer, 107 Florence
Hancock Wm, builder, 27 Locomotive
Hand & Co, firework manf (Prof W Hand, pres, H P Breay, sec) 20 Head
Hand Michael, moulder, bds 32 John n
Hand William, firework manf, 20 Head
Haney Mrs J H, confectioner, 149 York
Hanlan Mrs Margaret (wid Edward) 25 Macauley e
Hanley Martin, blacksmith, 37 Hannah e
Hanley Patrick, bricklayer, 34 Simcoe e
Hanley Mrs Rosanna, 294 John n
Hanley Timothy, laborer, 188 Robert e

Hanley William, laborer, 275 John n
Hanley William, blacksmith, 32 Bay s
Hanlon Mrs Ann M (wid Daniel) 81 Hunter w
Hanlon Patrick, grocer, Market cor Hess
Hann J W, printer, 56 Barton e
Hanna Mrs Sarah, nurse, 17 Grove
Hannaford Alfred (Hannaford Bros) 100 Robinson
Hannaford Bros (R Hannaford, A Hannaford) ornamental plasterers, 76 Merrick *See adv, page 3*
Hannaford Robert (Hannaford Bros) 76 Merrick
Hannah Alexander, bricklayer, 57 York
Hannah Elijah, laborer, 51 Canada
Hannah James, contractor, 125 James n
Hannah James, shoemaker, 151 John n
Hannah Street Methodist Church, Rev A C Crewes, pastor, Hannah nr Queen
Hannah Wm, 20 Stuart e
Hannam A W, clerk, bds 54 Hunter w
Hannon Emerson, 62 John n
Hannon John, laborer, 272 Mary
Hannon Mrs John, 231 Hughson n
Hanning Mrs Robert, 15 Murray w
Hapbush John, 47 Caroline s
Harbin Mrs Alice (wid Edward) 193 John n
Harcourt James, clerk, Bank of Commerce, bds 45 Charles
Hardiker George A, clerk G T R, 35 Bold
Hardikin Peter, laborer, bds 215 James n

Hardiman James, baker, 79 Hunter w
Hardiman Thomas, confectioner, 84 Market
Harding Henry, steam plumbing and gas fitting, 119 James cor Cannon
Hardman Mrs Alice (wid John) 10 Tiffany
Hardstaff Mrs Annie, 161 Victoria ave n
Hardy David, moulder, 24 Simcoe e
Hardy Edward, laborer, 13 Picton w
Hardy W R, sewing machines, 154 Mary
Hargrove & Sons (Joseph, W L and Henry) sewing machines and Domestic paper patterns, 118 King e, h 105 Emerald n
Harlow Thomas, grocer, 69 Young
Harman James, laborer, 165 Jackson w
Harney M J, manager Ontario Sewing Machine Co, 44 Victoria ave s
Harney —, porter, 44 King e
Harold John, glassblower, 348 James n
Harper A, butcher, 14 John s, h Main e
Harper Arthur J, plater, bds 116 Young
Harper Mrs Elizabeth (wid Richard) 16 O'Reilly
Harper George, laborer, 3 Florence
Harper Geo, printer, 20½ Ray n
Harper James, mail clerk G T R, 156 Market
Harper John, gardener, bds Argo
Harper Miss M, teacher, Main cor Burlington
Harper Richard, stove polisher, 113 Caroline s
Harper Robert, florist, 18-20 Wellington n
Harper Robert, carpenter, 66 Colborne
Harper Thomas, gardener, Burlington s
Harper Thomas J, plater, bds 116 Young
Harper William, printer, 128 Market
Harper Wm, 70½ Lower Cathcart
Harper Wm, fireman, 156 Market
Harper William, shoemaker, 113 King William
Harper William, laborer, 210 John n
Harrigan John, glassblower, 297 James n
Harris Benjamin, watchmaker, drill sheds, James n
Harris Duncan, clerk, 29 Hess n
Harris Edward, boarding, 140 Bay n
Harris Elliott, tobacco roller, 60 Bay n
Harris Fred J, clerk, bds 55 Park n
Harris George, com traveler, 215 King e
Harris George, 22 Strachan w
Harris Miss Henrietta, 53 Mary
Harris James, policeman, 39 Locomotive
Harris James, engine driver G T R, 47 Magill
Harris James, machinist, 20 Strachan w
Harris J M, clerk, 11 Cannon w
Harris John, laborer, 250 Jas n
Harris John, whitewasher, 69 John n
Harris John M, bookkeeper, 11 Cannon w
Harris Joseph, teamster, 250 James n
Harris Mrs Maggie E (wid Thos B) 40 Jackson w
Harris Mrs, bds 97 Hunter e
Harris R B, clerk, 11 Cannon w

Harris Mrs Susan (wid Alfred J) 92 Bold
Harris Thomas, stonecutter, 33 Strachan e
Harris William, messenger, 6 Steven
Harris William, laborer, 250 Jas n
Harris Mrs Wm, 139½ John s
Harris Wm, baker, 14 Market sq, h 55 Park n
Harris Wm, laborer, 182 King Wm
Harris Wm H, painter, 36 Cannon w
Harris Wm J, carter, 3 Inchbury s
Harris Wm J, clerk, bds 55 Park n
Harris W J, manager Wm Harris, 14 Market sq
Harris W J, caretaker drill shed, 144 James n
Harrison Mrs Amelia (wid Frank) dressmaker, 94 Hunter w
Harrison Mrs Anna (wid Henry) 84 Rebecca
Harrison Bros (F T and Jas) druggists, 36 James n and 274 James n
Harrison Charles W, teacher, 133 John n
Harrison Edward, hackman, 44 Locke s
Harrison F T (Harrison Bros) bds 133 John n
Harrison Geo, machinist, Garth
Harrison George P, manager Mason & Risch, 56 Wellington n
Harrison Henry, butcher, 51 James s
Harrison James, hackman, 40 Pearl s
Harrison James (Harrison Bros) bds 133 John n
Harrison J G, clerk, 37 Steven
Harrison John, plasterer, 107 Herkimer
Harrison John (Osler, Teetzel & Harrison) h 78 Bay s
Harrison John, screwcutter, Pine
Harrison John, plumber, bds 270 King e
Harrison Misses L & E, milliners, 178 King e
Harrison Luke, gymnast, 115 Hunter e
Harrison W H C, herbalist, 71 York
Harrison W S, painter, 270 King e
Harron Andrew, cab driver, 205 James n
Harron Wm, laborer, 205 James n
Hart Emery Wheel Co (limited) Samuel Briggs, manager, 19 Hunter w
Hart Machine Co, Samuel C Rogers, manager, 19 Hunter w
Harte Patrick, bookkeeper, 248 Hughson n
Hart Robert, hatter, 169 Mary
Harte R R, clerk, bds 7 Bold
Hart Solomon, teamster, 87 King William
Harter Joseph, moulder, 206 Cannon e
Hartford Fire Insurance Co, George McKeand, agent, 57 James n
Hartley Joseph T, laborer, 21 O'Reilly
Hartley Mrs Sarah (wid John) fancy goods, 131 James n
Hartnett Daniel, laborer, 215 Bay n
Hartnet Mrs Elizabeth (wid John) 148 King Wm
Harvey Allan, laborer, 127 Napier
Harvey Alex (Alex Harvey & Co) h 226 King w
Harvey Alex & Co, wholesale grocers, 21 King e
Harvey Alex, jr, clerk, 226 King w
Harvey Miss Annie, 43 Jackson e
Harvey A T, clerk, 34 Bay s
Harvey Mrs Ellen (wid James) nurse, Murray e

Harvey F L, journalist, bds 158 King Wm
Harvey G A, bds 59 John n
Harvey Henry, plumber, 44 Peter
Harvey Horace, carpenter, 64 Wellington n
Harvey James, laborer, 250 Jas n
Harvey James A, Excelsior Printing House, 26 Merrick, h 25½ Spring *See advt*
Harvey James S, clerk, bds 226 King w
Harvey John (John Harvey & Co) h Robinson cor Macnab
Harvey John & Co, wool merchants, 69 James n, warehouse 8, 10 Rebecca
Harvey Joseph, hotel, 350 Jas n
Harvey J S, clerk, 226 King w
Harvey Mrs Margaret (wid Wm) 34 Bay s
Harvey & Morgan, auctioneers, 13 Arcade
Harvey Samuel, auctioneer, 7 Baillie
Harvey Wm, stonecutter, Aikman's ave
Harvey Wm, com traveler, Herkimer
Harvey Wm C (Orr, Harvey & Co) h 7 Main w
Harvey Wm R, com traveler, 17 Barton w
Haskins G M, clerk, 226 King e
Haskins Wm, city engineer, 226 King e
Haskins Raymond L, manager Barton wine co, 226 King e
Haskin Robt, tobacco roller, 7 Park s
Haskins Robt, carpenter, 55 York
Haslem Charles, car driver, 266 James n
Haslett Thomas C, (Haslett & Washington) h 27 Hannah w
Haslett & Washington (T C Haslett, S F Washington) barristers, 20 James s *see card*
Hass Henry, hatter, bds 169 King e
Hastie Samuel, 41 East ave n
Hastings James, trunkmaker, 45 West ave n
Hastings James R, bookkeeper, bds 1 Main w
Hastings Philip, carpenter, 84 Wilson
Hastings Wm, cabinet maker, 171 King Wm
Hatchard Wm, cabinet maker, 13 Florence
Hatt —, laborer, 183 Main w
Hatt Mrs Oliver, 164 James n
Hattersley Miss Isabella, 109 Main e
Hatton Wm, laborer, 107 Caroline n
Hatts Mrs Sarah (wid John) r 13 Barton w
Hatzfeld L E, bookkeeper, 78 Hughson s
Havens James, ornamenter, 5 Cannon e
Havens Wm, painter, 32 Walnut s
Havers James, glassblower, 328 Macnab n
Havercroft William, messenger, Federal bank, King cor James
Haw Lawrence (Armstrong & Haw) 80 King w
Hawkes Edward, collector, 154½ John n
Hawkes Walter, machinist, part 22 Inchbury n
Hawkins David (G D Hawkins & Co) 6 Bay s
Hawkins George D (G D Hawkins & Co) h 4 Bay s
Hawkins G D & Co (Geo D and David Hawkins) shirt manfs, 2 George
Hawkins Henry, plasterer, 10 Cherry
Hawkins James, turnkey, h Barton e
Hawkins R J, carpenter, 283 King William

Hawkins Thomas, 18 O'Reilly
Hawkins William, policeman, 3 Wentworth n
Hawkins Wm, laborer, 11 Inchbury n
Hawthorn Hugh, spoke maker, 110 Strachan e
Hawthorn Mrs Rebecca (wid Robert) 110 Strachan e
Hawthorn Robert, finisher, Mill
Hay Alex, carpenter, 32 Canada
Hay Andrew, carpenter, 240 Jas n
Haydon James, tinsmith, York
Hayes Alexander, grocer, 44 Victoria ave n
Hayes John, 145 John n
Hayes John, machinist, 167 Mary
Hayes John, scalemaker, 297 John n
Hayes Matthew, hackman, 13 Sophia s
Hayes Michael, laborer, 13 Sophia s
Hayes Patrick, laborer, 112 Maria
Hayes Thomas, stonemason, Greig
Hayes Thomas, shoemaker, 303 John n
Hazet H J, butcher, 237 King e
Hayhoe Cornelius, fruiterer, 204, 208 King e
Haygarth Jacob, machinist, 102 Emerald n
Haygarth John, machinist, 102 Emerald n
Haygarth Thomas, machinist, 4 Grove
Haygarth W F, carpenter, 102 Emerald n
Haynes George, bookkeeper, 16 Murray e
Haynes Price, sawmaker, 129 West ave n
Haystead John, street car driver, 16½ James n
Hazell Wm, engineer, 44 Catharine s
Hazell Wm, porter, 8 Grove
Hazelton Hon John T, Consul of United States, G T R station, h 42 Murray w
Hazelwood Samuel, cabinet maker, Aikman's ave
Hazen George, tailor, 98 Wilson
Headland Harry, laborer, 92 Emerald n
Healey Egerton, grocer, Duke cor Bay
Healey J W, com traveler, 58 Emerald s
Healey M D, dry goods, 14 Macnab n, h 111 Bay n
Healey Thomas, 88 Hunter e
Hearne M S, manager A C Quimby & Co, h 87 Wellington n
Hearne Richard J, salesman, 87 Wellington n
Hearn Wm, watchman, 12 Margaret
Heath A J, dairyman, 293 King e
Heath Fred G, printer, 51 Pearl n
Heath James, blacksmith, 51 Pearl n
Heath James, clerk, 8 Pearl s
Heath Louis, bds 293 King e
Heath Samuel, blacksmith, 21 Florence n
Hebden Mrs Kate (wid John) Macnab cor Herkimer
Hebner Fred, laborer, 128 Jackson w
Heddle David, mason, 68 Maria
Hebden Thomas, blacksmith, 191 York
Hedley Thomas, upholsterer, 19 Macnab s, h 110 Herkimer
Heenan Very Rev E I, Vicar General diocese of Hamilton, the palace, 25 Sheaffe
Heeney Wm, bookkeeper, 36 Ferguson ave
Heilig George, builder, 95 John n
Heilig George Wm, bricklayer, 95 John n

Heim Mrs Jessie (wid Walter) 55 Kelly
Heime Samuel, tailor, 48 Walnut s
Heimbecker Henry, photographic stock dealer, 7½ Victoria ave n
Heins Mrs Kate, tailoress, 184 King e
Heitzmann J F, bartender Commercial hotel, 16 Sheaffe
Heitzman Joseph F, cigarmaker, 16 Sheaffe
Held Fred, laborer, 50 Magill
Heming G E, clerk, mountain top
Heming H P, clerk, mountain top
Heming Percy G, clerk, mountain top
Hemphill Z, manager A & S Nordheimer, h 101 Market
Hemsley Perry, second-hand dealer, 42 King Wm
Hempstock Andrew, brickmaker, Robinson w Locke
Hempstock Geo, laborer, 199 Main w
Hempstock Mrs Mary A (wid William, bds 156 Jackson w
Henderberry Andrew, laborer, 74 Locke n
Hendershot Morris, laborer, 81 Market
Hendershot Oscar, laborer, 66 Bold
Henderson Alex, carpenter, 1 Hess n
Henderson A S, boots and shoes, 184 King e
Henderson Dougald, clerk, 59 Herkimer
Henderson Miss Ellinor, mantle maker, Thomas C Watkins, 30 King e, h 29 Gore
Henderson George, boots and shoes, 45 Macnab n. *See advt*
Henderson George, printer, 25 Cannon e
Henderson James, laborer, 243 King e
Henderson James, 33 Emerald n
Henderson James, machinist, r 206 Catharine n
Henderson Mrs Janet (wid Andrew) bds 68 Bay s
Henderson John, laborer, 268 James n
Henderson John, laborer, King w
Henderson John, blacksmith, 17 Harriet
Henderson John, baker, 116 John s
Henderson John A, tobacco presser, 113 Cannon w
Henderson J M (J M Henderson & Co) Robinson cor Park
Henderson J M & Co (J M Henderson & Co) tailors 20 King w
Henderson Mrs Margaret (wid David) 58 Napier
Henderson Mrs Mary, 26 Strachan e
Henderson Mrs Mary (wid George) 117 King Wm
Henderson Robert, carpenter, 50 Steven
Henderson Wm, laborer, 159 Catharine n
Henderson Wm, tinsmith, 5 Margaret
Henderson W S, clerk, 68 Bay s
Hendrican James, moulder, 7 Simcoe e
Hendricks Frank, cigarmaker, bds Commercial hotel
Hendrie Alex, city foreman, 67 Pearl n
Hendrie & Co (Wm and Geo) cartage agents, 33 King w
Hendrie James, 23 Bold
Hendrie John, contractor, 23 Bold
Hendrie Wm (Hendrie & Co) h 23 Bold
Hendrie Wm jr, clerk, 23 Bold

Hendry A F, accountant, 19 Mulberry
Hendry Mrs Elizabeth (wid David) bds 72 Catharine s
Hendry John, pattern maker, 1 Rebecca, h Concession nr Queen
Henery John, governor jail, Barton e
Henery John, carpenter, 49 West ave n
Henigan James, gents' furnishings, hats, caps, etc, 108 King e
Hennessy Cornelius, tinsmith, bds 24 King Wm
Hennessey James, carpenter, 102 Florence
Hennessey Hugh, blacksmith, 19 Wilson
Hennessy Patrick, locksmith, 20 John n
Hennessy John, safe agent, 22 Hughson n, h 64 Macnab s
Henniger Mrs Mary (wid Geo) 50 Napier
Henning Mrs Janet (wid John) 71 Hunter w
Hennings Damartine, second-hand dealer, 102 James n
Henri Mrs Bridget (wid Cornelius) Dundurn
Henry Albert H, parcel express, Alexandria Arcade, h 87 Macnab n
Henry Daniel, grocer, Hannah cor Caroline
Henry Jas, fitter, 45 Magill
Henry James, boots and shoes, 22 York
Henry John, 235 King w
Henry John, laborer, 39 Florence
Henry John C, teamster, 47 Wellington n
Henry Michael, carpenter, 134 Emerald n
Henry Patrick, carpenter, 131 West ave n
Henry Philip, laborer, r 109 West ave n
Henry R, butcher, 121 James n
Henshaw William, hatter, 164 Wilson
Henstridge Alfred, painter, 34 Lower Cathcart
Henwood Thomas, grinder, 111 East ave n
Hepkins Lewis, blacksmith, bds 49 Stuart w
Herald Mrs Anna (wid Wm) 61 Queen n
Herald Chas, manager Greening's wireworks, 59 Queen n
Herald Joseph, pianomaker, 9 Peter
Herbert Thos H. stonecutter, 70 Mary
Herbert William, laborer, 88 Simcoe e
Heritage John, tailor, 132 Cannon w
Herman John, butcher, 142 Emerald n
Herman William, accountant and general agent, 16 James s, h 68 Main w
Herod Richard, bricklayer, bds 60 James s
Herriman Jeptha, mail contractor, 8 Bay s
Herring John H, com traveler, 28 George
Herrington Mrs Mary, 94 Walnut s
Herron G S, watchman, 21 Wentworth n
Herron Joseph, merchant tailor, 82 King e, h 67 Wellington s *See advt*
Herron Robert, bookkeeper, 205 James n
Hess Jacob, Hannah e
Hesse J R, grocer, 4 Liberty
Hetherington William. 70 Ferguson ave
Hewitt Alfred. pedler, r 79 Caroline n
Hewitt Chas J, brickmaker, 170 Jackson w

Hewitt John, bds 10 Stuart e
Hewitt Mrs Sarah (wid Henry) 150 Rebecca
Hewson George, carpenter, 20 Hunter e
Hewson George, cabinetmaker, 55½a Walnut s
Heyburn George, lithographer, 45 Jackson e
Heydeman Robert, blacksmith, 17 Locke s
Hickey John, brakesman, 253 Hughson n
Hickok H C, St Charles restaurant, 64 James n
Hicks Richard, carpenter, 168 James n
Hicks W S, carver, 34 James s, h 79 Stinson
Hibbard Mrs Ann (wid Orvill) 125 Dundurn
Hiby Charles, saloon, 90 James n
Hiesrodt C N, picture framer, 72 King e, h 33 Walnut
Higby Mrs Julia, 59 John n
Higgins Andrew, confectioner, 83 George
Higgins Edward M, M D, 74 Park n
Higgins James, machinist, 73 Locke n
Higgins Moore A, solicitor, 78 Park n
Higgins William, laborer, Pearl s
High Matthew, hotel keeper, 65-67 John s
Higham James, engine turner, G T R, 40 Locomotive
Higham Thomas, blacksmith, 131 Queen n
Highsted John, laborer, 160 Hughson n
Higley F H, salesman, bds Victoria hotel
Higley John, clerk, bds Victoria hotel
Hignell Albert R, printer, 62 Lower Cathcart
Hipkins Alfred, printer, 42 Hess s
Hildebrand Gottleib, laborer, 117 Napier
Hilder Edwin, shoemaker, 39 Inchbury n
Hiles, Louis, collector, Gore
Hiles W C, clerk, 5 Pearl n
Hill Mrs Ann (wid Henry) 178 Hughson n
Hill A S, saloon, 24 Hughson n
Hill Baldwin, com traveler, 102 James n
Hill Charles (Miller & Hill) h 15 Hunter e
Hill Edmund, grocer, 81 John, h 8 East ave n
Hill George H, butcher, 192 King w
Hill Henry, butcher, 98 Rebecca
Hill Henry, clerk P O, 15 Hunter e
Hill Henry, laborer, bds 56 Gore
Hill Harvey H, cabinet maker, r 3 Queen s
Hill James, blacksmith, 300 Macnab n
Hill Jasper, grocer, 86 Ferguson ave
Hill John, laborer. Jones
Hill Mark, baker and confectioner, 102 James n
Hill Richard, tobacconist, 172 King e and 26½ King w
Hill Richard A, cigarmaker, bds Victoria hotel
Hill R M, com traveler, bds 102 James n
Hill Robert, cabinetmaker, r 3 Queen s
Hill Rowland, dealer, 46 Ray n
Hill Mrs Sophia (wid John) 34 Vine
Hill Thomas, furniture, 21 Macnab n, bds Franklin House
Hill T S, watchmaker, 90 John s
Hill Miss Eunice, 126 York
Hill Mrs Wm, 28 Emerald n
Hill Wm, clerk, 15 Hunter e
Hill Walter, butcher, 104 James n

Hill Wm, butcher, 202 King e
Hillier Robert, salesman, hd Caroline s
Hilliard Mrs Mary (wid John) 106 Florence
Hilliard Thos, 2 O'Reilly
Hillman O S, 23 Jackson w
Hillman Peter, carpenter, 109 Robinson
Hillman T E, enginneer G T R
Hills C H, grocer, 142 Mary
Hills Jacob, insurance agent, 5 Pearl n
Hills J H, Mary cor Robert
Hills Lucian, architect, 12 King Wm, h 278 King w
Hills Mrs M, fancy goods, 8 Macnab n
Hills Roland, sec Canada Life Assurance Co, h 30 Jackson w
Hillyer Edward S, M D, 10 Main e
Hinchey Edward, moulder, bds 201 Mary
Hinchey Michael, laborer, 161 Catharine n
Hinchcliffe James, grocer, 299 York
Hinchcliffe Jas, machinist, Garth
Hinchcliffe Robert, machinist, 305 York, h 8 Inchbury s
Hinckley Chas, brakeman, bds 124 Cannon e
Hincks Henry, machinist, 156 Mary
Hindman Mrs, 9 Macnab s
Hinds John R, accountant, 30 Nelson ave
Hines Otis O, butcher, 229 York
Hinds Rudolphus, printer, 289 King Wm
Hinman Mrs Charles, milliner, 4 King Wm, h 12 King Wm
Hipkins Alfred, printer, 120 Napier
Hirst Jas, manf pain exterminator, 35 Park s
Hiscox James, chimney sweep, 138 Hunter e
Hislop Frank, laborer, 30 Strachan w
Hislop John, blacksmith, Park cor Merrick
Hitzroth Charles, shoemaker, 101 John s
Hoag Mrs (wid Thomas) 238 King Wm
Hobbs Alfred, tinsmith, 248½ Barton e
Hobbs James, carpenter, 170 Emerald n
Hobbs James, bricklayer, 59 Gore
Hobson Abram, glassblower, 61 Lower Cathcart
Hobson John S, engineer, 126 Napier
Hobson Joseph, civil engineer G T R, Concession cor Bay
Hobson Robert, chief clerk G T R, cor Bay and Concession
Hobson T Dudley, law student, 61 Lower Cathcart
Hockaday Joseph, cabinetmaker, 40 Maria
Hockbush John, laborer, 74 Locke s
Hodd George, salesman, 55 Tisdale
Hodd Wm, moulder, bds 55 Tisdale
Hodge George, teamster 105 John s
Hodge Miss, 98 Emerald n
Hodge T H, salesman, 17 Charles
Hodges —, moulder, bds 55 York
Hodges Humphrey, r 184 Macnab n
Hodges Wm, tobacco roller, r 213 King e
Hodgins Isaac, foreman rolling mills, 164 Catharine n
Hodgson Jeremiah, laborer, 331 Hughson n
Hodgins Mrs Maria (wid Alex) 50 Hughson s
Hodgson Wm, butcher, 327 Barton e

Haffer Fred, traveler, 13 Murray w
Hofsass Wm, jeweler, bds 169 King Wm
Hogan J H, 47 Park n
Hogarth George, carpenter, r 50½ Young
Holcomb Mrs Harriet (wid Wm H) 65 Caroline s
Holden George C, clerk, 241 King Wm
Holden Miss Margaret, 42 Cannon w
Holden Wm W, bottler, 209 King Wm
Holdsworth Charles, packer, 63½ Canada
Holdsworth Joseph, second-hand dealer, 221 James n
Holland Chas, agent, 126 Mary
Holland C J, machinist, bds 255 James n
Holland James, baker, 82 Maria
Holland James, boiler maker, 175 Bay n
Holland Jas, grocer, 48 Peter
Holland Jas, locksmith, 27 John n, h 36 Dundurn
Holland Thos J, hay and straw dealer, Mary, h 47 Mary
Holleran James, moulder, 49 Elgin
Holleran John, traveler, 61 Barton e
Holleran Mrs Kate, 219 Catharine n
Holleran Patrick, grocer, Barton e cor Catharine
Holloran Patrick, glassblower, bds 219 Catharine n
Hollinrake Wm, laborer, bds 205 John n
Holman John, prop Hamilton Gun Works, 79 James n
Holman John, brickmaker, bds West, King w, nr limits
Holmes A B, shoemaker, 34 Emerald n
Holmes Alex, painter, 4 Poulette
Holmes Alonzo, com trav, 200 East ave n
Holmes Asher, machinist, 10 West ave n
Holmes James, shoemaker, 140½ Main e
Holmes John, painter, 189 Main w
Holmes John, laborer, 107 Simcoe e
Holmes John, carter, 37 Wood w
Holmes Robert, 198 Cannon e
Holmes Wm, moulder, 48 Tisdale
Holmes Wm, bookkeeper, bds Bawden's hotel
Holmes Wm, laborer, 283 King w
Holmes Wm, brushmaker, 134 West ave n
Holt Frank, 80 Murray e
Holt John, carder, 206 Mary
Holt John, engineer, 276 James
Holt Samuel, laborer, 25 Murray e
Holtham George, tinner, 134 Macauley e
Holton Warren, gardener, Main e
Home of the Friendless, 72 Caroline s
Home John, tinsmith, 73 Bay n
Home John, market gardener, Ashley
Homer Mrs Mary, r Garth
Homer Wm, confectioner, 127 John s
Homiston Willis, burnisher, bds 62 Cannon e
Homewood John, carriage trimmer, 106 Bay n
Honeybourn George, carpenter, 36 O'Reilly
Honeycomb John, 28 Locomotive
Honeycomb Thos R, bricklayer, 24 Locomotive
Honeyford James, fitter, 41 Inchbury n
Honey W F, discount clerk Bank of British North America, 13 Bold

Hood & Bro (Thomas and John) props Royal hotel, 63 James n

Hoodless John (J Hoodless & Son) h 43 Jackson w

Hoodless J & Son (Joseph and John) furniture manufacturers, 51 King w, factory Catharine cor Main

Hoodless Joseph (J Hoodless & Son) Catharine cor Jackson

Hoodless J, fireman, 34 Hughson n

Hooker Joseph, gardener, 41 Aurora

Hooper Frederick, insurance agt, 50 Gore

Hooper F L (F L Hooper & Co) 50 Gore

Hooper F L & Co, ins brokers, Alexandra Arcade

Hooher George, shoemaker, 130 John n

Hooper George, blacksmith, 198 King Wm

Hooper George, shoemaker, 132 John n

Hooper H S, confectioner, 200 King e

Hooper James, com trav, 35 Victoria ave n

Hooper Wm C, printer, 56 Wilson

Hooper John, com trav, 350 Victoria ave n

Hope Adam & Co (C J & R K Hope) iron and hardware merchants, 102 King e

Hope A H (L D Sawyer & Co) h hd Macnab s

Hope Charles James (Adam Hope & Co) h 15 Duke

Hope George, book agent, 116 Market

Hope Geo, hardware merchant, 15 Duke

Hope Mrs Hannah wid Adam) 95 Macnab s

Hope John, tanner, 182 East ave n

Hope Mrs Margaret (wid John) 35 Ray n

Hope Mrs Martha (wid John) 65 Bold

Hope Robert Knight (Adam Hope & Co) h 15 Duke

Hope Robert J, printer, 35 Ray n

Hopgood E H, butcher, 69 Barton w, h cor Bay and Barton

Hopkin George H, boot and shoe dealer, 10 King Wm, h 202 Victoria ave n

Hopkin Joseph, carpet weaver, 166 Mary

Hopkin Robert, carpet weaver, 213 King e

Hopkins Israel, pedler, 28 Guise

Hopkins Jas, 100 Catharine n

Hopkins James, moulder, bds 134 Queen n

Hopkins Mrs Margaret (wid Patrick) 105 Macnab n

Hopkins Robt, bds King e

Hopkins S D, 104 Cannon w

Hopkins S F, pickle manf, 185 King Wm, h 9 Victoria ave n

Hopper John, clerk, 64 Hunter e

Hopwood Edward H, pork curer, 160 Bay n

Hore F W, jr, (F W Hore & Son) h 147 Victoria ave n

Hore F W, sr, (F W Hore & Son) h 155 Victoria ave n

Hore F W & Son, Hamilton Wheel Works, Elgin

Hore John R, painter, 193 Mary

Horn George, carpenter, 241 Hughson n

Horn Thomas, carpenter, 239 Hughson n

Horn Wm, messenger G T R, 153 Bay n

Hornby Thomas, brickmaker, bds 288 King w

Hornby Wm, machinist, 25 Magill

Horne Mrs Mary Ann (wid Jas) laundress, 73 Caroline n

Horne Thomas, engineer, 148½ Duke

Horning Edward, clerk, 47 Hannah e
Horning Joseph, clerk, 47 Hannah e
Horning —, finisher, Dundurn
Horsburg Mrs Helen (wid Jas) 124 Market
Horsfield William, laborer, 133 Jackson e
Horton Henry, laborer, 139 Locke n
Horspoole Wm, clerk, 45 Hess s
Horton Henry, laborer, r 183 Bay n
Horton Joseph, rag dealer, 95 King Wm, h 21 Wilson
Hoskins Frederick, fireman, 101 Simcoe e
Hossack James S, builder, 43 Hannah w
Hossock John, carpenter, 149 Macnab n, h Hannah w
Hotrum John, carpenter, 7 Murray e
Houghton —, prof hygiene, coll inst, bds 17 Main w
Houlden James, contractor, 156 John n
Houlden Mrs Margaret (wid Jefferson) 160 Catharine n
House J B, 111 Catharine s
House of Refuge, John cor Guise
Housden Charles, malster, 203 Catharine n
Housego Edward, fireman, 14 Crook
Houseman Louis, cooper, bds 39 John n
Houser David F, insurance agent, 119 Napier
Hover John, boilermaker, 29 Pearl s
Hover William, tailor, 29 York, h 179 Main w
How Edward J (How & Braid) h 204 King w
How & Braid (Edward J How, Alex Braid) pork butchers, 204 King w
Howard Charles, carpenter, 51 Victoria ave n
Howard Fred B, butcher, 208 King w
Howard James, bricklayer, 30 Chisholm
Howard John, bricklayer, 32 Emerald n
Howard & McVittie (R J Howard, A McVittie) blacksmiths, 16 Jackson e
Howard Mrs Mary (wid James) 54 Hunter w
Howard R J (Howard & McVittie) 99 Hunter e
Howard Samuel, carpenter, 80 Bold
Howard Thomas, bricklayer, 155 James n
Howard Wm, bricklayer, 155 James n
Howard W H, tailor, 17 Rebecca
Howard J J, laborer, 128 Macauley e
Howden J E, (Brethour & Co) h 190 King e
Howden John, carpenter, 83 Locke n
Howden Wm, laborer. 71 Market
Howe John, cigarmaker, bds Maple Leaf hotel
Howe Richard, gardener, Main e
Howell Fred J, lithographer, 112 Jackson w
Howell Lithographing Co, 18 James s
Howell William A, chemist, 1 Hunter w, h 62 Macnab s
Howells Mrs Victoria (wid Thos) 152 Macnab n
Howick Wm, grocer and butcher, 285 King w
Howitt Robert, butcher, 311 York
Hows James, butcher, King e, nr tollgate
Hoyle Jas, tailor, 45 Cathaine s

HubbardArthur,packer,114Maria
Hubbard Mrs E, milliner, 56 James n
Hubbard W L, tobacconist, King cor Mary
Hudson Edward, moulder, 96 Simcoe e
Hudson Edmund, clerk, 11 Charles
Hudson Geo, marble polisher, 152 Napier
Hudson Ormsby, cabinetmaker, 161 Main w
Hudson Wm, bds 83 Hess n
Hudson Wm, carpenter, 113 Park n
Hughes Charles, carpenter, 89 Lower Cathcart
Hughes Edward, springmaker, 25 Hess n
Hughes George, waiter, bds 159 James n
Hughes Wm, carpenter, 187 Mary
Hughes George, laborer, 31 Park s
Hughes James, 46 Wellington n
Hughes John, laborer, Caroline s
Hughes Patrick, laborer, 222 James n
Hughes Wm, machinist, r 14 Magill
Hull Chas, switchman, 49 Stuart w
Hull Charles, shoemaker, 327 Macnab n
Hull George, butcher, 146 Main e, h 20 Pearl s
Hull William, com traveler, 20 Pearl s
Hume Miss Isabella, 207 Main w
Hummel John, builder, 109 Robinson
Humphrey N, tanner, 184 John n
Humphrey & Newberry, tanners, 125 Jackson e
Humphrey George, moulder, 147 Ferguson ave
Humphrey Joseph, laborer, 138 Picton e
Humphreys Thomas, tinsmith, 66 West ave n
Hunt A E, stovemounter, 106½ Simcoe e
Hunt B, wagonmaker, bds 105 John s
Hunt Charles F, salesman, 101 Elgin
Hunt, Charles R, tinsmith, 101 Elgin
Hunt Daniel, 120 Main e
Hunt David, shoemaker, bds 55 York
Hunt Edmund, wagon maker, 105 John s
Hunt George, broom maker, 112 Caroline s
Hunt George M, Sun Life Association of Canada, Alexandra Arcade, 31 James n, h 69 George
Hunt James, brakeman, bds 101 Elgin
Hunt James, whipmaker, bds 126 Macnab n
Hunt Richard, moulder, 147 Robert e
Hunt William, butcher, 126 Macnab n
Hunt Wm, moulder, 12 Young
Hunt William, gardener, Inglewood, James s
Hunt Wm H, wood turner, 69 East ave n
Hunter Adam, bookseller and stationer, 52 James n, h 130 York
Hunter Alexander, laborer, 252 Mary
Hunter George, tailor, 64 Tisdale
Hunter George C, tinsmith, 93 John s
Hunter George S (Hunter & Hunter) 79 Bold
Hunter Hugh, porter, 40 Ray s
Hunter & Hunter, auctioneers, 24 Merrick
Hunter James, shipper, 75 Mary
Hunter John, grocer, 194 James n

Hunter John, policeman, 134 Cannon e
Hunter John jr, laborer, 105 Ferguson ave n
Hunter John sr, laborer, 103 Ferguson ave n
Hunter Mrs Joseph, 14 Steven
Hunter Mrs Mary (wid Laurence) caretaker, 46 Charles
Hunter Matthew, carpenter, bds 60 James s
Hunter Peter, carpenter, 272 Hughson n
Hunter Robert, packer, 65 Maria
Hunter Robert, (Hunter & Hunter) 129 Cannon w
Hunter Samuel, 162 King William
Hunter Rev W J, pastor Wesley Church, 56 Hughson n
Hunter Walter, B A, B C L, law student, mountain top
Hunter Wm, policeman, bds 134 Cannon e
Hunter Wm, brass founder, 38 Wellington n, h 19 Wellington s
Hunter Wm, porter, 56½ Lower Cathcart
Hunter William, collector, 27 Magill
Hunting Henry, fireman, 67 Main w
Hunting Miles, contractor, bds 123 Main e
Hurd Mrs Alice (wid Wilkins) 113 Catharine n
Hurd Hiram H (Hurd & Roberts) 10 Bay n
Hurd John, laborer, Main e
Hurd & Roberts (H H Hurd, D E Roberts) marble and granite, cor Bay and York
Hurley David, engineer, 109 Macnab n
Hurley Jas, moulder, 285 John n
Hurley John, bartender, 73 Stuart w
Hurley Peter, laborer, 73 Stuart w
Hurly James, moulder, 152 Emerald n
Hurrell Jasper, printer, 61 Robert
Hurst A R, carpenter, 153 Wilson
Hurton Chas, janitor Collegiate Institute, 69 Main w
Husband George E, M D, 75 Main w
Husband R J (Drs R J and T H Husband) h 62 East ave s
Husband Drs R J and T H, dentists, 10 King w
Husband T H (Drs R J and T H Husband) h 42 Vine
Hussel Mrs Mary (wid John) fancy goods, 128 James n
Husted Daniel, glassblower, 261 Macnab n
Hutcheson James Happle, merchant tailor, 118 King e
Hutchings John F, clerk, 93 Hunter e
Hutchinson George, painter, 44 West ave s
Hutchinson Henry, nr toll gate, York
Hutchinson Thomas, laborer, 142 Market
Hutchison Alex, gardener, 17 Cannon w
Hutchison Daniel, laborer, 176 Hughson n
Hutchison James, merchant, 61 Herkimer
Hutchison & Pilkey (R A Hutchison, Joseph B Pilkey) organs, pianos, etc, 10 King e
Hutchison Robert A (Hutchison & Pilkey) h 61 Herkimer
Hutchison Thomas, painter, 37 Alanson
Hutchison Thomas, engineer, 196 Hughson n
Hutchison Thomas, laborer, 290 Macnab n

Huton Charles, merchant tailor, 80 King e, h 103 Market
Hutton Amos, machinist, 31 Steven
Hutton David, laborer, 201 Wellington n
Hutton Francis R, builder, 5 Augusta
Hutton Gilbert, machinist, 4 Crooks
Hutton Mrs Mary Jane, tailoress 248 Barton e
Hutton Wm, laborer, Maple
Hutty Frederick, gardener, 40 Hannah w
Huxtable John, shoemaker, 200 James
Hyatt Henry, shoe laster, 131 Wellington n
Hyde E W, commission merchant, 38 Lower Cathcart
Hyde James, loom fixer, 151 Wellington n
Hyde James, section hand, 352 Hughson n
Hyde John, laborer, 276 Macnab n
Hyndman Mrs Hannah (wid James) 9 Macnab s
Hyndman Wm, blacksmith, 173 Park n
Hyndman Wm, blacksmith 10 Kinnell
Hyslop Cornell & Co (Wm Hyslop and S W Cornell) wholesale gents' furnishings and fancy goods, 7 James s and 6½ King William
Hyslop Robert, traveler, 36 Emerald n
Hyslop Wm (Hyslop, Cornell & Co) 27 Wellington s
Ibbetson Wm, tailor, 19 Railway
Ibbetson Wm jr, painter, 21 Railway
Ide Frank, laborer, 41 Alanson
Immigration Sheds (Dominion) John Smith, agent, 71 Stuart w
Immigration Sheds (Ontario) Stuart w
Imperial Mineral Water Co, J S Pearson, manager, 9 Jackson e
Inches James (Fraser & Inches) 141 John s
Ing Henry, watchmaker, 106 James n, h 68 Steven
Ing Mrs, 51 Tisdale
Ingleheart H F, 60 Vine
Ingles Wm, clerk, bds 36 Bay s
Ingles Wm, beamer, 90 Simcoe e
Ingram George, laborer, bds 81 Stuart w
Inkson Joseph, finisher, Dundurn
Inkson William, com traveler, Dundurn cor York
Inland Revenue Office, 1 Vine
Inman Steamship Line, Geo McKeand, agent, 57 James n
Insch James, fitter, 110 Bay n
Insch William V, moulder, 27 Simcoe
Insole James G, com traveler, 114 Catharine s
Inspector of Weights and Measures, Thomas H McKenzie, inspector, office James cor Vine
Insurance Co of North America (The Marine) Gillespie & Powis, agents, 31 King e
Iredale Miss Grace, 13 Bold
Iredale James, blacksmith, Main e
Iredale Walter, foreman rolling mills, 103 Locke n
Ireland Frank B, engraver, 24 Macnab n
Ireland Henry, fruit dealer, 127 King Wm
Irish Charles, shoemaker, 38 Emerald n
Ironside Alex, stonecutter, 309 King w
Ironside Bemus, painter, Dundurn
Irvine Mrs Helen (wid Alex) 66 Duke

Irvine James, teamster, 23 Guise
Irvine James, laborer, Ferrie e
Irvine John, mariner, bds 239 James n
Irvine Lendrum, com traveler, 73 John s
Irvine Mrs L L, milliner, 73 John s
Irvine Miss Sarah, 14 Markland
Irving Adam, picture dealer, 172 James n
Irving Æmilius, Q C, 137 James s
Irving Archibald, mariner, 293 Macnab n
Irving Franklin, clock maker, bds 4 Barton terrace, Wellington n
Irving John, mariner, 330 Jas n
Irving John, laborer, 210 Hughson n
Irving Mrs Sarah (wid Edward) 4 Barton terrace, Wellington n
Irving Wm, carpenter, Hess s
Irving Wm, machinist, 252 Bay n
Irwin John T (Thomas Irwin & Son) h 53 Herkimer
Irwin Richard, propr Victoria hotel, 79 King e
Irwin Richard, jr, clerk Victoria hotel
Irwin Robert, customs broker, 84 James n, h w side York nr Caroline *See card*
Irwin Robert, plater, bds 13½ Chisholm
Irwin Thomas, watchman, 211½ Mary
Irwin Thomas, laborer, 44 Chisholm
Irwin Thomas (Thomas Irwin & Son) h 53 Herkimer
Irwin Thomas & Son (Thos and John T) galvanized iron, felt roofing, tinware, etc, 12 Macnab s *See advt*
Irwin W H (W H Irwin & Co) h 53 Herkimer
Irwin W H & Co, directory publishers and publishers' agts, 14 Merrick and 12 Macnab s *See advt*
Irwin Wm H, tinsmith, 72 Ray s
Isbister John, contractor, 81 Wellington s
Israel Charles, confectioner, 187½ King e, h 154 King e
Israel Mrs Charles, confectioner, 154 King e
Issell George, shoemaker, bds 196 King w
Ives George, bank messenger, bds 28 King Wm
Ivory Mrs Nora (wid James) 105 Park n
Izzard Girdlestone B, com traveler, 80 Queen s
Jack Daniel, engineer, 19 Magill
Jack Wm, switchman, 71 Barton w
Jackman Thomas, fitter, 112 Florence
Jacques Robert S, machinist, 35 Margaret
Jackson Mrs Catharine (wid Sydney) 85 Wellington n
Jackson David, retinner, 9 Wood Market sq
Jackson David, laborer, 15 Simcoe w
Jackson Mrs Elizabeth (wid John) 65 Barton w
Jackson George, shipper, 90 Main e
Jackson George, salesman, 97 Robert
Jackson George, laborer, Markland
Jackson George, watchmaker, 134 King w
Jackson George N, shipper, 90 Main e
Jackson George W, salesman, 97 Robert
Jackson Henry, painter, Duke
Jackson Henry, grinder, r 22 Kelly

Jackson James, sailmaker, 91 Hughson n
Jackson James, carpenter, 170 East ave n
Jackson James R, carpenter, 72 Victoria hve n
Jackson John, laborer, 73 Emerald n
Jackson John, laborer, 93 Picton e
Jackson John, tailor, 100 West ave n
Jackson John, plater, 134 King w
Jackson John, shipper, 145 Locke n
Jackson Joseph, laborer, 96 Picton e
Jackson Joseph, brickmaker, Main w
Jackson Joshua, fireman G T R, Barton w
Jackson Mrs Mary (wid Joseph) Barton w
Jackson Mrs Mary (wid Joseph) 64 Peter
Jackson Richard, brakesman, bds 73 Stuart w
Jackson Robt, plasterer, 139 James n
Jackson Robert, carpet weaver, 23 Ferrie e
Jackson Thomas, contractor, 207 Main e
Jackson Thomas, foreman, 16 Ray n
Jackson Thos C, laborer, 99 George
Jackson Thos E, cabinet maker, 16 Ray n
Jacobson Joseph, rabbi, 78½ Hughson s
Jacobs Louis, cigarmaker, 104 John s
Jacobs Richard, cook, 91 King William
Jaggard Charles, polisher, r 22 Kelly
Jaggard Edward, fish dealer, James st market

Jaggard Edward, polisher, 83 John n
Jago John F, customs broker, 30 John n, h 81 Elgin
Jahn Robert, proprietor Germania hotel, 22 John s
James Alonzo T, fireman, 28 King William
James Alfred Thos, shipper, 58 Kelly
James A T, hotel and restaurant, 28 King Wm
James Charles, machinist, r 63 King Wm, h 37 Walnut s
James Rev C J, curate, Church of the Ascension, 37 James s
James Edward, laborer, 146 Rebecca
James Edwin, printer, bds 54 Ferguson ave
James George, staple dry goods, 8 King e, h 53 East ave s
James Henry, porter, 7 West ave n
James Rev John, D D, 49 Victoria ave s
James Mrs Sarah (wid Wm) 54 Ferguson ave
James Mrs Stephen, 7 West ave n
James Joseph, blacksmith, 259 Macnab n
James J W, bookkeeper, 149 York
James St Baptist Church, James cor Jackson
James Thomas, roller, 111 Locke n
James Thomas, saddler, 22 Catharine s
James Thomas, saddler, 4 Walnut n
James William, bricklayer, 29 Tisdale
James William, com traveler, 78 East ave s
James W H, letter carrier, 145 Wellington n
James Wallace T, fireman, 28 King William

Jamieson Archibald jr, clerk, 93 James s
Jamieson Mrs Archibald, 93 James s
Jamieson Charles, lineman, 152 Park n
Jamieson Mrs Isabella (wid Wm) 50 Caroline s
Jamieson Mrs Elizabeth, 243 Barton e
Jamieson James (Bowes, Jamieson & Co) h 284 King e
Jamieson James, pressman, Caroline s
Jamieson John, painter, 55 Locomotive
Jamieson John, telegraphist, 243 Barton e
Jamieson Samuel, stonecutter, 63 Market
Jamieson Wm, hat finisher, 243 Barton e
Jamieson Wm, moulder, 242 Hughson n
Jamieson Wm L, watchman, 162 East ave n
Jardine James, clerk, 98 Cannon w
Jardine James B, clerk, 98 Cannon w
Jariott Wm, York w
Jarrett Robert, engineer, 124 Queen n
Jarvis Æ, manager Farmers' & Traders' Loan Association, room 30 Canada Life Chambers
Jarvis Bold, clerk, 38 Ferrie w
Jarvis Bold, clerk G T R, 270 Bay n
Jarvis Frederick S, 71 Jackson e
Jarvis James, engineer, 257 York
Jarvis Mrs Jane (wid Chas) 70 Canada
Jarvis Mrs John, fancy goods, 186-8 King e
Jarvis John, laborer, 102 Strachan e
Jarvis R H, traveler, 60 East ave s
Jarvis Samuel, caretaker, 2 Augusta
Jarvis Samuel, brickmaker, 70 Canada
Jarvis Thomas, furniture, 21 Macnab n, and 99½ King w, h 81 Bay n
Jarvis Wm, confectioner, 262 King e
Jarvis William, cab proprietor, 13 Spring
Jarvis William, baker, etc, 262 King e
Jeffery Mrs Ann (wid Wm) 57 Park n
Jeffery Joseph, prop city laundry, 60 Main w, h 57 Park n
Jeffrey Ephraim, plasterer, 8 Steven
Jeffrey George, laborer, 33 Wellington n
Jeffrey John, laborer, 2 Markland
Jeffrey John, carpenter, 39 Cherry
Jeffs John, shipper, 99 East ave n
Jeffs Joseph B, machinist, 118 Jackson e
Jelfs G F (Gage & Jelfs) h 60 Herkimer
Jenkins Alfred, machinist, 140 Wellington n
Jenkins Charles, engineer, 34 Mulberry
Jenkins Chas, machinist, 84 Market
Jenkins George, new and second-hand furniture store, 140 King w
Jenkins John, carpenter, 133 Ferrie e
Jenkins J C N, machinist, 39 Kelly
Jenkins Mary A (wid Geo) 26 Canada
Jenkins Stephen, machinist, 102 Queen n
Jenkins Thomas, lather, 30 Bay s
Jenkins Wm, laborer, 54 Locomotive

Jennings David J, wood carver, 293 King w
Jennings John, moulder, 236 Cannon e
Jessop William, clerk G T R, 277 Bay n
Jewell Mrs Elizabeth (wid Thos) 107 West ave n
Jewell Wm, 107 West ave n
Jinks John, heater, 37½ Ray n
Job Wm J, shoemaker, Markland
Jobber Mrs Caroline, 315 James n
Jobson James, pork curer, 97 Caroline s
Jocelyn Joseph, plasterer, 37 Florence
Johnson Alfred, fireman G T R, 93 Caroline n
Johnson Allen W, clerk, Canada Life chambers
Johnston Amos, provision dealer, 49 Mary
Johnston Brent, carpenter, 199 Wellington n
Johnston Charles, bookbinder, bds Dominion hotel
Johnston Charles, brushmaker, 181 Main e
Johnson Rev Charles A, scientist, lecturer and journalist, 54 Herkimer
Johnstone Miss Emma, millinery, 108 King w
Johnston Fred (Fraser & Johnston) h Burlington s
Johnson Frederick G, wheelwright, 245 Mary
Johnston Fred W, moulder, 126 Cannon e
Johnson Freeman, laborer, 96 Ferrie e
Johnson George, carpenter, 238 Hughson n
Johnston & Gilmore (J Johnston and W J Gilmore) auctioneers 22 Merrick
Johnson G W, teacher, 167 John s
Johnson Henry, laborer, Greig
Johnston Henry, tender maker, 87 Victoria ave n
Johnston Jacob, tailor, 121 Hunter w
Johnston James, helper, 159 Wellington n
Johnson James, laborer, 19 O'Reilly
Johnston James, messenger Merchants Bank, 83 Victoria ave n
Johnston James (Johnston & Gilmore) 31 Victoria ave n
Johnson James, Capt Salvation Army, 164 King Wm
Johnson James, machinist, bds 267 King w
Johnson James, mariner, 201½ John n
Johnston James, laborer, 174 Catharine n
Johnston James, machinist, 89 Robert
Johnson James, music teacher, 14 Liberty
Johnston J H, furniture dealer, 128 King e, bds 46 Catharine n
Johnston John, moulder, 160 Victoria ave n
Johnson John, shoemaker, 174 John n
Johnston John, machinist, 47 Ferguson ave
Johnston John, engineer, 91 Tiffany
Johnson Mrs John, 16 Grove
Johnstone John, china store, 182 King William
Johnston Joseph, tinsmith, 58 Robert e
Johnson J P, agent American Express Co, h 7 Bold
Johnston Lewis, blacksmith, 180 Catharine n.
Johnston Mrs Mary (wid Wm) 117 Catharine n
Johnson Peter, cigarmaker, 255 Macnab n

Johnson Peter, cigarmaker, 277 John n
Johnston Robert, carpenter, 160 Victoria ave n
Johnston Robert, mariner, 37 Ferrie w
Johnston Thomas J, policeman, bds 36 Barton e
Johnston Thos, blacksmith, Aikman's ave
Johnston Thos, marble cutter, 29 Queen n
Johnston Thos, boiler maker, Jones
Johnson Walter, nailer, bds 140 Hess n
Johnson Wm, brushmaker, 99 John n
Johnston Wm, laborer, 203 Emerald n
Johnston Wm, painter, bds 117 Catharine
Johnson Wm, painter, 103 Hess n
Johnston Wm, blacksmith, Aikman's ave
Johnston Mrs Wm, 114 Catharine n
Johnston William, carpenter, 76 John n
Johnstone Wm L, blacksmith, 124 Bold
Joiner Thaddeus, laborer, 81 Caroline n
Jolly Chas, supt American nail works, 56 George
Jolley Chas Joseph (James Jolley & Sons) 17 Hunter e
Jolley James (James Jolley & Sons) 17 Hunter e
Jolley James & Sons, saddlers, 45 and 47 John s
Jolley W D (James Jolley & Sons) 17 Hunter e
Jones Albert, laborer, 28 Bay s
Jones Mrs Alexander, Ferguson ave n
Jones Chas J, steamship ticket agent, James cor Merrick, h 80 Ferguson ave
Jones C J, manager Can Mutual Telegraph Co, h 144 Bay s
Jones C K, roof painter, 76 East ave n
Jones Edward C, agent, 83 King w
Jones F V, hatter, 127 Wellington n
Jones George, carpenter Markland
Jones Hiram, bricklayer, 81 Macauley e
Jones James, moulder, 77 Catharine n
Jones James, 174 East ave n
Jones John, laborer, 235 John n
Jones John, bricklayer, 73 Macauley e
Jones John, laborer, bds 32 Ray n
Jones John, builder, n e cor Mary and Macauley
Jones John T, laborer, 53 Pearl n
Jones John W, LL B (Jones, McQuesten & Chisholm) h Maria cor Hughson
Jones Mrs Martha (wid John) 63 Ferguson ave
Jones Mrs Mary (wid Thomas) 45 Robinson
Jones, McQuesten & Chisholm (J W Jones, I B McQuesten, MA, Jas Chisholm, MA) barristers, Victoria Chambers, 31 James s
Jones Miss Minerva, 65 Hunter e
Jones Miss Nellie, 187 Wilson
Jones Patrick, quarryman, 34 Liberty
Jones Robert, whitewasher, 7 Hunter e
Jones Seneca, insurance agt, 59 James n, h 116 Main e *See card*
Jones Silas E, laborer, Wentworth s
Jones Stephen, laborer, 29 Alanson
Jones Thomas, quarryman, r 126 Hannah e

Jones Thomas, glassblower, 37 Burlington w
Jones Walter, moulder, bds 77 Catharine n
Jones Walter, laborer, 125 Napier
Jones Wm, moulder, 105 Catharine n
Jones Wm, laborer, 11 Stuart w
Jones Wm, car driver, bds 13 Strachao n
Jones W F, painter, 76 East ave
Jones Wm H, agent sewing machine, bds 9 Crooks
Jones W H, clerk, 26 Victoria ave n
Jones W J, tollgate keeper, Barton e
Jones Wm J, laborer, bds 45 Robinson
Jones Mrs, 13 Strachan e
Jones —, laborer, 235 John n
Jordan Mrs E B, 87 Macauley e
Jost Mrs Mary, hair works, 206 King w
Joy Edward, laborer, 35 Canada
Joy Wm, shoemaker, 67 Barton w
Joyce Edward, painter, 89 Caroline n
Joyce James, carpenter, bds 55 York
Joyce Philip, riveter, bds 36 York
Joyce Thomas, tobacco roller, 23 Queen n
Joyce Mrs (wid Michael) 10 Little Market
Judd Charles, clerk P O
Judd Hamilton W, manager Canada Fruit Preserving Co, 47 King Wm, h 138 Main w
Judd James P (W H Judd & Bro) 95 Florence
Judd Robert, painter, 24 Cherry
Judd Thomas, laborer, 117 Cannon e
Judd Wm Henry (W H Judd & Bro) h 72 Bay n
Judd W H & Bro (Wm H and James P) soap manufacturers, 71 Bay n
Julian Wm, laborer, 107 Hunter w
Jutten Thos W, carpenter, 95 Picton e
Kahn Ferd, salesman, 20 Stinson
Kane John, carpenter, 257 John n
Kane Wm, laborer, Aikman's ave
Kappelle Daniel, tailor, 54 West ave n
Kappelle George W, clerk, 50 Victoria ave n
Kartzmark Martin, blacksmith, 40 Robinson
Kavanagh Charles, laborer, 47 Robert
Kavanagh, Dennis, 16 Wood w
Kavanagh Edward, laborer, 41 Mulberry
Kavanagh Frank, 17 Mulberry
Kavanagh John, watchman, 13 Railway
Kavanagh John, laborer, 6 Tiffany
Kavanagh John F, grocer, 39 York, h 64 Bay s
Kavanagh Joseph, 64 Bay s
Kavanagh Matthew, boiler maker, 329 Catharine n
Kavanagh Thomas, laborer, 15 Burlington e
Kavanagh Terrence, moulder, 100 Barton e
Kavanagh Wm, 233 King w
Kay, Alex, machinist, 11 Canada
Kay Thos L, electrical works, 28 Bay n, h 11 Canada
Kaye Wm, laborer, 51 Markland
Keanan Michael, laborer, 162 Jackson w
Keale Mrs, bds 47 Walnut s
Keane Mark, laborer, 55 Main w
Kearney James, tobacco roller, bds Robinson
Kearney Mrs Johanna (wid John) Robinson
Kearley H J, 156 King e
Keating James, machinist, bds 28 O'Reilly

Keating William, confectioner, 59 Ferrie e
Keays Robert, laborer, 93 Young
Keays R S, real estate agent, 57 James n, h 17 West ave s
Keays Wm, machinist, 12 Ray n
Kee Sing, laundry, 87 King w
Keeble Arthur, teamster, 22 Tisdale
Keefe Alex, laborer, bds 350 James n
Keefer Rev B B, 11 West ave s
Keefer Robert, salesman, 30 Liberty
Keenan Andrew, laborer, 139 Napier
Keenan Mrs (Campbell) 49 Little William
Keewatin Lumbering and Manufacturing Co, R Fuller, Canada Life building, 1 James s
Kegan Wm, laborer, 94 Macauley e
Kehoe Lawrence, livery, 176 John n
Keith James, laborer, 304 King w
Kelk Frank G, tailor, 73 Lower Cathcart
Kelk Frederick, salesman, Maria
Kelk James, tinsmith, 207 John n
Kelk John G, paper bag manf, 72 Queen s
Kelk Wm, music teacher, 70 Maria
Kell Robert H, laborer, 57 Maria
Kell Wm, jr, hack drievr, 57 Maria
Kell Wm, 57 Maria
Kellar Francis, laborer, 42 Locke n
Keller Thos, agent, 6 Margaret
Kellar Wesley, 208 King w
Kellner John, tailor, 167 Robert e
Kellond Frederick, bookbinder, 2 Grove
Kellond George, shoemaker, 196 King w
Kelly Daniel, 198 Main e
Kelly Dennis, r 295 King Wm
Kelly Dennis, machinist, 47 Cherry
Kelly D J, wood and coal, 135 James n, h 44 Cannon e
Kelly D, jr, bricklayer, 13 Steven
Kelly Mrs Frances (wid Robert) 77 Main e
Kelly Harry, laborer, bds 181 Main w
Kelly James, cigar maker, bds Commercial hotel
Kelly James, laborer, 324 Macnab n
Kelly Jas, shoemaker, 95 Lower Cathcart
Kelly Jas, laborer, 31 Macauley e
Kelly Mrs Johanna (wid John) 29 Lower Cathcart
Kelly John, hotel keeper, 198 James n
Kelly John, laborer, 334 John n
Kelly J P, shoemaker, 13 Macnab n, h 38 Railway
Kelly Lawrence, laborer, 299 Macnab n
Kelly & Lockwood, British American laundry, 162 York
Kelly Mrs Maria (wid Bernard) 58½ Robert
Kelly Mrs Mary (wid Thomas) 83 Hunter w
Kelly Michael, moulder, bds 73 Stuart w
Kelly Patrick, laborer, 273 John n
Kelly P J, tailor, 138 Catharine n
Kelly Thomas, shoemaker, 247 Mary
Kelly Thomas, tailor, 138 Catharine n
Kelly Timothy, stovemounter, 92 Wilson
Kelly T M, grocer, 50 John s
Kemp Charles, fireman, 116½ Locke n
Kemp David, painter, 29 Barton e
Kemp George, tinsmith, 114 Queen n

Kemp George, grocer, 120 King e, h 71 Herkimer
Kemp John, laborer, r 142 King Wm
Kemp Mrs Mary (wid Rev Alex) 113 Jackson w
Kemp Richard, laborer, r 198 King Wm
Kemp Samuel, traveler, 63 Robert
Kemp Wm, painter, 120 Young
Kench William, fruiterer, 253 York
Kendall James, gardener, Concession, Highfield
Kendall Joseph, bds 58 Hunter e
Kendall Joseph T, butcher, 58 Hunter e
Kennard Edward, cabinet maker, 168 Emerald n
Kennard Henry, laborer, bds 27 Simcoe e
Kennedy Andrew, laborer, 33 Picton e
Kennedy Mrs Catharine (wid Owen) 76 Hughson s
Kennedy Donald, whipmaker, 13 Cannon w
Kennedy George, carpenter, 132 Jackson w
Kennedy Jas, blacksmith, Bowen, h 7 Canada
Kennedy Mrs Jessie (wid Donald) 80 George
Kennedy John, laborer, 132 Picton e
Kennedy John, boiler maker, 30 Macauley e
Kennedy John, car checker, 147 Hughson n
Kennedy John, foreman, 94 Barton e
Kennedy John, carpenter, 31 Queen n
Kennedy Mrs Margaret (widow Benj) 53 Strachan e
Kennedy Matthew, cooper, 138 Ferrie e
Kennedy Michael, hatter, 91 Mary
Kennedy Pat, laborer, 91 Mary
Kennedy Patrick, moulder, 116 Maria
Kennedy Reginald Æ, *Times* Printing Co, 8 Rae s
Kennedy R D, architect, provincial land surveyor and civil engineer, 42 James n, h 85 Main w
Kennedy T C, salesman, 48 Jas n
Kennedy W, clerk Bank British North America, 33 Bold
Kenny, David, seedsman, 13 York, h 73 Bay n
Kenny James, carpenter, 53 Steven
Kenny James, mail clerk, 211 Mary
Kenney S M, insurance agent, 78½ King e, h 9½ West ave s
Kenny S M, 78½ King e
Kenny Thomas, laborer, 24 Ferguson ave
Kenny Thomas, laborer, 232 Catharine n
Kenrick John, 159 John n
Kenrick John, grocer, 67 West ave n
Kent Mrs Elizabeth (wid George) 51 Elgin
Kent Geo T, city foreman 32 Queen s
Kent Henry, clerk, 34 Peter
Kent John, laborer, 120 Wood e
Kent John, moulder, 73 Stuart w
Kent Joseph, contractor, York w
Kent Joseph, clerk, bds 127 John n
Kent S H, assistant city clerk, 76 Bay s
Keough Rev John, chancellor diocese of Hamilton, 244 King e
Kerby Mrs M (wid And T) bds 114 Main w
Kern David W, grocer, 31 Canada
Kernan George, agent, 127 Market

Kerner Christian, hotel, 7 York
Kerner John, 48 Hunter w
Kern Mrs M (wid Jacob) 39 James s
Kerner Wm, agent, 18 Florence
Kerr Alexander, 81 Wellington n
Kerr Alfred, salesman, 81 Wellington n
Kerr A R (A R Kerr & Co) h 41 Charles
Kerr A R & Co, dry goods, 34 King w
Kerr C J, machinist, 264 Mary
Kerr George, caretaker Crystal Palace, Locke n
Kerr John, moulder, 265 Macnab n
Kerr John, 374 Hughson n
Kerr Murray A, Burlington Glass Works, h 63 East ave s
Kerr Robert, chemist, Winer & Co
Kerr Robert, salesman, 26 Main w
Kerr Thomas, moulder, Nightingale
Kerr W A, clerk, 81 Wellington n
Kerr Wm H, moulder, 123 Caroline n
Kerr Wm J, moulder, 123 Caroline n
Kerran John, carpenter, r 62 Locke n
Kerrigan Dennis, merchant tailor, 170 King e
Kerrigan John, druggist, bds 42 Vine
Kerrigan John, merchant tailor, 98 King w
Kerruish Mrs Ellen (wid Thomas) 119 Maria
Kerslake Joseph F, cabinet maker, 263 James n
Ketcheson Byron, moulder, 78 Lower Cathcart
Keyses James, 3 Emerald s
Keymer Harry, boiler maker, 217 James n
Kiah D A, mariner, 83 Park n
Kidd David, general agent Canada Life Assurance Co, 57 Bold
Kidd Samuel, fruit dealer, 65 Rebecca
Kidner Charles, printer, 99 Cherry
Kidner Edward, printer, 99 Cherry
Kidner Frank (Griffin & Kidner, 99 Cherry
Kidney Mrs Bridget (wid Wm) r 51 Young
Kievell Wesley, baker, bds 13 Cannon e
Kilgour Chas, laborer, 110 George
Kilgour James (J & R Kilgour) 83 Catharine s
Kilgour J & R, organ manfs, 64 John s
Kilgour Mrs Robert, 81 Catharine s
Killey J H (Osborne, Killey Manf Co) h 4 Hess s
Killey Wm, machinist, 4 Hess s
Kilroy Mrs John, second-hand dealer, 21 King Wm
Kilvert Francis E, M P, barrister, Canada Life Building, 1 James s, h 10 West ave s
Kilvington Thomas jr, florist, 254 King e
Kilvington Thomas sr, florist, 30 East ave n
Kime Wm H, laborer, 7 Park n
King Alfred, painter, e s Welling-n, n of G T R R
King Cyrus, grocer, 10 Market sq, h 122 Market
King Elias, porter, 16 Catharine n
King Mrs Elsie (wid Anthony) 74 Vine
King Francis E, rope maker, 245½ Mary
King George, painter, 145 Picton
King George, 150 Emerald n
King George, carpenter, 179 Rebecca

King George T, road master, 73 Elgin
King Harry, hostler Dominion hotel
King Hiram, 156 King Wm
King James, traveling agent, 42 Barton e
Kng John A, sewer pipe maker, 213 Main w
King Joseph, boot finisher, 96 Hunter w
King Mark, mason, 28 Spring
King Mrs Mary (wid Francis) 75 Barton
King Robert, laborer, 140 King William
King Robert sr, laborer, 36 East ave n
King Robert, jr, cigar maker, 36 East ave n
King Samuel S, building mover, Dundurn, h 2 Jones
King S V, moulder, 14 Elgin
King Thomas, engineer, 28 Tom
King Thomas, laborer, bds 77 Caroline s
King Thomas, laborer, Herkimer
King Thomas, stonemason, 33 Ray n
King Thos, machinist, 47 East ave n
King William, merchant tailor, 30 Main w
King Wm, engineer, 167 Jackson w
King Mrs, 77 Napier
King —, core maker, 9 Caroline n
Kingdon Mrs E, 177 King e
Kingdon James, tailor, 128 Mary
Kingdon James, blacksmith, 171 King e
Kingdon Wm J, printer, 36 Robinson
Kinleyside John, manager Hamilton Industrial Works Co, 3 Hess s
Kinrade Thomas, school teacher, Barton e

15

Kinsler Edward, grocer, 103 John n
Kinsler Wm, laborer, bds 175 Catharine n
Kinsella John, laborer, 89 Simcoe e
Kirby Thomas, painter, bds 379 John n
Kirk James, barber, 31 York
Kirk William, baker, 72 Vine
Kirk Wm, jr (Kirk & Truman) 72 Vine
Kirk & Truman (Wm Kirk and A E Truman) hairdressers, 18 Market sq
Kirkam Mrs John, 157 Catharine n
Kirkendall Mrs Euphemia (wid Samuel) 16½ Pearl s
Kirkendall Marshall, painter, 16½ Pearl s
Kirkendall Wesley, painter, 16½ Pearl s
Kirkham Luke, carder, 20 Picton e
Kirkness James, carpenter, 124 Cannon w
Kirkness John, cooper, 237 Barton e
Kirkpatrick John, hatter, bds 42½ West ave n
Kirkpatrick Henry, laborer, 256 James n
Kirkpatrick Joseph, grocer, 92 Emerald n
Kirkpatrick Neil, engineer, 355 James n
Kirkpatrick William, carpenter, 19 Simcoe w
Kirkwood John, laborer, 94 Ferrie e
Kirwin John P, shipper, 314 King William
Kitchen J B, photographer, 18 Augusta
Kite Harry, com traveler, 21 Mulberry
Kitten John, laborer, 102 Picton e
Kitts James, shoemaker, 5 Hilton

Kittson E C (Martin & Kittson) 16 Hughson s
Kittson H N, bookkeeper, 29 Wellington s
Kittyle Francis, collector *Times*, 44 Stuart e
Klager Michael, bricklayer, 54 Jackson w
Kleinstiber Hugo, cabinet maker, 103 Robinson
Klinger Herman, machinist, 108 James n
Klock John, packer, 53 Emerald n
Klock Rozell, cigar maker, 2 Tisdale
Klotz E W, buyer, 80 Robert e
Knags William, machinist, 99 Catharine s
Knapman Mrs A (wid John) 14 Emerald n
Knapman John, laborer, 108 Locke s
Knapman Wm, laborer, 2 Main w
Knapp Ethelbert, laborer, 42 Wellington n
Kneeshaw Joseph, lithographer, 46 Lower Cathcart
Knetsch August, tailor, 174 Cannon e
Knight Mrs Ellen, 232 Barton e
Knight Henry, car repairer, 45 Peter
Knights of Labor Co-operative Store (grocers) James Ailes, manager, 12 John n
Knott George, laborer, 99 Macnab n
Knott & Sons (John H and Chas) piano manfs, 98 James n h 49 Walnut s
Knott Thomas, clerk, 58 Bay n
Knotts Augustus, laborer, Herkimer
Knotts Mrs Sophia, Herkimer
Knowles E, laborer, 33 Macauley e
Knowles Mrs Caroline (wid Rainault) 7 Hess n
Knowles Henry, clerk, 194 King w
Knox Church (Presbyterian) James cor Cannon
Knox George, engine driver G T R, 93 Hess n
Knox John, policeman, 351 Jas n
Knox John (Knox, Morgan & Co) 7 King e
Knox, Morgan & Co (John Knox and Alfred Morgan) wholesale dry goods, 7 King e
Knox Mrs, tollgate keeper, King e
Koch Nicholas, moulder, 169 John n
Korn Wm, furrier, Markland nr Locke
Kouber Matthew, furrier, 15 Locke s
Kraft A A (E L Kraft & Son) Wentworth s of Main
Kraft E L (E L Kraft & Son) Wentworth s of Main
Kraft E L & Son (E L Kraft, A A Kraft) saddlery, 8-10 York
Kramer Mrs Barbara, Flamboro House, 53 Merrick
Kramer George, Eureka Hotel, 36 York
Krause Chas, buckle maker, 43 Queen s
Kronsbein Henry, tailor, 77 Jackson e
Kuntz Henry, brewer, 15 Bay n
Kuntz Jacob, brewer, 39 Bay n
Kuntz James, fireman, bds 122 Cannon e
Kurpieski Miss Agatha, 121 Jackson w
Kuskie William, machinist, bds Blaase hotel
Kyle Thos, laborer, 66 Locke s
Labatt John Agency, J H Linfoot agent, 35 King e
Labitzky Sebastien (Blumenstiel & Labitzky) bds 34 King William
La Chance Wm E, com traveler, 79 Main w

Lockie Thos, laborer, 112 Bold
Ladd Edward, baker, Ferguson ave n
Lafarelle James, fireman, bds 10 Stuart e
Lafferty James, M D, 27 Rebecca
Lagarie John, blacksmith, 130 Emerald n
Lagarie Octave, blacksmith, 186 Emerald n
Lahey Michael, bricklayer, 128 Hannah e
Lahey Thomas, messenger, 41 Catharine n
Lahey Wm, telegraphist, 41 Catharine n
Lahiff John, laborer, 144 Bay n
Laidlaw Adam (Laidlaw Manf Co) h 17 Wilson
Laidlaw George, brushmaker, 8 Elgin
Laidlaw James, carpenter, Ashley
Laidlaw James, machinist, bds 49 Stuart w
Laidlaw James, bookkeeper, 17 Wilson
Laidlaw Manuf Co, A Laidlaw managing director, 84 to 90 Mary
Laidlaw Thomas, clerk, 82 Mary
Laidlaw Robert, agent, 51 Walnut s
Laidlaw Rev R J, pastor St Paul's Church, 85 Hughson s
Laidman Richard, laborer, 9 Walnut n
Laing Edward, upholsterer, bds 79 Bay n
Laing Mrs Elizabeth (wid James S) 40 George
Laing H Hargreave, merchant, 70 Cannon w
Laing Mrs Isabella (wid George) 79 Bay n
Laing Jas B, bookkeeper, 73 Bay n
Laing John, bricklayer, 110 Caroline s
Laing John, machinist, Maple
Laing Wm, brakesman G T R, 19 Mill
Laing Wm J, grocer, Hannah w, cor Caroline, 47 Merrick
Laird Mrs Isabella (wid Joseph) bds 84 Queen s
Laird Thomas W, machinist, 245 Hughson n
Lake Albert, broommaker, 22 Barton w
Lakeland James F, artist, 34 Colborne
Lake & River Steamship Co, John Harvey & Co, 69 James n
Lalor Simon, hotel keeper (Thompson's hotel) 12 Market
Lalley Dominic, rougher, bds 73 Stuart w
Lalley Thomas, laborer, 270 Hughson n
Lamb F H, accountant, Ham Prov Chambers
Lambe Harold, com merchant, 24 Main e, h 87 Hughson s
Lambe T H, accountant, 58 Jackson w
Lambe W G, clerk, 61 George
Lambert Arthur, watchman, 18½ Simcoe e
Lambert Charles, manager Gore Coffee Tavern, 13 Hughson n
Lambert Frederick, pork packer, 140 Jackson e
Lambert George, teamster, 62 Robinson
Lambert Joseph, teamster, 62 Robinson
Lamont Alexander, lithographer, 140½ Mary
Lamont Miss Isabella, dressmaker, 140½ Mary
Lamont John, gardener, Main e
Lamonte —, laborer, Maple
Lamoreux Emile, shoemaker, 22 Upper Cathcart
Lamplough Jeremiah, watchman, 8 Inchbury n

Lampman Joseph, laborer, 69 Robert
Lampman William, laborer,, 69 Robert
Lampman Wm H, farmer, 20 Walnut s
Lampshire Mark, laborer, 106 Strachan e
Lamrock Mrs Nancy, 50 Chisholm
Lanaway R B, machinist, 111 West ave n
Lancashire Fire & Life Insurance Co, George A Young agent, 2 Merrick
Lancefield Mrs Agnes (wid Chas) 105 York
Lancefield C J, carriage trimmer, 105 York
Lancely Wm, engineer, 67 Hannah w
Land Allan, bookkeeper, 136 Hughson n
Land Mrs Helen (wid Wm) 159 Main w
Land Col John, Wentworth n
Land J H, sec Royal Templars, 296 Barton e
Land Peter, Wentworth n
Land Stephen, machinist, Smith Ave
Landon Frederick, com traveler, 121 John s
Landed Banking & Loan Co, Samuel Slater treasurer, Canada Life Building, 3 James s
Lane Edmund, carpenter, 62 Mulbery
Lane Edward, produce dealer, 154 Catharine n
Lane Wm, bricklayer, Hess s
Lane William, jr, bricklayer, bds Hess s
Laney James, 149 Ferguson ave
Lang Mrs Grace (wid William) 126 Catharine n
Lang Thomas, carpenter, 182 Robert e
Langberg Fred, cabinet maker, 85 King e
Langdon Daniel, 18 Stuart e
Langdon Joseph, engineer, 74 Canada
Langford Rev Alex, pastor King Sreet Methodist Church, 104 Main e
Langford John, carpenter, 74 Queen s
Langley Philip, watchman, 20 South e
Langlois Mrs Margaret (widow Thos) 59 Hunter w
Langlois Richard A, millwright, 19 Sophia n
Langton Mrs Julia (wid John) 134 Jackson e
Lanigan George, bookbinder, 68 Ferguson ave
Lannon Thomas, laborer, 97 Ferrie e
Lanton Rev Henry, 22 Sheaffe
Lappan Joseph, brakesman, 107½ Simcoe e
Large F W, agent *Mail*, 119 Catharine s
Lark W B, salesman, bds 17 Main w
Larkin Andrew, weaver, 100 Simcoe e
Larkin Francis, carpet weaver, 95 King w
Larkin Hall, 8 John n
Larkin Wm, moulder, 9 Elgin
Larkin Wm, moulder, 101½ Elgin
Larmer James, laborer, 59 Barton e
Larman William, brickmaker, 3 Sophia s
Larmer Wm, brickmaker, Jones
Larson J A, laborer, 31 Murray e
Larsen Lavis, shoemaker, 216 John n
Laskie Mrs Jeannette (wid Wm) 62 Ray n
Latham John, wagon maker, 137 Ferguson ave

Latham Shephard, machinist, 11 Crooks
Lathrop J M, manager Opera House, office 10 Gore
Latimer James, machinist 72 Locomotive
Lattimore Mrs Mary, 281 James n
Latimore Wm, blacksmith, 90 Bay n
Latremouille John, confectioner, 33 Sheaffe
Lauder Mrs Elizabeth (wid John) 146 Bay s
Lauder George, fireman, bds Court House Hotel
Laughlin Andrew, moulder, 47 Chisholm
LaVallee Charles, machinist, 293 James n
LaVallee D P, 297 James n
Lavell John, cigar maker, 24 Macnab n, h 22 Aurora
Lavell Mrs Kate (wid Michael) 172 Jackson w
Lavelle Mrs Ann (wid Owen) 63 Maria
Lavelle Anthony, laborer, bds 158 Rebecca
Lavelle John, laborer, 30 Ferguson ave
Lavelle Owen, laborer, 90 Maria
Lavelle Patrick, baker, 63 Maria
Lavelle Robert, tinsmith, 19 John, n, h 63 Maria
Lavelle Wm, tinsmith, 63 Maria
Lavery Henry, accountant, bds Royal hotel
Lavery James, carpenter, 31 East ave n
Lavery W J, solicitor, 4 Main, h 41 Hannah e
Lavin Mrs Ellen, 146 Catharine n
Laven J G, Canadian passenger agt M C R R, bds Royal hotel
Lavis Edward, carpenter, 105 Rebecca
Lavis Edward, 204 King Wm
Lavis Mrs Fanny (wid Wm) 37 Ferguson ave
Lavis James, carpenter, 2 Pine
Lawlor Mrs Ann, 20 Wood w
Lawlor John, cabinet maker, 69 Strachan e
Lawlor Patrick, carter, 16 Railway
Lawlor Thomas, machinist, 97 Cherry
Lawrason Mrs Hannah (wid Douglas) 162 Napier
Lawrence John, druggist's assistant, 21 Tom
Lawrence John, painter, 9 Wood e
Lawrence Mrs Sarah (wid John) 185 Napier
Lawrence Thomas, laborer, 356 John n
Lawrence Thomas, carpenter, 8 Emerald n
Lawrence Thomas, druggist, 81 James n
Lawrence Wm, polisher, 39 Emerald n
Lawrie James, salesman, 66 Ray s
Lawrie James, laborer, 66 Ray s
Lawrie John, clerk, bds 78 Market
Lawrie John, laborer, 143 Macauley e
Lawrie John S, clerk, bds 78 Market
Lawrie Robert, laborer, bds 99 Hunter w
Lawry Mrs A, 25 Augusta
Lawry Charles, hides and skins, 26 Merrick, res Dundas
Lawry Henry, butcher James st Market, h 13 Charles
Lawry Simon, advertising agent, 55 Young
Lawry Thomas & Son (Thos and Thos H) prop Hamilton Packing House, 14, 16 Macnab s and James st market, h 136 James s
Lawson A & Co, printers, 5 York
Lawson A J, manager Edison Electric Light Co, h 11 Park s

Lawson Alexander (A Lawson & Co) h 55 Macnab s
Lawson John, salesman, 78 John n
Lawson John, laborer, bds 55 Magill
Lawson Mrs Mary (wid Abraham) 55 Magill
Lawson Thomas, laborer, 18 Guise
Lawson William, traveler bds 37 Robert
Lawson Wm, carpenter, 33 Wellington s
Lay Andrew, saloonkeeper, 21 James n
Laycock Charles, blacksmith, 15 Wellington n
Layland Edwin, upholsterer, Robinson
Lazarus Geo J, wood turner, 14 Magill
Lazier, Dingwall & Monck (S F Lazier, M A, LL B, Kenneth Dingwall, B A, LL B, J F Monck) barristers, 42 James n *See card*
Lazier S F, M A, LL B (Lazier, Dingwall & Monck) barrister, h 67 Charles
Leary Wm, 17 Vine
Leask A R, 8 Maria
Leask R P, gents' furnishings, 24 King e, h 8 Maria
Leask Wm, watchman, 152 Bay n
Leather A T, clerk G T R, res Waterdown
Leather Henry R, fitter, 82 Hannah w
Leather Thomas E, com traveler, 97 Market
Leaver Uriah, 52 Strachan e
Leavers Geo, painter, 147 Jackson w
LeBarre Miss Fathama, 96 John n
Le Blanc Isaac, lineman, 32 Macauley w
Le Blanc Nil, lineman, 32 Macauley w
Lech Mrs Eliza (wid And) bds 41 Peter
Leckenby Francis J, com traveler, 9½ Park s
Leckie Campbell, machinist, South e
Leckie W R, bookkeper, 79 East ave n
Ledgerwood Mrs Myra (wid James) 45 Robert
Lee Charles, 373 Hughson
Lee Christopher, porter, 78 Jackson e
Lee Mrs Ellen (wid John) 77 Hunter e
Lee Miss Emma, 185 Catharine n
Lee George, 68 King w
Lee Harry, clerk, 11 Brock w
Lee Jacob, laborer, 21 Burlington w
Lee Joel, cabinet maker, 22 Emerald n
Lee Joseph, wood dealer, 176 York, h Burlington s
Lee Joseph, piano tuner, 138½ Main e
Lee Joseph, cabinet maker, 52 Gore
Lee Lyman, law student, 109 Macnab n
Lee Robert, fireman G T R, 20 Crooks
Lee Thomas, glass blower, s w cor John n and Picton
Lee Wesley, mariner, 380 Hughson n
Lee Wm, pedler, 152 Hughson n
Lee Wm, bricklayer, 191 Wellington n
Lee Wm G, 68 King w
Leegrice Mrs Charlotte, 68 John s
Leegrice Thomas, cabinet maker, r 77 Jackson e
Lees G H (G H Lees & Co) h 78 Napier
Lees G H & Co, watchmakers and jewelers, 114 King e

Lees Mrs Jane (wid George) 74 James s

Lees Thomas, watchmaker, jeweler and optician, 5 James n, h 143 Main w

Lees Wm (Walker & Scott) barrister, h 31 Main e

LeesWilliam,baker, 31 Main e

Lefevre Robt, carpet weaver, 11 Rebecca

Legarie John, wagon shop, 41 James s, h Emerald n

Legg James, pedler, 86 Bay n

Leggat John, clerk, 5 Duke

Leggat John, cabinet maker, bds 31 Gore

Leggat Matthew (Wood & Reggat) h 5 Duke

Legault Jacques, Smith ave

Legault Phœnix, shoemaker, Smith ave

Lehan Daniel, laborer, r 258 King w

Leighton Mrs A, temperance laundry) 6 Upper Cathcart

Leighton Augustus, laborer, 6 Upper Cathcart

Leishman Mrs Mary (wid Malcolm) 280 King e

Leister Charles, laborer, Garth

Leister Henry, laborer, Garth

Leitch Andrew (Leitch & Turnbull) h 18 Barton w

Leitch David G, clerk, 50 Hughson n

Leitch John, machinist, 50 Hughson n

Leitch John, machinist, 59 East ave n

Leitch & Turnbull (Andrew Leitch, Michael Turnbull) manfs hoisting machinery, 29 Rebecca

Leitch William, machinist, bds 50 Hughson n

Leith A, teller Stinson's Bank, 71 Main w

Leith Wm, clerk, David McLellan, 71 Main w

Le Messurier Daniel, painter, 59 Hunter w

Lemon Charles, barrister, 14 Hughson s, h 5 Young

Lemon Mrs Margaret (wid Wilson, dressmaker, 30 Wilson

Lemond George, laborer, 150 Jackson w

Lendon Mrs Mary Ann (wid John) 18 Sheaffe

Lendon Henry, machinist, 29 Crooks

Lendon Henry, machinist, 14 Harriet

Lennard Mrs George, 31 Stuart

Lennon Fred W, bartender Dominion Hotel

Lennon Rev James (Roman Catholic) 25 Sheaffe

Lennox John (W Griffith & Co) h 17 Pearl s

Lennox Wm, grocer, 53 Markland

Lentz August, laborer, 47 Tisdale

Lentz Fred, butcher, 47 Steven

Leonard, caretaker GTR offices, Stuart w

Leonard James, laborer, 67 Walnut s

Leonard Patrick, laborer, 1 Eliza

Le Page Pierre, shoemaker, 25 Liberty

Le Patourel Elias, shoemaker, 117 Main e

Le Riche George (J Winer & Co) h 102 Catharine s

Leslie James, MD, 37 Main w

Leslie Robert, shoemaker, 29 Florence

Leslie Robert, laborer, 97 Mary

Leslie Robert, bookkeeper, 44 Macauley w

Leslie Robert, fruiterer, 142 Rebecca

Leslie W L, clerk, 37 Main w

Lester B, Exchange Hotel, 12 Market sq

Lester J M, Canada Clock Co, h 75 East ave s

Lester Thomas W, real estate and insurance agent, 80 Emerald s
Level Wm, laborer, 61 Mary
Leveratt S, accountant, 2½ Jas n
Levi Abraham, rag dealer, 79 Macnab n
Levis John, laborer, 145 Catharine n
Levis William, carpenter, 241 King e
Leveque John, shoemaker, 34 Mulberry
Levy Abraham (Levy Bros & Scheuer) h 89 James s
Levy Bros & Scheuer (H & A Levy, E Scheuer) wholesale jewelers, 27 King e
Levy Herman (Levy Bros & Scheuer) h 89 James s
Levy Isaac, tailor, 99 Jackson e
Lewis Andrew, laborer, Burlington
Lewis Benjamin, 48 Cannon w
Lewis Benjamin, wool sorter, 36 Catharine n
Lewis David, laborer, Jones
Lewis Edward, plasterer, 62 Walnut s
Lewis Mrs Ellen (wid Robert) 15 Main w
Lewis Jas, machinist, 57 Young
Lewis Jas, carpenter, 61 Steven
Lewis J H, bartender Empire House
Lewis J H, bandmaster, 87 Park n
Lewis John, shoemaker, 89 King William
Lewis John, 95 Napier
Lewis John B, spring bed manf, 8 Wellington n
Lewis J L, city editor *Spectator*, 103 James s
Lewis Marvin, polisher, 2 Emerald n
Lewis Mrs Susan (wid Daniel) 83 Peter
Lewis Thomas, roller, 147 Locke n
Lewis Thomas, teamster, 118 West ave n
Lewis Thomas, cigar manf, 31 Maria
Lewis Thos S, machinist, 129 Simcoe e
Lewis William, plasterer, 43 Augusta
Lewis Wm J, carpenter, 120 East ave n
Leyden Charles, manager Duncan Lithographing Co, 13 Colborne
License Commissioners' Office, John I McKenzie, inspector, 4 James s
Life Association of Canada, John Cameron, manager, Wentworth Chambers, 25 James s
Life Association of Scotland, A F Forbes, agent, 2 Merrick
Lightfoot J L, shoemaker, 159 James n
Lillis J S, cigar manf, Centre, h 9 Cannon
Limin Charles, meat and provision dealer, 26 Jackson w
Limin William, bookkeeper, 26 Jackson w
Lindsay Wm, laborer, 116 Pictoh e
Lindsay W J, paying teller Bank of Hamilton, 114 Main w
Linfoot J H, agent John Labatt, 35 King e, h Victoria ave, cor Robert
Linfoot Leonard, salesman, 95 West ave n
Ling James, carpenter, 58 Chisholm
Ling John, 57 King Wm
Linger Jesse, sexton Christ church 166 James n
Linklater Andrew, 73 Peter
Linton Robert, carpenter, 49 Stuart w
Lipck Charles, brushmaker, 59 Steven

Lipkie Frank, laborer, 46 Hess s
Lister Jas, carpenter, 195 John n
Lister Joseph, office 42 James n, h 75 Victoria ave s
Lister W L B, law student, Stinson cor Victoria ave
Lithgow Jas, laborer, 210 King w
Little David, barber, 61 John s
Little Hector, grocer, 80 Barton e
Little Jas, laborer, bds 56 Burlington w
Little John, carpenter, King e
Little John M, bookkeeper, 5 Victoria ave n
Little M H, plumber, 240 Cannon e
Little Robert, laborer, 52 Locomotive
Little William, glassworker, 56 Burlington w
Little William, laborer, 145 Macauley e
Littlehales Mrs John, 234 Cannon e
Littlehales Thomas, engineer and manager gas works, 99 Park n
Littlejohn Chas, wood inspector G T R, 140 Queen n
Littlejohn Mrs M W (wid Alex) 90 Jackson e
Littlejohn Wm, bricklayer, 123 Emerald n
Littlewood George, machinist, 9 Murray e
Littlewood Thomas, brakesman, 227 Hughson n
Livernois Joseph, fruit dealer, 24 Spring
Livings Frank, grocer, 307 York
Livingston Stuart, law student, 100 Main w
Livingston T C sr, Dominion Land Surveyor, 18 James s, h 100 Main w
Livingston W Churchill (Staunton & Livingston) h 100 Main w

16

Lloyd Griffith, clerk, 116 Cannon w
Llyod H H, shipper, 45 Murray w
Lloyd James, laborer, Greig
Lloyd Joseph, bookkeeper, 116 Cannon w
Llyod Samuel, cabinet maker, 55 York
Lloyd's Plate Glass Insurance Co, Seneca Jones agent, 59 James n
Locke Charles, stovemounter, 84 Hannah e
Locke Mrs Margaret (wid Chas) 109 Jackson w
Locke Mrs Mary (wid Joseph) 109 Jackson w
Locke Wm J, clerk, Markland cor Caroline
Locke W J, clerk, 129 Ferguson ave
Lockhart James, 44 Victoria ave s
Lockhart Octaf, tobacco roller, 60 Hess n
Lockie Alex, printer, 36 Market
Lockie Mrs Isabella (wid Alex) 36 Market
Lockman Christopher F, 324 York
Lockman Wm, joiner, 36 Florence
Lockman Wm H, bridge builder, 40 Florence
Lockwood Miss Eliza (British American Laundry) 50 Robert
Lockwood Mrs Sarah, 50 Robert
Loemans Alex F, artist, 14½ King e, h 151 King w
Loftus James, laborer, 7 Harriet
Loftus James, laborer, 233 Macnab n
Logan J, excise officer, 198 Bay n
Logan John, coachman, Main w cor Hess
Logan Mrs Margaret (wid Adam) 8 Margaret
Logie James, 333 York

Logie Mrs M R (wid Alex) Markland
Lomas Joseph, laborer, Tiffany
London China House, 7 Market Square
London Guarantee & Accident Co, George A Young agent, 2 Merrick
London & Lancashire Fire Insurance, W J Findlay agent, 25 James s
London & Lancashire Life Insurance Co, J T Routh agent, 16 James s
Loney Alfred, shoemaker, 120 Maria
Loney Christopher, shoemaker, 107½ John s
Loney Thomas H, letter carrier, 42 Catharine s
Long & Bisby, wool merchants, 58 Macnab n
Long George, wood dealer, 32 Cherry
Long Horace J, bookkeeper, 60 Cannon e
Long Joseph, laborer, Evans
Long Philip, r 174 John n
Long Robert, blacksmith, 15 Park n
Long Thomas, engine driver, 255 King Wm
Long Walter, carriage painter, r 174 John n
Long Wm, laborer, 2 Chisholm
Long Wm D (Long & Bisby) 54 John n
Longhurst Henry (H Longhurst & Co) h 26 York
Longhurst Henry & Co, Stained Glass Works, 26 York
Longon Mrs Ellen (wid Wm) 134 King w
Lonsdale Frank, sec Young Men's Christian Association, Concession cor Queen
Loos Eugene, barber, 63 York
Loosley Edward, cutter, 20 Liberty
Lord Robert, tailor, 55 Gore
Lord Wm, dairyman, Queen s
Loretto Convent, Mount St Mary, King cor Ray
Lornie Thomas, machinist, 118 Wilson
Lorris Nathaniel, hay dealer, 40 Jackson e
Lottridge James M (P Grant & Sons) "Blackauton," Bay cor Herkimer
Lottridge Lewis, dairyman, 182 Emerald n
Lottridge Robt, 126 Bay s
Loucks Hilton, harness maker, 186 Main w
Loughrey S B, com traveler, 107 Victoria ave n
Love David, carpenter, 285 King William
Love Henry G, contractor, 108 Catharine s
Lovejoy James laborer, 66 Locke s
Lovejoy Thomas, builder 63 Emerald
Loveland Mrs Mary (wid Nathan) 37 Market
Lovell A R, clerk, 134 Mary
Lovell Henry, fireman G T R 43 Florence
Lovell Thomas, marble cutter, 14 Inchbury n
Lovering W J, proprietor Club Chambers, 16 Hughson s
Low Wm, carpenter, 23 Caroline n
Love David, wire weaver, 140 Market
Lowe George, fireman, 23 Caroline n
Lowe Harry, clerk, 104 Hess n
Lowe William, machinist, 208 Macnab n
Lowe Mrs Thomas, 183 Main e
Lowes John W, traveler, 278 King e
Lowrey Charles, machinist, 94 Market

Lowrey Jacob, 94 Market
Lowrey James, policeman, 124 Rebecca
Lowrey John, policeman, 143 Bay n
Lowrey Matthew, carpenter, Smith ave
Lucas Chas H, bookkeeper, 10 Crooks
Lucas J, restaurant, 11 Market sq
Lucas Luke, moulder, 85 Catharine n
Lucas, Park & Co (R A Lucas, John H Park, Geo E Bristol, Robert Steele) wholesale grocers, 59 Macnab n
Lucas R A (Lucas, Park & Co) h 23 Duke
Lucas Robert, moulder, 35 Tisdale
Lucas Robert, foreman E & C Gurney, 112 Rebecca
Lucas Robert N, moulder, bds 112 Rebecca
Lucas Thomas, laborer, 125 Picton e
Lucas Thos, farmer, 130 Picton e
Lucas Thomas O, butcher, 40 Catharine n
Lumgair W S, sewing machines and organs, 115 James n, h 175 Main w
Lumsden Bros (J A, W G & F A) wh grocers, 64 Macnab n, h 43 Cannon w
Lumsden Mrs Francis, 43½ Cannon w
Lumsden Paul, shipper, Wellington n
Lumsden William, 14 West ave n
Lunt Wm, blacksmith, 39 Robinson
Lutes Alonzo, salesman, 147 John s
Lutz John, teamster, 65 Pearl s
Luxton George, flour and feed, 12 York, h Barton township
Lyall Thomas F, teacher, 178 King w
Lydiatt John, gardener, Wentworth s
Lyght Joseph, pattern maker, 96 Jackson e
Lyle Mrs Andrew, 80 West ave n
Lyle John, plumber, 82 West ave n
Lyle Rev Samuel, pastor Central Presbyterian Church, 20 Jackson w
Lyle W J, machinist, bds 80 West ave n
Lynch Francis, teamster, 113 Barton e
Lynch James, printer, 132 Ferrie e
Lynch James, laborer, 132 Ferrie e
Lynch John, laborer, 254 Mary
Lynch John, brakesman G T R, 110 Locke n
Lynch John, laborer, 132 Ferrie e
Lynch Mrs Mary, 167 Wilson
Lynch Michael, laborer, 132 Ferrie e
Lynch Patrick, section foreman, Aikman's ave
Lynch Patrick, gardener, 167 Wilson
Lynch Mrs Patrick, 132 Ferrie e
Lynch Timothy, switchman, 214 John n
Lynch William, brakeman, 73 Stuart w
Lynd Mrs Eleanor (wid Wm) 79 Pearl n
Lyne John, shoemaker, 59 Little William
Lyne Wm, salesman, 59 Little Wm
Lyon Anthony, machinist, 115 Hess n
Lyon Mrs Isabella, 211 John n
Lyon Thomas, mariner, 9 Spring
Lyon Wm, carpenter, 9 Spring
Lyons Calvin, agent, 136 Robert e
Lyons Frederick, laborer, 8 Locke n

Lyons James, mariner, 9 Spring
Lyons John, shipper, Head
Lyons Townsend, laborer, 101 Cherry
Lyons William, laborer, 125 Simcoe e
McAdam Low, stonemason, Queen s
Macadams A H (Parkes & Macadams) barrister, h 130 Hughson n
Macadams Louis, quarryman, bds 70 Hughson s
McAdams Ninian, broommaker, 50 Young
McAdams William, teamster, 10 Stuart e
McAlden Mrs Harriet (wid Geo) 121 Market
McAllister Harmon J, grocer, 128 Macnab n
McAllister John, grocer 123 York, h 118 Macnab n
McAllister, John, laborer, 87 Bold
McAllister John, blacksmith, 250 James n
McAllister D, sewing machine agent, Pearl s
McAllister W J, lumber merchant, 232 Macnab n
Macallum Mrs Mary (wid Arch) 61 Bold
McAndrew Louis, finisher, 168 Mary
McAndrew William, printer, 153 King Wm
McAndrew Wm, cabinet maker, bds 158 Mary
McAndrews Patrick, laborer, 50 Stuart e
Macartney Mrs Eliza (wid Wm) 92½ Hess n
Macartney David, fruit dealer, 158 James n
Macartney Patrick, watchman, 85 Strachan e
McArthur Alex, switchman, bds 49 Caroline n
McArthur James (J McArthur & Co) 28 Wellington s
McArthur James & Co, hats and furs, 29 King w
McArthur John, prop Hamilton Straw work, 138 Hughson n
McArthur John, bookkeeper, 138 Hughson n
McArthur Robert, machinist, bds 49 Caroline n
Macaulay J A, fruiterer, 166 King e, h 191 King e
McAulay John, millwright, Greig
McAuley John, engraver, 160 King Wm
McAuliffe Denis, laborer, 17 Wood w
McAuliffe Jeremiah, saloon, 6 Hughson n
McAuliffe Mrs Julia (wid Patrick) 105 Market
McAvay Robert, gilder, 143 Ferguson ave
McBean John, pattern maker, 14 Kinnell
McBeth Peter, carpenter, 80 Napier
McBeth Sinclair, laborer, 118 Napier
McBeth Wm, machinist, 47 Hannah w
McBriar Mrs Alice, nurse, 379 John n
McBride Daniel, coal oil dealer, 227 Catharine n
McBride Denis, 218 John n
McBride John, moulder, 181 Catharine n
McBride John, policeman, 197 Wellington n
McBride Patrick, grocer, 220 John n
McBride Rich, packer, George
McBride Thomas, foreman Hendrie & Co, 30 Caroline n
McBride William, clerk, bds 60 James s
McBrien David, painter, 25 Cherry

McBrien David (Barker & McBrien) h Mountain top
McBrier Henry, laborer, 79 Caroline n
Macabe Mrs Agnes (wid James) 131 Market
McCabe Chas J, teacher, bds 33 Railway
McCabe John, com traveler, 32 Elgin
McCabe Patrick laborer, 108 Queen n
McCabe S, boots and shoes, 48 King e
McCabe Thomas, engineer, Main e
McCaffery, clerk, bds Dominion hotel
McCaffery Robert, laborer, 110 Maria
McCaghey Miss Elizabeth, milliner, 152 James n
McCallum Alexander, moulder, 42 Picton w
McCallum Mrs Caroline (wid Daniel) 46 Duke
McCallum & Hall (Thos McCallum and John T Hall) cabinet makers and upholsterers, 16 Macnab n
McCallum John, moulder, 228 Macnab n
McCallum Mrs Margaret (wid Wm) 113 Napier
McCallum Thomas jr (McCallum & Hall) h 111 Wellington n
McCamis Arthur, laborer, 236 Macnab n
McCandlish Peter, shipper, 112 Wellington s
McCann Mrs Ann (wid Henry) 9 Ferrie e
McCann Dennis, stove mounter, bds 83 Lower Cathcart
McCann Henry, confectioner, 62 West ave n
McCann John, shoemaker, 101 James n
McCann ,Thomas, moulder, 83 Lower Cathcart
McCann Thomas, vinegar manuf, 132 Cannon e
McCardell John, machinist, bds 25 Stuart w
McCardle Mrs Martha (wid Patrick) 130 John n
McCargow, Wm, M D, 16 Gore
McCarrol Robert, plumber, Walnut n
McCarter Mrs Mary (wid Arthur) 11 Walnut s
McCarthy Calahan, hackman) 20 Harriet
McCarthy Chas, laborer, 2 Dundurn
McCarthy Daniel, yardsman, 226 John n
McCarthy Daniel, boilermaker, 119 Locke n
McCarthy Dennis, gardener, 216 Victoria ave n
McCarthy James, foreman, 77 Hannah e
McCarthy J E, express messenger, 96 Wilson
McCarthy John, hackman, 57 Wood e
McCarthy John, laborer, 202 Hughson n
McCarthy Michael, laborer, 124 Hunter e
McCarthy Michael, moulder, 162 Mary
McCarthy Patrick, laborer, 26 Hess n
McCarthy Patrick, laborer, 39 Sheaffe
McCarthy Richard, laborer, 156 Duke
McCarthy Thomas, carter, 32 Burlington e
McCarty William, weaver, 284 John n
McCaul John, blacksmith, bds 71 Colborne
McCaul Thomas, laborer, 79 Market

McCauley William, ornamenter, 86 Wilson
McCauley Wm, buyer, e Hamilton
McClean John, boots and shoes, 22 King w, h Hess s
McClelland John, laborer, 229 Hughson n
McClelland Peter, printer, 31 Lower Cathcart
McClelland William, spice merchant, 26 Spring
McCloy Mrs Agnes, 54 Emerald n
McClure John, mason, bds 186 Catharine n
McClure Mrs Margaret, 46 Jackson w
McClure William, carpenter, 250 Bay n
McClusker Frank, provisions, James st market, h Napier nr Queen
McClusky —, laborer, 302 King w
McColl Hugh, driver American Express Co
McColl Mrs Jessie(wid Hugh) 17 Crooks
McCollum James, laborer, 120 Simcoe e
McComb Mrs Eliza (wid Thos) 126 Hess n
McComb John, tailor, 56 West ave n
McComb Wm, moulder, 7 Chisholm
McComb Louis, carpenter, 5 Nightingale
McComb Wm H, laborer, 111 Catharine n
McConnell John, caretaker St Mary's Cathedral, 44 Mulberry
McCowell Mrs Ann (wid John) 63 Ray n
McCowell Bernard, laborer, 12 Dundurn
McCowell Bernhard, baggage master G T R, 63 Ray n
McCowell John, grocer, 85 Hess n
McCoy Alexander, lithographer, 146 Cannon e
McCoy Archibald, laborer, 24 Guise
McCoy James, salesman, 97 Wellington n
McCoy Jeremiah, carpenter, 24 Bay n
McCoy John, asst inspector Ham-Prov and Loan Society, 15 West ave n
McCoy Wm, machinist, bds 97 Wellington n
McCormick Robert, teamster, 55 Hannah e
McCracken John, tailor, 218 Hughson n
McCracken John, moulder, 46 Market
McCrae Mrs Mary A, grocer, 241 John n
McCreath James, blacksmith, 12 Hunter e
McCue James, engine driver, 110 Locke n
McCulloch D W, clerk James Turner & Co
McCulloch Mrs Harriet (widow Robert) 122 Hughson n
McCulloch James, engine driver G T R, 18 Locomotive
McCulloch Matthew, clerk, 109 Market
McCullough Mrs David, 162 Main w
McCullough Fred, clerk, 269 King w
McCullough George, blacksmith, Walnut n, h 120 Bold
McCullough J D (Davis & McCullough) h 70 Jackson w
McCullough John, carpenter, 70 Jackson w
McCullough John, salesman, 70 Jackson w
McCullough Peter, laborer, 165 Bay n

McCullough Peter, com traveler, 70 Jackson w
McCullough Wm, bds 54 Hannah
McCully Alex, shoemaker, 144 Hughson n
McCully B, machinist, 15 Steven
McCully G A, custom bootmaker, 93 James n
McCurdy Wm, carpenter, 208 King Wm
McCurly Frank, 200 Main e
McCusker, Francis, dealer, 111 Napier
McCusker Wm, produce dealer, 131 Cannon w
McCutcheon Wm, carpenter, 107 Robinson
McDaide William, laborer, 132 Locke n
McDearmid Mrs Bertha, 61 George
McDermott Miss Catharine, 32 Wellington n
McDermott Daniel, painter, 123 Hunter w
McDonagh Frank, laborer, bds 106 Maria
McDonagh William, laborer, 106 Maria
McDonald Alex, traveler, 101 Rebecca
McDonald Alex, com traveler, 5 Erie ave
McDonald (A & J W McDonald) h 4 Wellington n
McDonald Angus, metal spinner, bds 100 Park n
McDonald Arch, shipper, 140 West ave n
McDonald A & W J, builders, 116 King Wm
Macdonald Charles, com traveler, 93 James s
McDonald David, grocer, 77 York
McDonald D B, com traveler, 93 James s
McDonald Mrs Ellen, 43 Burlington w
McDonald Mrs Esther (widow Patrick) 26 Aurora
McDonald Francis, machinist, 24 Locke s
Macdonald Frederick, moulder, 10 Railway
McDonald Mrs Grace (wid Duncan) 6 Florence
MacDonald Hugh, laborer, 368 James n
McDonald James, foreman J McPherson & Co, 79 Wellington s
McDonald Jas, 209 Hughson n
McDonald Mrs Janet, bds 78 Caroline n
McDonald John, shoemaker, 133 Hunter e
McDonald John, inspr weights and measures, 9 Simcoe e
Macdonald John, laborer, 58 Maria
McDonald John R, ticket agent, 63 Victoria ave n
Macdonald John D, M D, 10 Duke
McDonald Lewis, laborer, Tiffany
McDonald John D, clerk P O
Macdonald Mrs Mary, 292 Jas n
McDonald Nicholas A, carpenter, 88 Caroline n
McDonald Roderick, salesman, 18 King e
McDonald Mrs Sarah (wid Bernard) 89 Strachan e
McDonald W H (McDonald & Co) h 23 Augusta
McDonald W H & Co, clothiers, 20 James n
Macdonald Wm, laborer, 161 York
McDonald W J (A & W J McDonald) h 8 Emerald s
Macdonald W R, barrister, 13 Main e, h 12 Herkimer
McDonald Wm, timekeeper, 180 Mary
McDonnell Chas, basket maker, 271 King w
McDonnell John, flour and feed, 156 King w

Macdonnell Wm, asst inspector weights and measures, 42 Burlington w
McDonough James S, news agt GTR, 62 Cannon e
McDonough John, teamster, 48 Augusta
McDonough Michael, rougher, 60 Locomotive
McDougall Albert, blacksmith, 30 Inchbury n
McDougall Duncan, railway contractor, 39 Main w
McDougall Hugh, mason, 63 Walnut s
McDougal Mrs J, coal oil and lamps, 10 Macnab n
McDougall John, car checker, 270 Macnab n
McDougall William, fitter, 133 Locke n
McDowell Alex, laborer, 92 Hess n
McDuff Daniel, music teacher, 134 Park n
McEachern A, teller Ham Prov & Loan Society, 131 Macnab n
McEachern Malcolm, boilermkr, 59 Locomotive
McElcheran W H, ornamenter, 56 Barton e
McEwen John, laborer, Duke
McFadden John, 329 John n
McFadden W J, grocer, 342 Hughson n
McFarland Arthur, laborer, 4 Little Market
McFarland Armour, tobacco manf, 64 Canada
McFarlane Alex, flour and feed, 196 King e, h 61 Wellington s
McFarlane David, jeweler, bds Victoria hotel
McFarlane Miss Jane, matron Orphan asylum, Wellington s
McFarlane John, laborer, Ferguson ave n
McFarlane John A, laborer, 168 Park n
McFarlane Miss Margaret, matron Aged Women's Home, hd Wellington s
McFarlane Mark, machinist, 31 West ave n
Macfarlane Robt, dairyman, Concession
Macfarlane William, machinist, 79 Walnut s
McFarlane Wm, teamster, hd Queen s
McFedries Wm, salesman, 81½ Bay n
McFerran Mrs M, teacher, 96 Victoria ave n
McGarell James, hairdresser, 7 Macnab n
McGargle Ann (wid Francis) 35 Strachan e
McGargle Henry, r 109 West ave n
McGee Matthew, carpenter, Robinson
McGibbon Frank, clerk, 121 Rebecca
McGibbon Wm, baker, 121 Rebecca
McGibney Andrew, painter, bds 55 York
McGill John, blacksmith, bds 39 James s
McGillicuddy B, laborer, foot Caroline n
McGilvray Alex, cleaner, 75 Elgin
McGilvery George, conductor, 75 Lower Cathcart
McGilvary John, clerk, 48 East ave n
McGilvary Kenneth, carpenter, 194 Emerald n
McGilvary W J, clerk, 46 East ave n
McGinley John, laborer, 86 Simcoe e
McGinnis John, stovemounter, 12 Jackson e
McGinnis Wm, saloonkeeper, 29 James n

McGinty James, laborer, 337 John n
McGiverin Emma (wid Wm S) 100 Queen n
McGiverin Walter, laborer, 30 Colborne
McGiverin Wm F, sec-treas Hamilton Industrial Works Co, 115 Macnab s
McGoff John, machinist, 23 Ferguson ave
McGorlick Henry, malster, 71 Barton e
McGorman David, laborer, bds 25 Stuart w
McGorman Ogilvie, laborer, 230½ James n
McGovern John, laborer, 68 Ferrie e
McGovern Patrick, woodworker, 55 Steven
McGovern William, laborer, 87 Hess n
McGowan Arch, machinist, 77 Hess n
McGowan Francis M, artist, 22 Macnab s
McGowan Hugh, butcher, 33 Elgin
McGowan P, clerk G T R, 307 James n
McGowan Manus, butcher, 22 Dundurn
McGowan William, laborer, 58 Burlington w
McGrath Edward, wagonmaker, 23 Cherry
McGrath James, laborer, 91 Young
McGrath James, laborer, 66 Cherry
McGrath Joanna (wid Michael) 72 Canada
McGrath John, porter, bds 42½ West ave n
McGrath John, porter, 75 Victoria ave n
McGrath Patrick, laborer, 15 Burlington w
McGrath Patrick, laborer, 42 Robinson
McGrath Thomas, porter, bds 75 Victoria ave n
McGrath William, cabinetmaker, Argo
McGregor Chas K (McGregor & Parke) h 32 Victoria ave n
McGregor D G, manager Bank of BNA, 5 King e
McGregor Duncan, carriage builder, 215 King w
McGregor John, boilermaker, bds 11 Barton e
McGregor & Parke (Chas R McGor and Walter Parke) druggists, Market sq
McGregor Thomas, moulder, 87 Catharine n
McGrogan Mrs, 282 Hughson n
McGrogin John, laborer, 91 Lower Cathcart
McGuigan Mrs Catharine (wid Felix) 74 Caroline n
McGuire Francis, second-hand store, 95 King w
McGuire James, moulder, bds 41 John n
McGuire John, bookbinder, 134 Ferguson ave n
McGuire Patrick, 63 Charles
McGuirk John, carpenter, 44 Jackson e
McHaffie John (J Winer & Co) h 91 Cannon e
McHaffie Robert, traveler, 115 Rebecca
McHaffie Wm, com traveler, 43 Nelson ave
McHarg James, tree agent, 285 York
McHattie Thomas, engine driver G T R, 13 Mill
McHendrie James, carpenter, 7 Stuart w
McHendrie John, hotelkeeper, 239 James n
McHendry Emily (wid Ephraim) 249 Hughson n

McHendry Mary Ann (wid Peter S) 21 Hunter w
McHugh F J J, excise officer, bds 21 Macnab s
McIlroy Catharine (wid John) 4 Jones
McIlroy David, machinist, 17 Simcoe w
McIlroy James, watchman G T R, Barton w
McIlroy Mrs, Barton w
McIlroy Robert, bds Franklin House
McIlroy W H, clerk, res Bartonville
McIlwraith Elizabeth (wid Alex) 48 Lower Cathcart
McIlwraith J G (McIlwraith & McMaster) h 16 Augusta
McIlwraith & McMaster (J G McIlwraith, John McMaster) dry goods, millinery, mantles and dressmaking *See advt p* 3
McIlwraith Thomas, coal merchant, 54 Main e, h Cairnbrae, Macnab n
McIlwraith's Wharf, foot Macnab n
McIlwraith T F, clerk, Cairnbrae, Macnab n
McInerney John, laborer, 29 Devonport
McInerey John, moulder, 133 Catharine n
McInerey Michael, moulder, 133 Catharine n
McInnes Alexander, 173 John s
McInnes Hon Donald, Dundurn, York
McInnes Donald, com traveler, 37 Jackson w
McInnes Margaret A (wid Hugh) 37 Jackson w
McIntosh James, 27 East ave n
Mackintosh John, machinist, South
McIntosh John, merchant tailor, 3 Market sq, h Main e
Mackintosh R M, clerk, bds 125 John s
McIntyre E, clerk, 59 Charles
McIntyre J G, foreman boiler maker G T R, 46 Murray w
McIntyre John, tailor, 12 Hughson n, h 95 Wellington n
McIntyre William, silver plater, 59 Charles
McIsaac Alex, laborer, r 177 Bay n
McKay —, laborer, 13 Harriet
McKay Bros (Robert and Jas D) dry goods and carpets, 70 King e *See advt*
McKay A D, laborer, 145 Ferguson ave
Mackay Mrs Æ D, 379 James n
Mackay Æ D (estate of) wharfingers, coal, etc, R O Mackay, manager, ft James n, res 17 Wood e
Mackay A H, clerk, 80 King e
McKay Alexander, flour and feed, 4 John s, h 24 Grove
McKay Alex, clerk, 138 Murray
McKay Angus, machinist, 169½ John n
Mackay Augusta (wid James D) music teacher, 45 Duke
Mackay Miss Christina, bds 146 Bay s
McKay Daniel, painter, 83 Locomotive
McKay George, carpenter, 5 Florence
Mackay George, W, inland revenue, 174 Macnab n
McKay Grant, merchant, 84 Cannon e
McKay J B, foreman Flatt & Bradley, 3 Barton Terrace, Wellington n
McKay James, cutter, 45 Hannah w
McKay James, grocer, 118 Main e
McKay James D (McKay Bros) h 8 Maria
Mackay James, engraver, 2 King William, h 138 Mary

McKay John, conductor G T R, 38 Magill
McKay John, street inspector, bds 68 Hunter e
Mackay John, 232 Bay n
McKay John R, harness maker, 17 Queen n
Mackay Hugh A, bds 178 King w
Mackay Neil, vintner, 84 Hunter e
McKay Peter, packer, 80 Hunter
Mackay Richard, Dominion License Inspector, 100 James s
Mackay R O (Æ Mackay) forwarders, etc, 17 Wood e
McKay Mrs Robert, 8 Maria
McKay Robert, plasterer, 82 Caroline s
McKay Samuel, livery, 4 Jackson, h 73 Main e
Mackay Thomas, grocer, 48 King w, h 29 Victoria ave s
Mackay's Whafr, ft James n
Mackay Wm H, sewer inspector, 12 Grove
McKay Wm, conductor G T R, 95 Hess n
McKean David, accountant, 105 Hughson n
McKean Edward, machinist, bds 105 Hughson n
McKean John, clerk, 42 George
McKean John, law student, 42 George
McKeand George, insurance and steamship ticket agent, 57 James n, h 72 Hannah e *See card*
McKeand J C, issuer of marriage licenses, Registrar's office, Court House, h 88 Bay s
McKeand James, Concession, West Cottage
McKee Eliza (wid Wm T) bds 32 Caroline n
McKee Henry, laborer, 125 Catharine n
McKee T J, liveryman, bds Commercial hotel
McKee Wm, moulder, 73 Hunter e
McKee Wm W, nailer, 32 Caroline n
McKeegan Nicholas, plasterer, 12 West ave n
McKeever Bros (Wm and Robert) flour and feed, 91 James n
McKeever Eliza (wid P) 142 Wood e
McKeever James, laborer, 266 Bay n
McKeever Robert, butcher, 196 James n
McKeever Robert (McKeever Bros) James cor Barton
McKeever Wm, baker, 138 James n
McKeever Wm (McKeever Bros) 91 James n
Mackelcan Frank, QC (Mackelcan, Gibson & Gausby) h 52 Catharine n
Mackelcan, Gibson & Gausby (F Mackelcan, QC, J M Gibson, MA, LL B, J D Gausby) barristers, 16 James s *See card*
Mackelcan George L, MD, coroner, 14 Gore
Mackelcan H A, barrister, 20 Main e, h 54 Catharine n *See card*
Mackelcan John, MD, 38 Catharine n
McKellar Arch, sheriff, Court House, h 105 James s
McKellar Hugh (Mills & McKellar) h 9 Ontario
McKellar L, com traveler, 17 Victoria ave n
McKelvie Samuel, laborer, 95 Bold
McKenna George, fireman, bds 79 Peter
McKenna James, engineer, 79 Peter
McKenna John, yardman, 17 Tisdale

McKenna John, machinist, bds 183 Mary
McKenna John, broom maker, 47 Queen s
McKenna Mary Ann (wid Robert) bds 30 Caroline n
McKenna Morris, laborer, 148½ Mary
McKenna Thos, 55 Charles
Mackenzie A I, surveyor and acting collector customs, res Burlington village
McKenzie Alex, bds 7 Inchbury n
McKenzie Archibald, carpenter, 112 Emerald n
McKenzie Arch, painter, 84 Locke n
McKenzie A S, shoemaker, 94 King e
McKenzie Donald, burnisher, bds 205 Wellington n
McKenzie Donald, express agt G T R, 84 Hannah w
Mackenzie Dougall S, engineer, 43 George
McKenzie Duncan, wood yard, Wellington, h 205 Wellington n
Mackenzie Mrs Hester, 108½ Jackson e
Mackenzie Ian, detective, 79 John n
Mackenzie James, machinist, 46 Augusta
Mackenzie J F, salesman, 196 Macnab n
McKenzie John, carpenter, 7 Inchbury n
McKenzie John, coal and wood, 149 Macnab, h 1 Sheaffe
McKenzie John I, license inspector, 61 George
McKenzie Kenneth, laborer, 128 John n
McKenzie Kenneth, engineer, 11 Locomotive
McKenzie Kenneth, painter, 101 Bay n
McKenie Kenneth, grocer, 11 East ave n
McKenzie Malcolm, laborer, 184 Victoria ave
McKenzie T H, general insurance agent, 3 Market
McKenzie Thos H, inspector weights and measures, res Dundas
Mackenzie Robert, laborer, 79 Macauley e
McKenzie Wm, salesman, bds 32 Ray n
McKeown Mrs Ann, 233 Hughson n
McKeown Arthur H, tinsmith, 47 Robinson
McKeown Hugh, harness maker and grocer, 72 John s
McKeown Arthur (McKeown & Reddall) 112 King w
McKeown James, bartender, 4 King w
McKeown James, carriage maker, 61 Robinson
McKeown John, moulder, 7 Ontario
McKeown Joseph, prop Metropolitan hotel, 49 Stuart w
McKeown Neil, moulder, 120 Florence
McKerlie Alex, com traveler, 81 Peter
McKernan Peter, laborer, 74 Cherry
McKichan F R, paper bag manf, 8, 10 John s, h 53 West ave n
McKillop Alex, bds 52 Victoria ave s
McKillop David, machinist, 8 Upper Cathcart
McKillop Jane (wid John) confectionery, 218 James n
McKinty John, landing waiter customs, 21 Barton e
McKinty Mrs M (wid Thomas) groceries, 244 James n
McKittrick Samuel, laborer, 96 Park n
McKitirick William, moulder, 146 Victoria ave n

McKnight John, fireman, 155 Wilson
McLagan Alex, 182 Main e
McLaren Daniel, machinist, 231 Macnab n
McLaren Miss Harriet, accountant Thos C Watkins, 30 King e, h 47 Peter
McLaren Captain Henry, Balquhidder, 153 James s
McLaren James A, com traveler, bds 35 East ave n
Maclaren Mrs R G, 122 John s
McLaren Mrs W B, Oak Bank, 155 James s
McLaren W H, grocer, 6 King William, h 35 East ave n
McLaren Wm, shoemaker, 99 West ave n
McLaren Wm, dry goods, 226 James n
McLauchlan Alex, bds 68 Locomotive
McLaughlin Alexander, salesman, 140 Hunter e
McLaughlin Edward, civil engineer, 38 Hunter w
McLaughlin, Edward, clerk Public works, 38 Hunter w
McLaughlin David, laborer, 163 Wilson
McLaughlin Garret, laborer, 163 Wilson
McLaughlin Hugh, horse trainer, 144 Market
McLaughlin James, moulder, 149 Bay n
McLaughlin John, bookbinder, 41 John n
McLaughlin John, painter, 63 Colborne
McLaughlin Miss M, dressmaker, 1 Evans
McLaughlin Matthew, blacksmith, 61 Ray n
McLaughlin Morgan, moulder, 163 Wilson
McLaughlin —, laborer, 191 Victoria ave n
Maclean A A, bookkeeper, 61 Hunter w
McLean Alex, clerk, 88 Peter
Maclean Arch, 61 Hunter w
Maclean Mrs F, fancy goods, 4 King e, h 61 Hunter w
McLean George, moulder, bds 24 Caroline n
McLean Geo, shoemaker, 111 Bold
Maclean Hugh, baker, 76 Queen s
Maclean James B, cabinet maker, 70 Queen s
McLean John, tailor, 13 Head
McLean John, boilermaker, Aikman's ave
McLean John, blacksmith, Aikman's ave
McLean Neil, saloon keeper, 51 Gore
McLean Mrs Samuel, 166 John n
McLean Mrs Sarah (wid John) Simcoe e
McLellan David, agent Royal Insurance Co, 84 James, h 55 Herkimer *See advt, back cover*
McLellan Donald, book and stationery, Bible society and track depository, 28 King w
McLennan Kenneth, 165 Locke s
McLelland Andrew, laborer, 359 James n
McLelland Thoma J, engine driver, 18½ Elgin
McLelland Wm, collar maker, 34 Mary
McLennan Alex, gardener, York w
McLennan Andrew, laborer, 190 Robert e
McLennan George, laborer, 191 Bay n
McLennan Robert, 132 Young
McLeod Colin, cutter, 84 Merrick
McLeodColin, porter, 100 Cherry
McLeod Charles, dyer, 123 James n

McLeod David, moulder, 3 Sheaffe
McLeod Mrs Eborah (wid Angus) music teacher, 34 Caroline n
McLeod Mrs Elizabeth (wid Archibald) dyer, 123 James n
McLeod Geo H, salesman, 42 Vine
McLeod John, printer, 9 Napier
McLeod John, salesman, 36 Bay s
McLeod Mrs (wid Alex) 99 Wilson
McLeod Oliver, blacksmith, 26 Crooks
McLeod Robert, salesman, 70 Duke
McLeod William, printer, 79 Wilson
McLerrie James, local freight agent G T R, cor Bay and Strachan
McMahon Bernard, policeman, 71 Strachan e
McMahon Daniel, laborer, Robinson
McMahon H G, carpenter, 154 Hunter e
McMahon James, laborer, 6 Tiffany
McMahon John, laborer, 63 Wood e
McMahon John, dairyman, 27 Wilson
McMahon John, baker, 20 Cannon w
McMahon J S (J S McMahon & Co) h 46 Emerald
McMahon J S & Co (J S McMahon, George E Broadfield) crockery, glassware, lamp goods, wholesale only) 45 King w
McMahon Jeremiah, moulder, 53 Cherry
McMahon Thomas, clerk, 44 Walnut s
McMahon William, melter, 28 Ferguson ave
McMann John, nailer, 109 Florence
McManus James, shoemaker, 82½ Wellington n
McManus John, laborer, 334 Hughson n
McManus John, laborer, bds 143 Bay n
McManus John, traveler, 87 John n
McManus Robert, laborer, 10 Wood w
McMaster Daniel, mason, 100 Victoria ave n
McMaster John (McIlwraith & McMaster, h 14 Caroline s
McMaster John, carpenter, 16 East ave n
McMaster Mrs, 35 Wellington n
McMeekin John (Payne & McMeekin) 141 Robert
McMeekin William, carpenter, 54 Gore
McMenemy Edward, carpenter, 132 West ave n
McMenemy Hannah (wid Alex) 59 Florence
McMenemy James, painter, 132 West ave n
McMenemy James E, carpenter, 132 West ave n
McMenemy Wm, policeman, 39 Crooks
McMenemy William, laborer, 237 Wellington n
McMichael Calista (wid Isaac) 57 Catharine n
McMichael Chas N, bookkeeper, bds 54 Napier
McMichael C P, dairyman, 47 Jackson e
McMichael Isaac, whipmaker, 54 Napier
McMichael Judson, dairyman, 81 Jackson e
McMicken John, glassblower, 10 Wood e
McMicking Mrs (wid Thomas) 189 Cannon e

McMillan Alex, teacher, bds 178 King w
McMillan Charles, laborer, 158 Victoria ave n
McMillan James, carriage builder, 39 Catharine s
McMillan John, grocer, 210 King e
McMillan John, mason, 189 Hughson n
McMillan John, shoemaker, 202½ King w, h Robinson
McMillan Norman, plasterer, bds Commercial hotel
McMillan Roderick, carpenter, 27 Chisholm
McMonies & Ryan (James McMonies, James C Ryan) auctioneers, 7½ Market
McMullen Daniel, cooper, 228 John n
McMullen Daniel, cooper, 186 Victoria ave n
McMullen John, cooper, 142 John n
McMullen Louis, mason, 209 King e
McMurray James, machinist, bds 107 Hunter e
McMurray John, laborer, 82 Bay n
McMurtrie A B, salesman, bds Franklin House
McMurtrie David, com traveler, 67 Victoria ave n
McNab Alex, stonecutter, 202 Catharine n
McNab Charles, machinist, 178 John n
McNab Duncan, blind maker, 178 John n
McNabb Duncan A, 67 Elgin
McNab George, blacksmith, 178 John n
McNabb Peter, 67 Elgin
Macnab Street Presbyterian Church, Rev D H Fletcher, pastor, Hunter cor Macnab
McNab William, laborer, 42 Burlington w
McNab —, farmer, Concession
McNair Albert E, clerk, 26 East ave n
McNair & Bell, (Samuel McNair, Samuel Bell) constables, 4 Stinson's chambers, 1 King Wm
McNair Samuel, (McNair & Bell) h 89 West ave n
McNamara Daniel, prop Station hotel, 73 Stuart w
McNamara Luke, laborer, 27 Wood e
McNamee Peter, section boss, 125 Ferguson ave
McNaught Robt, pedler, 67½ Main w
McNeill Mrs Charlotte (wid Robert) 98 Hess n
McNeil James, wood carver, bds 31 Gore
McNeil John, laborer, 57 West ave n
McNeil Smith, laborer, 20 Elgin
McNeilly George, teamster, 119 Barton e
McNeilly Henry, salesman, bds 31 Bay n
McNeilly John, teamster, 119 Barton e
McNeilly Robert, teamster, 119 Barton e
McNeany Michael, laborer, Robinson
McNider Stanley, (R Spence & Co) h 225 Main e
McNichol Charles, glassblower, 320 John n
McNichol D, carpenter, 31 Barton e
McNichol John, laborer, 312 John n
McNichol Nichol, machinist, 211 Hughson n
McNire John D, cigarmaker, 135 Rebecca
McNoah Thomas, boarding, 209 Bay n
McPhail Miss Annie, dressmaker, 8 Macnab s

McPhail Hugh, bookkeeper, 294 King Wm

McPhail Hugh sr, agent, 294 King Wm

McPhail James, boots and shoes, 6 Market sq

McPhail Robert, clerk, bds 294 King Wm

McPherson A, book and job printer, 51 James n, h 140½ John n

McPherson Alexander, teamster, 69 Hunter e

Macpherson Edward, shoe cutter, 16 Pearl s

McPherson Elizabeth (wid And) 125 James n

Macpherson, Glassco & Co (T H Macpherson, John T Glassco) wh grocers, 67-9 King e

McPherson James (John McPherson & Co) h 45 East ave s

MacPherson J C, saloon keeper, 7-9 King Wm

McPherson John & Co, (James McPherson and R H Greene) manfrs boots and shoes, 51-3 King e

McPherson Malcolm, salesman, bds 97 Robert

Macpherson T H, (Macpherson, Glasscoe & Co)h 11 Duke

McPherson W O, com trav, 59 Macnab n

McPhie Donald, plumber, etc, King e, h 57 East ave s

McQuaid Mary Ann (wid John) Greig

McQueen James, carpenter, bds 154 Market

McQueen William, laborer, 128 Catharine n

McQuestenCalvin,MD,Jackson w

McQuesten I B, M A, (Jones, McQuesten & Chisholm) h 1 Bold

McQuillan Robert sr, carter, 110 West ave n

McQuillan Robert jr, carter, 110 West ave n

McQuinn Daniel, bookkeeper, bds 1 Sheaffe

McRae Colin, boots and shoes, 30-2 King w

McRae Colin, bookkeeper, 15 Cannon w

McRae Donald, salesman, 104 Barton e

McRae Joseph, farmer, bds 20 Hunter e

McRae Ronald, clerk, bds 104 Barton e

McRoberts Peter, contractor, bds 49 Stuart w

McSherry Margaret (wid Thomas) 108½ Jackson e

McStravick Grace (wid Henry) 135 Catharine n

McStravick Henry, laborer,, 62 Wellington n

McSwain Peter, carpenter, 19 Tisdale

McVeigh Hugh, moulder, 38 Guise

McVicar Jane (wid Angus) 23 Wilson

McWilliams Robert, machinist, 29 Macauley w

McViney Robert, laborer, 21 South e

McVittie Andrew (Howard & McVittie) h mountain

McVittie John, laborer, 157 East ave n

McVittie John, cooper, 128 Rebecca

McVittie George, coachman, 79 Caroline s

Mack Mrs Ann, 27 Burlington w

Mack George, teamster, bds 27 Burlington w

Mack John S, druggist, 92 Merrick

Mack Patrick, laborer, 27 Burlington w

Mackie Andrew, moulder, 47 John n

Mackie James, carpenter, 17 Hughson n
Mackie John A, salesman, 3 West ave s
Mackie Robert, engineer, 10 Greig
Macklem Miss Margaret, Locke s
Madden Mary (wid John) Lower 27 Cathcart
Madden Thomas, laborer, 149 Wellington n
Maddigan James, laborer, 102 Simcoe e
Maddigan J W, foreman tool works, 18 Mulberry
Maddock James, cabinet maker, 178 Catharine n
Maddock Samuel, shoemaker, 144 Rebecca
Maddocks George, blacksmith, 25 Tom
Maddocks William, blacksmith, 15 Locomotive
Maden John, spinner, 105 Mary
Madgett Clark, machinist, 122 Catharine n
Madgett John, machinist, 126 Macauley e
Madsen Peter, laborer, 336 John n
Maear Theodore, laborer, 281 King w
Magee Frank, flour and feed, 206 James n
Magee Henry, harness maker, 4 York, h 79 Jackson e
Magee James, coal dealer, 25 Burlington w
Magee Wm jr, ice and coal dealer, 206 James n, h 40 Barton w
Magee Wm, sr, flour and feed, 206 James n
Magee Christopher, butcher, Jas st market, h Main e
Mageurs Matthias, dairyman, 206 Catharine n
Magen Richard, butcher, 19 John s, h Main e
Magill Charles, 5 Jackson w
Magill Mrs Charles, 12 Main w

Magill Frederick, laborer, 87 Rebecca
Magill George, moulder, 51 West ave n
Magill Samuel, woodworker, 19 Gore
Magnus Robert, machinist, 5 O'Reilly
Maguire John, painter, r 38 Cannon w
Mahaffey James, machinist, 4 Wilson
Mahoney Andrew, stovemounter, 132 King Wm
Mahoney Dennis, shoemaker, 5 Tom
Mahony Dan, laborer, 58 Cherry
Mahony James, laborer, 17 Macauley w
Mahony J C, boots and shoes, 26 King e, res Saltfleet tp
Mahony Martin, mariner, 12 Wood w
Maidment & Co, tea dealers, 128½ King e
Mail, Toronto, F W Large, agt, 72 James n
Main Alex, rope manufacturer, Mary cor Strachan
Main James, grocer, cor John and Barton
Main William, rope maker, cor Mary and Strachan
Mair Miss Helen, matron Home for the Friendless, 72 Caroline s
Mair Henrietta (wid David) 77 Jackson w
Maitland Margaret (wid James) 200 King Wm
Maitland S, painter, 33 Spring
Makins Edward, boiler maker, 47 Locomotive
Makins Edward, machinist, 22 Little Market
Malamphy Susan (wid Thomas) 82 Hess n
Malcolm James, accountant, 38 Robinson

Malcolm James, stonecutter, 120 Caroline s
Malcolm James A (Malloy & Malcolm) h 246 York
Malcolm W, trustee Reid estate, 70 Hannah w
Malcolm Andrew, carpenter, 13 Ferrie e
Malcolmson Mrs E (wid George) 26 Ferrie w
Malcolmson Mrs George, 206 Macnab n
Malcolmson Hugh, carpenter, 27 Queen n
Malcolmson James, sailor, 49 Robert e
Malcolmson James, wire weaver, 27 Queen n
Malcolmson James, 140 Macnab n
Malcolmson J C, foreman Ham Glass Works, 21 Picton e
Malcomson John, carpenter, 27 Queen n
Malcolmson Samuel, mariner, 16 Ferrie w
Malcolmson Samuel E, mariner, 115 Macnab n
Male Charles, laborer, 51 Hess s
Male William, laborer, 129 Hunter w
Malins Wm, carter, 18 Tisdale
Malley Patrick, laborer, 73 Stuart w
Mallin John, general dealer, 185 Wilson
Malloch A E, M D, 70 James s
Malloch Elizabeth (wid George) 68 James s
Malloch Francis S, 72 James
Malloch Margaret (wid John) 57 Jackson w
Mallory Eli, hatter, 161 East ave n
Mallory Wm, broker, 107 John s
Malloy John (Malloy and Malcolm) h 39 Bold
Malloy & Malcolm (John Malloy, James A Malcolm) carriage builders, 9 Park n
Malloy Patrick, laborer, 290 Mary
Malone Martin (Martin & Malone) h 61 Colborne
Malone Michael, 124 Catharine n
Malone Michael jr, traveler, 124 Catharine n
Malone Michael, porter customs, 56 Catharine n
Malone Thomas, confectioner, 35 Mulberry
Maloney Edward, laborer, 243 John n
Maney William, laborer, 55 Stuart e
Mann Aaron, express messenger, 31 Gore
Mann Chas, mason, 30 Florence
Mann Henry H, laborer, 20 Pearl n
Mann Samuel, grocer, 256 and 258 King e
Mann William, carpenter, 29 Locomotive
Manning Catharine (wid John) 5 Devonport
Manning Fred, moulder, 90 Bay n
Mansergh Henry, salesman, 9 Wilson
Mansfield Alex, cabinet maker, 137 Park n
Mansfield George, engineer, 137 Park n
Manson Donald, bookkeeper, 24 Hannah e
Mantle Richard, laborer, 144 Picton e
Maplebeck John, laborer, 148 Jackson w
Mapplebeck William, engineer, 220 Macnab n
Marcham William, laborer, 144 Catharine n
Marchum John, moulder, 123 Mary
Marck Joseph, barber, 214 James n

Maria James, laborer, 37 Napier
Maricle John A, toll gate keeper, York
Marie James, laborer, 146 Jackson w
Marintee James, bookkeeper, 76 Napier
Markle David, agent, 10 King e
Markle Hiram, wheelwright, 243 Mary
Markle James, bender, 139 Wellington n
Marks Edward, moulder, 189 John n
Marlatt Rebecca (wid George) 51 Hunter w
Marriott Henry, machinist, 132 Emerald n
Marriott John, porter, 75 Market
Marriott Wm, carpenter, 64 Mulberry
Marris Henry, shoe cutter, 12 Queen n
Mars Alexander, bookbinder, 14 Hughson n
Marsden & Son (Thomas and Wm) manufacturers of mouldings and picture frames, agent Butterick's patterns, 46 James n
Marsden Thomas (Marsden & Son) 92 Jackson w
Marsden Wm (Marsden & Son) 48 Hannah w
Marsh Wm, blaoksmith, Markland
Marshall Bros, tea dealers, Alexandra Arcade
Marshall Christian (wid Butler) 72 Locke s
Marshall David, mason, 39 Park s
Marshall D G, law student, 70 Park n
Marshall Mrs George, 98 James s
Marshall Geo & Co, tea dealers, 56 Macnab n
Marshall Harry, gardener, Aikman's ave
Marshall Hubert machinist bds 39 Caroline
Marshall Jeannette (wid Henry) 20 Ray n
Marshall John, wire worker, 39 Caroline n
Marshall John, hemp dresser, 207 Mary
Marshall John, laborer, Wentworth n
Marshall Joseph, carpenter, 54 Ray n
Marshall Patrick, laborer, Stuart w
Marshall Thomas, tailor, 2 King William, h 95 Concession
Marshall Thomas, laborer, 278 James n
Marshall Thomas, laborer, Main e
Marshall Wm, sec-treas and manager Hamilton Vinegar Works Co, 10 Erie ave
Marshall Wm, salesman, 22 Victoria ave n
Marsten Samuel, machinist, 15 Tom
Martin Alex, laborer, 84 Peter
Martin Andrew C (P and A Martin) h 43 Young
Martin Archibald, moulder, 176 Robert e
Martin Benjamin, cabinet maker, 82 Main w
Martin Bernard, cabinet maker, 114½ King w, h 82 Main w
Martin Charles, tinsmith, 134 James s
Martin Charles H, foreman, 56 Hannah e
Martin Edward, QC (Martin & Kittson) h Ballynahinch, James s
Martin George E, law student, 58 Hunter w
Martin H, leather mrrchant, 3 King Wm, h 134 James s
Martin H A, printer, 13 John n
Martin Henry, Station hotel, 156 King e
Martin Henry, artist, 10 Hannah w

Martin H H, 12 Wellington n
Martin Mrs H H, dress and mantle maker, 12 Wellington n
Martin James, scalemaker, r 166 Mary
Martin Jas, laborer, 203 John n
Martin James, shoemaker, 92 Bay n
Martin James, baker, 96 Robinson
Martin J E, manager Adams Manufacturing Co, 114 Jas n
Martin John, bricklayer, 60 Tisdale
Martin John, upholsterer, 96 Robinson
Martin John, laborer, 123 Dundurn
Martin & Kittson (Edward Martin, QC, E E Kittson) barristers, Wentworth Chambers, 25 James s *See card*
Martin & Malone (Richard Martin, QC, Martin Malone) barristers, 2½ James s
Martin P & A, props Bordeaux packing house, cor John and King Wm and James st market
Martin Philip (P & A Martin) 54 King Wm
Martin Philip, sr, 31 Wellington s
Martin Richard, QC (Martin & Malone) hd John s
Martin Richard S, clerk, hd John s
Martin Robert, engine driver G T R, 15 Magill
Martin Stephen, 29 Elgin
Martin Thomas, mail clerk, 29 Elgin
Martin Thomas, enameler, r 22 Kelly
Martin Wm, clerk, 134 James s
Martin William H, machinist, 46 Tisdale
Marygold Mrs Harriet, 217 John n
Maslin George, sexton, 29 Steven
Maslin Richard, machinist, 84 Stinson
Maslin Samuel, 84 Stinson
Mason Charles, gardener, 116 Rebecca
Mason Christopher, fireman, 35 Emerald n
Mason G E, accountant G T R, 166 Main w
Mason Hadley, clerk, 21 Spring
Mason Jas, confectioner, 65 York
Mason J J, accountant, 86 James n, h 63 Hunter w
Mason Joseph, caretaker Masonic Hall, 90 Market
Mason Margaret (wid Ed) 114 Locke n
Mason & Risch, piano manfs (Hamilton branch) George P Harrison, manager, res 56 Wellington n
Mason Thomas, hats and furs, 13 James n, h 23 East ave n
Masonic Hall, 82 James n
Mass Wm, laborer, 16 Locke s
Massey Rev William, M A, St. Luke's Church, 305 John n
Massie Alexander, boatbuilder, 209 Macnab n
Massie Arch, timekeeper G T R, Barton w
Massie William, jr, machinist, 209 Macnab n
Matches Mrs John, 251 King Wm
Matchett Wm, laborer, 98 Ferrie e
Mathie Walter, tailor, 60 James s
Mathieson Donald, laborer, 4 Margaret
Mathieson George, wool buyer, 28 Railway
Mathieson John, porter, 75 Vine
Mathieson William, moulder, 71 Ray n
Mathesins Rudolph, artist, 118 Mary
Mathews Augustus, carpenter, 107 Ferrie
Matthews Fred C, caretaker cricket ground, Idlewild, Bold
Mathews George, mail clerk G T R, 74 Hunter e

Mathews George H, livery, 33 Market, h 37 Market
Matthews Henry, moulder, 149 Mary
Mathews James (James Mathews & Son) h 37 Victoria ave s
Mathews James E (James Mathews & Son) h 95 Victoria ave n
Mathews James & Son (James and James E) painters, 15 Hughson n
Mathews John, clerk, 18 Elgin
Matthews Joseph, carpenter, 188 Emerald n
Mathews The Misses, 35 Market
Mathews Oscar, carpenter, 107 Ferrie e
Mathews R V, assistant tax collector, 37 Victoria ave n
Mathews Walter, tailor James s
Mathews W C, student, 6 Augusta
Mathews William, clerk, 37 Victoria ave s
Matcom Peter, laborer, 336 John n
Matthewson Alex, moulder, 8 Locke s
Mattice James, nailer, 108 Market
Mattice J H, correspondent and business agent *Globe*, Alexandra Arcade buildings, 31 James n, h 70 Catharine n
Mattice Wm, porter, 108 Market
Mattice Wm H, 98 Locke s
Mawson Josiah, gas metre maker, 81 Cannon w
Max William, carpenter, 99 Robinson
Maxey Jackson, agent, 84 Rebecca
Maxham George, laborer, 91 Macauley e
Maxwell Francis, blacksmith, 124 Picton e
Maxwell James, engineer, 120 Macauley e
Maxwell John, machinist, Duke
Maxwell John, painter, 163 Main w
Maxwell Maggie (wid Wm) 3 Margaret
Maxwell Robert, bookkeeper, 34 Bay n
Maxwell Samuel P, moulder, 136 Macnab n
Maxwell Thomas G, policeman, 94 East ave n
May James E, carpenter, 34 Cherry
May Richard, laborer, 219 York
May Thomas, laborer, 26 Queen s
May Wm, finisher, bds 24 Caroline n
May Mrs, dressmaker, 10 Main e
May —, 208 Macnab n
Mayhew John, knitter, 152 King w
Mays Wm, fireman G T R, 126½ Queen n
Mead Joseph R & Co, shirt manfs, 10½ Market square
Mead Joseph R Joseph R Mead & Co) h 18 Nelson ave
Meade Miss Annie, 45 Charles
Meade Thomas, builder, 10½ Young
Meadows Hugh, spinner, 71 Simcoe e
Meadows Mary (wid Samuel) 120 Hess n
Meagher Thomas, engineer, 213 Hughson n
Meakin Carry (wid James) gents' furnishings, 190 James n
Meakins C W (Meakins & Sons) h 170 Main e
Meakins G H, machinist, 11 Erie ave
Meakins & Sons, brush manufs, King e, opp West ave
Meal John, laborer, 124 Hunter w
Maney Thomas, bookkeeper, ne w cor Vine and James
Mearce Joseph, teamster, 50 West ave n

Medley Samuel, stone cutter, 58 Victoria ave n
Medlock Annie (wid Wm) 16 Harriet
Meegan Patrick, laborer, 119 Jackson e
Meegan Peter, hotel, 14 John n
Meegen Thomas, moulder, 29 Mulberry
Meehan John, laborer, 329 Hughson n
Meek Matthew G, grocer, 88 Macnab n
Meekison Andrew (Sutherland & Meekison) bds Noble's Hotel
Megg Wm, pedler, bds 12 Market
Meikle Hannah (wid James) 25 Maria
Meiler John, tailor, 87 Florence
Mellon George, 98 Catharine s
Mellon Herbert, brakesman 49 Stuart w
Mellon John, builder, 6 Nightingale
Mellon Robert, bricklayer, 56 Steven
Mellon Thomas, machinist, 19 Liberty
Melody James, laborer, 38 Sheaffe
Melody Wm, carter, 58 Canada
Memory James, bds 60 Hughson n
Memory John, machinist, 164 Napier
Menard Peter, glassblower, 303 James n
Menary Robert, milk dealer, 29 Chisholm
Menorgon Margaret (wid John) 130 Cannon e
Menzie Mrs John, 61 Emerald n
Menzies Andrew, carpenter, 66½ King Wm
Mepham Thomas, plasterer, 203 Main w
Mepham Wm, laborer, 103 Caroline n
Mercer James, builder, 40 Ferguson ave
Mercer John, machinist, r 52 Hunter w
Merchants' Bank, J S Meredith manager, King cor John
Meredith Miss Elizabeth, music teacher, 46 Main w
Meredith J S, manager Merchants' Bank, bds 16 Hughson s
Merin Patrick, coal inspector, Stuart cor Macnab, h 242 Bay
Meriden Britannia Co, J E Parker, manager, Wellington cor Cannon
Merrick Miss Catharine, 96 Victoria ave n
Merriman James, laborer, 124 Locke n
Merryman Miss Ann, 29 O'Reilly
Mesle Frank, brushmaker, 23 Wentworth n
Meston Thomas, bookkeeper, 62 Cannon e
Messer W J, salesman, 88 Park n
Messmore —, tailor, Maple
Metcalf Arthur, carpenter, bds Queen s
Metcalfe George, painter, 65 Canada
Metcalfe Joseph, gardener, Main e, near tollgate
Metcalfe Mary (wid Wm) grocer, 26 Ray n
Mewburn L T, manager J Turner & Co, 60 Macnab s
Mewburn S C, law student, 148 Main w
Mewburn Thos C, inspector customs, 148 Main w
Meyers William E, shoemaker, 48 Young
Michael Wm, laborer, 189 Victoria ave n
Michael Wm jr, teamster, 6 Augusta
Michigan Central Railway, W J Grant, city ticket agent, Arcade, 33 James n

Midford Thirza (wid Wm) 3 Caroline s
Middleton Arthur, bookkeeper, 138 John n
Middleton John, moulder, bds 53 Gore
Middleton J T, wh marble dealer, 138-140 John n, h East Hamilton
Middleton Walter S, com traveler, bds 48 James n
Midgley Geo, shoemaker, 172½ James n
Midgley George jr, printer, 172½ James n
Midgley Peter, laborer, 119 Simcoe e
Midgley W H, japanner, 171½ James n
Midwinter Job, carpenter, 153 Park n
Midwinter Joseph, machinist, 131 Park n
Milburn John, scalemaker, 15 Little William
Miles Alexander G, plumber, 72 Merrick
Miles Mrs Mary, 16 Ray s
Miles John, carpenter, 57 East ave n
Miles Thomas W, laborer, 27 Macauley e
Miller A, harness maker, 63 John s
Miller Adam J, stovemounter, 134 Jackson w
Miller Adolf, glassblower, 12 Ferrie e
Miller Alex, butcher, Wentworth n
Miller Alfred, shoemaker, 124 Jackson w
Miller A J, porter, 109 Walnut s
Miller Andrew, laborer, 201 Main w
Miller Rev And E, Church of England, 66 Bay s
Miller Arthur, laborer, 8 Wood e
Miller August, machinist, 202 East ave n
Miller Catharine (wid Andrew) 58 Ferguson ave
Miller Frank (Miller & Hill) h Hannah cor Wellington
Miller Fred, butcher, 64 West ave n
Miller George, policeman, 42 East ave n
Miller George, bellman, 5 Hunter e
Miller Henry, glassblower, 7 Macauley w
Miller & Hill (F Miller, C Hill) carpenters, 81 James s
Miller James, grocer, 71 Elgin
Mitchell James, stovemounter, 208 Cannon e
Miller James, laborer, 176 Rebecca
Miller Mrs Jane, 58 Ferguson ave
Miller John, spicemaker, 143 James n
Miller John, laborer, 246 Catharine n
Miller John, plasterer, 85 Young
Miller John, cigar maker, 13 Market sq
Miller John E, moulder, 105 Wood e
Miller Louisa (wid William) Walnut n
Miller Miss M B, Markland
Miller Nichol, moulder, 32 John n
Miller Peter, machinist, 59 Young
Miller Robert, 56 Park n
Miller Thomas M D, 181 King w
Miller Wm, tinsmith, 218 King Wm
Miller Wm, switchman, 146 Robert e
Miller Wm, shoemaker, 3 Hilton
Miller —, carpenter, bds 166 Bay n
Miller —, 194 East ave n
Miller —, machinist, bds 44 Vine
Milliard J W, cashier, 128 Hughson n

W. G. TOWNSEND,

CUSTOM HOUSE BROKER,

IMPORTERS' MANUFACTURERS' AND COMMISSION AGENT,

FORWARDER AND SHIPPER.

OFFICE:

No. 33 Stuart Street West (Next Door to Custom House),

HAMILTON, ONTARIO.

P. O. Box 285.

CITY AND COUNTY DIRECTORIES.

The following are now ready, and will be sent on receipt of price:

City of Hamilton	$2 50
City of Kingston, including Frontenac county	2 00
City of St. Catharines, including Lincoln and Welland	2 00
City of Brantford, including Brant county	2 00
County of Simcoe	2 00
County of Wentworth	2 00

WE ARE ALSO AGENTS FOR THE

City of Guelph	$2 00
County of Wellington	3 00
County of Waterloo	3 00
City of Quebec	2 50
City of Ottawa	2 50
City of Montreal	3 00

All books are recent editions.

W. H. IRWIN & CO.,

12 MACNAB ST. SOUTH, HAMILTON, ONTARIO.

PETER BRASS, ARCHITECT.

Furnishes Plans and Specifications for every description of buildings, and having been a Mechanic and Contractor for a number of years, all work will be superintended in a practical and proper manner. Also measurement and Valuation of every description of buildings, either new or old, or of any works connected with buildings, made up in a correct and reliable manner.

OFFICE, 52 HUNTER ST WEST, OPP CENTRAL SCHOOL.

Residence, 49 Bay St. South, HAMILTON, ONT

Millican W J, law student, 11 West ave s
Milligan Ed, laborer, 22½ Little Market
Milligan John, driller, 8 Poulette
Milligan John, laborer, 276 Hughson n
Milligan Mrs Samuel, 63 Merrick
Milligan Thomas, dealer, 122 Locke n
Milligan Thomas J, laborer, 115 Cannon w
Milligan William, laborer, 63 Merrick
Milligan W, barrister, 11 West ave s
Milligan Wm J, baker, 21 Pearl n
Millman James, carpenter, 31 Chisholm
Millman John. clerk, 34 Bay n
Millman J J, photographer, 76 King w, h 145 John s
Millman —, salesman, bds 34 Bay n
Millmine Charles, gardener, 9 Wentworth n
Mills Mrs A, dressmaker, 114 King e
Mills Mrs Ann, 349 John n
Mills Mrs Anson, 12 O'Reilly
Mills Mrs Aurora (wid Samuel) 20 Charles
Mills Charles, com traveler, 89 Macnab n
Mills Charles, grocer, 142 Main e
Mills Chas, 106 Jackson w
Mills E J, law student, 286 King e
Mills Francis H, 35 Main w
Mills F W, salesman, bds 286 King e
Mills F W, telegraph operator, 286 King e
Mills George, 292 King e
Mills George, grocer, 26 Stuart e
Mills Geo, packer, 62 Peter
Mills Geo A, salesman, 7 James n
Mills George E, bricklayer, 8 Wilson
Mills George H, barrister, Wentworth chambers, 25 James s, h 73 George
Mills Isaac, electrician, 320 York
Mills James, laborer, 42 Ray n
Mills Jas B, com traveler, 12 Sophia n
Mills Jas D, fireman G T R, 115 Locke n
Mills J D (J D Mills & Co) h 139 York
Mills J D & Co, paper boxes, 4 Macnab n
Mills James H, 113 Main w
Mills John, builder, 31 Crooks
Mills John, box maker, bds 139 York
Mills Joseph & Son, hatters and furriers, 7 James n
Mills & McKellar (John Mills, Hugh McKellar) builders, 2 Caroline
Mills Miss, 42 Queen s
Mills William, carpenter, 286 King e
Mills Wm H, 151 Main w
Mills W R (Joseph Mills & Son) 76 Jackson w
Milne Alex, builder, 28 Victoria ave s
Milne G H, builder, 45 Mary
Milne James, gardener, Caroline s
Milne John (Burrow, Stewart & Milne) 45 Elgin
Milne Robert A, carpenter, 28 Victoria ave s
Milne Thomas, laborer, 121 Locke n
Milne W, manf native wine, Wentworth n
Milne William, packer, 123 Locke n
Miner Cyrus E, cabinet maker, 37 Magill
Mines Fred, laborer, Main e
Mines James, moulder, 197 Mary
Minke Frederick, stovemounter, 1 Grove

Minnes James, blacksmith, 132 Bold
Minnes John, hammersmith, 126 Locke n
Minty Francis C, cashier, 47 Wellington s
Minty Henry T, clerk, 47 Wellington s
Mitchell Alfred, harnessmaker, 41 Catharine s
Mitchell Bradfield, fireman, bds 24 Hunter e
Mitchell Chas, broom manf, 25 Inchbury n
Mitchell Chas A, clerk, 28 Caroline n
Mitchell Chas W, laborer, 64 Locke s
Mitchell David, shoemaker, 9 King w, res Burlington
Mitchell D A, bookkeeper, 17 West ave s
Mitchell Daniel, plumber, 28 Caroline n
Mitchell E, manager Canadian Bank of Commerce, res Main, East Hamilton
Mitchell Geo, machinist, 117 Locke n
Mitchell George, cabinet maker, 49 Maria
Mitchell James, stove fitter, 25 Walnut s
Mitchell James, teamster, 91 Robert
Mitchell James, laborer, 78 Hannah w
Mitchell Capt James, 40 Ferrie w
Mitchell James, bailiff, 37 East ave n
Mitchell John, stonemason, 100 Bay s
Mitchell John, 27 Main w
Mitchell John, cigar maker, 209 Main w
Mitchel John, shoemaker, 31 Sheaffe
Mitchell John, laborer, 142 Jackson w
Mitchell Joseph, plasterer, 48 Ferguson ave
Mitchell Joseph R, salesman, 90 Hunter e
Mitchell Mrs L (Cook & Mitchell) Franklin House
Mitchell Mrs S A, nurse, bds 34 Hughson s
Mitchell Thomas, brooms and woodenware, 31 King w, h 37 Queen s
Mitchell Thomas, plasterer, 141 Hunter w
Mitchell William, machinist, 265 York
Mitchell Wm, stonecutter, 61 Pearl n
Mitchell W B, tailor, 64 John s, h 48 Hunter e
Mitchell —, moulder, 226 Hughson n
Mitchell —, yardsman G T R, 226 Hughson n
Mitchenor Chas, laborer, 3 Poulette
Mitchkum Marks, com traveler, 121 Macnab n
Mittiff Joseph, whipmaker, 43 Hannah e
Mockridge Rev Chas, D D, rector Christ Church Cathedral, 156 Macnab n
Modlin John (Davison & Modlin) 26 Margaret
Moffat John A, machinist, 118 Bay n
Moffat Sophia (wid Robert) 118 Bay n
Moffatt Thomas, mail carrier, 77 Market
Moffat Willoughby, marble cutter, 118 Bay n
Moffat Wm, laborer, 7 Florence
Moir William, painter, 72 Market
Molsons Bank, J M Burns, manager, James s, cor King w
Monger David, porter, 59 Chisholm
Monks Jas, tailor, bds 48 James n

Monck J F (Lazier, Dingwall & Monck) h 25½ East ave n
Monk William, clerk waterworks, 89 Locke n
Monro Hugh, grocer, 269 James n
Montague Michael, laborer, 34 Ferguson ave
Monteith John, moulder, 104 Emerald n
Montgomery Edgar, blacksmith, bds 12 Market
Montgomery Gabriel, pedler, 28 Peter
Montgomery J W, M D, assistant medical supt Asylum for Insane
Montgomery John, salesman, hd Locke s
Montgomery Mary (wid Wm) 116 Young
Montgomery Robert, boarding, 51 Hughson s
Moodie James R (J Moodie & Son) h 63 George
Moodie John (John Moodie & Sons) h 65 George
Moodie John, jr (John Moodie & Sons) h 65 George
Moodie John & Sons (John, James R and John, jr) wh and retail fancy goods, 16 King w
Moody Charles, carpet weaver, 25 Wood w
Moody Christopher, jeweler, 27 York
Moody Miss F E, fancy goods, 162 King e
Moody R W, accountant, 162 King e
Mooney Albert J, glassblower, 43 Burlington w
Moody Charles, laborer, 126 Emerald n
Mooney Luke, laborer, 15 Railway
Moore Alex H, manager Stinson's Bank, h 126 Hughson n
Moore Alfred, policeman, 56 East ave n
Moore Arthur, watchman, 48 Wellington n
Moore Charles, file maker, 190 Victoria ave n
Moore & Davis, real estate agents, 2 King Wm
Moore D & Co, iron founders, manufacturers and importers, 98, 100 King e, foundry Catharine cor Robert
Moore Dennis (D Moore & Co) h 12 Hannah e
Moore Edward, salesman, 50 Hannah w
Moore E E W, clerk, 61 Napier
Moore E J, bookkeeper, 24 Victoria ave n
Moore Elizabeth (wid William) 134 Main e
Moore Emma (wid Hugh) dressmaker, 7 Murray w
Moore Frederick, bricklayer, 15 Spring
Moore George, 197 John n
Moore George, carpenter, 37 Catharine n
Moore Geo, refreshment rooms G T R, 14 Murray w
Moore George, 123 Macnab n
Moore George, laborer, 117 Ferrie e
Moore G H, 134 Hughson n
Moore James, dyer, bds 88 Robinson
Moore John, laborer, Dundurn
Moore Mrs John, 61 Napier
Moore John, potter, 163 Locke s
Moore John, laborer, 65 Locke s
Moore J H, clerk, 160 Mary
Moore J H (Bowman & Moore) h 238 King e
Moore Lawrence, 8 Florence
Moore Lyman, 33 Jackson w
Moore Louis, cabinet maker, 167 Catharine n
Moore Peter, shipper, 26 Hunter e
Moore Robert, tailor, 129 Hunter e

Moore S G, bookkeeper, 3 Wellington Terrace, Wellington n
Moore Samuel J, machinist, 43 Victoria ave n
Moore Thomas, laborer, 124 Wood e
Moore Thomas, engineer, bds 30 Guise
Moore Wm, bookkeeper,bds 134 Main e
Moore Wm, laborer, 76 Ferguson ave
Moore W G (Moore & Davis) h 71 Victoria ave s
Moore W J, painter, 1 Chisholm
Moore W P (Moore & Davis) h 241 Main e
Moore Wm R, clerk, h Main e
Moore W S, salesman, 41 East ave s
Moran Antoine, hotel keeper, 134 James n
Moran Mrs Catharine, 274 Jas n
Moran Edward, japanner, 230 Bay n
Moran Michael, laborer, 103 Picton e
Moran Nap, shoemaker, bds 9 Park s
Moran Patrick, laborer, 77 Caroline n
Morin Joseph, shoedealer, 224 James n
Moran Mrs, Aikman's ave
Mordan Jacob, 21 Sheaffe
Mordan John, 21 Sheaffe
Mordan John D, 17 Magill
Morden J W (W & J Morden) h 27 West ave s
Morden W J (W & J Morden) h 8 Crooks
Morden W & J, commission merchants, 7 Market sq
Morgan Alfred (Knox, Morgan & Co) h 3 West ave s
Morgan B J (Morgan Bros) h 51 East ave s
Morgan Bros, grain merchants, 27, 29 John s
Morgan Charles E, exchange office and general railway and steamship ticket agency, 11 James n, h 191 Macnab n
Morgan E P, teacher phonography, 158 King Wm
Morgan Richard, carriage trimmer, 134 York
Morgan R R (Morgan Bros) 77 Emerald s
Morgan Thomas, fireman GTR, 88 Hess n
Morgan Thomas, tanner, 14 Victoria ave s
Morgan Wm S (Morgan Bros) 227 Main e
Morgan William, machinist, 44 Barton w
Moriarty John, laborer, 108 Simcoe e
Moriarty Michael, laborer, 134 Bay n
Morley Jonn, blacksmith, 19 Margaret
Morley Jonathan, carpenter, 133 Wood e
Morley Thomas, laborer, 16 Crooks
Moroney Michael, laborer, foot Caroline n
Morphy Wm, machinist, 69½ Main w
Morris Charles, machinist, 27 Inchbury n
Morrris Chas F, clerk Bank of Commerce, bds 61 George
Morris George, butcher, 18 Locke s
Morris George, grocer, 270 York
Morris H H, accountant Bank of Commerce, King cor Hughson
Morris Isaac, tailor, 12 Macnab n, h 123 Market
Morris James, grocer, 225 Macnab n
Morris Jas, cutter, 129 James n
Morris John, bds 28 Market
Morris John, boat builder, Wentworth n

Morris John, fruiterer, 25 James n
Morris John M, engineer, Duke
Morris Joseph, clerk, 41 Robert
Morris Louis, butcher, King e
Morris M, second-hand dealer, 12½ King Wm
Morris Moses, laborer, 124 Macauley e
Morris Philip, grocer, 129 John n
Morris Thomas, flour and feed, 21 Wellington n, h 26 Wellington n
Morris Thomas, baker, 178 James n
Morris Wm, market gardener, Wentworth n
Morris Wm, baggage expressman, 26 and 28 Market
Morris Wm, brass founder and pattern maker, 64 Ray n
Morris William, grocer, 122 Macnab n
Morrissey Mrs Michael, 12 Victoria ave s
Morrison Alex, grocer, 86-88 John s
Morrison Alexander, grocer, 14 Wood Market square
Morrison Alex, fireman, 141 Catharine n
Morrison A R, agent, 132 Hughson n
Morrison Fred, temperance hotel, end York
Morrison Francis, shoemaker, 63 Robinson
Morison Fred S, bookkeeper, 2 Nelson
Morrison George C, engine and boiler works, foot Caroline n, h 35 Picton w
Morrison John, grocer, 66 Main w
Morrison J A, wood turner, 183 East ave n
Morrison Mrs J M, 97 Hughson n
Morrison Patrick, shoemaker, Burlington n
Morrison Samuel, agent, 83 Elgin
Morrison Thomas, 98 John s
Morron Charles, mason, 58 Wilson
Morrow John, policeman, 170 James n
Morrow Maria (wid James) confectioner, 170 James n
Morrow Wm, laborer, 17 Lower Cathcart
Morse Fred, officer Salvation Army, bds 164 King William
Morson Alfred, M D, 90 Bay s
Morson Alfred E, bookkeeper, 90 Bay s
Mortimer Edgar, teamster, 45 Alanson
Mortimer James, moulder, 57 Tom
Mortimer Joseph, stovemounter, 126 Maria
Morton Ann (wid Andrew) 56 Kelly
Morton Crooker, teamster, 13 Cannon e
Morton David sr, soap manuf, 186 Main e
Morton David jr, traveler, 186 Main e
Morton David, 36 Markland
Morton Edward, painter, 49 Hunter e
Morton George, barber, 87 John s
Morton George, laborer, 52 Herkimer
Morton James, grocer, 54 Hannah w, h 52 King w
Morton Rev John, 66 Victoria ave s
Morton John, shipper, 35 Railway
Morton John, soap manf, 12 Emerald s
Morton John, grocer, 11 Lower Cathcart
Morton John, salesman, 52 King w
Morton John, grocer, Wilson cor Cathcart

Morton John G, machinist, 42 Magill
Morton Robert, clerk, 186 Main e
Morton Wm (Dixon & Morton) h 52 King w
Morton Wm, 13 Cannon e
Morton Wm, teacher, bds 7 Bold
Morty John, laborer, 68 Market
Moses Mrs M, second-hand dealer, 51 John s
Moshier Edward, laborer, 107 Hunter e
Moss Charles, shoemaker, York
Mossman Mark, shoemaker, 23 Gore
Mostyn John, tinsmith, 150 Hunter w
Mottashed Charles, builder, 17 West ave n
Mottashed Lezetta (wid Joseph) 18 East ave n
Moyes George, 19 Walnut s
MoylenThos,shoemaker,37Napier
Moynahan Cornelius, broommaker, 250 Hughson n
Mowat Andrew, mason, 57 Erie ave
Mowat Mary (wid Wm) 85 Mary
Mugford Richard, painter, Ferguson ave n
Muir Andrew, bookkeeper, 48 Markland
Muir D A, contractor, 158 Mary
Muir James, baggageman, 177 Emerald n
Muir J G, bricklayer, 170 West ave n
Muir John, MA (Crerar, Muir & Crerar) h 37 Duke
Muir J P, bookkeeper, Mountain top
Muirhead Walter, butcher, James st market, h Mountain
Mulcahy Daniel, laborer, 45 Strachan e
Mulcahy Dennis, stovemounter, 59 Wood e
Mulholland Henry (J & H Mulholland) h 17 Barton e
Mulholland J & H, props Union wood and coal yard, Cannon cor Cathcart
Mulholland James, boxmaker, 73 Young
Mulholland John (J & H Mulholland, h 259 Bay n
Mulholland Mrs Margaret, 162 Catharine n
Mulholland Peter, laborer, 103 Hunter e
Mulholland Samuel, laborer, r 51 Young
Mulhurn James, moulder, bds 41 John n
Mullaney John, filecutter, bds 153 King e
Mullen Miss Sarah, 82 Jackson e
Mullen Thomas, carpenter, 13 Chisholm
Mulligan C W, architect, Court House, h 17 Main w
Mullin David, bds 123 Main e
Mullin Henry, carpenter, 75 Ray n
Mullin John A, MD, 124 Jas n
Mullin Mrs Mary, 123 Main e
Mullin Mrs Peter, 382 James n
Mullings Mrs E (wid Abraham) grocer, Locke s cor Robinson
Mullins Thomas, carpenter, 278 Mary
Mullins Wm, laborer, 65 Park n
Mulroy Michael, laborer, 116 Bold
Mulvale Wm, laborer, Clark ave
Mulvihill Thomas, engineer, 135 Wellington n
Munc Mrs Louisa (wid Jake) 52 Main w
Munday Miss M P, 147 James s
Mundell E D H, com traveler, 15½ Elgin
Mundie Margaret (wid William) 1 Robinson
Mundy Angus, grocer, 125 Park n
Munday Henry, machinist, 72 Ray n

Mundy Israel, 6 Hess s
Mundy Mark, druggist, 164 King e
Mundy William, letter carrier, 6 Hess s
Munn James, laborer, 101 John n
Munn Mrs William, 79 Maria
Mundt Adolphus, laborer, 68 Locke s
Mundt Charles, laborer, 111 Robinson
Munro Alex, com traveler, 61 Caroline s
Munro Colin, tinsmith, 89 Cannon e
Munro Eliza (wid Henry) Robinson
Munro Isaac, stovemounter, bds 250 James n
Munro James, foreman W E Sanford & Co, 33 East ave n
Munro Mary (wid John) 26 Guise
Munroe Alex, com traveler, Knox, Morgan & Co
Munro Emma (wid Malcolm) 53 Gore
Munroe James, laborer, 60 Ray s
Munsie Herbert, mechanical accountant G T R, 210 Victoria ave n
Munson Guy, fireman, 122 Cannon e
Munson Sarah (wid Ephraim) 134 King Wm
Muntz Robert, laborer, 44½ Robinson
Munzinger John M, bookbinder, 23 York
Murdock Andrew, com traveler, 29 Victoria ave n
Murdoch James, porter G T R, 14 Florence
Murison George, health inspector, Herkimer
Murphy Ann (wid John) 26 Picton w
Murphy Catharine (wid John) 53 Young
Murphy Catharine (wid William) 72 Rebecca
Murphy Cornelius, laborer, 130 Bay n
Murphy Edward, laborer, 293 John n
Murphy Edward, laborer, 5 Macauley w
Murphy Edmund, tailor, 32 Aurora
Murphy Edward, sign painter, 106 James n, h 57 York
Murphy James, cigar maker, 10 O'Reilly
Murphy John, supt letter carriers, P O
Murphy John, laborer, 130 Bay n
Murphy Mrs Joseph, fancy goods, 74 King w, h 129 John s

Murphy Lawrence, laborer, 217 Bay n
Murphy Matthew, teamster, 43 East ave n
Murphy Matthew, marble polisher, 223 Main w
Murphy Maurice, blacksmith, 68 Caroline n
Murphy Michael, shoemaker, 122 Emerald n
Murphy Michael, laborer, 72 Cherry
Murphy Michael, saloon, 35 Jackson e
Murphy & Murray (Wm Murphy, Hugh Murray) grocers, 66 King e
Murphy Patrick, laborer, r 185 Bay n
Murphy Patrick H, glassblower, 38 Macauley w
Murphy T D, manager Ham Whip Co, h 31 Wellington s
Murphy Timothy, moulder, 34 Macauley e
Murphy Wm, carpenter, 142 Duke
Murphy Wm (Murphy & Murray) h 53 Ferguson ave
Murray A & Co, im of staple and fancy dry goods, manfs of millinery, mantles and dresses, 18, 20 King e

Murray Alex (A Murray & Co) Arlo House, Main w
Murray Andrew, cigar maker, 148 King w
Murray Anthony, 188 King Wm
Murray David, blacksmith, 139 West ave n
Murray Miss Ellen, 2 South e
Murray David, gardener, 76 Emerald n
Murray Duncan, flour and feed, 16 York
Murray Mrs Eliza, 92 Maria
Murray Mrs Elizabeth, 139 York
Murray Hugh, clerk customs, 88 Main e
Murray James, tailor, 121 Ferguson ave
Murray James, clerk, Main cor Hess
Murray Jas H, cigar dealer, 81 George
Murray J H, tobacconist, 36 Peter
Murray John, rag carpet weaver, 148 King w
Murray John, salesman, Arlo house, Main w
Murray John, printer, 139 York
Murray Miss Kate, 102 John n
Murray R B, whip mounter manf, 47 King Wm, h 26 Rebecca
Murray Robt, shoemaker, 41 Robinson
Murray Thomas, contractor, 23 O'Reilly
Murray Thomas, salesman, 39 Macnab n
Murray Walter, saddler, 121 Queen n
Murray William, paper bag maker, 71 Merrick
Murray Wm, 49 Caroline n
Murray Wm, collecter, 115 Jackson w
Murray Wm, paper bag manuf, 35 Park n
Murray Wm, acconntant, Athol Bank, Queen cor Herkimer
Murton Miss Alice, private school, 182 John n
Murton J W, (Murton & Reid) h East Hamilton
Murton & Reid, (J W Murton, W Reid) coal dealers, 44 John n
Murton Wm A, bookkeeper, 182 John n
Musgrove Mrs Caroline, 55 York
Muskoka Lakes Steamship Line, W J Grant, agent, 33 James n
Myers Adolph, grocer, 68 Hess n
Myers Benjamin, engineer, 47 Caroline n
Myers Mrs Catherine (wid Geo) 18 Devonport
Myers Charles, 48 Victoria ave n
Myers Edgar, cooper, 9 Macnab s
Myers Henry, engineer, 11 Chisholm
Myers John, laborer, 111 Cannon w
Myers Joseph, laborer, 306 King e
Myers I W, 48 Victoria ave n
Myers Wm, tobacco roller, 33 Queen s
Myers Wm, tinsmith, 84½ West ave n
Myers Wm J, undertaker, 51 Macnab s
Myles Alfred, coal dealer, 146 John n
Myles C J (Thomas Myles & Son) 7 Elgin
Myles John, laborer, 61 Walnut s
Myles Thomas (Thomas Myles & Son) h Victoria ave cor Hunter
Myles Thomas & Son (Thomas and C J) coal merchants, Hughson cor Main
Myles William, laborer, 96 Walnut s
Myles Wm, laborer, 54 Caroline s
Myrick J H, picture framer, 107 James n
Nadin Samuel, bookkeeper, 116 Catharine s

Nall Susan (wid Thomas) 61 Merrick
Nangle Edward, plumber, 176 Catharine n
Napier James, machinist, 82 Robinson
Nash Alfred, expressman, 260 James n
Nash Arthur, laborer, 60 Barton w
Nash David, laborer, 183 Hughson n
Nash Elvin, fireman, 162 Ferguson ave
Nash George, pattern maker, 166 King Wm
Nash William, bricklayer, 122 Maria
Nash Wm, engineer, 54 Barton e
National Assurance Co, (of Ireland) Richard Bull, agent, 55 James n
National Fire Insurance Co of Ireland, Forbes & Brown, agents, 2 Merrick
National Steamship Line, Charles E Morgan, agent, 11 James n
National Hotel, S & J Wilson, proprs, 248 York
Naylor J, fancy goods, 147 York
Neal Edward, brickmaker, 151 Jackson w
Neal Fred, salesman, 50 James s
Neal Robert, laborer, New
Nealin Mary Ann (wid Thos) 100 Bold
Neelon Helen (wid John) boarding, 172 Bay n.
Neelon Wm, tinsmith, bds 155 John n
Neff Helena (wid Abram) 126 Wellington n
Negle Miss Ellen, boarding house, 234½ James n
Neill Andrew, asst tax collector, room 28, Canada Life chmbrs
Neilson Eliza (wid James) bds 83 Main w
Neilson George, bookkeeper, 83 Main w
Neilson John, shipper, bds 9 Napier
Neilson John E, salesman, Markland
Neilson Wm, baker, bds 83 Main w
Nelles W P, com traveler, 67 King e
Nelligan Bartley (G & B Nelligan) bds 192 James n
Nelligan Catherine (wid Patrick) fancy goods, 192 James n
Nelligan George (G & B Nelligan) 192 James n
Nelligan G & B, gents' furnishings, 230½ James n
Nelligan John, machinist, bds 192 James n
Nelligan J B, clerk, 234 Macnab n
Nelligan Mrs Margaret, 265 Hughson n
Nelligan Michael, wagonmaker, 263 Hughson n
Nelligan M D, wagon maker, James n, h Hughson n
Nelligan Thos, laborer, Breadalbane
Nelson Douglas, 53 Barton e
Nelson Edward, traveler, 64 Cannon w
Nelson Frank J, reporter *Times*, bds 64 Cannon w
Nelson Ira, laborer, Herkimer nr Queen
Nelson Mrs Jane, 223 King e
Nelson Joseph, car driver, 10 Murray e
Nelson Patrick, track master, cor South and Victoria ave
Nelson S U, salesman, bds Commercial hotel
Nelson Wm, lumber measurer, 177 Rebecca
Nelson William, waiter Royal, 13 Cannon e
Nelson William, laborer, 101 Hunter e

Nep Schaun, presser, bds 167 Catharine n
Nesbitt J W (Fuller, Nesbitt & Bicknell) 16 Hughson s
Neville Joseph, machinist, 24 Inchbury n
New Edward, brickmaker, 307 King w
New Eliza (wid Dan) 228 Main w
New Henry, sec-treas Campbell Sewer Pipe Co) 250 Main w
New James, brickmaker, 106 Market
Newbigging William, 104 Cherry
Newberry C E (Humphrey & Newberry) h 80 Robert
Newcomb William, laborer, 30 Augusta
Newcomb Wm, engine driver G T R, 51 Magill
Newcombe Wm, machinist, 1 Devonport
Newcombe Wm, iron finisher, Dundurn
Newell Charles, clerk, 70 Wilson
Newington Daniel, gunsmith, 114 Simcoe e
Newlands Jas, machinist, Robinson
Newman Charles J, organist, 101 Main e
Newman Edward, carpenter, 133 Macauley e
Newman Frederick, laborer, 83 Ferrie e
Newman Maitland, com traveler, 55 Hunter w
Newman Margaret (wid Tim J) boarding, 105 King w
Newport Wm, confectioner, 180 King e
New Raymond Sewing Machine, Hargrove & Sons, agts, 118 King e
Newsom Wm, trunk maker, 14 Pearl n
Newton David, agent Canada Sugar Refining Co (limited) 9 Main e, h 38 Nelson ave
New York Central & Hudson River Railroad, W J Grant, 33 James n
New York Mutual Marine Insurance Co, A F Forbes, agent, 2 Merrick
New Williams Sewing Machine, W S Lumgair, agent, 115 James n
Nex —, laborer, bds 100 Robinson
Nex Wm, laborer, 99 Hunter w
Niblock George, teamster, Murray e
Niblock Moses, laborer, 16 George
Niblock Wm, teamster, Murray e
Nichol Mrs C J (wid R) bds 90 Catharine s
Nichol George, agent, King e
Nichol James, porter, 129 King Wm
Nichol James, woodworker, end King e
Nichol Mrs James, 67 Jackson e
Nichol Mrs Margaret, 70 Ray s
Nicholl George, laborer, bds 34 Market
Nichol Walter C, reporter *Spectator*, 90 Catharine s
Nicholls John R, clerk G T R, 94 Catharine s
Nicholls Wm, brickmaker, King w nr limits
Nichols Thos E, wire and iron works, 59 York, h 117 Hess n
Nichols W H, butcher, 267 King e
Nicholson Edward, hide buyer, 89 Rebecca
Nicholson Mrs Elizabeth, 25 Inchbury s
Nicholson George, pedler, bds 182 Hughson n
Nicholson George (J & G Nicholson) 47 George
Nicholson Mrs H (wid Donald) Markland
Nicholson H, driver, bds Dominion hotel

Nicholson John (J & G Nicholson) h 17 Florence

Nicholson J & G, wood yard, 110 York

Nicholson Richard, laborer, 205 Catharine n

Nicholson Robert, cutter, bds 89 Rebecca

Nicholson Thomas, butcher, 113 King w, h 15 Caroline s

Nicholson Wm, coal and wood dealer, 111 King w, h George cor Ray

Nickling James, machinist, 13 Magill

Nichol James, laborer, 12 Market

Nicol Peter, machinist, 70 Hunter e

Nicolls Frank, coal and wood dealer, Main cor Lock, h Garth s of Concession

Nicolls Willoughby H, farmer, Garth

Nie Arthur J, machinist, 31 Inchbury n

Nieghorn Albert, clerk, 96 Florence

Nieghorn Charles, marble cutter, 96 Florence

Nieghorn Wm, music teacher, 103 Bay n

Nimmo Susan (wid James) 103 James s

Nisbet Mathew, gents' furnishings, King cor Walnut and 6 James n

Nixon Edward, saloon, 20 King Wm

Nixon George S, 47 Catharine n

Nixon John, laborer, 187 James n

Nixon Thomas, policeman, 345 James n

Nixon William, quarryman, 120 Catharine s

Nixon William A, laborer, 75 Jamess

Nixon W S, bailiff 1st Division Court, 72 Wellington n

Noble A W, chair caner, 130 James n

Noble James, machinist, 9 Macnab s

Noble John, express messenger, bds 49 Stuart w

Noble John, bricklayer, 86 Stinson

Noble Wm, prop Noble's hotel, James cor Cannon

Noblett Robert, dyer, 48 Victoria ave s

Nolan James, laborer, 235 Victoria ave n

Nolan John, laborer, bds 73 Stuart w

Nolan John, machinist, 3 Little Wellington

Nolan Michael, 3 Little Wellington

Nolan Michael Oliver, bds 26 Sheaffe

Nolan S, laborer, Mary

Noonan Patrick, shoemaker, 327 Macnab n

Noonan Patrick, laborer, 245 Wellington n

Nordheimer A & S, piano manfs, 80 James n

Norman Henry, 93 Lower Cathcart

Norman John W, laborer, 1 Florence

Norris Margaret (wid Patrick) 151 Macnab n

North British and Mercantile Fire and Life Co, J T Routh agent, 16 James s

North Chas, stonemason, Elizabeth

North John, teamster, 35 Spring

North J W, letter carrier, 93 John n

Northern Fire Assurance Co (London Eng) Seneca Jones agent, 59 James n

Northern and Northwestern Railways, W J, Grant, city ticket agent, Arcade, 33 James n

Northern & Northwestern Passenger Station, King cor Cherry
Northern & Northwestern R R Co, offices Ferguson ave, cor Cannon
Northey Diggory, engineer, Hannah e
Northey Henry, 46 Hannah w
Norwich & London Accident Insurance Association, Payne & McMeekin agents, 97 James n
Norwood Geo, laborer, Duke
Nottle J T, Wentworth s
Nowlan Owen, livery, 12 Rebecca, h 35 Rebecca
Nowlan John, laborer, 140 Rebecca
Noyes E F, bookkeeper, 12 Hannah w
Noyes Francis, salesman, 18 Wilson
Noyes George W, hair dresser, 122 King e
Noyes James, hair works, 116 King e
Nugent Thomas, laborer, 292 James n
Nunn James, teamster, 26 Elgin
Nurden J H, driver, 55 John n
O'Brien Charles, cigarmaker, 55 Walnut s
O'Brien Charles, blacksmith, bds 136 Jackson e
O'Brien D J, professor of music, 28 Sheaffe
O'Brien Edward, laborer, Burlington n
O'Brien Ed, laborer, bds 80 Locke n
O'Brien Henry, gunsmith, 57 Gore
O'Brien Hugh, fancy goods, 8 York
O'Brien James, laborer, 50½ Young
O'Brien James, flour and feed, 127 James n
O'Brien James, moulder, 37½ East ave n
O'Brien John, machinist, 247 James n
O'Brien John, laborer, bds 97 Strachan e
O'Brien John, cigarmaker, 55 Walnut s
O'Brien J F, excise officer, 21 Evans
O'Brien Michael, laborer, 168 John n
O'Brien Michael, laborer, 97 Strachan e
O'Brien Malcolm, laborer, bds 97 Strachan e
O'Brien Margaret (wid John) 55 Walnut s
O'Brien Mary Ann (wid Eugene) 4 Stuart e
O'Brien Patrick, laborer, 87 Young
O'Brien R, caretaker Loretto Convent, Ray n
O'Brien Samuel, printer, 57 Gore
O'Brien Thos, hair dresser, 202 King e
O'Brien Thomas (Canary & O'Brien) 157 James n
O'Brien Thomas, machinist, bds 4 Stuart e
O'Brien Wm, scale maker, 109 George
O'Brien Wm, moulder, 21 Evans
O'Brien Wm, clerk, bds 168 John n
O'Callaghan Frank, inspector, 179 Park n
O'Connell Daniel, laborer, 9 Locomotive
O'Connell John, laborer, 63 Marke
O'Connell Patrick, laborer, 94 Maria
O'Connell Thomas, riveter, 36 Barton e
O'Connor Bridget (wid John) 160 King w
O'Connor Daniel, laborer, 104 Maria

O'Connor Francis, wagon maker, 160 King w, h 146 Duke
O'Connor Jas, painter, 17 Devonport
O'Connor Jas, dairyman, 149 Locke n
O'Connor John, painter, 147 Mary
O'Connor John, freight tracer, 278 Hughson n
O'Connor Martin, engine driver, bds 17 Devonport
O'Connor Michael, moulder, 55 Strachan e
O'Connor Patrick, laborer, Herkimer
O'Connor Thomas, glassblower, 61 Wood e
O'Connor Thos, carriage painter, 160 King w
O'Dea Michael, blacksmith, Burlington n
O'Donnell Dennis, gardener, 57 Little William
O'Donnell James, glassblower, 16 Stuart w
O'Donnell J E, bookkeeper, 161 Hunter e
O'Donnell P J, clerk P O, 161 Hunter e
O'Driscoll Martin, 82 Wellington n
O'Grady Catherine (wid John) 26 O'Reilly
O'Grady James, moulder, 178 Robert e
O'Grady John, moulder, 139 Robert e
O'Grady Martin, laborer, 140 Picton e
O'Grady Michael, Hamilton Marble works, Hess n, cor York
O'Grady Thomas, moulder, 165 Wellington n
O'Heir Arthur, barrister, 4 Main e, h 54 Wellington s
O'Heir James, machinist, 124 Catharine s
O'Heir Peter, landing waiter, 54 Wellington s
O'Holleran Patrick, grocer, 155 Catharine n
O'Hara John, laborer, 180 Wilson
O'Keefe David C, land surveyor, 117 Maria
O'Lachlan Jas, baker, 14 Ray n
O'Leary Elizabeth (wid James) 136 Locke n
O'Malley Honora (wid Timothy) 66 Maria
O'Mara Martin, laborer, 370 James n
O'Neil Arthur, tailor, 95 Hannah e
O'Neil Daniel, painter, r 206 Catharine n
O'Neil Denis, laborer, r 61 Jackson e
O'Neil Felix, hackman, 54 Hunter e
O'Neil James, wagonmaker, 179 King e
O'Neil Jas, painter, bds Dundurn
O'Neil John, manager *Spectator* job department, 122 Jackson e
O'Neil John, tinsmith, 58 Hannah e
O'Neil John, cutter, bds 95 Hannah e
O'Neill John, laborer, 88 Jackson e
O'Neill John, laborer, 122 Young
O'Neil John, engineer, 175 Catharine n
O'Neil Martin, moulder, bds Evans
O'Neil Mrs Mary, 35 Wood e
O'Neil Matthew, bds 56 Park n
O'Neil Patrick, bricklayer, Clark ave
O'Neil Patrick, 150 Market
O'Neil Patrick, teamster, 327 Catharine n
O'Neil Robert, laborer, 55 Wood e
O'Neil Thos, blacksmith, Dundurn
O'Neil Thomas, laborer, 335 Hughson n
O'Neill Mrs Bridget, 287 John n

O'Neil Wm, mason, 147 Catharine n
O'Neill Michael, moulder, 291 John n
O'Neill Michael, glassblower, 315 Macnab n
O'Neill Patrick, laborer, 199 Bay n
O'Neill Thos, baker, 68 Bold
O'Regan Mrs Mary, grocer, 230 Hughson n
O'Reilly Catherine (wid Wm) bds 64 Macnab s
O'Reilly Frank, plumber, 117 Macnab n
O'Reilly J E, master in chancery, court house, h 53 Catharine s
O'Reilly Miles, local master supreme court at Hamilton, court house, h 73 Catharine s
O'Reilly Patrick, laborer, 4 Locomotive
O'Reilly Peter J, brushmaker, 179 Macnab n
O'Rourke Mrs James, 46 Jackson e
O'Sullivan Francis J, gardener, bds Burlington s
O'Sullivan Maurice, moulder, Burlington s
O'Toole John scalemaker, 103 Strachan e
O'Toole Stephen, laborer, 13
O'Toole William, cigarmaker, bds 36 York
Oak Hall, Wm Farrar, manager, 10 James n
Oakes Edward, tailor, 57 Barton e
Oakes Fred, butcher, 126 Wilson
Oaten Walter, salesman, 45 Wellington s
Obermeyer Henry M, printer, 18 Pearl s
Obermeyer Mattern, piano maker, 18 Pearl s
Oddfellows' Hall, 24 John n
Oddy Joseph, carpenter, 113 Wood e
Odell E W, bread pedler, 138 Jackson e
Odell John, laborer, 180 Hunter w
Odell Robert S, machinist, 50 Robinson
Oder Hugo, 61 Wellington n
Odery Rev Joseph, pastor Simcoe street Methodist ch, 131 John n
Ogilvie James, station master N & N W R, 55 Ferguson ave
Ogilvie Robert, tailor, 20 King w simcoe w
Old Albert, bricklayer, Murray e
Old Thomas, laborer, 132 Hunter e
Old Wm, laborer, 25 Lower Cathcart
Olde Horace, hatter, bds 159 West ave n
Oliver Cyrus, cutter, Markland
Oliver D M, mariner, 95 Hughson n
Oliver Edward, shoemaker, 231 James n
Oliver Hamilton, clerk, 125 King Wm
Oliver Jas M, com traveler, 20 Erie ave
Oliver Mrs John, 80 Jackson e
Oliver Thos, tailor, 122 Bold
Oliver Thomas, shoemaker, 158 Bay n
Oliver Mrs Thos, 280 King w
Oliver Thomas, buyer for Sanford, 79 Emerald s
Olmsted Bros, founders, cor York and Queen
Olmsted Charles, engineer, bds 93 King Wm
Olmsted Russell G (Olmsted Bros) 41 Bay s
Olmsted Sarah (wid Samuel) 11 Hess s
Olmsted W H (Olmsted Bros) bds Hunter e, nr John
Olsen Charles, shipper, 1 Cherry
Olsen Michael, shoemaker, Tisdale

Omand James, bds 140 Hughson n
Omand James A, fireman, 140 Hughson n
Omand Joseph, mariner, 11 Wood e
Omand William, 140 Hughson n
Omand William, machinist, 28 Murray e
Omand W O S, machinist, 28 Murray w
Omnium Securities Co, John F Wood, manager, 20 James s
Ontario Brewery, J Gomph, proprietor, 360 John n
Ontario Broom Factory, Walter Woods, proprietor, 62 Macnab n
Ontario Canning Co, J N Waddell, manager, office Court House, factory, Young cor Liberty
Ontario Cotton Mills Co, Macnab cor Simcoe
Ontario Havana Cigar Manufactory, John Lavell, Macnab cor Market square
Ontario Pharmacy, C G Warren, manager, G Wheeler, assistant, King cor Ferguson ave
Ontario Rolling Mill Co, foot Queen n
Ontario Sewing Machine Co, F M Wilson, pres, James Lockhart, sec treas, Wm Vassie, mechanical supt, James cor Hunter
Orange James, laborer, 117 Mary
Orme Ernest V, clerk, 43 Market
Orr Annie (wid Wm) 45 Catharine n
Orr Chas E, cagemaker, bds 116 Young
Orr James, yarn dresser, 209 Mary
Orr James, laborer, 59 Maria
Orr John, laborer, 149 Catharine n
Orr John A (Orr, Harvey & Co) h 82 James s
Orr, Harvey & Co (John A Orr, Wm C Harvey) wholesale boots and shoes, 21 King w
Orr William, carpenter, 102 Main e
Orton Ann (wid Henry) Beulah
Orton Thos, glassblower, bds 365 James
Orttopin Capier, tailor, 47 Hunter e
Osborne A G, bookkeeper, 10 Herkimer
Osborne R Bryson (Osborne, Killey Manf Co) bds cor Macnab and Robinson
Osborne C, machinist, 62 Robert
Osborne Francis, laborer, 72 Main w
Osborne James (Jas Osborne & Son) h 10 Herkimer
Osborne James, engineer, 41 Cherry
Osborne James & Son (James and John Y) grocers, 4 James s
Osborne John, bds 168 Mary
Osborne John, grocer, bds 10 Herkimer
Osborne John T (James Osborne & Son) h 10 Herkimer
Osborne-Killey Manf Co, successors to J H Killey & Co, 117 Barton e
Osborne Sarah (wid Friel) bds 169 Bay n
Osborne William, Osborne, Killey Manf Co, h cor Macnab and Robinson
Osborne W W, law student, 89 Macnab s
Osier Stanislas, telephone builder, 167½ East ave n
Osler A E, accountant, 5 West ave s

Parker's Steam Dye Works.

ROBERT PARKER & CO.

Ladies' and Gents' Outside Wearing Apparel, Ostrich Plumes, Damask Curtains, Kid Gloves, Cleaned and Dyed.

Robert Parker and Co. are prepared to do the very best work, employing only first-class artizans, using the most approved dyes and chemicals, and having the latest and most approved machinery for finishing goods.

HEAD HAMILTON OFFICE:

4 JOHN ST. N., LARKIN HALL BLOCK.

Hamilton, Ontario.

TORONTO OFFICES:

203 Yonge St., and 339 and 225 Queen St. West.

Osler Frank, file cutter, 25½ Tisdale

Osler, Teetzel & Harrison (B B Osler Q C, J V Teetzel, John Harrison) barristers, etc, Canada Life Building, 1 James s

Otter John, laborer, bds 208 Macnab n

Otto Albert H, carver, 205 Mary

Otto A (wid George) 153 John n

Ouimet Francis, shoemaker, 26 Mulberry

Overell Edward (E Overell & Co) 24½ King w

Overell E & Co, booksellers and stationers, 24½ King w

Overend Miles, deputy registrar, 57 Jackson w

Overend Miles A, clerk, 1 Queen

Overholt Jerome, cutter, 44 West ave s

Overholt Moses, tailor, 41 Victoria ave n

Owen Henry, laborer, 134 Queen n

Owen James, laborer, 49 Ray n

Owen James, plate polisher, 43 Ray n

Oxley Elizabeth (wid Philip) 18 Lower Cathcart

Oxley Frederick, grocer, etc, 69 York

Packham Thos, laborer, Garth

Padden Michael, cellarman, bds 143 Bay n

Paddon Patrick, laborer, 86-88 Maria

Padfield Herbert, watchmaker, 119 King

Page James, 36 Steven

Page Sarah A (wid Isaac) 192 Main w

Page Mrs S, 30 Catharine s

Pain Albert (Bowering & Pain) 21 Main w

Paine Thos B, bookkeeper, 166 James n

Painter Jas E, fireman G T R, 9 Crooks

Painter John M, pedler, Robinson

Palladium The, of Labor, Co-operative Printing Co, props, 92 King e

Palm Wm, 94 Bay s

Palmer Benjamin, moulder, 99 Locke n

Palmer John, tobacco roller, bds 20 Napier

Palmer Josiah, teacher, 48 Florence

Palmer J C, machinist, 56 Gore

Palmer Wm B, com traveler, 157 Main w

Panter Benjamin, stonecutter, bds 103 Catharine n

Panter George, stonecutter, 103 Catharine n

Panter Joseph, pattern maker, 119 Caroline n

Papps George S, barrister, 13 Main e, h 3 Robinson

Papps L L (wid Henry) 178 King w

Paquin Joseph, grocer, 287 Macnab n

Paradile Thomas, sexton, 82 Catharine s

Park Mrs Elizabeth, Markland cor Ontario

Park J D, asst inspector weights and measures, 155 Wellington n

Park John H (Lucas Park & Co) h Markland cor Park

Park Margaret (wid Wm) 38 Ferguson ave

Park Robert H (John Garrett & Co) h s s Hannah w, nr Macnab

Parke Walter(McGregor & Parke) bds 42 Vine

Parker Charlotte (wid Francis) 28 Elgin

Parker David, carpenter, 106 Emerald n

Parker Edward, coachman, bds 96 Main e

Parker James, laborer, Eliza

Parker J E, manager Meriden Britannia Co, cor Herkimer and Macnab

Parker L H, professor of music, bds 11 Charles

Parker Robert & Co, steam dyers and cleaners, 4 John n *See advt*

Parker Robert (Robert Parker & Co) res 32 Louther ave n, Toronto

Parker William, laborer, 20 Strachan w

Parkes James (Parkes & Macadams) bds Royal hotel

Parkes & Macadams (James Parkes, A H, Macadams) barristers, Hamilton Provident & Loan Building, 1 Hughson s *See card*

Parkhill Andrew, porter, 84 West ave n

Parkhill Thomas, carpenter, 84 West ave n

Parkinson Irene (wid John) 28 Ray n

Parks David, shoemaker, 146 King Wm

Parks Nelson, sergeant police, 94 Victoria ave n

Parks —, machinist, 127 Ferguson ave

Parmenter Amos W, agent, 1 Main w

Parmenter Charles, baker, 249 King Wm

Parnell George, clerk, 45 Park n

Parnell Samuel, painter, 120 Hughson n

Parrott Benjamin, carter, 24 Steven

Parry John, laborer, bds 23 Barton e

Parry Thomas, carpenter, 70 Park n

Parslow Mrs, Burlington n

Parsons Stephen, foreman, 88 Park n
Partridge John, moulder, 146 Emerald n
Partridge Richard, engineer, 83 Simcoe e
Partridge Thos, pattern maker, 147 Ferrie e
Paskey Wm H, machinist, 78 Maria
Passmore Edward, bds 215 John n
Passmore Francis W, painter, 105 Catharine s
Pastine August, fruit dealer, 150 King w
Patten L H, law student, 34 Bay n
Patterson Agnes (wid Peter) 72 Park n
Paterson Andrew, teacher, end King e
Patterson A B, ledger keeper, Merchants' Bank, 2 Hess s
Patterson Bros (John and Thos) lumber merchants and builders, foot Lower Cathcart
Patterson Donald, laborer, 46 Caroline s
Paterson George, laborer, foot Ferguson ave
Patterson H C, clerk, bds 44 Main w
Patterson James, carpenter, 123 John s
Paterson James, woolgrader, 100 Cherry
Paterson James S, bookkeeper, 74 Bay s
Patterson John (Patterson Bros) bds 88 Ferguson ave
Patterson John, cutter, 29 Inchbury n
Patterson John sr, merchant tailor, 41 John s, h 105 Cherry
Patterson John jr, cutter, h 76 Maria
Patterson John, moulder, bds 7½ Florence
Patterson John, cutter, 11 Magill
Patterson John, 2 Hess s
Patterson John, machinist, 30½ Magill
Patterson John B, foreman shirt factory, Duke
Paterson Mark, landing waiter, 4 Kelly
Patterson Peter, carpenter, 48 Steven
Patterson Robert, laborer, 372 Catharine n
Patterson Thomas (Patterson Bros) h 112 East ave n
Patterson Thomas, blacksmith, 74 Macnab n, h 33 Catharine n
Patterson Thos, salesman, 48 James n
Patterson Thomas, watchman, 221 Victoria ave n
Patterson T R, accountant Farmers & Traders Loan Association 2 Hess s
Patterson Walter, brakesman N & NWR, 43 Main w
Patterson —, com traveler, 33 Tisdale
Paterson —, laborer, 56 Locke s
Patrick Robert, laborer, 100 Young
Patten Andrew, moulder, 57 Victoria ave n
Pattison Zaccheus, manufacturing confectioner, 71 and 73 King w and 65 Cannon w
Pattle Wm, 144 King w
Patton Andrew J, deputy inspector post office dept, hd Queen s
Patton Mrs Geo, 23 West ave s
Patton James, carpenter, 276 York
Patton James, machinist, 240 Mary
Patton Robert, laborer, 46 Strachan e
Paull John, laborer, 224 John n
Paulley Joseph, carpenter, 328 Hughson n
Pawling Thomas, laborer, hd York

Pawson Daniel, gardener Undermount, John s
Payne Charles, painter, 135 Picton e
Payne Elford G, (Payne & McMeekin) h 49 East ave n
Payne John, gardener, Ferguson ave n
Payne & McMeekin, (Elford G Payne, John McMeekin) agents Commercial Union Assurance Co, 97 James n; *see card*
Payne Wm, canvasser, bds 146 Rebecca
Payne Wm, wood and coal dealer, cor Mary and Cannon, h 119 Cannon e
Payne Wm, engine driver GTR, 23 Pearl n
Payne —. laborer, 84 Lower Cathcart
Pazius Alex, upholsterer, 34 Stuart e
Peace Daniel, tobacconist, 72 James n, h 67 Vine
Peace D J, tobacconist, 88 King e, h 67 Vine
Peace Daniel J, 43 Picton w
Peace John, iron worker, 103 Locke n
Peace Wm, mariner, 39 Ferrie w
Peace Wm, carpenter, 101 East ave n
Peacock Arthur, butcher, 304 King e
Peacock Mrs Eliza, dry goods, 75 John s
Peacock John, inspector, 148 Cannon e
Pearce Edward, organist, bds 86 George
Pearce Fred, clerk, bds 86 George
Pearce Geo, laborer, 32 Locke n
Pearce John, laborer, 44 Wellington n
Pearce Joseph, laborer, hd Queen s
Pearce Louis, laborer, Ferguson ave n
Pearce Samuel, clerk, bds 86 George
Pearce Wm, engine driver GTR, 86 George
Pearman Wm, cook, 163 Mary
Pearson George, carter, 10 Victoria ave s
Pearson G L, agent, 212 Victoria ave n
Pearson Charles, glassblower, 327 James n
Pearson Frederick, laborer, 23 Burlington w
Pearson Henry, cutter, 136 Hunter e
Pearson Henry, saloonkeeper, 113 York
Pearson James, manager Imperial Mineral Water Co, 65 Hunter w
Pearson James, 33 Napier
Pearson John, accountant, real estate, rent, insurance and commission agent, 8-10 Hughson s, h Concession cor Queen *See card*
Pearson John, cab driver, 260 Hughson n
Pearson Joseph, laborer, r 124 Wood e
Pearson Thomas, laborer, 237 John n
Peason Thomas, glassblower, bds 327 James n
Pearson William, fish dealer, James St market, h Wentworth n
Peart Albert, machinist, 11 Pine
Peart Joseph, machinist, bds 11 Pine
Pease Walter R, bookkeeper, 46 Market
Pease Wm, barber, 4 Hughson n h 34 John n
Peat Thos G, 108 Hess n
Pecover F C, salesman, Copp's Block, King e
Pecover H J, upholsterer, Copp's Block, King e

Pecover Joseph, cabinet maker' Copp's Block, King e
Peden John, fruit dealer, 291 King Wm
Peden J, fruiterer, Steven cor King Wm
Peden Thomas, baggageman G T R, 126 Queen n
Pedlar Edward, clerk, bds 12 Liberty
Peebles C H, family grocer, 39 Macnab n
Peebles & Hamilton, carpenters, 220 King Wm
Peebles John, watchmaker, 192 King e, h 113 Hunter e
Peebles Robert, carpenter, 113 Hunter e
Peebles Robert jr, salesman, 113 Hunter e
Peebles Wm, carpenter, 85 East ave n
Peel William, machinist, 9 Inchbury n
Peeler Edward, painter, 178 Rebecca
Peene Alfred S, contractor, 24 Sheaffe
Peene Mrs F M, milliner, etc, 11 York, h 24 Sheaffe
Peer Philip, laborer, 32 Murray w
Pegler Emma (wid Thos) laundress, 18 George
Pegler William, shirt ironer, 18 George
Pegram Nathaniel, boot and shoe maker, 137 James n, h 38 Jackson e
Peirce Chas E, manager clothing department Pratt & Watkins, bds Dominion hotel
Peirce Henry, painter, 17 Park n
Peirce Jane M (wid Wm) 27 Jackson w
Peirce Julia P (wid George) 27 Jackson w
Pellon Thomas, brakesman, bds 73 Stuart w
Penfold Fred, bar tender, Walker house
Penney William, machinist, Maple
Pennell William jr, laborer, Bruce
Pennell William, soap maker Bruce
Pennington J D (J D Pennington & Co) h 11 Upper Cathcart
Pennington J D & Co, window and door screen manuf, 11 Upper Cathcart
Pennington M A, insurance and real estate agent, 30 James s, h 37 Hannah w
Pennington Printing Co, 30 James s
Pentecost Albert L (Campbell & Pentecost) h 142 Cannon e
Pentecost Richard, painter, 296 York
Pentecost Robert, com traveler, 9 Bold
Penzer Alfred, brakesman, bds 49 Stuart w
Peppitt John, dairyman, 113 Robinson
Perkins C R (F E Skelly & Co) bds 215 York
Perkins Mrs (wid Wm) 133 West ave n
Perrin James, laborer, 1 Margaret
Perry Arthur, silver solder, 145 West ave n
Perry George, foreman, 41 Ferrie w
Perry William, hostler, bds 45 York
Perry W H, solder, 152 Wilson
Perry W H A, polisher, bds 84 Park n
Pesel William, laborer, 118 Caroline s
Pessell William, watchman, 105 Jackson e
Peters Andrew S, basket maker, Maple
Peters Charles, clerk, 58 Barton w

Peters George, salesman, 5 Upper Cathcart
Peters Rudolph, machinist, etc, 76 Macnab n
Peterson G A, laborer, 20 East ave n
Pett James, mat manuf, Murray e, h 65 Lower Cathcart
Pett Joseph, tanner, 93 Mary
Pettigrew Ellen (wid Henry) Rebecca
Pettigrew John, carter, 71 West ave n
Pettinger George, 97 Bay n
Pew Walter, teamster, 98 Strachan e
Pfann George, cabinet maker, 96 Caroline s
Pfeifer Frederick, laborer, 9 Harriet
Pfeifer John, laborer, Duke
Phelan James P, steward Royal hotel, 66 Catharine n
Phœnix Insurance Co (Marine) J B Fairgrieve, agent, 59 James n
Phibbs George B, wheelwright, 99 Elgin
Philip David, machinist, 49 Markland
Phillips Alexander, blacksmith, 11 Cherry
Phillips Charles, blacksmith, bds 39 James s
Phillips David, carpenter, 20 Ferguson ave
Phillips Ellen (wid Joseph) 54 Ferrie e
Phillips Miss Esther, 134 Catharine n
Phillips George, merchant tailor, 192 King e, h 159 West ave n
Phillips Henry, shoemaker, 57 Ray n
Phillips James, carpenter, 11 West ave n
Phillips John, laborer, Garth
Phillips John, sail maker, 33 Macauley w
Phillips Joshua A, contractor, 124 King Wm
Phillips Martin, laborer, 231 Wellington n
Phillips Samuel, laborer, bds 146 Rebecca
Phillips William, butcher, 256 York
Philp Frank, salesman, bds 15 Barton e
Philp F W (J Philp & Son) 40 Young
Philp Harry, bookkeeper, 15 Barton e
Philp Harry, tinsmith, 12 Macnab s
Philp James (J Philp & Son) 40 Young
Philp James & Son (James and F W) saddlers, etc., 3 York
Philp Joseph, salesman, 15 Barton e
Philp T Frank, salesman, 15 Barton e
Philp William, M D, cor York and Hess
Philps John, stovemounter, 110 Wood e
Phelps William, laborer, 136 Picton e
Phœnix Fire Insurance Co, Gillespie & Powis, agents, 31 King e
Phœnix William, pattern maker, 120 Ferrie e
Pierce James, laborer, 44 Wilson
Pierce James, laborer, 44 Kelly
Piercy Charles, printer, 27 Steven
Piercy Christopher, carpenter, 35 Steven
Piercy Mrs James, bds 92 Wellington s
Piesel Ernst, laborer, 2 Poulette
Piggott Charles, cabinet maker, bds 17 Hunter e
Pigot Michael H, com traveler, 95 Macnab n
Pilgrim Bros (R A & S F) soda water, 1 Spring

Pilkey A, agent, 37 East ave n
Pilkey Joseph B (Hutchison & Pilkey) 127 Bay s
Pillman Thomas, butcher, 75 York
Pilton William, laborer, r 241 Bay n
Pim Mrs Hannah (wid Wm H) 10 Bay s
Pinch Edmund, machinist, 23 Wellington s
Pinch James, policeman, 85 West ave n
Pinch John, machinist, 18 Sheaffe
Pinkett James, laborer, 159 Hunter w
Pirie John, laborer, 121 Jackson w
Pitcher —, carpenter, bds 60 James s
Pitt Clarissa (wid William) 130½ Macnab n
Plair James, train despatcher G T R, 120 Jackson w
Plank John, grocer, 314 Macnab n
Plant John, wood dealer, 15 Cherry
Plant Richard, carpenter, 118 Wellington n
Plastow Charles A, carpenter, 205 Main w
Plastow Joseph, caretaker Court House, h 34 Hughson s
Pater Charles, shoemaker, 163 Bay n
Platt Thomas, fancy goods, 73 York
Platts Michael, 7 Kelly
Pocock John, stonecutter, 15 Florence
Pocock Stephen A, saw manf, 129 West ave n
Pointer James, E, com traveler, 42 West ave s
Poland William, fitter G T R, 39 West ave n
Poland Wm, jr, civil engineer, 39 West ave n
Police Court, James Cahill, police magistrate, Thos Beasley, clerk, King Wm cor Mary
Police Stations, No. 1, City Hall, James n; No. 2, 243 Jas n; No. 3, King Wm, cor Mary
Pollard Lawrence, laborer, 129 Queen n
Pollett John, draughtsman, bds Exchange hotel
Pollington Noah, laborer, 154 Jackson w
Pollitt John B, designer, 244 Hughson n
Poluke Antoine, cabinet maker, 14 Pearl s
Pomfret John, Mary nr Simcoe
Pope George, cabinet maker, 160 James n
Pope Wm, laborer, bds 102 Hannah w
Porteous James, machinist, 228 York
Porteous John, 50 Murray w
Porteous Thomas, butcher, 40 Bay n
Porter Edward, collar maker, 91 West ave n
Porter George, machinist, 84 Robinson
Porter Samuel, baker, 83 Cherry
Porter Wm, laborer, 94 Simcoe e
Porter Wm, machinist, 99 Robinson
Posal Theodore, laborer, 42 Canada
Post Charles, laborer, 96 Catharine s
Post Chas, carpenter, 24 Young
Post Francis, 133 John s
Post Justus, boiler tender, 128½ John n
Postoffice, 68 James n
Pothier William, burnisher, 63½ East ave n
Potter Bessie (wid Wm) 205 John n
Potter Frederick, laborer, bds 90 Bay n

Potter James, moulder, 185 Jas n
Potter James, brickmaker, 27 Wellington n
Potter John, farmer, 8 Wood w
Potter John, market gardener, 208 Main e
Potter John, 154 King Wm
Potter Walter, r 205 Catharine n
Potter Wm, ropemaker, 11 Cannon e
Potter Wm, machinist, 26 Locke n
Pottruff Jonathan, salesman, 97½ Hunter e
Pottruff Levi, porter, 42 Hunter e
Poulter Alfred, bookkeeper, 136 Wellington n
Pounden Mrs John W, 24 Main w
Povey Wm H, painter, 33 Barton e
Powell Charles, machinist, 54 Erie ave
Powell C W, window shades, 176½ King e
Powell Richard, machinist, 68 Lower Cathcart
Powell Robert, butcher, Main e
Powell R T S, florist, Hughson cor Hunter, h Mountain
Powell Wm, machinist, bds Robinson nr Macnab
Powell William, laborer, bds 16 Vine
Powell W R, builder, 68 Wellington n
Powers Ann (wid John) 97 Hunter e
Power Nicholas, 71 Markland
Powers Mrs Mary, 27 Strachan e
Powis Alfred (Gillespie & Powis) h Hess cor Concession
Powis Charles, ledger keeper, 118 Catharine s
Powis F A, accountant, 118 Catharine s
Poynton Joseph, painter, 43 Canada
Poyton Joseph, packer, 101 Picton e
Pratt T H (Pratt & Watkins) h 6 East ave n
Pratt & Watkins (T H Pratt and F W Watkins) dry goods and clothing, 16–18 James n
Pratt Wm J, barber, 3 John n, h 10 Macnab s
Pray Richard (Pray & Son) h 80 Hughson
Pray & Son (Richard W R) undertakers, 9 Macnab n
Pray W R (Pray & Son) h 9 Macnab n
Precore Joseph (Ten Eyck & Precore) 97 James s
Preddie Henry, watchmaker, 93 James n
Prentice Joseph, sergeant police, 81 George
Presnell Alfred, blacksmith, end Barton w
Press Richard, builder, 95 Elgin
Preston Joseph, watchman, 143 Bay n
Preston William, laborer, 41 Park n
Price John, carpenter, Hess s w s
Price Wm, bricklayer, bds 192 King Wm
Priestland Henry, 139 Park n
Priddis Mrs John, 122 East ave n
Priestland Thomas, second-hand dealer, 82 John s
Priestman James, butcher, 164 Macnab n
Prince Wm, laborer, 32 Peter
Prindiville John, carpenter, 69 Cherry
Prindiville Sarah (wid John) 47 Young
Pringle A, teller Merchants' Bank, 4 Hannah e
Pringle Mrs Phoebe, 4 Hannah e
Pringle Robert, broommaker, end Emerald n
Pringle Robert, bookkeeper, 158 Rebecca
Pringle R A, barrister, 16 James s, h Hannah e *See card*

Prior Joseph, laborer, 44 Gore
Pritchard Charles J, shoemaker, 152 York
Proctor Henry, 36 Wellington n
Proctor James, boilermaker, 138 Robert e
Proctor John, merchant, Cedar Grove, King e
Proctor John & Co, hardware, 4 James s
Proctor Mrs, 88 Ferguson ave
Proctor Wm J, manufacturer, h 179 Main e
Pronguey John C, carriage manf, 96 James n
Prout Mrs J C, confectioner, 58 James n, h 42 Catharine n
Provan David (Allen & Proven) h 54 Walnut s
Providence Washington Insurance Co, David McLellan, agent, 84 James n
Provost Andrew, barber, 47½ Young
Prowse Henry J, carpenter, 42 Emerald n
Pryke John, shoemaker, 124 Wellington s
Pugh Thos, carter, 90 Bold
Pugh Wm H, shoemaker, 134 Barton e
Pulkingham A (wid James) 152 King Wm
Pulling Mark, clerk, 21 Napier
Pumfrey Thomas, moulder, 7 Inchbury s
Purdy R J, carpenter, 91 Ferrie e
Purrott Geo, painter, 148 Duke
Purvis James, carpenter, 229 Victoria ave n
Pyle David, 89 York
Pyle David, clerk, 44 Market
Pyle George, machinist, 44 Market
Qua James, 28 East ave n
Quarrier John, millers' agent, 20 Wilson
Quarry Joseph H, com traveler, 39 Market
Queen (Fire and Life) Insurance Co, George A Young agent, 2 Merrick
Quigley Matthew, laborer, Wellington n
Quilter Thomas, laborer, r 185 Bay n
Quimby Mrs A, 16 Vine
Quimby C & Co, tobacconists, 27 James n
Quinlan Jeremiah, laborer, 204 Hughson n
Quinlan Michael, foreman G T R, 113 Simcoe e
Quinlan William, laborer, 128 Picton e
Quinn Alex, moulder, 63 West ave n
Quinn Charles, moulder, 18) John n
Quinn Frank, pattern maker, 268 King e
Quinn John sr, pattern maker, Barton w
Quinn Joseph, machinist, 61 Stuart w
Quinn Mary (wid Patrick) 315 York
Quinn Mrs, laundress, r 104 Bay n
Quinn Richard, hotel, 307 Jas n
Quinn Thomas, storekeeper Asylum, 7 Nelson ave
Quintar Thomas, laborer, r 185 Bay n
Quirk John, varnisher, Barton w
Robitoy Mrs Cary, 16 Napier
Rackley John, laborer, 103 George
Radford Henry, baker, 50½ Hunter e
Radford Wm, baker, 19 Stuart w
Radigan John, tinsmith, 44 Wilson
Rae Carus, turnkey jail, Barton e
Rake James, shoemaker, 21 Simcoe w
Ralph Richard, stonecutter, 55 York
Ralph Robert, clerk, 135 Robert e

Ralph Wm, Wentworth n
Ralston Thomas, caretaker Central School, 40 Bold
Ram Alfred, carpenter, 162 Hunter w
Ram Alfred G, printer, 162 Hunter w
Ramage W G, salesman, 85 Main e
Ramsay A G, F I A, president and managing director Canada Life Assurance Co, h Dunedin, 157 James s
Ramsay Alex, supt Canada Life Ass Co, h 134 Bay s
Ramsden George, machinist, 12 Little Market
Randall James, farmer, 45 Wellington s
Randall James, com traveler, 17 Elgin
Randall J W, 45 Wellington s
Randall Ralph W, carpenter, 42 Tisdale
Ranger Charles, carpenter, 215 James n
Rankin James J, clerk Bank of Montreal, cor Bay and Jackson
Rankin John, tobacco manf, West, King w
Rankine John, teller Bank of Montreal, 19 Nelson ave
Raphael Isaac, tailor, 96 John s
Rastrick F J, architect, 22 Maria
Ratfield Charles, laborer, r 109 Macnab n
Rattenbury John, carpenter, 112 John s
Rattray M L, principal Hamilton Commercial College, 48 James n
Raw Robert A, bookkeeper, 23 Bay s
Raw Robert, jr (R Raw & Co) h 94 Park n
Raw Robert & Co, book and job printers, 30 John n
Ray Arthur, laborer, 43 Hunter e
Ray Peter, city fireman

Raycroft Richard, grocer, 233 Barton e
Rayment James, gardener, Caroline s, w s
Raynor J G, grocer, 9 Steven
Raynor Mrs, 282 King e
Rayson Thomas, porter, bds Commercial Hotel
Rea Joseph, buffer, 155 East ave n
Read Geo, carpenter, 115 King w
Read George, hackman, 10 Main w
Read Mrs Mary (wid Robert R) 115 King w
Read Robert, machinist, 33 Peter
Read S, jr, asst accountant Bank of Commerce, 45 Charles
Reader Robert, moulder, 202 Wellington n
Reardon Mrs Catharine (wid Cornelius) 29 Sheaffe
Reardon Dennis, carpenter, 82 Peter
Reardon John, boiler maker, 356 Hughson n
Reardon John, moulder, 49 Cannon w
Reardon Michael, baker, 51 Inchbury n
Reardon Michael, 356 Hughson n
Reardon Terence, mariner, 48 Guise
Reaston John, laborer, 166 Bay n
Reche J A (R N Taylor & Co) h 119 Mary
Reche Thomas, carpenter, 119 Mary
Reddall & McKeown, stoves, tinware, etc, 112 King w
Reddall Thomas (Reddall & McKeown) h 51 Hunter e
Redden Matthew, laborer, St. Mary's Lane
Redfield James E, silver plater, 84 Wellington n
Redman Mrs Mary Ann (wid Robert) r 79 Caroline n
Reece Mrs Richard, 21 Tisdale
Reed James, hotel, 32 John n

Reed Nathaniel, carpenter, 22 Hunter e
Reeves Arthur L, baker, 190 King w
Reeves Arthur L, jr, groceries and liquors, 212 King w
Reeves Charles, engineer, 130 Cannon e
Reeves Richard, baker, 190 King w
Reeves Samuel, baker, bds 13 Cannon e
Reeves Samuel, pedler, 181 Main w
Reeves Wm, baker, 12 Charles
Regan Miss Emma R, 170 Bay n
Registry Office, Court House
Registry office for servants, Edward Britt, propr, 109½ King w
Rehder Christian, plater, 34 Little Wm
Reid A C, MD, 55 Hughson n
Reid Alex, bookkeeper, 171 Main w
Reid Alex, gardener, hd York
Reid Alex, machinist, 85 Locke n
Reid Alex E, cutter, 169 Main w
Reid & Barr Manuf Co of Ontarin (limited) steam engines and boilers, 64 Rebecca
Reid Charles, whipmaker, 26 Wilson
Reid Donald, gardener, hd York
Reid Eliza (wid James) 107 Rebecca
Reid Eliza (wid John) 82 Jackson e
Reid Estate of, W Malcolm, trustee, furniture and carpets, 67-69 King w
Reid Fletcher, laborer, 37 Young
Reid George, teamster, 52 Hughson s
Reid George, wood worker, 45 Hughson n
Reid George, express messenger, 66 Vine
Reid, Goering & Co (W J Reid, Wm Goering, G F Bireley) cigar manfs and dealers in wines and liquors, 104 King e
Reid & Halliday (W J Reid, W Halliday) carpenters, 131 Main e
Reid Henry, machinist, 149 King Wm
Reid Isabella (wid Peter) 8 Liberty
Reid James, carpenter, 100 Caroline s
Reid James, shipper, 51 Hunter e
Reid James, butcher, 41 Wellington n
Reid Mrs Jane (wid Robert) 143 Robert e
Reid John, glassblower, 44 Picton w
Reid Joseph, 201½ John n
Reid Joseph, conductor, bds 8 Magill
Reid Joseph W, carpenter, 116 Locke n
Reid Robert, bds 38 Ferrie w
Reid Thomas, carpenter, 8 Cherry
Reid W G (Reid, Goering & Co) h 31 Victoria ave s
Reid William, teamster, 60 Hughson s
Reid William, carpenter, 43 Macauley w
Reid William, policeman, 46 Emerald n
Reid Wm, clerk, bds 223 James
Reid William, engineer, 75 Cannon e
Reid William (Murton & Reid) h 75 Cannon e
Reid Wm, 206 East ave n
Reid Mrs William W, 46 West ave n
Reid W J, compositor, 107 Rebecca
Reid W J (Reid & Halliday) 131 Main e

ALASKA.

The Alaska Spectacles and Eyeglasses are specially adapted to remedy defective sight. For sale in this city by

FRED CLARINGBOWL,

Jeweler AND Optician,

WHO IS THE SOLE AGENT.

Also, a Fine Stock of Watches and Jewelry on hand.

Remember the address is

158 KING ST. EAST, HAMILTON.

ROBERT IRWIN,

Customs Broker, Forwarder and Shipper,

FREIGHT AGENT FOR THE

Chicago, Milwaukee & St. Paul R'wy.

To all points in Manitoba and the Northwest.

84 JAMES ST. NORTH.

Reilly Denis, nailer, bds 49 Stuart w
Reilly James, laborer, 92 Walnut s
Reilly John, moulder, 84 Jackson e
Reinholt Mrs Christiana (wid Henry) 85 Markland
Reinholt Herman, carpenter, 85 Markland
Reinholt Robert, presser, 48 Ray s
Reliance Hall, 1 Rebecca
Relph Walter, fitter, 117 Robinson
Rendell W H, blacksmith, 92 John s
Renner Charles, carder, bds 106 Walnut s
Rennie Mrs Gertrude (wid Alex) 71 George
Rennie Robert, carpenter, 173 East ave n
Rennie William, letter carrier, 247 Bay n
Renton Thomas, semaphore inspector, 239 Bay n
Renwick Mrs Elizabeth, 62 Locke n
Renwick Thomas, engineer, 133 Wellington n
Renwick Wm, porter G T R, 147 Hunter w
Resner W R, salesman, Main cor Erie
Reuben Louis, button hole maker, bds 56 Gore
Reuben L, pedler, 45 Cherry
Reuben Nelson, cigar maker, bds 21 Gore
Rewbury Wm, checker, 20 Tisdale
Reynolds Geo, butcher, Robinson
Reynolds Mrs Helena, 45 Chas
Reynolds Isaac, polisher, bds 14 Young
Reynolds James, laborer, 35 Napier
Reynolds James D, painter, 175 Hunter w
Reynolds John, lumberman, 14 Young
Reynolds M A, canvasser, bds Dominion hotel
Reynolds T W, M D, 122½ James n
Reynolds Robert, baker, 31 Tisdale
Reynolds William, broom maker, 14 Young
Rhynd James, fireman G T R, 142 Hess n
Riach George, printer, 115 Maria
Riache James, clerk, Main, e Hamilton
Riach John, general dealer, 54 James n and 62 King w, h 61 Park n
Riach Wm, clerk, 61 Park n
Rice Frederick, laborer, 82 Caroline n
Rice James, caretaker, James cor Vine
Rice William, teamster, 32 Stuart e
Rich Charles F, harness maker, 30 Merrick
Richards E T, packer, 13 Park n
Richards Fred J, coffin maker, 28 Locke n
Richards G H, painter, 160 Macnab n
Richards Geo W, sec-treas Reid & Barr Manuf Co, bds American hotel
Richardson Byron, carpenter, 140 Main w
Richardson Mrs Amelia S (wid Arthur) 56 Jackson w
Richardson Andrew, foreman G T R, 37 Picton e
Richardson George, second-hand dealer, 36-40 King William
Richardson Mrs Jessie (wid Wm) 58 George

Richardson John, machinist, bds 91 Rebecca
Richardson Mrs Mary (wid Wm) 28 Hess n
Richardson Matthew, boots and shoes, Copp's Block, King e
Richardson Robt, heater, 69 Locomotive
Richardson Theophilus H, com traveler, bds 54 Pearl s
Richardson Thomas, boilermaker, 13 Burlington w
Richardson William, bricklayer, 353 Hughson n
Richardson William, patent medicines, 2 Catharine s
Richardson Wm, laborer, 13 Macnab s
Richelieu & Ontario Navigation Co, George McKeand, agent, 57 James n
Richmond Alfred,grocer,72 Duke
Richmond George, moulder, 177 Cannon e
Richmond George H, printer, 63 Wellington n
Richmond John, butcher, bds 72 Duke
Richmond Thomas, grocer, s w cor James and Burlington
Richter T, propr Richter's saloon, 43 James n
Richards Joseph, com traveler, 63 East ave n
Ricketts Frederick, painter, 72 Main w
Riddel Mrs Catharine, 164 Hughson n
Riddel James, laborer, 312 King William
Riddel John, stockbroker, 4 Main e, h 141 James s
Riddel John E, tinsmith, 170 King e, h 26 East ave n
Riddell Joseph, tinsmith, 28½ East ave n
Riddel Thos, moulder, 164 Hughson n
Riddell Thomas, carpenter, 9 Clark ave
Riddel Thomas, carpenter, 74 Victoria ave n
Riddell Thomas, merchant, bds 51 Hunter e
Riddel Wm, moulder, 110 Victoria ave n
Riddle Mrs Ann, r 51 Young
Riddle Mrs Ellen, grocer, 146 Bay n
Rideout Arthur, grocer, 146 Bay
Rideout Arthur, clerk, bds King e
Rideout —, clerk, 36 Bay s
Ridler Wm, shoemaker, 156 Jackson w
Ridley Henry T, M D, 31 Main w
Rieger Alfred, blacksmith, 32 Hess n
Rieger Charles, bartender, 26 Peter
Rieger Henry W, laborer, 122 Hess n
Rigg William, car inspector, 196 Macnab n
Riggs John & Co, dry goods, 40 James n
Riggs Stanley, salesman, bds 91 Market
Rigsby John, builder, 133 King William
Riley Thomas, laborer, 29 Margaret
Ringer Ephraim, melter, 170 Catharine n
Ringrose Horace, stovemounter, 9 Mulberry
Ripley Abraham, moulder, 128 Victoria ave n
Ripley James, moulder, 128 Victoria ave n
Ripley John, carpenter, 20 Locke s
Rissman Rudolph, emigration agent, 1 Barton Terrace
Ritchie Mrs McKercher (wid James) registry office, 26 Charles

Ritchie Thomas, laborer, 35 Crooks
Roach Andrew P, Roach's hotel, 67 Stuart w
Roach Benjamim, moulder, bds 53 Gore
Roach David, blacksmith, 42 Hughson s
Roach Mrs Ellen, 109 Catharine n
Roach George, 43 Barton w
Roach John, mariner, 40 Burlington w
Roach John, laborer, 312 Hughson n
Roach Michael, laborer, 104 Picton e
Roach Patrick, laborer, 2 Brock w
Roach Richard, blacksmith, bds 328 Macnab n
Roach Thomas, porter, 34 King w
Roantree Charles, broommaker, 107 Macnab n
Robb Andrew, engineer, Hess s nr Robinson
Robb Louis, carder, 275 Hughson n
Robb William, printer, 135 Jackson e
Robins Alfred, engine driver, 123 Wellington n
Robbins Harry, polisher, 187 King e
Robins James, butcher, 72 Lower Cathcart
Robins John, tinsmith, bds 95 Robert
Robbins Joseph, shoemaker, bds 13 Florence
Robbins Joseph, compositor, 15 Little Peel
Robbins N B, grate manuf, 68 Mary, h 38 Wellington s
Robbins Samuel, tinsmith, 24 Wilson
Robbins Mrs Sarah, Royal Laundry, 187 King e
Robbins William, carpenter, 28 Wilson
Robins Wm, tailor, 95 Robert
Roberton Alexander, carpenter, 10 Augusta
Roberts David E (Hurd & Roberts) 172 Main e
Roberts George R, "Canadian Baptist," 3 Young
Roberts Rev J B, minister A M E Church, 82 John n
Roberts Capt John, 106 Catharine s
Roberts Mrs Robert, 7 Wilson
Roberts Sidney, fireman G T R, 26 Locomotive
Roberts William, laborer, 3 Walnut s
Lobertson Mrs Agnes (wid James) 69 Wellington n
Robertson Alex, stonecutter, 28 Tisdale
Robertson Archibald, shipbldr, 23 Brock w
Robertson A W, bookkeeper, 135½ Park n
Robertson Charles, teacher Collegiate Institute
Robertson Donald, bds 84 Merrick
Robertson Duncan, carpenter, 12 Barton w
Robertson Duncan, machinist, 19 Pearl s
Robertson & Henderson (P T Robertson, Alex Henderson) wholesale commission merchts, Merrick cor Macnab
Robertson H H (Robertson & Robertson) barrister, h Rannoch Lodge, hd John s
Robertson Hugh, brass moulder, 35 Little Wm
Robertson James, moulder, 124 Rebecca
Robertson John G, journalist, 3 Liberty
Robertson Malcolm, teamster, 14 Mill

Robertson Mrs Margaret (wid James) 25 O'Reilly
Robertson P T (Robertson & Henderson) h 20 Victoria ave n
Robertson R A, clerk, 127 King e
Robertson Robert, watchmaker, 69 Wellington n
Robertson Robert, engineer, 86 Peter
Robertson & Robertson (Thomas, Q C, and H H) barristers, Court House *See card*
Robertson Seath, com traveler, 79 Wellington n
Robertson Thomas, Q C, M P (Robertson & Robertson) Rannach Lodge, hd John s
Robertson Wm, ship builder, 50 Burlington w
Robertson William, bookkeeper, 183 Macnab n
Robertson William, tailor, r 87 Hughson n
Robertson Wm, birch beer manf, 44 Hess n
Robertson William, salesman, 96 Queen s
Robinson Miss Annie, matron jail, Barton e
Robinson Chas, laborer, Pine
Robinson Edward, broommaker, 92 Elgin
Robinson Elwood, com traveler, 23 West ave n
Robinson George, bandmaster, 133½ Park n
Robinson I A, discount clerk, Merchants' Bank, 10 Main e
Robinson James, moulder, 200 Barton e
Robinson James, brickmaker, 20 Inchbury s
Robinson John, tinsmith, bds 64 Main w
Robinson John, insurance agent, 168 West ave n
Robinson Mrs Julia, 282 Macnab n
Robinson Mrs Mary (wid Chas) Pine
Robinson R G, cutter, 11 Wilson
Robinson Robert, bricklayer, 91 Wilson
Robinson Samuel, butcher, 37 Wellington n
Robinson Thos, 47 Merrick
Robinson W A, 6 Hannah e
Robinson W H, clerk, 133½ Park n
Robinson Wm, sr, laborer, 72 Catharine s
Robinson Wm, jr, laborer, 70 Catharine s
Robinson Wm, mechanical supt N & N W R, 53 Wilson
Robinson Wm, shoemaker, 58 John s
Robinson Wm, brakeman, 106½ Emerald n
Robinson Wm, policeman, 116 Emerald n
Robinson Wm, bricklayer, 46 Walnut s
Robinson Wm, woodworker, bds Court House hotel
Robinson W W, manager D Moore & Co, h 39 East ave s
Robson Andrew, bricklayer, 148 John n
Robson James, brakeman, 73 Colborne
Robson Mrs James, 39 Picton w
Robson Robert, laborer, 83 Market
Robson Robert E, painter, 170 Bay n
Robson Wm, carpenter, 166 Victoria ave n
Robitaille Frederick, laborer, 291 James n
Rock Thomas, druggist, 124 Wilson
Rock Michael, harness maker, 76 Caroline n
Roderick John, tailor, 136 John n
Rodgers Alex, boiler maker, Maple

Rodgers James H, baker, 117 York
Rodgers John, blacksmith, 26 Bay n, h 48 Market
Rodgers Patrick, laborer, 168 Catharine n
Rodgers Samuel, laborer, Ferrie e
Rodway, Wm, bds 51 Ray s
Rodwell Wm, painter, 41 Hunter e
Roe George, tailor and clothes cleaner, 185 King e
Roehm Lawrence, tailor, 110 John s
Roehmer Mrs Amelia (wid Louis) 70 Cherry
Rogers Charles, laborer, 110 Queen n
Rogers Henry, gardener, Wilson, e Wentworth
Rogers James, plasterer, 128½ Emerald n
Rogers Joseph, nail cutter, bds 81 Stuart w
Rogers Robt, blacksmith, 46 Magill
Rogers Samuel C, manager Hart Machine Co, 75 Hunter w
Rogers Mrs Sarah, 92 West ave n
Rogers Mrs Sarah, 137 John s
Rogers Wm, 17 Elgin
Rohr Mrs K (wid Fred) 28 Canada
Rolls Samuel S, carriage trimmer, 130 Hunter e
Rolls W T, laborer, 237 Hughson n
Rolston Alexander, bds 18 Gore
Rolston Joseph, collector, bds 50 West ave n
Rolston Wm, Bell Telephone operator
Roman Catholic Bishop's Palace, 25 Sheaffe
Roman Henry, brickmaker, King w
Roman James, broom maker, 63 Rebecca
Rome George, cabinet maker, bds Court House hotel
Ronald John W, carpenter, 150 Napier
Ronald William, grocer, 20 York, h 37 Bay n
Ronald William, engineer, 127 Cannon e
Ronan John, grocer, Cannon cor Wellington
Ronan Patrick, flour and feed, 2 Market Square, h 136 Cannon e
Roney Albert E, tailor, 52 Walnut s
Rooks David, melter, 99 Wellington n
Rooney John, hostler, Dufferin House
Roos Louis, com traveler, 53 James s
Roper Mrs Elizabeth Ann (wid John H) 130 Bay s
Rose Christian, furrier, bds 24 Hunter e
Rose Miss F A M, agent Parker's steam dye works, 4 John n
Rose James, toll gate keeper, Main e
Rose Silas, hair dresser, 7 Macnab n
Rose Solomon, traveler, 30 East ave s
Rosebrugh J W, M D, 52 James s
Rosenstadt Mrs T, second-hand dealer, 32 King Wm
Rosenthal Barnard, button hole operator, bds 103 Main w
Ross Alex (Ross Bros) h 68 Colborne
Ross Andrew, com traveler, 143 Main e
Ross Andrew, carriage maker, 167 King e, h 39 Victoria ave n
Ross Bros (Alex, James W and Joseph T) decorative and plain painters) 1 Main w
Ross C H, clerk, 16 Ray s
Ross David, 67 Queen n

Ross David, bricklayer, 42 West ave n

Ross David, compositor, 42 West ave n

Ross Mrs E, dressmaker, 9 Cannon e

Ross E D, salesman, 83 Wellington n

Ross Fred, shoemaker, 73½ West ave n

Ross Fred B, student, bds 16 Ray s

Ross Fred H, bookkeeper, 83 Wellington n

Ross Frederick L V, shoemaker, 73 West ave n

Ross George, clerk P O, 24 Emerald n

Ross James, laborer, 282 King w

Ross James W (Ross Bros) h Bartonville

Ross John, laborer, 39 Victoria ave n

Ross John, head master Victoria school, 83 Wellington n

Ross John, blacksmith, 14 Inchbury s

Ross Joseph, blacksmith, 173 King e

Ross Joseph T (Ross Bros) h King, e Hamilton

Ross R M, painter, 66 Wellington n

Ross Mrs Sarah (wid Louis) 34 Barton e

Ross S F, deputy collector Inland Revenue, 16 Ray s

Ross Wm L, law student, bds 16 Ray s

Rosseaux J B, bookkeeper, 42 Vine

Rosseaux John B, detective, 42 Kelly

Rousseaux J M (J M Rousseaux & Co) h 101 James s

Rousseaux J M & Co, grocers, 76 King e

Rostadt Edward, com traveler, bds 53 John s

Roth George, cabinet maker, 97 King e

Roth Mrs Kate, 147 Wellington

Rothwell Benjamin, moulder, 112 Victoria ave n

Rotterdam Steamship Line, Wm Herman, agent, 16 James s

Roupell Lawrence, laborer, 227 Main w

Rous James, boiler maker, bds 133 West ave n

Rouse Alfred, fireman, 37½ Steven

Rouse John, porter, 44 King e

Rouse John, shipper, 37 Steven

Routh Mrs E R, 55½ Mary

Routh John T, insurance ag't, 16 James s, h 194 Macnab n

Rowan Anthony, laborer, 64 Young

Rowan Mrs Catharine (wid Thos) bds 26 Hess n

Rowan John, pedler, 28 Charles

Rowan John, barber, 6 Merrick, h 25 Catharine n

Rowan Martin, laborer, 101 Maria

Rowan Robert, laborer, 62½ Young

Rowe Mrs Elizabeth (wid Morton) 135 Park n

Rowe Frank, polisher, 143 Mary

Rowe James, florist, bds 65 Hannah w

Rowe Jeremiah, mason, Ashley

Rowe John N, stonecutter, Locke s

Rowe Miss L, milliner, 90 King e, h 51 Catharine n

Rowe Mrs Mary, (wid Richard) florist, 65 Hannah w

Rowe Richard, grocer, cor Ferguson and Ferrie

Rowe Mrs Sarah (wid William) 51 Catharine n

Rowe W H, manager Co-operative Printing Co, 92 King e, h 23 Steven

Rowe William, stonecutter, bds Locke s
Rowland Wm, lumber measurer, 121 Wellington n
Rowlin Francis, sausage casing manf, 261 Barton e
Roy Alex W, accountant Ham Prov and Loan Society, 7 Duke
Roy Mrs Annie (wid Robert) 7 Duke
Roy Ormiston G, clerk, 7 Duke
Royal Canadian Fire Insurance Co, Seneca Jones, agent, 59 James n
Royal Canadian Insurance Co (Marine) J B Fairgrieve, agent, 59 James n
Royal Hotel, Hood & Bro, props, 63 James n
Royal Insurance Co, David McLellan, agent, 84 James n, *See advt back cover*
Royal Mrs Jane (wid Edward) bds 52 Ray n
Royal Laundry, 14 Arcade
Royal Wm, carriage maker, 52 Ray n
Royal Templars of Temperance, Dominion Council, J H Land, sec, head office, James corner Vine
Royal Templars of Temperance, Ontario, J H, Land, sec, head office, James cor Vine
Rubin Louis, button hole maker, 56 Gore
Rule John R, cutter, 172 York
Rumple Ernest G, carpenter, 16 Sophia n
Rumsey Thomas, polisher, 119 Catharine n
Rush Mrs Elizabeth (wid John) 38 Pearl n
Rush Thomas, laborer, 298 Hughson n
Russ Ami, ragman, bds Robinson
Russ Levi, ragdealer, Robinson w of Locke
Russell A G, jeweler, 94 Wilson
Russell & Dunn (Wm Russell, John Dunn) general agents, 9 Market
Russell Miss Ellen, organist, bds 60 James s
Russell Felix, laborer, 172 Hunter w
Russell George E, saddler, 73 Markland
Rnssell George, foreman Walker's soap works, 2 Wilson
Russell Henry C, saddler, 74 Markland
Russell James, bookkeeper, 2 Wilson
Russell James, laborer, 86 Macauley e
Russell James, stonecutter, 75 Pearl n
Russell James, bookkeeper, Mary cor Wilson
Russell John, laborer, West, King w
Russell John, laborer, 127 Hunter
Russell Mrs Mary (wid Moses) Maple
Russell Richard, manf jeweler, 15 King w, h hd James s
Russell Richard, jr, com traveler, hd James s
Russell S M, polisher, 101 Victoria ave n
Russell Victor, carpenter, 20 Barton w
Russell Westlake, glassblower, bds 365 James n
Russell Wm, laborer, Robinson
Russell Wm, tobacco manf, King
Russell Wm, laborer, 86 Caroline n
Russell Wm, (Russell & Dunn) general agent, 188 Hughson n
Rutherford Adam (Rutherford & Lester) h 80 Emerald s
Rutherford Adam, laborer, York
Rutherford Mrs Alex, 12 (a) Grove
Rutherford Andrew (Garland & Rutherford) h 144 James s

Rutherford George (J Winer & Co) h Main, e Hamilton

Rutherford James, barber, 69 Stuart w, h 281 James n

Rutherford James A, clerk, bds 12 (a) Grove

Rutherford James B, moulder. 54 Hess n

Rutherford J R, clerk G T R, East Hamilton

Rutherford & Lester (Adam Rutherford, Thos W Lester) insurance agents, 80 King e

Ruthven Andrew, propr Atlantic House, 29 Macnab n

Rutley John, stovemounter, ft Wellington n, w s

Rutredge John, cellarman, bds 143 Bay n

Rutter Theodore, stovemounter, 74 Main w

Ryall Isaac, MD, 71 Main e

Ryan Albert, shoemaker, 131 Rebecca

Ryan Dennis, laborer, Burlington n

Ryan James, tailor, Greig

Ryan James, laborer, 163 Catharine n

Ryan James C, agent, bds 51 Park n

Ryan Jno. librarian Court House, bds 158 Rebecca

Ryan Mrs Mary Ann (wid John) 55 Barton e

Ryan Michael, bricklayer, Burlington n

Ryan Michael, laborer, 65 East ave n

Ryan Mrs, 32 Young

Ryan Philip, shoemaker, 298 John n

Ryan Wm, shoemaker, 71 Peter

Ryan Wm, porter, John n

Ryan —, 23 Elgin

Ryckman David, moulder, 86 West ave n

Ryckman Ed, laborer, 10 Devonport

Ryckman F S, contractor, 35 Walnut s

Ryckman Samuel, conductor G T R, 125 Locke n

Ryckman S S (W H Ryckman & Co) cor Hughson and Augusta

Ryckman W H (W H Ryckman & Co) h 20 Hess s

Ryckman W H & Co, grocers, 62 John s

Ryerson James, carpenter, 46 Locomotive

Rykert Henry, clerk, King e

Rymal Ed, bds 63 Wellington s

Rymal John, com traveler, 60 Bay n

Rymal Miss Margaret, 51 Hess n

Rymal M B, manager Trade association, 24 Macnab n, h 6 Crooks

Rymal Milton, checker G T R, 28 Strachan w

Rymal Mrs Nelson, 63 Wellington s

Rymal Stephen, cooper, bds Court House hotel

St Charles Restaurant, H C Hickok, propr, 64 James n

St James' Reformed Episcopal Church, Hunter cor Park

St John's Presbyterian Church, Rev Thomas Goldsmith, pastor, Emerald cor King

St Joseph's Church, (Roman Catholic) Jackson cor Charles

St Luke's Church, Rev Wm Massey, M A, curate, John cor Macaulay

S Mark's Church, (Episcopal) Rev R G Sutherland, rector, Bay cor Hunter

St Mary's Church, (Roman Catholic) Park cor Sheaffe

St Mary's Orphan Asylum, Park cor Colborne

St Nicholas Hotel, Alex Dunn, propr, 33-41 James n

St Patrick's Church, King cor Victoria ave
St Paul's Presbyterian Ch, Rev R J Laidlaw, pastor, James cor Jackson
St Thomas' Church, Rev W B Curran, rector, Main cor West ave
Sachs Adam, grocer, 55 Locke s
Sadleir C A, barrister, 8 Main e
Sage James, carpenter, 18 Blythe
Sala Claude, draughtsman, 127 Locke n
Sallaway George, telegraph operator, 39 Ray n
Salisbury Benjamin, saddler, 2 Elgin
Salisbury Benjamin, saddler, 61 Locomotive
Salmon George, caretaker Canada Life building
Salter Francis, laborer, 62 Locomotive
Salter George, laborer, 9 Hunter w
Salvation Army barracks, 1 Ferguson ave
Sammons Martin, gardener, 45 Hess n
Sandercock John, tinsmith, 21 Locomotive
Sandercock Thomas, machinist, 8 Magill
Sandercock Wm, boilermaker, 28 Inchbury n
Sanders Brownlow, organist, 286 Bay n
Sanders James W, japanner, 47 Elgin
Sanders John, laborer, Nightingale
Sanders Mrs Sarah (wid Henry) 286 Bay n
Sanders Wm A, baker, 73 East ave n
Sandyford Place, s s Duke, bet Macnab and Park
Sanford W E, (W E Sanford & Co) h Jackson cor Caroline
Sanford W E & Co, manufacturers of clothing, 45-9 King e
Sanger Eli, laborer, 53 Stuart e
Sangster J W, com traveler, 118 James n
Sangster Mrs Mary (wid Wm) 130 Wellington n
Santee E B, tinsmith, 87 King Wm
Santry Mrs Margaret, 12 Aurora
Santzburg Charles, 147 John n
Sarginson Mrs Elizabeth (wid John) 66 Walnut s
Saunders John, painter, 151 Bay n
Saunders J H, cook, 50 Cannon w
Saunders Mrs Kate, 230 Cannon e
Saunders Philip, laborer, 217 Main w
Saunders Samuel, traveler, 9 Caroline n
Saunders W C, saloon keeper, 14 King w
Saunders —, carpenter, 144 Rebecca
Savage Edmund, bookkeeper, 95 Bay s
Savage John, machinist, 117 Wellington n
Sawyer Mrs Jane (wid Samuel) 30 Jackson w
Sawyer L D (L D Sawyer & Co) 114 Macnab s
Sawyer L D & Co (L D Sawyer, Henry P Coburn, Jonathan Ames and A H Hope) n e cor Wellington and G T R
Sawyers Elzer, shoemaker, 242 Cannon e
Sayman Aaron, umbrella maker, 147 James n
Sayers Albert, musician, 141 John n
Sayman Charles, carpenter, 186 King Wm
Sayers Charles, shipper, Hannah w

Sayers Chas H, stove polish and extracts manfr, 32 Ray n
Sayers E A, clerk, cor King and Emerald
Sayers H R, bookkeeper, King cor Emerald
Sayers Jas, laborer, 1 Jones
Sayers Mrs —, 282 King e
Sayley Stephen, laborer, 35 Picton e
Sayers Wm. laborer, Oxford
Sayers Wm, laborer, 220 York
Sayers —, laborer bds 167 Macnab n
Saxby Stephen, laborer, 118 Wood e
Saxton Francis, laborer, cor Ferguson ave and Simcoe
Seadding Mrs Marianne, 27 Main w
Scantlon Patrick, laborer, bds 250 James n
Scarlett David, tobacco roller, 58 Ray n
Schadel Fred, blacksmith, 188 Main w
Schadel Henry, tobacco roller, r 81 Caroline n
Schaer H F, machinist, 85 Jas n, h 59 Ray n
Schaffer Miss Louisa, 83 Rebecca
Scheck August, piano maker, bds 26 Devonport
Scheck Louis, carpenter, 26 Devonport
Schelling Bernhardt, machinist, 126 Rebecca
Schelter Frederick, grocer, cor Ferguson ave n and Picton
Scheuer Benno, bookkeeper, 21 Augusta
Scheuer Edmund (Levy Bros & Scheuer) h 88 James s
Schierstein Mrs Catharine M (wid John F) 66 Robinson
Schlessing Carl, machinist, 255 James n
Schneider Peter, broommaker, 71 Vine
Schrader Frederick J, tobacconist, 91 Bay n
Schrader J C, cigar maker, 95 Cannon w, h 95 Bay n
Scragg George, moulder, 22 Inchbury s
Scragg John, moulder, 22 Inchbury s
Schram John, com traveler, 114 York
Scriven P L, engraver, 2½ James s, h 111 Jackson w
Scriven Mrs Mary J (wid Benjamin) 117 Market
Scriver Robert, boiler maker, 26 Canada
Schou Andrew, laborer, 43 Tisdale
Schuler Christian, whip maker, 51 Robert
Schwab Jacob, laborer, Bruce
Schwarz & Co, tobacconists, 4 James n
Schwarz Edward, shoemaker, 36 Walnut s
Schwarz Ernst L (Frederick Schwarz & Son) h 82 Market
Schwarz Frederick (Frederick Schwarz & Son) h 82 Market
Schwarz Frederick & Son (Frederick and Ernst L) cigar manfs, 3 Bay n
Schwarz John, com traveler, 43 Bay n
Schwarz Louis, tobacconist, 48 James n, h 50 Catharine n
Schwarz Wm, cutter, 36 Walnut s
Schevling Henry, laborer, bds 230 Bay n
Schwendau A J, clerk, 14 East ave n
Schwendau Alphons, trimmer, bds 14 East ave n
Scofield Julius, bookkeeper, 109 John s
Scollard John, butcher, 10 West ave n, h 1 Wentworth n
Scott Mrs Agnes (wid Robert) 73 Hunter w

Scott Alfred, clerk, bds 184 Robert e
Scott Mrs Christina (wid John) 75 Market
Scott C S (John Stuart, Son & Co) 104 Park s
Scott Ephraim, civil engineer, bds 127 John n
Scott George, porter, 54 Hannah w
Scott Isaac, horse trainer, bds Bawden's hotel
Scott James, painter, 127 Emerald n
Scott James, fancy goods, 54 King e, h 50 Ferguson ave
Scott John, porter, bds 70 Duke
Scott John J (Walker & Scott) barrister, h 35 Jackson w
Scott Richard, miller, 118 Hunter w
Scott Richard, teamster, 31 Guise
Scott Robert, machinist, Robinson
Scott Samuel, grocer, 184 Robert e
Scott Somner, 105 Park s
Scott S R, grocer, 184 Robert e
Scott Thos L, clerk, 73 Hunter w
Scott Terence, teamster, Jones
Scott T W, Empire House, 16 Market sq
Scott Walter, engineer, 261 Bay n
Scott W, shoemaker, 32 James s
Scott Wm, porter, 44 Hess s
Scott Wm, porter, 89 Hannah w
Scott Wm, shirt cutter, 65 Ray s
Scott Wm, bartender, bds 158 King w
Scottish Union National Insurance Co, James Walker, 20 Main e
Scoular Rev Thos, pastor Erskine Church, 160 Main w
Scully Kenneth, bds 81 Park n
Schultz Ernest, tinsmith, 16 Lower Cathcart
Schultz Maximilian, engineer, 84 Macauley e
Schumacher Geo, cabinet maker, 78 Macnab n
Sealey W A, carpenter, 25 Barton w
Sealey Wm, laborer, Maple
Seaman John, mason, bds 259 King Wm
Seaman Shadrick, 29 West ave n
Searle Henry, machinist, 219 John n
Searle Stephen, carpenter, 159 Mary
Searles George, laborer, Clark ave
Searles Henry, laborer, Ferrie e
Searles Thos C, wood turner, 127 Queen s
Seaton Wm, machinist, 20 Hughson n, h 22 Little Market
Seavey J R, artist, 7 King w
Seddon James, dyer, Picton e
Seelbech Mrs B (wid Wm) 82 Murray e
Sehwenger Chas, carpenter, bds 216 King w
Schwinger John, baker, 44 Ray s
Seitz John, telegraph operator, 138 Macnab n
Selback Louis, biscuit maker, 132 Catharine n
Seldon R W, grocer, 86 Cannon e
Sellar James, laborer, r 71 Wellington s
Selvin Mrs Jane, 202 Barton e
Selwood Thomas W, machinist, 36 Charles
Semmens Arthur W (Semmens Bros) h 44 Markland
Semmens Bros, coffin manfrs, Sophia n
Semmens Jas (Semmens Bros) h 3 Tom
Semmens Mrs Mary (wid John) 86 Florence
Semmens Thos, painter, 7 Pearl n
Sendell Wm S, carpenter, 10 Charles, h 31 Napier

Senn George, foreman, 52 Park n
Serbert Charles, cigar maker, bds 37 Robert
Service Joseph R, fireman, 120 Emerald n
Servos Ethelbert, bailiff, 127 Main w
Servos Joseph, fireman, 120 Emerald n
Servos Miss Mary, 92 Robert e
Servos Wm, 115 Main e
Servos W G, brakeman, 75 East ave n
Setzkorn Frederick, engineer, 116 Caroline s
Sevier Edward, letter carrier, 93 Jackson e
Sewell Bros (Henry, Wm and John A) grocers, 32 James n
Sewell Henry W (Sewell Bros) h. 47 Bay s
Sewell John A (Sewell Bros) 47 Bay s
Sexsmith George S, cutter, 50 Emerald s
Sexton Matthew, laborer, 37 Strachan e
Seymour Mrs Isabella (wid Robt) 12 Colborne
Shadbolt John, cabinet maker, 48 Queen s
Shadbolt Thomas, carpenter, 48 Queen s
Shackle Thomas, conductor, 236 Bay n
Shackleton Freeman, laborer, 95 Ferrie e
Shaldrick Richard, carter, r 68 Caroline n
Shambrook George, bookkeeper, 9 Erie ave
Sharkey Geo. caretaker R C cemetery, Head
Sharp Arthur, cabinet maker, 99 Lower Cathcart
Sharpe F H, machinist, 22 Erie ave
Sharp George, builder, 147 Park n
Sharp George, carpenter, 49½ Hunter e
Sharp Henry, carpenter, 46 Cherry
Sharp John W, carpenter, 144½ Bay n
Sharp Mrs Martha (wid William) 43 Lower Cathcart
Sharp William, baker, 106 John s
Sharp William, assessor, 5 Queen s
Sharples James, yardsman, 134 Robert e
Shaughnessy Martin, machinist, 101 Strachan e
Shaughnessy Wm, laborer, 177 Wilson
Shaver W H (W H Tallman & & Co) res Ancaster
Shaw Andrew, laborer, 296 John n
Shaw Mrs Elizabeth (wid James) 18 Grove
Shaw George, M D, 122 James n
Shaw George, gardener, 99 Caroline s
Shaw James, machinist, 59 Chisholm
Shaw Mrs John, 13 Gore
Shaw Joseph W, plasterer, 219 Main w
Shaw Mrs; matron Boys' Home, Stinson
Shaw Wm, bds 20 Hunter e
Shawcross Wm, tea merchant, 1 King Wm, h Garth
Shea Mrs Ann (wid John) 36 Strachan e
Shea James, staple and fancy dry goods. 42 King e, h 124 Hughson n
Shea James, shoe cutter, 6 Ferguson ave
Shea John, machinist, 109½ John s
Shea John, laborer, bds 95 George
Shea Mrs, 74 West ave n

Shea John F, boots and shoes, 40 King e, h 124 Hughson n
Shea Michael, laborer, bds 146 Bay n
Shea Patrick, blacksmith, 48 Emerald n
Shea Patrick, grocer, 258 York
Shea Thomas, laborer, 95 George
Shearer James, carpenter, 117 Rebecca
Shearer J H, file grinder, 163 Wellington n
Shearer Samuel, laborer, 273 Macnab n
Shearsmith F G, carpenter, 77 Wilson
Shearsmith Wm, com traveler, 275 King e
Shedden Co (The) James Hamilton, agent, 9 King w
Sheehan John, com traveler, 5 Little Peel
Sheehan John, 124 Young
Sheehan John, teamster, 306 John n
Sheehan Patrick, machinist, 5 Little Peel
Sheehan Timothy, laborer, 96 Maria
Sheen Miss Mary, 115 Caroline n
Sheet George, moulder, 74 Emerald n
Sheppard Alfred, bds 133 Park n
Shepard Mrs Catharine (wid Wm L) bds 99 Market
Sheppard Edward, bds 82 Hughson n
Sheppard Edward, ,carpenter, 137 Catharine n
Sheppard Francis, custom officer, 133 Park n
Shepard Mrs Harriet E (wid Gideon R) boarding, 49 Caroline n
Shepard H C, salesman, 99 Market
Shepherd Mrs Jane (wid Ralph) 40 Bay n
Sheppard Mrs John, Barton w nr Caroline
Sheperley Joseph, potter, 48 Pearl s
Sheppard Mrs Mary, 132 Macnab n
Sheridan Mrs Ann (wid Patrick) boarding, 185 Bay n
Sheridan John, laborer, 183 Mary
Sheridan T J, spring beds and sewing machines, 184 King e
Sheriff Mrs Margaret (wid Alex) 96 Bay n
Sheriff Wm, grocery, 96 Bay n
Sherman Jas, 160 Rebecca
Shetman Knighton, button hole maker, 104 Jackson e
Sherren Robert, coachman, 107 Jackson w
Sherring John C, plasterer, 97 Caroline n
Shibley Mrs Emily (wid Edwin) 35 Catharine n
Shields Mrs Charles, 52 Catharine s
Shields Charles, pedlar, 11 George
Shields James, com traveler, 273 King e
Shields John, 97 West ave n
Shields John, laborer, 41 Caroline n
Shields J W, com traveler, h King e
Shields Thomas, blacksmith, 86 Bold
Shields William, laborer, r 44 Jackson e
Shine Patrick, hair dresser, 7 Macnab n
Shipton Mrs Maggie (wid John) 7 Cherry
Shipley Vincent, laborer, Duke
Shoots George, carriage painter, 67 Merrick, h 153 Cannon e
Shoots James, carriage trimmer, 97 Lower Cathcart
Short Mrs M A, 45 Macauley w
Short William, machinist, 31 Catharine n
Shouldice J H, hotel, 99 John s

Shuttle James, fitter, 132 Macauley e
Shuttleworth William, salesman, 16 Grove
Shuttleworth Wm, upholsterer, bds Walker House
Siddell Hiram, laborer, 304 Hughson n
Siddell Hiram, laborer, 135 Macauley e
Siddel James, joiner, 104 East ave n
Sievert Augustus W, cabinet maker, 58 Pearl n
Sillett George, cooper, 70 Rebecca
Sillett Jasper, 70 Rebecca
Silver Charles J, bookkeeper, 124 John n
Silver Creek Brewery, C A Burdon, agent, 11 Jackson e
Silver William, manf boots and shoes, 83 Macnab n, h 27 Murray e
Simcoe Street Methodist Church, Rev Joseph Oderey, pastor, John cor Simcoe
S'me James, plater, 167 West ave n
Simkins George, painter, South w
Simmnnds John, laborer, 223 John n
Simmons Oliver, moulder, 10 Chisholm
Simmons —, 7 Wood e
Simms David, laborer, 67 East ave n
Simon Abram, confectioner, 210 James n
Simon Henry, cigar manf, 36 Merrick, h 12 Augusta
Simon Mrs M, grocer, 62 James s
Simonds Mrs H C (wid Harry) 151 Main w
Simons Charles, laborer, 1 South
Simons Charles, tailor, 242 York
Simons Mis Gharles, confectioner, 242 York
Simons Richard, laborer, 235 John n

Simons Thomas, 115 Wellington n
Simple William, laborer, 32 Macauley e
Sims Samuel, shoemaker, 12 West ave n
Simpson Arch T, clerk, 62 Merrick
Simpson Charles W, carpenter 8 O'Reilly
Simpson Frank, clerk G T R, 20 Locomotive
Simpson Mrs Francis (wid Rev M) 29 Jackson w
Simpson George, moulder, 70 Emerald n
Simpson James, porter, Maple Leaf hotel
Simpson James & Son (James and James, jr) brokers and com merchants, 22 Main e, h 62 Merrick
Simpson Mrs Jeannette (wid Wm) part of Bawden's house, Canada
Simpson John, baker, 68 Lower Cathcart
Simpson John, cigar maker, 84 Cherry
Simpson John, laborer, bds 49 Caroline n
Simpson John, salesman, 30 King w
Simpson Joseph B, conductor G T R, 2 Canada
Simpson J W, com merchant, 4 Hughson n, h 55 Hughson n
Simpson M, bookkeeper, h Beulah
Simpson Maltyward, accountant, Beulah
Simpson Philip H, law student, 29 Jackson w
Simpson Samuel, engineer, 96 Catharine n
Simpson Thomas, moulder, Duke w Locke
Simpson Thos, 171 Park n
Simpson W G, salesman, 30 King w

Simpson Wm, checker GTR, 100 Hunter w
Simpson Wm, moulder, 37 Stuart e
Simpson —, laborer, 41 Tisdale
Sinage Wm, shoe cutter, 43 Mary
Sinclair Alex,painter,bds 12 Little William
Sinclair Duncan, clerk Bank of Montreal, 33 Hannah e
Sinclair David, janitor Hamilton Provident & Loan Society, 1 Hughson n
Sinclair Duncan, student, 54 Hannah w
Sinclair Edward, brakesman, 106 Hess n
Sinclair George, carpenter, r 51 Hunter e
Sinclair James S, county judge, Court House, h 23 Herkimer
Sinclair J G, D D S, dentist, 22 King e, h 19 Maria
Sinclair J Herbert, law student, 23 Herkimer
Sinclair Jas W, grocer, 59 Canada
Sinclair J W, painter, 124 East ave n
Sinclair John, caretaker, 12 Little William
Sinclair Mrs Maria (wid Joseph) 115 Catharine n
Sinclair Mrs Mary (wid George) 51 Hunter e
Sinclair Peter, laborer, 14 Grove
Sinclair Peter G, gardener, 55 Charles
Sinclair William, laborer, 8 Devonport
Singer Manufacturing Co, 10 John n
Sinker John, laborer, 127 Queen n
Sinnott James, moulder, 81 Main e
Sintzel John, tailor, 12 John s, h 18 Liberty
Sintzel Thomas, 49½ Augusta
Sieuter Anderew, bds Franklin House
Skelly Dennis, 59 Ferguson ave
Shaftesbury Boys' Home, Robert Ward, supt, King e near toll gate
Skelly E J, clerk, 61 Ferguson ave
Skelly Frank E (F E Skelly & Co) 215 York
Skelly F E & Co (F E Skelly, C R Perkins, J E Skelly) dry goods, 215 York
Skerritt John, boots and shoes, 64 King w, h 226 Main w
Skilling John, carpenter, bds 60 James s
Skimin James, iron founder, Queen n, h 57 Queen n
Skinner Mrs A F, Fairleigh Park, Main e
Skinner Edward, laborer, 71 Cherry
Skinner Hugh, clerk, Fairleigh Park, Main e
Skinner James A & Co, wholesale crockery, 9 King e
Skinner John, watchmaker and jeweler, 79 King w
Skinner R B (Jas A Skinner & Co) h Fairleigh Park, Main e
Skinner R H, clerk, Fairleigh Park, Main e
Skinner Seymour, laborer, 14 Margaret
Skinner Thomas, laborer, 112 Cherry
Skirrow Frederick, laborer, 100 Ferrie e
Skolv Mrs Francis (wid Anthony) 151 Catharine n
Skuce Geo, laborer, 6 Kinnell
Slaght Charles, teamster, 51 Sheaffe
Slaght Freeman, agent, 136 Main
Slater James, merchant tailor, 54 King w, h 78 George

Slater John, carpenter, 320 Macnab n
Slater John S, inspector sewers, 110 Wellington s
Slater Mrs Robert, 52 Victoria ave s
Slater Robert, tailor, bds 84 Merrick
Slater Samuel, treasurer Landed Banking & Loan Co, h 129 Bay s
Slatterie James, machinist, bds 109 Bold
Slaughter John, 38 Mulberry
Slee William, carpenter, Ferguson ave n
Slider George, porter, Wood & Leggat
Sloen James, laborer, 28 Magill
Slone Thomas, 36 Elgin
Smale John, 166 Ferguson ave
Smale Wm sr, 86 Elgin
Smale Wm jr, 86 Elgin
Small Alex, shipper, 33½ Tisdale
Small Alex, clerk, mountain top
Small A W, porter, Knox, Morgan & Co
Small Mrs Eliza (wid James) 288 King w
Small Jas, butcher, 320 King w
Small J D, carpenter, Clark ave
Small Thomas, butcher, King e
Small Wm, laborer, King w nr limits
Smallwood George, tobacconist, 118 James n
Smart W L, 114 Park s
Smee Edmund, shoemaker, 44 Young
Smethurst William G, Markland
Smiley Miss Rebecca, Concession cor Queen
Smith A B, telegraph operator, 21 Walnut s
Smith Albert N, printer, 2 Wellington n
Smith Alex, police sergeant No 2 Station
Smith Alex K, teamster, 314 King w
Smith Alfred E, bricklayer, 18 Margaret
Smith Alfred W, bookkeeper, 15 East ave n
Smith Alonzo, blacksmith, 2 Little William
Smith Arthur, laborer, 68 Tisdale
Smith Beverley, student, 31 Bay n
Smith Charles, blacksmith, 13 Cannon w
Smith Charles city messenger, 2 Wellington n
Smith Charles, lithographer, 68 Walnut s
Smith Charles, moulder, 46 Market
Smith Charles, stove polisher, 32 Breadalbane
Smith Charles, tailor, 39 Catharine n
Smith Charles, jr, paper boxes, 5 King w, h 2 Wellington n
Smith Mrs Charles, 176 East ave n
Smith C L, builder, 84 Elgin
Smith C R, commission merchant, 8 John n, h 25 West ave s
Smith Chas W, 30 Magill
Smith Mrs Charlotte (wid James) 66 Ray n
Smith D B, tailor, 116 Rebecca
Smith D Day, MD, druggist, 214 King e
Smith Donald, mercht tailor, 14 James n, h Avon Cottage, Main e
Smith Mrs E, 16 Steven
Smith Edward, whip maker, 109 Cannon w
Smith Edward, 2 Wellington n
Smith Edwin J, carpenter, 162 Macnab n
Smith Mrs Eliza, 172 Hughson n
Smith Mrs Eliza (wid David A) 48 West ave s

Smith Miss Elizabeth, MD, physician and surgeon, 16 Main w
Smith E P, com traveler, 14 Emerald s
Smith Erskine, bricklayer, 5 Chisholm
Smith Mrs Esther (wid Joseph) 159 King Wm
Smith Francis, moulder, 18 Simcoe e
Smith Frank W, clerk Ham Prov and Loan Society, 14 Emerald s
Smith Frank, glassblower, 311 John n
Smith Frank, laborer, 95 King e
Smith Frank, porter, 37 Kelly
Smith Fred J, packer, 196 Main w
Smith & Findlay (W G Smith, John Findlay) saloon keepers, James cor Merrick
Smith G A, bricklayer, 56 Lower Cathcart
Smith George B, wood and coal dealer, 6 Mary, h 297 Barton e
Smith George, carpenter, 11 Colborne
Smith George, dealer, 61 Rebecca, h 15 East ave n
Smith George, cigar maker, 142 West ave n
Smith George, cigar maker, 62 Cannon e
Smith George, laborer, Wilson e Wentworth
Smith George, laborer, 76 Murray e
Smith Geo, laborer, 26 Tom
Smith George, painter, 144 King William
Smith George, shoe cutter, 45 Napier
Smith George, tinsmith, bds 105 King w
Smith George, 15 East ave n
Smith H, crockery, end King e
Smith H, stove dealer, 66 John s, h 57 Robert e
Smith H E, laborer, 196 Robert e
Smith Mrs Helen (wid James) 81 Maria
Smith Henry, laborer, 36 Stuart e
Smith Henry, shoemaker, Wentworth n
Smith Henry, tinsmith, 57 Robert
Smith Mrs Hugh, 35 Burlington w
Smith Jacob, engine driver, 65 Napier
Smith Jacob J, foreman W G Reid & Co, 34 East ave n
Smith James, blacksmith, 279 Hughson n
Smith James, boot crimper, 27 Peter
Smith James, carpenter, Beulah
Smith James, carpenter, 59 Pearl n
Smith James, gilder, 66 Hannah w
Smith James, machinist, 25 Cannon w
Smith James, moulder, 43 Peter
Smith Jas, moulder, 163 John n
Smith Mrs James, Turkish baths, 145 James n
Smith Mrs James, 74 Wilson
Smith James Blois, day and evening school, 1 Rebecca
Smith James B, laborer, 326 York
Smith James O, blacksmith, 65 Emerald n
Smith Mrs Jane (wid Samuel) 40 Market
Smith John, baker, 75 Jackson e
Smith John, blacksmith, bds 90 Bay n
Smith John, bricklayer, 20 Chisholm
Smith John, immigration agt, Stuart w, h 131 Bay s
Smith John, laborer, 31 Wood e
Smith John, laborer, 230 Bay n
Smith John, tailor, Concession
Smith John, teamster, 69 Lower Cathcart

Smith John, tinsmith, 43 Hughson n
Smith John J, laborer, Herkimer w
Smith Mrs J L, 23 Main w
Smith John M, carpenter, 308 James n
Smith John S, laborer, York w of toll gate
Smith John W, foreman Imperial Mineral Water Co, 54 Pearl s
Smith Joseph, confectioner, 97 Emerald n
Smith Joseph, cabinet maker, 30 Charles
Smith Levis, stovemounter, 86 Hannah e
Smith Mrs Louisa, 204 Barton e
Smith L C, barrister, 34 James n, h 8 Nelson ave
Smith Mrs Margaret (wid David) 27 Peter
Smith Mark, confectioner, 154 York
Smith Mrs, 51 Macnab s
Smith Mrs, caretaker, Wentworth Chambers, 25 James s
Smith Mrs Martha (wid John) variety dealer, 225 James n
Smith Mrs Mary (wid George) 25 Cannon w
Smith Mrs Mary (wid John) 191 James n
Smith Mrs Mary (wid John) 154 Rebecca
Smith Mrs Mary (wid Peter) 90½ Hess n
Smith Philip, barber, 172 Hughson n
Smith Richard, whip maker, 112½ East ave n
Smith R J, com traveler, 27 Tisdale
Smith Robert, baker, 60 John s
Smith Robt, carpenter, 43 Ferrie w
Smith Robert, laborer, 109 West ave n
Smith Robert, laborer, 28 Macauley e
Smith Robert, polisher, 281 King William
Smith R T, baggageman, 168 Mary
Smith Samuel, glassblower, 310 John n
Smith Samuel, laborer, Main e, opp toll gate
Smith Stephen, laborer, 9 Picton w
Smith Mrs Sarah M (wid Geo) 60 Jackson w
Smith Mrs Sarah (wid Wm) 230 King w
Smith Sylvester, bds 16 Main w
Smith Mrs Susan (wid Thomas) 85 Rebecca
Smith Theodore, fireman, 30 Bay n
Smith Thomas, bookkeeper, bds cor Mary and Robert
Smith Thos, brakesman G T R, r 124 Queen n
Smith Thomas, builder, 74 Catharine n
Smith Thomas, feather dyer, 110 King William, h 93 King William
Smith Thomas, laborer, Garth
Smith Thomas, laborer, 278 Macnab n
Smith Thos, r 164 Wilson
Smith Mrs Thomas, 61 West ave n
Smith V, clerk Bank of Commerce, bds 61 George
Smith Vincent, broker, 95 King e
Smith William, accountant, 42 Emerald s
Smith William, clerk, bds 74 Catharine n
Smith William, dyer, 95 Robinson
Smith William, laborer, 105 Napier
Smith William, laborer, bds 21 Tisdale
Smith William, laborer, 275 (b) Hughson n

Smith William, laborer, 25 Railway
Smith William, moulder, 80 Caroline n
Smith William, rope maker, 148 Victoria ave n
Smith William, stonemason, 54 Lower Cathcart
Smith William, stovemounter, 102 Young
Smith William, teamster, 177 Rebecca
Smith William, traveler, 173 King Wm
Smith Wm, 31 Margaret
Smith Mrs William, 142 West ave n
Smith Wm A, high constable, 10 Little Peel
Smith W B, planer, 190 Emerald
Smith Williamm G, laborer, 32 Augusta
Smith W L, M D, druggist, 116 James n
Smith William P, packer, 133 Market
Smith Wm S, com traveler, 220 Catharine n
Smith Wright, harness maker, 143 Duke
Smye Joseph, wagon maker, 34 Hunter e, h 56 Catharine s
Smye William, collar maker, 99 Rebecca
Smyth J C, manager Canada Glass House, h 182 King e
Smyth J S, polisher, 39 Steven
Smyth Robert, tinsmith, 24 King William
Snaith William, butcher, 172 King e
Snaudee James, printer, 20½ Locke s
Snaudee Mrs Jane (wid James) 20½ Locke s
Snaudee David, plumber, 151 King Wm
Snider George H (G H Snider & Co) h 9 Kennell
Snider G H and J A, millers, 278 York
Snider George R, laborer, 113 Locke n
Snider James A (G H Snider & Co) h 12 Crooks
Snider Peter, laborer, 12 George
Snider Miss Sarah, 84 Merrick
Snider Thomas H, baker, 16½ Augusta
Snodgrass Mrs Jeannette (wid Wm) 72 Peter
Snodgrass Mrs, 70 Locke n
Snodgrass Robert, 99 York
Snow C B, manager Ontario Cotton Mills, 17 Robert
Snow David, burnisher, bds 32 John n
Snowden John W, bookkeeper, 48 Hess n
Snowdon Lemuel, cabinet maker, 66 Steven
Snowden Mrs Mary (wid Wm) 48 Hess n
Snowdon Thomas, blacksmith, foot Macnab n, h 19 Burlington w
Sodon Mrs Mary (wid Samuel) 65 Jackson e
Solvisburg John, laborer, Aikman's ave
Solvisburg Nicholas, Aikman's ave
Somers John, laborer, 106 Young
Somerset George, shoemaker, bds 67 Duke
Somerville Francis, laborer, 66 Mulberry
Somerville James, salesman, 158 Main w
Somerville James, painter, King e
Somerville James H, com traveler, 61 Bay s
Somerville Robert, carpenter, 61½ East ave n
Somerville William, bookkeeper, 158 Main w
Somerville William, jr, commission merchant, 158 Main w

Somerville Wm & Co, commission merchants, 8 Hughson n
Somerville Wm H, com traveler, 61 Bay s
Soper Robert, sail maker, 54 Burlington w
Souter Alex, cabinet maker, 80 Hannah w
Souter David, carpenter, 80 Hannah w
Souter William, cabinet maker, 80 Hannah w
South Daniel, laborer, 32 Hess n
Southam & Carey (William Southam, William Carey) managing directors *Spectator* Co, 18 James s
Southam William (Southam & Carey) h Bold
Southwell William, machinist, 154 West ave n
Spackman J R, 52 Cannon w
Spackman S G, 79 John n
Spanton Mrs Mary (wid John) 34 Sheaffe
Spectator (daily and weekly) Southam & Carey, managing directors, 18 James s
Speight Charles, carpenter, 9 Park s
Speirs Hamilton, laborer, cor Ferguson ave and Strachan
Spellecy Thomas, broker, 168 King e
Spence Mrs Elizabeth (wid Peter) grocer, 211 John n
Spence George, shoemaker, 46 Hunter e
Spence James, machinist, 131 King Wm
Spence John, bds 29 Gore
Spence Joseph, mariner, 143 East ave n
Spence Matthew, stonecutter, 79 Ferrie e
Spence T (R Spence & Co) h 176½ King e
Spence R & Co, file manfs, 176½ King e
Spence Thomas B, mariner, 20 Sheaffe
Spencer E V, com traveler, 44 Catharine n
Spencer James, tinsmith, 80 Walnut s
Spencer Josiah, stonecutter, 64 Hunter e
Spencer Robert, laborer, 71 Market
Spencer Samuel, laborer, 36 Sheaffe
Spencer Walter, organ builder, 13 Bay n, h 87 Main w
Spera R B, fancy goods, 198 King e
Spera Wm, grain buyer, 28 Liberty
Spera William, grain buyer, 115 Victoria ave n
Spies Rev Chas A, evangelical, 98 Market
Spittle Robert, carpenter, 43 Steven
Spone Warren, tailor, 3 Cherry
Sporr George, 35 Hughson n
Spriggs Charles, laborer, 34 O'Reilly
Spriggs John, shoemaker, 67 York
Spring Brewery, Bay cor Mulberry
Spring James, engine cleaner, 37 Caroline n
Springate George, letter carrier, 61 Ray s
Springate John, laborer, 215 Main w
Springer Lewis, manager street railway, h East Hamilton
Springer Mrs Oliver, 52 John n
Springstead Mrs Ellen, laundress, 124 Macnab n
Springstead Jacob, engineer, 98 West ave n
Springstead S, carpenter 105 Elgin
Springstead Wm, gardener, Burlington n
Squibb Frank, plumber, 39 John s

Stacey John, sawyer, 44 Magill
Stacy James B P, upholsterer, 82 Hunter w
Stacy John C, upholsterer, 99 Hess s
Stacy Mrs M J, 31 Catharine n
Stafford Mrs Catharine (widow Philip) 52 Ferrie
Stafford Mrs Theodore, 32 Jackson e
Stamp Wm, painter, 116 King Wm
Standard Life Assurance Co, David McLellan, agent, 84 James n
Standard Whip Co, H D Baker, 175 James
Stanfield Samuel, laborer, Markland
Stanley George, stovemounter, 121 Hannah e
Stannard William, carpenter, 193 Hughson n
Stanton Green A, tobacco roller, King e
Stanton Thomas, painter, 43 Cherry
Stapleton George, laborer, 14½ Harriet
Stark John, stovemounter, 36 Wilson
Stark John, stovemounter, 208 Cannon e
Stark Wm G, M D, 149 King w
State Steamship Line, Chas E Morgan, agent, 11 James n
Staunton C F Lynch, clerk, Main cor Wentworth
Staunton F H Lynch, P L S, C E, surveyor, 18 James s, h Wentworth cor Main
Staunton & Livingston (Geo Lynch Staunton, W Churchill Livingston) barristers, 18 James s
Staunton Geo Lynch (Staunton & Livingston) h Wentworth cor Main
Staunton John, hotel keeper, 106 King e
Staunton Louis, blacksmith, bds 63 Rebecca
Steanger James, Temperance House, 79 Stuart w
Stebbins John, gardener, Barton e
Steedman James, machinist, 47 Napier
Steedman J P, bookkeeper, h 78 West ave n
Steele David, barrister, King cor James, over Federal Bank, h 51 Jackson w
Steele Mrs David, 54 Hunter w
Steele George, music teacher, 77 Park n
Steele George, dry goods, etc, 291 York
Steele James, laborer, 96 Strachan e
Steele John T, clerk, 80 Hughson n
Steele Robt T (Lucas, Park & Co) h 51 Jackson w
Steele Thos, teacher of vocal music, 105 Main w
Steele Wm, accountant, 67 Victoria ave n
Steer Edward, butcher, 23 South e
Stein James, laborer, Wentworth n
Stein M, jeweler, 68 King e, h 113 Catharine s
Steinberg Max, rag dealer, 106 York
Steinberg Nathan, rag dealer, 167 Main w
Steinmetz Valentine, tailor, 25 Emerald n
Stephens Henry, public accountant, Court House, h 5 West ave s
Stephens Isaac, r 104 Macnab n
Stephens James, moulder, 131 Ferguson ave

Stephens John, machinist, 85 Bold
Stephens Samuel, moulder, 88 Elgin
Stephens Mrs Sarah (wid Jefferson) 94 Elgin
Stephens Thos, machinist, 105 Hunter w
Stephens T L, tailor, 88 Elgin
Stephenson C D, lather, 86 Hunter e
Stephenson Isaac, moulder, 58 Locomotive
Stephenson John M, laborer, 139 Ferguson ave
Stephenson Robert, tinsmith, Ferguson ave n
Stephenson Thomas, harness maker, 58 Hughson s
Sterling Daniel, 7 Bold
Sterling George, 101 Main w
Sterling George A, cashier, 7 Bold
Sterling R N (Alex Harvey & Co) h 34 Jackson w
Sterling Wm, salesman, Bold
Stern Wm, com traveler, 31 Walnut s
Sterratt Wm, policeman G T R, 90 Hess n
Steven H S, assistant cashier Bank of Hamilton, 28 West ave s
Steven Robert, salesman, 15 Upper Cathcart
Stevens Mrs Ann, 126 Young
Stevens C A, porter, 15 Upper Cathcart
Stevens Mrs Eliza (wid John W) 2 Margaret
Stevens Jefferson, carpenter, 267 King w
Stevens Isaac, gardener, 120 James n
Stevens James, 126 Wood e
Stevens James, laborer, 109 Herkimer
Stevens John, painter, 13 Sophia n
Stevens John, baker, 148 Mary

Stevens Nelson, tobacco roller, 125 Mary
Stevens Philip, machinist, 32 Charles
Stevens Mrs Sarah, fancy goods, 120 James n
Stevens Silas, hotel, 352 John n
Stevens Thomas, porter, 7 Evans
Stevens Wm, engineer, 120 James n
Stevenson Alex, plumber, 60 James s
Stevenson Charles H, builder, 46 Wellington s
Stevenson George, baker, etc, 4 Hunter e
Stevenson Gervase, shoemaker, 9 Park s
Stevenson Hugh, salesman, Hughson s
Stevenson James, hay dealer, Duke
Stevenson James, 241 York
Stevenson Mrs Mary (wid And) 121 Market
Stevenson R C, bookkeeper, 15 Elgin
Stevenson Thomas, cabinet maker, 58 Hughson s
Stevenson Thomas, carpenter, 86 Duke
Stevenson William, carpenter, 59 Hunter e
Steward Thomas, salesman, 191 Main e
Stewart A A, bookkeeperr, 221 Main e
Stewart Alexander, tailor, 79 Main e
Stewart Albert A, student, 31 Bay n
Stewart A D, chief of police, 43 Bay s
Stewart Charles (Burrow, Stewart & Milne) h 122 John n
Stewart Charles, carpenter, 124 Cannon e
Stewart Charles, printer, 150 King Wm

Stewart Chas E, clerk, 25 Hunter w
Stewart David, moulder, 295 King William
Stewart Mrs E, millinery, 156 King e
Stewart Edward, hatter, 7 Grove
Stewart Frank, machinist, 21 East ave n
Stewart Gavin, tinsmith, bds 122 John n
Stewart George, laborer, 48 Napier
Stewart Hugh, grocer, 16 Ferguson ave
Stewart Jas, clerk, 81 Catharine s
Stewart James, com traveler, 130 Market
Stewart James, (Fairley & Stewart) h 130 Market
Stewart James (James Stewart & Co) bds Royal hotel
Stewart James & Co, (James Stewart, J F Stewart, W C Stewart, Thos Cook) ironfounders, 65-73 Macnab n
Stewart J D, com traveler, Lucas Park & Co
Stewart Mrs Jenny H, 75 Wellington n
Stewart John, accountant, 47 Duke
Stewart John, bookkeeper, 132 Market
Stewart John, carpenter, 54 Hannah w
Stewart John, clerk G T R, 139 Ferguson ave
Stewart John, 70 Bay s
Stewart John F, (James Stewart & Co) 55 Victoria ave s
Stewart John M, clerk, 88 Victoria ave s
Stewart Rev Joseph W A, Baptist, 107 Main w
Stewart, N L, com traveler, bds 55 Victoria ave s
Stewart Norman, packer, 12 Grove
Stewart Robert, bottler, 27 West ave n
Stewart Robert, (R Stewart & Co) h 186 King e
Stewart Robert, laborer, bds 134 Cannon e
Stewart Robert & Co, grocers, 186 King e
Stewart Robert C, civil engineer, 11 West ave s
Stewart Thomas, 3 East ave n
Stewart Thomas C, com traveler, 7 West ave s
Stewart W F, clerk, 55 Victoria ave s
Stewart W H, clerk, 33 East ave s
Stewart William jr, brushmaker, 7 Grove
Stewart Wm, carpenter, 51 Steven
Stewart Wm, laborer, 57 Pearl n
Stewart William, watchman, 7 Grove
Stewart Wm, watchman, 88 Ferguson ave
Stewart W C, (James Stewart & Co) 25 Hunter w
Stibbs Jesse, laborer, 59½ Wood e
Stickle C H, letter carrier, 50 Wellington n
Stier George, engraver, bds Victoria hotel
Stiff Charles, supt G T R, 140 James s
Stiff George W, clerk, 155 Park n
Stiff James, bookkeeper, 155 Park n
Stillman Charles, machinist, bds 23 Barton e
Stilwell C F, supt Edison Lamp factory, 26 King Wm, h 34 East ave s
Stilwell —, Concession
Stinder Wm, moulder, 25 Chisholm
Stinson's Bank, A H Moore, manager, 10 Hnghson n
Stinson's Chambers, King William cor James

Stinson Frank, porter, 86 Victoria ave n
Stinson James, banker, 100 Queen n
Stinson S C, 195 King e
Stinson T H, solicitor, Stinson's Chambers, 1 King Wm, h 5 Herkimer and 100 Queen n
Stinson Mrs, 116 Macnab s
Stirling Thomas, farmer, 135 Main e
Stirton Thomas, stonecutter, 221 John n
Stirton John, printer, 221 John n
Stits James, moulder, bds 112 Bay n
Stock David, foreman city yard, 16 Emerald n
Stockdale Arthur, tanner, Wentworth n
Stockwell Edward, dyer, 81 King w
Stockwell Mrs Mary (wid Caleb) 81 King w
Stodler Peter, carpet weaver, 53 Tisdale
Stokes Henry, 55 Pearl n
Stokes Thos, carpenter, 1 Hess n
Stokes Thos, carpenter, 5 Margaret
Stokes William, laborer, r 110 Young
Stokes William, mail clerk, 3 Barton Terrace, Wellington n
Stokinger Karl, 105 King Wm
Stone Charles, car cleaner, 56 Ferrie w
Stone Henry H, japanner, 166 West ave n
Stone J C, traveler, 26 Emerald n
Stone J H, manufacturer, h 12 East ave n
Stone Peter, bds 39 John n
Stoneham Job, plasterer, 78 Hunter e
Stoneham Joseph, machinist, 241 Cannon e
Stoneham William, plasterer, 78 Hunter e
Stonehouse Andrew, blacksmith, 36 Lower Cathcart
Stonehouse Michael, shoemaker, 25 Ferguson ave
Stoneman Charles, stonecutter, 35 Queen s
Stoneman Charles P, printer, 59 Young
Stoneman John, com traveler, 42 Victoria ave n
Stoneman Robert R, moulder, 59 Young
Stoner Frank, laborer, 2 Main w
Stoney John L, insurance agent, 44 Herkimer
Storm Edmond A (Storm & Green) 31 Elgin
Storm & Green (Edmond A Storm, Fred A Green) tea merchants, 128½ King e
Storm Mrs Jane (wid Jacob) 31 Elgin
Storror Mrs Ann (wid Wm) 21 Macnab s
Stott Peter, fireman, 184 Catharine n
Stout Thomas, engineer, 7½ Cherry
Strachan Alexander, agent, 167 King Wm
Strachan Thomas, switchman, bds 124 Cannon e
Strachan Thomas, grocer, 119 James n, h 19 Barton e
Strathdee John, salesman, 69 King Wm
Strathroy Knitting Co, Jas Watson, pres; Rupert Watson, sec, 69 James n
Strain George, laborer, 173 Macnab n
Strampel George, laborer, 32 Guise
Stratton Albert H, carpenter, 52 Ferguson ave
Stratton Robert, letter carrier, 52 Ferguson ave
Stratton S J, clerk, 55 Lower Cathcart

Strauss Henry, grocer, 101½ John s
Straws James, machinist, 68 Hunter e
Street John, bricklayer, Wilson e Wentworth
Strickland Arthur, carriage bldr, 19 Napier
Strickland W P, machinist, 31 Emerald n
Stringer —, plater, bds Victoria hotel
Strom Charles, tailor, 93 James n
Strong Wm, insurance agent, Arcade, James n, h 149½ John n *See card*
Strongman Wm, policeman, 76 Hunter e
Strongman Wm, carpenter, 127 Dundurn
Stroud Alfred, hotel, 37 Macnab n
Stroud Alfred (Alfred Stroud & Son) h 7 Cannon w
Stroud George, tanner, 214 Victoria ave n
Stroud John, bartender, 37 Macnab n
Stroud Mrs Mary Ann, 288 York
Stroud's Tannery, Alfred Stroud & Son, props, Ferrie e
Stroud Wm, hide buyer, 62 Vine
Stuart A A, bookkeeper, 221 Main e
Stuart Alex, city chamberlain, 56 Victoria ave s
Stuart Alex, jr, asst treas, city 43 Alanson
Stuart Andrew, ornamenter, r 55 Catharine n
Stuart Mrs Catharine (wid Wm) 92 Wellington s
Stuart Mrs Donald, 90 Hunter e
Stuart James (John Stuart, Son & Co) 9 West ave s
Stuart James M (J M Stuart & Co) 92 James s
Stuart James M & Co, wholesale grocers, 23 Macnab n
Stuart Mrs Jane (wid Peter) Pine
Stuart John (John Stuart, Son & Co, res Inglewood, James s
Stuart John, com traveler, Hunter cor Victoria ave
Stuart John, moulder, Concession
Stuart J H, accountant Bank of Hamilton, 5 Bold
Stuart J J (John Stuart, Son & Co) Ravenswood, 8 Hannah e
Stuart John, Son & Co (limited) wholesale grocers, 37 John s
Stuart Lewis, salesman, 56 Victoria ave s
Stuart Mrs Mary (wid And) 5 Bold
Stuart Paul, wood inspector, 120 Hunter e
Stuart P H, accountant, 5 Bold
Stuart Robert, sexton Knox Ch, 128 West ave n
Stuart W R, grocer, 60 Emerald n
Studdart I A, sec Ham Homestead Loan and Savings Society, Court House
Studholme Allen, stove mounter, 42 Wilson
Stull Mrs Jane (wid George) 68 Park n
Sturdy Frank, machinist, 215 James n
Sturdy James, laborer, 40 Barton w
Sturdy Thomas, tinsmith, 26 Catharine s
Sturt Miss Margaret, 58 Wellington s
Sturt W P, com traveler, 64 Stinson
Sturtz Richard, hatter, 169 King e
Suhl Peter, laborer, 92 Picton e
Sullivan Mrs Catharine (wid Pat) 11 Caroline n
Sullivan Daniel, grocer, 71 Walnut s
Sullivan Daniel, livery, 5 Charles, h 11 Caroline n

Sullivan Daniel, laborer, 6 Locke n
Sullivan Edward T, cooper, 18 Railway
Sullivan Mrs Ellen (wid Michael) 25 Aurora
Sullivan Mrs Ellen (wid John) 81 Cherry
Sullivan Dennis, laborer, 77 Pearl n
Sullivan Dennis D, laborer, 99 Young
Sullivan James, laborer, 37 Wood e
Sullivan James, laborer, Aikman's ave
Sullivan James, laborer, 55 Cherry
Sullivan John, livery, 52 Main e, h Caroline n
Sullivan John, brakeman, 32 Lower Cathcart
Sullivan John, laborer, Burlington e
Sullivan John, helper, 129 Catharine n
Sullivan John laborer, 342 John n
Sullivan John, laborer, 114 Emerald n
Sullivan John, cigar maker, bds Maple Leaf hotel
Sullivan Joseph, blacksmth, 131 Catharine n
Sullivan Mrs Kate (wid John) 117 Hunter e
Sullivan Mrs M, King e of limits
Sullivan Mrs Margaret, 286 John n
Sullivan Mrs Mary (wid John) 110 Cherry
Sullivan Michael, melter, 29 O'-Reilly
Sullivan Michael, laborer, 61 Young
Sullivan Michael, hotel keeper, 186 King e
Sullivan Patrick, laborer, Greig
Sullivan Mrs Sarah (wid Michael) 99 Maria
Sullivan Tate, laborer, 9 Cherry
Sullivan Thomas, laborer, 106 Wellington s
Sullivan Thomas, J, laborer, 132 Queen n
Sullivan Timothy, laborer, 216 Hughson n
Sullivan Timothy, laborer, 73 Stuart w
Sullivan Timothy, laborer, 217 Cannon e
Sullivan Timothy, moulder, 11 Caroline n
Sullivan Wm, laborer, 71 John n
Sullivan Wm, laborer, 108 Cherry
Summers Mrs Eliza, r 126 Catharine n
Semmers Stephen, porter, 28 Hughson s
Summers Mrs W, 50 Main w
Sun Accident Assurance Co, David McLellan, agent, 84 Jas n
Sun Life Association of Canada, George M Hunt, agent, Arcade, 31 Jamesn
Sunderland, Michael, polisher, 99 Strachan e
Suter David, clerk, 80 Hannah w
Suter R W, ins agent, 20 James s, res Dundas
Sutherland Alexander, turnkey jail, Barton e
Sutherland A F, inspector Ham Prov and Loan Society, 141 Victoria ave n
Sutherland Angus, family grocer, 56 King w, h 81 Jackson w
Sutherland Charles H, chief draughtsman G T R, 168 Main
Sutherland D, grocer, 100 Rebecca
Sutherland J B, salesman, 81 Jackson w
Sutherland John, brakesman G T R, 20 Railway
Sutherland John, stove polisher, 21 Gore
Sutherland John W, lumber merchant, 113 Hughson n

Sutherland J W, chemist and druggist, 180 King w
Sutherland J S, clerk, 141 Victoria ave n
Sutherland The J W Manufacturing Co, patent medicines, J W Sutherland, mgr, 180 King w
Sutherland & Meekison (W J Sutherland, And Meekison) grocers, James cor Cannon
Sutherland Rev Robert G, rector S. Mark's Church, 49 Hunter w
Sutherland Wm, blacksmith, 29 Strachan w
Sutherland William, carpenter, Wentworth n
Sutherland W J (Sutherland & Meekison) h 20 Railway
Sutherland W M, teacher, bds 60 Emerald s
Sutterby John, gardener, Wentworth n
Sutton Henry, conductor, 30 East ave n
Sutton John, laborer, 129 Queen s
Sutton Philip, laborer, 213 York
Sutton William, carpenter, 129 Queen s
Sutton William, collar maker, 71 Emerald n
Swab Peter, teamster, 10 Ferguson ave
Swain Mrs Mary (wid John) 109 Hughson n
Swallow Isaac, mason, 105 Simcoe e
Swallow John, stonecutter, 235 King e
Swallow William, carpenter, 157 King Wm
Swales Michael, carpenter, 135 Robert e
Swan Edward, stovemounter, bds York w of tollgate
Swannell Frederick, mgr Globe Straw Works, 44 Hannah w
Swartzenburg George, shoemaker, 3 Elgin
Swartzenburg W J, whipmaker, 283½ King Wm
Swayzie Abram, 43 John n
Swayze Andrew, laborer, 51 Hannah e
Swayzie Albert, flour and feed, 174 King e
Sweeny Hugh, moulder, 55 John n
Sweeney James, tinsmith, 13 King Wm
Sweeney John, conductor, 74 Cannon w
Sweeney John M, burnisher, 113 Bay n
Sweeney Michael, com traveler, 113 Bay n
Sweeney Thos, moulder, 59 Mary
Sweet Geo, com traveler, Main e
Sweet O C, manf, 72 Catharine n
Sweet Walter, grain dealer, 81 Emerald n
Sweet Wm, boiler maker, 301 York
Sweetlove George, watchman, 56 Tisdale
Sweetlove James, carpenter, 137 Macauley e
Sweetman Harry, saloon keeper, 4 King w
Swift Wm, machinist, 88 John n
Swinton Charles, teamster, 34 Ray n
Swinton Jas, salesman, 56 Ray n
Swinton Wm, carpenter, 56 Ray n
Swinyard Leon, clerk, hd Bay s
Swinyard Thos, hd Bay s
Syer Harry (W Gillies & Co) 159 York
Syme Gibson, laborer, 22 South e
Syme Henry, laborer, 134 Victoria ave n
Symington John, laborer, 10 Poulette
Symington Robert, telegraph engineer, 42 George
Symmers James, clerk, 41 Florence

Sabb Silas W, laborer, 171 Emerald n
Taafe Francis, butcher, 40 Catharine s
Taafe Thomas, butcher, 117 King e
Taffe Joseph, moulder, 109 Strachan e
Taft William, engine packer, 22 Inchbury n
Taggart Alex, carpenter, 13 Cannon w
Taggart Samuel, laborer, 33 Little William
Tait John E W, tailor, 52 Victoria ave s
Tait Mrs Mary (wid David) 50 Napier
Tait William, butcher, Burlington n
Talbot Arthur, teamster, 274 Macnab n
Talbot James, 56 Robert
Talbot John, plumber, 279 John n
Tallman Edward, porter, 131 Ferrie e
Tallman Mrs Elizabeth (wid Enoch) 145 Mary
Tallman Nelson, moulder, 54 Wellington n
Tallman William, carpenter, 90 John n
Tallman W H (W H Tallman & Co) h 98 John n
Tallman W H & Co (W H Tallman, W H Shaver) wood and coal dealers, 43 Cannon e
Tandy Thos, general freight ag't G T R, 47 Charles
Tansley Henry, turner, 68 Jackson e
Tansley Mrs M (wid Robert) 68 Jackson e
Tarbox Edward, white metal smith, 30 Victoria ave n
Tarbox Mrs, 30 Victoria ave n
Tarrant Harry, tailor, bds Court House Hotel
Tarrant Thomas, second hand store, 289½ King w
Tate Frederick, hatter, 145 East ave n
Taufkirch Augustus, clerk, 68 Hughson n
Taulty Michael, laborer, end Ferrie e
Taverner Joseph, tinsmith, bds 79 John n
Taylor Alfred, stonecutter, hd Hess s
Taylor Alfred H, painter, 130 Bold
Taylor Alfred J, shirt manf and gents' furnishing, 40 King w, h 185 King w
Taylor C H, bookkeeper, 37 Mulberry
Taylor Dixon, shoemaker, bds 147 Main e
Taylor Edward D, carriagesmith, bds 73 Caroline n
Taylor Enoch, polisher, 133 Barton e
Taylor E B, laborer, 313 Macnab n
Taylor Francis H, laborer, 41 Wood e
Taylor Frederick; moulder, bds 4 Main w
Taylor F G, polisher, 46 Ferguson ave
Taylor Geo, laborer, 31 Locomotive
Taylor George, laborer, bds 7½ Florence
Taylor George, 4 Duke
Taylor Henry, grocer, 284 King e
Taylor James, bricklayer, 35 Caroline n
Taylor James, polisher, bds 133 Barton e
Taylor Mrs Jane (wid Wm) 215 Cannon e
Taylor J C, coal oil and lamp goods, wholesale and retail, 27 King w, h 36 Markland

Taylor John, checker GTR, 133 Picton e
Taylor John E, baker, 129 James n
Taylor John, flour and feed, 40 York
Taylor John, huckster, 14 O'Reilly
Taylor John, machinist, 4 Main w
Taylor John, blacksmith, 105 Emerald n
Taylor John, laborer, 322 King w
Taylor Josiah, laborer, 4 Nelson
Taylor Joseph, livery, 11 Market
Taylor Joseph, machinist, 10 Greig
Taylor Joseph, bartender, Court House Hotel
Taylor Joseph, watchmaker, 42 King w, h 6 Hughson n
Taylor Lachlan, emery worker, Beulah
Taylor S E, carpenter, 57 Steven
Taylor Mrs Maria (wid Thos) r 1 Queen s
Taylor Mrs Mary (wid Daniel) 295 John n
Taylor Mrs Mary Ann (wid John) 274 Hughson n
Taylor Mrs Mary J (wid Thos) 300 King w
Taylor Mrs, 6 Stuart e
Taylor Peter, baker, 56 Cherry
Taylor Robert, shoemaker, 147 Main e
Taylor R N & Co, druggists, 35 and 95 John s
Taylor Mrs R N, 26 Hannah e
Taylor Samuel, hotel, 21 Stuart w
Taylor Sellar, teamster, 119 Cannon w
Taylor & Simpson (A J Taylor, John Simpson) suspender manfs, 4 Macnab n
Taylor Thomas, laborer, 32 O'Reilly
Taylor Thomas, carpenter, 34 Steven
Taylor Thomas, 192 Wilson
Taylor Thos H, bookkeeper, 6 Nelson
Taylor Wm H, teamster, 112 King Wm
Taylor W J, inspector, 37 Mulberry
Tebbs C, collector, bds Walker House
Teene Mrs Denis, 113 Cherry
Teeter William E, dairyman, 269 Macnab n
Teetzel J V, (Osler, Teetzel & Harrison) h 106 Park s
Teiper Charles, manager Hamilton Bridge and Tool Co, h 15 Colborne
Temperance Dining Rooms, Mrs Wm Tocher, proprietress, 48 James n
Temple John, livery, 20 Catharine n, h 60 Gore
Temple Wm, machinist, 70 Victoria ave n
Templeman Peter, foreman, 126 John n
TenEyck Arthur, fireman, 196 King Wm
TenEyck J W (TenEyck & Precore) h 64 Catharine s
TenEyck Martin, 64 Catharine s
TenEyck M H, V S, livery, etc, 24 Jackson e, h 64 Catharine s
TenEyck & Precore, grocers, 97 James s
Terryberry Mrs Angelon, 68 Catharine s
Terryberry David, 5 Simcoe e
Terryberry Edward, weaver, 5 Simcoe e
Terryberry Heman, weaver, 5 Simcoe e
Terryberry Wellington, bookkeeper, 105 West ave n
Terryberry William, bartender, 32 Hunter e
Tew Mark L, 104 Robinson
Tew Richard (James A Skinner & Co) h Woodmount hd John s

Thatcher Geo, tobacco worker, 155 Hunter w
Thatcher Rudolph, laborer, 39 Canada
Theal A M, sewing machine agt, 83 King w, h hd Queen s
Therrier Peter, shoemaker, 51 Robinson
Thom John, tobacconist, 72 King w, h 74 Jackson w
Thomas Arthur, moulder, bds 50½ Hunter e
Thomas Charles, salesman, bds Court House hotel
Thomas Charles, law student, 29 Tom
Thomas Charles, com traveler, bds 52 Park n
Thomas C L, piano manfr, 92 King w, h 303 King w
Thomas Edward, bricklayer, 55 Robinson
Thomas Edward, clerk, 95 Jackson e
Thomas Geo H, messenger, 95 Jackson e
Thomas H N, marble work, hd York, h 29 Tom
Thomas Jas, stonecutter, 45 Ray n
Thomas John J, piano manfr, 243 King w
Thomas Mrs, 47 Augusta
Thomas Phliip J, contractor, 46 Markland
Thompson Alex, cabinetmaker, 29 Gore
Thompson Alex, plumber, bds 24 Hunter e
Thompson Amos, laborer, 24 Strachan e
Thompson Archibald, laborer, 117 Cannon w
Thompson Charles, machinist, 293 King W n
Thompson David, watchmaker and jeweler, 78 King e, h 123 Bay s
Thompson E J, com traveler, 57 King e

Thompson Geo, 118 Florence
Thompson George R, pedler, bds 93 Caroline n
Thompson Geo S, salesman, 98 Florence
Thompson Gregor, shoemaker, 53 Duke
Thompson Mrs H E (wid Hannibal) boarding, 93 Caroline n
Thompson Mrs Harriet (wid Richard) 10 Macnab s
Thompson Isaac, laborer, 246½ Mary
Thompson James, bookkeeper, 106 Hunter w
Thompson James, ironworker, 63 Napier
Thompson James, shoemaker, 106 Hunter w
Thompson James C, printer, 93 Caroline n
Thompson James R, wood carver, 95 Jackson w
Thompson John, laborer, bds 59 Young
Thompson John, clerk, bds 127 John n
Thompson John, grocer, 370 Hughson n
Thompson John H, boat builder, 368 Hughson n
Thompson John R, gilder, bds 4 Market sq
Thompson Joseph, laborer, 193 Emerald n
Thompson Mark, carpenter, 154 Victoria ave n
Thompson Matthew, boat builder, 222 Macnab n
Thompson Mrs, 302 Macnab n
Thompson Peter, grocer, 101 Emerald n
Thompson Robert, laborer, cor York and Queen
Thompson Thos, news agent, King cor Walnut s
Thompson Thomas, 42 James n
Thompson Wm, clerk, 30 Peter

Thompson William, engineer, 58 Ferrie w
Thompson William, blacksmith, 246 Mary
Thompson Wm H, nailer, 91 Hess n
Thoms Mrs Elizabeth (wid John) 214 Hughson n
Thomson Alexander, proofreader, 40 Emerald n
Thomson Alfred H, clerk, bds 7 Bay s
Thomson Chas, laborer, 126 Bay n
Thomson Chas, carpenter, 18 Magill
Thomson Charles A, com traveler, 7 Bay s
Thomson Ed W, carpenter, 40 Peter
Thomson Frederick, laborer, 6 Magill
Thomson George, law student, 16 Herkimer
Thomson Geo, bookkeeper, Ida
Thomson Mrs Helen (wid Alex) bds 7 Bay s
Thomson James (Thomson & Wright) 70 George
Thomson James, moulder, 82 Napier
Thomson James, laborer,, 253 James n
Thomson James, hotel, 12 Market
Thomson John, appraiser customs, cor Cannon and Elgin
Thomson John W, com traveler, 46 Hess n
Thomson Miss Martha, 28 Young
Thomson Peter, grocer, 190 King
Thomson Mrs Richard, 16 Herkimer
Thomson Richard, clerk, 12 Market
Thomson Robert, lumber dealer, 89 Stuart w, r Burlington village
Thomson R M, clerk Merchants' Bank, 127 John n
Thomson Thomas, shoemaker, 143 Hunter w
Thomson William C, patternmaker, 254 Bay n
Thomson & Wright (James Thomson, Robert Wright) 107 York
Thorne Frederick, moulder, 104 Bold
Thorp Henry, cigar maker, 37 West ave n
Thorley Horse & Cattle Feed Co (Thomas Shaw, prop) 48 John s
Thorne S (S Thorne & Co) h 160 King e
Thorne S & Co, dry goods, gents' furnishings, mantles and dressmaking, 160 King e
Thornton Mrs Delia (wid James) 129 Napier
Thornton James, switchman, 17 Pearl n
Thornton James, musical instruments, 19 Market square, h 123 King w
Thornton John, engineer, bds 13 Cannon w
Thornton Thomas F, mariner, bds 123 King w
Thorbe Alfred, pedler, 182 Hughson n
Thresher W J, baker, 35 West ave n
Thurling Mrs Agnes (wid Geo) 137 Napier
Thurling James, laborer, 237 York
Tice J W, laborer, 136 Young
Tice Wellington, teamster, 34 Hunter e
Tiderington Ralph, bolt maker, 157 Bay n
Tidswell W O, engineer G T R, 10 Main
Tilbury Christopher, butcher, 58 Steven

Tilden John H (E & C Gurney Co, limited) h 81 Catharine n
Tilley David, bookkeeper, 79 Hunter e
Tilley George, pattern maker, 38 Locomotive
Tilley George jr, clerk, 107 Catharine s
Tilley Geo sr, patternmaker, 107 Catherine s
Tilley John Henry, clerk, 39 Rebecca
Tilley Jesse, clerk, 79 Hunter e
Times Printing Co (R Æ Kennedy, John Eastwood, Lyman Moore) 1-3 Hughson n
Timmons Robert, brakeman, bds 140 Mary
Timson John, policeman, 81 Bold
Tindall Robert, moulder, bds 75 Cannon w
Tindill Mrs James, 127 John n
Tindill Wm, tavern keeper, 328 King e
Tinling Charles W (Archdale Wilson & Co) 66 Stinson
Tinsley Edwin, engineer, 1 Centre
Tinsley Joseph, compositor, 58 Walnut s
Tisdale V H, 8½ King e
Tichener Walter, coachman, "Ballynachinch," James s
Tobin John, cabdriver, bds 42 Hughson s
Tocher Wm, clerk, 48 James n
Todd Israel, whitewasher, 90 Rebecca
Tolmie Chas, station master, Harrisburg, G T R, 54 George
Toll Clemence, laborer, 108 Caroline s
Tomes Mrs Annie (wid Wm) seamstress, 4 Florence
Tomkins Joseph, shoemaker, 134 Hunter w
Tomlinson Charles T, saddler, 89 King e
Tomlinson Harry, fireman G T R, 44 Locomotive
Tomlinson Richard, clerk, 88 Queen s
Tompkins George D, plumber, 199 East ave n
Tompkins Riddel, laborer, 169 Hunter w
Tompkins Thos, cigarmaker, 76 Lower Cathcart
Toner Hugh, laborer, 61 Canada
Toner John, teamster, n s Duke nr Hess
Toomey Mrs Mary (wid James) 123 Hunter e
Tope Richard, bricklayer, 73 Robinson
Tope Samuel, fireman, 142 Picton e
Topping Robert, engineer, 39 Hannah w
Toronto "News" Office, W H Bews, agent, 2 Gore
Toronto Safe Works, C F Bush, agent, 17 Arcade
Torrance Hugh, 2 Simcoe e
Torrance Thos, 58 Wellington n
Torrance William, moulder, 12 Ferrie w
Tory Alfred, clerk, 115 West ave u
Tout William, machinist, Wentwortn n
Tout William, machinist, 313 Barton e
Tovel John E, gardener, Burlington n
Tovel Samuel A, gardener, Burlington n
Tower David, laborer, 62 Hannah e
Towers David, carpenter, 175 East ave n
Towers George, sailor, 206 Hughson n
Towers John J, furnace fitter, 2 Evans

Towers Thomas, carpenter, bds Centre
Towers Mrs (wid William) 173 East ave n
Towersey Joseph, watchmaker, 120 King e
Towersey Mrs J, milliner, 120 King e
Towler William, broommaker, 60 Young
Townsend E J, florist, 62 Park n
Townsend John, tragedian, 130 West ave n
Townsend Samuel W, clerk customs, 27 Bay n
Townsend Sherman E, accountant, 6½ James s, h 77 East ave s *See card*
Townsend W G, custom house broker, 31½ Stuart w, h 27 Bay n *See card*
Townsend William J, clerk, 27 Bay n
Toye W C, porter, 137 Robert e
Tracey Daniel, teamster, 185 Mary
Tracey John, clerk, bds 17 Elgin
Tracey J H, salesman, bds Elgin cor Kelly
Tracie Edward, 86 Locke n
Tracie Thomas, brakesman, 266½ Bay n
Trade Association (Toronto) M B Rymal, manager, 24 Macnab
Trafford John T, laborer, 69 Hunter e
Traill Allan, porter, 65 West ave
Traill James, 32 Liberty
Traill Mrs William, 94 Sackson e
Tramskosker Mrs Laura (wid John) 127 Rebecca
Traub Adam, glassblower, 32 Picton w
Travelers' Life & Accident Co, J T Routh, agent, 16 James s
Travers J N, manager Bank of Montreal, res bank, James cor Main
Traynor John, tailor, 53 Robert
Treble S G, gents' furnishings, 2 King e, h 43 Main w
Tregenza Charles, salesman, 20 Stinson
Tregenza Edward, laborer, 197 Bay n
Tremble Jacob, teamster, 54 Wood e
Tremble John, bridge repairer, 149 West ave n
Tremlett John, shoemaker, 219 James n
Tremlett William, boots and shoes, 25 Macnab n
Trenwith George, blacksmith, 2 Locke s
Trevaskis George, wagon maker, Breadalbane
Trevaskis John, wagon maker, 258 King w
Trevaskis William, blacksmith, 315 King w
Tribbeck Wm, packer, 118 Queen n
Tribute Fred, cutter, 152 Main w
Tribute Mrs Mary (wid Thos) 57 Locomotive
Tribute Thomas, machinist, 5 Inchbury n
Tristram George, bookkeeper, 41 Pearl n
Trotman John, polisher, 1 Tom
Troup Mrs Elizabeth (wid Rev Wm) 46 Hunter w
Troy Laundry, W H Glarke manger, 7 Market square
Truman A E (Kirk & Truman) h 178 King e
Truman Frank, hair dresser, 180 King e
Truman Fred, hair dresser, 178 King e
Truman Mrs J H, confectioner, 178 King e
Truman Samuel, printer, 60½ Hunter e
Truman William, printer, 60½ Hunter e

Truman William, bookkeeper, 60½ Hunter e
Trumbull Mrs Eliza (wid Geo) 57 John n
Truscott Charles, carpenter, 109 Wellington n
Truscott James, machinist, 66 Lower Cathcart
Truscott Mrs Jane (wid William) 109 Wellington n
Truscott John, carpenter, 78 East ave n
Truscott John, painter, 172 East ave n
Truscott Mrs Mary (wid James) 35½ Lower Cathcart
Trusdale Watson, bookkeeper, Main e
Truse William. laborer, bds 140 King Wm
Tryter Benjamin, cigarmaker, 39 Hunter e
Tshann Antoine, butcher, 79 John s
Tucker Henry, laborer, 20 Napier
Tuckett George, 207 King w
Tuckett Geo E (Geo E Tuckett & Son) tobacco manfr, 118 King w, h 217 King w
Tuckett Geo E & Son, tobacco manfrs, 118 King w
Tuckett George T (George E Tuckett & Son) tobbacco manfrs, 118 King w, h King w
Tuckett John E (George E Tuckett & Son) tobacco manfs, 118 King w, h 61 Hunter e
Tufford Isaac, carter, 18 Sophia n
Tufford Lemuel, tinsmith, 53 Hess n
Tufford Washington, laborer, 62 Market
Tulk Alfred, moulder, 234 King William
Tulk John G, moulder, 5 Hunter w
Tunstead John, manager Dominion Hat works, 310 King e, h 48 Emerald s
Turk William, laborer, 310 Macnab n
Turkish Baths, Mrs James Smith 145 James n
Turnbull Adam, machinist G T R, 56 Pearl n
Turnbull A C, bookkeeper, bds 10 Wilson
Turnbull Henry, sexton Central Presbyterian Church, 78 Hunter w
Turnbull James, bds 31 Gore
Turnbull James, laborer, 122 Napier
Turnbull J D, clerk, 10 Wilson
Turnbull Michael (Leitch & Turnbull) h 78 Elgin
Turnbull Walter C, printer, 91 Jackson w
Turnbull William, assessor, 10 Wilson
Turnbull William H, cabinet maker, bds 78 Hunter w
Turner Alex (James Turner & Co) h 86 Hughson s
Turner Alfred, Wickham Villa, Mountain top
Turner Alfred, gardener, Mountain top
Turner A D (James Turner & Co) h Highfield, Concession
Turner Duke, salesman, 135 Main e
Turner George T, carpenter, 40 Lower Cathcart
Turner Henry, gardener, 9 Hunter w
Turner James (James Turner & Co) h Highfield, Concession
Turner James, laborer, Simcoe e
Turner James, laborer, 108 Wood
Turner James & Co (James, Alex and A D) wholesale grocers, 3 Hughson s
Turner John, salesman, bds 1 Main w

Turner Joseph, boiler maker, bds 112 Bay n
Turner Richard, laborer, 91 Simcoe e
Turner Thomas, bricklayer, 43 Aurora
Turner ThosW,engineer, Ferrie e
Turner W J, clerk, Mountain top
Turpin James, com traveler, 38 Jackson w
Turpitt Mrs Susannah (wid Wm) 22 Devonport
Tuttle Lyman P, agent, 7 Spring
Twohy H D, assistant waterworks, 150 Macnab n
Tyler O H, butcher, 212 James n
Tyson Adam, feather and mattrass renovator, 8 Main w
Tyson George, timekeeper, G T R, 47 Macnab n
Tyson William, stonemason, 5 Little Wellington
Underhill John, laborer, 162 Wilson
Underwood Charles, engraver, 114½ East ave n
Union Wood & Coal Yard, J and H Mulholland, props, cor Cannon and Cathcart
United States Consulate, Hon John F Hazelton, consul, office GTR station
United Workman's Hall, 12 Macnab s
Unsworth A (E S Collins & Co) bds 53 Merrick
Unsworth George, painter, bds 203 John n
Upfield J J, com-traveler, 44 Maria
Upsdell Mrs Amelia A (wid Wm J) 4 Robinson
Urquhart John, carpenter, 211 Main w
Urry Walter, barber, 67 James n, h 11 Murray w
Usher C E E, bookkeeper, bds Royal hotel
Vail A S (A S Vail & Co) 88 Hughson n
Vail A S & Co, wholesale manfr ready-made clothing, 16-18 James n
Vail Lemanuel N, spring mattrasses, 17 York, h 48 Locomotive
Vail L N (Vail & Morris) 48 Locomotive
Vail & Morris, roof paint, 270 York
Vale William J, printer, 1 Elgin
Valentine Charles, laborer, 121 Ferrie e
Vallance George, cashier, Wood & Leggat, 50 Hunter w
Vallance James, carpenter, 14 Picton e
Vallance Wm (Wood & Leggat) 46 Hannah w
Vallee Francis X, broommaker, 87 King w
VanAllen Edwin, carpenter, 93 Bay s
VanAllen Eli, builder, Hannah w, h 5 Bay s
Vanatter John, policeman, 45 Hunter e
Vanderburgh Walter, asst baggage master, G T R, 125 Queen n
Vandusen Joseph, carpenter, 170 Wilson
Vanevery Chas W, painter, 313 King w
VanNorman Clara B, shipper, Wentworth s
VanNorman & Co, sewing machine agents, King cor Catharine
VanNorman Mrs E, 67 Cannon e
VanNorman W P, 67 Cannon e
VanOrder George R, conductor, 5 Barton Terrace, Wellington n
Vanstone Fred, cutter, 30 Emerald n

Vant David, laborer, 103 Hunter ter w
Vant Mrs Mary (wid Wm) 103 Hunter w
Vanwyck Gilbert, tailor, 91 Elgin
Van Wyck Rev Jas, pastor Gore st Methodist Church, 33 Gore
Vassie George, machinist, bds 79 James s
Vassie Wm jr, mec supt Ont Sewing Machine Co, bds 79 James s
Vassie William sr, foreman Ont Sewing Machine Co, 79 James
Vaughan Albert, laborer, 56 Canada
Veal T O, gardener, 33 Steven
Vedder George, painter, 65 Merrick
Veidenheimer Philip, baker, Ray s cor Bold
Veiger Mrs Mary (wid John) 322 King w
Venard James, laborer, bds 143 Bay n
Venator Albert, wood turner, bds 54 Main w
Venator Frederick, wood turner, 69 Colborne
Venator Jacob, wood turner, bds 54 Main w
Venator Wm, wood turner, 91 John n
Venator Wm A, wood and ivory turner, 56 Main w, h 54 Main w
Venes Daniel, carpenter, bds Markland
Verner Andrew, moulder, bds 7½ Florence
Vernon Elias, MD, 80 James s
Vernon Henry, manager W H Irwin & Co, 136 Park n
Vernon Walter, com traveler, bds 80 James s
Verral William, butcher, 168 Macnab n
Vert John R, com traveler, 8 Hess n
Victoria Chambers, 31 James s
Victoria Hotel, Richard Irwin, propr, 79 King e
Victoria Mutual Fire Insurance Co, W D Booker, sec-treas, Wentworth chambers, 25 James s
Vila Mrs Ann, grocer, 253 Bay n
Vila Augustine, chandler, 255 Bay n
Villiers Frederick, 64 Catharine n
Vincent Arthur (A Vincent & Co) druggist, 230 James n
Vincent A & Co, druggists, 230 James n
Viner Thomas, clerk, 56 Catharine s
Vint Chas, shoecutter, bds 31 Railway
Vint James, stonecutter, 45 Caroline n
Vint Wm, tobacco caser, 31 Railway
Vipond Eli, carpenter, bds 127 Dundurn
Virgint John D, laborer, 146 Hunter w
Virt A R, com traveler, Market
Voegele Charles, hatter, 169 East ave n
Voelker Jacob, tailor, 66 Hunter e
Veolk Joseph, moulder, 64 Walnut s
Volkeir Charles, packer, bds 122 Mary
Volkeir G, laborer, 122 Mary
Voll John, glassblower, 85 Macaulay e
Vollick John, wood turner, 76 Market
VonHoxar Alexander, printer, Jones
VonHoxar Henry G, teacher of languages, Jones
Vosper Charles, butcher, James St market, h Mountain top
Waddell Mrs Mary (wid Thos) 31 Hunter w

Waddell Mrs Mary (wid William) 122 John s
Waddell & Waddell, (R R, J N and F R) barristers, Court House, h 31 Hunter w
Waddleton Wm, tailor, Duke
Wade James, carpenter, 75 Locke n
Wade Robt, laborer, 23 Margaret
Wade Robt, laborer, 115 Bold
Wadland Thomas H, supt construction Bell Telephone Co, 1 Hughson s, h 11 Victoria ave n
Wagner James, tailor, 73 John n
Wagner Mrs Sarah A (wid Wm) 77 Bay n
Wagstaff Walter, tinsmith, 23 Magill
Wah Lee, laundry, 87 James n
Wah Sing, laundry, 81 King e
Waite George, painter, 7 Cannon e
Wakeham Alfred, cabinetmaker, 86 Caroline n
Wakeham John, carpenter, 52 Burlington w
Wakelin Frederick, pensioner, 119 Hunter e
Wakley Richard, carter, 31 Lower Cathcart
Waldhof Wm, hay and straw dealer, 28 Rebecca
Waldren Wm, laborer, 66 Market
Waldron Mrs Harriet (wid Thos) 58 Barton e
Walford John, packer, Markland
Walker Alfred E, 68 Cannon w
Walker Miss Alice, 79 West ave n
Walker Charles L, confectioner, 40 Victoria ave n
Walker Edward, machinist, 102 West ave n
Walker F, com traveler, 62 Cannon e
Walker Frank E, carpets, stoves and furniture, Copp's Block, King cor Walnut h 63 Hunter e
Walker George, grocer, 75 King w
Walker George, machinist, 240 King William
Walker George, shoemaker, 92½ Jackson e
Walker George J, painter, 119 Market
Walker House, J M Bauer, propr, King cor Ferguson ave
Walker Hugh, gardener, 62 Hannah w
Walker James, insurance agt, 20 Main e, h 58 Hunter w
Walker James, chandler, 19 Bay s
Walker Mrs Jane (wid James) 137 Hunter e
Walker John, blacksmith, 65 John n
Walker John, moulder, 41 Steven
Walker J P, clerk, 58 Hunter w
Walker Joseph, dairyman, King w, nr limits
Walker Miss, 236 King William
Walker Raymond, cashier E & C Gurney, 65 Wellington s
Walker Robt, laborer, 169 Bay n
Walker Robt, laborer, 177 Mary
Walker Robert, grocer, 257 York
Walker Mrs Sophia (wid Robert) 5 Walnut s
Walker T F, saloon keeper, 15 James n
Walker Thos D, tie inspector G T R, 62 Jackson w
Walker Thomas R, salesman, 205 York
Walker & Scott (W F Walker, M A, LL B, John J Scott, Wm Lees, B C L) barristers, 10 James s, *See card*
Walker W F, MA, LLB, (Walker & Scott) barrister, h 140 Bay n
Walker Mrs Wm, dairy, 69 Hannah w
Walker William, poulterer, James st market, h 146 Hughson n
Walker Wm, brakeman G T R, 53 Magill

Walkinshaw John, moulder, 173 East ave n
Walkinshaw Wm, moulder, 173 East ave n
Wall Charles, engineer, 135 Ferrie e
Wall James, blacksmith, 22 Jackson e, h 136 Jackson e
Wall James, hatter, 126 Park n
Wall James, jr, blacksmith, 136 Jackson e
Wall Morgan, laborer, 10 Ferrie w
Wall Robert, bookkeeper, 136 Jackson e
Wallace Hugh S (J Wallace & Son) 31 Gore
Wallace James, moulder, 49 Cannon e
Wallace J McL, MD, med supt Asylum for Insane
Wallace John (J Wallace & Son) 82 George
Wallace Joseph, chief clerk G T R, 66 Jackson w
Wallace J & Son (John and Hugh S) tinsmiths, 15 John n
Wallace Robert, com merchant, 77 John n
Wallace Robert, MD, 8 Cannon w
Wallace Robert S, clerk, 102 Park s
Wallace Wm, Markland
Wallace Wm, machinist, Ferguson ave n
Wallace William J, moulder, 180 King Wm
Walling James, Brock e
Wallington Thomas, painter, 207 Wellington n
Wallman Mrs Harriet (wid Andrew) 138½ Hunter e
Walls George, laborer, Dundurn
Walsh David, messenger P O, 143 John n
Walsh E A, gents' furnishings, 70 King w, h 15 Margaret
Walsh George, porter, 15 Margaret
Walsh Hiram, policeman, 356 Hughson n
Walsh John, 198 King w
Walsh John, shoemaker, 127 Young
Walsh John, shoemaker, 43½ York
Walsh Mrs Martha (wid James) 15 Margaret
Walsh Robert, cigar maker, bds Commercial Hotel
Walsh Samuel, tobacco roller, 18 Mill
Walsh Thomas,, com traveler, 236 James n
Walsh Thomas, shuttle maker, 189 James n
Walsh Thomas, tinsmith, 144 King William
Walsh Thomas, grocer, 217 York
Walsh Wm, nailer, 49 Stuart w
Walsh William, plumber, 44 West ave n
Walsh William, machinist, 101 Locke n
Walter Elijah, master mariner, 280 Hughson n
Walterhouse James, millwright, 49 Tisdale
Walters Augustus, laborer, Robert w
Walters Chris, laborer, Duke
Walters Frank, laborer, Robinson
Walters John J, tinsmith, 2 Margaret
Walton Mrs Elizabeth (wid Wm) 121 Hess n
Walon Joseph, salesman, 52 Lower Cathcart
Walton Wallace, laborer, 63 Caroline n
Walton Watson G, milk and ice dealer, 54 Napier
Walton William, laborer, 180 Wood e
Wand Neil, laborer, 115 Robinson
Wands Eben H, carpenter, 164 Main w

Wanzer Frank (R M Wanzer & Co) h 82 Victoria ave s
Wanzer R M (R M Wanzer & Co) h 47 West ave s
Wanzer [illegible]ng Machine Co (R [illegible]zer & Co) 91 Barton e
Wanzer Thoma[illegible] (R M Wanzer & Co) h 73 Victoria ave s
Ward Alfred, carpenter, 50 Ferrie e
Ward Mrs Ann (wid Joseph) 17 Hunter w
Ward George, machinist, 17 Hunter w
Ward John A, asst paymaster G T R, 16 Colborne
Ward Joseph, laborer,37 Picton e
Ward Mrs Margaret (wid James) 29 Mary
Ward Mrs Mary Ann (wid Wm) 181 Napier
Ward Patrick, laborer, 12 Lower Cathcart
Ward Patrick, coachman, 14 Lower Cathcart
Ward Richard B, laborer, 135 West ave n
Ward Robert, supt Shaftesbury Boys' Home, King e nr toll gate
Ward Thos, laborer, 11 Wood w
Warden Joseph, loborer, 3 Mill
Wardlaw Mrs Amelia (wid John) 6 Ontario
Ware E W (Gurney & Ware) h 9 Vine
Waring George, blacksmith, 123 Hess n
Wark David, policeman, 87 Emerald n
Wark John, salesman, 185 Macnab n
Warmington H G, carpenter, 154 Rebecca
Warmington George, plumber,81 Young
Warner John M, wood worker ,r 173 Bayn
Warner Mrs Mary Jane (wid Francis) laundress, 80 Macnab
Warnick Wm, 104 Young
Warnke Peter, tailor, 25 Canada
Warren C J, manager Ontario Pharmacy, King cor Ferguson ave
Warren Donald, packer, 47 West ave n
Warren Edward, 52 Cherry
Warren Edward, 51 Catharine s
Warren George H, puddler, 212 Hughson n
Warren H R, clerk, 52 Cannon e
Warren Mrs Mary (wid James) 68 Strachan e
Warren Mrs M J, 93 King Wm
Warren Patrick, laborer, 83 Strachan e
Warren Robert, butcher, 16 Tisdale
Warren W H, bookkeeper, 62 Cannon e
Warron William, machinist, 77 Maria
Warwick William, carpenter, 51 Hunter e
Washington S F, (Haslett & Washington) h 11 West ave s
Waterloo Mutual Fire Insurance Co, Seneca Jones, agent, 59 James n
Waterman Ezra, upholsterer, 196 John n
Waterman Walter L, clerk, 196 John n
Waters A M, marble dealer, 39 West ave n
Waters Francis, teamster, 35 Catharine s
Waters Mrs Harriet, milliner, 58 York
Watkins Edgar H, merchant, 64 East ave s
Watkins F W, (Pratt & Watkins) h King e nr Burlington
Watkins Thomas C, dry goods, carpets, etc, 30-32 King e, h King cor Emerald

Watkins Wm T, merchant, 71 Emerald s
Watson Andrew, baker, 30 Walnut s
Watson Charles, hackdriver, 62 Young
Watson D A, druggist, 76 Napier
Watson Edward, cattle doctor, 25 Mary
Watson George, shoemaker, 77 Victoria ave n
Watson Geo, cabinetmaker, 108 Emerald n
Watson George, engineer, 10 Picton w
Watson Gordon, clerk, 9 Duke
Watson James, pres Strathroy Knitting Co, Sandyford Place, 9 Duke
Watson James, moulder, 71 Locomotive
Watson Jas, moulder, 16 Pearl n
Watson James, carpenter, 22 Locke s
Watson John W, porter G T R, 31 Simcoe e
Watson Rupert, sec Strathroy Knitting Co, 9 Duke
Watson Thomas, tinsmith, 136 Catharine n
Watson Thos J, policeman, 53 Wellington s
Watson Wm, hatter, 42½ West ave n
Watson Mrs Wm, 42½ West ave n
Watt John & Son, (John and Alex) merchant tailors, 15 Macnab n, h 112 West ave n
Watt John J, salesman, bds Victoria hotel
Watt P J, com traveler, Lucas, Park & Co
Watt Robert, packer, 19 Macnab
Watt Robt, porter, 67 Duke
Watts C W G, bookkeeper, 136 John s
Watts Mrs Elizabeth (wid Thos) 269 York
Watts John, laborer, 169 Bay n
Watts Thos, machinist, Markland
Waugh James, hatmaker, 230½ Bay n
Waugh John, b[illegible] 78 Bay n
Waugh W J, ge[illegible]nisher and hatter, 60 Ja[illegible]n
Wavell Th[illegible]nas, assignee and commissioner for the Province of Quebec, 12-14 Hughson s, h 26 Sheaffe
Way Bidwell, bursar Asylum for the Insane, Mountain top
Way Harry, butcher, 82 Emerald n
Way James, agent, 26 Mary
Way John, blacksmith, 15 Crooks
Waybrant Henry H, machinist, 84 Caroline n
Weager John W, laborer, 90 West ave n
Weakley Jacob, tinsmith, 39 Barton e
Weatherston Jas, carpenter, 21 Devonport
Weatherstone John, 33 Victoria ave n
Weaver Cyrus, laborer, 11 Picton w
Weaver Fred, switchman G T R, 21 Crooks
Weaver Mrs Elizabeth (wid John) 92 Elgin
Webb George, laborer, 150 Catharine n
Webb Geo N, shoemaker, 185 Main w
Webb Isaac, shoecutter, 76 Canada
Webb Jas W, shoemaker, 145 Jackson w
Webb John, carpenter, 99 Simcoe e
Webb John, contractor, Murray e
Webb John, engineer, 150 Catharine n
Webber Charles, bricklayer, 42 Maria
Webber B H, (Winslow & Webber) 106 Bold

Webber Emerson, liveryman, 28 Catharine s
Webber Frederick C, builder, 97 Catharine s
Webber Geo H, bricklayer, 103 Catharine s
Webber H C, 134 John s
Webber Henry, teacher, 42 Maria
Webber H S, clerk Bank of Hamilton
Webber J M, hardware, 27 Macnab n, h 66 James s
Webber John, clerk, 42 Maria
Webber Mrs John, 134 John s
Webber Joseph B, com traveler, 66 James s
Webber Mrs Maria A (wid Tillman C) dressmaker, 79 Napier
Webber O H, clerk, 121 East ave n
Webber P E, livery, 28 Catharine s
Webber Walter B, 13 Hess s
Webber W G, bricklayer, 42 Maria
Webster Archibald, machinist, 210 Catharine n
Webster Edmund, machinist, 46 Cannon e
Webster George, tailor, 26 John n, h 57 Walnut s
Webster Geo, machinist, 128½ King e, h Wentworth n
Webster James, florist, Wentworth n
Webster James, mason, 23 Lower Cathcart
Webster John, engine driver G T R, 22 Locomotive
Webster Joseph, flour and feed, 8 Market sq
Webster Robert, 142 Cannon e
Webster, William, flour and grain, 8 Market sq, h 53 Park n
Wedge Jas, carter, 200 Robert e
Weeks Mrs J A (wid George) Markland cor Caroline
Weeks William, whipmaker, 198 East ave n

Weights and Measures Office, cor James and Vine
Weir Frederick, stone cutter, York w of tollgate
Weir James, boatbuilder, Wentworth n
Weir James, baker, 75 Napier
Weir John, porter, 48 Strachan e
Weir Peter, lodging house, 49 Hnghson n
Weir Robert, baker, 55 York
Weir William, Nightingale
Welbey George, pattern maker, 94 West ave n
Welch Henry, machinist, 19 Barton w
Weller James, potter, 21 Little Market
Weller William, potter, 1 Poulette
Wellinger Thomas T, machinst, 258 James n
Wellington Thomas, porter, York
Wells Alfred, porter, 264 James n
Welsh J, machinist, 88 Ferguson ave
Welsh James A, emigration agt, Stuart w, h 97 Jackson e
Welsh Mrs Louisa (wid Walter) 33 Park s
Welsh Thomas, com traveler, 236 James n
Welsher Harvey B, carpenter, 173 Napier
Wennesheimer Mrs Mary, seamstress, 91 Caroline n
Wentworth Chambers, 25 James s
Wesleyan Ladies' College, Rev A Burns, DD, LLD, governor, 57 King e
Wesley Methodist Church, John cor Rebecca
West Charles, baker, 97 Cannon w
West David, laborer, 37 Catharine s
West David, laborer, 74 Hughson n
West Mrs E (wid William) 90 Victoria ave n

West George, planer, 129 Ferrie e
West John, baker, 76 Maria
West Robert, laborer, Markland
Westaway John, fireman, 72 Barton e
Westborough Cornelius, laborer, 28 Ferguson ave
Westbrook Mrs Nellie (wid O G) 7 Robert
West End Music Store, T J Baine, prop, 84 King w
Western Building Association, Seneca Jones, agent, 59 James n
Westfall John, laborer, 104 Market
Westfall William, laborer, 104 Market
Western Assurance Co'y (Ocean and Inland Marine) Toronto, W F Findlay, agent, 25 James s
Western Assurance Co'y (Fire) Toronto, Geo A Young, agent, 2 Merrick
Western Assurance Co'y (marine) J B Fairgrieve, agt, 59 James n
Western Henry B W, clerk, 67 Hughson s
Western John, shoemaker, 183 Main w
Westmore Albert, laborer, Locke s
Weston Mis Eliza (wid John) 21 Inchbury s
Weston George, watchman, 29 Little William
Weston John, shoemaker, 183 Main w
Weston W, shoemaker, 106 John n
Westphall Mrs —, 14 Florence
Westphal Franklin, laborer, 40 Ray n
Mestphal Mrs Minnie (widow August) 221 York
Wetherall Alex, dry goods, Copp's Block, 134 King e, h 354 Hughson n
Wetherall Henry, salesman, 354 Hughson n
Whalen James, laborer, 27 Stuart e
Whalen John, laborer, 376 Catharine n
Whalen Sylvester, silver smith, 183 Emerald n
Whalen Thomas, shoemaker, 111 Park n
Wharry Wm, blacksmith, Greig
Whateley Henry, barrister, 35 Hannah e
Whatley F L, bookkeeper, 98 Robinson
Wheaton Edward, conductor, 79 W Park n
heaton William, laborer, 36 Charles
Wheeler George, engine driver, 228 Catharine n
Wheeler Mrs H, 89 Macauley e
Wheeler Mrs Jane (wid Robin) 165 John n
Wheeler J S, carpenter, 93 Robert e
Wheeler Judson, asst man'gr Ontario Pharmacy, Victoria ave cor Barton
Wheeler Mrs M M (wid Samuel) York w of tollgate
Wheeler R N, grocer, 215 Barton e
Whelan James, shoemaker, 129 Main e
Whelan John, laborer, 367 John n
Whelan Michael, laborer, 55 Maria
Whipple E S, land agent and issuer of marriage licenses, 78½ King e, h 5 Walnut s
Whipple Herbert B, clerk, 55 Wellington n
Whitby John, fitter, 245 Bay n
White —, laborer, 25 Stuart w
White Alfred, bookkeeper, 3 Erie ave
White Charles, com traveler, 25 Young

White David, 109 Robert
White Frank A, laborer, Bruce
White George A, furnace builder, 311 King w
White H A, tinsmith, 44 Murray
White James, MD, coroner, 8 Cannon w
White Mrs Jane, matron old city hospital, Guise
White J C, fancy goods and regalia, 86 King e
White John, bricklayer, 98 Caroline s
White John, collector, 31 Queen s
White Mrs John, 15 Mulberry
White John, laborer, 155 King Wm
White John E, carpenter, 107 Emerald n
White J T, bookkeeper, 109 Robert
White Joseph, carpenter, Strachan e nr Wellington
White Mrs Maria (wid Eli) 11 Tom
White Michael, tailor, 73 Caroline n
White Nicholas, laborer, 250 James n
White Richard, carpenter, 144 Cannon e
White Samuel, 'bus driver, Dominion hotel
White Samuel, shoemaker, 94 John s
White Sewing Machine Co, H D Bassett, agent, 99 King e
White Mrs S G, 3 Erie ave
White Thos W, 83 Hess n
White W C, builder, 10 Burlington n
White Wm, blacksmith, 151 Wilson
Whitelock Frank, clerk, 228 Barton e
Whitehead Charles, gardener, Wentworth n
Whitehead E S, watchmaker, 161 John n
Whitehead Seth J, supt Ontario rolling mills, 7 Peter
Whitelock Wm John, bricklayer, 147 East ave n
Whiteside William, machinist, 82 Lower Cathcart
Whiting Benjamin, laborer, 207 James n
Whitmarsh James, laborer, 2 Little Market
Whitmore Daniel, porter, 72 Bay s
Whitney George, moulder, 16 Barton w
Whitney John, laborer, 115 Caroline n
Whitney Joseph, 235 Cannon e
Whitney Matthew, teamster, 22 Margaret
Whitney Thomas, hackman, 16 Barton w
Whittaker James, glassblower, 13 Wood e
Whittaker Thomas, clerk Wood & Leagatt
Whitwell C A, clerk, 25 East ave n
Wholton George, tinsmith, 158 West ave n
Wholton William, tinsmith, 158 West ave n
Whyte Arch, foreman Hendrie & Co, 73 Market
Whyte Andrew, baker, 11 Ferrie e
Whyte A R, bookkeeper, 12 West ave s
Whyte Geo. builder, 131 King e
Whyte Ralph L, chief clerk customs, 12 West ave s
Wickham James, stovemounter, 43 Wood e
Wickham John, laborer, 96 Macauley e
Wickham Michael, laborer, 113 Hannah e
Wickham Michael, foreman Jas Stewart & Co
Wickham Patrick, stovemounter, 85½ Macauley e

Wickham Wm, stovemounter, 284 Mary
Widger Mrs James, 43 East ave s
Widgery —, shoemaker, bds 55 York
Wilcock W P, butcher, 72 Wilson
Wilcox Charles A, piano agent, 31 Bay n
Wilcox George, cabinet maker, 51 Hunter e
Wilcox Mrs Nancy (wid William) 31 Bay n
Wilcox Richard, laborer, 25 Ferrie e
Wild Edward, laborer, Robert w
Wilde Edwin, valuator, Markland
Wild M B, clerk G T R
Wild Richard, laborer, 56 Chisholm
Wilde W C, printer, 95 Young
Wildman Edward, stonecutter, 211 King e
Wilds James, gardener, Barton e
Wilds George, gardener, Smith ave
Wiles Mrs (wid James) Wents nr King
Wilkes Charles, laborer, 156 Rebecca
Wilkes William, confectioner, 38 York
Wilkie John, engine driver, 46 Kelly
Wilkins H A, sculptor, 154 Park n
Wilkins Miss Harriet Ann, music teacher, 64 Main w
Wilkinson Frank, grain buyer, 98 Concession
Wilkinson Geo R, com traveler, 8 Hess n
Wilkinson John, engine driver, 82 Elgin
Wilkinson Samuel, porter St Nicholas hotel
Wilkinson Wm, butcher, 202 King Wm
Will Mrs Eliza (wid Geo) 122 Cannon e
Will Joseph, bookkeeper, 151 Hunter w
Will Ramsay, machinist, 151 Hunter w
Will Smith, clerk, 83 Hnnter e
Willard Henry H, Ontario Rolling Mills Co, 89 Jackson w
Willard L H, machinist, 109 Rebecca
Willer Samuel, butcher, 109 John s
William Henry, porter, 59 Hannah e
Williams Askett, gardener, Barton e
Williams Charles, plasterer, 51 Young
Williams Charles H, cierk, 318 King Wm
Williams C J, prop Canadian Oil Co, 18 Macnab n, h 42 Catharine n
Williams Daniel, laborer, 78 Cannon w
Williams Daniel, hotel, 211 James n
William E, 92 King e
Williams Edward, iron roller, 327 York
Williams Edward, laborer, 8 Macnab s
Williams Edward, engine driver, 164 West ave n
Williams George, stove polisher, 66 Robert
Williams George, carpenter, 16 Baillie
Williams Geo J, manager Dunn, Wiman & Co, mercantile agency, h Markland w of Queen
Williams Harry, laborer, 14 Cherry
Williams Henry D, teamster, 210 King Wm
Williams H R (J M Williams & Co) h hd Queen s
Williams H S, bookseller and stationer, Copp's block, King e

Williams Hugh, carpenter, 107 Bay n
Williams James, laborer, 268 Catharine n
Williams James, teamster, 20 Kelly
Williams James, heater, 33 Locomotive
Williams Mrs Jane (wid Vandolph) Queen s
Williams John, 87 Hughson n
Williams John, carpenter, 26 West ave n
Williams John, laborer, 118 John s
Williams John, confectioner, Copp's Block, King e
Williams John, brakeman GTR, 87 Bay n
Williams John, policeman, 20 Main w
Williams John B, hotel, 7 Market
Williams John C, gardener, 40 Walnut s
Williams J M, county registrar, Court House, h hd Queen s
Williams J M & Co (J M Williams jr, H R Williams, Wm Cook) stove manf, 59-63 Hughson n
Williams J M jr (J M Williams & Co) h hd Hess s
Williams Mrs Julia (wid Patk) 18 Mill
Williams Lenton, millwright, 43 Vine
Williams Mrs Mary, 117 King w
Williams Mrs Mary (wid Patrick) Greig
Williams Matthew, harnessmaker, 115½ Rebecca
Williams Michael, Clyde hotel, 49 Macnab n
Williams Patrick, laborer, Greig
Williams Robert, com traveler, 23 Bay n, cor Market
Williams Robert E, salesman, Copp's block, King e
Williamson A P, bookseller, 204 James n
Williamson Mrs Eliza (wid Peter) 16 Young
Williamson Miss Norah, 323 James n
Williamson Richard, ice dealer, 306 James n
Williamson Richard, 296 James n
Williamson Richard B, painter, 314 James n
Williamson Robert, laborer, 25 Ferrie w
Williamson Robert, mariner, 268 Hughson n
Williamson Thomas. laborer, 266 Hughson n
Williamson W B, ice dealer, 312 James n
Williamson William, carpenter, 23 Strachan w
Williamson William, teamster, 35 Sheaffe
Willis Frederick, moulder, 64 Locke n
Willman Mrs Annie (wid Fred) 103 Caroline s
Willmore Alfred, machinist, 12 Elgin
Wilmott Fred, photographer, 68 King e
Wilmot John, scale maker, 76 Elgin
Willoughby Frederick, dyer, 313 James n
Wills Charles, machinist, 124 Rebecca
Willis J, boot and shoe dealer, 54 John s
Wills R S, porter, Walnut
Wilson A McD, druggist, 44 Main w
Wilson Andrew, 27½ Tisdale
Wilson Archdale & Co (Archdale Wilson and Chas W Tinling) wh druggists, 19 Macnab n

Wilson Archdale (Archdale Wilson & Co) h 45 Bay s
Wilson Arch, hotel, 238 King w
Wilson Archibald, moulder, 33 West ave n
Wilson Mrs C, 54 Strachan e
Wilson Charles jr, bookbinder, 165 John n
Wilson Charles sr, contractor, 165 John n
Wilson Edwin, salesman, 27½ Tisdale
Wilson Mrs Elizabeth, dressmaker, 81 Main w
Wilson Mrs Emma (wid George) 26 Ferguson ave
Willson F J, sewing machines and organs, 24 John n, h 8 Hannah w
Willson F M, pres Ontario Sewing Machine Co, 61 East ave s
Wilson Geo, engine driver, 49 Florence
Wilson George, file cutter, 156 King e
Wilson Geo E, provision dealer, 6 York
Wilson Mrs Isabella, 61 Locke s
Wilson J, painter, 128½ King e
Wilson James, dyer, 8 Chisholm
Wilson Jas, painter, Crooks
Wilson James, National hotel 250 York
Wilson James, moulder, 183 York
Wilson James D (Wm Wilson & Son) h 9 Hess s
Wilson James I, clerk, 67 Hunter e
Wilson John, 122 Queen n
Wilson John, laborer, 35 Barton w
Wilson John, carpenter, 11 Bay s
Wilson John, carpenter, 3 Devonport
Wilson John, salesman, 18 King e
Wilson John (Hani & Wilson) 49 Ray s

Wilson John, dyer, Ferguson ave n
Wilson John, sectionman, Burlington n
Wilson John, painter, 83 Hunter e
Wilson John, stovemounter, 63 Rebecca
Wilson John, fireman city hospital, Barton e
Wilson John, grocer, 31½ West ave n
Wilson John, traveler, 287 King William
Wilson Joseph, provisions, James st market, h 122 Queen n
Wilson Joseph, letter carrier, 54 Wilson
Wilson Joseph H, pork packer, 99 Hess n
Wilson M & Co, hay tool manfs, Caroline, cor Barton
Wilson Matthew, manufacturer, 187 Macnab n
Wilson Miss Mary, 65 Hughson s
Wilson Peter, porter, 11 Strachan e
Wilson Robert, boots and shoes, 60 King e, h 118 Rebecca
Wilson Robert, fireman, 103 Napier
Wilson Robert, laborer, Brock e
Wilson Robert, laborer, 281 Hughson n
Wilson Ross, com traveler, 66 Queen s
Wilson Samuel, bds 250 York
Wilson Samuel, 98 Wellington s
Wilson T H, M D, 154 Main e
Wilson Thomas, provisions, James st market
Wilson Thomas, hotel keeper, 101 Wellington n
Wilson Thomas, foreman Bay st fire station, 116 Napier
Wilson Thomas, laborer, 93 Robinson
Wilson Thomas, carpenter, South

Wilson Thomas, 24 Walnut s
Wilson Thomas, saloon keeper, 135-137 Cannon e
Wilson Thos, messenger Bank of British North America, 5 King e
Wilson Thomas, laborer, 111 Wood e
Wilson William, laborer, 178 Wilson
Wilson William, cloth inspector, 201 East ave n
Wilson William, moulder, 100 Emerald n
Wilson William, carpenter, 83 Main e
Wilson William, porter, 44 King e
Wilson William, spinner, 85 Ferrie e
Wilson William L, boarding, 103 King w
Wilson William & Son, merchant tailor, 44 King w
Wilston Joseph D, carpenter, Herkimer
Winckler Adolph, cooper, 120 Rebecca
Winckler Chas H, cutler, 97 King w
Winckler Julius, faucet maker, 68 Hughson s
Winer John, 96 Main e
Winer J & Co, wholesale druggists, 23-25 King e
Winfield Thomas, carpenter, 92 Caroline n
Winfield Thos, grocer, 142 Hunter w
Wing George, loom fixer, 23 Barton e
Wing John E, machinist, 128 Hunter w
Wingfield Alex, landing waiter, 8 Queen n
Winn Geo, shoemaker, 10 Elgin
Winn George, shoemaker, 137 Wellington n
Winn J H, dyer, Ontario Cotton Mills
Winn Richmond, laborer, 40 Chisholm
Winnifrith B, grocer, 246 King e
Winniscroft Geo, laborer, Ferguson ave n
Winslow Mrs A, (Winslow & Webber) h 31 Hess n
Winslow & Webber, carriage hardware, 56 King e
Winstone Daniel, laborer, r 61 Jackson e
Winter Edward, blacksmith, cor York and Dundurn
Winter Timothy, fireman G T R, 9 Inchbury s
Wise John, laborer, 152 Emerald n
Wise John, machinist, 105 Locke n
Wishart James, blacksmith, 63 King Wm, h 13 Tiffany
Witherby H F, watchmaker, 60 Jackson w
Witherspoon Mrs Elizabeth, (wid Harry) 152 Catharine n
Witherspoon R W (Cameron & Witherspoon) 152 Catharine n
Witton H B, canal inspector, 12 Murray w
Wodehouse Arthur, Wentworth s
Wodehouse T F, clerk, 31 West ave s
Wodell F W, night editor *Spectator*, 136 York
Wolfe Mrs E, 257 James n
Wolf Joseph R, pawnbroker, 53 John s
Wolfe Michael, Tremont House, 65 Stuart w
Wolfe Mose, cigarmaker, 257 James n
Wolfe Nathan, varieties, 78 King w, h 257 James n
Wolf Patrick, watchman, 32 Simcoe e
Wolfe Patrick, bartender, 65 Stuart w

Wood A T, (Wood & Leggat) 151 James s
Wood Cornelius, carter, 46 Canada
Wood Fred L, bookkeeper, 18 Erie ave
Wood James, clerk, 181 Macnab n
Wood John, brakesman, 124 Cannon e
Wood John F, manager Omnium Securities Co, res Copetown
Wood & Leggat (A T Wood, Matthew Leggat, W A Wood, William Vallance) wh hardware, 44 King e
Wood Mrs Margaret (wid Wm) boarding, 41 Bay n
Wood Thomas, builder, 72 Cannon w
Wood Capt William, mariner, 181 Macnab n
Wood William A (Wood & Leggat) 151 James s
Woodall Wm, builder, 2 Nightingale
Woodbine John, laborer, Greig
Woodcroft Levi, Hannah w
Woodhall Wm, builder, 12 Chisholm
Woodhouse Wm H, timekeeper, 85 George
Woodley Samuel, boots and shoes, 22 James n, h 49 Jackson w
Woodley William, laborer, 34 Strachan e
Woodman John, machinist, 98 Hess n
Woodman John, baggageman, 80 Lower Cathcart
Woodman Thomas, clerk, 140 Robert e
Woodruff R E, piano tuner, 45 Hess n
Woods George, laborer, 185 Victoria ave n
Woods Henry, laborer, 107 Bay n
Woods John, tinsmith, 36 York
Woods Joseph, carpenter, 35 Hughson n
Woods Robt, furniture finisher, 10 Napier
Woods Walter, broom manfr, 60-2 Macnab n, h 154 Macnab n
Woods William, manager Walter Woods, 48 Cannon w
Woodson Washington, laborer, 115 Catharine n
Woodward Frederick, upholster, 18 Cherry
Woodward Henry, accountant, 242 King e
Woodward H W, clerk customs, 242 King e
Woolcot Charles, enginedriver G T R, 45 Queen s
Wooley Wm, stave factory, Little William, h South
Woolley Mrs M (wid Wm) 105 Bay n
Wooley Robert, spinner, 130 Macaulay e
Woolverton Algernon, M D, coroner, 153 James n
Woolverton Mrs Eunice W (wid Allen) homeopathic pharmacy, 85 King w
Woolverton F E, M D, 119 King e
Worthington George, brakeman, 22 Kelly
Work Donald, 9 Grove
Work John, laborer, 21 Magill
Work Thomas, salesman, 35 Barton e
Worrall William, carpenter, 6 Hunter e
Worril Walter, stove polisher, 1½ Queen s
Wragg Alfred G, laborer, 146 Picton e
Wren Alfred, blacksmith, 71 Market
Wren John, porter, 118 Cherry
Wren Maurice, tinsmith, 122 Wellington s

Wren Morris, tinsmith, 34 Aurora
Wright Mrs Clara (wid Charles) 7 Peter
Wright Mrs Alex, 7 Mulberry
Wright Alfred, locksmith, 38 Cherry
Wright Alfred W, second hand dealer 18 King Wm
Wright Elijah, 306 King w
Wright Mrs Eliza (wid Thomas) 75 Bay n
Wright Emerson, supt Bridge and Tool works, 16 Mulberry
Wright E T, manufacturer, 92 Catharine s
Wright E T & Co, japanners, 68 Mary
Wright Henry G, com traveler, 75 Bay n
Wright James, mariner, 4 Tisdale
Wright John, blacksmith, Wilson e Wentworth
Wright John, butcher, 286 York
Wright John, stove dealer, 48 King Wm, Little Wellington
Wright John, weaver, s w cor Mary and Picton
Wright Leslie, baggage master, 10 Grove
Wright Lewis, pedler, Locke s
Wright Matthew, cotton broker, 2 Duke
Wright Mrs James,279 King Wm
Wright Peter, stove driller, 52 Florence
Wright Robert (Thomson & Wright) h 42 Main w
Wright Robert, laborer, 154 Market
Wright Robert, spinner, 90 Macauley e
Wright Samuel, whipmaker, 140 Robert e
Wright Mrs S McB (wid D) 19 Augusta
Wright Thomas O, gunsmith, 25 York
Wright William, moulder,65 Colborne
Wright Wm, laborer, 36 Crooks
Wright William, machinist, 60 Locke s
Wright William, machinist, 2 Concession
Wright Wm G, machinist, 5 West ave n
Wurst Frederick, carpenter, 145 King William
Wurst John, bricklayer, 145 King Wm
Wurst William, machinist, 145 King Wm
Wyatt Thomas, laborer, Robinson
Wylie James, 36 Main w
Wyllie A A, asst appraiser customs, 158 Macnab n
Wyllie Allison, foreman Ontario Cotton Mills, 227 Macnab n
Wyndham Wm, packer, King e
Wynn Hugh, saloon, 165 Macnab n
Wynn John, heater, 36 Colborne
Wynn Michael, laborer, 238 Catharine n
Wynn Percy A, shoemaker, 262 York
Wynn Thomas, 61 Maria
Wyth Eleazar, carpenter, 261 York
Yaldon Mrs Margaret (wid Richard) 16 Cannon w
Yaldon R W, hotel keeper, 105 James n
Yaldon Wm, City Arms Hotel, 23 Murray w
Yarl Thomas, laborer, 23 Little William
Yates Albert, stove mounter, bds 251 Macnab n
Yates Charles R, bds 37 Tisdale
Yates George H, laborer, 169 Bay n
Yates Thomas, shoemaker, bds 251 Macnab n
Yates Walter, laborer, 37 Tisdale
Yates Wm, bricklayer, 68 Emerald n

Yates Wm H, laborer, bds 169 Bay n
Yearsley Samuel F, painter, bds 293 King w
Yeomans John W, druggist, 40 George
York Frank, clerk, 80 Robert
Young Miss Agnes, 184 Macnab n
Young Albert, machinist, bds 204 Macnab n
Young Albert, salesman, bds 34 Bay n
Young Alexander, laborer, bds 81 Stuart w
Young Mrs Ann (wid John) Ferguson ave n
Young Miss Annie, dressmaker, 84 Bay n
Young & Bro (Robert and William) chandelier manufacturers, dealers in lamp goods, 17 John n and 135 King Wm
Young Albert H, clerk, 101 Lower Cathcart
Young Charles, agent, 116 Cannon e
Young David, bds Locke s
Young Edward, salesman R Evans & Co
Young Edward, plasterer, 86 Ferrie e
Young Frederick, laborer, bds 204 Macnab n
Young Geo, clerk, 45 Jackson w
Young George A, insurance agent, 2 Merrick, h 11 Young
Young George A, clerk, bds 45 Jackson w
Young Hamilton, manager Ham Cotton Mills, h 41 Duke
Young Henry, carpenter, 62 Emerald n
Young Jacob, painter, 186 Catharine n
Young James, carpenter, 272 James n
Young James, veterinary surgeon, bds 139 York
Young James, bookkeeper, 88 Napier
Young James, laborer, 168 East ave n
Young James D, plumber, Cannon e nr Wentworth
Young James M, Hamilton Cotton Co, 91 Macnab s
Young John, gardener, bds 103 King w
Young John, engineer, 56 Wellington s
Young J H H, clerk, res Burlington
Young John B, bookkeeper, 33 Hannah w
Young John B, accountant and marriage licenses, 20 Charles
Young Jno H, architect, 26 Merrick, h 145 Park n
Young Maitland, sec N & N W By, res Burlington
Young Mrs Margaret (wid Hugh) 16 Locomotive
Young Mrs Margaret (wid Henry) 107 Catharine n
Young Men's Christian Association, 38 King e
Young P F, law student, 77 Mary
Young Miss Mary, dressmaker, bds 84 Bay n
Young Robert (Young & Bro) h 3 East ave s
Young Robert, brassfinisher, 98 Park n
Young Samuel, timekeeper, 204 Macnab n
Young Thomas, saloon, 7 Gore, h 64 John n
Young Thomas, porter, 137 Hunter w
Young Thos, heater, 129 Locke n
Young Wallace, foreman Young & Bro, 55 East ave n
Young Wm (Young & Bro) h 45 Jackson w
Young Wm, bookkeeper, bds 33 Hannah w
Young W A, plater, 14½ King e

Yuker C, com traveler, 26 Liberty
Yule James, clerk American hotel
Yunganger George, sausage mkr, 118 East ave n
Zachau Frederick A, furrier, 37 Wellington s
Zalinsky Maregin, laborer, bds 121 Jackson w
Zealand Mrs Edwd, 16 Murray w
Zealand E G, deputy sheriff, court house, h 16 Murray w
Zealand's Wharf, E Zealand, propr, Brock w
Zealand Capt Wm, 257 Bay n
Zimmerman A, merchant tailor, 50 James n, h 31 Caroline n
Zimmerman J, dentist, 38 King e, h 75 Emerald s
Zimmerman S, MD, DDS, dentist, cor King and Macnab
Zimmerman W E, salesman, 22 Liberty
Zingsheim Jacob, furniture manf, 225 Mary, h 33 Murray e
Zion Tabernacle, Rev Mr. Snider, pastor, Pearl cor Napier
Zoeller John, sr, tailor, 47 Catharine s
Zoller John, cigar maker, 230½ Bay n
Zwick W H, accountant and real estate agency, 26 Merrick

CITY AND COUNTY DIRECTORIES

The following will be sent on receipt of price.

City of Hamilton	$2 50
City of Kingston, including Frontenac county	2 00
City of St. Catharines, including Lincoln and Welland	2 00
City of Brantford, including Brant county	2 00
County of Simcoe	2 00
County of Wentworth	2 00

WE ARE ALSO AGENTS FOR THE

City of Guelph	2 00
County of Wellington	3 00
County of Waterloo	3 00
City of Quebec	2 50
City of Ottawa	2 50
City of Montreal	3 00

ALL BOOKS ARE RECENT EDITIONS.

W. H. IRWIN & CO.,

12 MACNAB ST. SOUTH. *Hamilton, Ontario.*

HAMILTON STREET DIRECTORY.

Aikman's Avenue, from Wentworth south, runs east

James Freed, gardener
Patrick Lynch, sectionman
Mrs Mary Duggan
Wm Kane, laborer
John McLean, boilermaker
Nicholas Solvesburg
James Sullivan, laborer
John Davis, fishmonger
John Solvisburg, laborer
Walter Davis, laborer
M Begley, conductor
Thos Johnston, blacksmith
J A Gold, piano maker
Wm Johnston, blacksmith
S Hazelwood, carpenter

Burlington-st intersects

John McLean, blacksmith
Harry Marshall, gardener
Mrs Morin

Wentworth-st intersects

Wm Harvey, stonecutter
Chas Anderson, stonecutter

Alanson-st from west of Erie ave east to Wentworth

Blythe-st intersects

30 Jeremiah O'Connors, laborer

Erie-ave intersects

29 Stephen Jones, laborer
31 Charles Anstey, letter carrier
33 Alex Stuart, clerk
35 Vacant
37 Thomas Hutchinson, painter
39 G W Cooper, blacksmith
41 Frank Ide, laborer
43 James Barle, lamplighter
45 Edgar Mortimer, teamster
47 Alex R Grant, carpenter

Ardvolich-st, from Dundurn west

No houses

Argo Street, from end Main east

Wm McGrath, cabinetmaker
Edward Earley, pedler

Ashley-st, from end King east north to Barton

John Home, dealer
J C Granger, pedler
Jeremiah Rowe, mason
James Laidlaw, carpenter

Augusta-st, north side, from 85 James south to Catharine

5 F R Hutton, builder
Vacant lots
15 Vacant

Hughson-st intersects

19 Mrs Sarah Wright
21 Benno Scheuer, bookkeeper
23 W H McDonald, merchant
25 James Cooper, barber

John st intersects

39-41 Ballentine Bros, grocers
43 Wm Lewis, plasterer
47 Mrs Thomas
49 Joseph Barry, artist
49½ Thomas Sinzel

Catharine-st intersects

Augusta-st, south side

2 Samuel Jarvis, caretaker
6 Wm Mitchell, jr, teamster
8 Hugh Daley, whipmaker
10 Alex Robertson, carpenter
12 Henry Simon, manf
14 P F Barber, P O clerk
16 J G McIlwraith, merchant
16½ Thos H Snider, baker
18 J B Kitchen, photographer
20 R S Ambrose, music teacher

Hughson-st intersects

28 J Dublin, whitewasher
30 Wm Newcomb, laborer
32 Wm G Smith, laborer
34 Hiram Denum, whitewasher

John-st Intersects

38 Frank Farrish, whipmaker
46 James McKenzie, machinist
48 John McDonough, laborer
48½ Mrs Michael Garvey

Catharine-st intersects

Aurora-st, east side, from 116 Young to Hannah

12 Mrs Margaret Santry

Young-st intersects

22 John Lavelle, cigar manf
24 Wm Berry, harnessmaker
24½ Daniel Sheen, baker
26 Mrs Patrick McDonald

Maria-st intersects

32 Edmund Murphy, tailor
34 John Foley, cooper
38 Thomas Mahony, laborer

Hannah-st intersects

Aurora Street, west side

19 Mrs Julia Fitzmaurice
25 Mrs Michael Sullivan

Maria-st intersects

41 Joseph Hooker, gardener
43 Thomas Turner, bricklayer

Hannah-st intersects

Baillie-st, from 72 Hunter east

4 Samuel Harvy, auctioneer
10 John Cline, marble cutter
16 George Williams, carpenter

Barton-st east, north side from 196 James north to City Limits

11 David Brown, carpenter
13 Vacant
15 Joseph Philp, salesman
17 Joseph Foquett, laborer
19 Thomas Strachan, merchant
21 John McKinty, customs
23 Mrs Alex Boyd

Hughson-st intersects

25 Mrs Thos Callon
29 David Kemp, painter
31 Daniel McNicol, carpenter
33 Wm H Povey, painter
35 Thomas Work, laborer
39 Jacob Weakley, tinsmith

John-st intersects

53 Douglas Nelson
55 Mrs John Ryan
57 Edward Oakes, tailor,
59 James Larmer, laborer
61 John Holleran, traveler
65 Patrick Holloran, grocer

Catharine-st intersects

71 Henry McGolrick
73 Thomas Finn, laborer
75 Mrs Mary King
79 John Ford

Mary-st intersects

91 Wanzer Sewing Machine Co

Elgin-st intersects

County jail

Ferguson-ave intersects

113 Frank Lynch, teamster
117 Osborne, Killey manf Co
119 George McNeilly, laborer
131 John Brennan, machinist
133 Enoch Taylor, polisher

Wellington-st intersects
Flatt & Bradley, lumber
City hospital
Victoria-ave intersects
215 R N Wheeler, grocer
217 Vacant
219 R W Crooks, teamster
221 James Gross, carpenter
223 Mrs Mary Burt
225 G M Cannon, mechanic
233 Richard Raycroft, grocer
East-ave intersects
237 John Kirkness, cooper
239 James Bews, clerk
243 Mrs Elizabeth Jamieson
Emerald-st intersects
Vacant lots
261 F Rowlin, butcher
297 G B Smith, wood dealer
309 Vacant
311 Vacant
313 Wm Tout, engineer
Little William-st intersects
319 John Graham, grocer
327 Wm Hodgson, butcher
329 David Buick, watchman
Wentworth-st intersects
Wm J Jones, tollkeeper
Askett Williams, gardener

Barton Street east, south side

6 John Cahill, blacksmith
32 Vacant
Hughson-st intersects
34 Mrs S Ross
36 Thos O'Connoll, laborer
38 Isaiah Audett, blacksmith
40 Edmund Davis, teacher
42 James King, agent
John-st intersects
54 Wm Nash, engineer
56 W H McElcheran, painter
58 Mrs Harriet Waldren
Catharine-st intersects
70 Vacant
72 John Westway, fireman

74 Thomas Adams, sailor
80 H Little, grocer
Mary-st intersects
Private grounds
92 Wm C Barnfather, engineer
94 John Kennedy, foreman
Elgin-st intersects
98 Martin Burns, machinist
100 T Kavanagh, moulder
102 John E Davis, machinist
104 Mrs G Allan
106 J A Griffin, printer
Ferguson-ave intersects
Round house
134 W H Pugh, shoemaker
136 Charles Edwards, clerk
138 James Dufton, bricklayer
140 Alex Campbell, policeman
142 Wm Blackburn, wheelwright
Wellington-st intersects
Vacant lots
West-ave intersects
198 Fred Beaumert, hatter
200 James Robinson, moulder
202 Mrs Jane Selvin
204 Mrs Louisa Smith
Victoria-ave intersects
226 Vacant
228 Frank Whitelock, clerk
230 Mrs Ellen Knight
232 Wm Cunnington, hatter
234 — Chambers, dyer
236 Vacant
East-ave intersects
John Fleming, grocer
Emerald-st intersects
248 Mrs M J Hutton, tailoress
248½ Alfred Hobbs, tinsmith
250 Mrs Edwards
Chisholm-st intersects
254 Edward Goff, traveler
Mrs Isabella Lewis
Smith-ave intersects
296 John H Land
298 Vacant

Wentworth-st intersects

Barton Street west, north side, from 125 James north to Locke

12 D Robertson, carpenter
14 Wm Allan, contractor
16 Thos Whitney, hackman
18 Andrew Leitch, machinist
20 Victor Russell, carpenter
22 Albert Lake, broommaker

Macnab-st intersects

40 Wm Magee, ice dealer
42 Wm Geldhart, finisher
44 Wm Morgan, machinist
52 John Black, butcher

Park-st intersects

58 Charles Peters, clerk
60 Arthur Nash, laborer

Bay-st intersects

Vacant lots to Locomotive street
A Massie, time keeper
Vacant lots to end

Barton Street west, south side

13 Mrs Blake
r13 Mrs John Hatts
15 Mrs Edwin M Coventry
17 Wm R Harvey, traveler
19 Henry Welch, machinist
25 W A Sealey, carpenter

Macnab-st intersects

35 Horace Brown, teamster
43 George Roach

Park-st intersects

65 Mrs John Jackson
67 Wm Joy, shoemaker
67½ Alfred Crist, glassblower
69 E H Hopgood, butcher
71 Wm Jack, laborer

Bay-st intersects

Caroline-st intersects

Mrs Jennie Sheppard
Vacant lots

Greig-st intersects

Alfred Presnell, blacksmith
John Cannon, fitter
Mrs Margaret Girouard
Miss M A Fletcher
John Dunn, laborer

Locomotive-st intersects

Vacant

Magill-st intersects

James McIlory, watchman
Joshua Jackson, fireman
John Daly, yardsman
Mrs Richard Crooks
James Black, conductor

Crook-st intersects

John Quinn, pattern maker
John Quinn, varnisher
John Qnirk, varnisher
V Byrne, laborer

Locke-st intersects

Bay-st north, east side, from 128 King west to Macnab

8 R Buskard, carriagemaker
10 Hiram Hurd, marble dealer

Market-st intersects

26 John Rodgers, blacksmith
28 Thos L Kay, machinist
30 George W Alderson, plasterer
34 Andrew A Cook, trimmer
36 John Armstrong
38 Dyer Durphey, carpenter
40-44 Thos Porteous, butcher
50 David McDonald, grocer

York-st intersects and Merrick-st ends.

58 Thomas Knott, clerk
60 John Rymal, traveler
62 Craven & Son, blacksmiths
Hurd & Roberts, marble-y'd

Vine-st ends

72 Wm H Judd, soap manfr
76 George Dew, soap boiler
78 John Waugh, carpenter
80 James Ailles, salesman
82 John McMurray, teamster

84 Miss A Young, dressmaker
86 James Legg, teamster
88 Thomas Ford, baker
90 Wm Lattimore, blacksmith
92 James Martin, shoemaker
Cannon-st intersects
94-96 Wm Sheriff, grocer
98-100 Wm Geiss, machinist
104 Mrs Thomas Bradfield
r 104 Mrs Quinn, laundress
106 John Homewood, carriage trimmer
108 William Ashby, foreman
110 James Insch, fitter
112 John Augus, pattern maker
114-116 Gas works
Mulberry-st intersects
118 Mrs Robert Moffatt
124 Adam Crossman, butcher
126 Charles Thomson, laborer
130 Cornelius Murphy, laborer
132 John Cloughley, melter
134 Michael Moriarty, laborer
136 Thomas Bowden, laborer
Sheaffe-st intersects
140-142 Edwin Harris, boarding
144 John Lahiff, laborer
144½ John W Sharp, carpenter
146 Mrs James Riddle, grocer
150 Wm Aikins, machinist
Colborne-st intersects
152 Wm Leask, watchman
154 Wm B Evans, meter maker
156 Pierce Grace, melter
158 Thos Oliver, shoemaker
160 Ed W Hopwood, pork curer
Barton-st intersects
162 M J Dillon, hotel keeper
166 John Davidson, collector
168 Vacant
170 Miss C R Regan
170 Robert E Robson, painter
172 Mrs John Neelon, boarding
174 Miss M Enwright, dressmkr
176 John Hall, foreman G T R
Murray-st intersects
Hamilton Industrial Wks Co
196 Wm Baker, supt Street R R
198 John Logan, inland revenue
204 James McKeown, hotel
Stuart & Strachan-sts intersect
Vacant lots
Simcoe-st intersects
230 Edward Moran, japanner
230½ John Zoller, cigar maker
232 John Mackay
234 Wm, Cowan, platelayer
236 Thos Shackell, conductor
238 George Clark, driver
240 Jeremiah McCoy, carpenter
242 Patrick Merrin, inspector
Ferrie-st intersects
250 Wm McClure, carpenter
252 Wm Irving, machinist
254 Wm C Thomson patrn mkr
256 Wm Campbell, checker
258 Capt Robert Hamilton
260 Captain John E Burrows
Picton-st intersects
266 James McKeever, laborer
266½ Thos Tracie, brakeman
268 Samuel Bennett, brassfinisher
270 Wm Durdon, engineer
274 Jos Charlton, glassblower
Macauley-st intersects
284 Mrs Augusta Grant
286 Mrs Henry Sanders
Burlington & Brock-sts intersect

Bay-st north, west side

1 T B Fairchilds, hotel
3 F Schwarz, cigarmaker
5 Vacant
7 Vacant
9 Vacant
11 Thos Devenport, gardener
13 Walter Spencer, tuner
15 Henry Kuntz, brewer
17 Vacant
19 Vacant
21 A T Davis, G T R
23 Robert Williams, traveler
Market-st intersects

25 Vacant
27 Sam W Townsend, customs
29 Wm Fitzgerald, miller
31 Chas A Wilcox, agent
33 T D Boyes, checker G T R
35 Mrs Wm Armitage, dressmkr
37 Wm Ronald, grocer
39 Jacob Kuntz, brewer
41 Mrs Wm Wood, boarding
43 John Schwarz, traveler

Napier-st commences

51 Vacant

York-st intersects

Copp Bros foundry
71 W H Judd & Bro, soap mfr
73 John Home, tinsmith
75 H G Wright, com traveler
77 Mrs Wm Wagner
79 Mrs George Laing
81 Thos Jarvis, furniture dealer
81¼ Wm McFedries, salesman
82 Fred Edworthy, butcher
85 Robert Ackland, patrn mkr
87 John Williams, brakeman
89 Mrs Margt Byrne, dressmkr

Cannon-st intersects

92 F J Schrader, tobacconist
93 Wm Aitchison, hotel
95 John C Schrader, cigar mkr
97 George Pettinger
101 Kenneth McKenzie, painter
103 Wm Nieghorn, music teacher
105 Robert Gray, conductor
107 Hugh Williams, carpenter
109 Wm B Croy, com traveler
111 M D Healey, dry goods merch
113 Michael Sweeney, traveler
115 Fred Filgiano, clerk
117 Vacant
119 Michael Arland
121 John D Evans, brewer
123 Wm L Cummer, brewer

Mulberry-st intersects

Spring Brewery

Sheaffe-st intersects

143 Joseph Preston, watchman
145 Wm Dowd, laborer
147 A Berryman, telegraphist
149 James McLaughlin, moulder
151 John Saunders, painter
153 Wm Horn, messenger GTR
155 Robert Amos, salesman
157 Ralph Tiderington, boltmkr
159-161 John Dillon, grocer

Barton-st intersects

163 Charles Plater, shoemaker
165 Peter McCullough, laborer
169 Wm Dillon, laborer
169 George H Yates, laborer
173 Mrs Elizabeth Chambers
r173 John M Warner, woodwkr
175 James Holland, boiler mkr
177 Alex McIsaac, laborer
179 James Fitzgerald, laborer
101 John Desmond, laborer
183 Hector Dodson, whipmaker
r183 Henry Horton, laborer
r183 Maurice Cummings, laborer
185 Mrs M Sheridan
r185 Patrick Murphy, laborer
r185 Thos Quinton, laborer
187 Matthew Burns, teamster
189 Mrs Mary Gleason
191 George McLennan, laborer
193 James Chambers, conductor
195 Jas Berryman, shoemaker
197 Ed Tregenza, laborer
199 Patrick O'Neil, laborer
Alison House

Stuart-st intersects

207 G T R engineer's office
Gillesby's grain warehouse

Strachan-st intersects

209 Thos McNoah, boarding
213 John Dobson, stovemounter
215 Daniel Hartnett, laborer
217 Lawrence Murphy, laborer

Simcoe-st intersects

239 Thos Renton, carpenter
241 James Falls, switchman
r241 Wm Pilton, laborer
243 James Forest, laborer
245 John Whitby, fitter
247 Wm Rennie, letter carrier

Ferrie-st intersects

J Massie's boathouse
253 Mrs Ann Vila, grocer
255 Augustin Vila, chandler
257 Capt Wm Zealand
259 John Mulholland, fireman
261 Walter Scott, engineer

Picton-st intersects

265 L H Bastien, boatbuilder

Macaulay-st intersects

277 Edward Brunt, stovemonnter
285 Robert Soper, sail loft
287 James Doyle, mariner

Wood-st intersects

Sweet's warehouse

Brock-st intersects

Bay-st south, east side, from 98 King west to the mountain

1 G C Briggs, drugs, etc
3 Wm Atkinson
5 Eli VanAllen, builder
7 Chas A Thomson, com trav
7½ Wm Birkett, manf
9 David Aitchison
11 John Wilson, cabinetmaker

Main-st intersects

19-21 J Walker, soap manf
23 R N Raw, bookkeeper
25 Hose reel house

Jackson-st intersects

39 C H Bamfylde, clerk
41 R G Olmsted, founder
43 A D Stewart, chief of police
45 A Wilson, druggist
47 H W Sewell, grocer
49 Peter Brass, architect
51 George Bristol, grocer

Hunter-st intersects

Central school grounds

Bold-st intersects

61 J H Somerville, com trav
69 C S Chittenden, dentist

Duke-st intersects

Vacant lots

Robinson-st intersects

93 Edwin VanAllen, carpenter
95 Edmund Savage, bookkeeper

Hannah-st intersects

109 Henry W Glassco, hatter
121 A R Gates, bookkeeper

Herkimer-st intersect

123 David Thompson, jeweler
127 J B Pilkey, merchant
129 Samuel Slater, banker
131 John Smith, emigration agt

Markland and Concession-sts intersects

Thomas Swinyard

Bay-st south, west side

4 G D Hawkins, shirt manf
6 David Hawkins, shirt manf

George-st commences

8 J Heriman, stage driver
10 Mrs Wm H Pim

Main-st intersects

24 Walker's soap factory
28 Albert Jones, laborer
30 Thos Jenkins, lather
32 Wm Hanley, blacksmith

Jackson-st intersects

34 Mrs Wm Harvey
36 John McLeod, clerk
46 Chas Doolittle, manf

Hunter-st intersects

St Mark's Church of England

Bold-st intersects

60 Mrs Alex Ewing
64 Joseph Kavanagh
66 Rev A E Miller
68 Wm Henderson, bookkeeper
70 John Stewart
72 Daniel Whitmore, porter

Duke-st intersects

E Healey, grocer
John Duff
74 James Paterson, bookkeeper
76 S H Kent, clerk

78 John Harrison barrister
80 Vacant
82 John Catchpole, clerk P O
84 Vacant
86 Vacant
88 J C McKeand, merchant
Robinson-st intersects
90 Alfred Morson, M D
92 Walter Ambrose, clerk
94 Wm Palm
96 Mrs Chas Freeman
98 Henry H Fuller
100 John Mitchell, mason
104 Vacant
Hannah-st intersects
James M Lottridge, brewer
Herkimer-st intersects
126 Robert Lottridge
128 Wm Gatenby, tailor
130 Mrs Eliza Roper
132 Wm Carey, publisher
Markland-st intersects
134 Alex Ramsay
140 W F Walker, barrister
144 C J Jones, telegraph co
146 Mrs Elizabeth Lauder
148 F Wm Gates, manf
Concession-st intersects

Bauer's Lane, from 360 John n
6 Wm Gompf, teamster
8 John Brown, laborer
Ontario Brewery

Blyth-st, from 72 Stinson south to Alanson
14 Josiah Baker, carpenter,
16 John Butterworth, carpenter
18 James Sage, carpenter
26 George F Fisher, harness mkr

Bold-st, north side, from 78 James south to Queen
2 Elias Vernon, M D
4 H F Gardiner, journalist
Macnab-st intersects
Vacant grounds
Charles & Park-sts intersect
Central school grounds
40 Thos Ralston, janitor
Bay-st intersects
66 Oscar Hendershot, laborer
68 Thos O'Neil, baker
Caroline-st intersects
76 George Curry, laborer
78 George Green, butcher
80 Samuel Howard, carpenter
82 James Goodale, laborer
84 John Dowrie, carpenter
86 Vacant
88 Thos Butler, blacksmith
90 Thos Pugh, carter
92 Mrs Susan Harris
96 James Baxter, teamster
98 Mrs Mary Cullen
100 Mrs Mary Ann Nealin
102 Wm Ballantine, laborer
Hess-st intersects
104 Fred Thorne, moulder
106 B H Webber, merchant
110 Henry Clark, publisher
112 Thos Lackie, laborer
114 Kenneth Campbell, laborer
116 John Coyne, laborer
118 Vacant
120 G McCullough, blacksmith
122 Thos Oliver, tailor
124 Wm L Johnstone, blacksmith
Queen-st intersects
128 Matt T Carroll, bricklayer
A H Taylor, painter
130 James Minnes, blacksmith
Ray-st intersects
Wm Gardner, scalemaker
1 I B McQuesten, barrister
3 Rev Thos Baker
5 P H Stuart, clerk
7 Daniel Sterling, traveler
9 Robert Pentecost, com trav
11 Mrs James Fisher
13 Mrs Gracie Iredale
Macnab-st intersects

23 Wm Hendrie, contractor

Park-st intersects

31 David Dow, plasterer
33 George Dickson, principal Coll Ins
33½ Wm Southam, publisher
35 George Hardiker, clerk
37 John W Bickle, broker
39 John Malloy, carriage maker

Bay-st intersects

57 D Kidd, cashier Can Life
61 Mrs A Macallum
65 Mrs John Hope
67 John Cole

Caroline-st intersects

E B Feast, grocer
77 N Frolich, bricklayer
79 Geo S Hunter, auctioneer
81 John Timson, policeman
83 Geo Baxter, teamster
85 John Stevens, machinist
87 John McAllister, laborer
95 Samuel McKelvie, laborer

Hess-st intersects

100 Samuel Coulter, shoemaker

Queen-st intersects

111 G McLean, shoemaker
115 Robt Wade, baker
F C Matthews, caretaker

Bowen-st from 48 Main east to Jackson

James Kennedy, blacksmith
P E Webber, livery
Joseph Hoodless & Son, warehouse

Breadlebane, from Jones to Galt

Thos Nelligan, laborer
Geo Trevaskis, wagonmaker
Charles Smith, laborer
Alfred Cheesman, laborer

Brock-st east, north side, from foot of Bay to Macnab

Robertson's shipyard
Zealand's wharf
J Anderson, teamster
Patrick Roach, laborer

Brock-st, south side

23 Arch Robertson, shipbuilder
11 H Lee, clerk

Brock-st west, from Hughson to Mary

46 Robert Wilson, laborer
51 James Walling, laborer
Timothy Holland, laborer

Bruce-st, from Markland bet Bay and Caroline, south to Concession

Jacob Schwab, machinist
Frank A White, laborer
Sam Bailey, carpenter
Wm Pennell, jr, laborer
Wm Pennell, sr, laborer

Concession-st intersects

Burlington-st north, Tp of Barton, east side

John S Beer, butcher
George Greig, gardener
W C White, builder

Wilson st intersects

Wm Springstead, gardener
Harry Atwell, porter
Mrs Patrick O'Dea
Joseph Wilson, laborer
Michael O'Dea, blacksmith
Wm Tait, butcher
Andrew Lewis, laborer
Michael Ryan, bricklayer
Dennis Ryan, laborer
Edward O'Brien, laborer
Robert Bow, tinsmith
Mrs Parslow
John Ellis, laborer
Patrick Morrison, shoemaker

Burlington-st, west side
Samuel A Tovel, gardener
John E Tovel, gardener

Burlington-st south, Tp of Barton, east side
Henry E Elliott, cutter
Thos Harper, gardener
M O'Sullivan, moulder
E S Whipple, real estate agt

Burlington-st south, west side
Fred Johnston, merchant
Alex Fraser, merchant

Burlington-st east side from 368 James n to John
Vacant
13 James Ennis, laborer
15 Thos Kavanagh, machinist
Hughson-st intersects
Vacant lots to end

Burlington-st east, south side
Hughson-st intersects
32 Thos McCarthy, carter
John-st intersects
John Sullivan, laborer

Burlington-st west, north side from 347 James n to Bay
Private grounds
Macnab-st intersects
Burlington Glass works
40 John Roach, sailor
42 Wm McNab, laborer
44 Mrs Robert Graham
46 Mrs Ellen Macdonald
48 Fred Bootham, mariner
50 Wm Robertson, shipbuilder
Wood-st intersects
52 John Wakeham, carpenter
54 Robert Soper, sailmaker
56 Wm Little, glassblower
58 Wm McGowan, laborer
Bay-st intersects

Burlington st w, south side
e13 Thos Richardson, boilermkr
15 P McGrath, laborer
17 M Hamilton, laborer
19 Thos Snowdon, blacksmith
21 Jacob Lee, laborer
23 Fred Pearson, laborer
25 James McGee, carter
27 Mrs A Mack
Macnab-st intersects
33 Vacant
35 Mrs Hugh Smith
37 Thos Jones, glassblower
39 Wm Cunningham teamster
41 A J Mooney, laborer
43 John Dolman, sailor
Wood-st intersects
53 Wm Griffin, sailor
57 D Barker, carpenter
63 Andrew Donovan, laborer
Bay-st intersects

Canada-st, north side, from Queen south to western limits
2 J B Simpson, conductor
4 George Crockford, jeweler
8 John B Faulkner, bricklayer
Ray-st Intersects
18 Moses Dow, plasterer
20 John D Campbell, enameler
24 Geo Ennis, cabinetmaker
26 Robert Scriver, boilermaker
28 Mrs Fred Rohr
Pearl-st intersects
34 Wm Ford, salesman
36 Wm Fickley, moulder
42 Theo Posal, laborer
44 Geo A Burke, varnisher
46 Cornelius Wood, carter
Locke-st intersects
52 John Dennis, painter
56 Albert Vaughan, laborer
58 Wm Melody, carter
62 Wm J Dyer, bookkeeper
Poulette-st intersects
64 A McFarlane, tobacconist
70 Thos Collins, potter
72 Mrs Michael McGrath
74 Joseph Langdon, engineer

76 Isaac Webb, shoe cutter
78 John Bawden, brickmaker
82 Alex Hay, carpenter
86 Aaron Bawden, brickmaker

Garth-st intersects

Canada-st south side

3 Richard Haigh, bookbinder
4 Jas Kennedy, blacksmith
11 Alex Kay, machinist

Kay-st intersects

25 Peter Warnke, tailor
29-31 David W Kern, grocer

Pearl-st intersects

35 Edward Joy, carpenter
39 Rudolph Thatcher, laborer
43 Joseph Poynton, painter

Locke-st intersects

49 Vacant
51 Elijah Hannah, laborer
57 Wm Earl, brickmaker
59 Jas W Sinclair, grocer
61 Hugh Toner, laborer
63 Thos Brown, teamster
63½ Chas Holdsworth, packer
65 George Metcalfe, painter

Poulette-st intersects

Vacant lots
79 Walter Etherington, carpenter
83 Robert Budge, laborer
89 Vacant

Garth-st intersects

Cannon-st east, north side. from 118 James north to Wentworth

Knox Church
Cannon street school

Hughson-st intersects

Vacant
Malleable Iron Works

John-st intersects

42 P J Cnlhane, bill poster
44 Daniel Kelly, coal dealer
46 Ed Webster, machinist
48 Mrs Ann Black

Catharine-st intersects

62 G Bilton & Co, pop manfs
84 G McKay, merchant
86 R W Seldon, grocer

Mary-st intersects

John Thomson, customs

Elgin-st intersects

N & N W Railway offices

Ferguson-ave intersects

114 John Garrison, engineer
116 Charles Young, agent
118 John Glassford, fireman
120 S Cunningham, conductor
122 Mrs George Will
124 Chas Stewart, carpenter
126 F W Johnston, moulder
126½ Wm Clear, machinist
128 Mrs E Degarmo
130 Mrs John Menorgan
132 Thos McCann, vinegar manf
134 John Finlayson, saddler

Cathcart-st intersects

136 P Ronan, flour dealer
138 Geo Allan, telegraphist
140 J G Currell, barrister
142 Albert Pentecost, merchant
142 Robert Webster
144 R White, carpenter
146 Alex McCoy, lithographer
148 John Peacock, inspector
152 John Ronan, grocer

Wellington-st intersects

158 Walter Bastedo, furrier

West-ave intersects

174 Augustus Knetsch, tailor

Victoria-ave intersects

198 Robert Holmes

East-ave intersects

204 Vacant
206 Joseph Harter, moulder
208 John Stark, stovemounter

Emerald-st intersects

226 J Burton, cabinet maker
228 Joseph Cripps, laborer

Chisholm-st commences

234 Mrs John Littlehales
236 John Jennings, moulder

240 M H Little, plumber
242 Elzer Sawyers, shoemaker
Smith-ave intersects
James D Young, plumber
Wentworth-st intersects

Cannon-st east, south side

1 Albert Armstrong, bartender
3 Wm Nelson, waiter
5 James Haven, ornamentor
7 George Waite, painter
9 Mrs E Ross, dressmaker
11 Wm Potter, ropemaker
13 Wm Morton
Hughson-st intersects
Congregational Church
25 George Henderson, printer
27 Wm Dixon, needlemaker
John-st intersects
43 W H Tallman & Co, wood
45 Charles Egener, nickel plater
47 Wm Curry, laborer
49 James Wallace, moulder
Catharine-st intersects
57-63 Thomas Doherty, coffee mills
65 John Dunbar, porter
67 W P VanNorman, agent
75 Wm Reid, machinist
Mary-st intersects
87 E B Cunningham
89 C Mnnroe, tinsmith
91 John McHaffie, merchant
Elgin-st intersects
N & N W premises
Ferguson-ave intersects
117 Thos Judd, laborer
119 Wm Payne, wood dealer
123 Union wood and coal yard
Cathcart-st intersects
127 Wm Ronald, engineer
127 Donald Graham, fireman
131 Wm Chappell, builder
137 Thomas Wilson, saloon
Wellington-st intersects
153 Geo Shoots, painter
155 Alex Boyd, painter
West-ave intersects
175 John Corigle, carpenter
177 George Richmond, moulder
179 W Goodfellow, patternfitter
181 Wm Goodfellow, stovemntr
183 E A DeWitt, butcher
Victoria-ave intersects
189 Mrs M McMicking
191 George Broadbent, engineer
193 Mrs Henry Coulter
195 Henry Filgiano, clerk
197 Peter Foreman, shoemaker
East-ave intersects
215 Mrs Wm Taylor
Emerald-st intersects
217 Timothy Sullivan, laborer
221 Mrs Patrick Fitzgerald
223 Vacant
225 George Blake, laborer
227 William Elder, shoemaker
Tisdale-st intersects
235 Joseph Whitney
239 Albert Dowling, machinist
241 Joseph Stoneham, machinist
243 Vacant
Steven-st intersects

Cannon-st west, north side, from 119 James north to Hess

8 James White, M D
16 Mrs M Yaldon
20 John McMahon, baker
22 A Bell, tailor
Macnab-st intersects
30 Bay Horse Hotel
32 Arch Coutts, livery
36 Wm H Harris, painter
38 James Dumfrie, laborer
r38 John McGuire, painter
40 Miss Margaret Holden
42 A Cunningham, fireman
44 Robt D Cowan
46 Vacant
48 Benj Lewis, foreman
50 J H Saunders, cook
52 J R Spackman

Park-st intersects

64 Edward Nelson, traveler
68 A E Walker
70 Henry H Laing, merchant
72 Thomas Wood, builder
74 John Sweeney, conductor
78 Daniel Williams, laborer
80 Geo Dick, painter

Bay-st intersects

90 J C Schrader, tobacconist
98 Mrs Helen Gay
98 James Evel, foreman

Railway-st intersects

104 S D Hopkins
Vacant lots

Caroline-st intersects

108 J Burns, grocer
110 A S Cruickshanks, teacher
112 John Flynn, baker
114 Mrs Alfred Feast
116 Joseph Lloyd, bookkeeper
120 Thos Egan, fitter
122 John Gore, letter carrier
124 James Kirkness, carpenter
126 Vacant
132 John Heritage, tailor
134 Wm Grey, foreman GTR

Cannon-st west, south side

1 Wm Noble, hotel
7 Mrs Sarah Gray
9 J S Lillis, cigar manf
11 John M Harris, clerk
13 Alex Taggart, carpenter
15 Colin McRae, bookkeeper
17 Alex Hutchison, gardener
19 Jas Eagleshan, porter
25 Mrs George Smith

Macnab-st intersects

41 J M Byrens, builder
43 W G Lumsden, grocer
43½ Mrs Francis Lumsden
45 Mrs Wm Fogwell
Geo Sharp, carpenter
47 George Callahan, butcher
49 John Reardon, moulder

Park-st intersects

65-71 Z Pattison, confectioner
73 Joseph Clark, salesman
75 Thos Ford, machinist
77 Geo Davis, confectioner
79 Daniel Coughlin, carpenter
81 Jos Mawson, gasmeter mkr

Bay-st intersects

95 J C Schrader, cigar manf
97 Charles West, baker

Caroline-st intersects

107 Wm Grahman, grocer
109 E Smith, whipmaker
111 John Myers, laborer
113 J A Henderson, tobacconist
115 Thos J Milligan, laborer
117 Arch Thompson, laborer
119 Sellar Taylor, teamster
121 Patrick Griffin, laborer
123 Mrs Wm Connor
125 Wm Clucas, builder
127 Wm Ede, clerk
129 Robert Hunter, auctioneer
131 Wm McCusker, speculator

Hess-st intersects

Caroline-st north, east side, from 168 King west to Stuart

2 Mills & McKellar, builders

Market-st intersects

24 John Anderson
26 George Grayson, spring mkr
28 Rees Evans, printer
30 Thos McBride
32 Wm W McKee, nailer
Mrs Angus McLeod, teacher

Napier-st intersects

46 George Carlislie, carpenter

York-st intersects

Fred Gottoroff, marble cut'r
68 John Brown, blacksmith
r68 Richard Shaldrick, carter
70-2 Wm Evans, planing mill
74 Mrs C McGuigan
76 Michael Rock, harnes
78 Robert Boles, laborersmkr

80 Wm Smith, moulder
82 Fred Rice, laborer
84 H H Waybrant, machinist
86 Andrew Grey, checker

Cannon-st intersects

88 N A McDonald, carpenter
90 John Elliott
92 Thomas Winfield, carpenter
Vacant lots
G C Morrison, engine works
Hamilton Bridge & Tool Co

Stuart-st intersects

Caroline-st north, west side

7 James Foster, cutter
9 Samuel Saunders, traveler
11 Mrs P Sullivan

Market-st intersects

23 Wm Low, carpenter
31 Adam Zimmerman, tailor
33 Wm Aitchison, manf

Napier-st intersects

36 James Taylor, bricklayer
37 James Spring, laborer
39 J Marshall, wire rope maker
41 John Shields, laborer
43 J Brundle, letter collector
45 James Vint, stonecutter
47 Benj Myers, enginner
49 Mrs Shepard
51 B M Danforth, nailer

York-st intersects

71 H Granger, agent
73 Michael White, tailor
r 73 Mrs James Horan
Patrick Moran, laborer
79 Mrs James McBrier
r 79 Alfred Hewitt, clerk
r 79 Mrs Mary Redman
81 Thaddeus Joiner, laborer
r 81 H M Arthur
r 81 H Schadel, tobacconist
83 Wallace Walton, laborer

Cannon-st intersects

89 Edward Joyce, painter
89 Wm Russell, laborer
91 Mrs Mary Wenneshimer,
93 Mrs H E Thompson
95 David Flintoft, teamster
97 John G Sherring, plasterer

Mill-st intersects

99 Nicholas Cullinan, laborer
101 Vacant
103 Wm Mepham, bricklayer
105 Wm Cuseck, laborer
107 Wm Hatton, laborer
109 Richard Bolton, laborer
111 Vacant
113 Vacant
115 Miss Mary Sheen
115 John Whitney, laborer

Harriet-st intersects

119 Joseph Panter, carpenter
121 John Dawson, laborer
123 W J Kerr, moulder

Ellen-st intersects

M Wilson & Co, manfrs

Barton-st intersects

B McGillicuddy, laborer
Mrs Elliott
Laurence Grill, laborer
Michael Moroney, laborer
Jeremiah Connor, laborer

Eliza-st intersects

Caroline-st south, east side, from 141 King west to Concession

M Charlesworth
3 W H Dean, com traveler
5 J W Gerrie, druggist
7 E Freeman, ins agent
W J Field, merchant
11 D R Dewey, publisher
11 D Dewey, ice dealer

George-st intersects

Collegiate Institute

Main-st intersects

15 Thomas Nicholson, salesman
17 Mrs Richard Field
19 John Donaldson, engineer

Jackson-st intersects

W E Sanford, merchant

Hunter-st intersects

47 John Hapbush
51 Mrs P Butler

Bold-st intersects

53 Isaac Coombs, patternmaker
61 Alex Munro, com traveler
63 Mrs Thos Flack
65 Mrs Wm Holcomb

Duke-st intersects

77 Samuel Aylett, gardener
79 Geo McVittie, coachman
81 Anthony Belau, tailor

Robinson-st intersects

97 James Jobson, pork curer
99 George Shaw, gardener
101 Geo Brettingham, fitter
Mrs F Willman

Hannah-st intersects

113 Rich Harper, machinist

Herkimer and Markland-sts intersect

John Hughes, laborer
Alex Gardener, carter

Concession-st intersects

Caroline-st south, west side

American Bracket Works

George and Main-sts intersect

14 John McMaster, merchant

Jackson-st intersects

Private grounds

Hunter-st intersects

38 James Dodman, grocer
46 Donald Paterson, laborer
48 Robert Bulley, tailor
50 Mrs Wm Jamieson
52 Mrs Samuel Blair
54 Wm Myles, laborer
56 A B Baxter, butcher

Bold-st intersects

58 Edwin B Feast, grocer
66 Mrs J F Davidson
72 Home of the Friendless

Duke-st intersects

78 Rev A C Crews
78 Andrew J Cox
80 Mrs Wm Chisholm
82 Robt McKay, plasterer

Robinson-st intersects

96 Geo Pfann, cabinetmaker
98 John White, bricklayer
100 Jas Reid, carpenter

Hunter-st intersects

108 C Toll, laborer
110 John Lang, bricklayer
112 Geo Hunt, broommaker
114 Mathew Gair, pianomaker
116 Fred Setzkorn, laborer
118 Wm Pesel, laborer
120 Jas Malcolm, mason

Herkimer-st intersects

Jacob F Ellsurerth, grocer
John Cardwell, plasterer
James Milne, gardener

Market-st intersects

James Rayment, gardener
Robert Hillier, clerk

Concession-st intersects

Catharina-st, now called Young, north side, from 105 James s to Wellington

1 Bennoi Daniels, merchant
3 G D Roberts, printer
5 Chas Lemon, barrister

Hughson-st intersects

11 Geo A Young, ins agent
13 Chas Dempster, manf

John-st intersects

21 David Barton, bookkeeper
23 Geo S Findlay, com trav
25 Mrs Evan Davis

Catharine-st intersects

37 Fletcher Reid, laborer
39 Patrick Booth, shoemaker
41 Vacant
43 Andrew C Martin, merchant
45 Wm J Fitzgerald, carpenter
47 Mrs John Prinderville
47½ Andrew Proost, barber

49 Peter Fobert, tinsmith
51 Dennis Corcoran, carpenter
r " Mrs Ann Riddle
r " Mrs Bridget Kidney
r " Mrs Charles Dabbs
r " Samuel Mulholland, laborer
r " James Brown, carpenter
r " Charles Williams, plasterer
53 Mrs Catharine Murphy
55 Simon Laury, agent
57 James Lewis, machinist
59 Mrs Wm Dicker
61 Michael Sullivan, laborer
63 Charles Evans, lamplighter
67 Herbert Cotton, plasterer

Walnut-st intersects

69 Thos Harlow, grocer
71 James Callan, laborer
73 Peter Mulholland, box maker
75 Wm Burgess, laborer
77 John Cauley
79 Mrs C Campbell
81 George Warmington, plumber
83 Robert Barrett, laborer
85 John Miller, plasterer
87 Patrick O'Brien, laborer
89 Mrs John Anketell
91 James McGraw, laborer
93 Robert Keays, laborer
95 W C Wilde, printer

Cherry-st intersects

97 J Donovan, shoemaker
99 Dennis D Sullivan, laborer
Ontario Canning Co

Liberty-st intersects

Vacant lots

Aurora-st intersects

117 Alex Finlayson, salesman
127 John Walsh, shoemaker
129 Addison & Sons, builders

Wellington-st intersects

Catharina-st, south side

Vacant lots

Hughson-st intersects

8 Mrs Maria Dalley
10 Vacant
12 Thos Mead, builder
12½ Wm Hunt, moulder
14 John Reynolds, lumberman
16 Mrs Elizabeth Williamson

John-st Intersects

18 J G Buchanan, editor
20 David Dunlop, harnessmak'r
22 Simon Doak, blacksmith
24 Charles Post, carpenter
26 Miss Mary A Carry
28 Miss Martha Thompson
30 Wm Francis, pedler
32 Mrs Ryan

Catharine-st intersects

40 James Philp, saddler
44 Edmund Smee, shoemaker
46 Wm F Hammond, shoemkr
48 Wm E Myres, shoemaker
50 N McAdams, broommaker
r " George Hogarth, carpenter
50½ James O'Brien, laborer
52 Philip Fenton, grocer
54 Mrs Adam Allan
56 Vacant
58 John Geary, gardener
60 Wm Towler, broom mkr
62 Chas Watson, hackman
62½ Robert Rowan, laborer

Walnut-st intersects

64 Anthony Rowan, laborer
76 Vacant
78 John Coates, dairyman
80 Michael Carroll, shoemaker

Cherry-st intersects

100 Robert Patrick, laborer
102 Wm Smith, stovemounter
104 Wm Warnick
106 John Somers, laborer
108 Chas H Gracie, laborer
110 John Flemming laborer
r " Wm Stokes, laborer
r " John Connelly
116 Mrs Wm Montgomery

Aurora & Liberty-sts intersect

120 Wm Kemp, painter
122 John O'Neil, laborer
124 John Sheehan
126 Mrs Ann Stevens

128 Wm Flynn, clerk P O
130 Michael Dwyer, shoemaker
132 Robt McLennan
136 J W Tice, laborer

Wellington-st intersects

Catharine-st n, east side, from 104 King east to the Bay

King Wm-st intersects

16 Elias King, porter
20 John Temple, livery
22 Peter Armstrong, carriage maker
24 Vacant
26 Vacant

Rebecca-st intersects

30 Vacant
32 Wm Gordon, cooper
34 Geo Barr, engineer
36 Benj Lewis, wool sorter
38 John MacKelcan, M D
40 T O Lucas, butcher
42 C J Williams, oil manfr
44 Mrs John Atkinson
46 Geo S Coulson, grain dealer
48 James S Amos
50 Louis Schwarz, tobacconist
52 Frank MacKelcan, barrister
54 H A MacKelcan, barrister
56 Vacant
58 Vacant
58½ Vacant
60 Vacant
62 Vacant
64 F Villiers
66 James Phelan
70 J H Mattice, agent Globe
72 O C Sweet, manfr
74 Thos Smith, carpenter

Cannon-st intersects

94 A C Anderson, jeweler
94½ T E Brown, checker
96 Samuel Simpson, engineer
100 James Hopkins
102 Joseph Champagne, harness maker
110 D Moore, & Co, founders

Robert-st intersects

114 Mrs Wm Johnston
116 Fred Daugal, shoemaker
118 Joseph Dodson, printer
120 Vacant
122 Clark Madgett, machinist
124 Michael Malone
126 Mrs Wm Lang
r " Mrs Eliza Summers
128 Wm McQueen, laborer
130 James Connell, milk dealer
132 Louis Selback, biscuit baker
134 Miss Esther Phillips
136 Thos Watson, tinsmith
138 Patrick J Kelly, tailor
144 Wm Marcham, laborer
146 Mrs Ellen Laven
150 Geo Webb, laborer
152 Mrs Hy Witherspoon
154 Edward Lane, produce dealer
160 Mrs Margaret Houlden

Barton-st intersects

162 Mrs M Mulholland
164 Isaac Hodgins, engineer
166 Robert Bennett, moulder
168 Patrick Rodgers, laborer
170 E Ringer, melter
172 James Buntin, painter
174 James Johnston, laborer
176 Ed Nagel, machinist
178 Jas Maddock, cabinet maker
180 Lewis Johnson, blacksmith
182 Mrs Edward Devine
184 Peter Scott, engineer
186 Jacob Young, painter

Murray-st intersects

202 Alex McNab, stonecutter
204 James Govey, laborer
206 M Mageurs, dairyman
r " Daniel O'Neill, machinist
r " J Henderson, painter

G T R track intersects

210 Arch Webster, machinist

Strachan-st intersects

220 Wm S Smith, traveler

Simcoe-st intersects

228 George Wheeler, engineer

Thomas Falihee, car checker
Thomas Kenny, car exam'er
Ferrie-st intersects
238 Michael Wynn, laborer
Picton-st intersects
246 John Miller, laborer
Macaulay-st intersects
268 Jas Williams, teamster
Wood-st intersects
329 Chas Frank, glue manf
Brock-st intersects
370 Geo Freeborn, laborer
372 Robt Patterson, laborer
374 James Black, laborer
376 John Whalen, laborer
Vacant lots to end

Catharine-st n, west side

1-5 Adam Hope & Co, hardware
King Wm-st intersects
19 Gurney's warehouse
Rebecca-st intersects
25 John Rowan, barber
27 David Boyd, cooper
29 Vacant
31 Mrs M J Stacy
33 T Patterson, blacksmith
35 Mrs Ellen Shibley
37 George Moore, carpenter
39 Charles Smith, tailor
41 Thos Lahey, messenger
43 H T Boyle, clerk
45 Mrs Wm Orr
49 Geo S Nixon
Gore-st ends
51 Mrs Wm Rowe
53 C Delorme, carriage maker
55 Henry Beare, laborer
55½ A Stewart, ornamenter
57 Mrs C T McMichael
59 Mrs Ellen Fields
61 Wm Frier, dry goods
63 Ed Bethune, bookkeeper
65 Rev Solomon Leogon
67 Owen Catharine, smelter
69 James Babb, iron melter
71 Wm Gunner, tea dealer
75 Patrick Allen, laborer
77 James Jones, moulder
Cannon-st intersects
79 James M Byrens, builder
81 W H Belnap, tinsmith
85 Luke Lucas, moulder
87 Thos McGregor, moulder
89 Nicholas Buck, tailor
95 Wm Bowsted, machinist
99 John Freeth, sr
103 George Panter, stonecutter
r " John Appleyard, machinist
105 Wm Jones, moulder
107 Mrs M Young
109 Mrs Ellen Roach
111 Wm H McCornus, laborer
113 Mrs W Hurd
115 Washington Woodson, laborer
117 Mrs Wm Johnson
Robert-st intersects
119 Thos Rumsey, polisher
123 Steven Chapman
125 Henry McKee, laborer
129 Joseph Sullivan, blacksmith
131 Joseph Sullivan, blacksmith
133 Michael McInerney, moulder
135 Mrs Henry McStravick
137 Edward Sheppard, carpenter
141 Alex Morison, fireman
143 Patrick Barrett, tinsmith
145 John Levis, laborer
147 Wm O'Neil, mason
149 John Orr, laborer
151 Mrs Francis Skoly
153 Wm Cameron, hotel
Barton-st intersects
155 P Holleran, grocer
157 Mrs John Kirkham
159 Wm Henderson, laborer
161 Michael Hinchey, laborer
163 James Ryan, laborer
165 Mrs John Burns
167 Louis Moore, cabinetmaker
175 John O'Neil, engineer
181 Mrs Ann McBride
185 Mrs Emma Lee

Murray-st intersects

199 Vacant

Stuart-st ends

201 James Barry, laborer
203 Charles Honsden, malster
205 Richard Nicholson, laborer
r " Wm Bolton, carpenter
r " Thomas Best, laborer
Walter Potter
G T Railway bridge

Strachan-st intersects

219 Mrs Kate Holleran
Wm Bragg, yardsman
223 Francis Hamburg, loom fixer
225 John Flahaven, painter
227 Daniel McBride, pedler

Simcoe-st intersects

John Callaghan, driver
225 John Christie, blacksmith

Ferrie-st intersects

249 Patrick Coughlin, laborer

Picton and Macauley-sts intersect

253 Wm Gerrie, moulder

Wood-st intersects

327 Patrick O'Neil, teamster
329 M Kavanagh, boilermaker
331 H Becker, laborer
Gompf's brewery

Burlington and Brock-sts intersect

367 J H Ainsborough, moulder

Guise-st intersects

Catharine-st s, east side, from 73 King e to the Mountain

Main-st intersects

Joseph Hoodless' factory
Lumber yard

Jackson-st intersects

27 J Hoodless, cabinet maker
32 Vacant
33 James Bridgewood, fruit
35 Francis Waters, teamster
37 David West, laborer
39 J McMillan, carriage maker
41 A Mitchell, harness maker
45 Jas Hoyle, tailor

45½ Michael Allan, shoemaker

Hunter-st intersects

47 John Zoeller, tailor
47½ John Almas, farmer
49 Isaac Eisenberg, tailor
51 Edward Warren
53 J E O'Reilly, barrister
65 S E Gregory
73 Miles O'Reilly, Q C
77 Henry Braid, foreman
79 Vacant
81 Mrs Robert Kilgour
83 James Kilgour, music dealer
Vacant lots

Young-st intersects

97 F C Webber, builder
99 Wm Knags, machinist
101 Vacant
103 Geo H Webber, bricklayer
105 F W Passmore, painter
107 Geo Tilley, pattern maker
109 Frank B Halliday, com trav
111 J B House
113 Simon Stein, jeweler
115 W A Bellhouse, clerk

Maria-st intersects

117 H C Bliss, patent medicines

Hannah-st intersects

Catharine-st s, west side

2 W Richardson
Wanzer & Co's foundry

Main-st intersects

McIlwraith's coal yard
20 Vacant
22 Thos James, saddler
24 Edwin Grigg
26 Thos Sturdy, tinsmith
28 E Webber, livery
30 Geo Flette, tailor

Jackson-st intersects

30 James Dowden, whitewasher
36 Mrs S Page
40 Francis Taafe, butcher
42 Thos H Loney, mail carrier
44 Wm Hazell, engineer

Hunter-st intersects

52 Mrs Charles Shields
54 Vacant
56 Joseph Smye, wheelwright
58 Mrs H Beaton
60 S Davis, jr, clerk
62 A W Andrews, laborer
64 Martin TenEyck
68 Mrs A Terryberry
70 Wm Robinson, jr, laborer
72 Wm Robinson, laborer

Augusta-st intersects

76 Charles Barlow, carpenter
80 Mrs Hannah Bell
82 Thos Paradine, sexton
88 John Burkholder, engineer
90 Mrs C Nichol
92 Edward T Wright, japanner

Young-st intersects

94 John R Nicholls, clerk
96 Charles Post, laborer
98 George Mellon
102 George LeRiche, druggist
104 G Haas, nurseryman
106 Capt John Roberts
108 H G Love, contractor
110 H Barnard
112 F W Large, agent Mail
114 Jas G Insole, com traveler
116 Samuel Nadin, bookkeeper

Maria-st intersects

118 Charles Powis, bank clerk
120 Wm Nixon, quarryman
122 Robert Berryman, merchant
124 James O'Heir, machinist

Cathcart Lower-st, east side, from 166 Rebecca to Barton

Wilson-st intersects

12 Patrick Ward, laborer
14 Vacant
16 Ernest Schultz, tinsmith
18 Mrs Philip Oxley
20 Joseph Acheson, machinist
Hamilton clock works

Kelly-st intersects

32 John Sullivan, brakeman
34 A Henstridge, painter
36 Andrew Stonehouse, blksmith
38 E W Hyde, news agent
40 G Turner, carpenter
46 Jossph Kneeshaw
48 Mrs E McIlwraith

Cannon-st intersects

52 Joseph Walton, clerk
54 Wm Smith, stonemason
56 G A Smith, bricklayer
56½ Wm Hunter, porter
58 Peter Boniface, tinsmith
60 Fred Aldridge, printer
62 A R Highnell, printer
64 Thomas Ham, printer
66 James Truscott, machinist
68 Wm Simpson, baker
70 Wm Baylie, laborer
70½ Wm Harper
72 James Robins, butcher
74 Michael Gallagher, shoemkr
76 Thos Tompkins, cigarmkr
78 B Ketcheson, moulder
80 Jno Woodman, baggageman
82 Wm Whiteside, machinist
84 — Payne, laborer
Patterson Bros, lumber

Cathcart Lower, west side

1 Vacant

Wilson-st intersects

11 John Morton, grocer
13 Luke Cuzner, tinsmith
15 Edward Denroche, carpenter
15 Wm Morrow, laborer
19 John Groves, brakeman
21 Mrs James Hampson
23 James Webster, mason
25 Wm Old, laborer
27 Mrs John Madden

Kelly-st intersects

29 Mrs John Kelly
31 Richard Wakely, teamster
33 Thos Anderson, machinist
35 John Barnes, livery
35½ Mrs James Truscott
37 A D Parks, inspector
39 Mrs Mary Bennetto
Mrs Wm Sharp
Union wood and coal yard

Cannon-st intersects

53 James Carter, bricklayer
55 S J Stratton, clerk
r 55 John Booth, signalman
57 David Congo, porter
59 Jas Eltsworth, carpenter
61 Abe Hobson, glassblower
69 John Smith, teamster
71 Jas Pett, tanner
73 Frank G Kelk, tailor
75 Geo McGilvrey, conductor
81 Francis Elder, tailor
83 Thos McCann, moulder
85 Walter Butler, turner
87 Stanley Arnold, upholsterer
89 Charles Hughes, carpenter
91 John McGarrigle, laborer
93 Henry Norman
95 Jas Shoots, carriage trimmer
97 James Kelly, shoemaker
99 Arthur Sharp, cabinetmaker
101 Albert H Young, clerk

Barton-st intersects

Cathcart, Upper, east side from 198 King e to King William

2-4 Vacant
6 A Leighton, laborer
8 David McKillop, machinist
10 Jovide Filiatrault, laborer
12 Mrs Evans Griffiths
16 Vacant
20 Lawrence Beltz, tailor
22 Amale Lamoreaux, shoemkr
Brennen's lumber yard

King Wm-st intersects

Cathcart, Upper, west side

1 Mrs Jarvis
5 George Peters, clerk
7 Thos Bogges, broker
9 John Christian, porter
11 J D Pennington & Co, manfs
15 C A Stevens, porter
17 Joseph Chapman, laborer

King Wm-st intersects

Centre-st, from 11 Colborne-st

1 Edwin Tinsley, engineer
J S Lillis, cigar maker

Charles-st east side, from 57 King-st w, south to Bold

3 Vacant
5 Daniel Sullivan, livery
7 Mills & McKellar, carpters
Thos Lawry's warehouse
11 Edmund Hudson, clerk
13 Henry Lawry, butcher
15 Robert Addison, carpenter
17 Dan LeMessurier, painter
23 Murton & Reid, coal dealers

Main-st intersects

Vacant grounds

Jackson-st intersects

39 Robert Duncan, merchant
41 A R Kerr, merchant
43 Alex Gartshore, manf
45 Miss Ann Meade
47 Thomas Tandy, G T R
53 Fred G Foster, florist
55 Mrs Jane Page
" Thos McKenna
" Peter G Sinclair, gardener

Hunter-st intersects

57 Lewis D Birely
59 Mrs Peter McIntyre
63 Patrick Maguire
67 S F Lazier, barrister

Bold-st intersects

Charles-st, west side

American hotel
10 Wm S Sendall, carpenter
12 Wm Reeves, baker
14 C F Abraham, grain dealer

Main-st intersects

20 John B Youug, accountant
26 Mrs James Ritchie
28 John Rowan, pedler
30 Joseph Smith, cabinetmaker
32 Philip Stevens, laborer
34 Mrs Richard Foquet
36 Thos W Sellwood, machinist

38 John Early, laborer
40 Mrs James Flynn

Jackson-st intersects

46 Mrs Mary Hunter
48 Vacant
50 Robert Evans, seedsman
54 Nursery

Hunter-st intersects

66 David Gillies, merchant

Bold-st intersects

Cherry-st, east side, from 116 Main east to Mountain

1 Charles Olsen, shipper
3 Warren Spone, tailor
5 John Bradley, contractor
7 Mrs John Shipton
7½ Thos Stout, engineer
11 T Sullivan, laborer
11 Alex Phillips, blacksmith

Jackson-st intersects

15 John Plant, wood dealer
23 Edwd McGrath, wagonmakr
25 David McBrien, painter

Hunter-st intersects

35 G Fickley, shoemaker
39 John Jeffrey, carpenter
41 James Osborne, engineer
43 Thos Stanton, painter
45 L Reuben, pedler
47 Dennis Kelly, machinist
49 Mrs John Donnelly
51 Wm Dodds, mason
53 J McMahon, moulder
55 Jas Sullivan, laborer

O'Reilly-st intersects

65 Joseph Gayette, porter
67 Ed Costello, laborer
69 John Prindiville, carpenter
r " James Canary, laborer
71 Edward Skinner, laborer
73 Mrs Patrick Doyle

Young-st intersects

77 Mrs Edward Gale
79 Thos Burns, laborer
81 Mrs E Sullivan
83 Samuel Porter, baker
85 Wm Foster, moulder
87 P G Cowil, salesman
93 Walter Crossland, cigarmaker

Maria-st intersects

97 Thomas Lawlor, machinist
99 Chas Kidner, printer
101 T Lyons, laborer
103 Chas Farrell, clerk
105 John Patterson, tailor
113 Mrs Dennis Teene
115 James Flaherty, laborer
High level pumping station

Cherry-st, west side

N & N W station

Main-st intersects

8 Thos W Reid, carpenter
10 Henry Hawkins, plasterer
12 Fred Cornell, plasterer
14 Henry Williams, laborer
16 John P Cline, marble cutter

Jackson-st intersects

18 Fred Woodward, upholsterer
20 Vacant
22 Thos Brick, carter
24 Robert Judd, painter

Hunter-st intersects

32 George Long, wood dealer
34 James E May, carpenter
38 Alfred Wright, locksmith
42 Robert Fitzmorris, moulder
44 Chas E Dunbar, moulder
46 Hy Sharpe, carpenter
48 John Campbell, watchman
52 E Warren
54 Miss B Burke, tailoress
56 P Taylor, baker
58 Dan Mahony, laborer
60 T H Baine, hotel

O'Reilly-st intersects

66 James McGraw, laborer
68 Robt C Bland, machinist
70 Mrs Louis Rohmer
72 Michael Murphy, laborer
74 Peter McKernan, laborer

Young-st intersects

84 John Simpson, cigarmaker
86 Vacant
88 Vacant

Maria-st intersects

98 D C Connell, gardener
100 James Patterson
104 Wm Newbigging
108 Wm Sullivan, laborer
110 Mrs Mary Sullivan
112 Thomas Skinner, laborer
114 Donald Foley, laborer
116 John Goodfellow, painter
118 John Wren, laborer

Hannah-st intersects

Chisholm-st, east side, from 225 Cannon e, north to Barton

2 Wm Long, laborer
2½ Mrs Catharine Gage
4 Michael Dunbar, carpenter
8 James Wilson, dyer
10 Oliver Simmons, moulder
12 Wm Woodall, builder
14 Arthur Duggan, brickmaker
16 Joseph Cole, laborer
18 Fred Arnat, tailor
20 John Smith, bricklayer
24 James Howard, bricklayer
28 Samuel Fisher, laborer
34 James Ling, carpenter
36 Vacant
40 Richard Winn, laborer
44 Thomas Irwin, laborer
48 George Miller
50 Mrs James Lamrock
56 Richard Wild, laborer
58 James Ling, carpenter
74 Frank Campaign, laborer

Barton-st intereects

Chisholm-st, west side

1 W J Moore, painter
3 P Dunbar, carpenter
5 Erskine Smith, bricklayer
5½ Wm Derby, buffer
7 Wm McCombe, moulder
9 John Connor, sawyer
11 Henry Myers, engineer
21 Thomas Mullens, carpenter
23 B Boreham, carpenter
25 Wm Stinder, moulder
27 R McMillan, carpenter
29 Robert Menary, dairyman
31 James Millman, carpenter
33 James Brock, whipmaker
37 T Beardmore, brassfinisher
39 Chas Berry, pattern maker
41 James Allan, moulder
47 Andrew Laughlin, moulder
51 Richard Hammond, laborer
53 S Freeman, laborer
57 James Fisher, polisher
59 D Monger, porter

Barton-st intersects

Clark ave, east side, between Wellington and Victoria-ave, off Simcoe

John Connell, bricklayer
John Freeborn, laborer
Wm Barclay, pattern fitter
Patrick O'Neil, bricklayer
J D Small, carpenter
George Searles, laborer

Clark-ave, west side

Wm D Goodman, moulder
G Grundy, gardener
Thomas Riddell, carpenter
Thomas Freeborn, laborer
Wm Mullvale, laborer

Colborne-st, north side, from 185 James n, west to Bay

2 Gurneys & Ware, scale mfs
12 Mrs R Seymour
14 B J Conway, excise officer
16 John A Ward, accountant

Macnab-st intersects

30 Walter McGiverin, laborer
32 Vacant
34 James F Lakeland, artist
36 John Wynn, iron worker

Park-st intersects

64 Daniel Graham, carpenter
66 Robert Harper, carpenter
68 Alex M Ross, painter

Bay-st intersects

Colborne-st, south side

11 George Smith, carpenter

Center-st intersects

13 Chas Leyden, lithographer
15 Casper Teiper, manfr
17 C M Belknap, lumber dealer

Macnab & Park-sts intersect

61 Martin Malone, barrister
63 John McLaughlin, painter
63 Charles H Egg, clerk
65 Wm Wright, moulder
67 Mrs N Bell
69 Fred Venator, turner
71 Hopkin Hamilton, moulder
73 James Robson, brakeman

Bay-st intersects

Concession-st, north side, from James to city limits

Wm Wright, machinist
David C Dowrie, letter car'r
M Dawson, letter carrier
Wm Cook, coachman
George Catchpole, salesman
W H Gillard, merchant

Bay-st intersects

Joseph Hobson, C E
John Alexander, merchant

Hilton & Caroline-sts intersect

Carl Dormer
Vacant

Bruce & Hess-sts intersect

F Wilkinson, grain dealer
John Hendry, pattern mkr
Frank Lonsdale

Queen-st intersects

John Pearson, accountant

Kent and Locke-sts intersect

Robt McFarlane, dairyman
John Smith, tailor
Alfred Grigg, clerk

Garth-st intersects

— Stillwell

Concession-st south side

John Stuart, merchant
Wm Hunt, gardener
James Turner, merchant
Wm J Copy, manfr
Thos Marshall, tailor

Hess-st intersects

A Powis, com traveler

Queen-st intersects

Joseph Grimes, laborer
James Findlay, roofer

Mountain-ave intersects

James Keand

Locke-st intersects

Garth-st intersects

Capt Nichol's farm
— McNab, farmer
John Stuart, moulder

Crooks-st, east side, from York to Barton

2 John Binkley, farmer
4 G Hutton, machinist
6 Alex E Davis, telegraphist
8 W J Morden, com agent
10 Chas H Lucas, bookkeeper
12 James A Snider, miller
12½ Vacant
14 E Housego, laborer
16 Thos Morley, laborer
18 Samuel Gage, laborer
20 Robert Lee, fireman
22 George Cook, watchman
26 Oliver McLeod, blacksmith
32 James Wilson, painter
36 Wm Wright, laborer

Crooks-st, west side

9 James E Painter, fireman
11 Shephard Latham, machinist
15 John Way, blacksmith

17 Mrs J McColl
19 Alex Elder, fitter
21 Fred Weaver, switchman
23 John Clayton, painter
29 Henry Lendon, machinist
31 John Mills, builder
33 John Goddard, laborer
35 Thos Ritchie, laborer
37 Jas Badger, shoemaker
39 Wm McMenemy, policeman

Barton-st intersects

Devenport-st, east side, from 337 York to Tom

6 John Copeland, carpenter
8 Wm Sinclair, laborer
10 Edward Ryckman, laborer
18 Mrs Geo Myers
22 James Garrett, moulder
26 Louis Scheck, cabinetmaker

Tom-st intersects

Devonport-st, west side

1 Wm Newcombe, machinist
3 John Wilson, carpenter
5 Mrs John Manning
7 Frank Baker, laborer
9 George Carson, laborer
15 Robert Douglas, moulder
17 James O'Connor, painter
19 Jarvis Abey, boilermaker
21 Jas Weatherston, carpenter
29 John McInerney, laborer

Tom-st intersects

Duke-st. north side, from 100 James s to western limits

M Wright, cotton broker
4 Geo Taylor, bookkeeper
10 Dr J D Macdonald

Macnab & Park-sts intersect

36 Alex Bruce, barrister
40 St Clair Balfour, merchant
42 James Angus, sr
44 James Angus, jr, hatter
46 Mrs C McCallum
46 Ed Furlong, barrister

Bay-st intersects

58 D Doyle, wagonmaker
62 Wm Dickson, carpenter
64 Rev John Gauld
66 Mrs M J Davidson
68 Vacant
70 Robert McLeod, clerk
72 Alfred Richmond, grocer

Caroline-st intersects

John Toner, teamster
86 Thos Stevenson, carpenter

Hess-st intersects

John M Morris, engineer

Queen-st intersects

140 Alfred Best, gardener
142 Wm Murphy, carpenter
144 Levi Buckingham, moulder
146 Frank Connor, carriagemakr
148 George Purrott, painter
148½ Thos Horne, laborer
150 Richard McCarthy, laborer
152 Wm Foulis, packer
154 Henry Blankstein, carpenter

Ray-st Intersects

Cricket grounds

Locke-st intersects

Daniel Buckley, laborer
Thos Franey, blacksmith
Charles Burgess, laborer
Mrs Eliza George
Jas Stevenson, hay dealer
Vincent Shipley, laborer
John Pfeiffer, laborer

Garth-st intersects

Duke-st, south side

1 Vacant
5 Matthew Leggat, merchant
7 Alex W Roy, accountant

Macnab-st intersects

Sandyford Place:
6 James Watson, president knitting company
11 T H Macpherson, merchant
13 D G Greer, estate agent
15 Charles J Hope, merchant

23 R A Lucas, merchant

Park-st intersects

37 John Muir, barrister
41 Hamilton Young, manfr
43 R Dunlop, manfr
45 Mrs A Mackay, teacher
47 John Stewart, accountant

Bay-st intersects

Egerton Healey, grocer
53 Gregor Thompson, shoemkr
67 Robert Watt, porter
69 Henry Hamill, gardener
73 James Castell, policeman

Caroline-st intersects

75 Jas Fraser, moulder
John B Pattison

Hess & Queen-sts intersect

143 Wright Smith, harness mkr
145 Louis Banks, laborer
147 Wm Duncan, gardener
149 Wm Dunsmore, porter
151 W H Clarke

Ray & Locke-sts intersect

Jas Cook, painter
Henry Jackson, painter
John Maxwell, machinist
John A Craven, blacksmith
Thos Simpson, moulder
Geo Norwood, brickmaker
John McEwen, laborer
Christopher Walters, laborer
Wm Waddleton, tailor

Garth-st intersects

Dundurn-st, east side, from end of King west to York

Tom-st intersects

Ben Ironside, painter
John Foreman, laborer
Thos O'Neil, blacksmith

Dundurn-st, west side

2 Edward Duncan, laborer
George Walls, laborer
12 Bernard McCowell, laborer

Ardavolich-st intersects

22 M McGowan, butcher

Florence-st intersects

John Martin, laborer
Mrs Ann Hibbard
Wm Strongman, carpenter

Tom-st intersects

Wm H Buscombe, bricklayer
Wm Newcombe, finisher
John Moore, laborer
Chas McCarthy, laborer
Samuel King, building removing
W Inkson, traveler
James Holland, locksmith

Jones-st Intersects

York-st intersects

East-ave north, east side, from 258 King east to South

6 Thos H Pratt, merchant

King Wm-st intersects

8 Edmund Hill, grocer
12 J H Stone, manfr
14 John Schwendau, tailor
16 John McMaster, carpenter
18 Mrs Joseph Mottashed
20 G A Peterson, laborer
22 Gustave Brizzie, moulder
24 J E Riddell, tinsmith
26 Albert E McNair, clerk
28 James Qua, G T R
28½ J Riddell, tinsmith
30 Henry Sutton, conductor
32 Thos Kilvington, sr, florist
34 J J Smith, foreman

Wilson-st intersects

36 Robert King, laborer
38 John Duffy
40 F Crawley, machinist
42 George Miller, policeman
44 Thomas Bailey, carpenter
46 J McGilvray, clerk
48 John Black, brushmaker
50 E Bezanson, photographer
54 Robert Christie, supt
56 Alfred Moore, policeman

58 Mrs Samuel Anderson
60 Hy Bennett, printer
66 Henry Angold, machinist

Evans-st intersects

70 Mrs John Burk
76 C K Jones, roofer
76½ Wm Davis, blacksmith

Cannon-st intersects

78 John Truscott, carpenter
88 Dennis Connors, gardener
90 Wm D Broach, engineer
92 — Greasley, gardener
94 Thos G Maxwell, policeman
96 C W Flanders, brakeman
104 Jas Siddell, carpenter
108 Wm Burgess, machinist

Robert-st intersects

112 Thomas Patterson, manf
112½ Richard Smith, whipmaker
114 Arthur Catchpole, laborer
114½ Chas Underwood, engraver
116 Vacant
116½ Vacant
118 George Yunganger, sausage maker
120 W J Lewis, carpenter
122 Mrs John Priddis
124 John W Sinclair, painter
126 Geo Coleman, painter
128 Martin Allen, laborer

Barton-st intersects

130-2 Vacant
162 W L Jamieson, watchman
168 James Young, laborer
170 James Jackson, carpenter
172 John Truscott, painter
174 Jas Jones
176 Mrs Charles Smith
182 John Hope, tanner
182 Robert Faulks, carpenter
194 — Miller
196 J Elfving, basket maker
198 Wm Weeks, whipmaker
200 Alonzo Holmes traveler
202 August Miller, machinist
204 Thomas Brydges, laborer
206 Wm Reid

South-st intersects

East-ave north, west side

1 John Cameron, clerk
3 Thomas Stewart
9 Jas Brown, hide inspector

King Wm-st intersects

11 K McKenzie, grocer
13 Miss Mary Gregg
15 Geo Smith
17 Mrs Jane Burns
21 Francis Stewart, machinist
23 Thos Mason, hatter
25 C A Whitman, clerk
25½ J F Monck, barrister
27 James McIntosh
29 Samuel Bell, constable
31 James Lavery, carpenter
33 James Munroe
35 W H McLaren, grocer
37 Alfred Pilkey, agent
37 James Mitchell, bailiff

Wilson-st intersects

37½ James O'Brien, moulder
41 S Hastie, stovemounter
43 Matthew Murphy, teamster
45 Thos King, machinist
49 E G Payne, ins agent
55 Wallace Young, manf
57 John Miles, carpenter
59 John Leitch, machinist
63 Ed W Cuttriss, carpenter
65 John W Blakely, policeman
67 Robert Somerville, carpenter
69 J Richards, traveler

Evans-st intersects

63a Wm Pothiea, burnisher
65a M Ryan, laborer
67a David Simms, laborer
69a Wm H Hunt, turner
73 Wm A Sanders, baker

Cannon-st intersects

75 W G Servos, brakeman
77 Napoleon Badean, shoemkr
79 W R Leckie, bookkeeper
81 J H Hamilton, builder

83 Andrew Begg, laborer
85 Wm Peebles, carpenter
89 H C Breckin, spinner
91 Andrew Cowan, clerk
97 Clarence Forester, turner
99 John Jeffs, shipper
101 Wm Peace, carpenter
105 John Alexander, moulder
107 George Adams, stove fitter
111 Thos Henwood, laborer

Robert-st intersects

121 O H Webber, bookkeeper
123 J Graham, shoemaker
125 Samuel Groves, blacksmith
137 James Franks, painter
129 Mrs O Edgebombe
143 Joseph Spence, sailor
145 Fred Tate, hatter
147 Wm J Whitelock, mason

Barton-st intersects

155 Joseph Ray, buffer
157 John McVittie, laborer
161 James R Greenwood, hatter
167 Fred Dittrick, bender
167½ Tanis Osier
169 Chas Voegeler, hatter
173 Mrs Wm Towers, boarding
179 John Booth
183 J A Morrison, turner
195 Wm Albins, machinist
197 Vacant
199 Geo D Tompkins, plumber
201 Vacant

South-st intersects

East-ave s, east side, from end of King e to Stinson

1 Jas Elliott, agent
3 Robert Young, manf

Main-st intersects

31 David Dexter
33 J D Climie, merchant
35 Wm Dixon, fruiterer
37 James Dixon, fruit dealer
39 W W Robinson, manager D Moore & Co
41 George Black, Northwestern Tel Co
43 Mrs James Widger
45 James McPherson
51 B J Morgan, flour dealer

Hunter-st intersects

53 George James, merchant
55 Joseph Culham, barrister
57 Donald McPhie, plumber
61 Fred W Wilson, manfr
63 M A Kerr, manfr
73 D W Gitchell
75 J M Lester
77 S E Townsend, accountant
79 Chas H Foster, merchant

Stinson-st intersects

East-ave south, west side

St Patrick's Church

Main-st intersects

30 S Rose, traveler
32 H H Findlay, traveler
34 C F Stillwell
38 Andrew W Gage, merchant
40 John G Bowes, manf
42 Wm S Moore, merchant
44 Samuel Davis, sr

Hunter-st intersects

60 R H Jarvis, ins inspector
62 R J Husband, dentist
64 Edgar Watkins, merchant
66 Mrs Richard Greene
72 F C Fearman
78 Wm James, traveler
80 Vacant

Elgin-st, east side, from 16 Wilson north to Barton

2 Benj Salisbury, saddler
4 H Geiss, turner
6 Caleb Buchanan, printer
8 Mrs S Cole
10 George Winn, shoemaker
12 Alfred Willmore, machinist
14 S V King, moulder

Kelly-st intersects

16 Samuel Arthur, builder
18 J Mathews, clerk post office
18½ T McLelland, engineer

20 S McNeil, laborer
22 Richard Clark, moulder
24 Ed Crofton, painter
26 James Munn, teamster
28 Mrs Charles Parker
30 Joseph Gates
32 John Macabe, traveler
34 E A Dalley, druggist
36 Thos Sloan

Cannon-st intersects

Vacant grounds

Robert-st intersects

68 Vacant
70 John Wilmot, scalemaker
72 James Gilchrist, carpenter
72½ Mrs James Foster
74 Dan Curell jr, machinist
76 Thos Beasley, conductor
78 M Turnbull, machinist
80 W Freeman, coal dealer
82 John Wilkinson, engineer
84 C L Smith, builder
86 Wm Smale, sr
88 Samuel Stephens, moulder
90 C Dallyn, barber
92 Mrs John Weaver
94 Mrs Jeff Stephens
96 John Burns, printer
98 M Dwyer, machinist
George Elliot, expressman

Barton-st intersects

County jail
Hamilton Wheel Works

Elgin Street, west side

1 Wm J Vale, printer
3 G Swartzenburg, whip maker
7 Charles Myles, coal dealer
9 Wm Larkin, moulder
11 Joseph Beddoe, shoemaker
13 James Connolly, grocer

Kelly-st intersects

15 R C Stevenson, bookkeeper
15½ E D H Mundell, traveler
17 Wm Rogers
23 — Ryan
25 Elwood Cooney, laborer
27 Mrs Elizabeth Crawford
29 Thos Martin, mail clerk
31 Mrs Jacob Storm
33 Hugh McGowan, butcher

Cannon-st intersects

45 John Milne, manfr
47 J W Sanders, japanner
49 James Holleran, moulder
51 Mrs G Kent
63 D A MacNabb

Robert-st intersects

69-71 James Mills, grocer
73 Geo T King, roadmaster
75 Mrs Donald McGillivray
77 Joseph Greenfield
79 Mrs E I Cusack
81 John F Jagoe, broker
83 S Morrison, agent
87 Thomas Glass, moulder
89 T Hall, engine driver
91 Gilbert Vanwyck, tailor
93 Wm Carroll, polisher
95 R Press, builder
97 Ed Burniston, carpenter
99 G B Phibbs, wheelwright
101 Chas R Hunt, tinsmith
101½ Wm Larkin, moulder
103 E H Dunnett, clerk
105 Simon Springstead, grocer

Barton-st intersects

R M Wanzer & Co's factory

Elizabeth-st, from New to Garth

Charles North, mason

Eliza-st, commencing on the west side of Caroline north of Stuart

Patrick Leonard, laborer
James Parker, laborer

Ellen-st, from 133 Caroline n, west to Hess

Not built upon

Emerald-st n, west side

Vacant lots

King Wm-st intersects

23 E Furneaux, carpenter
25 V Steinmetz, tailor
31 Wm P Strickland, machinist
33 James Henderson
35 Christopher Mason, enginr
39 Wm Lawrence, laborer
Emerald Street Methodist Church
45 Rev J H Collins

Wilson-st intersects

53 J Klock, cigar maker
55 Richard George, shoemaker
57 Alfred Charlesworth, shoemr
59 Samuel Griffith, porter
61 Mrs John Menzie
63 Thos Lovejoy, mason
65 James D Smith, blacasmith
67 George Croal, blacksmith
71 Wm Sutton, collar maker
73 John Jackson, laborer
75 John Dow, laborer

Evans st intersects

77 Matthew Collins, wool carder
79 Vacant
81 Walter Sweet, grain dealer
83 Thos Bale, com traveler

Cannon-st intersects

87 David Wark, constable
97 Joseph Smith, confectioner
99 Thomas Cline
101 P Thompson, grocer
103 John J Cline, grocer
105 John Taylor, blacksmith
107 John E White, builder
119 Jos Hargrove, agent

Robert-st intersects

123 Wm Littlejohns, builder
125 Wm Chiswell, moulder
127 James Scott, painter
129 Thos Armitage, machinist
133 Chas Britt, laborer
135 Alfred Coleman, carpenter

Barton-st intersects

171 Silas W Tabb, carpenter
177 James Muir, baggageman
179 Wm Ayers, carpenter
183 Sylvester Whalen, silversmith
185 John Batstone, baker
193 Joseph Thompson, laborer
203 W Johnston, laborer

South-st intersects

Emerald-st n, east side, from 258 King e to the Bay

St. John's Church
2 M Lewis, polisher
4 James Anderson, stonecutter
8 Thos Lawrence, carpenter

King Wm-st intersects

14 Mrs John Knapman
16 David Stock, city foreman
18 Robert Clohecy, carpenter
20 Wm Brown, shoemaker
22 Joel Lee, cabinet maker
24 George Ross, clerk P O
26 John C Stone, traveler
28 Mrs Wm Hill
30 Fred Vanstone, cutter
32 John Howard, bricklayer
34 A B Holmes, shoemaker
36 Robert Hyslop, com trav
38 Charles Irish, shoemaker
40 Alex Thomson, reporter
42 H J Prowse, patternmaker
44 Wm Reid, policeman

Wilson-st intersects

48 Patrick Shea, blacksmith
50 J A Durfey, laborer
52 Hy Way, butcher
54 Mrs Agnes McCloy
58 Mrs Wm Dixon
60 W R Stuart, grocer
62 Henry Young, carpenter
64 Richard Gray
66 Duncan Graham, laborer
68 Wm Yates, bricklayer
70 George Simpson, moulder
74 George Sheet, moulder
r 74 Henry Fuller, tailor
r 74 Thos Aldridge, shoemaker
76 David Murray, gardener

80 Alex Clark, mason
82 James Flight, mason
84 Thos B S Austin, letter car'r
90 George Bailey, lamplighter
92 Henry Headland, miller

Cannon-st intersects

92 Jos Kirkpatrick, grocer
94 Robt Ashbaugh, hotelkeeper
96 H Braid, jr, shoemaker
98 Miss Hodge
100 Wm Wilson, moulder
102 Jacob Haygarth, machinist
104 John Monteith, moulder
106 Geo Parker, carpenter
106½ Wm Robinson, brakeman
108 Geo Watson, cabinetmaker
112 Arch McKenzie, carpenter
114 John Sullivan, laborer
116 Wm Robinson, constable
118 Eric Bowers, shoemaker
120 Joseph Servos, fireman
122 Michael Murphy, shoemaker
126 Charles Mooney, laborer
126½ James Hampson
128 Wm Forster, turner
128½ James Rogers, plasterer
130 John Legarie, blacksmith
132 Henry Marricott, machinist
134 Michael Henry, carpenter
136 Thos Cain, shoemaker
142 John Herman, butcher
146 John Partridge, moulder
150 Geo King
152 John Wise, carpenter
154 Wm Baddams, mason
148 James Hurley, moulder

Barton-st intersects

168 Edward Kennard, cabinet maker
170 James Hobbs, carpenter
172 James Frith, blacksmith
174 Simon Buchanan, carpenter
182 Lewis Lottridge, dairyman
186 O Lagarie, blacksmith
188 Joseph Mathews, carpenter
190 W B Smith, planer
192 Burton Smith, carpenter
194 K McGilvray, carpenter
196 Vacant
198 E H Austin, carpenter

South-st intersects

Emerald-st s, east side, from King e to Stinson

3 James Heyes
9 Geo H Gillespie, merchant

Main-st intersects

43 David Morton, soap factory
55 A N Barber
57 Vacant
71 Wm T Watkins, merchant
73 R Fuller, contractor
75 J Zimmerman, dentist
77 R R Morgan, flour and feed
79 Thomas Oliver, buyer

Stinson-st intersects

Emerald-st s, west side

Vacant grounds
8 W J McDonald, builder
10 Josias Bray, ins agent
12 John Morton, soap manf
E P Smith, traveler

Main-st intersects

40 P S Campbell, teacher
42 Wm Smith, accountant
44 C A Davis, dentist
46 J S McMahon, merchant
48 John Tunstead manf
50 G S Sexsmith, cutter
52 Vacant
54 E H Watkins
56 Vacant
58 John W Healey, traveler

Hunter-st intersects

60 Geo E Bradfield, merchant
74 H D Cameron, Ham Prov and Loan Society
80 Adam Rutherford

Stinson-st intersects

Erie-ave, east side, from end of Main south to Alanson

8 Thomas Franklin
10 Wm Marshall manf

12 Geo Crites, manf
18 Fred L Wood, bookkeeper
22 F H Sharpe, machinist
24 Isaac Christian, printer
J M Oliver, trav

Stinson-st intersects

55 John Connors, laborer
57 Andrew Mowat, mason

Alanson-st intersects

Erie-ave, west side

Vacant lots
3 Mrs S J White
5 A McDonald, com trav
9 Geo Shambrook, bookkeeper
11 Geo H Meakins, machinist

Stinson-st intersects

54 Charles Powell, machinist
56 Jno Ferguson, shoemaker

Alanson-st intersects

Evans-st, north side, from 87 Wellington north, east to Emerald

1 Miss M McLaughlin, dressmaker

West-ave intersects

3 Samuel Bowes, machinist
5 — Brandon, broommaker
7 Thomas Stevens, porter

Victoria-ave intersects

James Jackson, carpenter
21 Wm O'Brien, moulder

East-ave intersects

Joseph Long, laborer

Emerald-st intersects

Evans-st, south side

2 J J Towers, fitter

West-ave intersects

6 Geo Glass, shoemaker

Victoria-ave intersects

Mission Sabbath School

East-ave intersects

Ferguson-ave, east side, from 164 King e to the Bay

2 David Cullum, carpenter
4 Mrs Charles Dickinson
6 Jas Shea, cutter
8 John Cousins, messenger
10 Peter Swab, teamster

King Wm-st intersects

16 Hugh Stewart, grocer
22 David Phillips
24 Thomas Kenny
26 Mrs Geo Wilson
28 Wm McMann, melter
30 John Lavelle, laborer
32 Mrs A McGoff
34 Michael Montague, laborer
36 John Canty, laborer

Rebecca-st intersects

36½ Wm Heeney, accountant
38 Mrs Wm Park
40 James Mercer, builder
40½ J R Camboden, butcher

Wilson-st intersects

44 R Blair, grocer
46 F G Taylor, polisher
48 Joseph Mitchell, plasterer
50 James Scott, merchant
52 Robert Stratton, letter carrier
54 Mrs Sarah James
58 Mrs Andrew Millar

Kelly-st intersects

64 James Hamilton, agent
68 George Lanigan, bookbinder
70 Mrs Ruth Armstrong
76 Wm Moore, laborer
78 M C Dickson, freight agent
80 Chas T Jones, broker

Cannon-st intersects

86 Jasper Hill, grocer
90 Mrs M Proctor
100 Vacant
N & N W R shops and stores

Barton-st intercects

162 Elvin Nash, fireman
164 Fred Gough, fioreman

166 John Smale
168 Thos A Green, mariner
170 Mrs Susan Greenaway
Railway Crossing
Hamilton Straw Hat works
Strachan-st intersects
Hamilton Speer, laborer
Joshua Dossett, polisher
John McFarlane, laborer
Simcoe-st intersects
F Saxton, laborer
Mrs Jane Miller
Thos Allison, machinist
Mrs John Young
104 John Payne, gardener
106 Alfred Anson, cigarmaker
Richard Mugford, painter
Richard Rowe, grocer
Ferrie-st intersects
Louis Pearce, laborer
R Stephenson, tinsmith
Picton-st intersects
Fred Schelter, grocer
Edward Ladd, baker
Macaulay & Wood-sts intersect
Jas Devine, carpenter
Burlington-st intersects

Ferguson-ave, west side

1 P W Freeman, coal dealer
Salvation Army Barracks
3 E S Cummer
5 J G Gibson, conductor
7 James Aldridge, shoemaker
King Wm-st intersects
23 Mrs John Gidley
25 Michael Stonehouse
25 Charles Carey, dealer
John R Camben, butcher
Rebecca-st intersects
37 Mrs Wm Lavis
Wilson-st intersects
45 H B Haight, yardmaster
47 John Johnston, machinist
49 Richard Dynes, moulder
51 Mrs Mary Byrne
53 Wm Murphy, grocer
55 Jas Ogilvie, station master
59 Dennis Skelly
61 E J Skelly, clerk
63 Mrs John Jones
Kelly & Cannon-sts intersect
N & N W R offices
Robert-st intersects
121 James Murray, tailor
123 Walter Catton, car builder
125 Peter McNamee, sectionman
127 — Parks, machinist
129 W J Locke, clerk
131 James Stephens, moulder
133 Mrs Peter Barr
135 A W Dunnett, brakeman
137 John Latham, wagonmaker
139 John M Stephenson, laborer
141 Wm Beatty, engineer
143 Robert McAvay, gilder
145 A D McKay, laborer
147 Geo E Humphrey, moulder
149 James Laney
Barton-st intersects
G T Railway
Strachan-st intersects
Mrs Alex Jones
Simcoe-st intersects
John Wilson, dyer
John Hunter, sr, laborer
John Hunter, jr, laborer
Michael Cussen, laborer
Ferrie and Picton-sts intersect
Geo Winniscroft, laborer
Wm Slee, carpenter
John McGuire, bookbinder
Macauley & Wood-sts intersect
George Patterson, laborer

Ferric-st e, north side, from 298 James north to Victoria avenue

5 David Audette, clerk
7 Jeremiah Behan, glassblower
9 Mrs Henry McCann

11 Andrew White, baker
13 Andrew Malcolmson, carp'r

Hughson-st intersects

23 Robert Jackson, carpet wvr
25 Richard Wilcox, laborer
27 Charles Cartwright, laborer

John-st intersects

Patrick Burns, glassblower

Catharine-st intersects

59 Wm Keating, confectioner
67 James Geddes, clerk G T R

Mary-st intersects

79 Matthew Spence, stonecutter
83 Fred Newman, laborer
85 Wm Wilson, spinner
89 Thos Furey, nail cutter
91 R J Purdy, carpenter
93 Edward Bodden, painter
95 Freeman Shackelton, laborer
97 Thomas Lennon, laborer
99 Vacant
101 Joseph Badeau, shoemaker
103 Patrick Cosgrove
105 J Buskard, blacksmith
107 Oscar Mathews, carpenter
109 John Dolan, carter

Ferguson-ave intersects

117 Geo Moore, laborer
121 Chas Valentine, laborer
125 Michael Cahill, glassblower
129 Ceo West, carpenter
131 Ed Tallman, porter
133 John Jenkins, carpenter
133½ Charles Carter, laborer
135 Chas Wall, engineer
139 Wm Gleason, laborer
143 Solomon Butler, tinsmith
147 Thos Partridge, pattern mkr

Wellington-st intersects

Stroud's Tannery

Victoria-ave intersects

James Irving, laborer
Thos W Turner, engineer
Samuel Rodgers, laborer
Thomas Carter, engineer
Henry Searles, laborer

Clark-ave intersects

Ferrie-st e, south side

12 Adolph Miller, glassblower

Hughson-st intersects

26 James C Duggan, tailor
28 Arthur Cullen, laborer
30 Vacant
32 Vacant

John-st intersects

Wm Blaine, laborer
48 Vacant
50 Alfred Ward, carpenter
52 Mrs Philip Stafford
54 Mrs Joseph Philips

Catharine-st intersects

60 Michael Taulty, laborer
68 John McGovern, laborer

Mary-st intersects

86 Edward Young, plasterer
94 John Kirkwood, laborer
96 Freeman Johnson, laborer
98 Wm Matchett, laborer
100 Fred Skirrow, weaver
102 M Gill, boilermaker
104 Vacant

Ferguson-ave intersects

114 Richard Rowe, grocer
120 Wm Phenix, pattern mkr
126 Thos Freel, laborer
132 Mrs Patrick Lynch
134 Francis Fagan, ropemaker
138 Matthew Kennedy, cooper

Wellington-st intersects

John Pomfret, foreman
229 John Beveridge, laborer
231 Isaac Bernard, tanner

Victoria-ave intersects

Ferrie-st w, north side, from 281 James north to the Bay

10 Morgan Wall, laborer
12 Wm Torrance, moulder
16 Samuel Malcolson, sailor
26 Mrs Elizabeth Malcomson

Macnab-st intersects

34 John Cowan, laborer
36 John Dillon, machinist
38 Bold Jarvis, clerk
40 Capt James Mitchell
42 Vacant
44 Wm Blake, butcher
46 Thomas Clark, laborer

Bay-st intersects

56 Charles Stone, laborer
58 Wm Thompson, engineer
Burlington yacht club
Massie's boat house

Ferrie-st w, south side

Ontario Cotton Mills Co
25 Robt Williamson, laborer

Macnab-st intersects

31 Hugh Gillespie
37 Robt Johnson, mariner
39 Wm Peace, sailor
41 Geo Perry, foreman
41 Robt Smith, carpenter

Bay-st intersects

Florence-st, north side, from 72 Bay north to west of Dundurn

4 Mrs A Tomes
6 Mrs D McDonald
8 Lawrence Moore
14 James Murdoch, porter
16 Wm Kerner, com trav
20 Wm Armstrong, laborer

Pearl-st intersects

30 Chas Mann, mason
36 W Lockman, carpenter
40 Wm H Lockman, builder
44 Wm Brenston
46 Mrs Eliza Braund
48 Josiah Palmer, teacher
50 Robert Fisher, painter
52 Peter Wright, driller
54 Mrs D Durant

Locke-st intersects

56 Stephen Carter, blacksmith

Inchbury-st intersects

Semmens' factory

Sophia-st intersects

86 Mrs John Semmens
88 E S Gilbert, laborer
90 John Attle, tinsmith
94 Wm Bateman, laborer
96 Charles Neighorn, marble cutter
98 Geo S Thompson, salesman
102 James Hennesy, carpenter
104 Henry Fisher, laborer
106 Mrs John Hilliard
110 John Craig, carpenter
112 Thos Jackman, fitter
118 George Thompson
120 Neil McKeown, moulder

Dundurn-st intersects

Florence-st, south side

1 J W Norman, laborer
3 Geo Harper, laborer
5 Geo McKay, carpenter
7 Wm Moffat, laborer
7½ Wm Dyer, laborer
9 Joseph Fletcher
11 Vacant
13 Wm Hatchard, cabinetmkr
15 John Pocock, mason
17 John Nicholson, wood dealer
19 John Fox
21 S Heath, blacksmih

Pearl-st intersects

25 Alex Anderson, blacksmith
27 Thos Farmer, photographer
29 Robt Leslie, shoemaker
31 James Gavey, salemaker
33 Wm Cathchpole, machinist
35 Mrs Hannah Catchpole
37 Joseph Jocelyn, plasterer
39 Robt Henry, laborer
41 James Symmers, salesman
43 Henry Lovell, fireman
45 Geo Kerr, watchman
47 Vacant
49 George Wilson, engineer
51 George Brand, laborer

Locke and Sophia-sts intersect

86 John Meiler, tailor
95 Jas Judd, soap manf
107 Samuel R Hancock, laborer
John McMahon, salesman
Dundurn-st intersects

Garth-st. east side, from end of King w to Mountain

Thomas Smith, laborer
Henry Cooper, laborer
Geo Cooper, laborer
Thos Packham, laborer
Main and Robinson-sts intersect
John Philips, laborer
Concession-st intersects
Wm Shawcross, traveler

Garth-st, west side

Charles Leister, laborer
James Hinchcliff, machinist
Geo Harrison, machinist
Main-st intersects
Fred Childs, brickmaker
Robinson-st intersects
Wm Burke, dairyman
Concession-st intersects
Wm Gillard, moulder
Mrs A W Addock
Wm Dow, moulder
John Gibson, carpenter
W H Nicolls, farmer

George-st, north side, from 6 Bay s to Locke

2 G D Hawkins & Co, shirt manfs
12 Peter Snider, laborer
14 M G Cornish, porter
16 Moses Niblock, laborer
18 Wm Pegler, laborer
Caroline-st intersects
26 John Gillard, merchant
28 John H Herring, traveler
30 G G Hacker, clerk
32 Wm Armstrong, com trav
38 Chas Foster, inspector
40 Mrs Elizabeth Laing
42 John McKean, clerk
44 Vacant
Hess-st intersects
54 Chas Tolmie. agent
56 Chas Jolley, manf
58 Mrs Wm Richardson
Queen-st intersects
70 John Thomson
— Nicholson, merchant
Ray-st Intersects
78 Jas Slater, merchant
80 Mrs Donald Kennedy
82 John Wallace, tinsmith
86 Wm Pearce, engine driver
Pearl-st intersects
92 David Bates, teamster
Richard McBride, packer
Wm Evans, bricklayer
108 Charles Coleman, laborer
110 Charles Kilgour, laborer
Locke-st intersects

George-st, south side

3 Samuel Bennett, turner
5 A J Goodwin, porter
7 Samuel Brunt, laborer
11 Charles Shields, pedler
13 Mrs Mary Case
13½ Arthur S Brunt, barber
15 Dewey & Sons, ice dealers
Caroline-st intersects
35 Henry Blue, laborer
39 F C Bruce, seedsman
41 C Cooper, carriage painter
43 D S McKenzie, engineer
45 Edmund Browne, builder
47 G Nicholson, wood dealer
49 Geo Dodd, piano finisher
Hess-st intersects
59 Vacant
61 Mrs B McDearmid
63 Robert Moodie, merchant
65 John Moodie, merchant
Queen-st intersects
69 Geo M Hunt, ins agent
71 Mrs A Rennie

73 Geo H Mills, barrister

Ray-st intersects

77 Industrial school
79 Vacant
81 Jos Prentice, serj police
83 And Higgins, confectioner
85 Wm Woodhouse, timekeeper

Pearl-st intersects

95 Thos Shea, laborer
99 Thomas C Jackson, laborer
103 John Rackley, laborer
109 Wm O'Brien, scalemaker

Locke-st intersects

Gore-st, north side, from 90 James n, east to Catharine

2 C Hiby, billiard room
4 Toronto "News" office
6 Grand Opera House
8 Garrick Club
10 J M Lathrop, manager
14 G L MacKelcan, M D
16 Wm McCargaw, M D
18 E H Dilliabough, M D

Hughson-st intersects

Lutheran Church
28 Mrs Mary Bates
30 Moss Freeman, laborer

John-st intersects

44 Joseph Prior, laborer
50 F L Hooper, ins agent
52 Joseph Lee, cabinet maker
54 Wm McMeekin, carpenter
56 J C Palmer, machinist
60 John Temple, livery keeper

Catharine-st intersects

Gore-st, south side

5 Hamilton Bottling Co
7 Thos Young, saloon
13 Mrs John Shaw, boarding
15 Vacant
17 Vacant
19 Samuel Magill, woodworker
21 George Colwell, machinist

Hughson-st intersects

23 Mark Mossman, shoemaker
29 Alex Thompson, cabinet mkr
31 Aaron Mann, clerk
33 Rev James VanWyck
Methodist Church

John-st intersects

51 Neil McLean, saloon keeper
53 Malcolm Munroe
55 Robert Lord, tailor
57 Henry O'Brien, machinist
59 James Hobbs, bricklayer

Catharine-st intersects

Greig-st, east side, from Queen north

Robert Mackie, engineer
Joseph Taylor, machinist
Edward Flynn, laborer
Edgar H Dickson, porter
David Gillespie, furniture
James Ryan, tailor

Greig-st, west side

1 Patrick Williams, laborer
3 Thomas Duffy, moulder
5 Patrick Snllivan, laborer
7 James Gee, fitter
9 Henry Johnson, laborer
11 John B Clark, puddler
13 James Lloyd, puddler
15 John Cardwell, laborer
19 Thomas Hayes, shearsman
John McAulay, millwright
Timothy Corbett
Wm Wharry, blacksmith

Grove-st, north side, from 3 Liberty east to Wellington

1 Fred Meinke, stove mounter
3 Vacant
7 Wm Stewart, watchman
9 Donald Work, laborer
11 Jacob Gould, joiner
13 Peter Freeman, wood dealer
15 Ed Cuckow, packer
17 Mrs L Hanna, nurse
19 D W Abell, machinist

Wellington st intersects

Grove-st, south side

2 Fred Kellond, bookbinder
4 Thos Haygarth, machinist
8 Wm Hazell, porter
10 Leslie Wright, baggage mast
12 Wm H McKay, inspector
12a Mrs Alex Rutherford
12b Norman Stewart, machinist
14 Peter Sinclair, laborer
16 Wm Shuttleworth, salesman
18 Mrs E Shaw
24 Alex McKay, merchant

Wellington-st intersects

Guise-st north side, from 383 James north to the Bay

23 James Irvine, teamster
25 Laurence Connelly, teamster
31 Richard Scott, teamster

John-st intersects

Myles' coal yard
Murton & Reid's coal yard

Guise-st, south side

18 Hugh Guy, brewer
12 Vacant
14 Thos Fuerd, laborer
16 Mrs Nancy Cross
18 Thos Lawson, laborer
20 Vacant
22 Mrs John Amor
24 Arch McCoy, watchman
26 Mrs J Munro
28 Israel Hopkins, pedler
30 Richard Green
32 G Strampel, laborer

Hughson-st intersects

34 James Berry, grocer
38 Hugh McNeigh, moulder
40 Henry Fahagan, laborer
42 Mrs Daniel Callaham
44 Patrick Earles, laborer
46 Vacant
48 T Reardon, laborer
50 Vacant
56 John Berry, teamster

John-st intersects

58 Vacant
House of Refuge

Hannah-st e, north side, from 137 James south to Wellington

Hughson-st ends

Ch of Ascension S school

John-st intersects

25 John Dobie, bookbinder

Catharine-st ends

29 Rev H Birkenthal
31 Vacant
33 D Sinclair, clerk
35 Henry Whately, barrister
37 Martin Hanley, blacksmith
39 George Campbell
41 W J Lavery, solicitor
43 Joseph Mittiff, whipmaker
45 Mrs Ann Barclay
47 Edward Horning, clerk
51 Andrew Swayzie, laborer
53 John Barry, painter
55 Ralph McCormick, teamster
59 Henry William
61 A Blakemore, brass finisher
63 Michael Dwyer, laborer

Walnut-st ends

67 Patrick Connell, laborer
71 Mrs Mary Cusha
77 Jas McCarty, laborer
79 James Adams, laborer
81 Leo Blatz, tailor

Cherry-st intersects

93 Patrick Dillon, laborer
95 Arthur O'Neil, tailor
99 Alex Davidson, gardener
101 Joseph Dent, upholsterer

Aurora-st intersects

113 Michael Wickham, laborer
119 Timothy Foley, laborer
121 George Stanley, stovemountr

Wellington-st intersects

Hannah-st e, south side

4 R A Pringle, barrister

6 W A Robinson
8 John J Stuart, merchant
12 Dennis Moore, founder

John-st intersects

22 Joseph Hancock
24 Donald Manson, bookkeeper
26 Mrs R N Taylor
28 R L Gunn, clerk 9th division court

Catharine-st intersects

46 John Baylis, gardener
56 Chas H Martin, teamster
58 John O'Neil, tinsmith
John Carnahan, brushmaker
62 David Tower, laborer
r 62 James Fenton, bailiff

Walnut-st ends

64 Vacant
66 Timothy Cashmere, laborer
84 Charles Locke, stove fitter
86 Lewis Smith, stovemounter

Cherry-st intersects

120 D Northey, engineer
122 Vacant
126 Thos Byron, broommaker
r " Fred Clark, laborer
r " Thos Jones, laborer
Frank Miller, carpenter

Welliugton-st intersects

Hannah-st west, north side, from James south to Locke

8 Fred J Willson, manf
10 Henry Martin, artist
12 Edward Noyes
14 A T Freed, journalist
16 Adam Burns
18 John Garry, bookkeeper

Macnab & Park-sts intersect

Fred Swannel, manf
Wm Vallance, merchant
James Balfour, architect
E Van Allen, builder

Bay-st intersects

Peter Balfour
44 A Boyle, shoemaker
46 Henry Northey
48 Wm Marsden, merchant
50 George Barr, salesman

Caroline-st intersects

54 James Morton, grocer
54 George Scott, porter
60 Alex Crooks, dairyman
62 Hugh Walker, gardener
64 John Broadley, carpenter
66 James Smith, gilder
68 T A Aitchison, bookkeeper
70 Wm Malcolm, clerk
72 George McKeand, ins agent

Hess-st intersects

76 Hugh Gorman, porter
78 James Mitchell, laborer
80 David Souter, carpenter
84 H R Leather, fitter

Queen-st intersects

Levi Woodcroft, gardener
John Woodcroft, piano mkr

Locke & Garth-sts intersect

Hannah-st west, south side

Private grounds

Macnab-st intersects

Rev Hartley Carmichael
Robt H Park, merchant
Thos C Haslett, barrister
H P Coburn, manfr

Park-st intersects

35 John B Young, bookkeeper
37 M A Pennington, real estate agent
39 Robert Topping, engineer
James McKay, cutter
Robert Brackenbury

Bay-st intersects

Chas Sayers, shipper
Ed Appleby, stovemounter
41 Samuel Cottrell
43 James Hossack, builder
45 James McKay, cutter
47 Wm McBeth, machinist
49 Fred Hutty, gardener
Daniel Henry, grocer

Caroline-st intersects

Mrs Richard Rowe, florist

Wm Lancely, engineer
Wm Walker, dairyman
Hess-st intersects
Methodist Church
Queen-st intersects
Wm Scott, porter
Vacant
Locke & Garth-sts intersect

Harriet-st, north side, from 115 Caroline n, west to Hess

14 Vacant
14½ George Stapleton, laborer
16 Mrs Wm Medlock
18 George Childs, carpenter
20 C McCarthy, hackman
Hess st intersects

Harriet-st south side,

1 Vacant
3 Vacant
5 Wm Alderman, helper
7 James Loftus, laborer
9 Fred Pfeifer, laborer
11 Vacant
13 — McKay, laborer
13 John Coppins, tailor
15 Francis Brohman, brewer
15 X Dolmheirn, laborer
17 Jno Henderson, blacksmith
Hess-st intersects

Head-st, from Sophia

Hand & Co, fireworks
John Lyons, shipper
John McLean, tailor
Dundurn-st intersects
John Cotter, carter
George Sharkey, caretaker

Herkimer.st, north side, from James west to Queen

10 James Osborne, grocer
12 W R Macdonald, barrister
Argyll Terrace { J M Burns, banker
Mrs Kate Thomson
Mrs Fanny Chapman
Park-st intersects
44 John L Stoney, ins agent
46 J B Brown, manf
Bay-st intersects
52 Geo Morton, whitewasher
54 Rev C A Johnson
60 Geo Jelts, barrister
62 James Davidson, jeweller
64 A H Baker, watchmaker
Caroline-st intersects
70-72 Vacant
Chas Bremner, grocer
Hess-st intersects
110 Thos Hedley, upholsterer
Queen-st intersects
Ira Nelson, laborer
John Bond, laborer
Kent & Locke-sts intersect
G W Collins, mason
Baptist Mission Church
A F Drew, carpenter
P O'Connor, laborer
D Dolman, teamster
Thos King, laborer
C Clark, laborer
Garth-st intersects

Herkimer-st. south side, James west to Queen

Burlington Terrace { 1 Chas M Counsell
3 H C Baker
5 Thos H Stinson, solicitor
7 F W Gates, pres Gas Co
Macnab-st intersects
11 John E Parker, manf
13 Adam Brown, merchant
21 A Gaviller
Park st intersects
23 Judge Sinclair
Bay-st intersects
53 Thos Irwin, manfr
55 David McLellan, ins agent
57 Vacant
59 D Henderson, salesman
61 Robt A Hutchison

Caroline-st intersects

Jacob Ellsworth, grocer
69 Thos Clappison, booksell'r
71 George Kemp, grocer
73 J Crossley, dry goods
75 John Barry, barrister
77 Vacant
79 Vacant

Hess-st intersects

107 John Harrison, plasterer
109 James Stevens, laborer
111 Alex Doston, tobacco roller

Queen-st intersects

G Murison, health inspector

Kent & Locke-sts intersect

Wm Harvey, traveler
Henry Anderson, machinist
Wm Garton, shoemaker
Mrs Sophia Knotts
Joseph D Wilson, carpenter
John J Smith, laborer

Garth-st intersects

Wm Boswell, gardener

Hess-st n, east side, from 183 King w to Stuart

8 John R Vert, traveler

Market-st intersects

26 P McCarthy, teamster
28 Mrs Mary Richardson
30 Thomas Addison, laborer
32 Alfred Rieger, blacksmith
34 Daniel South, laborer

Napier-st intersects

44 Wm Robertson, birch beer manfr
46 John W Thomson, traveler
48 John Snowden, clerk
50 Adam Clarke, machinist
52 Wm Brooks, bookkeeper
54 Jas B Rutherford, moulder

York-st intersects

Central Drug Store
56 Wm Philp, M D
58 Matthew Dunn, stonecutter
60 O Lockhart, tobacco roller
62 Thos Duncan, machinist
64 Wm Angus, tinsmith
66 Mrs Mary Colbeck, grocer

Cannon-st intersects

68 Adolphus Myers, grocer
70 Vacant
72 James Brugger, carpenter
82 Mrs Thos Melampy

Mill-st intersects

84 Danford Evans, agent
86 James Bowen, tobacco roller
88 Thomas Morgan, fireman
90 Wm Sterrett, policeman
92 Alex McDowell, laborer
92½ Mrs Wm McCartney
98 Mrs Charlotte McNeil

Harriet-st ends

104 H Lowe, salesman
106 Edward Sinclair, brakeman
108 Thos G Peat
120 Mrs Samuel Meadows
122 H W Rieger, laborer
124 John Connors, conductor
126 Mrs T McComb
140 John Cousens, carpenter
142 James Rhynd, fireman

Stuart-st intersects

Hess-st n, west side

1 Thomas Stokes, carpenter
5 George Clark, machinist
7 Mrs R Knowles
9 Mrs James Gray
11 Mrs Mary Doran
13 Patrick Hanlon, grocer

Market-st intersects

25 Edward Hughes, spring mkr
29 D Harris, salesman
Mrs A Winslow

Napier-st intersects

43 J J Daley, grocer
45 Martin Sammons, gardener
51 Miss Margaret Rymal

Peter-st commeuces

53 Samuel Tufford, tinsmith
55 Elijah Beckerson, laborer

York-st intersects

Public school
75 Vacant
77 Arch McGowan, machinist
79 Robert T Brown, merchant
81 John Brown, machinist
83 Arthur Goulding, caretaker
85 John McCowell, grocer
87 Wm McGovern, laborer
89 Thos Farrow, carpenter
89½ George Copley, clerk
91 Mrs Mary Smith
91½ W H Thompson, nailer
93 Geo Knox, engineer
95 Wm McKay, conductor
97 James Connor, machinist
99 J H Wilson, pork dealer
103 Wm Johnson, painter
105 Henry Greenway, laborer
107 Vacant
109 Andrew Cameron, G T R
109½ Mrs James Butler
111 Robert Dickson, carpenter
113 John F Anderson, moulder
115 Anthony Lyon, machinist
117 Thos E Nichols, wireworker
119 Mrs Emma Goddard
121 Mrs Wm Walton
123 George Green, laborer
127 James Brass, laborer

Stuart-st intersects

Hess-st s. east side, from 185 King w to Mountain

1 Vacant
3 John Kinleyside, manfr
5 Joseph H Killey, manfr
9 James Wilson, merchant
11 Mrs S M Olmstead

George-st intersects

13 W B Webber
15 And Dalton, moulder
17 Thos B Greening, merchant

Main & Jackson-sts intersect

41 John Dow, wood dealer

Hunter-st intersects

45 Wm Horspoole, clerk
47 John Fahey, shoemaker
49 Vacant
51 Chas Male, laborer
53 Vacant

Bold-st intersects

Vacant lots

Duke & Robinson-sts intersect

99 J C Stacey, upholsterer
101 George Graham, tailor

Hannah-st intersects

Wm Flitcroft, blacksmith

Herkimer-st intersects

John Hislop, blacksmith

Markland and Coucesiion-sts intersect

James M Williams, manfr

Hess-st s west side

2 John Patterson
4 Herbert Dixon, customs
6 Wm Mundy, letter carrier
12 C Carpenter, merchant

George-st intersects

14 Vacant
16 Vacant

Main-st intersects

20 Wm Ryckman, grocer
22 Wm Colville, clerk

Jackson-st intersects

W D Booker, sec Vic ins Co
42 Alfred Hipkins, printer
44 Wm Scott, packer
46 Frank Lipkie, laborer

Hunter-st intersects

50 Felix Russell, laborer
Vacant lots

Bold, Duke, Robinson, Hannah & Herkimer-sts intersect

Alfred Taylor, stonecutter

Markland-st intersetts

Wm Irving, carpenter
Wm Clark, laborer
Wm Lane, bricklayer
John Price, carpenter

Concession-st intersects

John McLean, merchant

Hilton-st, east side, from Markland s to Concession

2 Daniel A Bedwell, cutter
6 Vacant
8 Mrs Peter Brass
Concession-st intersects

Hilton-st, west side

3 Wm Miller, shoemaker
5 James Kitts, shoemaker
Concession-st intersects

Hughson-st n, east side, from 34 King e to Guise

Wm Pease, barber
6 Jeremiah McAuliffe, saloon
8 Wm Somerville & Co, com agents
10 Stinson's bank
12 John McIntyre, tailor
14 Alex Mars, bookbinder
16 J H Bland, barber
18 John Clayton, painter
20 Wm Seaton, machinist
22 John Hennessy
22 W C Barnes & Son, stained glass
22 J Adam, plumber
24 A S Hill, saloon
King Wm-st intersects
34 Central fire station
42 Mrs Ann Drenin
44 Wm Elrington, printer
46 Joseph Taylor, jeweler
48 S F Hopkins, pickle manfr
50 John Leitch, machinist
Rebecca-st intersects
52 Vacant
56 Rev W J Hunter
58 Thos Bale, sexton
60 Andrew Goddard, engineer
64 J W Simpson, com agent
66 Thos Greenaway, moulder
68 A Taupkirch, clerk
70 Wm Critchley, teamster
72 Thos Bale, machinist
Gore-st intersects
74 David West, laborer
78 George Dennison, clerk
80 John T Steel, clerk
82 Edward Clary, shoemaker
84 Thos Bottle
88 Albert S Vail, merchant
Congregational church
Cannon-st intersects
120 Samuel Parnell, painter
122 Mrs Robert McCulloch
124 J Shea, merchant
126 A H Moore, banker
128 J W Millard, clerk
130 Alex Macadams, banker
132 A R Morris6n, agent
134 G H Moore
136 Allen Land, bookkeeper
Robert-st intersects
138 J W McArthur
140 Wm Omand
142 H M Coates, letter carrier
144 A McCully, shoemaker
146 Wm Walker, poultry dealer
148 P J Downing, whitewasher
150 Vacant
152 Wm Lee, pedler
154 John Baker, laborer
156 Thos Applegate, laborer
158 Joseph Carroll, laborer
160 John Highsted, laborer
162 Alex Dingwall, mason
164 Mrs Catharine Riddle
166 David Gilbert, polisher
168 Mrs Fossett
170 Thos Applegate, hackman
172 Mrs Eliza Smith
174 Wm Cumbers
176 Daniel Hutchinson, laborer
178 Mrs Ann Hill
180 Geo Carmichael, cab driver
Barton-st intersects
182 Alfred Thorpe, pedler
188 Wm Russell, traveler
190 John Dunn, traveler
196 Thos Hutchinson, engineer
Murray-st intersects
202 John McCarthy, laborer
204 Jeremiah Quinlan, laborer

206 George Towers, sailor
208 John Brennan, carpenter
210 John Irving, laborer
212 Geo H Warren, puddler
214 Mrs John Thomas
216 Timothy Sullivan, laborer

Stuart-st intersects

218 Thos McCracken, tailor
220 Fred Childs, brickmaker
222 Mrs J Bowers
224 John Carroll, moulder
226 — Mitchell, yardsman
228 Mrs E Griffiths
230 Mrs O'Regan, grocer

Strachan-st intersects

238 Geo Johnson, carpenter
242 Wm Jamieson, moulder
242 John Politt, designer

Simcoe-st intersects

248 Patrick Harte, clerk
250 Cornelius Moynahan broommaker
252 Michael Duffy, moulder
256 Mrs L Hadley
258 Thos Grace, wood dealer
260 John Pearson, hackman
266 Thos Williamson, teamster
268 Robert Williamson, laborer

Ferrie-st intersects

270 Thos Lally, laborer
272 Peter Hunter, carpenter
274 Mrs Mary A Taylor
274½ Geo W Belling, carpenter
276 John Milligan, laborer
278 John O'Connor, clerk
280 Elijah Walter, mariner
282 Mrs McGrogan
284 James Clarke, carpenter
286 Thos Furlong, laborer
288 Robert Gray, laborer

Picton-st intersects

298 Thomas Rush, laborer
300 Thos Beatty, boilermaker
302 Henry Free, engineer
304 Hiram Siddell, laborer
306 Joseph Cahill, glassblower
310 Robert Ball, laborer
312 John Roach, laborer

Macauley-st intersects

326 Vacant
328 Joseph Paulley, carpenter
330 Mrs E Bowles
332 Patrick Bennett, laborer
334 John McManus, laborer
336 Daniel Flynn, laborer
338 David Findlay, moulder

Wood-st intersects

342 W J McFadden, grocer
348 Wm Bolton, teamster
350 H Walsh, policeman
352 James Hyde, section hand
354 Mrs S Wetherall
356 John Reardon, boiler mkr
360 Michael Reardon, laborer

Burlington-st intersects

368 J H Thompson, boatbuilder
370 John Thompson, grocer
374 John Kerr
380 Wesley Lee, mariner

Guise-st intersects

Hughson-st north, west side

J A Clark, druggist
1 Times editorial rooms
3 Times Printing Company
13 Gore Coffee Tavern
15 J Matthews & Sons, painters
17 James Mackie, carpenter
19 Fred De Lacy, saloon
21 John Barnes, livery

King Wm-st intersects

31 James' hotel
33 Robert Allan, broker
35 Mrs McCrooks
43 John Smith, tinsmith
45 George Reid, carriage maker
49 Peter Weir, coffee rooms

Rebecca-st intersects

55 Dr Alex C Reid
55 J W Simpson, com agent
J M Williams & Co, manfs

Gore-st intersects

77 Mrs Samuel Cann

85 Robert Bow, tinsmith
87 John Williams
87 Wm Robertson, tailor
89 Thos Greening, moulder
91 James Jackson, sailmaker
93 Thos Cauley, laborer
95 D M Oliver, mariner
97 Mrs J M Morrison

Cannon-st intersects

Public school
105 David McKean, accountant
107 James Chisholm, barrister
109 Mrs J Swain
111 A E Carpenter, contractor
113 J W Sutherland, lumber merchant
117 Henry Dunnett, painter

Robert-st intersects

143 E Bissonnette, moulder
145 Louis Fraser, clerk
147 John Kennedy, clerk

Barton-st intersects

183 David Nash, laborer
185 Jas Bartholomow, moulder
187 John Duffy, laborer
189 John McMillan, mason
193 Jas Stannard, carpenter
195 John Gillespie, machinist
197 Wm Burrow, founder
199 Mrs Wm Ambrose

Murray-st intersects

203 John Cartney, blacksmith
205 Louis Burnett, laborer
207 Morris Devine, laborer
209 James McDonald
211 N McNichol, boilermaker
213 Thos Meagher, engineer
215 Chris Clark, hatter

Stuart-st ends

G T R bridge
225 Wm Fowler, foreman
227 Thomas Littlewood, brakeman
229 John McClelland, laborer

Strachan-st intersects

231 Mrs John Hannon
233 Mrs T McKeown
235 Thomas Brady, coal inspec'r
237 Wm T Rolls, laborer
239 T Horn, carpenter
241 George Horn, carpenter
243 Patrick Carroll, laborer
245 Thos W Laird, machinist
249 Mrs E McHendry

Simcoe-st intersects

251 Chas Blackburn, carder
253 John Hickey, brakeman
255 Mrs David Creighotn
Primary school
261 Patrick Dalton, laborer
263 M Nelligan, wagonmaker
265 Mrs M Nelligan

Ferrie-st intersects

275 Wm Smith, laborer
r " Louis Robb, carder
277 Patrick Donnelly, laborer
279 James Smith, blacksmith
281 Bobert Wilson, laborer
283 John Anderson, laborer
285 James Valance, carpenter

Picton-st intersects

305 Hamilton Glass Works

Macauley-st intersects

315 Mrs George Andrews
317 Vacant
329 John Meehan, laborer
331 J Hodson, laborer
335 Thos O'Neil, laborer
Vacant lots

Wood-st intersects

351 Moses Blondin, engineer
353 Wm Richardson, bricklayer

Burlington-st intersects

367 Henry Gillam, laborer
369 Thos Doyle, laborer
373 Chas Lee
381 Vacant

Guise-st intersects

Hughson-st s, east side, from 117 King e to Hannah

Hamilton Provident and Loan Society Chambers:
Bell Telephone Co
1 Cameron & Witherspoon barristers
1 Crerar, Muir & Crerar, barristers
F H Lamb, accountant
Parkes & Macadams, barristers
J Dunn, tea and sugar broker
3 Dun Wiman & Co, mercantile agency

5 W H Gillard & Co, grocers
7 Vacant
Thos Myles & Son, coal dealers

Main-st intersects

Court House
Prince's Square
Registry office

Jackson-st intersects

J & R Kilgour, organ manfr
R T S Powell, florist

Hunter-st intersects

51 R Montgomery, Wood market
63 Harry Green merchant
Miss Mary Wilson
67 H B W Western, clerk
69 Vacant
71 S S Ryckman, grocer

Augusta-st intersects

Synagogue
83 Alex Turner, merchant

Young-st intersects

85 Rev R J Laidlaw
87 Harold Lambe, broker
89 Richard Green, merchant
Vacant lots

Maria and Hannah-sts intersect

Hughson-st south, west side

Bank of Commerce
James Turner & Co, wholesale grocers

Main-st intersects

Chancery Chambers:
10 John Pearson, accountant and ins agent
D G Ellis, broker

Equity Chambers:
12 Charles Lemon, barrister
14 T Wavell, offi'l assignee Dom license office

16 Club Chambers
28 Stephen Summers, shoemkr

Jackson-st intersects

30 Z B Choate, carpenter
34 Joseph Plastow, caretaker
42 David Roach, blacksmith

Hunter-st intersects

50 Mrs Maria Hodgins
52 George Reid, teamster
54 John Burns, laborer
56 H J Hampton, machinist
58 Thomas Stevenson, finisher
60 Wm Reid, teamster
66 James Gay, bookkeeper
68 Julius Winckler, machinist
70 John Brundle, tinsmith

Augusta-st intersects

76 Mrs Owen Kennedy
78 Wm Birnie, miller
78½ Rev Joseph Jacobson
80 Richard Pray, undertaker

Young & Maria-sts intersect

98 John Calder, merchant
102 W H Glassco, merchant

Hannah-st intersects

Hunter-st e, north side, from 61 James s to Emerald

1 Mrs Mary Carr
3 Vacant
5 George Miller, bellman
7 R Jones, whitewasher
9-11 James Cheyne, builder
15 Charles Hill, carpenter
19 James Jolley, merchant

Hughson-st intersects

Hotel stables

John-st intersects

30 Benj Tryter, cigarmaker
41 Wm Rodwell, painter
43 Arthur Ray, laborer
45 John Vanatter, policeman
47 C Orttopin, tailor
49 Ed Morton, painter
49½ George Sharp, builder
51 Wm Warrick, carpenter
53 Mrs George Sinclair
53 John Allan, grocer

Catharine-st intersects

55 Michael Allen, grocer
59 Wm Stevenson, carpenter
61 John Tuckett, tobaçconist
63 Frank E Walker
65 Mrs M Jones
67 James Dunlop, merchant
69 Alex McPherson, teamster
73 Wm McKee, moulder
75 Charles Dunbar, moulder
77 Mrs John Lee, grocer
79 David Tilley, bookkeeper
81 Mrs John Fraser
83 Smith Will, clerk

Walnut-st intersects

93 J E Hutchings, bookkeeper
95 John Hachett, polisher
97 Mrs John Powers
97½ J Pottruff, salesman
99 R J Howard, blacksmith
101 Wm T Nelson, laborer
103 Peter Mulholland, laborer
105 Mrs Sarah Brick, grocer

Cherry-st intersects

107 Edw Moshier, miller
113 Robert Peebles, carpenter
115 Luke Harrison
117 Mrs Kate Sullivan
119 Fred Wakelin, pensioner
121 Mrs Patrick Gorman
123 Mrs James Toomey
127 Vacant

Spring-st ends

129 Robert Moore, tailor
131 Vacant
133 John McDonald, shoemaker
135 Peter Adams, tailor
137 Mrs James Walker

Wellington-st intersects

Vacant lots

West-ave intersects

161 P J O'Donnell, clerk P O
Vacant grounds

Victoria-ave intersects

Vacant grounds to Emerald street

Hunter-st e, south side

4 G Stevenson, baker
6 Wm Worrall, carpenter
8 James Atkins, barber
12 James McCreath, blacksmith
14 Richard Bull, ins agent
16 Mrs M Adams
18 George Garner
20 George Hewson, carpenter

Hughson-st intersects

22 N Reed, carpenter
24 Mrs Amy Disher
26 PMoore, shipper
28 Wm Terryberry, bartender
30 Joseph Smye, wagon maker
34 Simeral Doak
34 W Tyce, clerk

John-st intersects

40 Vacant
42 Levi Potruff, porter
44 Mrs Levi Pottruff
46 George Spence, shoemaker
48 W B Mitchell, tailor
50 Wm Gosgrove, agent
50½ Adam Almas, laborer
52 William Bews

Catharine-st intersects

54 Felix O'Neil, hackman
58 Joseph T Kendall, butcher
60 Vacant
60½ Wm Truman, bookmaker
64 Josiah Spencer, stonecutter
66 Jacob Voelker, tailor
68 James Straus, carpenter
70 Peter Nicol, laborer

Baillie-st intersects

74 Geo Matthews, clerk
76 Wm Strongman, policeman
78 Wm Stoneham, mason
80 Peter McKay, packer
82 R F Dodd, valuator
84 Neil McKay, wine maker
86 C D Stephenson, lather
88 Thomas Healey

Walnut-st intersects

90 Mrs Donald Stuart
90 J R Mitchell, salesman
94 S R Hamill, teamster
104 Long's wood yard

Cherry-st intersects

St Patrick's school

Liberty-st intersects

120 P Stuart, wood inspector
124 Michael McCarthy, laborer
126 Henry Burrows, laborer
130 S S Rolls, carriage trimmer
132 Thos Old, laborer
134 Mrs Wm Gow
136 Henry Pearson, cutter
138 James Hiscox
138½ Mrs Andrew Wallman
140 Alex McLaughlin, salesman
142 W A Edwards, architect
144 Donald Dawson, tax col

Wellington-st intersects

154 H G McMahon, carpenter
Primary school

West, Victoria and East-aves intersect

Hunter-st w, north side, to Garth

Private grounds

Park -st intersects

St James R E Church
36 J C Burrows, builder
38 E McLaughlin, civil engineer
40 Alex Gillies, com trav
42 Alex Anderson
44 Wm Acres, furrier
46 Mrs Wm Troup
48 John Kerner
50 George Vallance, cashier
50 Peter Brass, architect

Bay-st intersects

52 Wm G Bailey, miller
r " J Mercer, cabinet maker
54 Mrs M Howard
56 Wm Bowman, merchant
58 James Walker, agent

Caroline-st intersects

78 Henry Turnbull, sexton
80 D D Campbell, clerk P O
82 James B P Stacey, cabinet-maker
90 John Gilmore, cabinetmaker
94 Mrs Frank Harrison, dresser
96 Joseph King, tinsmith
98 Vacant

Hess st intersects

100 Wm Simpson, checker
104 Arthur Fell, machinist
106 James Thompson

Queen-st intersects

118 Richard Scott, miller
124 John Meal, laborer
126 Wm Cooke, laborer
128 John E Wing, machinist

Ray-st intersects

134 Jos Tompkins, shoemaker
136 James Glass, shoemaker
138 Richd Fairhurst, wire weaver
142 Thomas Winfield, grocer
146 John D Virgint, laborer
150 John Mostyn, tinsmith

Pearl-st intersects

160 Fred Bateman, laborer
162 Alfred Rain, carpenter

Locke-st intersects

180 John Odell, laborer
182 Vacant
190 George Fitzgerald, laborer

Hunter-st w, south side

1 Wm A Howell, druggist
5 J G Tulk, moulder
7 George Finlayson, baker
9 George Salter, laborer
9 Henry Turner
11 Robert Chisnell

13 Michael Donovan, hackman
15 R Chisnell, cooper
17 Mrs Joseph Ward
19 Hart Emery Wheel Co
21 Mrs P S McHenry
25 Wm C Stewart, founder

Macnab-st intersects

Presbyterian Church

Charles-st intersects

31 R R Waddell, barrister

Park-st intersects

Central School

Bay-st intersects

49 Rev R G Sutherland
51 Mrs R Marlatt
53 David Graham, hatter
55 M Newman, com traveler
59 Daniel Le Messurier, painter
61 A Maclean, merchant
63 J J Mason, accountant
65 James Pearson, manfr
67 Mrs Martha Fell

Caroline-st intersects

69 James Dodman, grocer
71 Daniel Comfort, paper bag manfr
71 Mrs John Henning
73 T L Scott, clerk
75 S C Rogers, manfr
77 Wm Bromley, barber
79 James Hardiman, baker
81 Mrs John Duggan, laundress
83 Mrs Thos Kelly
85 James Falconer, carpenter
87 James Cutt, cutter
89 B Dickinson, laborer
91 George Beach, traveler
95 George Feasel, gardener

Hess-st intersects

99 Wm Nex, laborer
103 Mrs Wm Vant
r 103 James Carrol
105 Thomas Stevens, machinist
107 Wm Julian, laborer

Queen-st intersects

119 Congr'l Sabbath School
121 Jacob Johnson, tailor
123 Daniel McDermott, painter
125 Mrs Thos Conklin
129 Wm Male, laborer

Ray-st intersects

137 Thos Young, porter
139 Vacant
141 Thomas Mitchell, plasterer
143 Thomas Thomson, shoemkr
145 A C Best, clerk
147 Wm Renwick, porter
151 Ramsay Will, laborer

Pearl-st intersects

155 G Thatcher, tobacco worker
157 John Clapham, plasterer
159 James Pinkett, laborer
167 John Cruickshanks, mason
169 Riddel Tompkins, laborer
171 Thos Exley, printer
175 James D Reynolds, painter

Locke-st intersects

Ida-st, commences at Wentworth south and runs east

Geo Thompson, bookkeeper

Inchbury-st n, east side, from 296 York to St Mary

6 Robt Binnington, laborer
8 J Lamplough, watchman
14 Mrs Thos Lovell
18 Thos Adams, carpenter
22 Wm Taft, engineer
24 Joseph Neville, machinist
24½ Ed Connors, baggage master
26 Michael Gleason, boilermaker
28 Wm Sandercock, boilermaker
30 A McDougall, blacksmith
32 T Daley, turner
50 Thos Blackburn, engineer
52 Ed Buscombe, bricklayer

St Mary's Lane intersects

Inchbury-st n, west side

5 T Tribute, machinist
7 John McKenzie, carpenter
9 Wm Peel, machinist
11 Wm Hawkins, laborer

13 Thos Hall, fitter
15 Wm Bankes, artist

Kennel-st intersects

25 C Mitchell, broommaker
27 Chas Morris, machinist
29 John Patterson, tailor
31 A J Nie, machinist
33 Richard Buscombe, bricklayer
35 George Daniels, fireman
37 Geo Gallagher, boilermaker
39 E Hilder, shoemaker
41 James Honeyford, fitter
43 Wm Dundin, laborer
51 M Reardon, baker

St Mary's Lane intersects

Inchbury-st s, east side, from 305 York to Florence

8 Robt Hinchcliffe, machinist
14 John Ross, blacksmith
16 Thos G Gaston, wireweaver
18 Wm Broughton, fireman
20 James Robinson, brickmaker
22 George Scragg, moulder

Florence-st intersects

Inchbury-st south, west side

3 Wm J Harris, laborer
5 John Bickell, carpenter
7 Thos Pumfrey, moulder
9 Timothy Winter, fireman
21 Mrs E Weston
23 Joshua Audette, laborer
25 Mrs Elizabeth Nicholson

Jackson-st e, north side, from James s to Wellington

7 Henry Kronsbein, tailor
7 Imperial Mineral Water works
11 Silver Creek Brewery

Hughson-st intersects

Court House

John and Bowen-sts intersect

37 Michael Murphy, hotel

Catharine-st intersects

43 Miss Annie Harvey
45 Geo Heyburn, lithographer
47 C P Michael, milk dealer
55-57 Robt Cruickshank & Co, planing mills
59 James Findlay, shoemaker
r 61 Daniel Winstone, laborer
r " Dennis O'Neil, laborer
r " Mrs M Burns
r " Stephen Donohue, laborer
John Fanagh, laborer
61 George Brooks, boxmaker
63 Wm Emerson
65 Mrs Samuel Sodon
69 Mrs James Nichol
71 F S Jarvis
73 Henry C Duval, barber
75 John Smith, baker
77 George Bartman, tailor
r 77 Thomas Leegrice, cabinet maker
79 Henry Magee, saddler
81 Hamilton Dairy Co
83 Vacant

Walnut-st intersects

91 John Callaghan, laborer
93 Edward Sevier, letter carrier
95 G H Thomas, messenger
97 James A Welsh
99 Isaac Levy, tailor
105 Wm Pessell, watchman
105½ Moses Cross, carter

Cherry-st intersects

107 Robert Gimblett, shoemaker
111 Thos Beatty, laborer
113 Simeon Beedom, laborer
117 Wm Hallisey, policeman
119 Patrick Meegan, laborer
125 Humphrey & Newberry, tanners

Spring-st intersects

133 Wm Horsefield, laborer
135 Wm Robb, printer

Wellington-st intersects

Jackson-st e, south side

4 Mrs Alex Dwyer
12 John McGinnis, stovemntr

Hughson-st intersects

14 Burkholder & Co
16 Howard & McVittie, horse shoers
18 Bell Telephone Co's storehouse
20 Vacant
22 Jas Wall, blacksmith
24 M H TenEyck, V S

John-st intersects

32 Theo Stafford, inspector
34 Charles Caldwell, moulder
36 D J Fraser, laborer
38 Henry Griffin
40 Nathaniel Norris, haydealer
42 James Douden, whitewasher

Catharine-st intersects

44 John McGuirk, carpenter
r " Wm Shields, laborer
46 Mrs M O'Rourke
48 Miss M Griffin, dressmaker
50 James Cleary, laborer
52 Colin Campbell, tailor
54 John Burns, laborer
56 F N Farner, hay dealer
58-60 Cruikshank's lumber yd
68 Mrs Robert Tansley
70 Mrs S McCullough
72 Geo H Dennis, teamster
78 Christopher Lee, porter
80 Mrs John Oliver, candies
82 Mrs Eliza Reid
84 John Reiley, moulder
86 Vacant

Walnut-st intersects

88 John O'Neil, laborer
90 Mrs Alex Littlejohn
92 Vacant
94 Mrs Wm Trail
94½ George Walker, shoemaker
96 Joseph Lyght, pattern mkr
98 Robert Brick, machinist
100 John Brick, lithographer
102 John Cronn, laborer
104 Knighton Sherman, buttonhole maker
106 John Brehany, shoemaker
108 Richard Crozier, laborer
108½ Mrs H Mackenzie

108½ Mrs M McSherry
110-112 Mrs J Grant, grocer

Cherry-st intersects

118 Joseph Jeff, laborer
120 Henry Gurner, bricklayer
122 John O'Neil, printer
124 Miss Eliza Barr
126 Henry Callowhill, tinsmith
128 George Canning, plasterer

Spring-st intersects

134 Mrs J Langton
136 Jamel Wall, blacksmith
138 E W Odell, pedler
140 Fred Lambert, porkpacker

Wellington-st intersects

Jackson-st w, north side, from James s to Garth

St Paul's Church
4 Samuel McKay, livery
Wood yard

Macnab-st intersects

Central Presbyterian Church
20 Rev Samuel Lyle

Charles & Park-sts intersect

28 Charles Limin, butcher
30 R Hills, sec Canada Life
30½ Ford Brownfield, clerk
32 W E Brown, bookkeeper
34 Robert Sterling
36 Robert Angus
38 Jas Turpin, com trav
40 Mrs Thomas B Harris
42 F F Dalley, manfr
44 J W Bowman, merchant
46 Mrs Margaret McClure

Bay-st intersects

50 John Connors, dairyman
52 Vacant
54 Michael Klager, bricklayer
56 Mrs A S Richardson
58 T H Lambe, accountant
60 H F Witherby, jeweler
62 T D Walker, inspector
64 N H Davis
66 Joseph Wallace, clerk
68 W R Davis, jeweler

70 John McCullough, carpenter
74 John Thom, tobacconist

Caroline-st intersects

76 Mrs L H Brooks
80 Henry A Eager, clerk P O

Hess-st intersects

88 W D Booker, sec Vic Mut Ins Co
90 Richard Coleman, traveler
92 Thos Marsden, merchant

Queen-st intersects

100 Samuel Ecclestone
102 Wm Bremer, com traveler
104 John D Clarke, editor "Times"
106 Charles Mills
108 Robert Campbell, potter
Fred J Howell, lithographer
120 James Blair, train despatcher
122 Vacant

Ray-st intersects

124 Alfred Miller, shoemaker
126 H W Craft, salesman
128 Fred Hebner, laborer
130 Geo S Board, blacksmih
132 George Kennedy, cabinet maker
134 Adam J Miller, stovemounter
136 Joseph Embling, laborer

Pearl-st intersects

138 Wm Combes, moulder
140 James Hamilton, tobacco presser
142 John Mitchell, laborer
144 Wm R Baker, fireman
146 James Marie, laborer
148 — Maplebeck, laborer
150 George Lamond, laborer
154 Noah Pollington, laborer

Locke-st intersects

156 Wm Ridler, shoemaker
160 Vacant
162 Michael Keagan, laborer
164 Miss R Cresswell

Poulette-st intersects

170 Chas J Hewett, brickmaker
172 Mrs Michael Lavelle
176 Ed Downing, carpenter
178 James Garner, finisher
184 Wm Auld, watchman
186 Thos Ellis, laborer
Campbell Sewer Pipe Co

Garth-st intersects

Jackson-st w, south side

3 John Billings
5 Charles Magill

Macnab-st intersects

Dr Calvin McQuesten

Charles-st intersects

German Roman Catholic Church
21 Mrs A Buntin
23 Oliver Hillman, merchant
25 Mrs Alex Duncan

Park st intersects

27 Mrs George Pierce
29 Mrs F Simpson
31 Mrs E Dewar
33 Lyman Moore
35 John J Scott, barrister
37 Mrs Hugh McInnes
39 Mrs Christina Aitken
41 W M Goodwin, telegraphist
43 John Hoodless, manfr
45 Wm Young
49 Samuel Woodley, shoemaker

Bay-st intersects

51 Robert T Steele, merchant
51 David Steele jr, barrister
53 Mrs Daniel Campbell
55 John Campbell, merchant
57 Miles Overend, depuly registrar
65 W E Sanford, merchant

Caroline-st intersects

75 Mrs T B Fuller
77 Geo H Bull, clerk P O
79 John Armour, C E
81 Angus Sutherland, grocer
83 Richard Brierley, druggist
85 Vacant
87 Vacant

Hess-st intersects

87½ Miss Mary Ann Briggs

89 G S Counsell, Co clerk
89 H H Willard
91 W C Turnbull, printer
95 J R Thompson, carver

Queen-st intersects

109 Mrs M Locke
111 P L Scriven, engraver
113 Mrs Alex Kemp
115 Wm Murray, collector

Ray-st intersects

121 Mrs Agatha Kurpieski
129 F Flaherty, laborer
131 Owen Doyle, carpenter

Pearl-st intersects

145 James W Webb, shoemaker
147 Geo Leavers, painter
149 James Gavey, scalemaker
151 Ed Neal, brickmaker

Locke-st intersects

165 James Harman, laborer
167 Wm King, engineer

James-st n, east side, from King to the Bay

2 Geo M Barton, barrister
T LeP Filgiano, dentist
4 E L Schwartz, tobacconist
6 M Nisbet, hatter
8 Vacant
10 Oak Hall, clothing
12 McIlwraith & McMaster, dry goods and millinery
14 Donald Smith, mercht tailor
14 Caledonian Hall
16 Pratt & Watkins, dry goods
18 A S Vail & Co, clothiers
20 W H McDonald & Co, clothiers
22 S Woodley, boots and shoes
24 C P Edwards, boots & shoes
26 Vacant

King Wm-st intersects

28 John Crossley, dry goods
30 John W Gerrie, druggist
32 Sewell Bros, grocers
34 J G Curell, barrister
Anderson & Bates, oculists and aurists
34 Josias Bray, ins agent
34 J C Smith, barrister
36 Harrison Bros, druggists
38 Ferres & Co. hardware
40 John Riggs & Co, dry goods
42 Lazier, Dingwall & Monck, barristers
" R D Kennedy, architect
" E Bezanson, photographer
" Joseph Lister
" Misses Graham, hair jewelry
44 Vacant
46 Thos Marsden & Son, gilders
48 Temperance dining rooms
" Louis Schwarz, tobacconist
50 A Zimmerman, tailor
52 A Hunter, bookseller
54 John Riach, general dealer
56 Mrs E Hubbard, millinery
58 Mrs Wm Prout, fruits, etc
60 W J Waugh, gents' furnish'gs

Rebecca-st intersects

62 T K Foster, tailor
64 St Charles restaurant
66 Atkinson Bros, news dealers
68 John Peden, fruiterer
68½ F A Ford, barber
70 Post office
" Vacant
" E Burns, lumber dealer
72 Daniel Peace, tobacconist
" Mail (Toronto) agency
74 Vacant
78 Thos Burrows, auctioneer
80 Nordheimer & Co, pianos
82 Vacant
84 David McLellan, ins agent
84 Robert Irwin, custom broker
86 Masonic Hall
88 J J Mason, grand sec grand lodge A F & A M
88 Vacant
90 Vacant

Gore-st commences

92 Thomas Clappison, booksel'r
Grand Opera House

J Chapman, hotel
Wm Carroll, barber
Vacant
94 Vacant
96 J C Pronguey, coachmaker
100 Davison & Modlin, agents
100 John Foster, fishmonger
102 Mark Hill, baker
104 Walter Hill, butcher
106 Henry Ing, watchmaker
106 Edward Murphy, painter
108 W J F Gordon, coal and lime
108 Foresters' Hall
108 Samuel Chapman, druggist
108b Cumming Bros, grocers
112 C Blaase, hotel
110 Wm Farmer, plumber
112 Richard Brochelsbey, confectioner
114 American Wgriner Co
116 W L Smith, M D, druggist
118 George Smallwood, tobacconist
120 Mrs Sarah Stevens, fancy goods
122 Miss Esther Edwards, millinery
124 James Dwyer, undertaker
126 Sutherland & Meekinson, grocers

Cannon-st intersects

Knox Church
122 G M Shaw, M D
122½ T W Reynolds, M D
124 Dr John A Mullin
126 W Barrett, painter
128 Mrs M Hussell, fancy goods
130-32 A W Noble, caner
134 Anthony Moran, hotel
136 J Colvin, grocer
138 Wm McKeever, baker
W J Harris, caretaker
146 Drill Shed

Robert-st intersects

152 Miss McCaghey, milliner
154 John Chappel, tinsmith
156 Vacant
158 J McCartney, confectioner
160 Geo Pope, cabinetmaker
162 D H Gould, boots and shoes
164 Mrs John Hatt
164 Mrs Francis Arnold
164½ John Haystead, driver
166 T B Paine, bookkeeper
Christ Church Cathedral
Jesse Linger, sexton
168 Mrs R Hicks, fancy goods
170 Mrs M Morrow, confectioner
170½ Mrs Ann Dallyn
172 Adam Irving, fancy goods
172½ Geo Midgely, shoemaker
174-6 John Field, crockery
178 Thos Morris, baker
180 Peter Furnidge, butcher
182 L Hemmings, broker
184 Mrs H Feast, confectioner
186-188 H C Chapple, tinsmith
190 Mrs Jas Meakins, dry goods
192 Mrs Nelligan, fancy goods

Barton-st intersects

194 John Hunter, grocer
196 Robert McKeever, butcher
198 John Kelly, saloon
200 John Huxtable, shoemaker
202 Miss Mary Gleason, dressm'r
204 A P Williamson, stationer
206 Wm McGee, flour dealer
208-10 A Simon, confectioner
212 Thos Clarke, butcher
214 Joseph Marck, barber
216 Paul Dame, fishmonger
218 Mrs Jane McKillop, conf'r
220 Jas E Doyle, grocer
222 Joseph Cook, butcher
224 Jos Morin, boots & shoes
226 Wm McLaren, dry goods
228 Dake's hotel

Murray-st intersects

230 A Vincent & Co., druggists
230½ G & B Nelligan, gents' furnishings
232 Mrs Hugh Moore, dressmkr
O M Gorman, laborer
232 L A Edick, spinner
234 C H Fields, barber
234½ Mrs Ellen Negle, boarding

236 Thos Welch, com traveler
240 Andrew Hay, carpenter
244 Mrs Thos McKinty, grocer

Stuart-st intersects

248 M D Nelligan, wagon mkr
G T Railway bridge
250 John Harris, boarding

Strachan-st intersects

252 Thos Dickinson
254 Wm Hamburg, carpenter
256 Henry Kirkpatrick, laborer
258 Thos T Wellinger, fitter
260 Alfred Nash, expressman
262 Adam Clark, fitter
264 Alfred Wells, laborer
266 Chas Haslam, driver
268 John Henderson, laborer
270 John Hafner, glassblower
272 James Young, carpenter
274 Mrs Catharine Moran
274½ John Holt, engineer
274 Harrison Bros, druggists

Simcoe-st intersects

276 Wm Buckingham, butcher
278 Thos Marshall, laborer
280 John Day, shoemaker
282 J Gant, barber
284 Stephen Cleary, porter
286 Theo Le P Filgiano, dentist
288 Vacant
288½ Levi Cassell
290 Vacant
292 Thos Nugent, laborer
266 R Williamson, ice dealer

Ferrie-st intersects

298 Joseph Dorman, machinist
300 Oliver Beatty, hotel
304 Joseph Guttridge, boarding
306 Richard Williamson
308 John Smith, carpenter
312 Wm B Williamson, ice dealer
314 R B Williamson, laborer

Picton-st intersects

Hamilton Glass Works

Macauley-st intereects

326 Joseph Clinton, laborer
328 James Farrell, laborer
330 John Irving, laborer
342 Geo M Brown, laborer
344 Isaac Blowes, laborer
346 Nicholas Daly, laborer
348 John Harold, glassblower
348½ Wm Burnett, glassblower
350 Joseph Harvey, hotel

Wood-st intersects

364 Mrs Catharine Blowes
366 Lawrence Dunn, laborer
368 Hugh Macdonald, laborer
370 Martin O'Mara, laborer

Burlington-st intersects

376 Vacant
378 John Campbell, packer
382 Mrs Peter Mullin
390 Mrs Oliver Gagnier, grocer

Guise-st intersects

394 Stephen Dunn, foreman
McKay's wharf

James-st n, west side

1 A Hamilton & Co, druggists
3 David Graham, hatter
5 Thos Lees, watchmaker
James Davidson, manfr jeweler
7 Joseph Mills & Son, hatters
9 J Bowes, dentist
" W A Edwards, architect
" E S Collins & Co, painters
" E Crockford & Son, jewelers
11 C E Morgan, broker
13 Thos Mason, hatter
15 Thos Fred Walker, saloon
17 Robt Duncan & Co, books, etc

Market Square

City Hall
21 Andrew Lay, saloon
23 Samuel Easter, saloon
25 John Morris, oyster parlors
27 A C Quimby & Co, tobacconists
29 Wm McGinnis, saloonkeeper
31 Carroll's American watch house

Canada Business College
Alexandra Arcade
Globe (Toronto) Agency
31 Wm J Grant, ticket agent
32-41 St Nicholas Hotel
43 T Richter, saloon
45 Frank England, barber
47 Vacant
49 P Grossman, music dealer
51 Alex McPherson, printer
53 Alhambra Saloon

Merrick-st commences

55 Richard Bull, ins agent
55 C T Jones, ticket agent
57 G McKeand, ins agent
57 R F Keayes, real estate agn't
57 Ontario Mutual Life Association
59 J B Fairgrieve, coal dealer
" Senecca Jones, ins agent
61-63 Royal Hotel
65 Vacant
67 Walter Urry, barber
69 John Harvey & Co, wool brokers
69 Strathroy Knitting Co
71 W Armstrong
73 Geo A McCully, shoemaker
75 Vacant
77 Peter Carnegie, tailor
79 John Holman, gunsmith
81 Thos Lawrence, druggist
83 James Cannon, barber
85 Joseph Donders, fruiterer
87 Chinese Laundry
89 Thos Appleton, pawnbroker
91-93 McKeever Bros, flour & feed
95 Inland revenue office
Gas inspector
Weights and measures

Vine-st commences

97 Federal Life Association
Payne & McMeekin, insurance agents
Royal Templars of Temperance
99 John Gorvin, sewing machi's
99 F F Dalley & Co, patent medicines
H F Schafer, machinist
101 John McCann, shoemaker
103 R W Yaldon, hotel
107 J H Myrick, picture framer
109 Queen's Laundry
113 O C Evans, window shades
115 Wm S Lumgair, sewing machines
117 Wm Ford, barber
119 Thos Strachan, grocer
Wm Noble, hotel

Cannon-st intersects

119 Henry Harding, plumber
121 R Henry, butcher
123 Mrs Chas McLeod, dyer
125 Mrs Andrew McPherson
127 James O'Brien, flour and feed
129 John E Taylor, confectioner
131 Mrs S Hartley, knitter
131½ Alfred Defour, provisions
133 James Hannah, contractor
133½ James Morris, cutter
135 D J Kelly, wood dealer
137 Horace Brown, laborer
137½ Nath'l Pegran, shoemaker

Mulberry-st commences

139 Robt Jackson, plasterer
141 Vacant
143 John Miller, foreman
145 Turkish Baths
147 Aaron Sayman, umbrella maker
151 Mrs A E Edson
153 Dr A Woolverton, coroner
155 Mrs Wm Howard, fancy goods
157 Wm McKay, hotelkeeper
159 J L Lightfoot, shoemaker
165 R J Dunstan, com trav
167 Mrs Jane McKillop
169 W A Freeman, coal and wood
173-5 H D Baker, whip manfr
175 John A Chadwick, metal spinner
173 A M Forster, brass founder

Colborne-st commences

177-183 Gurneys & Ware, scale manfrs
185 James Potter, moulder
187 John Nixon, laborer
189 Thos Walsh, machinist
191 Mrs Mary Smith

Barton-st intersects

203 W Doran, vinegnr manfr
205 Andrew Herron, hackman
207 Benj Whiting, laborer
211 Daniel Williams, hotelkeeper

Murray-st intersects

213 Vacant
215 Frank Sturdy, machinist
217 Henry Keymer, boilermaker
219 John Tremlet, shoemaker
221 Joseph Holdsworth, broker
223 Mrs Ellen Dowler, grocer
225 Mrs John Smith, varieties
227 R Featherstone, butcher
229 Julia Carnotta
231 Edward Oliver, shoemaker
235 Wm Halcrow, mason
239 John McHendrie, hotel

Stuart-st intersects

243 Police Station, No 2
245 Samuel Crist, glassblower
247 John O'Brien, machinist

Strachan-st intersects

249 Daniel Cronyn, carter
253 Jas Thomson, laborer
255 Carl Schlessing, machinist
257 Mrs C Wolfe
259 Peter Commerford
461 Wm Beare, dairyman
263 Joseph F Kerslake, cabinet maker
265 Owen Budgen, dairyman
267-9 Hugh Monro, grocer

Simcoe-st intersects

Ontario Cotton Mills

Ferrie-st intersects

281 Mrs Mary Lattimore
283 Thos Bard, glassblower
289 Mrs Richard Green
291 Fred Robitaille, laborer
293 Chas Lavalle, machinist
297 John Harrington, glassblower
297 D P Le Valle, dry goods
303 P Menard, glassblower
305 E Cherrier, butcher

Picton-st intersects

307-9 R Quinn, hotel
311 Vacant
313 Fred Willoughby, dyer
315 Mrs Caroline Jobber
317 Mrs M Barr
319 Mrs Sarah Fairbairn, grocer
321 M Bracken, glassblower
323 Miss Norah Williamson
325 Thomas Farrell, glassblower
327 Thomas Pearson, glassblower
331 Joseph Carson, grocer

Macauley-st intersects

345 Thos Nixon, policeman
347 Mrs John Arthur

Wood-st intersects

351 John Knox, policeman
355 Neil Kirkpatrick, engineer
357 Holden Barker, carter
359 Andrew McLellan, laborer
363 Vacant
365 Wm Gardener, musician
369 Thos Richmond, grocer

Burlington-st intersects

379 Mrs Æ D Mackay
381 R O MacKay, wharfinger MacKay's wharf

James-st s, east side, from King to Mountain

1 Canada Life Assurance Co

Canada Life Chambers:
- Osler, Teetzel & Harrison, barristers
- F E Kilvert, barrister
- Edison Electric Light Co
- Keewatin Lumbering and Manfr Co
- Bruce, Burton & Culham, barristers
- Duggan & Ambrose, barristers

3 Landed Banking & Loan Co
5 Brown, Balfour & Co, wholesale grocers
7 Hyslop, Cornell & Co, fancy goods

Wentworth Chambers:
- Victoria Mutual Fire Ins Co
- Life Association of Canada
- W F Findlay, ins agent
- Martin & Kittson, barristers
- James Balfour, architect
- Wm Bell, barrister
- George H Mills, barrister

Main-st intersects

Victoria Chambers:
- Jones, McQuesten & Chisholm, barristers
- W A H Duff, barrister
- T J C Greene, barrister

33 Barker & McBrien, painters
37 Miss Mary Fitzgerald
39 Miss M Kern

Jackson-st intersects

41 John Legarie, wagonmaker
52 Henry Harrison, butcher
53 Louis Roos, traveler

Hunter-st intersects

61-73 Ontario Sewing Mach Co
75 Wm A Nixon, laborer
77 P E J Fitzpatrick, bookkeeper
79 Wm Vassie, machinist
81 Easter & Purrott, painters
81 Miller & Hill, carpenters
85-87 Hamilton Vinegar Works
89 Herman Levy, merchant
91 Rev Wm Curran
93 Mrs Archibald Jameson
95 Mrs Agnes Buchanan

Augusta-st commences

97 TenEyck & Precore, grocers
101 J M Rousseaux, grocer
103 Mrs S E Nimmo
105 Mrs E Hamilton
107 Rev W W Carson, Methodist

Young-st intersects

Vacant lots

Maria-st intersects

135 Vacant
137 Æmilius Irving, Q C

Hannah-st intersects

139 Wm Griffith, merchant
141 John Riddle, broker
143 Mrs Thos J Chestnut
147 Miss M L Munday
149 P D Crerar, solicitor
151 A T Wood, merchant
153 Henry McLaren
155 Mrs McLaren, Oak Bank
157 A G Ramsay, Canada Life
159 K J Dunstan, Telephone Co
161 Mrs S B Freeman

James-st s, west side

2 Molson's Bank
2½ Hamilton Commercial College
" Martin & Malone, barristers
" D Steele, barrister
" P L Scriven, wood engraver
" S Leveratt, accountant
4 License Commissioners' office
4 John Proctor & Co, hardware
4 James Osborne & Son, grocers
6 Vacant
6½ S E Townsend, accountant
8 Canada Mutual Telegraph Co
10 Walker & Scott, barristers
12 H T Bunbury, clerk 1st Div court
12 D R Dewey, coal dealer
14 C M Counsell, banker
16 J T Routh, ins agent
" Wm Herman, com agent
" MacKelcan, Gibson & Gausby barristers
" R A Pringle, barrister
18 Great Northwestern Tel Co
" American Express Co
" Canadian Express Co
" Spectator Printing Co
" Staunton & Livingston, barristers
" T C Livingston, Dom Land surveyor

20 Haslett & Washington, barristers

Commercial Chambers:
- Omnium Securities Co
- Fuller, Nesbitt & Bicknell, barristers
- R W Suter, ins agent
- D G Greer, real estate agent

22 F W Gates, manfr
26 W C Baker, commission
28 Morton & Dixon, fruiterers
30 M A Pennington, real est agt
32 Wm Scott, shoemaker
34 W S Hicks, carver
36 Adam Clark, plumber

Main-st intersects

Bank of Montreal
Wm Angus, letter carrier
St Paul's church

Jackson-st intersects

Baptist church
52 Dr John W Rosebrugh

Hunter-st intersects

Wm A Howell, druggist
60 Mrs E H Davis
62 Mrs M Simon, grocer
66 J M Webber, merchant
68 Mrs E Malloch
70 Dr A E Malloch
72 F S Malloch
74 Mrs Geo Lees
78 James Ferres, merchant
80 Dr Elias Vernon

Bold-st intersects

82 John A Orr, merchant
84 J E P Aldous, B A
86 Vacant
88 Edmund Scheuer, merchant
90 Mrs Wm Bellhouse
92 J M Stuart, merchant
94 Vacant
96 S W Cornell, merchant
98 Mrs George Marshall
100 Richard Mackay

Duke-st commences

Vacant

Robinson-st commences

36

134 Hubert Martin, merchant
136 Thos Lawry, merchant

Hannah-st intersects

140 C Stiff, supt G T R
144 A Rutherford, druggist

Herkimer-st intersects and Markland commences

Edward Martin, barrister

Concession-st intersects

John Stuart, merchant
Richard Russell, manfr

John-st north, east side, from 70 King east to the Bay

McKay Bros, dry goods
4 Robt Parker & Co, dye wks
6 Evans & Co, tailors
8 Larkin Hall
8 C R Smith, grain dealer
8 Collins & Leigh, collectors
12 Co-operative grocery store
14 Peter Meegan, saloon
18 Fairley, Stewart & Co, plumbers
20 P Hennessy, safes
22 Vacant
24 F J Willson, sewing mach's
24 Odd Fellows' Hall
26 George Webster, tailor
28 Dominion Suspender manf Co
30 Robert Raw & Co, printers
30 J F Jago, custom hourse broker

King Wm-st intersects

32 James Reed, hotelkeeper
34 Wm Pease, dealer
36-42 E & C Gurney, founders

Rebecca-st intersects

44 Murton & Reid, coal dealers
46 T J Derrick, laborer
48 Chas Faustman, cooper
50 Mrs Wm Boice
52 Mrs O Springer
54 J H Bisby, wool dealer
56 Vacant

58 B E Charlton

Gore-st intersects

62 Emerson Hannon
64 Thos Young, saloonkeeper
66 Wm Dillon, moulder
68 J E Halloran, livery
76 Wm Johnston, carpenter
78 W P Campbell, printer
80 B M E Church
82 Rev J B Roberts
84 Mrs George Allen
88 Mrs W R Swift
90 Wm Tallman, carpenter
96 Miss F Le Barre
98 W H Tallman, wood dealer
100 Wm W Anstey, plumber

Cannon-st intersects

102 Miss Kate Murray
106 W Weston, shoemaker
116 Fred Brown, laborer
122 Chas Stewart, founder
124 Charles Silver, bookkeeper
126 Peter Templeman, foreman
128 K McKenzie, laborer
128½ Justus Post, boiler tender
130 Mrs M McCardle

Robert-st intersects

132 George Hooper, shoemaker
136 John Roderick, tailor
138 Arthur Middleton, bookkpr
140 Donald Crerar, tailor
140 J T Middleton, marble dealer
140½ Alex McPherson, printer
142 John McMullan, cooper
144 Vacant
146 Alfred Myles, coal merchant
148 Hy Robson, bricklayer
150 George M Dexter, canvasser
152 F Cameron, shoemaker
154 Mrs Mary Burns
154½ Edwd Hawkes, collector
156-8 James Houlden, carpenter

Barton-st intersects

164 M A Broderick, grocer
166 Mrs Samuel McLean
168 Michael O'Brien, watchman
174 John Johnson, shoemaker
174 Philip Long
176 Lawrence Kehoe, hackman
178 Duncan McNab, painter
180 W J Crankshaw, bookkeeper
182 Wm A Murton, clerk
184 Nelson Humphrey, manfr
186 Vacant
188 George Bible
190 Vacant
192 Geo Gardner, conductor
194 Walter Armstrong, painter
196 Ezra Waterman, upholsterer

Murray-st intersects

202 J A Chadwick, manfr
208 Wm Drake, shoemaker

Stuart-st intersects

210 Wm Harper, laborer
214 Timothy Lynch, laborer
G T R bridge
216 L Larsen, shoemaker
218 Dennis McBride
220 Patrick McBride, grocer

Strachan-st intersects

224 John Paull, laborer
226 Daniel McCarthy, yardsman
228 Daniel McMullin, cooper

Simcoe-st intersects

Simcoe St Methodist Church
260 St Lawrence Catholic School

Ferrie-st intersects

280 Peter Johnson, cigarmaker
282 Joseph Gormley, cigarmaker
284 Wm McCarthy, weaver
286 Mrs Margaret Sullivan
288 Wm Grant, printer
290 Mrs M Geddes

Picton-st intersects

292 Alex Graham, grocer
294 Mrs Rosanna Hanley
296 Andrew Shaw, laborer
298 Philip Ryan, shoemaker
300 Wm Dermody, laborer
302 St Luke's Church

Macauley-st intersects

306 John Sheehan, teamster
310 Samuel Smith, glassblower

314 John McNichol, laborer
316 Vacant
320 Chas McNichol, glassblower
Wood-st intersects
324 John Campbell, machinist
334 John Kelly, laborer
336 Peter Matson
342 John Sullivan, laborer
Burlington-st intersects
350-2 S Stevens, hotel
354 Patrick Connors, boatbuilder
356 Thos Lawrence, laborer
358 Henry Bond, teamster
360 John Gompf, brewer
Brock-st intersects
Corporation weighing house
370 Samuel Berry, carpenter
Old City Hospital
Guise-st intersects
Murton & Reid's wharf
Myles' wharf

John-st n, west side

3 W J Pratt, barber
5-7 Vacant
9 Fraser & Johnson, saddlery
11 Vacant
13 H A Martin, printer
15 J Wallace & Son, tinsmiths
17 Young & Bro, plumbers
19 Robert Lavelle, stoves, tins
21 Andrew Dillon, hotel
King Wm-st intersects
23 Martin Bros, pork packers
27 J H Holland, locksmith
29 Wm Dodson, painter
31 C Delorme, carriage maker
37 E & C Gurney's pattern shop
39 Alex Anderson, laborer
41 Michael Dwyer, moulder
43 Abram Swazie
Rebecca-st intersects
Wesley Church
45 Ernest Faustman, cooper
47 Andrew Mackie, moulder
49 George Foreman, moulder
51 James Hall, moulder
55 Hugh Sweeney, machinist
57 Mrs George Trumbull
59 Mrs Julia Higby
Methodist Episcopal church
Gore-st intersects
65 John Walker, blacksmith
67 Mrs Sarah Estress
69 J Harris, whitewasher
71 Wm Sullivan, laborer
73 Mrs Benjamin Wagner
75 Mrs James Brennan
77 Robert Wallace
79 S G Spackman
81 Warren Davis, stonecutter
79 James Barron, policeman
79½ R O Biglow, carpenter
81 John A Davis
83 Edward Jaggard, polisher
85 Robert Curran, dyer
87 John McManus, com trav
89 George Brown, livery
91 Wm Venator, turner
93 W North, letter carrier
95 George Heilig, livery
97 Edwd Kinsler, grocer
99 Wm Johnson, brushmaker
101 James Munn, laborer
103 Amos Cassidy, carpenter
103 Edward Kinsler, grocer
Cannon-st intersects
Malleable Iron Works
121 C K Domville, G T R
127 Mrs James Tindill
Robert-st intersects
129 Philip Morris, grocer
131 Rev Joseph Odery
133 Chas W Harrison
135 Andrew Dougall, machinist
137 Geo Childs, moulder
139 John Bird, machinist
141 Albert Sayers, musician
143 D Walsh, messenger P O
145 John Hayes
147 Charles Santzburg
147½ Wm Strong, ins agent
151 James Hannah, shoemaker
153 Mrs George Otto
155 Thomas Glackin, cutter

157 Wm Albery, shoemaker
159 John Kendrick
161 E S Whitehead, watchmaker
163 James Smith, moulder
165 Charles Wilson, contractor
167 Wm Hall, patternmaker
169 Nicholas Koch, moulder
163a Dennis Buckley, laborer
165a Mrs Jane Wheeler

Barton-st intersects

167a James Main, grocer
169a Vacant
169½ Angus McKay, machinist
Vacant
173a Mrs Edward Harbin
189 Chas Quinn, moulder
189 Edward Marks, moulder
191-3-3½ Vacant

Murray-st intersects

195 James Lister, carpenter
197 Geo Moore
199 Chas Bolton, carpenter
201 Henry Bleeze, machinist
201½ James Johnson, sailor
203 James Martin, laborer
205 Mrs Wm Potter
207 James Kelk, tinsmith
209 James Hammond, grocer

Stuart-st intersects

211 Mrs Elizabeth Spence, grocer
215 Sydney Brenton, polisher
G T bridge
217 Mrs H Marigold
219 Henry Searle, machinist
221 Thos Stirton, stonecutter

Strachan-st intersects

223 John Simmonds, laborer
235 John Jones, laborer
" Richard Simons, laborer
237 Thos Pearson, laborer
241 Mrs M A McCrae, grocer

Simcoe-st intersects

243 Edward Malone, laborer
245 Patrick Donnelly, laborer
247 Robert Gill, boilermaker
249 John Corrigan, laborer
251 Chas Capperne, marble cutter
257 John Kane, carpenter
259 Vacant
261 J S Dillon, grocer

Ferrie-st intersects

265 Edward Crofton, grocer
267 John Kane, carpenter
269 James Ford, health inspector
273 Patrick Kelly, laborer
275 Wm Hanley, laborer
277 Peter Johnson, cigarmaker
279 John Talbot, plumber
281 John Gallaghan, carpenter
285 James Hurley, moulder
Thos Lee, glassblower

Picton st intersects

287 Mrs Bridget O'Neil
291 Michael O'Neil, moulder
293 Ed Murphy, laborer
295 Mrs Daniel Taylor
297 John Hayes, scalemaker
303 Thos Hayes, shoemaker

Macauley-st intersects

305 Rev Wm Massey, M A
311 Frank Smith, glassblower

Wood-st intersects

325 Patrick Connors. laborer
329 John McFadden,
337 James McGinty, laborer
339 John Gorman, teamster
341 Malcolm Conbrough, laborer

Burlington-st intersects

349 Mrs Ann Mills
351 Thomas Drever, carpenter
353 Fred Alexander, laborer
353 Wm Dryden, teamster
367 John Whelan, laborer

Brock-st intersects

375 Mrs John Boyd
379 Mrs Alice McBriar, nurse
383 Chas Blackburn, weaver
385 David Coulter, policeman

Guise-st intersects

John-st s, east side, from 43 King east to Mountain.

Merchants' Bank
13-15 W E Sanford & Co
17 George Goering, hotel
19 Richard Magen, butcher
21 Jacob Burges, fruit dealer
23 Paul Deutschur, hotelkeeper
25 Vacant
27-29 Morgan Bros, millers
31 Vacant
33 Henry Belz, tailor
35 R N Taylor & Co, druggists

Main-st intersects

37 John Stuart, Son & Co
39 Frank Squibb, plumber
42 John Patterson, tailor
43 Vacant
45-47 Jas Jolley & Sons, saddlers
49 I Blumensteil, broker
51 Mrs M Moses, clothing
53 J R Wolf, pawnbroker
55 Gage & Jelfs, barristers
55½ H J Halford, barber
57 Court House Hotel
61 David Little, hairdresser
63 A Miller, harness maker
65 Matthew High, hotel

Jackson-st intersects

67 Vacant
69 Vacant
73 Lendrum Irvine, traveler
75 Mrs Eliza Peacock, fancy gds
77 Wm Goodwin, watchmaker
79 A Tshann, butcher
81 Edmund Hill, grocer
83 C J Fenton, dry goods
83½ James Barker, fruiterer
85 Mrs P Dowling, dry goods
87 George Morton, barber
89 Daniel Barry, hotel

Hunter-st intersects

91 James Dunlop, flour & feed
93 George C Hunter, tinsmith
95 R N Taylor & Co, chemists
95½ David Dunlop, saddler
97 Thos Backus, shoemaker
99 James H Shouldice, hotel
101 Chas Hitzroth, shoedealer
101½ H Strauss, grocer
103 Mrs H Arless, confectioner
103½ Ed Hunt, blacksmith
105 George Hodge, teamster
107 Wm Mallory, broker
107½ Chris Loney, shoemaker
109 S Willer, pork butcher
109½ John Shea, machinist
111 Mrs Geo Garner, dressmaker
115 George Ashby, furniture
117-119 Ballentine Bros, grocers

Augusta-st intersects

131 Fred Landau, traveler
123 James Patterson, carpenter
125 James F Farmer, blacksmith
127 Wm Homer, confectioner
129 Mrs Sarah Murphy
133 Bryant & Post, grocers

Young-st intersects

135 James Dingle, butcher
137 Mrs Sarah Rogers
139 James Forrest, locksmith
139½ Mrs William Harris
141 James Inches, merchant
143 Robert Griffith, com traveler
145 J J Millman, photographer
147 Alonzo Lutes, clerk
149 H G Greig

Maria-st intersects

Col C C Grant
153 Mrs Isabella Alexander

Hannah-st intersects

167 G W Johnson, teacher
169 Alex McInnes, merchant
Richard Martin, Q C
Richard Tew, merchant
Thos Robertson, barrister
Chas Gurney, manfr
Mrs Edward Gurney
Samuel Barker

John-st south, west side

2 New postoffice
4 Alex McKay, flour dealer
6 Wm Gillesby, grain dealer

8-10 J R McKichan, paper bags
12 John Sintzel, tailor
14 A. Harper, butcher
16 Leo Platz, tailor
18 Frazer & Inches, grocers
20 H C Duval, barber
22 Robert Jahn, hotel

Main-st intersects

Court House

Jackson-st intersects

48 Thorley Cattle Food Co
50 T M Kelly, grocer
52 J T Bronson, hotelkeeper
54 James Wills, shoemaker
56 John Caddocks, harnessmkr
56½ George Allan, moulder
58 Wm Robinson, shoemaker
60 Robert Smith, baker
62 W H Ryckman & Co, grocers
64 J & R Kilgour, organ manfs
64 W B Mitchell, tailor
66 H Smith, stove dealer
68 Mrs Leegrice, baker
70-72 Hugh McKeown, saddler
74 James Burges, hotel

Hunter-st intersects

76 Vacant
78 Connell & Cross, dressmkrs
82 Thos Priestland, furniture
84 John Buckingham, laborer
86-88 Alex Morrison, grocer

Wood Market Square.
12 Miss Susan Feaver, hotel
9 D Jackson, retinner
7 Geo Goodale, laborer
R Montgomery, boarding

90 Thos S Hill, butcher
92 W H Rendell, blacksmith
94 Samuel White, shoemaker
96 Isaac Raphael, tailor
98 Thos Morrison
102 Robert George, tailor

Augusta-st intersects

104 Louis Jacobs, cigarmaker
106 Wm Sharp, baker
110 Lawrence Roehm, tailor
112 John Rattenburg, carpenter
114 L Blumensteil, cigar manf
116 John Henderson, baker
118 John Williams, laborer
122 Mrs Wm Waddell

Young-st intersects

124 Robert Gallagher, tailor
126 James Garson, carpenter
128 Mrs Amanda Forrest
130 Vacant
132 W F Findlay, accountant
134 Mrs John Webber
136 C W Watts, bookkeeper

Maria-st intersects

Church of Ascension

Hannah-st intersects

Edward Browne, wharfinger

Jones-st, north side, from Dundurn west to city limits

S S King, mover
Mrs J McElroy
David Lewis, laborer
H G Von Hoxar, linguist
John Hill, laborer
Thomas Frawley, laborer
Michael Frawley, laborer
Terrence Scott, teamster
Thos Johnstone, laborer
James Hamilton, laborer

Jones-st, south side

James Sayers, ruffler
James Gaskin, laborer

Kelly-st, north side, from 82 Mary east to Wellington

Laidlaw Manuf Co, founders
4 M Paterson, custom officer
6 Mrs Thos Davison, teacher
8 Geo E Mills, bricklayer

Elgin-st intersects

20 James Williams, teamster
22 George Worthington, brakeman
r 22 Charles Jaggard, laborer
r 22 Henry Jackson, laborer
r 22 Michael Conley

Ferguson-ave intersects

42 John B Rousseaux
44 James Pierce, laborer
46 John Wilkie, engineer
48 Robert Bennet, blacksmith

Cathcart-st intersects

56 Mrs Andrew Morton
58 A T James, shipper

Wellington-st intersects

Kelly-st, south side

3 George Forbes, teamster
5 John W Emery, scalemaker
7 Michael Platts
13 James Conley, grocer

Elgin-st intersects

17 Daniel Downs, carriagemaker

Ferguson-ave intersects

31 Samuel Beeston, laborer
33 M Gahagen, shoemaker
35 Thos Edwards, laborer
37 Frank Smith, porter
39 J C N Jenkins, machinits

Cathcart-st intersects

53 Canada Clock Co
55 Mrs Walter Heim
57 Thomas Canary, driver

Wellington-st intersects

Kent-st, from Hannah w, to Concession

No houses

King-st e, north side, from James to Delta

2 S G Treble, gents' furnishings
4 Mrs F McLean, fancy goods
6 Garland & Rutherford, drugs
8 George James, dry goods
8½ S C Chittenden, dentist
" Thomas Farmer
" C O Oddfellows' hall
10 Hutchison & Pilkey, pianos
12 Wm Acres, hatter
14 Richard Brierley, druggist
14½ Wm Bruce, patent agent
" A F Yoemans
" W A Young, plater
16 J Eastwood & Co, books &c
18-20 A Murray & Co, dry goods
22 I O F hall
22 J G Sinclair, dentist
24 R P Leask, gents' furnishings
26 J C Mahony, boots and shoes
28 J D Climie, boots and shoes
30-32 Thomas C Watkins, dry goods
34 John A Clark, druggist

Hughson-st intersects

36 Farmers' and Traders' Loan Association
36 J Zimmerman, dentist
38 Y M C Association
40 J F Shea, boots and shoes
42 James Shea, dry goods
44 Wood & Leggat, hardware
46 China Palace
48 Simon McCabe, boots
50 Henry Blandford, gilder
52 Canada Glass House
54 Bowman & Moore, hardware
56 Winslow & Webber, hardw're
58 Geo Gage, boots and shoes
60 Robert Wilson, boots & shoes
62 H Arland & Bro, boots and shoes
64 J V Dynes, clothier
66 Murphy & Murray, grocers
68 C A Davis, dentist
68 Fred Wilmott, photographer
68 M. Stein, jeweler

John-st intersects

70 McKay Bros, dry goods
72 C N Hiesrodt, picture framer
74 Bews Bros, tailors
76 J M Rosseau & Co, grocers
78 John B Gay, stationer
78 D Thompson, jeweler
78½ E S Whipple, land agent
" Richard Hill, cigar manfr
" Rutherford & Lester, ins agents
80 Charles Huton, tailor
82 Jos Herron, merchant tailor
84 Globe Hotel
86 J C White, fancy goods

88 D J Peace, tobacconist
90 Miss L Rowe, milliner
90 Palladium of Labor office
92 Vacant
94 A S McKenzie. shoemaker
96 Mrs Eliza Burns, fancy gds
98-100 D Moore & Co, tinware, stoves, etc
102 Adam Hope & Co, hardware

Catharine-st intersects

Reid, Goering & Co, general merchants
104 N D Galbreath, grocer
106 John Staunton, hotel
108 James Henigan, hatter
112 B Cauley, tobacconist
114 G H Lees & Co, watchmkrs
118 Joseph Hargrove & Son, sewing machine dealers
120 George Kemp, grocer
116 J Noyes, hair worker
118 J Happle Hutcheson, tailor
Mrs Joseph Towersey
120½ Geo W Noyes, barber
122 E Battram
124 N G Eckerson, photographer
124 W L Hubbard, tobacconist

Mary-st intersects

Copp's Block.
126 P D Carse, gents' furnishings
128 J H Johnston, furniture
128½ Maidment & Co. teas
" Jos M Clark, tailor
" Geo Webster, machin't
" R B Burt, dentist
" Storm & Green, tea
J Wilson, painter
130 Alex Wetherall, drygoods
130 Vacant
132 Vacant
134 Vacant
J Pecover, cabinetmaker
Vacant
J Finagin, merch't tailor
H S Williams, stationer
Charles Black, hardware
Alfred Baylis, grocer

Copp's Block, continued
John Williams, confectioner
134 M Richardson, boots and shoes
136-8 J Scott, fancy goods
140 Mrs E Stewart, milliner
F Claringbowl, jeweler
S Thorne & Co, drygoods
F E Moody, fancy goods
M Mundy, druggist
Frank E Walker, house furnishings

Walnut-st north intersects

M Nesbit, hatter
170 Dennis Kerrigan, tailor
172 R Hill, cigar manuf
174 W T Bell, confectioner
176 A T Collyer, hat manfr
178 Misses L & E Harrison, milliners
180 Mrs E Newport, confectioner
182 J C Smyth, merchant
184 Vacant
186 Robert Stewart & Co, grocers
188-190 Brethour & Co, merchants
192 J Peebles, watchmaker
194 Mrs Chas Israel, confectioner
196 Henry Martin, hotel
198 Robert B Spera, dry goods
200 H S Hooper, confectioner
202 Thos O'Brien, barber
204 Ontario Pharmacy
204 G S Bingham, M D

Ferguson-ave intersects

164 Walker House
166 J A Macaulay, fruiterer
168 Thos Spellacy, broker
180 J E Riddell, stoves
172 Wm Snath, butcher
174 A Swazie, flour and feed
174½ C W Powell, window shades
174 E Taylor, grinder
176 Vacant
R Spence & Co, file workers
178 Vacant
178 Mrs J H Truman, confectioner
180 Frank Truman, barber

182 Hamilton Universal Agency
184 T J Sheridan, spring beds
186 Michael Sullivan, hotelkeeper
184 Miss Kate Heins
188 Mrs John Jarvis, furniture

Upper Cathcart-st commences

190 Peter Thompson, grocer
192 Geo Phillips, tailor
194 R M McCline, fish dealer
198 Alex McFarlane, flour and feed
200 E W Bateman, baker
202 Wm Hill, butcher
204 C Hayhoe, confectioner
204½ Geo Biggar, M D
210-212 Dominion Hat Co
R Leslie, truiterer
210 John McMillan, grocer
212 James Dennis, bootmaker
214 D D Smith, M D, druggist

Wellington-st intersects

Corporation lumber yard
226 Wm Haskins, city engineer

West-ave intersects

238 J H Moore, merchant
240 W F Burton, barrister
242 Menry Woodware, customs
244 Rev John Keough

Victoria-ave intersects

246 B Winnifrith, grocer
250 T Arthur, carpenter
254 Thos Kilvington, jr, florist

East-ave intersects

256 Samuel Mann, fancy goods
260 Fred Clarke, boots and shoes
262 W Javis, confectioner
262-280 New houses
280 Samuel Chapman, druggist
282 James Jameson, founder

Emerald-st intersects

Laidlaw, Bowes & Co, founder

Tisdale-st intersects

268 Frank Quinn, pattern-worker
270 W S Harrison, painter
274 Arthur Awty, clerk

37

276 R C Grant, agent
278 John W Lowes, com trav
280 Mrs Mary Leishman
282 Mrs P Raynor
182½ John Galvin, machinist
284 Henry Taylor, grocer

Steven-st intersects

286 Wm Mills, carpenter
288 Fred Frewing, plasterer
292 George Mills

Ashley-st intersects

304 Arthur Peacock, laborer
306 Joseph Myers, laborer
308 H P Bonny, clerk
324 Job Angle, laborer
326 Samuel Angle, laborer

Wentworth-st intersects

Wm Tindill, tavern
Green A Stanton, cigarmakr
H Smith, crockery
Thos Fitzgerald, laborer
Vacant
— Howard, laborer
Mrs M Sullivan, rag dealer
Michael Curran, laborer

Burlington-st intersects

Thos Small, butcher
Louis Morris, butcher
Samuel Burner, gardener
Wm J Anderson, butcher
Joseph Ross, painter
Alex Glove, dairyman
Andrew Patterson, teacher
Robert Hopkins, merchant

Toll Gate

A C Case, farmer
George Gage
Delta, Simon James

King-st east, south side

1-3 Canada Life Assurance Co
5 Bank British North America
7 Knox, Morgan & Co, wh dry goods
9 J A Skinner & Co, crockery
11 W H Glassco & Sons, hats, etc
13 Vacant

15 Canadian Bank of Commerce

Hughson-st intersects

17-19 Hamilton Provident and Loan Society
21 Alex Harvey & Co, wholesale grocers
23-25 J Winer & Co, wholesale druggists
27 Levy Brothers & Scheuer, wholesale jewelers
29 Vacant
31 Gillespie & Powis, brokers and ins agts
31 Canadian Pacific Railway office
33 Dixon Bros, wh fruiterers
35 Atkinson Bros, stationers
35 J H Linfoot, agent

John-st intersects

45 Merchants' Bank
47-9 W E Sanford & Co, wholesale clothiers
51-53 J McPherson & Co, wholesale boots and shoes
55 A C Anderson & Co, whole-jewelers
57 A W Gage & Co, wholesale jewelers
57 Wesleyan Ladies College
67-69 Macpherson, Glassco & Co, wholesale grocers
71 Duncan Bros, wholesale grocers
73 Vacant

Catharine-st intersects

75 VanNorman & Co, agents
79 Victoria hotel
81 Wah Sing, laundry
81½ Wm Dicker, shoemaker
83 Fred Langberg, cabinetmkr
87 Robt Coulter, shoemaker
89 Chas T Tomlinson, saddler
91 Thos Evans, varieties
93 D McPhie & Co, plumbers
95 Vincent Smith, broker
97 George Routh, furniture
99 H D Bassett, machinist
101 James Cahill, police magistrate
113 Wm I A Case, MD
113 Wm H Case, MD

Walnut-st intersects

115 Chas Brennan, grocer
117 Thos Taafe, butcher
119 F E Woolverton, M D
121 Vacant
123 Francis Beer, butcher
125 James Amess, carpenter
127 Miss Mary Clark, dressmaker
131 George Whyte, carpenter
135 R R Ashbaugh, hotel
N & N W station
143 D J Burkholder, wood dealer
151 Vacant
153 Jos J Aynsley, green grocer
155 Edward Breheny, shoemaker
167 A Ross, carriage maker
169 Thos Baxter, wire worker
171 James Kingdon, blacksmith
175 Joseph Ross, blacksmith
177 Mrs A Kingdon
179 James O'Neil, wagonmaker
181 Mrs Mary Hall
183 E J Case, pedler

Spring-st commences

185 George Roe, clothes cleaner
187 Mrs Sarah Robbins, laundress
187½ Chas Israel, confectioner
189 James Garrioch, mason
191 John McCauley, fruiterer
195 S C Stinson

Wellington-st intersects

First Methodist Church
207 Geo Fisher, harness maker
209 L McMullen, mason
211 Edwd Wildman, stonecutter
213 Robert Hopkins, weaver
r213 Wm Hodgers, tobacco wrkr
215 Geo Harris, traveler
221 Vacant
223 Mrs Jane Nelson
Meakins & Sons, brush mfrs
225 Geo Buckingham, laborer
227 Frank Fullen, laborer

235 John Swallow, mason
237 H J Hazet, butcher
241 WmLewis, carpenter
243 James Henderson, laborer
245 Patrick Cummings, laborer

Vict ria-ave intersects

St. Patrick's Catholic church

East-ave intersects

267 W H Nichols, butcher
271 Thomas C Watkins, merch't

Emerald-st intersects

273 James Shields, com traveler
275 Wm Shearsmith, traveler
277 Chas Cutler, carpenter
293 A J Heath, dairyman
295 Vacant
297 Mrs Peter Grant

Wentworth st intersects

John Little, carpenter
George Nichol, agent
James Nichol
James Somerville, painter
Wm Wyndham, packer
John Fowler, tailor

Burlington-st intersects

Henry Rykert, clerk
Michael Geary, gardener
Colin Arthur, butcher
F W Watkins, merchant
John Proctor, merchant
Robert Ward, Boys' Home
Mrs Knox

King-st west, north side, from James to city limits

2 A Hamilton & Co, druggists
4 Harry Sweetman, restaurant
6 Wm Drayton & Co, fruits, etc
8-10 Farmer Bros, photographers
" Francis Fitzgerald, barrister
" Drs R J & T H Husband, dentists
12 Davis & McCullough, jewelers
14 W C Saunders, saloon
16 John Moodie, fancy goods
18 Finch Bros, dry goods
20 J M Henderson & Co, tailors
22 J McLean, boots and shoes
24 James Angus, jr, hatter
24½ E Overell G Co, booksellers
26 Vacant
26½ Richard Hill, tobacconist
28 Donald McLellan, bookseller
30-32 Colin McRae, boots and shoes
34 A R Kerr & Co, dry goods
36 P B Barnard, dry goods
38 J Crawford, confectioner
40 A J Taylor, gents' furnishings
42 Joseph Taylor, jeweler
44 Wm Wilson & Son, tailors

Macnab-st intersects

48 Thos MacKay, grocer
50 H S Case, druggist
52 Dixon & Morton, fruiterers
54 James Slater, tailor
56-58 A Sutherland, grocer
60 Richard Haigh, bookbinder
62 John Riach, fancy goods
64 A S Henderson, boots and shoes
66 Geo Lee
70 George A Mills, gents furnisher
72 John Thom, tobacconist
74 Mrs Joseph Murphy, fancy goods
76 Eckerson & Millman, photographers
78 N Wolfe, varities
82 Dominion Hotel
82½ James Cooper, barber
84 T J Baine, West end music store
86 Edward Green, furniture
88 M W Attwood & Son, watchmakers
90 Hamilton House Furnishing Co
92 C L Thomas, piano manfr
94 Franklin House

Park-st intersects

96 Thos Crooks, hotel

98 John Kerrigan, tailor
100-2 B Edwards, confectioner
104 Chas P Edwards, boots
106 Vacant
108 Miss E Johnstone, millinery
108 Vacant
109½ E Britt, labor agency
110 Oliver Hancock, tobacconist
112 Reddall & McKeown, hardware
114 Vacant
114½ B Martin, cabinetmaker
116 Richard Allen, bootmaker
118 Tucket & Sons, tobacco manfrs
124 R Buskard, carriage maker

Bay-st intersects

130 T B Fairchild, hotel
132 Samuel Crawford, grocer
134 T H Beveridge & Co, plumbers
136 Ed Bates, upholsterer
140 George Jenkins, broker
142 Vacant
144 Wm Pattle, fruiterer
146 D J Garrick, varities
148 J Murray, rag carpet weaver
150 A Pastine, fruiterer
152 John Mayhew, knitter
156 J McDonnell, flour and feed
158 Vacant
160 T O'Connor, carriage painter
162 Peter Gorman, blacksmith
164 T & G Broadbent, machinery brokers

Caroline-st intersects

168 Wm Garner, fruit dealer
178 Mrs Laura Papps, boarding
180 Jas W Sutherland, druggist
182 John Johnstone, china, etc
202 Mrs J Chambers, dressmakr
202½ John McMillan, shoemaker
204 Nathaniel Goddard, fishmonger
208 Fred B Howard, butcher
210 Alex Cuthbertson, grocer

Hess-st intersects

190 A L Reeves, baker
192 G H Hill, butcher
194 H Knowles, clerk
196 G Kellond, shoemaker
198 John Walsh
200 Mrs David Almond, dairy
204 How & Braid, butchers
206 Mrs Mary Jost, hairworker
208 Wesley Kellar
210 James Lithgow, laborer
212 A L Reeves, jr, grocer

Queen-st intersects

216 John H Geiger, saloon
218 Albert Geiger, baker
220 Wm Geiger, flour aud feed
226 Alex Harvey, merchant
230 Mrs Sarah Smith

Ray-st intersects

238-242 Loretto Convent
246 Vacant

Pearl-st intersects

248 Jas Bremner, grocer
258 John Trevaskis, wagonmaker
r258 Daniel Lehan, laborer
278 Lucian Hills, architect
280 Mrs Thos Oliver
292 James Ross, laborer
284 Alfred Causewell, painter
282 Stephen Bull, laborer
288 Arch Wilson, hotelkeeper

Locke-st intersects

Crystal Palace and grounds

Sophia-st intersects

298 Wm Bradley, blacksmith
300 Mrs Mary J Taylor
302 — McCluskey, laborer
304 James Keith, laborer
306 Elijah Wright
308 George Fudge, engineer
310 Hand & Co, fireworks
314 A K Smith, teamster
318 Wm Baker, laborer
320 Thos Charters, laborer
322 Mrs Mary Veiger

Dundurn-st intersects

330 John Cheesman
336 Vacant
Cemetery

Samuel Cheesman, brickmaker
Wm Nichols, bricklayer
John Rankin, tobacco manf
John Russell, laborer
Francis Dean, brickmaker
Peter Fletcher, laborer
Wm Small, laborer
Henry Roman, laborer
Wm Russell, tobacco manfr
John Henderson, laborer

Kingt-st w, south side

5 Star Box factory
5 J R Seavey, artist
7 Carscallen & Cahill, barristers
9 David Mitchell, shoemaker
9 The Shedden Co
13 John Alexander, leather
15 Rich Russell, manf jeweler
17-19 Bank of Hamilton
21 Orr, Harvey & Co, boot and shoe manfs
23 T B Greening & Co, teas
25 G C Briggs & Sons, patent medicines
27 James C Taylor, coal oil, etc
29 J McArthur & Co, hatters
31 Thos Mitchell, wooden ware
33 Hendrie & Co, cartage agts
35 Wm Farmer, photographer

Macnab-st intersects

37-9 J A Bruce & Co, seeds
41-3 Buntin, Gillies & Co, wholesale stationers
45 McMahon, Broadfield & Co, crockery
47 Blachford & Son, undertakers
49 Jesse Chapman, funeral emporium
51 Joseph Hoodless & Son, furniture
53 Wm Griffith, wholesale boots and shoes
55-7 John Garrett & Co, shoe manufacturers

Charles-st intersects

59-63 American Hotel
65 J Elliott, barber
67-69 James Rid estate

Park-st intersects

71-73 Z Pattison, confectioner
75 George Walker, grocer
77 J Fielding, hatter
79 John Skinner, watchmaker
81 Ed Stockwell, dye works
83 E C Jones, agent
83 A M Theal
85 Mrs E Woolverton, homœopathic
87 N Guillet, tobacco roller
87 Sing Kee, laundry
89 Bowering & Pain, butchers
91-3 E & D Carr, flour and feed
95 F McGuire, broker
97 Chas H Winckler, cutler
99 Richard Catchpole, china
103 Thos Jarvis, furniture dealer
95 Francis Larkin, weaver
101 R J Hamilton

Bay-st intersects

103 Wm L Wilson, boarding
105 Mrs Margaret Newman
111 Wm Nicholson, wood dealer
113 Thos Nicholson, butcher
115 Geo Read, carpenter
117 Mrs James Williams
119 I C Chilman, baker
121 John Cumming, cutter
123 James Thornton, manfr
131 Geo H Geldart, gilder
139 Wm Cox, pork curer

Caroline-st intersects

141 T & G Broadbent, machinery brokers
141 Hiram Broadbent, agent
145 American Bracket Co
149 Wm G Stark, M D
151 Alex T Loemans, artist
181 Thomas Miller, M D
185 Alfred Taylor, merchant

Hess-st intersects

All Saints Church

Queen-st intersects

207 George Tuckett, manfr
215 D McGregor, carriagemaker
217 G E Tuckett, manfr

Ray-st intersects

229 P B Barnard, merchant
233 Wm Kavanagh
235 John Henry
237 C Fortier, col in revenue
241 W H Ballard, school insp'r
243 John J Thomas, piano mkr
245 Arthur Doherty, grocer

Pearl-st intersects

267 Jefferson Stevens, carpenter
269 Fred McCullough, clerk
271 C McDonnell, basketmaker
277 Edward Winter, blacksmith
281 Theo Macar, laborer
283 Wm Holmes, laborer
r283 John Beckman, laborer
285 William Howick, butcher and grocer

Locke-st intersects

289 Vacant
289½ Thomas Tarrant, broker
291 George Bridgewood
293 David J Jennings, carver

Margaret-st commences

295 John Eydt, teamster
303 C L Thomas, piano manfr
307 Edward New, brickmaker
309 Alex Ironside, stonecutter
311 Geo A White, bricklayer

New-st intersects

313 Chas W Vanevery, painter
315 Wm Trevaskis, blacksmith
317 Bristol Barber, brickmaker

Garth-st intersects

337 John Bridges, laborer
Samuel Cheesman, laborer
Joseph Walker, dairyman

King William-st, north side, from 28 James north, to Wentworth

2 Moore & Davis, estate agts
2 Jas G McKay, engraver
2 Chas G Booker, merchant tailor
2 Thos Marshall, tailor
2 Chas Sylvester, tailor
4 Mrs Chas Hinman, milliner
4½ G W Counihan, barber
6 W H McLaren, grocer
6½ Hyslop, Cornell & Co's shirt factory
8 R C Burkholder, printer
10 Hopkin & Son, boots and shoes
12 D B Bowman, law office
12½ M Morris, broker
14-16 Allen & Proven, second-hand dealers
18 A W Wright, broker
20 E Nixon, saloon
24 Robert Smyth, tinsmith
26 Edison Lamp Co
28 A T James, hotel

Hughson-st intersects

30 James B Bishop, tinsmith
34 Mrs T Rosenstadt, broker
36-40 Geo Richardson, broker
42 P Hemsley, furniture
44-46 Fire engine station
48 John Wright, gunsmith
54 Martin Bros, pork packers

John-st intersects

56 James Reed, hotel
66 E & C Gurney, pattern shop
66½ And Menzies, carpenter
68 Mrs Mary Ann Cuzner

Catharine-st intersects

A Hope & Co, store houses
Police station

Mary-st intersects

110 Thomas Smith, dyer
112 Wm H Taylor, laborer
114 Franks & O'Neil, painters
116 A & W J McDonald, carptrs
116 Wm Stamp, painter
122 Alex Gibb, paper boxes
124 Joshua A Phillips, carpenter
126-8 Vacant
130 George Begg, clerk

132 And Mahoney, stovemounter
134 Mrs E Munson
136 Wm Allan, carpenter
138 Walter England, barber
140 Robert King, laborer
142 Henry Fowler, shoemaker
r142 John Kemp, laborer
144 George Smith, painter
146 David Parks, shoemaker
148 Mrs E Hartnett
150 Charles Stewart, printer
152 Mrs Jas Pulkingham
154 John Potter
156 Hiram King
158 E P Morgan
160 John McAuley, engraver
162 Samuel Hunter

Ferguson-ave intersects

164 James Johnston
166 George Nash, carpenter
168 Vacant
170 Brennen's lumber yard
178 Mrs Osborne Allen
180 Wm J Wallace, moulder
182 Wm Harris, laborer
184 Robert Alder, teamster
186 Charles Sayman, carpenter
188 Anthony Murray
190 Jeremiah Donohue, moulder
192 Alfred Emberson, coal oil
194 Esau Carter, harness maker
196 Arthur Teneyck, fireman
198 George Hooper, blacksmith
198 Richard Kemp, laborer
200 Mrs M Maitland
202 Wm Wilkinson, butcher
204 Edward Lavis
206 James Ennis, printer
208 Wm McCurdy, carpenter
210 H D Williams, laborer

Wellington-st intersects

218 Wm Miller, tinsmith
226 Peebles & Hamilton, carpenters
228 Vacant

West-ave intersects

230 James Ainslie, tanner
232 Mrs Joseph Gill
234 Alfred Tulk, moulder
236 Miss Walker
238 Mrs Thos Hoag
240 Geo Walker, machinist

Victoria-ave intersects

Public School

East-ave Intersects

Vacant grounds

Emerald-st intersects

Johnson Bros, carpenters

Tisdale-st intersects

290 John Gardiner, postman

Steven-st intersects

294 Hugh McPhail, sr, agent
302 E Fearnside, gardener

Ashley-st intersects

310 Alfred Burgess, laborer
312 James Riddle, laborer
314 John P Kirwin, shipper
318 Chas H Williams, clerk
328 John Curran, stovemounter
330 Andrew Barr, butcher

Wentworth-st intersects

King Wm-st, south side

T H Stinson, solicitor
1 McNair & Bell, constables
1 Wm Shawcross, teadealer
3 H Martin, leather dealer
9 J C Macpherson, saloon
11 Thos Fowkes, dry goods
13 Jas Sweeney, tinware
15 John Carruthers, flour and feed
17 Wm Gell, broker
19 T Bogges, broker
21 Mrs John Kilroy, second-hand dealer
23 Wm Gell, broker
25 T Boggess, broker

Hughson-st intersects

41 Wood & Leggatt, warehouse
47 R B Murray, whip mounter
47 George Dempsey, manf
47 Griffin & Kidner, printers

Canada Fruit Canning Co
49 Brayley & Dempster, machinist
55 Andrew Dillon, saloon

John-st intersects

57 John Ling
63-7 M Brennen & Sons
r " P Fraser, spring beds
r " C James, machinist
69 John Strathdee, salesman

Catharine-st intersects

85 G T R stables
87 E B Santee, tinsmith
89 John Lewis, shoemaker
93 Mrs M J Warren
95 Joseph Horton, rag dealer

Mary-st intersects

101 C W Attwood, saloon
105 Karl Stokinger
107 John Chapman, laborer
109 Mrs Nicholas Carroll
111 Mrs Dodd
113 Wm Harper, shoemaker
115 A Carson, carpenter
117 Mrs Geo Henderson

Walnut-st intersects

125 Hamilton Oliver, clerk
127 H Ireland, fruiterer
129 Jas Nicol, porter
131 Jas Spence, machinist
133 John Rigsby, builder
135 Young & Bros, manfs
145 Fred Wurst, carpenter
147 Mrs James Cox, dressmaker
149 Henry Reid, machinist

Ferguson-ave intersects

151 David Snoddy, plumber
153 Wm McAndrew, printer
155 John White, laborer
157 Wm Swallon, carpenter
159 Mrs Joseph Smith
161 John Hampson, shoemaker
163 Mrs Jane Allan
165 Vacant
167 Alex Strachan, agent
169 John Close, carpenter
171 Wm Hastings, cabinetmaker
173 Wm Smith, traveler
175 James Briar, lather
181 Mrs S Chester
185-189 S F Hopkins, pickle manf

Wellington-st intersects

Robert Harper, florist
209 Wm W Holden
211 Wm Fraser, grocer
231 S Battram, shoemaker
241 Geo C Holden, clerk

Victoria-ave intersects

247 Samuel Gillespie, contractor
249 Charles Parmenter, baker
251 Mrs John Matches
255 Thomas Long, engineer

East-ave intersects

259 Charles Carson, cigarmaker
261 John Armstrong, printer

Emerald and Tisdale-sts intersect

279 Mrs James Wright
281 Robert Smith, polisher
283 Robert J Hawkins, carpenter
283½ W J Swartzenburg, whipmkr
285 David Love, carpenter
287 John Wilson, traveler
289 Rudolphus Hinds, printer
291 John Peden, fruiterer

Steven-st intersects

293 Charles Thompson, machinist
r 293 Dennis Kelly, laborer
295 David Stewart, moulder

Ashley & Wentworth-sts intersect

Kinnel-st, north side, from Inchbury

6 Geo Skuice, laborer
8 David Craig, machinist
10 Wm Hyndman, blacksmith
14 Jno McBean, patternmaker

Kinnell-st, south side

8 G H Snider, miller
11 Robt Allen, carter

Liberty-st, east side, from 120 Hunter east, south to Catharina

3 Wm Costie, carpenter

Grove-st intersects

17 Wm Anderson, pumpmaker
19 Thos Mellon, machinist
21 Wm Fallis, watchman
23 Albert Case, engineer
23 Vacant
25 Peter LePage, shoemaker

Young-st intersects

Liberty-st, west side

Grove-st commences

4 J R Hesse, grocer
6 James Armstrong, painter
8 Mrs I Reid, dressmaker
10 Mrs Wm Allison
12 Mrs Harry Gillard
14 J Johnson, music teacher
16 Mrs Wm Foreman
18 John Sintzel, tailor
20 Edward Loosley, cutter
22 W Zimmerman, salesman
24 Alex Campbell, druggist
26 C Tuker, traveler
28 Wm Spera, grain buyer
30 Robt Keefer, clerk
32 James Traill, clerk
34 Patrick Jones, laborer
36 Michael Lahey, mason
38 Wm Bramford, plasterer

Young-st intersects

Ontario Canning Co

Little Market-st, north side, from Pearl north west to Locke

2 James Whitmarsh, laborer
4 Arthur McFarland, laborer

Little Wellington-st intersects

8 George Dorning, laborer
10 Mrs Michael Joyce
12 Wm Goodram, harnessmkr
20 James Dora, laborer

Little Peel-st intersects

22 Ed Makins, machinist
22½ Ed Milligan, laborer
24 Patrick Doyle, tailor

Locke-st intersects

Little Market-st, south side

21 James Weller, laborer

Locke-st intersects

Little Peel-st, east side, from 20 Little Market to Napier

4 Chas Eicoff, cigarmaker
8 Robert Edgar, laborer
10 Wm A Smith, high constable

Napier-st intersects

Little Peel-st, west side

3 John Craig, tool keeper
5 John Sheehan, com agent
7 John Dyke, laborer
9 Donald Fraser, tailor
15 Jos Robbins, compositor

Napier-st intersects

Little Wellington-st, from Little Market to Napier

1 Walter Gordon, moulder
3 Michael Nolan, laborer
5 Wm Tyson, builder
7 John Dean, laborer

Napier-st intersects

Little William-st, east side, from Barton e north to G T R track

2 Alonzo Smith, blacksmith
12 J Sinclair, caretaker
14 Christian Reahder, plater
22 Michael Flannigan, laborer
32 Vacant
Wm Woolley, cooper

South-st intersects

Little William-st, west side

5 Wm Garvin, machinist
13 John Graham

15 John Milburn, scalemaker
21 Joseph Halter, butcher
25 R G Darby, machinist
27 Herbert Brown, machinist
29 George Weston, watchman
33 Samuel Taggart, laborer
35 Hugh Robertson, moulder
37 John Burns, laborer
39 A W Darby, laborer
41 James Catlin, laborer
43 Edward Beckingham, laborer
45 Thos Bradley, butcher
47 David Forbes, laborer
49 Mrs Mary Keenan
51 Wesley Cooper, laborer
53 Thos Yarl, laborer
55 Mrs C Bradley
57 Dennis O'Donnell, gardener
59 John Lyne, shoemaker

South-st intersects

Lockearne-st, runs from Dundurn to Breadalbane

Mrs E Burns

Locke-st n, east side, from 288 King w to G T R workshops

6 Vacant
8 Fred Lyons, laborer
12 Edwad Duffy

Little Market-st ends

26 Wm Potter, machinist
28 Fred J Richards, coffin mkr
32 George Pearce, laborer

Napier-st ends

42 F Kellar, tobacco worker
Crystal Palace View Hotel

Peter-st ends

62 Mrs Elizabeth Renwick
r62 John Kerran, carpenter
64 Fred Willis, moulder
Vacant lots

Florence-st intersects

70 Mrs Snodgrass
72 Patrick Duffy
74 Andrew Henebery, laborer
76 John Durphey, carpenter
78 Charles Blackman, porter
80 Mrs John Bentis
82 Fred Ball, moulder
84 Arch McKenzie, painter
86 Edward Tracie
88 Vacant
90 Robt Gowanlock, engineer

York-st intersects

110 Jas McCue, engine driver
112 Frank Evans, blacksmith
114 Mrs Margaret Mason
114½ Vacant
116 Joseph Wm Reid, carpenter
116½ Chas J Kemp, fireman
118 Joseph Foster, engine driver
120 Donald Campbell, carpenter
122 Thomas Milligan, dairyman
124 Jas Merriman, laborer
126 John Minnes, blacksmith
130 Sidney Brown, laborer
132 Wm McDade, laborer
134 Mrs Francis Hamilton
136 Mrs Elizabeth O'Leary
138 W J Hamill, laborer

Barton-st ends

152 Patrick O'Reilly, laborer

Locke-st n, west side

Crystal Palace and grounds
George Kerr, caretaker
Engine house

Florence-st intersects

71 Peter Dingman, shoemaker
73 James Higgins, machinist
75 James Wade, carpenter
81 G Cook, machinist
83 John Howden, carpenter
85 Alex Reid, machinist
87 Thos Gordon, shipper
89 Wm Monk, bookkeeper
91 Mrs Edward Hall, music teacher
93 Thos Hall

York-st intersects

99 Benj Palmer, moulder

101 Wm Walsh, machinist
103 Walter Iredale, machinist
105 John Wise, machinist
111 Thomas James, roller
113 George R Snider, laborer
115 James D Mills, fireman
117 Geo Mitchell, machinist
119 Daniel McCarthy, boiler-maker
121 Thos Milne, laborer
123 Wm Milne, packer
125 Saml Ryckman, conductor
127 C Sala, draughtsman
129 Thos Young, heater
133 Wm McDougall, machinist
135 Arthur Cline, hackman
139 Henry Horton, laborer
143 John Peace, iron worker
145 John Jackson, shipper
147 Thos Lewis, roller
149 Jas O'Connor, dairyman
153 Chas Booth, heater
155 Vacant

Locke-st s, east side, from 287 King w to the Mountain

3 David Hall, blacksmith

George-st ends

15 Matthew Kouber, furrier
17 Robert Heydeman, helper
19 John Barnard, manufacturer

Nelson, Main, Jackson aud Canada-sts intersect

55 Adam Sachs
61 Mrs Isabella Wilson

Hunter-st intersects

Vacant lots

Bold-st intersects

John N Rowe, stonecutter
65 John Moore, laborer
John Montgomery, salesman
163 John Moore, potter

Herkimer-st intersects

165 K McLaren, builder

Locke-st s, west side

2 Geo Trenwith, blacksmith
8 Alex Matthewson, moulder
10 Wm Finchamp, moulder
16 Wm Mass, laborer
18 G Morris, laborer
18 G Morris, butcher
20 John Ripley, carpenter
20½ Jas Snaudee, printer
22 James Watson, carpenter
24 Francis McDonald, machinist
26 Wm Davidson, tailor

Main-st intersects

J C Boligan, grocer
44 Edw Harrison, hackman

Jackson-st intersects

46-52 R Campbell's pottery

Canada-st intersects

58 John Doherty, laborer
60 Wm Wright, machinist
62 Vacant
64 Chas W Mitchell, laborer

Hunter and Duke-sts intersect

66 James Lovejoy, laborer
66 Thomas Kule, laborer
68 Adolphus Mundt, laborer
70 Michael Fanning
72 Mrs Christian Marshall
74 John Hockbush, laborer
T Fanning, grocer

Robinson-st intersects

Mas A Mullings
John W Blasdell, carpenter
Miss Margaret Macklem

Maple-st intersects

98 Wm H Mattice

Herkimer-st intersects

108 John Knapman, laborer

Locomotive-st, east side, from 230 York north to Barton

2 John Kavanagh, laborer
4 Patrick O'Reilly, laborer
6 Richard Batterton, laborer
8 D Edgar, lumber merchant
10 Josh Chapman, actor
16 Mrs Hugh Young
18 J McCulloch, engine driver

20 F Simpson, clerk
22 John Webster, laborer
24 T R Honeycomb, bricklayer
26 Sidney Roberts, fireman
28 John Honeycomb
32 J W Clifton, engineer
34 Edward Egan, fitter
36 Andrew Fox, millwright
38 Geo Tilley, pattern maker
40 J Higham, turner
44 Harry Tomlinson, fireman
46 James Ryerson, carpenter
48 S N Vail, painter
50 Wm Byer, fitter
52 Robert Little, laborer
54 Wm Jenkins, laborer
56 Vacant
58 Isaac Stephenson, moulder
60 Michael McDonough, laborer
62 Francis Salter, laborer
64 John Brace, nailer
66 Adam Grotz, nailer
68 Wm Clunas, machinist
70 David Cashion, moulder
72 James Latimer, machinist

Barton-st intersects

Locomotive-st, west side

Vacant lots
9 D O'Connell, laborer
11 K McKenzie, foreman
15 W Maddocks, blacksmith
19 Thos Cockburn, wireworker
21 John Sandicock, tinsmith
23 Patrick Gray, laborer
27 Wm Hancock, builder
29 Wm Mann, carpenter
31 Geo Taylor, laborer
33 Jas Williams, heater
37 C S Griggs, policeman
39 Jas Harris, policeman
47 Edward Makins, boilermkr
49 Wm Conley, laborer
51 Joseph Campbell, laborer
53 Francis Cochner, laborer
55 John Jamieson, painter
57 Mrs Mary Tribute
59 M McEachern, boilermaker
61 B Salisbury, saddler
63 Wm R Allan, blacksmith
69 Robert Richardson, heater
71 Mrs Charlotte Bridgewood
73 Vacant
75 Vacant
81 Wm Hamilton, carpenter
83 David McKay, painter

Barton-st intersects

Macnab-st n, east side, from 40 King w to the Bay

6 J D Mills, paper box maker
6 American Suspender Co
8 Mrs Mary Hills, fancy goods
10 Mrs James McDougall, oil and lamps
12 Isaac Morris, tailor
14 M D Healey, dry goods
16 McCallum & Hall, cabinet makers
18 Canadian Oil Co
20 G M Bell, machinist
22 T & J Beckett, flour and feed
24 John Lavell, cigar manf

Market Square

Merrick-st intersects

56 Geo Marshall & Co, tea dealers
58 Long & Bisby, wool dealers
60-62 Ontario Broom Factory
64 Lumsden Bros, grocers
74 T Patterson, blacksmith

Vine-st intersects

76 R Peters, machinist
78 G Schumacher, cabinet mkr
80 Mrs Francis Warner
82 Wm Carter, plasterer
84 R Gwyder, whitewasher
86 Mrs Mary Dunn
88 Matthew G Meek, grocer
92 Dodson Bros, brass founders
94 H E Bucklen & Co

Cannon-st intersects

104 Mrs Daniel Gray
r " Mrs George Flagley
" Isaac Stephens

106 Baptist Church
r " Mrs Jacob Arnick
108 Isaac Buchanan, plasterer
110 Wm Britt, shoemaker
112 J J Fitzpatrick, painter
114 James Chisholm, builder
116 H Collingwood, laborer
120 David Cobb, laborer
122 Vacant

Mulberry-st intersects

124 Mrs Ellen Springstead, laundress
126 Wm Hunt, butcher
128 John J McAllister, builder
r " Mrs Jane Daniels
130 C Delorme, carriage maker
130½ Mrs Wm Pitt
132 British American Dying Co
134 Chris Halliday, laborer
136 S P Maxwell, moulder
138 John Seity, telegraphist
140 Capt J Malcomson
150 H Twohy, collector
152 Mrs V Howells
154 W Woods, manf
156 Rev C H Mockridge, DD
158 A A Wyllie, customs clerk
160 G H Richards, painter
160½ John Finagin, merchant

Colborne-st iutersects

162 Edwin J Smith, carpenter
164 James Priestman, butcher
168 Wm Verral, butcher
170 Thos Anderson, baker
172 Wm T M Crowther, music teacher
174 Geo W Mackay, excise offi'r
176 Vacant

Barton-st intersects

182 Mrs Phœbe Dummer
184 Miss Agnes Young
r " Humphrey Hodges
186 Vacant
188 Vacant
190 A D Drake, foreman
192 James Anderson, M D
194 J T Routh, ins agent
196 Wm Rigg, car inspector
198 Wm Yaldon, tavern

Murray-st intersects

204 Samuel Young, bookkeeper
206 Vacant
208 Wm Lowe, machinist

Stuart-st intersects

Vacant lots
218 H March, baggageman GTR
G T R track
210 Wm Maplebeck, engineer
222 Matt Thompson, boat bldr

Strachan-st intersects

226 Robt Archibald, brakeman
228 John McCallum, moulder
230 Richard Dowle, clerk
232 W J McAllister, lumber
234 John B Nelligan, clerk
236 Arthur McCanns, laborer
244 Joseph Donderi, fruiterer

Simcoe-st intersects

250 Ontario Cotton Mills Co
256 Lawrence Dunn, laborer
r " Thos Dunn, laborer
r " R Fuerd, laborer
r " Robert Baker, laborer
r " Mrs Nora Backus
James Dillon, hotel

Ferrie-st intersects

264 James Andress, carpenter
266 Mrs Geo Malcolmson
268 W Brenton, mould maker
270 John McDougall, clerk
272 John Blain, painter
274 Arthur Talbot, teamster
276 John Hyde, laborer
278 Thos Smith, laborer
280 Henry Dean, dryer
282 Mrs Julia Robinson
286 James Begley, laborer

Picton-st intersects

288 Wm Betzner, laborer
290 Thos Hutchison, laborer
294 Hugh Doherty, mariner
296 Dennis Donahue, laborer
300 James Hill, blacksmith

Macauley-st intersects

302 Mrs Thompson
304 Henry Booker, machinist
306 Geo Frank, carpenter
308 Thomas Drever, laborer
310 Wm Turk, laborer
312 James Blizzard, laborer
314 John Plank, grocer

Wood-st intersects

320 John Slater, carpenter
324 James Kelly, laborer
326 Thomas Fowles, teamster
328 James Havers, glassblower

Burlington-st intersects

332 Vacant
" Thos McIlwraith, Cairnbrae

Macnab-st n, west side

1-3 Thos McKay, grocer
5 S Zimmerman, M D, dentist
7 Patrick Shine, barber
9 R Pray & Son, undertakers
11 Wm Alford, crockery
13 J P Kelly, shoemaker
15 Jno Watt & Son, mcht tailors
17 F W Fearman, provisions
19 Archdale Wilson & Co, wh druggists
21 Thos Jarvis, furniture
23 James M Stuart & Co, wh grocers
25 Wm Tremlett, shoemaker
27 J M Webber, paints, oils, etc
29 Andrew Ruthven, hotel

Market-st commences

21 R C Cooper, grocer
33 Robert Evans & Co, seed merachnts

York-st intersects

35 John A Barr & Co, druggists
37 Alfred Stroud, hotel
39 C H Peebles, grocer
41 John A Dresser, hotel
43 Campbell & Pentecost, dry goods
45 Geo Henderson, boots and shoes
47 Miss M B Fiset
49 Michael Williams, hotel
51 John Davis, china and glass
53 Mrs E Duffy, fancy goods
55 Peter Duffy, hotel

Merrick-st intersects

57 John Calder & Co, wholesale clothiers
59 Lucas, Park & Co, wholesale grocers
61 Vacant
75 Jas Stewart & Co, foundry

Vine-st intersects

77-79 Abraham Levy, rag dealer
83 Wm Silver, boot and shoe manfr
85 Vacant
87 A H Henry, expressman
89 C D Mills, traveler
95 M A Pigott, builder

Cannon-st intersects

97 Arch Coutts, livery stable
99 George Knott, laborer
101-3 Francis Burdett, brushmaker
105 Mrs Patrick Hopkins
107 Charles Roantree, broommaker
109 David Hurley, engineer
r 109 Charles Ratfield, laborer
111 Arthur Arkell, miller
113 Robert Chisholm, builder
115 James Chisholm, builder
117 Frank O'Reilly, plumber

Mulberry-st intersects

119 Vacant
121 Vacant
123 Geo Moore
127 Henry Fernihough, shipper
129 Francis Edgar, carpenter
131 Arch McEachern, teller
139 Mrs S J Evans
141-7 R C Model school
149 Jno McKenzie, wood dealer
" J S Hossack, carpenter
151 Mrs Margaret Morris
153 Wm Clinton, pattern fitter
155 Mrs M Browne

157 Thomas Gribbon, carpenter

Colborne-st intersects

163 Joseph Canute
165 Hugh Wynn, saloon
167 Wm Ferguson, teamster
169 Henry Creel
171 James Cotter, tailor
173 George Strain, laborer

Barton-st intersects

179 Peter J O'Reilly, brushmkr
181 Capt Wm Wood, mariner
183 Wm Robertson, bookkeeper
185 John Wark, clerk
187 Matthew Wilson, manf
189 R D Coles, traveler
191 C E Morgan, ticket agent

Murray-st intersects

209 Mrs Wm Massie

Stuart-st intersects

G T R bridge
221 Samuel Church, laborer

Strachan-st intersects

225 James Morris, grocer
227 Allison Wyllie, foreman
231 Daniel McLaren, machinist
233 Vacant
235 Chas Beatty, broker

Simcoe-st intersects

251 Henry Hale, laborer
253 Thos Nugent, laborer
255 Peter Johnson, cigarmaker
247 R C Guerin, clerk
259 Joseph James, blacksmith
261 Daniel Husted, glassblower
263 Hugh Gillespie, grocer

Ferrie-st intersects

263½ Wm G Fairweather, grocer
265 John Kerr, butcher
267 Wm Teeter, dairyman
269 Wm Teeter, dairyman
271 Mrs Mary Moody
273 Samuel Shearer, laborer
275 Robert Cowie, carpenter
279 Patrick Burke, laborer

Picton st intersects

287 Joseph Paquin, grocer
293 Arch Irving, sailor
295 Moses Furlong, hackman
299 Lawrence Kelly
303 Mrs Wm Fletcher
r " Miss E Adamson

Macauley-st intersects

309 James Arrol, moulder
311 Joseph Fretman, glassblower
313 E B Taylor, laborer

Wood-st intersects

315 Michael O'Neill, glassblower
317 L Fitzgerald, boilermaker
319 Mrs Mary Armstrong
321 Vacant
323 Vacant
327 Patrick Noonan, shoemaker

Burlington-st intersects

Burlington glass works

Brock-st intersects

Charles Hamilton, foreman
Browne's wharf

Macnab-st s. east side, from King w to Markland

7 Wm G Crowley, dealer
9 James Noble, machinist
13 Wm Richardson, laborer
15 Edgar Myers, cooper
19 Thos Hedley, upholsterer
21 Mrs Wm Storror

Main-st intersects

27 Benj Coombs, laborer
29 John Bower, lithographer

Jackson and Hunter-sts intersect

51 Mrs Smith
51 Wm J Myers
53 Mrs Charlotte Daville
55 Alex Lawson, printer
61 John Fairgrieve, coal merchant

Bold-st intersects

63 Vacant
65 J D Macdonald, M D

Duke & Robinson- sts intersect

91 James M Young, manf

93 George Grover, supt American Express Co
95 Mrs Adam Hope
Hannah-st intersects
John Crerar, barrister
Herkimer-st intersects
113 John Bradley, cabinetmaker
115 Wm F McGivern, bookkeeper
117 Cameron Bartlett, accountant

Macnab-st s, w side

John A Bruce & Co, seedsmen
6 Vacant
8 Edward Williams, laborer
10 Mrs H Thompson
12 Thos Irwin & Son, tinsmiths
14-20 Thos Lawry & Son, pork packers
22 David Bewick, printer
" F M McGowan, artist
" James Fletcher, jeweler
Main-st intersects
24 Mrs Horace Aylwin
Central Presbyterian ch
Jackson-st intersects
Calvin McQuesten, MD
Hunter-st intersects
Macnab st Presbyterian ch
58 Rev D H Fletcher
60 Lloyd Mewburn
62 Wm A Howel, druggist
64 John Henessey, safe dealer
Bold, Duke, Robinson & Hannah-sts intersect
Mrs John Hebden
Herkimer-st intersects
Luther Sawyer, manfr
John T Glassco, merchant
Markland-st intersects

Macauley-st e, north side, from Glass Works, James n, to Wellington

Hughson-st intersects
25 Mrs Edward Hanlan
27 Thos W Miles, laborer
31 James Kelly, laborer
33 Emanuel Knowles, weaver
35 James Burn, laborer
John, Catharine and Mary-sts intersects
73 John Jones, bricklayer
75 R Finch, bricklayer
77 Hugh Churchill, laborer
79 Robert Mackenzie, laborer
81 H Jones, bricklayer
85 John Voll, glassblower
87 Mrs Ellen Jordan
89 Mrs H Wheeler
91 George Maxham, laborer
93 Pat Conlon, laborer
Ferguson-ave intersects
129 W H Bodden, bricklayer
131 George Crossland, laborer
133 Edw Newman, carpenter
135 Hiram Siddell, laborer
137 James Sweetlove, carpenter
143 John Laurie, carpenter
145 Wm Little, laborer
Wellington-st intersects

Macauley-st e, south side

Hamilton glassworks
Hughson-st intersects
28 Robert Smith, laborer
30 John Kennedy, boilermaker
32 Wm Simple, laborer
34 Timothy Murphy, laborer
John, Catharine and Mary-sts intersect
80 Michael Conway, glassblower
82 Michael Cullen, laborer
84 M Schultz, engineer
84½ Patrick Wickham, stovemtr
86 James Russell, watchman
90 Vacant
92 Wm Keegan, laborer
96 John Wickham, laborer
Ferguson-ave intersects
120 James Maxwell, engineer
124 Moses Morris, laborer

126 John Madgett, machinist
128 J J Howarth, boilermaker
130 Robert Wooley, spinner
132 James Shuttle, machinist
134 George Holtham, tinner
136 Wm E Carless, carter
138 Thomas Garrett, moulder
Wellington-st intersects

Macaulay-st w, north side, from 331 James n to Bay

13 Ed Daley, laborer
15 Robert Barker, laborer
17 J Mahoney, laborer
Macnab-st intersects
29 Robt McWilliams, machinist
33 John Phillips, sailmaker
35 Wm Batzmer, teamster
37 Thos Elliott, engineer
41 Peter Davis, sailor
43 Wm Reid, carpenter
45 Mrs Richard Short
47 John Fell, machinist
49 Thos Boothman, sailor
Bay-st intersects

Macaulay-st w, south side

5 Edward Murphy, laborer
7 Henry Miller, glassblower
Macnab-st intersects
32 Isaac Leblanc, laborer
36 Mrs John Brown
38 P H Murphy, glassblower
40 Thos Beavers, laborer
42 Wm B Griner, glassblower
44 Robt Leslie, bookkeeper
Bay-st intersects

Magill-st, east side, from 250 York north to Barton

4 John C Cooper, blacksmith
6 Fred Thomson, laborer
8 Thos Sandercock, fitter
10 George Tollett, machinist
14 George J Lazarus, turner
18 Chas Thomson, carpenter
22 Vacant
24 Mrs Wm Flock
28 James Sloan, laborer
30 C W Smith
30½ John Patterson, machinist
32 James Flynn, laborer
36 George C Byerns
38 John McKay, conductor
40 James Baines, fitter
42 John G Morton, fitter
44 John Stacey, laborer
46 Robert Rogers, blacksmith
50 Fred Held, policeman
52 Donald Campbell, policeman
Barton-st intersects

Magill-st, west side

Arthur Boyle, chemist
11 John Patterson, cutter
13 James Nickling, machinist
15 Robert Martin, engineer
17 John D Morden
19 Daniel Jack, engineer
21 John Work, laborer
23 W Wagstaff, tinsmith
25 Wm Hornby, machinist
27 Wm Hunter, collector
35 Geo Dawe, blacksmith
37 C E Miner, cabinetmaker
39 Jas R Allan
45 James Hendry, fitter
47 James Harris, engineer
51 Wm Newcomb, engineer
53 Wm Walker, brakeman
55 Mrs Abraham Lawson
Barton-st intersects

Main-st e, north side, from 26 James s to city limits

9 R Benner, com agent
9 David Newton, agent
11 John W Bickle, grocery broker
11 Edward Furlong, barrister
11 David Blackley, accountant
13 W R Macdonald, barrister
" G S Papps, barrister
J Turner & Co's warehouse

Hughson-st intersects

Thos Myles & Son, coal dealers
J Winer & Co
29 Chas Cook, shades saloon
31 Wm Lees, baker
33 Vacant

John-st intersects

43 N Taylor & Co, druggists
49 Morgan Bros, flour mills

Catharine-st intersects

71 Isaac Ryall, MD
73 Samuel McKay, livery
77 Mrs R Kelly
79 Alex Stewart, tailor
81 James Sinnott
83 Wm K Wilson, carpenter
85 Wm Ramage, salesman
89 S H Ghent, dep clerk crown

Walnut-st intersects

101 Charles J Newman, organist
103 R S Beasley
107 Chas Black, merchant
109 Miss Isabella Hattersley
115 Wm Servos
115 Secretary's office H & N W R R

Cherry-st intersects

117 E Lepatourel, engineer
123 Mrs Mary Mullin
129 James Whelen, shoemaker
131 Wm J Reid, carpenter
131½ Wm Halliday, carpenter
133 Vacant
135 Thomas Sterling
137 Daniel Gallivan, laborer
139 James Gosnay, filesmith
141 Mrs Robert Gilmore
143 Andrew Ross, grain buyer
145 Mrs Joseph Ford, dressmkr
147 R Taylor, shoemaker
149 James Fox, tinsmith
151 Mrs Patrick Dermody
153 Arthur Boond, filecutter
155 George Duncan, merchant

Spring-st intersects

163 to 177 Vacant
179 Wm J Proctor, manf

Wellington-st intersects

First Methodist Church
181 Alex Drysdale, com trav
183 Mrs Patrick Bain
185 Mrs Margaret Baine
187 Mrs Jane Christian
191 Thomas Steward, salesman
205 J G Geddes, agent
207 Thos Jackson, contractor

Victoria-ave intersects

St. Patrick's Church

East-ave intersects

219 P W Dayfoot
221 A A Stewart, bookkeeper

Emerald-st intersects

225 Stanley McNider, manf
227 Wm Morgan, merchant
239 J G Davis
241 W P Moore, estate agent
243 Henry Carscallen, barrister
245 John Campbell, pork packer

Wentworth-st intersects

Chris Magen, butcher
Jas M Iredale, blacksmith

Burlington-st intersects

Samuel Smith, laborer
Richard Howe, gardener
Frank Rainor, gardener

Toll Gate

Warren Holton, nursery
Mrs John Field
Thos Beasley, city clerk
Donald Smith, tailor
Thos Barnes

Mountain-ave intersects

J A Bruce & Co, seed farm

Main-st e, south side

2 Hamilton club house
4 John Riddell, stock broker
" A O'Heir, barrister
" Wm J Lavery, solicitor
6 R Benner, broker
8 C A Sadlier, barrister

10 Dr Hillyer
12 Albert Bauer, artist
14 Mrs Henry Bauer, wine mcht
16 Hamilton & Dundas Railway Co
20 H A Mackelcan, barrister
20 James Walker, ins agent
22 James Simpson& Son, brokers
24 Ennis & Cook, printers
24 Harold Lambe, broker

Hughson-st intersects

Prince's Square
Registry office
Hamilton Protective Collection Association
Court House
Miles O'Reilly, Q C, Master's office
J E O'Reilly
G S Counsell, county clerk
John Stock, Co treasurer
Hon A McKellar, sheriff
S H Ghent, dep clerk of the crown
Waddell & Waddell, barristers
H Stephens, accountant
Æ Irving, barrister
C W Mulligan, architect
Ninth Div Court
Hamilton Homestead Loan and Savings society
Matthew Broadbent, engin'r

John-st intersects

John Stuart. Son & Co

Bowen-st intersects

52 John Sullivan, livery
54 T McIlwraith, coal dealer

Catharine-st intersects

62-64 Joseph Hoodless & Son, mattress shop
72 Casey & Sons, planing mill
76 Stables
80 Fred Bearn, tailor
86 Wm Casey, sr, manfr
88 Hugh Murray, customs
90 Geo Jackson, shipper
96 John Winer

Walnut-st intersects

102 Wm Orr, carpenter
104 Rev A Langford, Methodist
106 Vacant
116 D B Galbreaith, customs

Cherry-st intersects

118 Jas McKay, grocer
120 Daniel Hunt
124 Arch Davis, printer
126 F A Cutler, cabinetmaker
132 Jas S Dalrymple, clerk
134 Mrs Wm Moore
136 Freeman Slaght, agent
138 Geo Cuttriss, engraver
138½ Joseph Lee, tuner
140 Wm Gilmore, butcher
140¼ Jas Holmes, shoemaker
142-4 Chas Mills, grocer

Spring-st intersects

146 Vacant
156 T H Wilson, M D
158 J Cummings, tax colleetor

Wellington-st intersects

St Thomas' Church

West-ave intersects

168 P Grossman, music dealer
170 C W Meakins, brush manf

Victoria-ave intersects

172 D E Roberts, marble dealer
178 N D Galbraith, grocer

East-ave intersects

182 Alex McLagan
184 Mrs N F Birely

Emerald-st intersects

186 David Morton, soap manf
188 Wm Barr
192 M Brennen, merchant
194 Jonathan Davis
196 W R Reasnor, clerk

Erie-ave iutersects

198 Daniel Kelly
200 Frank McCurly
208 John Potter, gardener
214 Alex Bain, cabinetmaker

220 Wm Blair
224 Henry Blandford, gilder

Wentworth-st intersects

Thos McCabe, engineer
John Fuller, gardener
D Lamont, gardener

Burlington-st intersects

Mrs Andrew Harper
John Fisher, fireman
Thos Marshall, laborer
Fred Mines, laborer

Argo-st intersects

John McIntosh, tailor
John Hurd, laborer
Robert Powell, butcher
James Rose, toll-keeper
Mrs Andrew Skinner
Geo Rutherford, druggist
Edward Mitchell, banker
John Eastwood, bookseller
J W Murton, coal dealer
Lewis Springer
J T Middleton, marble de'lr
George Sweet, traveler
Watson Trusdale, bookkeepr
Chas Carpenter
R R Gage, barrister
Simon James, Delta hotel

Main-st w, north side, from 36 James south to city limits

2 Mrs Butler
4 John Taylor, machinist
6 Vacant
Adam Tyson, renovator
Centenary Church
10 George Read, hackman
12 Mrs Chas Magill
14 Vacant
16 Miss Elizabeth Smith

Macnab-st intersects

18 C VanNorman Emory, M D
20 John Williams, policeman
22 John H Caddy
24 Mrs John W Pounden
26 Wm P Bruce
28 Alfred Bowditch, clerk
30 Wm King, merchant tailor
32 James H Davidson, trav
Murton & Reid's coal yard

Charles-st intersects

36 James Wylie

Park-st intersects

40 Thos Cook, founder
42 Robert Wright, lumber mcht
44 Mrs John Davis
46 Vacant
48 John H Fernside, clerk P O
50 W W Summers
52 Mrs Jake Mune
54 Wm A Venator, turner
56-58 Aitchison & Co, planing mill
60 Joseph Jeffery, city laundry
62 Chas H Bamfylde
62 Miss H A Wilkins, teacher
66 John Morrison, grocer

Bay-st intersects

66 Wm Herman, merchant
70 David Garson, brushmaker
72 Fred Ricketts, painter
74 Theo Rutter, stovemounter
76 Richard Congdon, bricklayer
78 John Hall, laborer
82 B Martin, cabinetmaker
84 Hamilton Cooper, carriage builder
Collegiate institute

Caroline-st intersects

100 Thos C Livingstone, surveyor
102 John M Gibson, barrister
104 Alex Hamilton, druggist
108 Peter Blaicher, druggist
112 George Dempsey, ins agent
114 W J Lindsey, clerk

Hess-st intersects

116 Alex Murray, merchant
138 H W Judd, manfr
140 Miss Botts
142 Adam Clark, plumber
144 Vacant
148 T C Mewburn, insp customs

150 Vacant
152 Fred Tribute, cutter

Ray-st intersects

154 Mrs Wm Campbell
156 Vacant
158 Wm Somerville, agent
160 Rev Thos Scoular
162 Mrs D McCulloch
164 Thos D Beddoe, manf
166 George E Mason, accountant
168 Charles H Sutherland
174 Nathan Sternberg, rag dealer

Pearl-st intersects

Vacant lots
Frank Nicolls, coal dealer

Locke-st intersects

184 E H Wands, carpenter
186 Hilton Loucks, harnessmkr
188 Fred Schadel, blacksmith
190 R W Campbell, potter
192 Mrs Isaac Page
196 F J Smith, packer

Margaret st intersects

226 John Skerritt, shoe dealer
228 Mrs Eliza New

New-st intersects

250 Henry New, manufacturer

Garth-st intersects

Main-st w, south side

1 Ross Bros, painters
1 Amos W Parmenter
7 Wm C Harvey, merchant
15 Mrs Ellen Lewis
17 Ed Evans, laborer

Macnab-st intersects

21 Albert Pain, merchant
23 Mrs J L Smith
27 John Mitchell
31 Dr Henry T Ridley

Charles-st intersects

35 F H Mills
37 Jas Leslie, MD

Park st intersects

39 D McDougall, contractor
41 Vacant
43 Walter Patterson, brakeman
45 Dow Bros, wood, etc
55 Mark Keane, laborer
57 W G Dunn & Co, spice mills

Bay-st intersects

67 Henry Hunting, fireman
" Robt McNaught, pedler
69 Wm Morphy, machinist
" Chas Hurton, caretaker
71 Mrs Wm Leith
73 Miss Sarah A Feast
75 Dr Geo E Husband
79 Wm E LaChance, traveler
81 Mrs E Wilson, dressmaker
83 G Nielson, clerk
85 R D Kennedy, architect
87 Walter Spencer, piano tuner
89 Alex Aitchison, chief fire department
91 Vacant
93 Robert Burns

Caroline-st intersects

101 George Sterling
103 Harris Fischer, button hole
105 Thos Steele, music teacher
107 Rev Joseph W A Stewart
109 Mrs H A Armstrong
111 Robert Campbell, manfr
113 Jas H Mills

Hess-st intersects

127 Ethelbert Servos
Primary School

Queen-st intersects

141 Walter Bailey
" Joseph, Best, porter
143 Thos Lees, merchant
145 Mrs John Green
147 Vacant
149 Byron Richardson, carpenter
151 Wm H Mills

Ray-st intersects

155 John Cameron, editor Spectator
157 W B Palmer, com trav
159 Mrs Wm Land
161 O Hudson, cabinet maker

163 John Maxwell, painter
Mrs B Holmes
167 Nathan Stanberg, rag dealer

Pearl-st intersects

169 A E Reid, cutter
171 Alex Reid, bookkeeper
175 W S Lumgair, agent
177 Wm Brend, fitter
179 Wm Hover, tailor
181 Alfrrd Barnard, bookkeeper
" Samuel Reeves, pedler
183 John Western, shoemaker
185 Geo N Webb, shoemaker

Locke-st intersects

John C Bolegan, grocer
189 John Holmes, painter
191 Jesse Coombes, laborer
193 John Davis, brickmaker
197 Henry Allcock, laborer
203 Thos Mepham, plasterer
205 Chas A Plastow, carpenter
207 Miss I Hume, seamstress
209 J Mitchell, cigarmaker
211 John Urquhart, carpenter
213 H P Breay, manf

Poulette-st intersects

213 J A King, potter
215 John Springate, laborer
217 Philip Saunders, laborer
219 Joseph W Shaw, plasterer
221 Geo Frid, brickmaker
221 Geo Bray, carriage trimmer
223 Matthew Murphy, polisher
227 Lawrence Roupelle, laborer
229 Geo R Alladice, stonecutter
231 Henry Hall, teamster

Garth-st intersects

Leonard Foster, potter
Joseph Jackson, brickmaker
— Brannigan, brickmaker

Maple-st, south side

John Bell, machinist
Thos Dunford, laborer
Wm Hutton, laborer
David Duncan, machinist
— Fair, laborer
— Merimore, tailor
Charles Bevan, laborer

Maple-st, north side

Public sehool
— Lamonte, laborer
Wm Penney, machinist
Alex Rodgers, boiler maker
Alber E Darling, brickmkr
John T Laing, fitter
Andrew S Peters, basketmkr
Mrs And Gardner, laundress
Mrs Mary Fisher, laundress

Maple-ave, from Stinson to Mountain.

James Carson, moulder
W L Billings, M D

Margaret-st, east side, from 293 King w to Main

1 James Perrin, laborer
3 Miss M Maxwell, dressmkr
5 Thos Stokes, carpenter
9 Thos Fee, hackman
15 Mrs James Walsh
17 Wm H Chilman, confec'r
19 John Morley, blacksmith
23 Robert Wade, laborer
25 Alfred Haines, potter
27 Vacant
29 Thomas Riley, laborer
31 Wm Smith, laborer
33 Michael Gallivan, laborer
35 Robert S Jacques

Main-st intersects

Margaret-st, west side

2 Mrs John Stevens
4 Donald Mathieson, laborer
6 Thomas Keller, agent
8 Mrs Adam Logan
12 Wm Hearn, watchman
14 Seymour Skinner, laborer
16 Isaac Atkins, sailor
18 A E Smith, mason
20 John Gentle

22 Matthew Whitney, teamster
24 Vacant
26 John Modlin
28 Mrs John Campbell
Main-st intersects

Maria-st, north side, from James s, east to Wellington

Vacant lot
Hughson-st intersects
19 J W Jones, barrister
23 George French, gardener
25 Mrs James Meikle
27 Mrs Charles Ambrose
John-st intersects
31 Thos Lewis, manfr
Catharine-st intersects
47 Robt Cruickshank, manfr
49 Geo Mitchell, cabinetmaker
51 John Donaldson, engineer
55 Michael Whelan, laborer
57 Wm Kell, sr
59 James Orr, laborer
61 James Hancock, whipmaker
63 Mrs Ann Lavel
65 Robert Hunter, packer
Walnut-st intersects
75 John Patterson, tailor
77 Wm Warren, machinist
79 Mrs C Munn
81 Mrs James Smith
Cherry-st intersects
99 Mrs John Benton
101 Martin Rowan, laborer
103 John Bingham, laborer
105 Thos Archibald, laborer
Aurora-st intersects
111 A Doyle, laborer
115 Geo D Rioch, printer
117 D C O'Keefe, surgeon
119 Mrs Thos Kerruish
Wellington-st intersects

Maria-st, south side

8 Mrs Robert McKay
Hughson-st intersects
20 Mrs M Davis
22 F J Rastrick, architect
Church of Ascension
John-st intersects
Thos Lewis, cigar manf
Catharine-st intersects
40 Joseph Hockaday, cabinetmaker
42 Wm G Webber, bricklayer
44 J J Upfield, traveler
46 Mrs Thos Capes
56 Geo Coombs, moulder
58 John McDonald, stonecutter
60 John Beal, baker
62 Mrs Day Dundon
64 M T Evans, brewer
66 Mrs H O'Malley.
68 David Heddle, mason
70 Wm Kelk, music teacher
Walnut-st intersects
72 Josiah Beare, moulder
74 C Donovan, inspector
76 Mrs John West
78 Wm H Paskey, machinist
80 Robert Forbes
82 Mrs Jas Holland
Cherry-st intersects
86-88 Patrick Padden, laborer
90 Owen Lavelle, laborer
92 Mrs Eliza Murray
94 Patrick O'Connell, laborer
96 Timothy Sheehan, laborer
104 D O'Connor, laborer
106 Wm McDonagh, laborer
108 Fred Clark, galvanizer
110 Robert McCaffrey, laborer
Aurora-st intersects
112 P Hayes, laborer
114 Arthur Hubbard, packer
116 Patrick Kennedy, moulder
118 Wm Aspell, clerk
120 A Loney, shoemaker
122 Wm Nash, bricklayer
124 Daniel Barrett, laborer
126 Joseph Mortimer, stovem'ter
Wellington-st intersects

Market-st, north side, from 31 Macnab n to Ray

2 Philp & Son, saddlers
4 A Lawson & Co, printers
6 C Kerner, saloon
12-14 Simon Lalor, hotel
16 Hiram E Bush, pumpmaker
18 Market stables
22 J Craig, V S
24 Vacant
26-28 Wm Morris, grocer
Park-st intersects
34 J Craig, vet surgeon
36 Alex Lockie, printer
38 Robert Ferguson, printer
40 Mrs Jane Smith
42 H E Bush, pump manfr
44 George Pyle, machinist
46 W R Pease, bookkeeper
48-54 John Rodgers, blacksmith
Bay-st intersects
58 Vacant
62 Washington Tufford, laborer
64 Thos Farrell, laborer
66 Wm Waldren, teamster
68 John Morty, teamster
70 Hendrie & Co, shops
72 Wm Moir, ornamenter
74 John Cummings, laborer
76 John Vollick, wood turner
78 Thos N Best
80 Dennis Gleason, agent
82 Fred Schwartz, tobacconist
84 Thos Hardiman, confectioner
86 Mrs Jas Gilchrist
88 John Gilmore, organ builder
Caroline-st intersects
90 Joseph Mason, caretaker
92 Wm Brass, carpenter
94 Jacob Lowery
96 Primary School
98 Rev Charles Spiers
Evangelical Church
100 T S Bell, civil engineer
102 Mrs James Flett
104 John Westfall, laborer
106 James New, brickmaker
108 Wm Mattice, porter
110 Thomas Dawe, forgeman
Hess-st intersects
114 Walter Anderson, bookkeeper
116 Vacant
118 John Cook
120 R E Gallagher, principal Canada Business College
122 Cyrus King, grocer
124 Mrs James Horsburg
126 Rev L DesBrisay
128 Wm Harper, printer
130 James Stewart, traveler
132 John Stewart, bookkeeper
Queen-st intersects
140 David Lowe, wire weaver
142 T Hutchinson, teamster
144 Hugh McLaughlin, horse-trainer
150 — O'Neil, gardener
154 Robert Wright, laborer
156 Wm Harper, fireman
158 James Fairclough, carpenter
160 James Burns, porter
162 Mrs Ann Bailey
164 Peter Gorman, blacksmith
Ray-st intersects

Market-st, south side

1 Robt Berryman, wool dealer
3 T H McKenzie, wool dealer
5-7 J B Williams, hotel
7½ McMonies & Ryan, auctioneers
11 Russell & Dunn, gen agents
13 Joseph Taylor, livery
Wm Fitzgerald, flour mill
Park-st intersects
33-35 Mathews' livery stable
The Misses Mathews
37 George H Mathews, livery
39 Joseph H Quarry, com trav
41 Tuckett's warehouse
43 E V Orme, clerk
Bay-st intersects
63 John O'Connell, laborer
69 Hendrie & Co.'s stables

71 Robert Spencer, laborer
73 Arch Whyte, foreman
75 John Mariott, porter
77 Thomas Moffatt, mail carrier
79 Morris Hendershott, laborer
81 Robert Robson, laborer

Caroline-st intersects

91 Robt H Climie, merchant
93 John Billington, shoemaker
95 I Armstrong, grain buyer
97 Thos E Leather, traveler
99 H C Sheppard, clerk
101 Z Hemphill, agent
103 Charles Huton, tailor
105 Mrs Patrick McAuliffe
107 Wm W Godard, traveler
109 M McCulloch, bookkeeper
111 Adolph Egener, excise office

Hess-st ends

117 Mrs Benjamin Scriver
119 G J Walker, painter
121 Mrs Andrew Stevenson
123 Isaac Morris, tailor
125 Thos A Duggan, clerk
127 George Kerner, agent
129 H T Drope, printer
131 Mrs James Macabe
133 Wm P Smith, packer

Queen-st intersects

Market Square, from 17 James n to Macnab

1 McGregor & Parke, druggists
2 P Ronan, flour and feed
3 John McIntosh, tailor
4 Wm Felf, engraver
5 J & C J Brennan, grocers
6 James McPhail, boots and shoes
7 London China House
7 W H Clarke, laundry
7 W & J Morden, produce and commission
8 Joseph Webster, flour and feed
9 Carpenter Bros, grocers
10 Cyrus King, grocer
10½ Joseph R Meade & Co, shirt manf
11 J Lucas, restaurant
12 Benj Lester, hotel
13 Henry Goold, hotel
14 Wm Harris, baker
15 F L Cherrier, grocer
16 Thos W Scott, Empire House
17 Patrick Crilly, tailor
18 Kirk & Truman, hairdress'rs
19 Jas Thornton, musical instruments
20 J Crawford, confectioner

Macnab-st intersects

Markland-st, south side

Macnab-st intersects

Mrs D Nicholson

Ontario-st intersects

J H Park, merchant
Mrs M R Logie

Bay-st intersects

Wm Ainslie, trunk maker
Edmund Gilbert, laborer
Benj Brass, carpenter

Hilton-st intersects

W R Job, shoemaker
F E Gadsby, shoemaker
Ed Wilde, valuator

Caroline-st intersects

W J Locke, salesman
Geo Jones, carpenter
Thos Briers, painter

Bruce-st intersects

David Phillips, machinist
Wm Kay, laborer
Wm Lennox, grocer

Hess, Queen and Kent-sts intersect

Locke-st intersects

Richard Graham, dyer
Cyrus Oliver, cutter
Thos Watts, machinist
Geo Russell, harnessmaker
H C Russell, saddler

Geo Collis, coppersmith
John Hahan, mason
Chas Bishop, carpenter
Wm Marsh, blacksmith
J W Korn, furrier

Markland-st, north side

John Jeffrey, laborer

Macnab-st intersects

Thos Irvine

Park-st intersects

Wm Wallace

Bay-st intersects

John Walford, packer
Jas C Taylor, merchant

Caroline-st intersects

David Morton
Geo Jackson, laborer
P J Thomas, contractor
Andrew Muir, bookkeeper
John Croft, laborer
Miss Mary Miller

Hess-st intersects

Robt West, laborer

Queen st intersects

G J Williams
Vacant
Vacant lots

Kent and Locke-sts intersect

Wm Knapman, laborer
Sidney Brown, laborer
N Power
H Reinholt, carpenter
Mrs C Reinholt
Vacant house

Mary-st, east side, from 124 King e to the Bay

8 G B Smith, wood yard
10 Burn & Robinson Manf Co
16 Vacant
18 Arthur Gee, tailor
20 James Arthurs, laborer

King Wm-st intersects

26 James Way
34 Wm McLelland, collarmaker
38 Wm Smye, collarmaker

Rebecca-st intersects

46 Vacant
Public school

Wilson-st commences

68 N B Robbins, grate manf
68 Star Augur Co
70 Thos H Herbert, stonecutter
74 M A Gallagher, traveler
76 J Carruthers, flour dealer
78 John Forbes, boxmaker
80 Jas Farr, bricklayer
82 Thos Laidlaw, clerk

Kelly-st intersects

84-88 Laidlaw Manfr Co
W Payne, coal and wood
Bain & Colville, machinists

Cannon-st intersects

108 Vacant
118 Rudolph Mathesins, artist
122 Ginder Volkeir, laborer
124 Chas Holland, agent
128 Jas Kingdon, tailor
134 A R Lovell, clerk
136 Jas F Chamberlain, machinist
138 Alex McKay, clerk
140 J W Brown
140½ Miss Isabella Lamont
142 Chas H Hills, grocer

Robert-st intersects

148 John Stevens, baker
148½ Morris McKenna, laborer
152 A P Boam, cabinetmaker
154 W R Hardy
156 H Hincks, machinist
158 D A Muir, contractor
160 J H Moore, clerk
162 Michael McCarthy, moulder
166 Joseph Hopkins, weaver
r 166 Jas Martin, scalemaker
168 R S Smith, baggageman
170 Wm Rymal
172 Ed Fearman, plasterer
172 F L Cherrier, grocer

Barton-st intersects

180 Wm McDonald, timekeeper
184-204 Hamilton Cotton Co
206 John Holt, carder
208 Wm Fairley, plumber
210 Joseph Fairley, carpenter
G T R bridge
238 Alex Main, rope manfr

Strachan-st intersects

240 Jas Patton, machinist
242 T H Buckingham, mechanic
244 John Gorman, laborer
246 Wm Thompson, blacksmith
246½ Isaac Thompson, laborer
252 Alex Hunter, laborer

Simcoe-st intersects

254 John Lynch, laborer

Ferrie-st intersects

264 C J Kerr, machinist
266 Wm Davis, laborer
270 Alfred Bates, carpenter
272 John Hannon, laborer

Picton-st intersects

276 Peter Carroll, carpenter
278 Thos Mullins, carpenter
280 Mrs John Clellan
282 Chris Connoly, boilermaker
284 Wm Wickham, stovefitter
288 Vacant
290 Patrick Malloy, laborer
292 Vacant

Macauley-st intersects

John Jones, builder

Wood-st intersects

Mary-st, west side

15 John Burt, caretaker

King Wm-st intersects

25 John Watson, cattle doctor
27 Wm Gillespie, whipmaker
29 Mrs Jas Ward
31 Mrs Thos Barnes
33 P Armstrong, carriagemaker
W S Gully, hotel keeper

Rebecca-st intersects

H Hill, butcher
43 Wm Linage, shoe cutter
45 Geo H Milne, builder
47 Thos J Holland, hay and straw
49 Amos Johnston, huckster
51 Louis Bennett, waiter
53 Miss Henritta Harris
55 Ira Buchner, tailor
55½ Mrs Ed R Routh
57 John Hammond, laborer
59 Mrs Susan Sweeney
61 Wm Level, laborer
63 Thos J Holland, hay and straw
73 Vacant
75 James Hunter, salesman
77 P Young
79 J G Cloke, bookseller
81 Hamilton Whip Co (limited)
83 James Adams, packer
85 Mrs Wm Mowat
87 Geo Bilton, soda water manf
89 Wm Farrar, merchant
91 Patrick Kennedy
93 Joseph Pett, tanner
95 Vacant
97 Robert Leslie, laborer
99 Vacant

Cannon-st intersects

111 Richard Seldon, grocer
117 James Orange, laborer
119 John Riche, druggist
121 Peter Fitzpatrick, carpenter
123 John Marchum, moulder
125 Nelson Stevens, tobacco roller

Robert-st intersects

143 Frank Rowe, polisher
145 Mrs E Tallman
147 John Connor, painter
149 Henry Mathews, moulder
151 John Carmichael, laborer
153 Martin Good, cabinetmaker
157 Duncan Brown, bookkeeper
159 Stephen Searle, carpenter
161 Alfred Crowe, machinist
163 Wm Pearman, cook
165 John Farr, teamster
167 John Hayes, machinist

169 Robt Hart, hatter
171 Vacant
173 Thos Church, moulder
175 Ed Armstrong, laborer
177 Robert Walker, laborer
179 H Little, grocer

Barton-st intersects

183 John Sheridan, laborer
185 Dan Tracy, teamster
187 Wm Hughes, carpenter
193 John R Hore, painter
195 John Maden, spinner
197 James Mines, moulder
199 James Dalton, laborer
201 John Baine, laborer
203 Mrs Mary Grace
205 A H Otto, wood carver
207 J Marshall, ropemaker
209 J Orr, yarn dresser
211 James Kenny, mail clerk
211½ Thos Irwin, watchman
213 John Connors, laborer

Murray-st intersects

225 J Zingsheim, cabinet manfr
227 Robert Gordon, clerk
229 Jacob Culp, wheelmaker
233 Peter O'Connor, teamster
G T R bridge

Strachan-st intersects

243 H Markle, ropemaker
245 Fred G Johnson, wheelwright
245½ Francis E King, ropemkr
247 Thos Kelly, shoemaker
249 P Croty, carpenter

Simcoe-st intersects

255 Jas Blake, grocer
257 Geo Askew, shoemaker
Vacant
— Nolan, laborer

Ferrie-st intersects

John M Ferguson, dyer
Vacant
John Wright, weaver

Picton and Macauley-sts intersect

Vacant lots

Wood-st intersects

Merrick-st, north side, from 55 James n to Bay

2 A F Forbes, ins agt
2 G A Young, ins agt
2 Walter Brown, ins agt
6 John Rowen, barber
8-12 Royal hotel
14 City Directory office
16 Vacant
18 Vacant
20-22 Johnson & Gilmore, auctioneers
24 Hunter & Hunter, actioneers
26 W H Zwick, collector
26 John H Young, architect
26 Jas A Harvey, printer
Chas Lawry, hide dealer
28 Woodbine saloon, J Gully
30 C F Rich, harnessmaker
32 Geo M Bailey, restaurant
34 Vacant
36 Henry Simon, cigarmaker
Gospel Hall
36 Hamilton Laundry
38 Vacant
38 Robertson & Henderson, commission

Macnab-st intersects

62 Jas Simpson

Park-st intersects

72 A G Miles, plumber
74 Wm Dodd, feather dyer
76 Hannaford Bros, plasterers
78 Vacant
80 Abner Fraser, bookkeeper
82 John Baillie, bookkeeper
84 Miss Sarah Snider
86 R A Allardice & Co, furniture
90 Vacant
92 A Galder, druggist
94 Vacant
96-98 Hurd & Roberts, marble works

Bay-st intersects

Merrick-st, south side

1-7 Billiard rooms
Market square

Macnab-st intersects

49 Thos Robinson, hotel
53 Flamboro house
57 Daniel Doyle, blacksmith
59 Thos Clohecy, harnessmkr
61 Mrs Nall
63 Mrs Samuel Milligan
65 George Vedder, painter
67 George Shoots, painter

Park-st intersects

71 Wm Murray, paper bag mkr
73 Miss Bridget Grimes, dressmaker
75 A C Foster, tailor
77 Vacant
79 Vacant
83-85 Alex Campbell, grocer
87 W F Farmer, watchmaker
89 A Calder, d.uggist

York-st intersects

Mill-st, north side, from 95 Caroline n, west to Hess

8 Vacant
20 Wm Coutts, laborer
14 Vacant
16 Richard Beckerson
18 Sam Walsh, tobacco roller

Hess-st intersects

Mill-st, south side

1 Robert Hawthorne, finisher
3 Joseph Warden, laborer
7 Wm H Childs, machinist
9 Wm H Connor, laborer
11 Vacant
13 Thos McHattie, engineer
15 Mrs John Dryland
17 Wm Butler, brakeman
19 Wm Laing, brakeman

Hess-st intersects

Mulberry-st, north side, from 159 James n to Caroline

6 M J Dingman, excise
16 E Wright, supt
18 J W Madigan, foreman
18½ Hiram Cleary, shoemaker
20 Peter Gordon, moulder
22 Mrs Duff
24 John Banrick, laborer
26 Francis Ouimette, shoemaker

Macnab-st intersects

30 P Hennessey, locksmith
32 Chas Jenkins, engineer
34 John Levique, shoemaker
38 John Slaughter
40 Mrs Patrick Gavin
44 John McConnell, caretaker

Park-st intersects

62 Edmund Lane, carpenter
64 Wm Marrott, carpenter
66 Francis Somerville, laborer
New gasometer
82 John W Childs, laborer
84 Vacant

Bay-st intersects

P Grant & Son's brewery

Railway-st intersects

Mulberry-st, south side

7 Mrs Alex Wright
9 Horace Ringrose, stovemounter
11 Mrs M J Cusick
13 Chas Bennett
15 Mrs John White
17 Frank Kavanagh
19 Alex Hendry, accountant
21 H Kite, com trav

Macnab-st intersects

25 Thos Meegan, moulder
33 John Cowturie
35 Thos Malone, confectioner
37 W J Taylor, inspector
39 S F Egan
41 Edward Kavanagh, laborer

Park st intersects

66-67 Hamilton Gas Light Co

Bay-st intersects

103 Wm Goodyer, malster

Railway-st intersects

Murray-st east, north side. from 228 James north to Wellington

7 John Hotrum, carpenter
9 George Littlewood, machinist
15 Geo Anderson, carpenter
17 Patrick Dillon, laborer

Hughson-st intersects

25 Samuel Holt, laborer
27 Wm Silver, manf
29 Wm Forsyth, tinsmith
31 J A Laroon, laborer
33 J Zingsheim, manfr
35 Isaiah Beer, builder

John-st intersects

Vacant lots

Catharine-st intersects

87 Jas Danley, brass founder
91 Arch Forster
93 Herbert Hall, fireman

Mary-st intersects

Mrs Ellen Harvey
Miss Mary Edwards
John Webb, bricklayer
Albert Old, bricklayer
A J Cox, cork cutter

Wellington-st intersects

Murray-st east, south side

10 Joseph Nelson, driver
Mrs Edward Andrews
16 Geo Hayness, bookkeeper

Hughson-st intersects

20 Geo Burton, engraver

John-st intersects

74 R J Day, inspector G T R
76 George Smith, laborer
80 Frank Holt
82 Mrs Wm Seelbeck, tailoress

Catharine, Mary and Ferguson-ave intersects

J Pett, sheepskins
Wm Niblock, teamster
Peter Austin, carpenter

Wellington-st intersects

Murray-st west, north side from 213 James north to Bay

12 H B Witton
16 Mrs Capt Edward Zealand

Macnab-st intersects

28 Wm Omand, machinist
30 Wm Fardy
32 Philip Peer, laborer
Primary school
42 J F Hazelton, U S Consul
44 H Lee, bookkeeper
" H A White, tinsmith
46 J G McIntyre, boilermaker
48 Robt Archibald, machinist
50 John Porteous

Bay-st intersects

Murray-st w, south side

1 D Williams, hotel
7 Mrs Emma Moore, dressmkr
9 Mrs John H Greer
11 Walter Urry, barber
13 Fred Haffer, traveler
15 Mrs Robert Hanning
23 Wm Yaldon, hotel

Macnab-st intersects

29 Vacant
41 Geo Moore, restaurant
45 Vacant

Park-st intersects

Napier-st, north side, from 43 Bay north, west to Locke

2-8 Vacant
10 Robt Woods, finisher
14 Poutien Filliatrault, tobacon't
16 Mrs Jas Rabitoy
18 Robt Edwards, tinsmith

20 Henry Bennett, foreman
22 Thos Freeborn, shoemaker
30 Mrs Thos Drew, tinsmith

Caroline-st intersects

48 Geo Stewart, teamster
50 Mrs David Tait
52 Vacant
54 I McMichael, whipmaker
54 W G Walton
58 John Edmonston, conductor

Hess-st intersects

John J Daly, grocer
74 Wm Elvin, traveler
76 Miss Mary Clement
78 Geo H Lees, merchant
80 Peter McBeth, contractor
82 Jas Thomson, moulder
88 Jas Young, bookkeeper

Queen-st intersects

112 Mrs Joseph Fletcher
114 Julius Breternitz, tailor
116 Thos Wilson, fireman
118 Sinclair McBeth, laborer
120 Alfred Hipkins, printer
122 Jas Turnbull, laborer
124 Geo Edmondson, butcher
126 John S Hobson, engineer

Ray-st intersects

150 John W Ronald, carpenter
152 G Hudson, marble polisher
154 Wm Dorning, carter
156 Miss Helena Gourlay
158 John Bayne, moulder
160 Jas Brennan, grocer
162 Mrs Douglas Lawrason
164 John Memory, machinist

Pearl-st intersects

172 Zion Sunday School
174 Mrs M Bauer
178 Mrs Harriet Hall
180 Mrs Gilbert Anderson
180 Mrs Sarah Drysdale

Locke-st intersects

Napier-st, south side

9 John McLeod, printer
11 Fire engine house
17 Mrs Martin Fitzpatrick
19 Arthur Strickland, carriage builder
21 Mark Pulling, salesman
23 John Dixon, carpenter
31 Wm S Sendall, carpenter
33 James Peason
35 James Reynolds, laborer
37 Thos Moylan, shoemaker

Caroline-st intersects

45 George Smith, shoemaker
47 James Steedman, machinist
53-55 James Baker
59 Thos Dixon
61 Mrs John Moore
63 James Thompson, ironworker
65 Jacob Smith, engineer
67 Thos Frazer, butcher
69 Thos Fraser, butcher

Hess-st intersects

71 H Fisher, machinist
73 John Easson, broommaker
75 James Weir, baker
77 Mrs King
79 Mrs Webber, dressmaker
89 Aaron Carr, messenger
91 Fred A Ashbaugh, traveler
93 J M Dingwall, fitter
95 John Lewis

Queen-st intersects

103 Robert Wilson, fireman
105 Wm Smith, laborer
107 Thos Cookson, machinist
111 Francis McCusker, dealer
113 Mrs Margaret McCallum
117 G Hilderbrandt, laborer
119 David F Houser, agent
121 Rev F Coleman
125 Walter Jones, laborer
127 John Cash, laborer
129 Mrs James Thornton
131 Wm Crawford, bricklayer
135 Vacant
137 Mrs Agnes Thurling
139 Andrew Keenon

Ray-st intersects

157 Joseph Faulknor, builder

Pearl and Little Wellington-sts intersect

173 H B Welsher, carpenter
175 Nathan Everton, laborer
179 Mrs John Haines
181 Mrs Mary Ward
183 Mrs Wm Debus
185 Mrs John Laurence

Little Peel aud Locke-sts intersect

Nelson-ave, north side, commences at Queen 's, and runs west to Locke

4 Irving Crossley, merchant
8 L C Smith, barrister
18 Joseph R Mead, manfr

Kent-st intersects

30 John R Hinds, accountant
38 David Newton, agent

Locke-st intersects

Nelson-ave, south side

7 Thos Quinn, storekeeper
19 John Rankin, teller

Kent-st intersects

31 James Bicknell, accountant
43 Wm McHaffie, com traveler

Locke-st intersects

Nelson-st, commences at Pearl north of George, and runs west to Locke

2 Fred S Morrison, bookkeeper
4 J Taylor, bookkeeper
6 Thos H Taylor

New-st, east side, from King w, to Main

Robert Neal, laborer
Wm Fletcher, laborer
Charles Beveridge, carpenter
Thos Alexander

New-st, west side

James Carroll, bricklayer

Nightingale-st, from 31 Steven to Wentworth

2 Wm Woodall, sen, builder
5 Louis McCombs, carpenter
6 John Mellon, builder
Thos Kerr, moulder
John Landers, laborer
Wm Weir

Wentworth-st intersects

Oak-st, from Locke south to Pearl

Geo Green, laborer

Ontario-st, from Concession to Markland, west to James

5 Henry Derby, accountant
6 Mrs John Wardlaw
7 John McEwen, moulder
8 Benj Fowler, laborer
9 Hugh McKellar, carpenter

Oxford-st, from York, between Queen and Locomotive

Wm Sayers
G E Tuckett & Son's warehouse

O'Reilly-st, north side, from west of Walnut to Cherry

1 Leo Blatz, tailor
3 Adam Bartman, tailor
5 Robt Magness, machinist
7 Wm Anderson, boot crimper

Walnut-st intersects

17 Thos Baker, baker
19 Jas Johnson, laborer
21 Joseph T Hartley, laborer
24 Thos Murray, contractor
25 Mrs Jas Robertson
29 Miss Ann Merryman
29 Michael Sullivan, melter

Cherry-st intersects

O'Reilly-st, south side

2 Thos Hilliard
4 Mrs Hamilton
6 Alex Fleck, painter
8 C W Simpson, carpenter
10 Jas Murphy, cigarmaker
12 Mrs Anson Mills

Walnut-st intersects

14 John Taylor, huckster
16 Mrs Richard Harper
18 Thos Hawkins
20 Patrick Brady, laborer
22 John Dwyer, laborer
26 Mrs Catharine O'Grady
28 Thos Curtis, tailor
32 Thos Taylor, teamster
34 C Spriggs, laborer
36 Geo Honeybourne, carpenter

Cherry-st intersects

Park-st north, east side, from 94 King w to Murray

Franklin house
10 Wm Fitzgerald, miller

Market-st intersects

28 Samuel Groves, blacksmith

York-st intersects

36 John Hislop, blacksmith

Merrick-st intersects

50 Jas Stewart & Co, warehouse
52 Geo Senn, foreman
54 Vacant
56 Robt Miller

Vine-st intersects

64 E J Townsend, florist
68 Mrs George Stull
70 Thos Parry, builder
72 Mrs Peter Patterson
74 E M Higgins, M D

Cannon-st intersects

84 Wm Ball, baker
86 Wm Coiley, lithographer
88 Stephen Parsons, foreman
90 Edward Baker, foreman
92 Wm Crawford, bridge ins
94 Robt Raw, jr, printer
96 Samuel McKitrick, laborer
98 Robt Young, brassfinisher
100 Thomas Evans, laborer

Mulberry-st intersects

St Mary's school
Roman Catholic Cathedral

Sheaffe-st intersects

125 Jas Wall, hatter
128 John Beaufort, carpenter
130 Miss Sarah Armstrong
132 Vacant
234 D McDuff, music teacher
136 Henry Vernon, manager W H Irwin & Co
138 St Joseph's Orphan Asylum

Colborne-st intersects

152 Chas Jamieson, operator
154 H A Wilkins, sculptor

Barton-st intersects

162 John Black, butcher
164 Vacant
168 John A McFarlane, laborer
170 John Edmunds, laborer

Murray-st intersects

Park-st n, west side

7 Wm H Kime, laborer
9 Dominion Carriage Factory
13 E T Richards, packer
15 Robert Long, carriage blacksmith
17 Henry Pierce, painter

Market-st intersects

21 J B Bagwell
29 David Cook, hotelkeeper
29½ James Garland, painter
31 Commercial Hotel

York-st intersects

33 Wm Crombie, barber
35 Wm Murray, paper bag manf

Merrick-st intersects

45 Mrs Robt Wm Blanney
47 J H Hogan
49 Vacant
51 Mrs H Harrison, boarding

53 Wm Webster, flour and feed
55 Wm Harris, baker

Vine-st intersects

57 Joseph Jeffery
61 J Riach, general dealer
63 Wm Edgar, carpenter
65 Wm Mullins, laborer
67 Henry Arland, shoemaker
69 Henry Bradford, laborer
73 Geo Brown
75 John Clark, butcher

Cannon-st intersects

77 George Steele, music teacher
79 Edward Wheaton, conductor
81 Mrs Mary Scully
83 David Kiah, mariner
87 Wm Curtis
89 Miss M L Bruce
91 Gas Works office
99 T Littlehales, manager gas works

Mulberry-st intersects

105 Mrs James Ivory
109 James Clark, stovemounter
111 Thos A Erly, agent
113 Wm Hudson, carpenter
119 Wm M Davey, laborer
121 Richard Coleman, moulder
123 Mrs Daniel Gilmore
125 Angus Mundy, grocer

Sheaffe-st intersects

129 John Allan, machinist
131 Joseph Midwinter, machinist
133 Francis Sheppard, customs
133½ George Robinson, bandmaster
135 Mrs Morton Rowe
135½ Arthur Robertson, bookkeeper
137 George Mansfield, engineer
139 Henry Priestland
141 Vacant
143 Mrs Edward Boyle
145 J H Young, architect

Colborne-st intersects

147 George Sharp, builder
153 J Midwinter, carpenter
155 James Stiff, accountant
157 Vacant
159 Vacant
161 Vacant

Barton-st intersects

171 James Egan, traveler
173 Wm Hyndman, blacksmith
179 Frank O'Callanhan, inspector

Murray-st intersects

Park-st s, east side, from 69 King w to Concession

1-5 Vacant
7 Geo Boardman
9 Mrs John Corey
9½ F J Leckenby, traveler
11 A J Lawson, engineer
13 Louis Edworthy, patternmkr
17 Chas F Abraham, merchant

Main-st intersects

29 Wm Evans, foreman
31 Geo Hughes, sawyer
33 Mrs Walter Welsh
35 Jas Hirst
37 Wm Crombie, cutter
39 David Marshall, mason
41 Wm Preston, laborer
43 Calvin Campbell, cook

Jackson-st intersects

Vacant lots

Hunter aud Concession-sts intersect

Park-st s, west side

2 Z Pattison, confectioner
6 H G Cooper & Co, coach factory
8 Edwin A Gaviller, M D
10 John Bowes, dentist
12 Mrs M W Brown
14 L Garland, druggist
16 F Armstrong, station agent G T R

Main-st intersects

Vacant lots

Jackson-st intersects

Reformed Episcopal Church

Hunter-st intersects

Central school

Bold & Duke-sts intersect

Samuel Briggs, manf
Geo F Glassco, furrier

Robinson-st intersects

Skating rink
Vacant

Hannah-st intersects

102 Robt Wallace, clerk
104 Somer Scott
106 J V Teetzel, barrister

Herkimer-st intersects

Henry Bunbury
W L Smart, barrister

Pearl-st n, east side, from 264 King w to York

14 Wm Newson, trunk maker
16 Jas Watson, moulder
18 Wm Brown, tailor
20 Jas H Mann, laborer

Napier-st intersects

38 Mrs John Rush
40 Jas P Gay, clerk
42 Samuel Crawford, grocer
Primary school

Peter-st intersects

52 W H Cliffe, printer
54 F J Greenway, ornamenter
56 Adam Turnbull, machinist
58 A W Sievert, joiner

Florence-st intersects

68 Jas Greenley, carpenter

York-st intersects

Pearl-st n, west side

Jas Bremner, grocer
5 Jacob Hills, agent
7 Thos Semmens, painter

Little Market-st commences

17 Jas Thornton, switchman
r " Mrs H Fitzpatrick
21 Wm J Milligan, baker
23 Wm Payne, engineer
25 Thos G Furnivall, tailor

Napier-st intersects

Zion Tabernacle
41 Geo Tristam, clerk
41½ Jas Gould, stone cutter
43 John Crawford, moulder

Peter-st intersects

51 Jas Heath, blacksmith
53 John T Jones, laborer
55 H Stokes
57 Wm Stewart, laborer
59 Jas Smith, carpenter
61 Wm Mitchell, mason

Florence-st intersects

65 Alex Barron, grocer
67 Alex Hendrie, foreman
69 Walter Chapman, moulder
71 Erskine Presbyterian Church
75 Jas Russell, stonecutter
77 Dennis Sullivan, laborer
79 Mrs Wm Lynd
r " Thos Fulton, laborer
83 Patrick Gleason

York-st intersects

Pearl-st south, east side, from 241 King w to Hunter

George-st intersects

17 John Lennox, traveler
19 Duncan Robertson, machinist
23 Vacant
25 John Cox, spice manf
29 John Hover, boilermkr
35 Nathan Steanberg, dealer

Main-st intersects

41 W J Blackbrough, carpenter

Jackson-st intersects

Geo P Dunn, laborer
Eli Allins, whitewasher
65 John Lutz, teamster

Canada-st intersects

Vacant lots

Hunter-st intersects

Pearl-st, south, west side

6 Wm Higgins, laborer

8 Jas Heath, clerk

George-st intersects

14 A Polucco, coffin maker
16 E Macpherson, cutter
16½ Mrs Samuel Kirkendall,
18 M Obermeyer, pianomaker
20 Wm Hull, traveler

Nelson and Main-sts intersect

40 Jas Harrison, hackman
44 M W Attwood, watchmaker

Jackson-st intersects

46 Wm T Fell, machinist
48 Joseph Sheperley, potter
52 Vincent Edwards, baker
54 John W Smith, foreman
56 John T Gilbert, machinist

Canada-st intersects

66 Geo Fleck, laborer

Hunter-st intersects

L D McAllister, agent

Bold-st intersects

Peter-st, n side, from 53 Hess n to Locke

Queen-st intersects

26 Chas Rieger, bartender
28 G Montgomery, pedler
30 Wm Thompson, clerk
32 Wm Prince, laborer
34 Henry Kent, clerk
36 J H Murray, tobacco dealer
40 C W Thomson, carpenter
42 Jas Belling, jeweler
44 Henry Harvey, plumber
46 Robert Burns, heater
48 J W Halloran, grocer

Ray-st intersects

58 Wm Dean, shoemaker
62 Geo Mills, shipper
64 Mrs Mary Jackson
68 Jas Branston, bricklayer
72 Mrs Janet Snodgrass
74 Mrs Henry Bailey

Pearl-st intersects

82 Dennis Reardon, carpenter
84 Alex Martin, laborer
86 John Robertson, engineer
88 Alex McLean, clerk

Locke-st intersects

Peter-st, south side

7 Seth J Whitehead, supt
9 Joseph Herald, pianomaker
Dunlop & Feast, sewing machine mfrs

Queen-st intersects

27 Jas Smith, laborer
29 Mrs Christina Da[illegible]
31 Charles Carter, laborer
33 Robert Read, machinist
35 Wm Dossett, polisher
37 Arthur Buggy, tobacco roller
39 Fred Foyster, tobacconist
41 Stephen Balmer, laborer
43 James Smith, moulder
45 Henry Knight, car repairer
47 Mrs C Bailey
53 Henry Cook, baker

Ray-st intersects

59 Vacant
61 Mrs Samuel Burchill

Pearl-st intersects

71 Wm Ryan, shoemaker
r 71 Alfred Boult, fitter
73 Andrew Linklater
75 Mrs John Andrews
79 James McKenna, engineer
81 Alex McKerlie, traveler
83 Mrs John Duffy
85 Harry Bawden, hotel

Picton-st e, north side, from 314 James north, to Wellington

21 J C Malcolmson, foreman

Hughson-st intersects

31 Kennedy Connor, shoemaker
33 Andrew Kennedy, laborer
35 Stephen Sayley, laborer
37 Andrew Richardson, checker

John-st intersects

Vacant lots

Catharine and Mary-sts intersect

92 Peter Surl, laborer
94 Vacant
96 Joseph Jackson, laborer
102 John Kitton, laborer
104 Michael Roach, laborer
114 John Bayley, blacksmith
116 Wm Lindsay, laborer

Ferguson-ave intersects

124 Francis Maxwell, blacksmith
126 Wm Culm, laborer
128 Wm Quinlan, laborer
130 Thos Lucas, farmer
132 John Kennedy, laborer
134 John Gray, laborer
136 Wm Phelps, laborer
138 Joseph Humphreys, laborer
140 Martin O'Grady, laborer
142 S Topp, engineer
144 Richard Mantle, laborer
146 A G Wragg, laborer

Wellington-st intersects

Picton-st e, south side

10 James Burnet, laborer
14 James Vallance, carpenter
20 Luke Kirkham, carder

Hughson-st intersects

34 A Bloomer, laborer
36 John Cahill, blacksmith
38 Wm Duston, weaver

John & Catharine-sts intersect

James Seddon, dyer

Mary-st intersects

89 Vacant
91 Henry Alexander, sawyer
93 John Jackson, laborer
95 T W Jutton, carpenter
97 Edward Bodden, painter
99 Robert Andrew, spinner
101 Joseph Poynton, packer
103 Michael Moran, laborer

Ferguson-ave intersects

123 Wm Ferguson, fitter
125 Thos Lucas, laborer
127 Mrs Edwd Forster, laundress
129 Ed Day, laborer
133 John Taylor, laborer
135 Charles Payne, painter
139 A J Anthony, plasterer
143 George King

Wellington-st intersects

Picton-st w, north side, from 307 James n to Bay

6 Robt Campbell, carpenter
10 George Watson, engineer
12 Peter Callaghan, laborer

Macnab-st intersects

26 Mrs Ann Murphy
32 Adam Traub, glassblower
34 Wm Evans, carpenter
42 Alex McCallum, moulder
44 John Reid, glassblower

Bay-st intersects

Bastien's Boat House

Picton-st w, south side

3 Michael Bracken, bricklayer
5 Thos Balch, fitter
7 Edward Brown, mariner
r " Michael Burke
9 Stephen Smith, laborer
11 Cyrus Weaver, laborer
13 Edward Hardy, laborer

Macnab-st intersects

35 Geo C Morrison, machinist
37 Joseph Ward, laborer
39 Mrs Jas Robinson, laundress
43 Daniel J Peace, tobacconist

Bay-st intersects

Pine-st, north side, from Locke s to Cricket Ground

Jas Lavis, carpenter
J Bertram, tobacconist

Pine-st, south side

11 Albert Peart, machinist
Chas Robinson, brickmkr
John Harrison

Poulette-st, east side, from end of Main e to Hunter

1 Wm Weller, potter
3 Chas Mitchenor, laborer

Poulette-st, west side

2 Ernest Piesel, laborer
4 Alex Holmes, painter
6 E Belleville, laborer
8 John Milligan, driller
10 John Symington, laborer

Queen-st n, east side, from 212 King w to Stuart

8 Alexander Wingfield, customs
10 John Malcomson, carpenter
12 Henry Morris, cutter
Market-st intersects
32 Thos K Foster, tailor
34 John Clifford, machinist
Napier-st intersects
Dunlop & Feast, sewing machines
Peter-st intersects
Jas Skimn, foundry
York-st intersects
100 Mrs Col McGivern
102 Stephen Jenkins, machinist
104 Edwin Griffiths, laborer
106 Mrs John Brown
108 Patrick McCabe, laborer
110 Chas Rogers, laborer
112 John Carroll, engineer
114 George Kemp, tinsmith
116 John Crooks, laborer
118 Wm Tribbeck, packer
120 Wm Collins, laborer
122 Joseph Wilson, pork dealer
122½ Vacant
124 Robt Jarrett, engineer
r " Thos Smith, brakeman
126 Thos Peden, baggageman
126½ Wm Mayo, fireman
128 Michael Guerin, laborer
130 Chas Littlejohn, inspector
132 Thos J Sullivan, laborer
134 Henry Owen
Barton-st intersects
Hamilton Forging Co
146 John Collins, culler
Stuart-st intersects

Queen-st n, west side

9 Wm Amor, clerk
Market-st intersects
17 John R Mackay, harness
19 Wm J Feaver, bartender
21 W Carlyon, blacksmith
23 Thos Joyce, tobacco roller
25 Peter Bayne, carpenter
27 John Malcolmson, carpenter
29 Thos Johnson, marble cutter
31 John Kennedy, carpenter
33 J H Faulkner, mason
35-7 Andrew Gage, butcher
Napier-st intersects
41-43 Greening's wire mill
45 Jas Alexander, carpenter
47 Mrs Agnes Allen
Peter-st intersects
57 Jas Skimin, founder
59 Chas Herald, manager
61 Mrs Wm Herald
63 S Greening, wire manfr
67 David Ross
69 Geo Anderson, carpenter
York-st intersects
West Lawn
Greig-st intersects
119 John Greig, bookseller
121 W Murray, harnessmaker
123 Wm D Curry, engineer
125 W Vandeburgh, baggageman
127 John Sinker, laborer
129 L Pollard, blacksmith
131 Thos Higham, blacksmith
133 Vacant
Barton-st intersects
Rolling mills
Stuart-st intersects

Queen-st s, east side, from 207 King w to Mountain

All Saints Church
M A Overend
1½ Mrs M Taylor
1½ Walter Worril, polisher
3 Jas Amor
r " Robert Hill, cabinetmaker
5 Wm Sharp, assessor
George and Main-sts intersect
29 — Davey, laborer
31 Vacant
33 Wm Myers, tobacco roller
35 Chas Stoneman, stonecutter
Jackson-st intersects
37 T Mitchell, merchant
43 Chas Krause, bucklemaker
45 Chas Woolcott, engineer
47 John McKenna
Hunter-st intersects
57 R J Faulknor, bricklayer
59 Wm Dowrie
61 David Dowrie, contractor
Bold, Duke aud Robinson-sts intersect
127 Thos C Searles, turner
129 John Sutton, upholsterer
Hannah-st intersects
Wm Murray, bookkeeper
Herkimer-st intersects
Wm Lord, dairy
Asylum engine house
Markland-st intersects
Thos Cassells, coachman
Joseph Pearce, carpenter
Concession-st intersects
A A Anderson, H & D S R
Andrew Patton
J H Farmer, photographer
H Williams, foundryman
J M Williams, county regist'r
Henry Boothby, engraver

Queen-st s, west side

Private grounds
George-st intersects
12 Mrs John Ferrie
Wm G Dunn, manfr
Main-st intersects
24 Geo W Complin, bookkeeper
26 Thos May, laborer
28 Vacant
30 Vacant
32 G T Kent, city foreman
Jackson-st intersects
34 V E Fuller, barrister
42 Miss Mills
Canada-st commences
46 David Bowman, barrister
48 Thos Shadbolt, cabinetmkr
54 T H Gilmore, cabinetmaker
Hunter-st intersects
56 P Costello, baker
Vacant lots
Bold-st intersects
64 Mrs Thos S Allan
OFFICE
66 Ross Wilson, traveler
68 Charles J Dixon, clerk
70 J B Maclean, cabinetmaker
72 J G Kelk, paper bag manfr
74 John Langford, carpenter
76 Hugh McLean, baker
78 Wm Bateman, baker
Duke st interects
80 G B Izzard, traveler
82 Vacant
84 Daniel Glover, bricklayer
88 Richard Tomilson, clerk
90 Wm Barber, gardener
93 W Greenhill, harnessmaker
94 Wm Robertson, salesman
Robinson-st intersects
Low McAdams, laborer
Rich Avis, laborer
Hannah-st, Nelsou-ave and Herkimer-st intersect
Vacant lots
Markland-st intersects
A Theal, agent

Concession-st intersects

Wm McFarlane, teamster

Railway-st, east side, from 38 Cannon w, north to Barton

10 Fred Macdonald, moulder
12 Robert Bryce
14 Thos Elwell, laborer
16 Patrick Lawlor, carter
18 Edward T Sullivan, cooper
20 John Sutherland, brakeman
28 Geo Mathieson, wool sorter
30 Joseph Kelly, shoemaker
32 Samuel Astle, machinist

Mulberry-st intersects

Railway-st, west side

13 John Kavanagh, watchman
15 Luke Mooney, laborer
17 Rice Carson, mason
19 Wm Ibbetson, tailor
21 Wm Ibbetson, painter
23 James Gartland, laborer
25 Wm, Smith, laborer
29 John Doyle, laborer
31 Wm Vint, tobaccoworker
33 John M Brown, machinist
35 John Morton, shipper
37 John W Coffee, lather

Mulberry-st intersects

Ray-st n, east side, from 234 King w to York

Private grounds

Market-st intersects

12 Wm Keays, machinist
14 James O'Lachlan, baker
16 Vacant
18 Mrs George Fox
20 Capt L B Barr
22 Mrs E Beck

Napier-st intersects

26 Mrs M Metcalf, grocer
28 Mrs I Parkinson
32 Chas H Sayers, manfr
34 Charles Swinton, teamster
40 Franklin Westphall, laborer
42 James Mills, laborer
46 Rowland Hill, dealer
48 James Branston, bricklayer
50 Henry Cook, baker

Peter-st intersects

50 James Holland, grocer
52 Wm Garner, dealer
52 Wm Royal, carriagemaker
54 Joseph Marshall, carpenter
56 Wm Swinton, carpenter
58 David Scarlet
" Samuel Gariety, customs
60 Thos Garrow
62 Mrs J Laskie
64 Wm Morris, patternmaker
66 Mrs James Smith
68 John Duffy, hatter
70 Patrick Duffy, blacksmith
72 Henry Mundy, machinist

York-st intersects

Ray-st n, west side

Loretto Convent

Napier-st intersects

33 Thos King, mason
35 R J Hope, printer
37 Vacant
37½ John Jinks, heater
39 George Sallaway, operator
41 Wm Boylan, laborer
43 Jas Owen, plater
45 Jas Thomas, stonecutter
47 Luke Donlay, cabinetmaker
49 Jas Owen, laborer

Peter-st intersects

53 Joseph Fletcher, shoemaker
55 Vacant
57 Henry Phillips, shoemaker
59 Henry Schaefer, agent
61 M McLaughlin, blacksmith
63 B J McCowell, baggageman

Florence-st intersects

71 Wm Mathieson, moulder
75 Henry Mullen, carpenter

York st intersects

Ray-st s, east side, from 217 King w to Hunter

49 John Wilson, tinsmith
51 Jas Bardwell, machinist
Canada-st intersects
63 John Springate, laborer
65 John Elwell, moulder
67 Mrs Wm Fagan
Hunter-st intersects
Wm Scott, cutter

Ray-st s, west side

6 T B Griffith, ticket agent
8 R Æ Kennedy
14 Robert B Ferrie
George-st intersects
16 S F Ross, dep col in rev
20 Robert Chisholm, builder
Main-st intersects
34 Robt Bible
36 Robt Dow, plasterer
40 Hugh Hunter, fitter
42 Chas Burns, laborer
Jackson-st intersects
44 John Schwinger, baker
48 Robt Reinholt, presser
50 Vacant
56 Wm Clayton, laborer
60 Jas Munroe
Canada-st intersects
66 Jas Lowrie, laborer
68 Thos Brooks, laborer
70 Mrs Margaret Nichol
72 Wm H Irwin, tinsmith
74 Wm Bridgewood, laborer
Hunter-st intersects
86 Vacant
88 Charles Bagot, traveler
Bold-st intersects
Philip Veidenheimer

Rebecca-st, north side, from 62 James n to Wellington

8-10 J Harvey & Co, wool dealers

12 Owen Nolan, livery
Hughson-st intersects
26 Robert Murray, plater
28 Wm Waldhoff, hay dealer
40 Wesley Church lecture room
John-st intersects
64-68 Reid & Barr manfr Co
70 Geo Sillett, cooper
Mrs Wm Murphy
Catharine-st intersects
82 Wm Gordon, cooper
84 Mrs Harrison, boarding
86 Wm Barringer
88 Wilson Barr, clerk
90 Israel Todd, whitewasher
" John Anderson, waiter
92 Wm Gilmore, shoemaker
98 Henry Hill, butcher
Mary-st intersects
100-2 D Sutherland, grocer
104 T J Carroll, jeweler
108 Harry Clayton, lithographer
112 Robert Lucas, machinist
114 Fred Domville
116 D B Smith, tailor
118 Robert Wilson, shoemaker
120 A Winckler, cooper
122 Wm Gugel, shoemaker
124 James Robertson, moulder
126 Bernhardt Schelling, machin't
128 John McVittie, cooper
130 John Chapman, laborer
136 Vacant
138 Wm Clark, packer
140 John Nowlan, laborer
142 Mrs Thos Darlington
142 Robert Leslie, fruiterer
144 Samuel Maddocks, shoemkr
146 Edward James, laborer
Ferguson-ave intersects
148 Joseph Horton, rag dealer
150 Mrs Henry Hewitt
150½ Henry Cowing, machinist
152 Henry Campbell, porter
152½ Arthur Cross tea dealer
154 Mrs J Smith
156 Chas Wilkes, laborer

158 Robert Pringle, bookkeeper
160 James Sherman
162 Wm Burrows, tailor
164 Mrs Geo Glass

Cathcart-st intersects

166 Chas Mason, gardener
170 Thos Chappell, butcher
172 Mrs H Pettigrew, dressmkr
174 John Basquel, tobacco roller
176 James Miller, laborer
178 Edward Peeler, painter

Rebecca-st, south side

1 Reliance Hall, I O G T
" J B Smith, teacher
" John Hendry, patent agent
3 Vacant
5 Vacant
7 Vacant
9 Vacant
11 R H Lefevre, weaver
13 Henry Fell, fireman
15 George Catchpole, umbrellas
17 W H Howard, tailor

Hughson-st intersects

27 Dr Lafferty
29 Gentral Iron Works
33 Philip Martin, sr
35 O Nowlan, livery keeper
37 Mrs A E Hamilton
39 John H Tilly, clerk

John-st intersects

61 George Smith, fancy dealer
63 James Roman, broommaker
65 S Kidd, fruiterer

Catharine-st intersects

73-75 Vacant
83 Miss Louisa Schaffer
85 Mrs Susan Smith
87 Fred Magill, laborer
89 E Nicholson, hide dealer
91 Mrs Thomas Richardson

Mary-st intersects

97 Wm Smye, collarmaker
101 Alex McDonald, traveler
103 Mrs Mary Fenton
105 Edward Lavis, carpenter
107 Mrs James Reid
109 L H Willard, machinist
111 T Boggess, broker
113 Mrs John Addison
115 Robert McHaffie, traveler
115½ M Williams, harnessmaker
117 James Shearer, joiner
119 George Combes, bricklayer
121 Wm McGibbon, baker
123 Thos Amey, carpenter
125 Thos Guthrie, poultry dealer
127 Mrs John Tramskoskee
127 Stephen Baker, laborer
129 Mrs Rebecca Burshaw
131 Albert Ryan, shoemaker
133 Wm Godfrey, baggageman
135 J D McNire, cigarmaker
137 John Cambden, butcher

Ferguson-ave intersects

Lumber yard
Pork factory
177 Wm Nelson, lumber measurer
179 Geo King, painter

Wellington-st intersects

Robert-st e, north side, from James n to East ave

7 Mrs O G Westbrook
9 Jas Austin, blacksmith
17 C B Snow, manfr

Hughson-st intersects

35 Wm Givin, accountant
37 Mrs Josiah Blanchard
39 Mrs Mary Halson
41 Philip Morris, grocer

John-st intersects

45 Mrs M Ledgerwood
47 Chas Kavanagh, laborer
49 Jas Malcolmson, sailor
51 Christian Schuler, whipmkr
53 John Traynor, tailor
57 Henry Smith, tinsmith
59 Thos S Dalton, boat builder
61 J Hurrell, printer
63 Samuel Kemp, com traveler
69 Joseph Lampman, foreman

Catharine-st intersects

73 Walter Crofton, moulder
75 Geo Brock, soda water manf
77 Vacant
79 Vacant
85 Thos Barrett, laborer

Mary-st intersects

89 Jas Johnston, machinist
91 Jas Mitchell, teamster
93 J S Wheeler, carpenter
95 Wm Robins, tailor
97 Geo Jackson, salesman

Elgin-st intersects

109 David White

Ferguson-ave and Cathcart-sts intersect

135 Michael Swales, carpenter
137 W C Toye, clerk
139 John O'Grady, moulder

Wellington-st intersects

141 J McMeekin, agent
143 Mrs R Reid
145 Albert Darche, conductor
147 Richard Hunt, moulder

West-ave intersects

167 John Kellner, tailor

Victoria-ave intersects

Robert-st e, south side

Drill Shed

Hughson-st intersects

Private grounds

John-st intersects

50 Mrs Sarah Lockwood
52 Mrs Wm Barrett
54 John Dundon
56 Jas Talbot
58 Joseph Johnston, tinsmith
58½ Mrs Maria Kelly
60 Vacant
62 C Osborne, machinist
64 Mrs John Duggan
66 Geo Williams, laborer

Catharine-st intersects

Moore's foundry
80 C E Newbery, tanner

Mary-st intersects

90 Jas Gibbons, gardener
92 Miss Mary Servos
94 Chas Fursdon, moulder

Elgin-st intersects

H & N W Sheds

Ferguson-ave intersects

134 Jas Sharples
136 Calvin Lyons, agent

Cathcart-st intersects

138 Jas Proctor, boilermaker
140 Thos Woodman, clerk

Wellington-st intersects

Vacant lots
146 Wm Miller, switchman
S R Scott, grocer

West-ave intersects

176 Arch Martin, moulder
178 Jas O'Grady, moulder
182 Thos Laing, carpenter
184 Samuel Scott, hotel

Victoria-ave intersects

186 Vacant
188 Timothy Hanley, laborer
190 Andrew McLellan, laborer
192 Horace Green, millwright
194 Oliver Christopher, laborer
196 H E Smith, laborer
198 Nelson Clark, laborer
200 Jas Wedge, carter
204 Joseph Brown, stonemason

East-ave intersects

Robert-st w, from Locke to Garth, between Hunter and Bold

1 Benj Brown, laborer
3 Edward Wild, laborer
4 A Walters, laborer

Robinson-st, north side, from James s west to limits

Private grounds

Macnab-st intersects

John Harvey, merchant
J M Henderson, merchant

Park-st intersects

Vacant lots

Bay-st intersects

36 Wm J Kingdon, printer
38 Jas Malcolmson, accountant
40 M Kartzmark, blacksmith
42 Patrick McGrath, laborer
44 Edw Burdett, brushmaker
44½ Robt Muntz, laborer
46 John Driscoll, laborer
48 Thos Copeland, carpenter
50 Robt S Odell, machinist

Caroline-st intersects

52 Robert Burns, laborer
54 Daniel McMahon, laborer
56 Thos Connors, carpenter
58 Jas Armstrong, plumber
62 Joseph Lambert, teamster
64 John J Lambert, clerk
66 Mrs Catharine Schrerstein

Hess and Queen-sts intersect

Mrs Henry Munro
John M Painter
John Carr, clerk
Fred L Whately, clerk
Alfred Hannaford, plasterer
Jas Fletcher, jeweler
Mark L Tew
G C Carlson, tailor
Cricket grounds

Locke-st intersects

Michael Fanning, grocer
Wm Rolph
P A Wynn, shoemaker
Geo Reynolds, butcher
Robert Chanter, laborer
Thos Wilson, laborer
Wm Smith, dyer
Matthew McGee, carpenter
Mrs J Hempstock
George Porter, machinist
Owen McMenemy, pedler
Jas Napier, machinist
Thos Wyatt, laborer
Robert Scott, laborer

Garth-st intersects

Robinson-st, south side

1 Mrs W Mundie
3 Geo S Papps, barrister
5 Wm Osborne, founder

Macnab-st intersects

Vacant

Park-st intersects

Curling rink
29 Geo M Bagwell, printer
31 John A Beattie, clerk

Bay-st intersects

39 Wm Lunt, blacksmith
41 Robert Murray, shoemaker
43 Richard Ferguson, tailor
45 Mrs Thos Jones
47 Arthur H McKeown, tin smith
49 Matthew Armstrong, clerk

Caroline-st intersects

51 Peter Therrier, shoemaker
53 Wm Burrows, carpenter
55 Edward Thomas, bricklayer
57 Andrew Cox
59 Vacant
61 Jas McKeown, carriage mkr
63 Francis Morris, shoemaker

Hess-st intersects

Andrew Robb, engineer
73 Richard Tope, mason
75 Chas Emboden, laborer

Queen-st intersects

Edwin Layland
Wm Porter, laborer
Henry Bustin, cabinetmkr
Vacant lots
H Kleinsteiber, cabinet mkr

Locke-st intersects

W Blaisdell, grocer
Mrs Mary Cornell, laundress
Wm Max, carpenter
Levi Russ, rag gatherer
Jas Newlands, machinist
Mrs John Kearney

James Fielding, blacksmith
109 John Hummell, bricklayer
111 Chas Mundt, laborer
113 Henry Eland, barber
115 Robt Crowe, machinist
115 John Rackley, laborer
115 James Vent, carpenter
117 Wm Bell, machinist
121 Wm S Russell, teamster

Garth-st intersects

St. Mary's Lane, from end of Locke n to Inchbury

D Davidson, gardener
Matthew Redden, laborer

Sheaffe-st, north side, from St. Mary's Cathedral, Park n, west to Caroline

Dewey's ice house

Park-st intersects

16 Joseph Heitzman, cigarmkr
18 John Pinch, fitter
20 Thos B Spence, mariner
22 Rev Henry Langton
24 Alfred S Peene, contractor
26 Thomas Wavell, accountant
28 D J O'Brien, music teacher

Bay-st intersects

34 Mrs John Spanton
36 Samuel Spencer, laborer
38 James Melody, laborer
40 George Friday, laborer
42 Wm Boyd, fireman

Sheaffe-st, south side

1 John McKenzie, wood dealr
3 David McLeod, moulder
St. Mary's Cathedral

Park-st intersects

17 Louis Cook, moulder
10 Wm Gray, stonemason
21 Jacob Morden, laborer
25 Bishop's Palace
27 Albert Campbell, moulder
29 Mrs C Reardon
31 John Mitchell, shoemaker
33 John Latremouille, confr
35 Wm Williamson, teamster
37 David Nutley, laborer
39 Patrick McCarthy, laborer

Bay-st intersects

41 T G Gully, soda water manf
47 Vacant
49 Thos Cook, fireman
51 Chas Slaght, teamster
53 Andrew Coleman, teamster
55 Alex Donald, bottler

Simcoe-st e, north side, from 276 James n to Wellington

5 David Terryberry
7 James Hendrican, moulder
9 John McDonald, inspector

Hughson-st intersects

25 Mrs David Grant
27 Daniel Butler, carpenter
29 Patrick Cosgrove, laborer
31 John W Watson, car checker
33 Maurice Cummings, laborer
Simcoe-st Church
Mrs John McLean
Jas Turner, laborer
71 Hugh Meadows, spinner

Mary-st intersects

83 R Partridge, engineer
85 R Fish, spinner
87 John Dowd, laborer
86 John Kinsella, laborer
91 Richard Turner
95 Jas Bigley, fireman
99 John Webb, carpenter
101 Fred Hoskins, fireman
103 Thos Briggs, laborer
105 Isaac Swallow, mason
107 John Holmes, pensioner
107½ Joseph Lappan, brakeman
109 Thos Fursdon, laborer
113 M Quinlan, trackman

Ferguson-ave intersects

119 Peter Midgley, laborer
121 Jas McCollum, laborer
125 Wm Lyones, laborer
129 Thos S Lewis, machinist

131 Peter Clark, laborer

Wellington-st intersects

Simcoe-st e, south side

2 Hugh Torrance, grocer
8 Wm Gillespie, patternmaker
10 Thos Allan, machinist
12 Charles Ducklos, laborer
14 H F Dummer, fireman
16 Vacant
18 Francis Smith, moulder

Hughson-st intersects

18½ Arthur Lambert, watchman
18 Wm Julian, laborer
22 Wm Ferguson, cigarmaker
24 David Hardy, moulder
28 Henry Allen, boilermaker
30 John Fletcher, machinist
32 Patrick Wolfe, watchman
34 Patrick Hanley, bricklayer

John-st intersects

Vacant lots

Catharine and Mary-sts intersect

84 Michael Canary, laborer
86 John McGinley, laborer
88 Wm Herbert, laborer
90 Wm Inglis, laborer
92 Samuel Cook, carpenter
94 Wm Porter, laborer
96 Ed Hudson, moulder
100 Andrew Larkin, weaver
102 Jas Madigan, laborer
102 Robert Batty, moulder
106 J J Alliss, laborer
106½ A E Hunt, stovemounter
108 Peter Doherty, mason

Ferguson-ave intersects

114 Daniel Newington, gunsmith

Wellington-st intersects

Simcoe-st w, n side, from 261 James n to Bay

Ontario Cotton Mills Co

Macnab & Bay-sts intersect

Simcoe-st w, south side

13 Stephen O'Toole, laborer
15 David Jackson, laborer
17 David McIlroy, machinist
19 Wm Kirkpatrick, carpenter
21 Jas Rake, shoemaker
23 John Flockton, fireman
25 Morse Enwright, laborer
27 Wm Daly, laborer
29 Jas Campaign, laborer

Bay-st intersects

Smith-ave, e side, from Barton to Cannon, between Emerald and Wentworth

Matthew Lowery, carpenter
Phenix Legault, shoemaker
Vacant
Sydney Forster, wood turner
Steven Land, machinist
George Wild, gardener

Smith-ave, west side

B Cox, shoemaker
Vacant

Sophia-st n, east side, from 319 York

12 James B Mills, traveler
14 Robt Britton, machinsst
16 Ernest G Rumple, cabntmkr
18 Isaac Tufford, carter
Ontario Planing Mill

Florence-st intersects

Sophia-st n, west side

13 John Stevens, painter
15 Samuel Fenton, shipper
17 Wm Evans, marble cutter
19 Richard Langlois, carpenter

Tom-st intersects

Private grounds

Florence-st intersects

Sophia-st s, from 293 King w, north to Palace Grounds

3 Wm Larmer, brickmaker
5 Edw Dowler, boilermkr
7 John Ceaser, laborer
9 Frank Blackwith, laborer

13 Michael Hayes, carter

South-st, from Locke to Garth

James Carter, mason
Peter Crerar, carpenter
John Mackintosh, machinist
George Simpkins, painter
Thos Wilson, carpenter

South-st e, from 199 Wellington n, east to Wentworth

1 Chas Simons, laborer
2 Miss E Murray
Victoria-ave intersects
20 Philip Langley, watchman
21 Robert McVvey, laborer
22 Gibson Syme, laborer
23 Edward Steer, butcher
24 John H Freed, traveler
28 Joseph Erwood, carter
East-ave intersects
Emerald-st intersects
Campbell Leckie, machinist
Wentworth-st intersects

Spring-st, east side, from 183 King e, south to Hunter

1 Pilgrim Bros, soda water mfs
Main-st intersects
7 L P Tuttle, agent
9 James Lyons, mariner
11 Mrs Harriet Armitage
13 Wm Jarvis, hackman
15 Fred Moore, bricklayer
17 Chas Davidson, finisher
19 Frank England, barber
Jackson-st intersects
21 Hedley Mason, hatter
23 H D Baker, whip manfr
25 Jas A. Harvey, printer
27 Vacant
33 Stuart Maitland, painter
35 John North, teamster
37 Vacant
Hunter-st intersects

Spring-st, west side

2 Chas Mills, grocer
6 John H Fell, laborer
8 Robert Ahern, polisher
Jackson-sts intersects
22 Alex Campbell, ins agent
24 Jos Livernois, fruit dealer
26 Wm McClelland, spice manf
28 Mark King, bricklayer
Hunter-st intersects

Steven-st, east side, from 286 King east to Cannon

6 Wm Harris, messenger
8 E Jeffrey, plasterer
12 John Anders, brushmaker
King Wm-st intersects
14 Mrs Joseph Hunter
16 Mrs E Smith
24 Benj Parrott, carter
Nightingale-st intersects
34 Thos Taylor, carpenter
36 James Page
Wilson-st intersects
46 George Carr, plater
48 Peter Patterson, carpenter
50 R Henderson, carpenter
52 Chas Cripps, bricklayer
54 Wm Bevis, machinist
56 Robert Mellon, bricklayer
58 Chris Tilbury, butcher
60 James Ditty, tinsmith
64 John Gee, laborer
66 L Snowden, cabinet maker
68 Henry Ing, watchmaker
Cannon-st intersects
9 J G Rayner

Steven-st, west side

King Wm-st intersects
13 D Kelly, bricklayer
15 B McCulley, machinist
17 John P Gardner, cutter
19 Mrs Ann Gaing
21 James Fallahey, gardener
23 W H Rowe, printer

25 Daniel Cripps, bricklayer
27 C Piercy, printer
29 Geo Maslin, laborer
31 Amos Hutton, tool maker
33 Thos O Veale, gardener
35 C Piercy, carpenter

Wilson-st intersects

37 John Rouse, shipper
39½ Alfred Rouse, fireman
39 J S Smyth, polisher
41 John Walker, moulder
43 Robert Spittal, carpenter
45 Chas C Farr, plasterer
47 Fred Lentz, butcher
49 Albert Carson, tailor
51 Wm Stewart, carpenter
53 James Kenny, carpenter
55 Patrick McGovern, carriage maker
57 L E Taylor, carpenter
59 Chas Lipek, brushmaker
61 James Lewis, carpenter
63 James Collins, carpenter
65 James Fletcher, jeweler

Cannon-st intersects

Stinson-st, north side, from 81 Wellington south, east to Wentworth

9 Samuel Cottrell, gardener

West-ave intersects

75 Michael Dougherty, shipper
77 Vacant
79 W S Hicks, carver
Boys' Home

Wentworth-st intersects

Stinson-st, south side

20 Chas Tregenza, clerk

Victoria-ave intersects

Joseph Lister
58 F W Fearman, pork dealer

Maple-ave intersects

64 Walter Sturt, com traveler
66 Chas Tinling, druggist
70 L Eckerson, photographer

Emerald-st intersects

72 Michael Doherty, laborer

Blyth-st intersects

84 Samuel Maslen
86 John Noble, bricklayer

Erie-ave intersects

F E Dallyn

Wentworth-st intersects

Strachan-st e, north side, from 252 James north to Wellington

9 Mrs Andrew Begley
11 David Farrar, constable GTR
13 Mrs Jones

Hughson-st intersects

31 Hugh Cassidy, laborer
33 Thos Harris, stonecutter
35 Mrs Frank McGargle
39 Patrick Connors, laborer

John-st intersects

45 D Mulcahy, laborer
47 Hiram Markle, wheelsman
53 Benj Kennedy, ropemaker
55 Michael O'Connor, moulder
61 John Fred Foster, plumber

Catharine-st intersects

Vacant lots
67 Pat Canary, engineer
69 John Lawlor, cabinetmaker
71 B McMahon, policeman

Mary-st intersects

83 Patrick Warren, laborer
85 Patrick Macartney, watchmn
89 Mrs Barnard McDonald
91 M Doyle, baggageman
97 Michael O'Brien, laborer
99 Michael Sunderland, polisher
101 M Shaughnessy, machinist
103 John O'Toole, scalemaker
107 Patrick Corbett, hatter
109 Joseph Taffe, moulder

Ferguson-ave intersects

Strachan-st e, south side

Hughson-st intersects

24 Amos Thompson, laborer
26 Mrs Mary Anderson
28 Mrs Wm Clarkson
32 Peter Anderson, laborer
34 Wm Woodley, laborer
36 Mrs John Shea
38 Mrs Ann Armitage
40 Michael Brady, laborer

John-st intersects

46 Robert Patton, laborer
48 John Weir, clerk
52 Uriah Leaver
54 Mrs Charlotte Wilson
60 Jas Fallahee, laborer

Catharine-sts intersect

68 Mrs Mary Warren

Mary-st intersects

96 James Steele, laborer
98 Walter Pew, teamster
102 John Jarvis, laborer
106 Mark Lampshire, laborer
108 Wm Green, laborer
110 Mrs Robert Hawthorne
112 Louis Boneny, laborer
114 Stephen Boney, laborer

Ferguson-ave intersects

Joseph Whyte, carpenter

Wellington-st intersects

Strachan-st w, north side, from 249 James n to Bay

16 Chas Cameron, laborer
18 Thos Allen, dyer
20 James Harris, machinist
120 Wm Parker, laborer
22 George Harris
24 George Fraser

Macnab-st intersects

28 Milton Rymal
30 Francis Hislop, laborer

Bay-st intersects

Thompson's boat house

Strachan-st w, south side

5 Mrs Ellen Boyd
7 James Delaney, laborer
23 Wm Williamson, carpenter
25 Robert Carr, laborer
27 Mrs Powers
29 Wm Sutherland, blacksmith

Macnab-st intersects

37 Henry Gray, customs officer
39 James McClere, freight agt

Bay-st intersects

Gillesby's warehouse

Stuart-st e, north side, from 244 James n, to Catharine

Vacant lots
23 Daniel Flynn, stovemounter
25 B Flemming, laborer

Hughson-st intersects

27 James Whalen, laborer
29 Mrs Robert Clen
31 Mrs George Lennard
33 John Galtrey
35 J Greenless, moulder.
37 Wm Simpson, moulder
39 John Coutts, patternmaker
41 Joseph Davis, butcher
43 Mrs B Hammond

John-st intersects

51 Wm Cooper, laborer
53 Eli Sanger, laborer
55 Wm Maney, laborer
57 John Gray, laborer

Catharine-st intersects

Stuart-st e, south side

4 Mrs Mary Ann O'Brien
6 Mrs Taylor
10 Wm McAdams, teamster
12 John Callaghan, cigarmaker
16 Vacant
18 Daniel Langdon
20 Wm Hannah, porter
24.26 Geo Mills, grocer

Hughson-st intersects

30 Vacant
32 Wm Rice, teamster

34 Alex Pazius, upholsterer
36 Henry Smith, laborer
38 Robert Aikins, scalemaker
42 Ed Bolus, patternmaker
44 F Kittyle, collector

John-st intersects

48 Thos Duffy, carpenter
50 Patrick McAndrews, laborer
52 Chas Coy, harnessmaker
54 Mrs Wm Doyle

Catharine-st commences

Stuart-st w, north side, from 239 James n, to Queen

14 Jeremiah McCoy, carpenter
16 James O'Donnell, glassmkr
City Weigh Scales

Macnab-st intersects

G T R general offices

Bay-st intersects

G T R station
J B Fairgrieve, coal office

Stuart-st w, south side

John McHendrie, tavern
7 James McHendrie, carpenter
9 Wm Jones, laborer
11 H Fuller, tailor
19 Wm Radford, baker
21 Mrs E Riddle, boarding
23-25 S Taylor, hotel

Macnab-st intersects

31 Doran Bros, vinegar works
33 W G Townsend, custom broker
35 Custom House
Street Railway office
49 Metropolitan hotel

Bay-st intersects

51 Allison House
61 Joseph Quinn, machinist
r 61 James Marshall, laborer
63 R England, fruiterer
63 M J Wolf, hotel
67 Ontario Emigration Agency
69 Roach's hotel
69½ Mrs Bent, refreshments
73 Dan McNamara, hotel

Tiffany-st intersects

79 J Steanger, temperance hotel
81 Immigrant sheds
89 Robt Thomson, lumber dlr

Caroline-st intersects

A Gartshore & Co

Hess & Queen-sts intersect

Tiffany-st, from 73 Stuart w to Barton

Dan McNamara, hotel
Mrs John Hardman
4½ Jas McMahon, laborer
6 John Kavanagh, laborer
6½ Joseph Lomas, laborer
8 Lewis McDonald, laborer
Jas Beardwell, carpenter
7 Wm Burniston, carpenter
Wm J Berryman, laborer
John Johnston, engineer

Barton-st intersects

Tisdale-st, east side, from 272 King e, north to Barton

2 R Klock, cigarmaker
4 Jas Wright, mariner
6 — Dawson, pedler

King Wm-st intersects

16 Robert Warren, butcher
18 Wm Malins, carter
20 Wm Rewbury, checker
22 Arthur Keeble, teamster
24 Alf Chidley, machinist
26 H Andrup, tinsmith
28 Alex Robertson, stonecutter
30 Geo Hamilton, stonecutter
42 R W Randal, carpenter
44 Geo Cartwright, blacksmith
46 Wm H Martin, machinist
48 Wm Holmes, moulder
50 Robert F Drake, gunsmith
54 Frank Booth, bookkeeper
56 Geo Sweetlove, watchman

Wilson-st intersects

58 Samuel Buscombe, shoemakr

60 John Martin, bricklayer
60½ W Flood, clerk
62 Jas Connor, burnisher
64 Geo Hunter, tailor
68 Arthur Smith, laborer
70 John Carson, laborer
72 Patrick Fitzgerald
Cannon-st intersects

Tisdale-st, west side

Vacant lots
King Wm-st intersects
17 John McKenna, yardsman
19 Peter McSwean, carpenter
21 Mrs Richard Reece
25 John Butterfield, stonecutter
25½ Frank Osler, filecutter
27 R J Smith, traveler
27½ Andrew Wilson
29 Wm James, builder
31 Robert Reynolds, baker
33 — Patterson, traveler
33½ Alex Small, shipper
35 Robert Lucas, moulder
37 Walter Yates, laborer
39 Martin Carson
41 — Simpson, laborer
43 Andrew Schon, laborer
47 A Lentz, laborer
Wilson-st intersects
49 Jas Walterhouse, millwright
51 Mrs Ing
53 Peter Stodler, weaver
55 Mrs Jas Hodd
57 John Clushman, moulder
Cannon-st intersects

Tom-st, north side, from Sophia to Dundurn

10 Henry Fitt, cabinetmaker
Devenport-st intersects
26 Geo Smith, laborer
28 Thos King, engineer
Dundurn-st intersects
56 Wm Ashburn, laborer

Tom-st, west side

1 John Trotman, polisher
3 J Semmens, carpenter
5 Dennis Mahoney, shoemaker
9 Wm Furniss, marble cutter
11 Thos Burrell, fireman
r " Mrs Eli White
15 Samuel Marsten, machinist
17 John Clegg, laborer
21 John Lawrence, clerk
25 Geo Maddox, blacksmith
29 Henry Thomas, marble dlr
33 Samuel Fiddler, sailor
37 Jos T Hartley, laborer
39 John Curran, printer
Dundurn-st intersects
57 James Mortimer, moulder
59 Vacant

Victoria-ave n, east side, from 244 King e to the Bay

Vacant lots
10 Chas C Foote, plater
King-Wm-st intersects
Public school
20 P S Robertson, merchant
22 Wm Marshall, salesman
24 E J Moore, bookkeeper
26 W H Jones, bookkeeper
28 Samuel Atkin, clerk
30 Mrs Tarbox
32 Chas McGregor, druggist
34 Joseph S Brennen, carpenter
36 Daniel Blackley, accountant
38 John P Bampfylde, ale bottlr
40 C L Walker, confectioner
42 John Stoneman, traveler
Wilson-st intersects
44 Alex Hayes, grocer
48 I W Myers
50 Geo Kappele, bookkeeper
58 Samnel Medley, stonecutter
60 John Arthur, polisher
64 David R Gibson, mason
66 Mrs Wm Findlay
70 Wm Temple, machinist
Evans-st intersects

72 J R Jackson, carpenter
74 Thos Riddell, carpenter
74½ Wm Blair, carpenter
78 Mrs Samuel Bradt

Cannon-st intersects

86 Frank Stinson, porter
90 Mrs Wm West
92 Nelson Parks, policeman
92½ Samuel Elliott, watchman
94 Simon Elliott, watchman
96 Miss Catharine Merrick
96 Miss M McFerran, teacher
98 James Foreman, brakeman
100 Daniel McMaster, mason
104 Robert Blake, watchman

Robert-st intersects

110 Benj Rothwell, moulder
114 Walter Bale, bookkeeper
118 James Farmer
124 Wm Farmer, photographer
128 Abraham Ripley, moulder
130 Joseph Bale, shipper
132 David Dick, fireman
134 Henry Syme, laborer

Barton-st intersects

146 Wm McKittrick, moulder
148 Wm Smith, ropemaker
154 Mark Thompson, carpenter
156 Jos Degan, shoemaker
158 Chas McMillen, laborer
160 Robt Johnson, carpenter
166 Wm Robson, planer
170 Jas Green, laborer
178 Walter Fowler, moulder
180 Vacant
184 M McKenzie, laborer
186 Daniel McMullen, cooper
190 C P Moore, file cutter

South-st intersects

200 G H Hopkins, merchant
202 Vacant

Barton-st intersects

208 Andrew Diamond, machinist
210 H Munsie, bookkeeper
212 G L Pearson, agent
214 George Stroud, tanner

Ferrie-st intersects

220 Dennis McCarthy, gardener
H & N W Ry wharf

Victoria-ave n, west side

3 Hy Bedlington, traveler
5 J M Little, bookkeeper
5½ Jas Brown, hide inspector
7 Henry Humbecker
9 L Hopkins, pickle manfr
11 Thos Wadland, inspector telephone Co

King Wm-st interects

S J Moore, manufacturer
17 L McKellar, traveler
19 Engine house
21 A D Cameron, barrister
25 W D Bews, merchant
23 Jas C Fairgrieve, merchant
27 E W Bateman, baker
29 A Murdock, com traveler
31 Jas Johnson, auctioneer
33 John Weatherstone
35 John Hooper, com traveler
39 John Ross, laborer
41 M Overholt, tailor
43 S J Moore, manfr

Wilson-st intersects

51 Chas Howard, carpenter
53 B D Bowron, tinsmith
55 Jas Dodson, brassfounder
57 Andrew Patton, moulder
59 D Graham, fireman
61 Fred Dodson, painter
63 John R McDonald
65 Wm Dodson, painter
67 Dan McMurtrie, traveler
69 John E Hampson, traveler
71 Vacant
73 Mrs Cooper
75 Jas Brock, whipmaker
77 Geo Watson, shoemaker

Evans-st intersects

83 Jas Johnston, caretaker
85 Jas F Bryant, plasterer
87 Henry Johnson, laborer

Cannon-st intersects

91 Vacant

95 Jas Matthews, painter
97 Wm Anderson, machinist
99 Jas Anderson, laborer
101 Stephen M Russell, polisher
103 Wm Anstey, shoemaker
107 S B Longhrey, traveler
111 C E Dyer, traveler
115 Wm Spera, grain buyer

Robert-st intersects

131 John Einfoot, agent
139 Wm Burns, tailor
141 J S Sutherland, clerk
143 Donald Gunn, painter
147 F W Hore, jr, manfr
155 F W Hore, manfr
159 Geo Brad, lather
161 Mrs A Hardstaff
City Hospital
183 Jos Curno, carpenter

Barton-st intersects

185 Geo Woods, laborer
189 Wm Michael, laborer
191 Wm McLaughlin, laborer

South-st intersects

G T R track intersects

221 Thomas Patterson, watchman
225 Wm H Finch, iron founder

Ferrie-st intersects

229 James Purvis, carpenter
235 Jas Nolan
Jas Walker, soap factory
Michael Coughlin, laborer
Geo Russell, soap boiler

Victoria-ave south, east side, from 246 King east to the Mountain

St Patrick's church

Main-st intersects

29 Thos McKay, grocer
31 Wm G Reid, merchant
37 Jas Matthews, painter
43 Wm Edgar, lumber dealer
49 Rev John James, D D
55 J F Stewart, manfr

Hunter-st intersects

57 Thos Myles, coal dealer
65 Rev John Morton
69 Miss Hattie Fields
71 Wm G Moore, land agent
73 Thos D Wanzer, manfr

Stinson-st intersects

Joseph Lister, Wood Lawn

Victoria-ave south, west side

10 Geo Pearson, carter
12 Mrs Michael Morrisey
14 Thomas Morgan, tanner

Main-st intersects

28 Alex Milne, builder
30 Vacant
38 John A Barr, druggist
44 James Lockhart
46 John A Clark, druggist
48 Robert Moblett, dyer
50 M Cohen, ins agent
52 Mrs Mary Slater
54 W Glennie, traveler
56 Alex Stuart, chamberlain

Hunter and Stinson-sts intersect

82 Francis Wanzer, manfr
88 J M Stewart, clerk
90 Vacant
94 Harry Dallas, traveler
96 Thos Burns, P O
100 John Farthing, sectionman

Vine-st, north side, from 95 James north to Bay

Standard Ins building
16 Mrs A Quimby
18 Vacant
24 Rudolph Peters, machinist

Macnab-st intersects

34 Mrs Sophia Hill
42 J B Rousseaux, bookkeeper
44 Donald Dallas, polisher

Park-st intersects

58 Thos Wilson, fireman
60 Hiram F Inglehart
62 W Stroud, hide dealer
66 George Reid, messenger

68 Mrs Richard Barrett
70 Wm Birrell, foreman
" Farmers Dairy Co
" Walton Ice Co
72 Wm Kirk, baker
74 Anthony King

Bay-st intersects

Vine-st, south side

1 Inland revenue office
5 Robt Chatto, teamster
9 E A Ware, scale manfr
15 John M Durward, marbleized slate manfr
17 Wm Leary

Macnab-st intersects

Stewart's foundry
43 Lenton Williams, millwright

Park-st intersects

65 John Glasgow
67 D J Peace, tobacconist
69 James Anderson, carpenter
71 Wm Gillies, steward
73 John Greening, agent
75 John Mathieson, porter

Bay-st intersects

Walnut-st north, east side, from King to King William

Charles Almas, barber
Robert McCarroll, plumber
George McCullough, black smith
4 Thos James, saddler

Walnut-st north, west side

Mrs Louisa Miller
The J H Stone Manf Co
7 John Armstrong, carpenter
9 Richard Laidman, laborer

Walnut-st south, east side, from 113 King e, south to Hannah

George Bartman, tailor
1 Thos Ferguson, shoemaker
3 Wm Roberts, laborer
5 Mrs Robt Walker
7 Wm Ferguson, tailor
7½ Wm Breheny, shoemaker
9 Vacant
11 Mrs Mary McCarter

Main-st intersects

15 H D Griffin, M D
17 Richard Ellicott, assessor
19 George Moyes
21 A B Smith, tel operator
23 Fire engine house
25 Jas Mitchell, stove fitter

Jackson-st intersects

31 Wm Stern, traveler
33 C N Heisrodt, gilder
35 F S Ryckman, contractor
37 Chas James, machinist
43½ Mrs F Bush, grocer

Hunter-st intersects

45 Wm Betcone
47 Miss E Ambrose
49 Miss Louisa Knott
51 Robert Laidlaw, agent
53 John Flynn, laborer
55 Mrs Margaret O'Brien
55½ M Birrell, porter
" Geo Hewson, cabinetmkr
57 George Webster, tailor
59 Chas L Ennis, tuner
61 John Myles, laborer
63 Hugh McDougall, mason
65 Joseph Burns, laborer
67 James Leonard, laborer
69 Mrs M Hamilton
71 D Sullivan, grocer

O'Reilly-st intersects

77 James Fenton, bailiff
79 Wm Macfarlane, machinist
81 Mrs James Butler

Young-st intersects

Jos Brace, shoemaker

Maria-st intersects

103 Vacant
105 Mrs John Fitzgerald
107 M Foley, moulder
109 A J Miller, porter
111 M J Forster, maltster
113 Jas Gallagher, watchman
117 Owen O'Connell, laborer

121 Vacant

Hannah-st intersects

Walnut-st s, west side,

Wm I Case, M D

Main-st intersects

John Winer
18 Joseph Conian, conductor
18½ I H Culp, machinist
20 Wm H Lampman, farmer
24 Thos Wilson

Jackson-st intersects

30 Andrew Watson, painter
32 Wm Havens, painter
34 Mrs Sarah Cleghorn
36 Edward Schwarz, shoemaker
38 Thos Bolton, laborer
40 John C Williams, gardener

Hunter-st intersects

44 Thos McMahon, clerk
46 Wm Robinson, bricklayer
48 Samuel Heim, tailor
48½ Matt Beckerson, teamster
50 Michael Flynn
52 Albert Rooney, tailor
54 Samuel Provan, merchant
56 John Balllie, salesman
58 Joseph Tinsley, printer
62 Edward Lewis, plasterer
64 Joseph Volk, moulder
66 Mrs E Sarginson, tailoress
68 Chas Smith, lithographer

O'Reilly-st intersects

80 James Spencer, tinsmith
82 John Halliday, laborer
84 Samuel White, bus driver

Young-st intersects

92 James Reilly, laborer
94 Mrs Mary Herrington
96 Wm Myles, laborer

Maria-st intersects

106 Mrs M Elz
110 Thos Coughlin, laborer

Hannah-st intersects

Wellington-st n, east side, from 216 King e to Burlington Bay

2 Chas Smith, messenger
4 Alex McDonald, carpenter
6 Jas G Foster, laborer
8 John B Lewis, manfr
10 Wm Connell, finisher
12 Hector H Martin
14 Vacant
16 Mrs Francis Croombie
18 Robt Harper, gardener

King Wm-st intersects

24 John Hancock, builder
26 Thos Morris, flour and feed
28 Thos Cathcart, baker
30 Wm Dewart, laborer
32 Miss Catharine McDermott
34 Wm Aiken, blacksmith
36 Alex Campbell, laborer
38 W Hunter, brass founder
40 W Glass, moulder
42 E Knapp, laborer
44 John Pearce, teamster
46 Jas Hughes
48 Arthur Moore, watchman
50 John Bull, laborer
52 A Bowron, tinsmith
54 N Tallman, moulder
56 George P Harrison, traveler

Wilson-st intersects

54 W P Willcock, butcher
56 Henry Proctor
58 Thos Torrance
60 Geo Broad, carpenter
62 Henry McStravick, laborer
64 Horace Harvey, carpenter
66 R M Ross, painter
68 W R Powell, builder
70 Vacant
72 Wm S Nixon, bailiff
74 H S Battram, clerk
80 Martin O'Driscoll, finisher
80½ Jas McManus, shoemaker
84 Jas E Redfield, burnisher
88 Wm Dingle, machinist

Evans-st intersects

Meriden Britannia Co

Cannon-st intersects

122 Alex Durand, carpenter
124 Jas Bovaird, carriagemaker
126 Mrs Abe Neff
128 R Bagnall
130 Mrs M Sangster
Lumber yard

Robert-st intersects

136 Jas Poulter, bookkeeper
138 Thos Foster, clockmaker
140 A Jenkins, machinist
142 Mrs S Bowes
144 T P Bates, clerk
150 Nicholas Carrier, shoemaker
152 P J Fenton, policeman

Barton Terrace:
1 Rudolph Rissman, agent
2 C Brown, laborer
3 J B McKay, foreman
4 Mrs E Irving
5 George R VanOrder, conductor

Barton-st intersects

202 Robt Reader, moulder
204 G S Copeland, ropemaker

South-st intersects

G T R Crossing
Canada Felt Hat Works
L D Sawyer & Co, agr implements
Alfred King, painter

Ferrie, Wood and Macauley-sts intersect

Wellington-st n, west side

1 Hamilton vinegar works
Swimming Baths
15 Chas Laycock, blacksmith
19 Vacant

King Wm-st intersects

21 Thos Morris, flour and feed
27 James Potter, brickmaker
29 Ed Beard, laborer
31 Nicholas Carroll, laborer
33 George Jeffrey, laborer
35 Mrs McMaster
37 Samuel Robinson, butcher

Rebecca-st intersects

39 C C Baird, grocer
41 James Reid, butcher
45 John R Burt, moulder
47 John C Henry, teamster
49 Thomas Campbell, moulder
51 H Gildon, general store

Wilson-st intersects

53 T B Haines, machinist
55 Herbert Whipple, agent
57 Vacant
59 John Campbell, moulder
61 Hugh Oder
63 George Richmond, printer
65 Wm Gilmore, shoemaker
69 Mrs James Robertson
71 John Ronan, grocer

Kelly-st intersects

75 Mrs J H Stewart
77 James Cumison
79 Seath Robinson, com traveler
81 Alex Kerr
83 John Ross, teacher
85 Mrs Sidney Jackson
87 Matthew Hearne, tobacconist
89 H Cummer, brewer
91 John Acheson
93 W P Crawford, excise officer
95 John McIntyre
97 James C McCoy, clerk
99 David Rooks, melter
99½ Richard Atkinson, shoemkr
101 Thos Wilson, hotel keeper

Cannon-st intersects

103 J Ronan, grocer
Primary School
109 Charles Truscott, carpenter
111 Thos McCallum, cabinetmkr
113 John Cook, bookkeeper
115 Thomas Simons
117 John Savage, machinist
119 Alex Durrand, carpenter
121 Wm Rowland, lumber measurer
123 Alfred Robbins, engineer
127 F V Jones, hatter
131 Henry Hyatt, shoelaster

Robert-st intersects

133 Thos Renwick, engineer
135 C H Brooks, brakeman
137 George Winn, shoemaker
139 James Markle, binder
141 Chas Goring, carpenter
143 John Edwards, hatter
145 W H James, mail carrier
147 Miss K Roth
149 Thos Madden, laborer
151 James Hyde, laborer
153 C Erdmen, laborer
155 J D Park, inspector
157 Alfred Cox, cork cutter
159 James Johnston, blacksmith
161 Fred Bell, shoemaker
163 J H Shearer, file grinder
165 Thos O'Grady, moulder
169 E Ecclestone, grocer

Barton st intersects

181 Alex Forbes, potash manf
187 Thos Fair, laborer
189 John Brodie, clerk
191 Wm Lee, mason
193 John A Cameron, fitter
195 Robert Barker, carriagemkr
197 John McBride, policeman
199 Brent Johnston, carpenter
201 David Hutton, laborer
203 Vacant
205 D McKenzie wood dealer

Murray-st intersects

207 Thos Wallington, painter
209 Henry Busby, morticer
219 John Cameron, laborer
221 Duncan McKenzie
D R Dewey & Co, coal
Railway crossing
231 Martin Philips, laborer

Strachan-st intersects

237 Wm McMenemy, laborer
239 John Conway, machinist
245 Patrick Noonan, laborer

Ferrie & Picton--sts intersect

Matthew Quigley, laborer

Macauley-st intersects

Wm H Clarke, machinist

Wood-st intersects

44

John Rutley, stovemounter

Wellington-st s, east side, from 191 King e to the Mountain

First Methodist Church

Main-st intersects

19 Wm Hunter, brass moulder
23 Edmund Pinch, machinist
25 Harry Duncan, merchant
27 Wm Hyslop, merchant
29 H N Kittson, bookkeeper
31 T D Murphy, manager whip Co
33 Wm Lawson, carpenter
37 Fred A Zachau, furrier
45 J W Randall
47 F C Minty, bank teller
49 Geo Canning, plasterer
51 Mrs Charlotte Day
53 T G Watson, policeman
55 Peter Ferres, policeman

Hunter-st intersects

61 A McFarlane, flour dealer
63 Mrs Nelson Rymal
65 Raymond Walker, bookke'r
67 Joseph Herron, tailor
71 P S Bateman, blacksmith
r " Jas Sellar, laborer
73 Thos Davis, com trav
75 Wm Barclay, piano maker
77 Wm Claringbowl, gardener
79 Henry Gayfer, manager A Murray & Co
81 John Isbister, contractor

Stinson-st intersects

Edward Gillett
Railway crossing
Aged Woman's Home
Hamilton Orphan Asylum

Hannah-st intersects

Wellington-st s, west side

Private grounds

Main-st intersects

28 Jas McArthur, furrier
30 John Campbell, merchant
36 W S Champ, paymaster GTR

Jackson-st intersects

38 J E Bull, salesman
44 John H Foster
46 Chas H Stephenson, builder
48 Wm G Flooks, letter carrier

Hunter-st intersects

54 Peter O'Heir, customs officer
56 Vacant
58 Miss M Sturt, dressmaker
64 D G Ellis, broker

Grove-st intersects

72 Robert Gordon, carpenter
84 Geo Wm Bartman, tailor
86 Jas Burgess, bookkeeper
90 Wm Addison, jr, builder
92 Mrs C Stuart
94 Wm Addison, sr, builder

Young-st intersects

98 Samuel Wilson
102 C Doyle, moulder
104 J J Armstrong, foreman
106 Thomas Sullivan, laborer
110 John S Slater, inspector
112 Peter McCandlish, shipper
Mission room

Maria-st intersects

118 Richard Plant, carpenter
122 Maurice Wren, tinsmith
124 John Prike, shoemaker

Hannah-st intersects

Wentworth-st n, east side, from King east to the Bay

Street Car Inn
John Sutterby, gardener
A Donohue, shoemaker

Nightingale-st intersects

John T Gully, groceries

Wilson-st intersects

Wm Ralph
Robert Acklan, carpenter
A Goodman, carpenter
Henry Smith, shoemaker
M B Burkholder

Cannon-st intersects

Wm Milne, wine manfr
Mrs E Brown
Alfred Brown
Arthur Brown
C Whitehead, gardener

Barton-st intersects

Col John Land
Peter Land
James Aikin, butcher
Mrs Collins

Railway Crossing

Thos Lawry, pork factory
John Egg, butcher
John Duffy, gardener
Wm Carry, ice dealer
P D Bates, fishmonger
George Webster, machinist
James Weir, boat builder
John Morris, boat builder

Wentworth-st n, west side

John Scollard, butcher
Wm Hawkins, policeman

King Wm-st intersects

Babtist Mission Church
5 Arthur Stockdale, tanner
Wm Sutherland, carpenter
9 Chas Millmine, gardener
11 Henry Cartmell, tailor

Nightingale-st intersects

Vacant
Vacant
21 Geo S Herron, watchman
23 Frank Mesle, brushmaker

Wilson, Cannon and Barton-sts intersect

Rev R Miller
John Marshall, laborer
Mission Sabbath School
John Arthur, porter
Alex Miller, butcher
Vacant
Wm Tout, machinist

South-st commences

James Stein, laborer
Ed Cain, laborer
Jno Bailey, market gardener

Wm Eagleshani, gardener
Wm Morris, gardener

Wentworth-st s, east side

Mrs George Wilds
S E Jones, laborer
James Freed, gardener
Aikmans'-ave intersects
C E VanNorman, packer
Chas Armstrong, N W R
F Lynch Staunton, surveyor
Main-st intersects
E Kraft, harnessmaker
Jacob T Nottle
Ida-st intersects
Wm Bell, barrister
J H Davis, merchant
G T Billington, farmer

Wentworth-st s, west side

Robert Hall, inspector
Main-st intersects
Arthur Woodhouse
Wm Gillesby
R J Duggan, barrister
Stinson-st intersects
Andrew Alexander

West-ave n, east side, from 238 King east to Barton

2 John Cotton, carpenter
8 Burnet Doherty, carpenter
10 Asher Holmes, machinist
12 Nicholas McKeegan, plaster'r
14 Mrs Etha Lumsden
15 Mrs James Govier
18 Sylvester Battram, grocer
King Wm-st intersects
20 John Scollard, butcher
26 John Williams. shipwright
28 Mrs Thomas Griffin
32 W J Edwards, carpenter
36 Wm Davey
38 Peter Carse
40 James Callan, laborer
42 David Ross, bricklayer
42½ Mrs William Ross
44 Wm Walsh, plumber
46 Mrs Wm W Reid
48 Thos Burrows, auctioneer
50 Joseph Mearce, teamster
52 Geo Barr, carpenter
54 D Kapelle, tailor
56 John McComb, tailor
62 Henry McCann, confectioner
Wilson-st intersects
64 Fred Miller, butcher
66 Joseph Day, porter
68 James Charters, filler
70 John Beatty, melter
74 Mrs Shea
78 J P Steedman, clerk
80 Mrs Andrew Lyle
82 John Lyle, plumber
84 Thomas Parkhill, carpenter
84½ Wm Myers, tinsmith
86 David Ryckman, moulder
90 John W Yeager, laborer
90 Mrs S Rodgers
94 Geo Welby, patternmaker
98 Jacob Springstead, laborer
Evans-st intersects
100 John Jackson, tailor
102 Ed Walker, machinist
104 Philip Gee, laborer
110 Robt McQuillan, jr, teamster
112 John Watt, merchant
Cannon-st intersects
116 Michael Donohue, tinsmith
118 Thos Lewis, carter
124 Richard Atkinson, shoemkr
124 J B Haines, conductor
128 Robert Stuart, sexton
130 John Townsend
132 James McMenemy, painter
134 Wm Holmes, brushmaker
136 Edward Flanery, moulder
138 James Groves, blacksmith
140 Arch McDonald, shipper
142 Mrs Wm Smith
S R Scott, grocer
Robert-st intersects
154 Wm C Southwell, fitter

156 Alex Beddie, mason
158 Wm Wholton, tinsmith
164 Edward Williams, engineer
166 H G Stone, japanner
168 John Robinson, ins agent
190 J G Muir, bricklayer

Barton-st intersects

West-ave n, west side

1 Andrew Boyd, laborer
3 James Boyd, plasterer
5 Wm G Wright, machinist
7 Mrs Stephen James
11 James Phillips, builder
13 Samuel Sims, shoemaker
15 John McCoy, bank inspector
17 Charles Mottashed, builder
19 James M Davis, machinist
21 W G Hall, com traveler
23 Elwood Robinson, traveler

King Wm-st intersects

27 Robert Stewart, bottler
29 Shadwick Seamen
31 M McFarlane, machinist
33 Joseph Wilson, grocer
35 W J Thresher, baker
37 Henry Thorp, cigarmaker
39 A M Waters, marble dealer
43 James Anderson, blacksmith
45 Jas Hastings, trunkmaker
57 Daniel Warren, packer
49 John Henry, carpenter
51 Geo Magill, moulder
53 John R McKichan, manfr
57 John McNeal, laborer
61 Mrs M E Smith
63 Alex Quinn, moulder
67 John Kendrick, grocer

Wilson-st intersects

71 John Pettigrew, carpenter
73 Vacant
73½ Fred W Ross, shoemaker
75 Fred Burrows, clerk
77 L H Buttrey, cabinetmkr
79 Miss Alice Walker
81 John S Fox, cabinetmaker
85 Jas Pinch, sergt police
87 Jas Duffy, machinist
89 Sam McNair, constable
91 Edw Potter, collarmaker
93 David Cullum, plumber
95 Leonard Lintoot, saloon
97 John Shields
99 Wm McLaren, shoemaker

Evans-st intersects

101 W V Ecclestone, salesman
103 Mrs Ann Evans
105 W Terryberry, barkeeper
107 Mrs Elizabeth Jewell
109 Robert Smith, laborer
109 Philip Henry, laborer
111 R B Lanaway, machinist
r " Thos Feaver, butcher
113 Jos Derby, grain buyer
115 Alfred Torry, clerk

Cannon-st intersects

129 Stephen H Pocock, sawmkr
131 Patrick Henry, carpenter
133 Mrs Wm Perkins
135 R B Ward, laborer
137 Walter Fricker, machinist
139 David Murray, blacksmith

Robert-st intersects

143 Thos Allen, contractor
145 Arthur Perry, mechanic
147 Emory Chagnon, turner
149 Jno Trimble, bridge repairer
151 J D Baine, machinist
153 R Armstrong
155 George Dow, plater
157 George Phillips, tailor
159 Eldridge Gerry, hatter
161 J R Dodson, brassfinisher
163 Wm Cook, machinist
165 J J Bennett, engineer
167 James Sime, plater

Barton-st intersects

West-ave s, east side, from St Thomas' Church, Main east to Stinson

1 James T Barnard, manfr
3 Alfred Morgan
5 Mrs E Dallas

7 Thos C Stewart, traveler
9 James Stewart, clerk
9½ S M Kenney, ins agent
11 Rev B B Keefer
13 W J Grant, ticket agent
15 Vacant
17 R F Keayes, land agent
19 Rev Thos Goldsmith
21 A L Burns
23 Mrs Mary Patton
25 C R Smith
27 J W Morden
31 Vacant

Hunter-st intersects

47 R M Wanzer, manfr

Stinson-st intersects

West-ave s, west side

Main-st intersects

St. Thomas' Church
6 Jonathan Ames, manf
10 F E Kilvert, M P, barrister
12 R L Whyte, customs officer
22 Julius Grossman, merchant
24 A Grossman, merchant
26 Mrs Ann Fox
28 Hugh H Stevens, bank inspector

Hunter-st intersects

42 Jas E Pointer, traveler
44 G Hutchison, painter
46 Thos Beckett, merchant
48 Mrs David A Smith
50 Mrs Jas Campbell
54 Mrs J W Gœring
54 Wm Gœring, merchant

Stinson-sts intersects

Wilson-st, north side, from 56 Mary to east of Burlington

2 George Russell, foreman
4 Jas Mahaffey, machinist
6 Chas Colville, machinist
10 Wm Turnbull, assessor

Elgin-st intersects

16 Chas Duncan, merchant
18 T H Butler, clerk
20 John Quarrier, agent
22 Miss Mary Golden, milliner
24 Samuel Robbins, tinsmith
26 Chas Reid, whipmaker
28 Wm Robbins, carpenter
30 Mrs M Lemon, dressmaker
32 Joseph Atkinson, painter

Ferguson-ave intersects

R Blair, grocer
32 Alfred Gilbert, machinist
34 Mrs Griffin
36 John Stark, stovemounter
38 J Fotheringham, wagonmkr
40 John Hall
42 A Studholme, stovefitter
44 Jas Pierce, laborer
44 John Radigan, tinsmith
50 Fred Abraham, tailor
52 Vacant
John Morton, grocer

Cathcart-st intersects

54 Joseph Wilson, letter carrier
56 Wm C Hooper, printer
58 Chas Morrow, bricklayer
r 58 Thos P Haines, machinist

Wellington-st intersects

68 Wm Arnold, polisher
70 Chas Newell, clerk
72 W P Wilcox, butcher
74 Mrs Jas Smith
76 Jacob Gebhard, shoemaker

West-ave intersects

84 Philip Hasting, carpenter
86 Wm McCauley, japanner
88 Thos Appleton, gardener
90 T E Davis, bricklayer
92 Timothy Kelly, stovemtr
94 R G Russell, jeweler
96 J E McCarthy, messenger
98 George Hazen, tailor

Victoria-ave intersects

Henry Glebe, tailor

East-ave intersects

118 Thos Lornie, machinist
120 Saml B Fuller, policeman

122 Thos Crow, machinist
124 Thos Rock, druggist
126 Fred Oakes, butcher

Emerald-st intersects

Vacant lots

Tisdale-st intersects

148 Samuel Buscomb, shoemaker
152 W H Perry, solderer
154 Geo Collins, carpenter

Steven-st intersects

162 John Underhill, laborer
164 Wm Henshaw, hatter
" Thos Smith
166 John Cox, carpenter
170 Joseph Vandusen, carpenter
174 Chas Bourque, brushmaker

Ashley-st intersects

176 Alfred Duffield, plasterer
178 Wm Wilson, laborer
180 John O'Hara, laborer
190 Henry Davis, carpenter
192 Thos Taylor

Wentworth-st intersects

John Booker, traveler
Henry Rogers, gardener

Burlington-st intersects

Ernest Barrow, surveyor
Job Greenaway, foreman
John Street, bricklayer
Henry Hamill, gardener

Wilson-st, south side

3 Miss Ann Eadie
7 Mrs Esther Roberts
9 Henry Mansergh, clerk
11 R G Robinson, cutter
17 Adam Laidlaw, founder
19 Hugh Hennessy, blacksmith
21 Joseph Horton, rag dealer
23 Mrs Angus McVicar
27 John McMahon, dairy

Ferguson-ave and Cathcart-sts intersect

53 Wm Robinson, foreman
57 Mrs Mathew Bell

Wellington-st intersects

77 F G Shearsmith, carpenter

West-ave intersects

91 Robert Robinson, bricklayer
93 Donald Currie, carpenter

Victoria-ave intersects

97 Geo Dunnett, moulder
99 Mrs Alex McLeod

East-ave intersects

118 Vacant

Emerald and Tisdale-sts intersect

149 Geo Axford, butcher
151 Wm White, blacksmith
153 A R Hurst, carpenter
155 John McKnight, engineer

Steven-st intersects

163 G McLaughlin, laborer
167 Mrs Mary Lynch

Ashley-st intersects

177 W O'Shaughnessy, laborer
185 John Mallin, dealer
187 Miss Nellie Jones
191 Jeremiah Gregg, laborer

Wentworth-st intersects

George Smith, laborer
John Wright, locksmith
Henry East, bricklayer

Burlington-st intersects

John Graham, cigarmaker

Wood-st e, north side, from foot James n to Wellington

7 — Simmons
9 John Lawrence, painter
11 Joseph Omand, sailor
13 Jas Whittaker, glassblower
15 William Doyle, laborer
17 R O Mackay

Hughson-st intersects

27 Luke McNamara, laborer
29 John Blake, teamster
31 John Smith, laborer
33 Patrick Curran, laborer
35 Mrs Mary O'Neil
37 James Sullivan, laborer
39 Wm Hall, dairyman

41 F H Taylor, laborer
43 Jas Wickham, stovemounter
John-st intersects
55 Robert O'Neill, laborer
59 John McCarthy, driver
59 Dennis Mulcahy, stovemntr
59½ Jesse Stibbs, laborer
61 Thos O'Connor, glassblower
63 John McMahon, laborer
Catharine and Mary-sts intersect
105 John E Miller, moulder
107 Thos Butler, laborer
111 Thos Wilson, laborer
113 Joseph Oddy, carpenter
Ferguson-ave intersects
129 Richard Glen, carter
133 George Fielding, warper
135 Edward Allen, blacksmith
137 Edward Fuller, laborer
141 Wm Aldrich, laborer
Wellington-st intersects

Wood-st e, south side

6 Samuel Blowes, glassblower
8 Arthur Miller, laborer
10 John McMicken, glassblower
Hughson-st intersects
24 Patrick Colvin
John-st intersects
52 Wm Daly, tailor
54 Jacob Tremble, teamster
56 Patrick Burns, laborer
60 Angustus Fickle, packer
64 Joseph Gilligan, glassblower
Catharine and Mary-sts intersect
108 Jas Turner, laborer
110 John Philips, stovemounter
114 Richard Franklin, machinist
118 Stephen Saxby, laborer
120 John Kent, laborer
Ferguson-ave intersects
124 Thomas Moore, laborer
r 124 Joseph Pearson, laborer
126 James Stevens
130 Wm Walton, laborer
132 Edward Carless, laborer
136 Vacant
142 Mrs P McKeever
Wellington-st intersects

Wood-st w, north side, from 239 James n to Macnab

8 John Potter, farmer
10 Robert McManus, grocer
12 Martin Mahony, sailor
16 Dennis Kavanagh, fireman
20 Mrs Mary Lawler
Macnab-st intersects
Jacob Burlinghoff, laborer

Wood-st w, south side

11 Thos Ward, laborer
13 John Dunn, laborer
15 Wm Braidswood, laborer
17 Dennis McAuliffe, laborer
23 Mrs John Doyle
25 Chas Moody, weaver
Macnab-st intersects
37 John Holm, carter
39 Jas Dilworth, laborer
Burlington-st intersects

York-st, north side, from Macnab n to city limits

2 John Greig, stationer
4 Henry Magee, harness
6 Geo E Wilson, provisions
6a John Davis, crockery
6½ H O'Brien, varieties
8-10 Kraft & Son, saddlery, hardware
22 Geo Luxton, flour, feed, etc
14 Wm Bangarth, confectioner
16-18 D Murray, flour and feed
20 Wm Ronald, grocer
22 J Henry, boots and shoes
24 Vacant
26 Hy Longhurst & Co, glasswks
28 Jas H Boggess, broker
30-32 Albert Brunke, furrier
34 Star Laundry
36 George Kramer, hotel
38 Mrs T Wilkes, fruiterer

40 John Taylor, flour and feed
42 Vacant

Park-st intersects

Cheapside Block {
Chas G Carlson, tailor
Vacant
Vacant
Thos Bowker, confectioner
J J Bigelow
George Dodd, finisher
}

50 Wm Craft, pork butcher
52 Tnos Ballantyne, plumber
54 Alex Campbell, grocer
56 Wm F Farmer, watchmaker
58 Mrs H Waters, milliner
60 A Calder & Co, druggists

Bay-st intersects

Copp Bros, founders
102 Vacant
104 Vacant
106 Max Steinberg, rag dealer
110 J & G Nicholson, wood dlrs
114 John Schram, carpenter
116 John Browne, blacksmith
118 Fred Gottorff, marble dealer

Caroline-st intersects

124 Ed Green, furniture dealer
126 Miss Eunice Hill
128 Mrs Bridget Duffy
130 Adam Hunter, stationer
132 Chas Brown, machinist
134 R Morgan, carriage trimmer
136 F W Wodell, journalist
144 146 John Duff, grocer
148 Vacant
150 Vacant
152 C J Prichard, shoemaker
154 Mark Smith, baker
156 J Philp, druggist

Hess-st intersects

160 David Gillespie, broker
162 British American Laundry
166 M O'Grady, marble works
168 Wm Cook, painter
172 John R Rule, cutter
174-76 Joseph Lee, wood dealer
178 Richard Beckerson, laborer
180 Hamilton Ornamental Iron Foundry

Queen-st intersects

West Lawn, A Copp

Oxford-st intersects

220 Wm Sayers, laborer
226 Jas Haydon, tinsmith
228 Jas Porteous, machinist
230 Henry Carson, shoemaker

Locomotive-st commences

240 Vacant
242 Mrs Charles Simon, confectioner
244 Edward Beatty, laborer
246 J A Malcolm, carriage mkr
250 National hotel

Magill-st commences

254 Arthur Boyle, druggist
256 Wm Phillips, butcher
258 Patrick Shea, laborer
260 Matthew Flynn, engineer
262-4 Percy A Wynn

Crook-st commences

270 Geo Morris, grocer
270 Vail & Morris, roofers
276 Mrs Jas Patton
278 Dundurn Flour Mills

Locke-st intersects

286 John Wright, butcher
Mrs Mary Ann Stroud
290 Wm Armstrong, tailor
296 Richard Pentecost, painter

Inchbury-st intersects

320 Isaac Mills
324 C F Lockman
326 J B Smith, laborer
Dundurn Castle
Joseph Kent, contractor
Henry Hutchison
J A Maracle, toll keeper
Henry Fairbank
Fred Weir, stonecutter
John S Smith, laborer

York-st, south side

1 R Evans & Co, seedsmen
3 James Philp & Son, saddlers
5 A Lawson & Co, printers

7 C Kerner, hotel
9 J H Carmichael, shoemaker
11 Mrs F M Peene, millinery
13 David Kenny, seedsman
15 Jas Cuzner, shoemaker
17 L M Vail, spring mattras maker
17½ R H Elliott, furniture
19 H Brazier, barber
21 J Belling, watchmaker
23 J M Munzinger, bookbinder
23½ Thos Ballantyne, plumber
25 Thos A Wright, locksmith
27 Chris Moody, watchmaker
29 Wm Hover, tailor
31 Jas Kirk, barber
33 P S Bateman, blacksmith
33½ M Fitzpatrick & Co, paint's
37 S Groves, blacksmith
39 John F Kavanagh, grocer

Park-st intersects

41 Commercial hotel
43 John Walsh, shoemaker
45 Mrs M A Earle
47 R Arroll, broker
51 E M Furniss & Son, marble works
53 C Carpenter & Co, hardware
55 Mrs Musgrove, boarding
57 Edward Murphy, painter
57½ Alex Hannah, bricklayer
57½ Vacant
59 Thos E Nichols, iron fence manfr
61-63 H Goering, hotel keeper
65 Jas Mason, fruiterer
67 John Spriggs, shoemaker
69 F Oxley, grocer
71 W H C Harrison, herbalist
73 Thos Platt, fancy goods
75 Thos Pillman, butcher
77 David McDonald, grocer

Bay-st intersects

79-83 Vacant
85 Vacant
87 Robert England, barber
91 Thos J Foulkes, barber
93-95 Geo Bradshaw
97 John Billington, shoemaker
99 Robert Snodgrass
99½ Chas Carey, confectioner
101 Vacant
103 Wm Fulton, laborer
105 Mrs Agnes Lancefield
105½ Vacant
107 Thomson & Wright, lumber dealers
113 H Pearson, hotel
115 John Dixon, knitter
117 Jas H Rodgers, baker
119 Mrs Laura Hedden, dressmaker
123 John McAllister, grocer

Caroline-st intersects

Robert Irwin, customs brok'r
127 Vacant
129 Vacant
131 Vacant
133 Corneluis Donovan, moulder
137 John English, carpenter
139 Mrs Ann Gillespie
141 Mrs W H Duffield
147 Jas Naylor, fancy goods
149 Mrs J H Haney, confectioner
151 Jas Christie, carpenter
153 Duncan Cameron, com trav
157 George Edmondson, butcher
159 W Gillies & Co, grocers

Hess-st intersects

161 Wm McDonald, laborer
183 Jas Wilson, moulder

Queen-st intersects

189 Miss Mary Dampier
207 Robt Walker, grocer
209 John Burrows, laborer
213 Philip Sutton
215 F E Skelly & Co, dry goods
217 Thos Walsh, grocer
219 Richard May, laborer
221 Mrs August Westphal
227 G Beaver, hotel

Ray-st intersects

226 O O Hinds, butcher
237 Jas Thurling, laborer
241 Jas Stevenson

245 John Barlow, laborer
253 Wm Kench, confectioner

Pearl-st intersects

255 Jas Bain, grocer
257 Jas Jarvis, engineer
261 E Wyth, carpenter
263 Geo Ellis, machinist
265 Wm Mitchell, machinist
267 Alex Bell, laborer
269 Mrs Thos Watts
271 Vacant
285 Jas McHarg, agent
289 Dundurn hotel

Locke-st intersects

291-3 Geo Steele, dry goods
299 Jas Hinchcliffe, grocer
301 Wm Sweet, boilermaker
305 R Hinchcliffe, machine shop

Inchbury-st intersects

307 Frank Livings, grocer
309 R C Cuff, butcher
311 Robert Howitt, butcher
315 Mrs Patrick Quinn
317 Edward Collins, painter
319 Mrs Johanna Boyle

Sophia-st intersects

327 Edward Williams, iron roller
333 Jas Logie
335 Vacant
337 Samuel Collyer, grocer

Devenport-st intersects

Thos Pawline, rag picker
Ed Winter, blacksmith

Dundurn-st intersects

Burlington Cemetery
James Brown
C Myss, shoemaker
H N Thomas, marble works
Wm Jarriott
Thos Wellington, porter
F Morrison, hotel
Peter Colvin, grocer
Burlington Cemetery
Alex Craig, caretaker cemetery
Adam Rutherford, laborer
Donald Reid, gardener
Alex Reid, gardener
Mrs M M Wheeler, hotel

Young-st, formerly Catharina.
See Page 237.

GOOD WORK. LOW PRICES.

A. McPHERSON,

FINE ✠ JOB ✠ PRINTER,

51 JAMES STREET NORTH,

HAMILTON, - - ONTARIO.

SPECIAL ATTENTION TO FINE COMMERCIAL AND SOCIETY PRINTING.

SUBSCRIBERS'
CLASSIFIED BUSINESS DIRECTORY

ACCOUNTANTS.

Blackley David, 11 Main e
Findlay W F, 25 James s
Herman William, 16 James s
Mason J J. Masonic hall
Moody R W, 162 King e
Pearson John, 8-10 Hughson s
Townsend S E, 6½ James s
Wavell Thos L, 12 Hughson s

AGENTS—COLLECTING (RENTS, DEBTS, ETC).

Hamilton Protective Collecting Agency, F R Ghent, Sec, room 9, Court House
McNair & Bell, constables, 1 King William
Moore & Davis, 2 King Wm
Pearson John Hughson s
Trade Association, M B Rymal, 24 Macnab n
Whipple, E S, 78½ King e
Zwick W H, 26 Merrick

AGENTS—LAND AND ESTATE.

Hamilton Universal Agency, 182 King e
Moore & Davis, 2 King Wm
Pearson John, 10 Hughson s
Whipple E S, 78½ King e

ARCHITECTS.

Balfour J, 25 James s
Brass Peter, 50 Hunter w
Edwards W A, 9 James n
Hills Lucian, 278 King w
Kennedy R D, 42 James n
Mulligan C W, court house
Rastrick F J, 22 Maria

AUCTIONEERS AND APPRAISERS.

Burrows Thos, 78 James n
Hunter & Hunter, 24 Merrick

BAKERS.

Bateman E W, 200 King e
Chilman I C, 119 King w
Dermody John, 151 Main e
Geiger H, 214 King w
Harris Wm, 14 Market Square
Hill Mark. 102 James n
Lees Wm, 31 Main e

BANKS.

Bank of British North America, 5 King e
Bank of Hamilton, 17 King w
Bank of Montreal, cor James and Main
Canadian Bank of Commerce, cor King and Hughson
Merchants' Bank, King cor John
Molsons Bank, cor James and King
Stinson's Bank, 10 Hughson n

BANKERS, EXCHANGE STOCK AND SHARE BROKERS.

Forbes A F, 2 Merrick
Morgan Chas E, 11 James n

BARRISTERS AND SOLICITORS.

Barton George M, 4 James n

Jones, McQuesten & Chisholm,

Barristers and Solicitors,

VICTORIA CHAMBERS,

31 James St. South,

HAMILTON, ONT.

J. W. Jones. LL.B., I. B. McQuesten, M. A., James Chisholm, M. A.

Mackelcan, Gibson & Gausby,

BARRISTERS,

Solicitors of the Supreme Court of Ontario,

16 James St. South,

HAMILTON, ONT.

F. Mackelcan, Q. C.; J. M. Gibson, M. A., LLB.; J. D. Gausby.

Lazier, Dingwall & Monck,

Barristers & Solicitors,

42 JAMES STREET NORTH,

S. F. Lazier, M.A., LL.B.; K. Dingwall, B.A., LL. B.; J. F. Monck.

ROBERTSON & ROBERTSON,

Barristers,

Solicitors, Notaries, Etc.,

Have removed to the

COURT HOUSE,

HAMILTON, - - CANADA.

Thomas Robertson, Q. C.; H. H. Robertson.

Money to lend at lowest rates of interest.

PARKES & MACADAMS,

Barristers and Solicitors,

In the Supreme Court.

ATTORNEYS and NOTARIES

OFFICES—Hamilton Provident Building, 1st flat; entrance on Hughson street.

J. PARKES, A. H. MACADAMS.

DUGGAN & AMBROSE,

Barristers, Solicitors, Etc.,

CANADA LIFE CHAMBERS,

HAMILTON, - - ONTARIO.

Money to Lend.

R. J. DUGGAN. A. W. AMBROSE.

SHERMAN E. TOWNSEND,

Accountant, Auditor, Assignee and General Attorney,

6½ JAMES ST. SOUTH, HAMILTON, ONT.

REFERENCES BY PERMISSION.

Alex. Turner, Esq., of Messrs. James Turner & Co. Wholesale Grocers; A. T. Wood, Esq., of Messrs. Wood & Leggat, Wholesale Hardware Merchants; Adam Brown, Esq., of Messrs. Brown, Balfour & Co., Wholesale Grocers; John W. Murton, Esq., of Messrs. Murton & Reid, Coal Merchants; Reid, Goering & Co., Wholesale Wine and Spirit Merchants; E. & C. Gurney & Co., Wholesale Stove Manufacturers, etc.; Fuller, Nesbitt & Bicknell, Barristers, etc.; John Winer & Co., Wholesale Druggists; Jas Watson, Esq., President Strathroy Knitting Company; Geo. H. Gillespie, Esq., President Hamilton Provident and Loan Society; A. G. Ramsay, Esq., President Canada Life Assurance Company; Edward Mitchell, Esq., Manager Canadian Bank of Commerce; Waterous Engine Works Company, Brantford.

MARTIN & KITTSON,

Barristers and Solicitors,

WENTWORTH CHAMBERS,

25 James St. South,

HAMILTON, CANADA.

Edward Martin, Q. C. E. E. Kittson.

HASLETT & WASHINGTON,

Barristers,

Solicitors, Conveyancers, Etc.

20 James Street South,

HAMILTON, - CANADA.

Thos. C. Haslett. S. F. Washington.

FRANCIS FITZGERALD,

Barrister, Etc.,

10 KING STREET WEST,

HAMILTON. ONTARIO.

W. A. H. DUFF,

BARRISTER, SOLICITOR,

NOTARY PUBLIC, ETC.,

VICTORIA CHAMBERS,

31 James Street South,

HAMILTON, - ONTARIO.

CAMERON & WITHERSPOON

BARRISTERS,

Solicitors in Supreme Court of Ontario.

NOTARIES, ETC.

Offices—Hamilton Provident Building, 1st flat, entrance on Hughson street

A. D. Cameron, LL.B. R. W. Witherspoon.

WALKER & SCOTT,

BARRISTERS, ETC.,

10 James Street South,

HAMILTON, - ONTARIO.

W. F. Walker, M.A., LL.B., John J. Scott
Wm. Lees, B. C. L.

EDWARD FURLONG, LL.B.,

Barrister and Solicitor,

NO. 11 MAIN ST. EAST,

Hamilton, Ont.

CHARLES LEMON,

Barrister and Solicitor,

NOTARY PUBLIC, ETC.

Money to Loan on Real Estate Security.

Collection of Accounts and Agency promptly attended to.

Office, No. 14 Hughson Street South

HAMILTON, ONT.

Bell Wm, Wentworth Chambers, 25 James s
Bruce, Burton & Culham, Canada Life Chambers, 1 James s
Cameron & Witherspoon, 1 Hughson s
Carscallen & Cahill, 7 King w
Haslett & Washington, 20 James s
Crerar, Muir & Crerar, 1 Hughson s
Curell J G, 34 James n
Duff W A H, 31 James s
Duggan & Ambrose, Canada Life Buildings, 1 James s
Fitzgerald Francis, 10 King w
Fuller, Nesbitt & Bicknell, 20 James s
Furlong Edward, 11 Main e
Gage & Jelfs, 55 John s
Irving Æmelius, Q C, court house
Jones, McQuesten & Chisholm, 31 James s
Lavery W J, 4 Main e
Lazier, Dingwall & Monck, 42 James n
Lemon Chas, 112 Hughson s
Macdonald Walter R, 13 Main e
MacKelcan, Gibson & Gausby, 16 James s
MacKelcan H A, 20 Main e
Martin & Malone, cor James and King
Martin & Kittson, 25 James s
Mills Geo H, 25 James s
O'Heir Arthur, 4 Main e
Osler, Teetzel & Harrison, Canada Life Chambers, 3 James s
Papps Geo S, 13 Main e
Parkes & Macadams, 1 Hughson s
Pringle R A, 16 James s
Robertson & Robertson, Court House
Sadleir C A, 8 Main e
Staunton & Livingston, 18 Jas s
Steele D, 2½ James s
Stinson T H, cor James and King William
Waddell & Waddell, court house
Walker & Scott, 10 James s

BOOKSELLERS AND STATIONERS.

Atkinson Bros, wh and retail, 66 James n and 35 King e
Buntin, Gillies & Co, wholesale
Clappison Thos C, James cor Gore
stationers, 41 King w
Duncan Robert & Co, cor Market Square and James
Eastwood John & Co, 16 King e
Hunter A, 52 James n
McLellan D, Bible depository, 28 King w
Overell E & Co, 24½ King w
Williams H S, Copp's Block, King e

BOOK-BINDERS.

Duncan Robert & Co, cor James and Market Square
Eastwood J & Co, 60 King e
Haigh Richard, 16 King w
Mars Alex, 14 Hughson n

BOOTS AND SHOES.

Arland H & Bro, 62 King e
Climie J D, 28 King e
Edwards C P, 104 King w
Garrett John & Co, wholesale, 55-7 King w
Griffith William, wholesale, 53 King w
Henderson A S, 64 King w
Henderson George, 45 Macnab n
McCully G A, 73 James n
McPherson John & Co, wholesale, 51-3 King e
McPhail James, 6 Market Square
Mahony John C, 26 King e
Pegram Nathaniel, 137 James n
Richardson Matthew, Copp's Block, King e
Wilson Robert, 60 King e

BREWERS.

Gomph John, 360 John n
Labatt John, office, 35 King e

H. A. MACKELCAN,

Barrister,

Solicitor of Supreme Court of Ontario,

NOTARY, ETC.

NO. 20 MAIN ST. EAST,

HAMILTON, ONTARIO.

Money to Loan on Land at Lowest Rates.

GEORGE M. BARTON,

BARRISTER, ETC.,

Law, Chancery, and Conveyancing Office.

Cor. James and King Streets,

Hamilton, Ont.

WILLIAM BRUCE

Solicitor of Canadian and Foreign

PATENTS,

Draughtsman and Engrosser.

14½ King St. East, opposite the Gore,

HAMILTON, CANADA.

R. A. PRINGLE,

BARRISTER, SOLICITOR,

ETC., ETC.,

16 James St. South,

HAMILTON, ONTARIO.

JOHN PEARSON,

Chancery Cambers, - Prince's Square,

8-10 Hughson-st. south.

ACCOUNTANT, COLLECTOR,

House, Real Estate and

Commission Agent,

MONEY TO LOAN.

R. D. KENNDEY,

ARCHITECT,

Provincial Land Surveyor and Civil

ENGINEER,

No. 42 James Street North,

GILLESPIE & POWIS,

BROKERS,

TOBACCOS, TEAS, COFFEES, SUGARS, &C

31 KING ST. EAST, HAMILTON, ONT.

Spring Brewery, P Grant & Sons, 119 Bay n

BROKERS.

Dunn J S, teas and sugars
Gillespie & Powis, teas, sugars, etc, 31 King e
Irwin Robert, customs, 84 James n
Townsend W G, customs, 33 Stuart w
Wavell Thos, teas, etc, 12 Hughson s

BROOM MANUFACTURERS.

Mitchell Thos, 31 King w
Woods Walter, 62 Macnab n

BRUSH MANUFACTURERS.

Meakins & Sons, 225-9 King e
Mitchell Thos, 31 King w

BUILDERS AND CONTRACTORS

Addison Wm & Sons, Wellington cor Young
Beer Isaiah, 35 Murray e
Chisholm Robert, 174 Macnab n
Clucas Wm, 123 Cannon w
Cruickshank Robt, 55 Jackson e
Hancock Wm, 27 Locomotive
Hannaford Bros, plasterers, 76 Merrick
Isbister John, 81 Wellington s
Meade Thos, 8 Young
Miller & Hill, 81 James s
Pigott M A, 95 Macnab n
Sharp Geo, 147 Park n
VanAllen Eli, 5 Bay s
Whyte Geo, 131 King e

BUILDERS' SUPPLIES.

Freeman W A, 169 James n
Gordon W J F, 108 James n

BUTCHERS.

Bowering & Pain, 89 King w
Harrison Henry, 51 James s
Hill Walter, 104 James n
How & Braid, 204 King w
Lawry Thos & Son, James-st Market
Limin Chas, 26 Jackson w

CABINET MAKERS AND UPHOLSTERERS.

Allardice R A & Co, Merrick
Hoodless & Son, 51 King w
Jenkins Geo, 140 King w
Johnson J H, 128 King e
McCallum & Hall, 16 Macnab n
Pecover Joseph, Copp's Block, King e
Keid estate of, King cor Park
Richardson George, 36 King William
Zingsheim Jacob, Mary nr Murray

CARPETS AND HOUSE FURNISHINGS.

Walker Frank E, King cor Walnut n

CARPET BEATER.

Brunt Samuel, 7 George

CARTAGE AGENTS.

Armstrong Chas, (N & N W R) 33 James n
Hendrie & Co (G W R), 35 King w
Shedden Co (G T R). 9 King w

CHINA, GLASS AND EARTHENWARE

Canada Glass House, 52 King e
London China House, 9 Market square
McMahon, Broadfield & Co, 45 King w
Skinner J A & Co, 9 King e

CIGARS, TOBACCOS, ETC.

Ontario Havana Cigar manufactory, office 12-4 Hughson s

Pattison Z, 65 Cannon w
Reid, Goering & Co, cor King and Catharine
Schrader J C, cor Bay and Cannon

CLOTHING.

Calder John & Co, Macnab cor Merrick
Sanford W E & Co, 47 King e
Vail A S & Co, 18 James n

COAL OIL, LAMPS, ETC.

Canada Glass House, 52 King
Farmer Wm, 114 James n
OFFICE
Taylor J C, 27 King w
Williams J C, manf, 18 Macnab n
Young & Bro, 17 John n

COAL AND WOOD.

Browne E & Son, ft Macnab n
Dewey D R & Co, 12 James s
Dow Bros, 45 Main w
Fairgrieve J B, 59 James n
Freeman W A, 169 James n
Kelly D J, 135 James n
McIlwraith Thos, cor Main and Catharine
McKenzie John, 149 Macnab n
Mulholland J & H, Union wood and coal, yard, Cannon cor Cathcart
Murton & Reid, cor John and Rebecca, and Main cor Charles
Myles Thomas & Son, cor Main and Hughson
Nicholson Wm, 111 King w
Nicholls Frank, Main cor Locke
Payne W, Mary cor Cannon
Smith G B, 8 Mary

COFFEE AND SPICE MILLS.

Canada—W G Dunn, 59 Main w

COMMISSION.

Benner Richard, 9 Main e
Gillespie & Powis, 31 King e
Hamilton Universal Agency, 182 King e
Morden W & J, 7 Market sq
Robertson & Henderson, Merrick cor Macnab

CONFECTIONERS.

Chilman I C, 117 King w
Edwards Benjamin, 102 King w
Pattison Z, wholesale, cor King and Park s

CONSULS.

Hawaii Kingdom, Adam Brown, 5 James s
Norway & Sweden, S E Gregory 55 Catharine s
United States, J F Hazelton, G T R station

COTTON FACTORIES.

Hamilton Cotton Factory, Mary
Ontario Cotton Mills Co, 250 Macnab n

DENTISTS.

Bowes John, 9 James n
Chittenden G S, 8½ King e
Husband Drs R J & T H, 10 King w
Zimmerman S, M D, King cor Macnab

DINING ROOMS.

Arcade Coffee Room, Alexandra Arcade, James n
Gore Coffee Tavern, 13 Hughson n
Temperance Dining Rooms, 48 James n

DRUGGISTS.

Barr John A & Co, 33 Macnab n
Boyle Arthur, York cor Magill
Brierley Richard, 14 King e
Case H Spencer, 50 King w

Calder A & Co, 58 York
Central Drug Store, York cor Hess
Doherty Arthur, 245 King w
Gerrie John, 30 James n
Hamilton A & Co, cor King and James
Harrison Bros, 36 James n
Ontario Pharmacy, King cor Ferguson ave
Smith W L, 116 James n
Sutherland James W, 180 King w
Taylor R N & Co, 35 and 95 John s
Vincent A & Co, 230 James n
Wilson Archdale & Co, wholesale, 19 Macnab n
Winer J & Co, wh, 25 King e

DRY GOODS, MILLINERY, ETC.

Barnard P B, 36 King w
Campbell & Pentecost, 43 Macnab n
Crossley John, cor James and King Wm
Finch Bros, 18 King w
Kerr A R & Co, 34 King w
Knox, Morgan & Co, wh, 7 King e
James George, 8 King e
McIlwraith & McMaster, 12 James n
McKay Bros, cor King and John
Mann Samuel, 258 King e
Murray A & Co, 18-20 King e
Pratt & Watkins, 16 James n
Shea James, 42 King e
Thorne & Co, 160 King e
Watkins Thomas C, 30-32 King e

DYERS AND CLEANERS.

Howard W H, 17 Rebecca
Parker Robt & Co, 4 John n
Roe G, 185 King e

EMPLOYMENT BUREAUS

Britt E, 109½ King w
Hamilton Universal agency, 182 King e

ENGROSSER.

Bruce Wm, 14½ King e

EXPRESS COMPANIES

American & Canadian Express Cos, 18 James s

FANCY GOODS

Levy Bros & Scheuer, 17 King e
Maclean Mrs F, 4 King e
Moodie John & Sons, 16 King w
Moody Miss F E, 162 King e

FELT AND GRAVEL ROOFERS

Irwin Thos & Son, 12 Macnab s

FILE MANUFACTURER

Spence R & Co, 176½ King e

FISH DEALERS.

Cline R M, 194 King e

FLORISTS AND NURSERYMEN

Hamilton Nursery, W Holton, Main e
Harper Robert, 18 Wellington n
Townsend E J, cor Park and Vine

FLOUR AND FEED.

Carr E & D, 91-93 King w
Dunlop James, 91 John s
Geiger Wm, 220 King w
McFarlane Alex, 196-8 King e
Morris Thomas, 21 Wellington n

FOUNDERS, MACHINISTS, IRON WORKS, ETC.

American Nail Works, foot Queen n
Bowes, Jamieson & Co, King cor Tisdale
Brayley & Dempster (wrought iron, etc), 47 King Wm

Burrow, Stewart & Milne, corner Cannon and John
Copp Bros, Empire Foundry, cor York and Bay
Gartshore Alex, Stuart w
Gurney E & C Co, 36-42 John n
Hamilton Bridge & Tool Co, foot Caroline n
Hamilton Iron Forging Co, cor Barton & Queen
Hart Emery Wheel Co, Samuel Briggs, manager, 19 Hunter w
Hart Machine Co, S E Rogers, manager, 19 Hunter w
Killey, Osborne & Co, Barton e
Laidlaw Manfr Co, Mary cor Kelly
Moore Dennis & Co, Catharine n
Morrison George, foot Caroline n
Ontario Rolling Mills, Queen n
Olmsted Bros, ornamental, cor York and Queen
Ontario Rolling Mills, Queen n
Sawyer L D & Co, foot Wellington n
Stewart J & Co, cor Macnab and Vine

FORWARDERS.

Browne Edw & Son, Browne's wharf
Mackay R O, Mackay's wharf

FRUIT, FISH, OYSTERS, GAME, ETC.

Dixon & Morton, 52 King w
Drayton & Co, 6 King w
Hayhoe C, 204 King e

FURRIER.

Brunke Albert, 30 York

GENTS' FURNISHINGS, ETC.

Henigan Jas, 108 King e
Hyslop, Cornell & Co, wh, 7 James s
Leask R P, 24 King e
Taylor A J, 40 King w
Treble S G, 2 King e

GILDERS.

Blandford Henry, 50 King e
Marsden T & Son, 46 James n

GROCERS

Blake Jas, 254 Mary
Bremner Jas, 248 King w
Brennan J & C J, 5 Market sq
Brown, Balfour & Co, wholesale, 5 James s
Carpenter Bros, 9 Market square
Cherrier F L, 15 Market square
Cooper Robt C, 31 Macnab n
Cumming Bros, 108 James n
Doherty Arthur, 245 King w
Duff John & Son, 144 York
Duncan Bros, 71 King e
Feast Edwin B, 58 Caroline s
Galbreaith N D, 104 King e
Gillard W H & Co, wholesale, 5 Hughson s
Harvey A & Co, wholesale, 21 King e
Hunter John, 194 James n
Kemp Geo, 120 King e
King Cyrus, 10 Market square
Lucas, Park & Co, wholesale, 59 Macnab n
Lumsden Bros, wh, 64 Macnab n
Macpherson, Glassco & Co, wh, 67 9 King e
McMillan John, 210 King e
Mann Samuel, 256 King e
Meekison Andrew, James cor Cannon
Morrison Alex, 86-8 John s.
Murphy & Murray, 66 King e
Osborne Jas & Son, 4 James s
Peebles C H, 39 Macnab n
Reeves A L, jr, 212 King w
Stuart John Son & Co, wh, cor John and Main
Sutherland Angus, 56-58 King w
Thomson Peter, 190 King e
Turner Jas & Co, wh, 3 Hughson s

Winnifrith B, King cor Victoria ave

GUNSMITHS

Hamilton Gun Works, J Holman, 79 James n

HAIRDRESSER.

Rutherford James, 69 Stuart w

HARDWARE.

Hope Adam & Co, wholesale, 102 King e
Kraft E & Son, saddlery, 8-10 York
Winslow & Webber, carriage, 56 King e
Wood & Leggat, 44 King e

HARNESS, SADDLES AND TRUNKS.

Jolley Jas & Sons, 47 John s
Kraft E & Son, 8-10 York
Philp Jas & Son, 3 York

HAT MANUFACTURER.

Dominion Hat Co, John Tunstead, 210 King e

HATS AND CAPS

Acres Wm, 12 King e
Leask R P, 24 King e
Mills Joseph & Son, 7 James n
Nisbet Matthew, King cor Walnut and 6 James n
Taylor A J, 40 King w
Treble S G, 2 King e

HOT AIR FURNACES.

Copp Bros, cor York and Bay
Gurney E & C Co, 36-42 John n
Irwin Thos & Son, 12 Macnab s
Stewart Jas & Co, cor Macnab and Vine

HOTELS, SALOONS AND RESTAURANTS.

Allison, Wm T Allison, 51 Stuart
American, F W Bearman, corner King and Charles
Atlantic House, Andrew Ruthven, 29 Macnab n
Blaase Chas, 112 James n
Brunswick, James C Macpherson, 7-9 King Wm
Central, R R Ashbaugh, 135 King e
Columbia Thos Crooks, King w
Commercial, cor York and Park
Continental, J McHenry, cor Stuart and James
Court House, Wm Gowland, 55-9 John s
Crystal Palace View, Harry Bawden, cor Peter and Locke
Dominion, Armstrong & Haw, props, 80 King w
Fairchild T B, cor King and Bay
Franklin, Cook & Mitchell, King cor Park
Goering, Henry, 61-3 York
Grand Opera House Restaurant
Germania, J Jahn, 33 John s
High Matthew, 65 John s
James A T, 28 King William
Lay Andrew, 21 James n
Noble W, cor James and Cannon
Office Restaurant, Harry Sweetman, 4 King w
Richter T, 43 James n
Royal, Hood & Bro, 61-63 James n
St Charles Restaurant, H C Hicock, 64 James n
St James Restaurant, Fred DeLacy, propr, 19 Hughson n
St Nicholas, Alex Dunn, 37 James n
Victoria, Richard Irwin, 79 King e
Walker House, M Bauer, 166 King e
Western, John Callane, 81 Stuart w

ICE DEALERS.

Dewey D & Son, 15 George
Walton Ice Co, 70 Vine

INSURANCE CO'S AND AGENTS

Accident of North America, Seneca Jones, 59 James n
Ætna of Hartford, fire, W F Findlay, Wentworth Chambers, 25 James s
Agricultural fire (Watertown, NY) Payne& McMeekin,97 James n
British America Assurance Co, fire and marine, A F Forbes, 2 Merrick
British & Foreign Marine Insursurance Co, (Liverpool), W F Findlay, 25 James s
British Empire Life Assurance, M A Pennington, 30 James s
Caledonian Fire, (Edingburgh), M A Pennington, 30 James s
Canada Guarantee Co, Seneca Jones, 59 James n
Canada Life, A G Ramsay, F I A, manager, head office, cor. King and James
Canadian Millers' Mutual Fire Co, Seneca Jones, 59 James n
Citizens Insurance Co, James Walker, 20 Main e
Citzens Insurance Co (Accident branch) Richard Bull, 55 James n
City of London Fire Co, Richard Bull, 55 James n
Commercial Union Assurance Co (London, Eng,) Payne & McMeekin, 97 James n
Confederation Life Association, Seneca Jones, 59 James n
Dominion Plate Glass Insurance Co, David McLellan, 84 James n
Economical Mutual Fire, Wm. Strong, Arcade
Fire Insurance Association, J T Routh, 16 James s
Glasgow & London Insurance Co, Wm Strong, Arcade
Guarantee Co of North America, Seneca Jones, 59 James n.
Guardian Fire and Life Assurance of London, (Eng) Gillespie & Powis, 31 King e
Hartford Fire, Geo McKeand, 57 James n
Insurance Co of North America, (the) Marine, Gillespie &Powis, 31 King e
London & Lancashire Fire Insurance Co, W F Findlay, 25 James s
London & Lancashire Life Co, J T Routh, 16 James s
Lancashire, fire and life, Geo A Young, 2 Merrick
Life Association of Canada, John Cameron, manager, 25 James s
Life Association of Scotland, A F Forbes, 2 Merrick
Lloyd's Plate Glass Insurance Co, Seneca Jones, 59 James n
London Guarantee & Accident Co, Geo A Young, 2 Merrick
National Assurance Co, (Ireland) Richard Bull, 55 James n
National Fire Insurance Co, Forbes & Brown, 2 Merrick
New York Mutual Marine insurance Co, A F Forbes, 2 Merrick
Northern Fire Assurance Co, Seneca Jones, 59 James n
North British & Mercantile, fire and life, J T Routh, 16 James s
Norwich & London Accident Ins Association, Payne & McMeekin, 97 James n
Pearson John, general agent, 10 Hughson s
Phœnix Ins Co, marine, J B Fairgrieve, 59 James n
Phœnix Fire, of London (Eng) Gillespie & Powis, 31 King e
Providence Washington Insurance, David McLellan, 84 James n
Queen, Fire and Life, R Benner, 9 Main e

INSURANCE AND SHIPPING DIRECTORY.

The following are among the Principal Companies represented in the City. See also Insurance and Steamship agents.

SENECA JONES,

General Insurance Agent

COMPANIES REPRESENTED:

Fire—Northern Assurance Co. of London, Eng.
" Royal Canadian Insurance Co. of Montreal.
" Waterloo Mutual Ins. Co. of Waterloo.
" Canadian Millers' Mutual Insurance Co.
Life—Confederation Life Association of Toronto.
Accident—Accident Insurance Co. of North America, of Montreal.
Guarantee—Guarantee Co. of North America, of Montreal.
Plate Glass—The "Lloyds" of New York.

OFFICE---ROYAL HOTEL BUILDINGS,

59 James St. North, Hamilton.

W. F. FINDLAY,

Public Accountant and Adjuster

Financial and Estate Agent.

--AGENT FOR--

Ætna Insurance Co. (Fire).
London and Lancashire Fire Insurance Co.
British and Foreign Marine Insurance Co.
Western Assurance Co. (Marine).

Wentworth Chambers,

25 James Street South, - Hamilton.

RICHARD BULL,

Insurance and Real Estate Agent

No. 55 James St. N., Hamilton

FIRE, LIFE AND ACCIDENT.

Fire Insurance—For short periods, or for one or three years.
Life Assurance—On ordinary plan, or on TONTINE, Endowment or Partnership, or for a special number of years.
Accident Insurance—For the trip, one day, week, month or year, with weekly compensation in case of being disabled by an accident.
Fidelity Insurance—Guarantee Bonds issued at lowest rates.

A share of public patronage respectfully solicited.

FIRE!

Glasgow & London

INSURANCE COMPANY

Of Great Britain

Hamilton Dist. Agency, 15 Alexandra Arcade

WM. STRONG, Agent.

Commerc'l Union Assurance Co
of London, England.

Agricultural Insurance Co.,
of Watertown, N. Y,

Norwich and London Accident Insurance Association,
of Norwich, England.

Payne & McMeekin, Agents

Office 97 James St, North.

GEO. McKEAND,

57 James-st. N., Royal Hotel Buildings

—AGENT FOR—

Richelieu and Ontario Navigation Co., to Montreal, Quebec and Intermediate Ports.
Anchor Line, to Glasgow, via Londonderry.
Hartford Fire Insurance Company.
Inman Line, to Liverpool, via Queenstown.
R. & O. Steamers, run in connection with Intercolonial Railway to Maritime Provinces.

GEO. McKEAND,

57 James St N., Royal Hotel Buildings.

Queen, Fire and Life, George A Young, 2 Merrick
Royal Canadian, fire, life, Seneca Jones, 59 James n
Royal Canadian, Marine, J B Fairgrieve, 59 James n
Royal, Fire and Life, David McLellan, 84 James n
Scottish Imperial Fire Ins Co, M A Pennington, 30 James s
Scottish Union and National Ins Co, James Walker, 20 Main e
Standard Life Assurance Co, David McLellan, 84 James n
Sun Accident Assurance Co, David McLellan, 84 James n
Sun Life Association of Canada, Geo M Hunt, Arcade, 31 Jas n
Traveler's Life and Accident, J T Route, 16 James s
Victoria Mutual, Fire, W D Booker, sec-treas, 25 James s
Waterloo Mutual, Fire, Seneca Jones, 59 James n
Western Assurance Co, (ocean and inland marine, Toronto,) W F Findlay, 25 James s
Western, Fire, George A Young, 2 Merrick
Western, Marine, J B Fairgrieve, 59 James n

LAND COMPANIES.

Hamilton House Building Co, R L Gunn, Court House
Western Building Association, Seneca Jones, 59 James n

LANTERNS, ETC.

Burn & Robinson Manf Co, 12 Mary

LAUNDRIES.

City, J Jeffery, 60 Main w
Royal, Mrs S Robbins, 187 King e
Troy, W H Clarke, manager, 7 Market sq

LEATHER AND FINDINGS.

Alexander John, 13 King w

LIVERY AND SALE STABLES.

Craig Joseph, 24 Market
Coutts A, cor Macnab and Cannon
Matthews G H, 33 Market
Temple John, 20 Catharine n

LUMBER MERCHANTS.

Brennen & Sons, 63-67 King Wm
Flatt & Bradley, Barton cor Wellington
Patterson Bros, ft Lower Cathcart
Thomson Robert, 89 Stuart w
Thomson & Wright, 107 York

MARBLE WORKS.

Gottorff Fred, 118 York
Hurd & Robert, wholesale, 86-100 Merrick
Victoria Marble Works, E M Furniss & Son, 51 York

MARRIAGE LICENSES.

McKeand J C, 88 Bay s
McLellan David, 84 James n, h 55 Herkimer
Whipple E S, 78½ King e

MERCHANT TAILORS AND CLOTHIERS.

Barmann George, 1 Walnut s
Bews Bros, 74 King e
Booker Chas G, 2 King Wm
Carlson G C, 44 York
Carnegie Peter, 77 James n
Finagin John, 140 King e
Foster T K, 62 James n
Henderson J M & Co, 20 King w
Herron Joseph, 82 King e
Hutcheson James Happle, 118 King e

Huton Charles, 80 King e
McDonald W H & Co, 20 James n
McIntosh John, 3 Market sq
Oak Hall, 10 James n
Roe G, 185 King e
Slater James, 54 King w
Smith Donald, 14 James n
Watt John & Son, 15 Macnab n
Webster George, 26 John n
Wilson Wm & Son, 44 King w

MILLINERY.

Stewart Mrs E, 156 King e

MOODY'S NEW TAILOR SYSTEM.

Moody D W & Co, 176 King e

NEWSPAPERS.

Canadian Royal Templar, monthly, W W Buchanan, managing editor, James cor Vine
Globe (daily and weekly) J H Mattice, correspondent and agent, 31 James n
Mail (daily and weekly) F W Large, 72 James n
Palladium of Labor (weekly) 92 King e
Spectator (daily and weekly) 18 James s
Times (daily and weekly) 3 Hughson n

OPTICIAN.

Lees Thos, 5 James n

ORGANS, PIANOS, MUSIC AND MUSICAL INSTRUMENTS.

Baine T J, west end music store, 84 King w
Bell Organs, Hutchison & Pilkey, 10 King e
Canadian Piano Stool Co, T Wavell, manager, 12 Hughson s
Dominion Organ & Piano Co, Hutchison Pilkey, 10 King e
Grossman Peter, 49 James n
Heintzman Piano Co, Hutchison & Pilkey 10 King e
Lumgair W S, 92 James n
Mason & Risch (Hamilton Branch) Geo P Harrison, manager, 56 Wellington n
Nordheimer A & S, 80 James n
Rainer Piano Co, Hutchison & Pilkey, 10 King e
Thomas C L, manfr, 92 King w

PAINTS, OILS AND COLORS.

Hamilton A & Co, cor James and King

PAINTERS AND PAPER HANGERS.

LeMessurier Daniel, 17 Charles
Matthews James & Son, 15 Hughson n
Ross Bros, 1 Main w

PATENT MEDICINES.

Sutherland the J W Co, J W Sutherland, manager, 186 King w

PATENT SOLICITOR.

Bruce Wm, 14½ King e

PHOTOGRAPHERS.

Eckerson & Millman, 70 King w
Eckerson N G, 124 King e
Farmer Bros, 10 King w

PHYSICIANS.

Anderson James, 192 Macnab n
Anderson & Bates, 34 James n
Bigger G W, 204½ King e
Bingham G S, King cor Ferguson ave
Case Wm F A, 113 King e
Case W H, 113 King e
Cochrane J M, City hospital

Emory C VanNorman, 18 Main w
Gaviller E A, 8 Park s
Griffin H S, Walnut cor Main
Higgins Edward M, 74 Park n
Hillyer E S, 10 Main e
Husband Geo E, 75 Main w
Macdonald John D, 10 Duke
MacKelcan G L, Coroner, 14 Gore
MacKelcan John, 38 Catharine n
Malloch A E, 70 James s
Miller Thos, coroner, 181 King w
Mullin John A, 124 James n
Philp W, coroner, cor York and Hess
Reid Alex C, 55 Hughson n
Ridley H T, 31 Main w
Rosebrugh John W, 52 James s
Ryall Isaac, 71 Main e
Smith Daniel Day, cor King and Wellington
Smith Miss Elizabeth, 16 Main w
Shaw Geo M, 122 James n
Stark W G, 149 King w
Vernon Elias, cor James and Bold
White James, coroner, 8 Cannon w
Wilson T H, 156 Main e
Woolverton Algernon, coroner, 153 James n

PLANING, SASH, DOOR, BLINDS, ETC

Aitchison & Co, 56-58 Main w
Allardice R A & Co, 86 Merrick
Brennen M & Sons, 63-67 King Wm, and cor Mary and Cannon
Casey & Sons, 72 Main e
Cruickshank Robert, 55 Jackson e

PLATED WARE AND SILVER AND METAL PLATERS.

Moodie & Sons, 16 King w
Meridan Britannia Co, cor Wellington and Cannon

PLUMBERS, STEAM AND GAS FITTERS.

Adam James, 22 Hughson n
Clark Adam, 36 James s
Fairley, Stewart & Co, 18 John n
Farmer Wm, 110 James n
Harding Henry, cor James and Cannon
Squibb Frank, 39 John s
Young & Bro, 17 John n

PORK PACKERS.

Fearman F W, 17 Macnab n
Lawry Thos, 14 Macnab s

POTTERS.

Campbell Robt, cor Locke and Canada
Campbell Sewer Pipe Co, Henry New, sec-treas, end Jackson w

PRINTERS—BOOK AND JOB

(See also Newspapers)

Caxton Printing House, 22 Macnab s
Co-operative Printing Co, 92 King e
Griffin & Kidner, 47 King William
Harvey Jas, 26 Merrick
Lawson A, 5 York
McPherson Alex, 51 James n
Martin H A, 13 John n
Pennington Printing Co, 30 James s
Rowe W H, 92 King e

RAILWAYS AND AGENTS.

Canadian Pacific, W J Grant, 33 James n
Chicago, Milwaukee & St Paul, Robert Irwin, freight agent, 84 James n
Grand Trunk ticket agency, C E Morgan, 11 James n

Hamilton & Northwestern Railway, 113 Main e
Michigan Central, W J Grant, 33 James n
New York Central & Hudson River Railroad, W J Grant, 33 James n
Northern & Northwestern, W J Grant, 33 James n

SCALE MANUFACTURERS.

Gurneys & Ware, cor James and and Colborne

SEEDSMEN.

Bruce J A & Co, 37 King w
Evans Robt & Co, cor Macnab and York

SEWING MACHINE MANUFACTURERS AND DEALERS.

Davis, W S Lumgair, agent, 92 James n
Domestic, Hargrove & Sons, agents, 118 King e
Dunlop & Feast, Queen cor Peter
New Raymond, Hargrove & Sons, agents, 118 King e
New Williams, W S Lumgair, agent, 92 James n
Ontario Sewing Machine Co, James cor Hunter
Singer Mfg Co, 10 John n
Wanzer R M & Co, 91 Barton e
White, H D Bassett, 99 King e
VanNorman & Co, King cor Catharine

SHIRT MANUFACTURERS.

Mead Joseph R Co, 10½ Market sq
Treble S G, 2 King e

SLATERS.

Findlay J, 12 Macnab s
Irwin Thos & Son, 12 Macnab s

SOAP MANUFACTURERS.

Judd & Bro, 73 Bay n
Walker Jas, 19 Bay s

STEAMSHIP LINES AND AGENTS

Allan Line, J B Fairgrieve, 59 James n
Anchor Line, Geo McKeand, 57 James n
Bremen Line, Wm Herman, 16 James s
Canada Transit Co, W J Grant, 33 James n
Carr's direct Hamburg Line, Wm Herman, 16 James s
Dominion Steamship Line, David McLellan, 84 James n
Georgian Bay Transportation Co, W J Grant, 33 James n
Inman Line, G McKeand, 57 James n
Lake and River Steamship Co, John Harvey & Co, 69 James n
Muskoka Lakes, W J Grant, 33 James n
National Steamship Line, Chas E Morgan, 11 James n
Richelieu & Ontario Navigation Co, Geo McKeand, 57 James n
Rotterdam Line, Wm Herman, 16 James s

STAINED GLASS WORKS.

Longhurst H & Co, 26 York

STOVE POLISH AND EXTRACTS MANFR

Sayers Chas H, 32 Ray n

SUGAR REFINERS.

Canada Sugar Refining Co (Limited) David Newton, 9 Main e

SURVEYORS.

Kennedy R D, 42 James n
Livingston T C, 18 James s
Staunton F H Lynch, 18 James s

TANNERS.

Brown John E, 9 East ave n

TEA MERCHANTS.

Storm & Green, 128½ King e

TELEGRAPH AND TELEPHONE COS.

Canada Mutual Telegraph Co, 8 James s
Great North-Western Telegraph Co, 18 James s.
Bell Telephone Co, 1 Hughson s

TINSMITHS AND STOVE DEALERS.

Bowes, Jamieson & Co, cor King and Tisdale
Gurney E & C Co, 35-42 John n
Ham & Wilson, 35 York
Irwin Thos & Son, 12 Macnab s
Laidlaw Manufacturing Co, Mary
Moore Dennis & Co, 98-100 King e
Reddall & McKeown, 112 King w
Stewart Jas & Co, cor Macnab and Vine
Williams J M & Co, Hughson n

TOBACCO MANUFACTURERS

Tuckett Geo & Son, 118-124 King w

UNDERTAKERS.

Blachford & Son, 47 King w
Chapman's Sons, 49 King w
Pray & Son, 11 Macnab n

VINEGAR MANUFACTURERS

Doran Bros, Stuart w
Hamilton Vinegar Works Co, (limited) Wellington n and James s

WATCHMAKERS AND JEWELERS

Belling James, 21 York
Carroll T J & Co, 31 James n
Claringbowl F, King e
Davis & McCullough, 12 King w
Goodwin Wm, 77 John s
Lees G H & Co, 114 King e
Lees Thos, 5 James n
Levy Bros & Scheuer, importers, 27 King e
Russell Richard, manf'g, 15 King w
Skinner John, 79 King w

WHIP MANUFACTURERS.

Brown John E, whip lashes, 9 East ave n
Hamilton Whip Co, 81 Mary st

WIRE MILLS.

Greening B & Co, 41 Queen n
Nichols Thos E, 59 York

WOODEN AND WILLOW WARE

Hamilton Wooden Ware Co, 107 York
Mitchell Thos, 31 King w
Woods Walter, 60-62 Macnab n

WOOL MERCHANTS.

Harvey John & Co, 69 James n
McKenzie T H, 3 Market

WRINGERS AND WASHERS.

Adams Manfr Co, J E Martin, manager, 114 James n
Hamilton Industrial Works, cor Bay and Murray

COUNTY OF WENTWORTH.

☞County of Wentworth Gazetteer and Directory, including postal addresses and numbers of lots and concessions of the farmers. Price, $2.00. Sent to any address on receipt of price. W. H. Irwin & Co., publishers, 12 Macnab street south, Hamilton, Ont.

COUNTY OFFICERS.

J S Sinclair, Judge; Hon A McKellar, Sheriff; John Crerar, Clerk of Peace and County Attorney; G S Counsell, Clerk; John T Stock, Treasurer; S H Ghent, Clerk of Court, Deputy Clerk of the Crown and Registrar Surrogate Court; J M Williams, Registrar; T H A Begue, Warden

ALBERTON—A village in the Township of Ancaster, 14 miles from Hamilton

Kerr James A, P M, merchant
Muirhead Wm, blacksmith
Odell Henry, carpenter
Passmore Ed, butcher
Peer Nelson, wagon maker

ALDERSHOT—(Waterdown Station, G T R), 5 miles from Hamilton

Brown Alex W, P M, coal
Dickson H B, station agent

ANCASTER—A village in the township of Ancaster. Stage twice each day between here and Hamilton. Distance from Dundas 3 miles, and from Hamilton 7 miles. Population about 400

Ancaster Carriage Co
Brandon James, M D
Bristoll Rev E, Methodist
Cameron Mrs John, grocer
Chapman Alex, miller
Clarey Thos, store keeper
Clark Edwin, P M, grocer
Clark Rev W R, Episcopal
Donnelly Bolton W, druggist
Daniels J A, sawmills
Dyer Rev Jas E, Methodist
Egleston E F, foundry
Farr John, blacksmith
Findlay Samuel A, merchant
Forsyth Robert, tailor
Gurnett L A, Division Court Clerk
Gurnett L A & Son, merchants
Henderson Edward, hotel
Heslop John, township clerk
Hyslop & Garroch, merchants
Irwin Jas S, blacksmith
Jackson John, butcher
Johnston Rev T T, Presbyterian
Kenrick Edward, barrister
Lowry Morris, hotel
Moore Geo, cabinetmaker
O'Neil Henry, tinsmith
Orr Joseph, harnessmaker
Richardson Henry, M D
Smith J H, public school inspector
Thompson Geo, shoemaker
Tilman J, hotel keeper
Wilson Jas, shoemaker

BARTONVILLE—A village in the Township of Barton, four miles from Hamilton

Condy W. blacksmith
Durrand George, hotel
Ferguson Rev Geo. Methodist
Gage W J, postmaster
Oliver John, innkeeper
Skinner Geo, blacksmith
Webb Rev Jas, Methodist

BINBROOK—A village in the Townshih of Binbrook, 11 miles from Hamilton.

Alway Enoch, M D
Bailey Edward, saw mills
Barlow A, waggons
Bush Geo, harness
Gawley Jas, P M, blacksmith
Hall Wm W, grocer
Harris Rev S G, Baptist
McGann John, blacksmith
McKenzie J J, blacksmith
Russell Jas, M D
Taylor Jas T, clerk 8th Division Court
Wickett Robert, hotel
Wright Wm, tailor

BLACKHEATH — A Post Office in the Township of Binbrook.

Bain Alexander, postmaster
Gowland W G, merchant
Grassie Bros, wagon makers
Rees Rev W D, Presbyterian

BULLOCK'S CORNERS—A village in the Township of West Flamboro', near Dundas

Bullock Wm, sr, grocer
Clark A & J, woollen manfrs
Cochenour Jacob, saddler
Davidson A T, blacksmith
Frazer Morden, P M, merchant
Frederick & Bain, hotel
Geoghegan Rev T, ch of Eng'd
Hourigan John T, tavern
Lyons J, hotel
Morden W J, sr, P M, merchant
Webster Joseph, flour mills

CARLISLE—A small village in the Township of East Flamboro', 6 miles from Waterdown

Campbell Wm, miller
Cranston Geo, cooper
Duffy Michael, butcher
Galloway C E, butcher
Green F, woolens
Haws John, grocer
Koella Mrs, P M, general store
Wilden John, shoemaker
Zimmerman Peter, hotel

CARLUKE — A Post office situated in the Township of Ancaster, 11 miles from Hamilton

Calder John B, postmaster
Chisholm T C, merchant
Donald Thos, weaver
Mayhew R, merchant
Somerville Adam, miller
Wilson Wm, blacksmith

CLAPPISON P O—A Post Office in the township of East Flamboro

Barrett Robert, blacksmith
Curtis Wm, grocer
Clappison H, postmaster
Hunter Wm, hotel

CLYDE— A village in the Township of Beverly, 5 miles from Galt and 24 from Hamilton

Sippeel E M, P M, gen store

COPETOWN—A village and station on the G T R, 10 miles from Hamilton

Bowman Joseph, sawmill

Flannigan Wm, blacksmith
Horning John E, blacksmith
Howell G W, P M, storekeeper
McCarty Mrs C, hotel
Williams Wm, shoemaker

DUNDAS—A town and station on the Grand Trunk Railway, in the township of West Flamboro', in the centre of a rich agricultural region. A number of extensive mills and manufactories are in full operation. Distance from Hamilton, 5 miles; from Suspension Bridge, 45 miles. Population about 4,000.

Allen James, watchmaker
Babcock Wilder, hotel
Ball Geo, conductor H & D R
Barton G M, barrister
Batty Benj, watchmaker
Begue T H A, barrister
Bell T J, prop *Standard*
Bennett Alfred, restaurant
Bickell G, grocer
Billington J P, manufacturer
Biggs R L, drover
Black J, builder
Black Mrs J, fancy goods
Bowman Joseph, lumber
Boyd Mrs Geo, confectioner
Brady Patrick, tinsmith
Brady Peter, tinsmith
Brinkworth Wm, watchmaker
Brooke R S, photographer
Brown W G, barber
Brown John, basketmaker
Burns Mrs Mary, boots and shoes
Burrows Geo F, screw works
Burton J F, cabinetmaker
Byrns Thomas, saddler
Cain A S, grocer
Cain Patrick, hotel
Caldwell Thomas, nurseryman
Gampbell Wm F, butcher
Canada Screw Co, G F Burrows
Canadian Bank of Commerce
Canadian Gas Light Co
Cantwell James, dry goods
Clarke Edward, boots and shoes
Cody Richard, cooper
Conley Bernard, shoemaker
Cowper Willoughby, coal dealer
Davis John H, boots and shoes
Dingle R, butcher
Dixon J C & Bros, woolens
Dodds Miss, fancy goods
Doherty James, tobacconist
Doidge Bros, grocers
Dominion Card Clothing Co
Dundas Drug Co
Dundas Foundry, T Wilson
Dundas Manuf Co
Dundas Stove Co
Dundas Standard, T J Bell, editor
Dundas True Banner, James Somerville, editor
Elliott Mrs, hotel keeper
Enright John & Bro, livery
Feeny Rev J, Roman Catholic
Fisher John & Sons, paper mills
Fitzgerald Duncan, chief police
Forneret Rev George, Episcopal
Freeman Mrs A, confectioner
Fry & Wright, wagonmakers
Gillesby W, collector customs
Grafton J B & J S, dry goods
Graham Rev Jas, Methodist
Graham Wm, grocer
Grant Donald, clerk P O
Greening & Sons, wire weavers
Gray Wm R & Sons, card clothing
Gurney E & C, agri implements
Gwyn H C, barrister
Hardy Wm, saddler
Hefferman John, grocer
Henderson Mary E, hairworker
Kerwin John, grocer
Laing Rev John, Presbyterian
Laing P & R, grocers
Latshaw Fred A, cabinetmaker
Lawry Chas, tanner
Lawson James, blacksmith
Lees Geo, baker
Lennard & Sons, hosiery manfrs
Lennie Rev Robt, Baptist

Lightfoot G A, butcher
Lucas Benj, boots and shoes
Lumsden W W, baker
Lyon James D, tinsmith
McAdel C A, shoemaker
McArdle James, hotelkeeper
McKechnie & Bertram, tools
McMahon James, M D, MPP
McMillan D, photographer
McQueen James jr, postmaster
Mallet Wm, hotel
Mason Wm & Sons, tanners
Maw & McFarlane, machinists
Meacham J B, druggist
Millington Wm, pedler
Mitson Wm, painter
Morrish & Durrant, grocers
Morton James, butcher
Moss Joseph, baker
Mountain Thos, painter
Nelson Bros, blacksmiths
Newitt Wm, butcher
Niblett W C, druggist
O'Connor Patrick, blacksmith
Osler Rev F L, Ch of England
Palmer & Hickey, bricklayers
Parmenter A W
Patterson Charles, painter
Perry John R, supt Cotton Mills
Powell H F, grocer
Ramsey Miss Mary, dry goods
Riach George, tailor
Ross James, M D
Ross Miss J A, fancy goods
Seaman Thos, clothier
Shaw & Wilson, boilermaker
Smith J F, hardware
Smith Robert, butcher
Smyth Wm G, grocer
Somerville James, M P, *True Banner*
Somerville Roy, *True Banner*
Spittal L & Co, boots and shoes
Suter F D, clerk 2nd Div Court
Suter R W, ins agent
Swanson Mrs, confectioner
Tapp Philip, carpenter
Taylor E, cutter
Thayer & Judd, Paraffine Co
Vanevery Hugh, agent
Walker & Perks, M D
Wardell & Wyld, barristers
Webster James, flour and feed
Wheeler John, mason
White J B, hotel
Williams D, brewer
Williams Wm, blacksmith
Wilson J, mill owner
Wilson Mathew S, malster
Wilson R T, axe manfr
Wilson Thos, founder
Witherspoon David, boots & shoes
Woodsworth Rev R W, Methodist
Woodhouse Edwin, town clerk

ELFRIDA—A village in the Township of Saltfleet, 10 miles from Hamilton

Edmonds E, blacksmith
Quance Richard, miller
Staples John, butcher
Swayze H, P M, merchant
Walker Rev W P, Presbyterian

FLAMBORO' CENTRE—A post office in the township of East Plamboro'.

George Church, postmaster

FREELTON—A village in the township of West Flamboro', 16 miles from Hamilton

Brady John, waggonmaker
Burkholder Isaac C, blacksmith
Burns Samuel, hotel
Currie Geo, blacksmith
Duffy Chris, hotel
Hickson Wm, butcher
Hurst Edward, merchant
Johnston John J, waggonmaker
Metherall Geo, M D
Muirhead Walter, miller
O'Leary Rev J S
Ross John, P M, gen merchant

GLANFORD—(Formerly Mt Hope)—A post office in the township of the same name, 7 miles from Hamilton

Armstrong Bros, blacksmiths
Atkinson T, P M, grocer
Carroll N, hotel
Case D G, storekeeper
Dingwall A M, M D
Elliott Rev Robert, Methodist
Farewell A, M D
Finch Elijah, agent
Gillan D, blacksmith
Jerome Joel, agent
Livingston Rev H G, Methodist
McAllister Wm, painter
McClement J, clerk 7th Div court
Murphy R, blacksmith
Neal & Son, wagon makers
Smith Joel, undertaker
Smith W L, M D

GREENSVILLE — A village in the township of West Flamboro', 2 miles from Dundas, and 7 from Hamilton

Ballantyne Thos, cooper
Bear Fred, tailor
Black And, P M, gen merchant
Brennan John, gen storekeeper
Green Wm, blacksmith
Humphrey Richard, music teachr
Morden J, miller
Snasdell Joseph, township clerk
Soper Geo, carpenter
Steele Jas, malster
Williamson P, shoemaker

HANNON (Rymal Station)—township of Glanford, adjoining Rymal Station, 6½ miles from Hamilton.

Cowie Mrs Thos, P M, merchant

HAYESLAND—A village in the township of West Flamboro', 11 miles from Hamilton

Hayes Michael, P M, tavern

JERSEYVILLE — A village in the township of Ancaster, 4½ miles from Lynden and 15 from Hamilton. Population 250

Bishop Wm, planing mill
Bristol Rev B, Methodist
Cooley Rev J W, Methodist
Grant Rev W, Baptist
Hendershot A, P M, merchant
Howell Levi, merchant
Howell O, saw mill
Miller A K, blacksmith
Petrie Geo, blacksmith
Miller & Bigger, millers
Pitcher Chas, M D
Stenabaugh Harman, storekeeper
Stewart Rev S, Methodist
Swartz John, pumps
Vansickle J F, cheese

KIRKWALL — A village in the township of Beverly, 8 miles from Galt and 20 from Hamilton

Christie Geo, P M, storekeeper
Lapsley David, shoemaker
McQueen Wm, blacksmith
Tennant David, sawmills

LYNDEN — A village and station on the G T R, in the township of Beverly, 16 miles from Hamilton. Population 400

Baker John, hotel
Berrington John, station master G T R
Burbank J, merchant
Chapman Geo, shoemaker
Doherty S, blacksmith
Hanes Rinear, postmaster
Johnston Joseph, tinsmith
Lemon Wm, watchmaker
Moore Rev C A, Methodist
Pitton John, hotel
Rouse Henry W, harnessmaker
Thompson R, saw mill
Vansickle B, gen store
Wales Fred, butcher

MILLGROVE—A village in the township of West Flamboro', 8 miles from Hamilton

Berney Wm H, P M, gen store
Flatt John Ira, lumber merchant
Markle J R, blacksmith
Miller Thos, blacksmith
Ryckman Abe, fruitdrier
Shapland John, wagonmaker

MOUNT ALBION P O—Township of Saltfleet, 7 miles from Hamilton
Cook J R, miller
Davis Herbert, merchant
Galloway Andrew, wagonmaker
Grassie Chas, blacksmith
Martin Henry, merchant
Pottruff Jas, hotel keeper
Turner D, carpenter

MOUNTSBERG P O—East Flamboro

Connell John, blacksmith
Foster Wm, wagonmaker
Lakins Wm, sawmills
Revell Charles, P M

NORTH GLANFORD — A village in the township of Glanford, 6 miles from Hamiltom

Choate Thos, tp clerk
Dickenson Ed & Sons, brickmkrs
Dickenson John, P M
Terryberry Bros, hotel keepers

ORKNEY—(Thompson's corners)—Township of Beverley, 3 miles from Copetown

Anderson C, P M, gen store
Robinson R, hotel
Thompson Robert, lumber

RENFORTH —A post office in the township of Ancaster

Gritman Jacob, blacksmith
Mayhew R, P M, gen store

RENTON STATION P O—Township of Glanford

Thomas Wilkinson, P M

ROCKTON—A village in the township of Beverley, 15 miles from Hamilton

Atkins W & Sons, blacksmiths
Bannen Richard, bailiff
Bell David, organs
Cornell Benoni, P M, merchant
Jackson Daniel, wagonmaker
McDonald Wallace, J P, tp and div court clerk
McLane A, miller
Moss Wm, carpenter
Patrick Geo, hotel
Plastow J B, general merchant
Robinson Wm, blacksmith
Stuart John, wagons
Stockwell Wm, lime burner
Wood Wm, general merchant

RYCKMAN'S CORNERS—A village in the Township of Barton, 3½ miles from Hamilton

Allison Isaac, blacksmith
Bond John T, cattle dealer
Carr John, hotel keeper
Dawson Geo, wagons
Dawson Jonathan, wheelwright
Gillan John, blacksmith
Hess Samuel, butcher
McConnell Thos, blacksmith
Wells Wm, contractor

SHEFFIELD—A village in the township of Beverly, 19 miles from Hamilton

Bond Edwin & Son, P M, and produce dealers
Henning B, hotel
Laing C W & Co, storekeepers
Main Henry, wagonmaker
Reaman Chas, agr implements
Smith John W, M D
Steele W, blacksmith
Voaden Rev Thos, Methodist

SINCLAIRVILLE — A post office in the township of Binbrooh

Crawford R, grocer
Hewit Robert, sawmills
Hewitt John, blacksmith
Parker Joshua, blacksmith
Wilson James R, P M, gen store

STONEY CREEK—A village in the township of Saltfleet, 7 miles from Hamilton

Campbell D W, M D
Carpenter C, tinsmith
Clark Walter, carpenter
Gould Fred, mason
Hopkins Mrs T W
Howitt Rev F E, ch of England
Hull Fred, hotel
Jones Alva G, P M, clerk 5th div court, township clerk
Lee & Hamilton, blacksmiths
Mooney Rev James, Methodist
Moore J Charles, grocer
Springstead A C, wagon maker
Springstead John, shoemaker
Squire Rowland, mason
Thornton Wm, M D
Wallace Frank, fruitgrower
Whitcombe Rev C E, ch of Eng
Woodhouse W H, merchant
Woodhouse S C, hotelkeeper

STRABANE—A village in the township of Flamboro' West, 12 miles from Hamilton

Arthur Samuel, store keeper
Ballison Richard, carpenter
Fernally Fred, merchant
Hicks John, wagon maker
Lakins W, saw mills
Peebles Mathew, postmaster

TAPLEYTOWN—A village in the township of Saltfleet, 11 miles from Hamilton

Dewitt C W, agent
Duff Rev Robert, Methodist
Graham John, blacksmith
Harris John C, P M, dry goods
Harris & Miller, merchants
Pettit Wm, blacksmith
Smith Rev Thos, ch of England
White Wm, store keeper

TROY—A village in the townshsp of Beverley, 18 miles from Hamilton, and 3 from Lynden

Clark George, P M, merchant
Methers David, blacksmith
Misener Sidney, store keeper
Neff Samuel, carpenter
O'Reilly D, blacksmith
Parks Robert, blacksmith
Vinton H W, shoemaker
Webb Rev Jas, Methodist

TWEEDSIDE—A post office in the township of Saltfleet, 3 miles from Winona station

Buckbee James, store keeper
Johnson Thos S, P M, blacksmith

WATERDOWN—An Incorporated village and station on the Grand Trunk Railway, in the township of East Flamboro', 6 miles from Hamilton and 35 from Toronto. Population about 1,000.

Attridge Thomas, sawmills
Baker Henry, butcher
Baker John, undertaker
Balfour Bros, general store
Bemrose Joseph, wagon maker
Bremer John, towship clerk
Brown & Baker, cradles, rakes, etc
Clark Henry, tailor
Cook Samuel, hotelkeeper
Crooker Fred, grocer
Davis David, cooper
Docking W, agric implements

Doyle Michael, hotel
Eager J C & Co, gen merchants
Forstner John, grist mill
Foster Joseph, blacksmith
Francis Rev John, Episcopal
Garvin Thomas, shoemaker
Gilmore Wm, blacksmith
Goodson John, shoemaker
Green Samuel, blacksmith
Gross H, merchant
Hazelton Rev W P, Baptist
Howland W P, flour mills
Hunter D H, prin High School
Jarvis C M, agent
McGregor J O, M D
McMonies James jr, auctioneer
Misener W D, wagons
Robertson Rev W, Presbyterian
Robson Wm, man W P Howland
Rogers James, baker
Rymal Geo W
Rymal J W, agent
Seeley C
Simmons J, blacksmith
Stewart James, tailor
Stock John T, general merchant
Thompson Hugh, saddler
Thompson J B, postmaster
Trusdell Hiel, wagonmaker
Vanfleet A P, harness
Watson Rev W C, Methodist
Wilson W R, tinsmith
Yenny Rev John, Lutheran

WEST FLAMBORO'—A village in township of same name, distant from Hamilton, 8 miles

Clark Wm, woolen mills
Fisher Rev S, Presbyterian
Durrant J A, P M, merchant
Gibney A D & Co, merchant
Jackson Rev Thos W, Methodist
Jones Alfred, wagon maker
Peters John, merchant
Shaver A W, M D
Simmons John, tinsmith
Stutt James & Son, paper manfs
Taylor J W, blacksmith

WESTOVER—A village in the township of Beverley, 15 miles from Hamilton

Fletcher & Hanes, shingles
Law Thos, shoemaker
McDonald Jas, blacksmith
McDonough Jas, saw mills
McIntosh Benj, postmaster
Mills Jas, merchant
Skoyles B H, miller

WINONA—A station on the G T R, township of Saltfleet, 12 miles from Hamilton

Cline G W, fruit grower
Carpenter Joseph, P M
McNeilly John, shoemaker
Oakes George, blacksmith
Secord W K, merchant
Smith E D, fruit grower
Smith Wm H, scrap iron
Smith R R, township clerk
Smith & VanDuzen, nurserymen
Wilson J H, grain dealers

WOODBURN—A village in the township of Binbrook, 15 miles from Hamilton

Edmonds John, miller
Jarvis James E, merchant
McEvoy Wm, P M
Ptolemy Henry M, merchant
Roberts John, blacksmith

MISCELLANEOUS DIRECTORY.

CITY COUNCIL, 1885.

Regular meetings every alternate Monday, at 7:30 p. m.

J J Mason, Mayor.

Ward No 1—Wm Morgan, H Carscallen, James Addison. Ward 2—P C Blaicher, Alex McKay, Geo S Papps. Ward 3—F C Bruce, J V Teetzel, C L Thomas. Ward 4—Jas Stevenson, W J Morden, W H Judd. Ward 5—John Glasgow, Wm Doran, Wm Kavanagh. Ward 6—John Carruthers, J G Bowes, A H Moore. Ward 7—Thomas Allen, James Dixon, John Kenrick.

COMMITTEES

Board of Works—Ald Glasgow, chairman; McKay, Morden, Moore, Thomas, Allen and Addison.

Market, Fire and Police—Ald McKay, chairman; Carruthers, Stevenson, Morgan, Kenrick, Bruce and Kavanagh.

Hospital and House of Refuge—Ald Moore, chairman; Blaicher, Allen, Addison, Thomas, Judd and Doran.

Jail and Court House—Ald Morden, chairman; Carscallen, Blaicher, Thomas, Moore, Glasgow and Allen.

Waterworks—Ald Stevenson, chairman; Carruthers, Morgan, Papps, Teetzel, Kenrick and Kavanagh.

Board of Health—Ald Morgan, chairman; McKay, Bruce, Judd, Kerr, Carruthers and Allen.

Parks and Crystal Palace—Ald Bruce, chairman; Carscallen, Bowes, Papps, Dixon, Stevenson and Kavanagh.

Sewers — Ald Dixon, chairman; Papps, Morden, Bowes, Addison, Teetzel and Doran.

Finance—Ald Blaicher, chairman; Carscallen, Bruce, Judd, Bowes, Dixon, and Doran.

Assessors—Peter Balfour, head supervisor. Wards 1, Richard Ellicott: 2, Jos Kent; 3, Wm Sharp; 4, Lucian Hills; 5, J B Nelligan; 6, John Byrne; 7, Wm Turnbull.

Auditors—R L Gunn and S E Townsend.

BOARD OF EDUCATION.

Public Schools—B J Morgan, chairman; W H Ballard, inspector; Thos Beasley, secretary; A Stuart, treasurer; Charles Smith, messenger.

Ward 1—Jas. Cummings, B J Morgan. *Ward 2*—I B McQuesten, H McLaren. *Ward 3*—Roland Hills, Angus Sutherland. *Ward 4*—Joseph Fielding, Wm Clucas. *Ward 5*—F F Dalley, A M Ross. *Ward 6*—George Coumbe, H S Brennen. *Ward 7*—Thos Morris, W F Burton.

COLLEGIATE INSTITUTE

David McLellan, Louis Garland, Alex Turner, Wm Young, C R Smith, Wm Bell.

CHAIRMEN OF COMMITTEES.

Finance—David McLellan.

Internal Management—I B McQuesten.

Building—Angus Sutherland.

BOARD OF TRUSTEES, SEPARATE SCHOOLS

Very Rev E I Heenan, Chairman; James O'Brien, secretary; P Ronan, treasurer; Rev J Lennon, superintendent; Messrs A C Best, Rev Father Craven, M J Forster, Rev Father Cleary, Rev Father Bergmann, P J Kelly, J Duffy, J O'Brien, John Byrne, Charles Leyden.

OFFICERS OF THE CORPORATION

Jas Cahill, police magistrate; Thos Beasley, clerk; S H Kent, asst clerk; Alex Stuart, treasurer; Alex Stuart, jr, asst treasurer; William Haskins, city engineer and manager of the water works; James Cummings, tax collector; Donald Dawson, Andrew Neill, R V Mathews, asst collectors; Edward McLaughlin, clerk public works; Chas Foster, food inspector; John McKay, inspector streets; P Merin and Thos Brady, coal inspector; Charles Smith, messenger; J M Smith, M D, hospital physician; E Easterbrook, hospital steward; George Murison, health inspector; J Ford, asst health inspector; Isaac Ryall, M D, physician board of health; Paul Stuart, wood inspector.

POLICE.

The force consists of 45 men all told: One chief, three sergeants, four acting sergeants, two detectives, 35 constables. There are four stations: No 1 at City hall; No 2, corner James and Stuart streets; No 3, corner King William and Mary streets; and patrol wagon station at the central fire station. The department is governed by A D Stewart, chief, under the direction of the board of commissioners, which consists of mayor, police magistrate and county judge.

WATER WORKS

William Haskins, Manager.

William Monk, Henry D Twohy, W A Kerr, W R Campell — Clerks.

William Anstey, foreman mechanical department.

FIRE BRIGADE

A W Aitchison, chief; Thos Wilson, foreman.

LOCATION OF THE SIGNAL BOXES.

2 Corner Catharine and Jackson
3 " King and John
4 " Park and King
5 " Hess and King
6 " Locke and King
7 " Macnab and Picton
8 " Inchbury and York
9 " Queen and York
12 Corner Bay and York
13 " Bay and Mulberry
14 " James and Mulberry
15 " James and Gore
16 " Hughson and Barton
17 " Stuart and Macnab
18 " Guise and John
19 " Barton and Mary
21 " Catharine and Cannon
23 " Cathcart and Cannon
24 " Wilson and East Ave
25 " King and Steven
26 " Stinson and Victoria Ave
27 " King and Wellington
28 " O'Reilly and Cherry
29 " Catharine and Young
31 " James and Hannah
32 " James and Hunter
34 " Park and Hunter
35 " Bay and Robinson
36 " Hunter and Queen
37 " Pearl and Jackson
38 " Main and Caroline
42 Brennen's planing mill
43 Central Fire Station
45 Corner Rebecca and Ferguson Ave
46 " Emerald and Cannon
47 " Stuart and Caroline
51 City Hall Police Station
52 Corner John and Simcoe
53 " Ferguson ave and Ferrie

LICENSE COMMISSIONERS

John W Murton, John Proctor, Nelson Humphrey; John I Mackenzie, inspector. Office, 4 James street south.

HAMILTON POST OFFICE

Postmaster—H N Case; assistant postmaster, H Colbeck

Registration and foreign mail branch—H A Eager, P J O'Donnell, R M Fitzgerald

Money order and savings bank branch—Thomas Burns, G H Bull, Miss R A McKay

Accountant's office—George Ross, Henry Dinsse.

Clerks—Alfred C Crisp, John C Dempsey, John S Mathews, Ed H Dunnett, Benjamin F Barber, W R Ecclestone, Wm Smith, W Flynn, Donald D Campbell, Walter L Waterman, Harry Hill, John A Webber, Henry Ed J Filgiano, John D McDonald, Charles Judd, Oliver Beatty, J R Morden.

Letter Carrier's Branch—John Murphy, superintendent; John Catchpole, John H Fearnside, asst superintendents;

Thomas B S Austin, John Gore, Wm G Flooks, Henry M Coates, Chas W W Fielding, Josh Wilson, John Gardner, Robert Stratton, Wm Angus, John E S Baillie, Wm Rennie, Chas Anstey, David C Dowrie, Thomas H Loney, Andrew Griffin, Wm Dawe, Wm H James, Emil Frank, J W North, C H Stickle, Geo Springate, Meredith Dawson, Ed Sevier, Wm A Mundy.

Messengers—David Walsh, James Strauss.

Street Letter-box Collector—Joshua Brundle.

Letter-boxes are placed at the corners of the following streets: James and Market, York and Macnab, opp. Eastwood's, King east; Main and James, Macnab and King, Bay and York, John and King, Court House, John and Cannon, James and Hunter, Park and Mulberry, opp William's, Copp's block, Hess and York, James and Murray, John and Hunter, Caroline and King, Bay and Main, King and Ferguson ave, Cannon and Ferguson ave, Wilson and West ave, Mary and Barton, James and Hannah, Bay and Bold, King and Wellington, Pearl and York, John and Young, Cannon and Wellington, Queen and Main, James and Picton, King and Pearl, Wilson and Emerald, Park and Herkimer, Cherry and O'Reilly, Caroline and Hannah, Stinson and Victoria ave, Canada and Locke, Emerald and Hunter, Mary opp Kelly.

HAMILTON BOARD OF TRADE

T H McPherson. president; R Benner, secretary.

CUSTOMS

Custom House Stuart street.

John Thompson, appraiser; A A Wylie, assistant; A I Mackenzie, surveyor; R L Whyte, chief clerk; F Shephard, H W Woodward, Andrew Alexander, Hugh Murray, S W Townsend, D B Galbreaith, clerks; H L Dixon, chief landing waiter; J M Patterson, J McKindy, P O'Heir, A H Wingfield, landing waiters; Stephen Cleary, searcher; James Halcrow, locker and guager; H Gray, locker; Michael Malone and Samuel Garrity, porters; Alex Ferguson, messenger.

INLAND REVENUE

Corner James and Vine.

C G Fortier, collector; S F Ross, deputy collector; B J Conway, bookkeeper, John Logan, James B Blair, Francis J J McHugh, D W McKay, T S Gosnell, W P Crawford, William Amos, Joseph F O'Brien, N J Dingman, F J Barrett, A Egener, excise officers.

CHURCHES

Diocese of Niagara—Right Rev Chas Hamilton, M A, Lord Bishop.

Christ Church Cathedral, Rev Chas H Mockridge, D D, rector. Divine service on Sundays at 11 a m and 7 p m, and on Wednesday evenings at 8 p m. Sunday school at 3 p m. Baptism second Sunday in every month at 2.30 p m. Holy communion every Sunday; first and third Sundays at 11 o'clock service, and second, fourth and fifth (when occurring) at 8 a m.

St. Luke's Church, cor John and Macauley streets. Rev Wm Massey, M A, curate in charge. Services on Sundays at 11 a m and 7 p m

Church of Ascension, John street south—Rev Hartley Carmichael, M A; Rev Charles J James, B A. Divine service each Sunday at 11 a m and 7 p m. Litany, 4 p m. Holy communion celebrated

1st Sunday in each month, 11 a m.
3rd " " 11 a m.
Last " " 7 p m.

Sunday school, 3 p m. Divine service every Wednesday night at 7 30.

All Saints' Church, corner Queen and King streets. Rev Lestock Des Brisay, M A, rector. Services at 11 a m and 7 p m.

St. Thomas' Church, corner Main and West ave—Rev W B Curran, rector. Services at 11 a m and 7 p m.

S. Mark's Church, corner Bay and Rev Hunter stts—Rev R G Sutherland, B A, rector. Services at 8 a m, 11 a m, 4 p m and 7 p m.

REFORMED EPISCOPAL

St. James', cor Hunter and Park sts.

Bishop Edward Wilson, D D, in charge. Sunday services are held at 11 a m and 7 p m. Communion, first Sunday in every month after morning service. Sunday school at 3 p m; weekly service, Wednesday at 7.30 p m.

PRESBYTERIAN CHURCHES.

Hours of service 11 a m and 7 p m.

Central Church, corner Jackson and Macnab streets. Pastor—Rev Samuel Lyle.

Macnab Street Church, corner Hunter and Macnab streets. Pastor—Rev Donald H Fletcher.

St. Paul's Church, corner James and Jackson streets. Pastor—Rev R J Laidlaw.

Knox Church, corner Cannon and James streets.

St. John's Church, corner King and Emerald streets. Pastor—Rev Thos Goldsmith.

Erskine Church, Pearl street north. Pastor—Rev Thos Scoular.

METHODIST CHURCHES.

Hours of service, 11 a m and 7 p m, except otherwise stated. Sunday school at 2.30 p m.

Centenary Church, Main street west. Rev W W Carson, pastor

Wesley Church, John street, corner of Rebecca. Rev W J Hunter, pastor.

First Methodist Church, corner of King and Wellington streets. Rev A Langford, pastor.

Zion Tabernacle, Pearl street north. Rev Mr Snider, pastor.

Simcoe Street Church. Rev Joseph Odery, pastor.

Hannah Street Church. Rev Albert C Crews, pastor.

Gore Stret Church, corner John and Gore streets. Rev James Vanwyck, pastor.

Emerald Street Church. Rev J H Collins, pastor.

American M E Church, Rev J B Roberts, So John street north.

BAPTIST CHURCHES.

James Street Baptist Church, Rev J W A Stewart. Hours of service 11 a m and 7 p m. Weekly prayer meetings every Thursday evening at a quarter to 8 o'clock. Sabbath school at 2.30 p m.

Baptist Church (colored) Macnab street north. Hours of service, 10.30 a m and 6.30 p m.

Baptist Mission, Wentworth street north. Sabbath school, 2.30 p m. Preaching service every Sunday at 7 p m. Weekly prayer meetings every Wednesday evening at a quarter to 8 o'clock.

EVANGELICAL ALLIANCE.

Rev J W A Stewart, president; Rev J W Hunter, D D, vice president; Rev D H Fletcher, recording sec; Jas Walker, treasurer.

CONGREGATIONAL AND OTHER CHURCHES

Congregational Church. Hours of service, 11 a m and 7 p m. Rev J Morton, Hughson street north.

Brethren of the One Faith, corner of James and Rebecba. Each first day at 11 a m. Lecture on Bible subject at 7 p m.

Believers, cor Merrick and Macnab. Hours of service, 11 a m, 3 p m, and 7 p m.

Evangelical Lutheran Congregation, Rev D Dippel, pastor, Market street. Hours of service, 10.30 a m and 7 p m. Sabbath school at 3 p m.

Plymouth Brethren meet at their hall, Macnab street south. Services at 11 a m and 6. 30 p m. Sabbath school at 3 p m.

Mountain Mission. Meeting at 2 p m. Supplied by the pastors of the city.

Jewish Synagogue—Hughson street south. Services, Friday evening and Saturday at 10 a m. Rev Dr H Birkenthal, rabbi

ROMAN CATHOLIC CHURCHES

St Mary's Church—Pro Cathedral. Right Rev J J Carbery, D D, Bishop, O P, S T M; Very Rev E I Heenan, Vicar-General of Hamilton; Rev Fathers M J Cleary, James Lennon and M S Halm. Hours of service: 1st mass, 7.30 a m, 9 a m; high mass, 10.30 a m, vespers, 7 p m. Mass every day at 7 a m in summer, 7.30 a m in winter. Corner Park and Sheaffe streets.

St. Patrick's Church, King street east. Revs John Keough and J Craven. Mass 7.30 a m and 10 30 a m; vespers, 7 p m.

St. Joseph's Church, Rev Father R Bergman. Mass 10.30 a m, Sundays; vespers 7 p m. Corner Charles and Jackson streets. Mass every day, 7.30 a m.

EDUCATIONAL

SCHOOLS AND COLLEGES.

Hamilton Collegiate Institute—Geo Dickson, M A, principal.

PUBLIC SCHOOLS.

For school purposes the city is divided into four districts, in each of which there is a central school. Over each district is placed a head master, who has supervision not only of his own school, but also of the primary schools attached to the central school of the district.

District I includes Wards 1 and 7; head master, John Ross.

District II includes Wards 2 and 3; head master, G W Johnson.

District III includes Ward 4; head master, J S Cruickshank.

District IV includes Wards 5 and 6; head master, W C Morton.

Inspector of the four districts, W H Ballard.

COLLEGIATE INSTITUTE.

Geo Dickson, M A, Principal; O J Brown, M A, mathematical master; Chas Robertson, M A, modern languages; P S Campbell, M A, classical master; A Paterson, English master; W M. Sutherland, B A, commercial master; A McMillan, master lower second form, boys; Mrs M Davidson, upper second form, girls; T F Lyall, B A, lower first form, boys; Miss L Bell, upper first form, girls; E Byfield, lower first form, girls; W C Forster, drawing master; James Johnson, music master; E Houghton, drill master.

WESLEYAN LADIES' COLLEGE

King street east, incorporated 1861, Rev A Burns, D D, LL D, governor. Prof C W Harrison, M A, natural science and latin; Prof Henry Martin, O S A, drawing and painting; Prof R S Ambrose, music; Prof L H Parker, singing and vocal culture, and eleven lady teachers.

CANADA BUSINESS COLLEGE

Established 1861, Arcade building, 31-33 James street north. R E Gallagher, principal and proprietor; W H Dennis, first assistant; S F Lazier, M A, LL B, commercial law; F W Wodell, phonography.

HAMILTON COMMERCIAL COLLEGE.

2½ James street south, M. L. Rattray, Principal; E A Geiger, Secretary; David Steele, commercial law; Edward Morgan, phonography.

ROMAN CATHOLIC SCHOOLS.

Rev Father J Lennon, superintendent

St Mary's Model School, Sheaffe street—Charles J Macabe, principal; number of pupils on the roll 180.

St Mary's Central and St Mary's Training Schools, Mulberry street.

St Patrick's School, Hunter street; St Lawrence School, John street, and St Charles School, King street west—conducted by the sisters of St Joseph.

The number of pupils attending these schools (not including the Model School) is about 1,900.

Convent of Mount St Mary, King

street west—under the direction of the Ladies of Loretto; M Francis, lady superioress.

LITERARY AND SCIENTIFIC ASSOCIATIONS

Hamilton Association. Instituted 1857, incorporated 1883. Meets first and third Thursdays of the month. —President, J D Macdonald, M D; 1st vice-president, H B Witton; 2nd vice president, Rev C H Mockridge, D D; cor secretary, Geo Dickson, M A; rec secretary, Andrew Alexander; treasurer, Richard Bull; librarian and curator, Wm Turnbull.

Hamilton Law Association, 70 members—Æ Irving, Q C, president; Thos Robertson, Q C, vice-president; A Bruce, treasurer; R R Waddell, secretary.

Hamilton Athletic Park Company (late Hamilton Cricket Club Company) —E Martin, president; F H Mills, sec-treasurer.

Hamilton Medical and Surgical Society, meets 2nd Tuesday of the month at Royal hotel—James White, president; W G Stark, vice-president; T W Reynolds, sec-treas.

Collegiate Institute Literary Society —W J Fortune, president; F Langford, sec-treasurer.

St Thomas' Church Literary Society —Rev W B Curran, president; Richard Bull, secretary.

Young Men's Christian Association, 38 King street east—James Watson, president; Frank Lonsdale, secretary. A free reading room. Meetings Sundays at 4.15 and 8 30 p m

Women's Christian Association—Mrs James Watson, president; Mrs J D McDonald, 1st vice-presidant; Mrs D McLellan, 2nd vice-president; Miss J M Stewart, secretary; Mrs J M Burns, treasurer.

Garrick Club, Gore street—F Mackelcan, president; Campbell Ferrie, sec-treasurer.

Grand Opera House Co—C M Counsell, president; James H Mills, sec-treasurer.

CHARITABLE INSTITUTIONS.

City Hospital, cor Barton and Victoria avenue—J M Cochrane, resident physician; E Easterbrook, steward.

Asylum for the Insane, mountain top —J McL Wallace, medical supt; J W Montgomery, M D, assistant supt; Bidwell Way, bursar.

House of Providence, Dundas—Sisters of St. Joseph.

House of Refuge, foot of John street north—Under the patronage of the City Council.

Boys' Home—Jane McFarlane, matron, 59 Stinson street.

St. Mary's Orphan Asylum, Park street north—Under the supervision of the Sisters of St Joseph.

Hamilton Orphan Asylum and Ladies' Benevolent Society, Wellington street south—Misses M and J McFarlane, matrons.

Home of the Friendless, Caroline street south, Miss Matherson, matron.

Children's Industrial School, 77 George street—Incorporated by Act of Parliament. Miss Annie Raynor, matron.

Ladies' Benevolent Society, Roman Catholic—Mrs J T Routh, president; Mrs J Egan, secretary; Miss A Hogan, treasurer.

NATIONAL AND BENEVOLENT INSTITUTIONS.

St. George's Society—F Mackelcan, president; C H Egg, secretary.

St. Andrew's Society — Instituted December 29, 1835. James Angus, jr, president; D. McLellan, treasurer; John McMaster, secretary.

Caledonia Society—Ian McKenzie, chief; Wm Murray, secretary; Colin McRae, treasurer; meets 1st and 2nd Friday in Caledonia Hall, Arcade.

Irish Protestant Benevolent Society —Established in 1869. John Alexander, president; Geo Ross, secretary; H A Eager, treasurer; meets in I O O F Hall, John north, 2nd Thursday of each month.

Catholic Mutual Benefit Association No 3—Meets at 74 James n. John Ronan, president; John Byrne, sec-treasurer.

Emerald Beneficial Association, Sarsfield Branch No 1, Ont—George Nelligan, president; J Flahaven, secretary. Stated meetings, 1st and 3rd Wednesdays of each month.

Sarsfield Branch No. 16—John Smith, president; John Nelligan, secretary; meets 1st and 3rd Monday.

St Vincent de Paul's Society — H Arland, president; A C Best, secretary.

SONS OF ENGLAND

Britannia Lodge No 8—J B Buckingham, president; R Realf, secretary.

Acorn Lodge No 29—John Clayton, prersident; W S Harrison, secretary.

MILITARY

Hamilton Field Battery—Major H P VanWagner, commanding; Capt J S Hendrie, Lieuts Bankier and Copp.

Thirteenth Battalion A M—Lt-Col J A Skinner, commanding; Majors: Bt Lt-Col J M Gibson, M P P, and A H Moore; Adjutant, Capt J J Stuart; Captains: H McLaren, P B Barnard, James Adam, John Stoneman, W G Reid, E G Zealand; Lieutenants: W J Coulson, G McL Brown, E G W Moore, B R Osborne, J C Gillespie, S G Mewburn; 2nd Lieutenants: J W G Watson and H G Marquis; Paymaster, Hon Major C Armstrong; Quartermaster, Hon Major J J Mason; Surgeon, J Ryall; Asst Surgeon, H S Griffin.

TEMPERANCE SOCIETIES

Hamilton Temperance Reform Club—Robert Stratton, president; Edward Shepherd, secretary. Meetings at the Foresters' Hall every Saturday at 8 p m, and Sundays at 9 a m and 4 p m.

Woman's Christian Temperance Union—Mrs Pratt, secretary.

INDEPENDENT ORDER GOOD TEMPLARS

Excelsior Lodge No 6—George Lambert, L D; meets Tuesday, 9 King west.

Rescue Temple No 222—Wm Wilson, L D; meets every Monday evening, James cor King William.

Burlington Lodge No 470—Mrs A M Cummer, L D; meets Monday evening in the hall, 22 King street east.

Reliance Lodge No 518—George Turner, L D; meets Wednesday evening in Reliance Hall, corner James and Rebecca streets.

Ambitious City Lodge No 586—Peter Armstrong, L D; meets Monday evening, James corner King Wm.

Under the jurisdiction of the Right Worthy Grand Lodge of the World

International Lodge No. 1—F S Morison, D R W G T; meets every Tuesday evening at 8 o'clock in the International hall, 60 King street west.

Unity Lodge No 5—G Stanton, D R W G T; meets every Wednesday evening at 8 o'clock in International hall, 60 King street west.

Beaver Lodge No 6—J S Brend, D R W G T; meets every Monday evening at 8 o'clock in International hall, 60 King street west.

Pioneer Temple No 2 (Juvenile)—Mrs E James, superintendent; meets every Friday evening from 7 to 8 in International hall, 60 King street west.

Public meeting under the auspices of the city lodges held every Sunday afternoon at 4 o'clock in International hall, 60 King street west.

ROYAL TEMPLARS OF TEMPERANCE

Hall 97 James street north.

Imperial Council No 5—C Smith, jr, S C.; J S Knapman, sec; meets 2nd and 4th Thursdays in hall, 97 James north.

Sovereign Council No 9—Dr E Emory, S C; C H Stickle, sec; meets 1st and 3rd Thursdays.

Regina Council No 67—W J Kerr, S C; J Burns, R S; meets 2nd and 4th Tuesdays.

Wentworth Council No 149—James Catlin, sec; meets Wednesdays in Mission Church, Wentworth north.

SONS OF TEMPERANCE.

Hamilton Division, No 25—R McBride, D G W P; meets Thursday at 22 King street east.

SOCIAL ORGANIZATIONS

MASONIC

Hamilton District—Gavin Stewart, D D G M.

Barton Lodge No 6—H S Griffin, W M; W J Grant, sec; meets second Wednesday.

Strict Observance No 27—W C Morton, W M; T W Lester, sec; meets 3rd Tuesday.

St John's Lodge No. 40—E Hill, W M; Thos McCallum, sec; meets 3rd Thursday.

Acacia Lodge No 61—A Whyte, W M; A Poulter, sec; meets 4th Friday.

Temple Lodge No 324—John W Murton, W M; E H Browne, sec; meets 2nd Tuesday.

Doric Lodge No 382—Thos Irwin, W M; J C Cheyne, sec; meets 3rd Monday.

Hamilton Masonic Hall Association—Edward Mitchell, president; James Robertson, treasurer; J J Mason, sec.

Hamilton Masonic Mutual Benefit Association—R Brierley, president; J J Mason, sec-treas.

The Hiram R A C, No 2—E Comp C W Mulligan, Z; W J Grant, Scribe E; meets first Monday in each month.

St John's R A M, No 6—E Comp James A Malcolm, Z; C W W Fielding, S C; meets second Thursday in each month.

Harrington Conclave, No. 22, Kts R C R and C—Sir Kt H A Mackay, M P S; Sir Kt W Gibson, recorder; meets February, May, August and Nomber.

The Godfrey de Bouillon Preceptory—Em Comp Thomas Hood; C N McMichael, registrar; meets 1st Friday.

Murton Lodge of Perfection, No 1—Ill Bro John W Murton, 33°, T G P M. Sov Pr W H Ballard, 32°, secretary; meets 1st Tuesday.

Hamilton Sovereign Chapter Rose Croix No 1—Ill Bro R K Hope, 32°, M W S; Ill Bro W H Ballard, 32°, registrar. Meets 4th Tuesday.

Moore Sovereign Consistory, S P R S, 32°—Ill Bro John M Gibson, 33°, Ill Bro David McLellan, 33°, grand secretary; meets 2nd Friday.

Royal Order of Scotland, for the Provinces of Ontario and Quebec—Ill Bro H A Mackay, 33°, Prov G M; Ill Bro J W Murton, 33°, Sr Gr Warden Ill Bro W Reid. 33°, Jr Gr Warden; Ill Bro Hugh Murray, 33°, Prov Gr Secretary.

ODD FELLOWS

INDEPENDENT ORDER

Hamilton U D Camp No 2—John H McCabe, commander; P E Fitzpatrick, secretary.

Burlington Encampment No 7—P McCandlish, C P; W Hastings, R S.

Royal Encampment No 36—G E Wilson, C P; G E Heming, R S.

Excelsior Lodge, No 44—W Burrowes, N G; P Hastings, R S.

Unity Lodge, No 47—J M Iredale, N G; Robert Stewart, R S.

Victoria Lodge, No 64—George E Wilson, N G; Geo E Henning, R S.

Crescent Lodge, No 104—Fred Vannatter, N G; T Raycroft, R S.

Oak Leaf Lodge, No. 159—Frank Hutton, N G ; T McBride, R S.

Minerva Lodge, No 197—D Robertson, N G ; W Brooks, R S.

CANADIAN ORDER, MANCHESTER UNITY

Loyal Hamilton Lodge, No 7—Chas Blackman, N G ; Thos Parry, P S ; meets every other Wednesday.

Loyal Commercial Lodge, No 9—James McCulloch, N G ; J Philp, P S; meets every second Wednesday.

Loyal Strict Observance, No 48—E A P Cook, N G; C H Bampfylde, P S; meets every other Monday each month.

Royal Purple Encampment, No 1—C H Bampfylde, N G ; Thomas Parry, P S ; meets last Friday.

KNIGHTS OF PYTHIAS

Red Cross Lodge, No 3—William Massie, C C ; W H Tribute, K of R & S ; meets at the Odd Fellow's hall, John street north, Mondays at 8 p m.

Alpha Division, No 1- D J Peace, Sir Kt Commander ; Thos Knott, rec ; meets Wednesdays at 8 p m for drill, and first Monday at 8 p m, at 33 James street north.

Grand Orient, No 1—D J Peace, I S; Alex W Aitchison, H S ; meets last Monday at Odd Fellows' hall, John street north.

ANCIENT ORDER OF UNITED WORKMEN

Hall 14 Macnab south.

Hamilton Lodge, No 49—H McK Donaldson, M W ; A McPherson, recorder ; meets alternate Fridays.

Gore Lodge, No 88—A McLean, W M; E Hawkes, recorder ; meets alternate Fridays.

Wentworth Legion, So 3, Select Knights of A O U W—Robert Irwin, S R ; W H Woodhouse, S C ; meets alternate Tuesdays.

HOME CIRCLE

Pioneer Council, No 66 ; meets in I O O F hall, John street north, 2nd and 4th Thursdays. John Wallace, L : John A Morrison, secretary.

CANADIAN LEGION OF HONOR

Hall James corner King William.

Parthenon Lodge, No 1—G F N Birely, commander ; P Corridi, sec.

Monarch Lodge, No 2—W L Hubbard, commander ; H A Mackelcan, secretary ; meets alternate Wednesdays.

CHOSEN FRIENDS

Maple Leaf Council—Jas Summers, C C ; Charles Martin, secretary.

ROYAL ARCANUM

J M Byrens, D S R for Hamilton.

Kanawha Council, No 681—John McClean, regent ; W S Duffield, secretary ; meets first and third Thursdays in Odd Fellows hall, John street north.

Regina Council, No 757 - W E Brown, regent ; Alex Finlayson, sec ; meets second and fourth Thursdays, in A O U W hall.

Barton Council No 861—J F Monck, regent ; A T Neill, sec ; meets first and third Tuesdays in Odd Fellows hall, John street.

ANCIENT ORDER OF FORESTERS

Hall 110 James north.

Court Pride of Ontario, No 5,640—W J Emery, C R ; J B Buckingham, secretary. Alternate Thursdays.

Excelsior Court, No 5,743—C J McMillan, C R ; W J Vale, secretary. Alternate Thursdays.

Court Maple Leaf, No 5,690—H Martin, C R ; W Davis, secretary. Alternate Thursdays.

Marquis of Lorne, No. 6,490—Thomas Ramsay, C R ; Jas Barry, secretary.

Sanctuary, A O S—F W Hughes, P ; Thomas Rumsey, scribe.

KNIGHTS OF SHERWOOD FOREST.

Pioneeer Conclave, No. 21—J B Buckingham, commander ; Thomas Rumsey, Ad ; meets Wednesday.

INDEPENDENT ORDER O F

Court Oronhyateka, No 23 — W Griffith, C R ; John Anderson, R S ; E S Cummer, C D H C R. Meets first and third Fridays in each month, at 22 King street east.

Court Amity, No — W Taylor, C D H C R ; E Easterbrook, C R ; D Gleeson, secretary. Meets first and second Tuesday.

LOYAL ORANGE ASSOCIATION.

DISTRICT OF HAMILTON.

George Watson, D M ; Wm James, D S.

Royal Black Preceptory, No 148, G R I Encampment—Richard Ailles, W Sir Kt in command , Wm Aspel, registrar. Meets on the third and fourth Monday in the month, in the Orange Hall, King street east.

LOYAL ORANGE LODGES.

No 71—John Philips, W M ; R Lawson, R S. Meets on the first and third Tuesday in each month.

No. 286—John Tulk, W M ; Robert Steven, R S. First Wednesday.

No 312—John W Hotram, W M ; Wm Hay, R S. First Monday.

No 554—James H Smith, W M ; J Krug, R S. Second Monday.

No 779—Wm Richardson, W M ; E T Richards, R S. First Friday.

No 1,019—Hugh Hunter, W M ; Richard Smale, secretary. Fourth Thursday.

BANKS.

Bank of British North America—D G McGregor, manager ; F. Brownfield, accountant ; Wm Graham, teller ; W T Hony, discount clerk ; T Wilson, messenger.

Bank of Hamilton—E A Colquhoun, cashier ; H S Steven, assistant cashier : C Bartlett, accountant ; J H Stuart, assistant accountant ; W J Lindsay, teller ; E S Ambrose, W Butler, O S Clarke, J C Brown, J S Gordon, H S Webber, clerks. F Bennett, messenger.

Canadian Bank of Commerce—E Mitchell, manager ; O G Roy, teller ; H H Morris, accountant ; S Read, jr, assistant accountant ; John Cousins, messenger.

Bank of Montreal—J N Travers, manager ; George Drummond, accountant : John Rankin, teller ; G Thomas, messenger.

Merchants' Bank of Canada—J S Meredith, manager ; A Pringle, teller ; W A Bellhouse, accountant ; A B Patterson. ledger keeper ; J Johnston, messenger.

Molson's Bank—J M Burns, manager ; H A Ambridge, accountant ; A O N Beatty, teller ; W E Plant, ledger keeper ; W. Haverscroft, messenger.

Stinson's Bank, 10 Hughson street north—A H Moore, manager ; A Leith, teller ; W B Coles, ledger keeper

LOAN AND BANKING.

Farmers' and Traders' Loan Association—Æ Jarvis, manager ; Thos R Patterson, teller ; L Lambert, ledger keeper. 36 King street east

Omnium Securities Co—John F Wood, manager. 20 James street south.

Hamilton House Building Co—R L Gunn, sec. Court House.

Hamilton Provident and Loan Society, corner King and Hughson. Incorporated in 1871—H D Camer[illegible] treasurer ; A F Sutherland, inspe[illegible] A W Roy, accountant ; A McEach[illegible] teller.

Landed Banking and Loan Co—Samuel Slater, secretary - treasurer, 3 James street south.

DIVISION COURTS AND CLERKS

Wentworth — 1st, H T Bunbury, Hamilton; 2nd, F D Suter, Dundas; 3rd, J McMonies, jr, Waterdown; 4th, W McDonald, Rockton; 5th, Alva G Jones, Stoney Creek; 6th, L A Gurnett, Ancaster; 7th, John McClemont, Glanford; 8th, J S Taylor, Binbrook; 9th, R L Gunn, Hamilton.

RAILWAYS.

Grand Trunk Railway. — General Offices, Montreal — Joseph Hickson, general manager; L J Seargeant, traffic manager; Wm Wainwright, assistant manager; J Burton, general manager's assistant; J Stephenson, superintendent; E P Hannaford, chief engineer; Herbt Wallis, mechanical superintendent; R Wright, treasurer; John Porteous, general freight agent; W Edgar, general passenger agent; T B Hawson, auditor; H W Walker, accountant; John Taylor, general storekeeper.

Great Western Division, G T R.—Offices, Hamilton—Charles Stiff, superintendent; Joseph Hobson, chief engineer; Thos Tandy, general freight agent; C K Domville, mechanical superintendent; F J Domville, mechanical engineer; W S Champ, paymaster.

Hamilton and Northwestern Railway—John Stuart, president; John Proctor, vice-president; Maitland Young, secretary.

Northern and Northwestern Railway.—Head Office, Toronto—S Barker, general manager; James Webster, superintendent, Robert Quinn, general passenger agent; M C Dickson, agent, Hamilton; W C Schreiber, purchasing agent, Toronto.

CITY AND COUNTY DIRECTORIES

The following will be sent on receipt of price.

City of Hamilton	$2 50
City of Kingston, including Frontenac county	2 00
City of St. Catharines, including Lincoln and Welland	2 00
City of Brantford, including Brant county	2 00
County of Simcoe	2 00
County of Wentworth	2 00

WE ARE ALSO AGENTS FOR THE

City of Guelph	2 00
County of Wellington	3 00
County of Waterloo	3 00
City of Quebec	2 50
City of Ottawa	2 50
City of Montreal	3 00

ALL BOOKS ARE RECENT EDITIONS.

W. H. IRWIN & CO.,

12 MACNAB ST. SOUTH. *Hamilton, Ontario*

ADDENDA.

NAMES RECEIVED TOO LATE FOR REGULAR INSERTION, CHANGE OF RESIDENCE, AND BUSINESS LOCALITIES, NEW ARRIVALS, ETC.

Ambridge H A, accountant Molson's Bank, 31 West ave s

Ambrose A W (Duggan & Ambrose) h 199 Hughson n

Becker & Hughes, manfr jewelers, 130 King e

Bell W T, confectioner, 174 King e

Beveridge T H (T H Beveridge & Co) 134 King w, h 17 Barton w

Beveridge T H & Co, plumbers, 134 King w

Black H J, 48 Cannon e

Bowes Joseph, bookkeeper, 142 Wellington n

Brass Benjamin, 27 Markland

Bull Rev G A, rector Holy Trinity, Barton, res The Cliff, Mountain top

Clappison Thomas, bookseller and stationer, James cor Gore

Collins and Leigh (E W Collins, Jabez Leigh) general agents, 8 John n

Crockford C & Son, manf jewelers, 9 James n

Dermody John, baker, 151 Main e

Duggan & Ambrose, barristers, Canada Life Chambers, 1 James s *See card*

Duggan R J (Duggan & Ambrose) Wentworth cor Stinson

reeman W H, wood and coal and builders' supplies, 169 James n, h 80 Elgin

Grant & Furmidge, carriage builders, 100 James n

Henderson Alex (Robertson & Henderson) h 20 Victoria ave n

Henderson A S, boots and shoes, 64 King w

Hinman Mrs C A, milliner, 8 James n

Leigh Jabez (Collins & Leigh) 8 John n

Leslie R, fruiterer, 208 King e

Lumgair W S, sewing machines and organs, 92 James n

Limin Frederick, policeman

McKay Wm, hotel, 157 James n

McMahon, Broadfield & Co (J S McMahon, G E Broadfield) crockery, glassware, lamp goods; wholesale only, 45 King w

Meekison Andrew, grocer, James cor Cannon

Mills George A, gents' furnishings, hats and caps, etc, 70 King w

Moody D W & Co, dressmaker school and Moody's tailors' system of cutting, 176 King e

Morrison E W, 132 Hughson n

Murphy Mrs, laundress, 34 York

Olmsted W H (Olmsted Bros) h 11 Hess s

Plante W E, ledger keeper Molsons Bank, Duke cor Bay

Queen's Laundry, 107 James n

Reinholt Robert, manager D W Moody & Co, 176 King e

Rutherford & Lester, real estate agents, 6½ James s

Sawyer L D & Co (L D Sawyer, Henry P Coburn, Jonathan Ames and A H Hope) n e cor Wellington and G T R track

Snider Rev D W, pastor Zion Church, 270 York

Star Laundry, Mrs Murphy, 34 York

Taylor E, grinder, 174 King e

Trade Association, (Toronto) M B Rymal, manager, 24 Macnab n

City of Kingston and County of Frontenac

GAZETTEER AND DIRECTORY, 1885-6.

SECOND EDITION.

Including the Postal Addresses, Number of Lots and Concessions, Freeholder and Tenant of the farmers of the county. This book will be published and orders received, July 1st, 1885. **PRICE, $2.**

W. H. IRWIN & CO.,

PUBLISHER,

HAMILTON, - - - ONTARIO.

Directories of the city of St. Catharines (including Lincoln and Welland) and the county of Simcoe. Price, $2 each. Most recent publications.

THE

Hamilton Galvanized Iron Works

ESTABLISHED 1863.

THOS. IRWIN & SON, PROPRIETORS.

12 Macnab Street South,

HAMILTON, ONTARIO.

MANUFACTURERS OF ALL KINDS OF

GALVANIZED IRON WORK.

TIN AND COPPER WARE.

Iron, Tin and Gravel Roofing a Specialty. Also, sole manufacturers of the celebrated Acme Chimney Top, which has proved such a grand success—warranted to cure any smoky chimney.

JOHN MACDONALD & CO.,

WHOLESALE IMPORTERS OF

DRY GOODS, CARPETS,

WOOLLENS AND FANCY GOODS.

We beg to announce to the trade, that having every facility afforded us for purchasing which cash payments can command, we are in a position to offer in every department goods at prices that will prove profitable to close buyers.

Our permanent representatives, who are always on the alert to supplement our stock for the assorting trade, together with our staff of departmental buyers, who visit the British and Foreign Markets semi-annually, enables us to offer a very varied and complete stock, not only during the regular but also during the assorting season, giving the purchasers the advantages of filling in their stocks with the most seasonable goods required.

Believing that our true interests are identical with those of our customers, we carefully and continuously study the various changes of fashion, so that our clients may be in a position to place before their customers the latest choice novelties as they appear.

ORDERS BY MAIL, WIRE, OR THROUGH OUR TRAVELLERS, WILL RECEIVE MOST CAREFUL AND PROMPT ATTENTION.

DEPARTMENTS.

Staples. — Manchester Goods, Flannels and Blankets, Linens and Jute Goods.

Dress Goods.—Hosiery and Gloves, Ribbons and Corsets, Gents' Furnishings.

Mantles and Shawls.—Laces, Muslins, Embroideries, Silks, Satins, Crapes, British and German Knitted Goods.

Woollens.—Canadian Tweeds, Imported Woolens, Rubber Goods.

Haberdashery. — Wools and Wool Work, British and Foreign Fancy Goods, Japanese and Papier Mache Goods.

Carpets and Oil Cloths.—Brussels and Tapestries, Supers and Three-Ply Carpets, Dutch and Hemp Carpets.

Upholsterers' Goods.—Raw Silk and Jute Coverings, Damasks, Reps, Terries, Plushes, Piano and Furniture Felts, &c.

21, 23, 25, 27 Wellington Street East,
28, 30, 32, 34 Front Street East, } TORONTO.

31 Major Street, Manchester, England.

ROYAL INSURANCE CO'

OF ENGLAND.

FIRE AND LIFE.

Assets, - - - $28,000,00

The Royal Insurance Company has the Large Surplus of Assets over Liabilities of any Fire Insurance Co'y in the World.

STANDARD LIFE ASSURANCE CO.

Total Risks, - - - - - - - $100.000
Invested Funds, - - - - - - 30,000
Investments in Canada, - - - - 2,000.

Rates Liberal and Losses Promptly Settled.

DOMINION PLATE GLASS INSURANCE OFFICE

Insurance on Plate Glass Windows, Show Cases, etc. Stock held on hand for immediate replacemer in case of breakage.

Sun Accident Ins. Co.

Insures ag all classes of Accident.

DOMINION LINE OF STEAMSHIPS,

From Quebec or Portland every week.

ISSUER OF MARRIAGE LICENSES

For City of Hamilton and County of Wentworth. Good for part of the Province of Ontario.

Money to Loan on Real Estat

At Liberal Rates of Interest and Easy Terms of Payment.

DAVID McLELLAN,

House, 55 Herkimer street. Office, 84 James street nort

www.ingramcontent.com/pod-product-compliance
Lightning Source LLC
Chambersburg PA
CBHW030859270326
41929CB00008B/488

* 9 7 8 3 7 4 4 7 5 6 8 5 3 *